Rhyme and Reason

Rhyme and Reason

An Introduction to Minimalist Syntax

Juan Uriagereka

The MIT Press

Cambridge, Massachusetts

London, England

First MIT Press paperback edition, 2000

© 1998 Juan Uriagereka

This book was set in Stone Sans and Bembo by Graphic Composition, Inc. and was printed and bound in the United States of America.

Library of Congress Cataloging-in-Publication Data

Uriagereka, Juan.
    Rhyme and reason : an introduction to minimalist syntax / Juan Uriagereka.
        p.   cm.
    Includes bibliographical references and index.
    ISBN 0-262-21014-2 (hc : alk. paper), 0-262-71008-0 (pb)
        1. Grammar, Comparative and general—Syntax.   2. Minimalist theory (Linguistics)   3. Language and languages—Philosophy.   I. Title.
    P291.U75   1998
    415—dc21   98-18660
                                                                                                          CIP

A Javier, en memoria de otras vidas

Unha dama entrou aquí,	A lady entered here,
Un pícaro entrou con ela.	A knave entered with her.
Xa se foi, mais está aquí.	She left, yet she's still here.
Qué diremos que foi dela?	What ever happened to her?

—Old Galician riddle

Contents

Synopsis

To the reader: The bold-typed glosses refer to important or more established parts of the theory; italicized glosses indicate digressive or tentative material.

1

This dialogue is a gem. Rarely have I encountered, in an advanced and highly specialized field, a reconstruction that, like this one, is largely enjoyable by a novice, thought-provoking to the professional, and capable of illustrating with a delicate brush the rigorous internal logic of a whole domain. Language (or rather, our tacit knowledge of it) constitutes an unquenchable source of wonder. Children and adults alike take pleasure in exploring new subtle reverberations between sounds and meanings. In every culture, poems, rhymes, puns, limericks, riddles, jokes, and jeux de mots all testify to the multitude of enjoyments that are made possible, at varying degrees of depth, by the infinite use of a finite repertoire of linguistic materials. By reading this book, we fully realize exactly *why* this is so, and how far and how deep an explanation of this natural propensity can lead us. Also, thanks to a dazzling display of graphic inventiveness, Juan Uriagereka conducts in the universe of syntax and semantics an exploration not dissimilar from those to which we have grown accustomed in the universe of mathematics and pure logic. Readers who have been enthralled by *Gödel, Escher, Bach* may well like this syntactic companion as well, a sort of *Chomsky, Fibonacci, Bach* (the Fibonacci numbers, as explained in chapter 1, are the cornerstone of certain universal biological "harmonics").

Juan Uriagereka is a leading member of the (by now) large international community of linguists working in the domain known as generative grammar. This field was created some forty years ago by Noam Chomsky, one of the towering intellectual figures of our time. Of Chomsky—and of the collective Linguist of the dialogue, a convenient single label that subsumes a collective mind, a kind of Bourbaki of linguistics powerfully inspired by Chomsky's work—it can be said, according to the ancient tradition, "He solved the riddle of the Sphinx, and was a man most mighty." Indeed, this book allows us to participate in one of the most fascinating conceptual adventures of our time. I anticipate that many readers will share the feeling of excitement that pervades the profession. How elating it is to discover that so much is going on these days! And that what's in full progress affects our basic understanding of human nature.

The artful stratagem of the dialogue in fact allows the reader to accompany the discussants, step by step, through a systematic reconstruction of the foundations of modern scientific linguistics, all the way up to a very recent and still hotly debated theoretical turn called the "Minimalist Program." Many researchers have grappled for long months with the seminal technical articles (and now a whole book) presenting this program. The least that can be said is that not every aspect of the new theory is yet crystal clear to every professional linguist. Chomsky's recent technical work is particularly "bare" of glosses, dense, at times too rapid, at times allusive, occasionally somewhat disconcerting, and, as always, immensely stimulating. It is most welcome to be invited to explore the intricacies of this new theory under the patient guidance of an expert. Here and there we are also exposed to recent original contributions made by Richard S. Kayne, Howard Lasnik, Juan Uriagereka himself, and many more.

It is also fitting that the Linguist's partner in this exchange (the Other) be an encyclopedic physicist-mathematician, one of those intellectually omnivorous characters whom the French, with a faint shade of mockery, call a polymath. Conveniently, the Other is immensely smart; he is also immensely naive (at least at the outset) in all matters linguistic, but he happens to speak a vast number of languages. As the dialogue makes clear from the first day, the Other's relentless challenging of the Linguist is the engine that drives all motion—especially because the Minimalist turn makes linguistic theory resemble, strangely enough, more the theories we encounter in physics than the ones we encounter in biology. I say "strangely enough," because, as Chomsky has rightly stressed, and as the Linguist relentlessly reminds us here, the language faculty is part of the genetic makeup of our species; therefore, the principles that guide it would not be expected to possess so much elegance and allow for so much deductive power. The organization of other organs, shaped as it is by the vagaries of biological evolution, usually does not offer such elegance and compactness. The dialogue aptly opens with many acute and intriguing considerations on this all-important and unexpected (and still rather tentative) conclusion.

Chomsky's new turn is a refinement and a radicalization of ideas and presuppositions that have been at the very heart of generative grammar since its inception. This dialogue offers constant reminders of the deeper roots of the new theory, and dutifully monitors for us what is new, what is not, and what represents a daring reinterpretation of antecedent positions. In fact, many ideas are genuinely novel and illuminating. Despite substantial continuity, the Minimalist Program is indeed a revolution within a revolution. This dialogue is both a general introduction to the field as a whole and a sophisticated series of advanced lectures on the most elusive ramifications of Minimalism. I, for one, learned much from it and found in it excellent reasons to reread the technical texts in a new light.

2

I know through long and often frustrating experience how difficult it is to explain to hard-nosed scientists what generative grammar is all about. Physicists and biologists often assume that linguistics is, by its very nature, destined to be the study of a class of behaviors, namely, "communicative" behaviors. Since linguistics deals with symbolic communication, and since behaviorism is a relic of the past, perhaps these scientists want to concede, by making this assumption, that linguistics cannot be a straightforward description of behaviors as such, but rather an inquiry into the "causes" of these behaviors. Moreover, in this era of sophisticated brain imaging, they guess that linguistics must somehow eventually link up with detailed explorations of neuronal structures, natural or artificial, and, presumably, with artificial intelligence. These scientists are somewhat baffled when one stresses that the main body of generative grammar in fact links up only occasionally and only rather peripherally with the study of the neural correlates of language. These may represent, mostly in cases of inborn or traumatic deficits, confirming or disconfirming indirect evidence, but not the kind of central data with which the discipline is concerned. The core of generative grammar, qua natural science of language, deals not with the causes of verbal behaviors but with in-depth analyses of a kind of *knowledge:* humans' tacit and internally caused knowledge of language. It is not easy, either, to explain to a nonlinguist that the overlap with the most popular variants of artificial intelligence is at best slim, and more often than not highly conflicting. Now and then, generative grammar has something to gain from a machine model of the workings of its principles and parameters, but in the main such artificial embodiments are neither necessary nor sufficient. I cannot see it as an accident that the high priests of the most popularized brands of artificial intelligence often take pride in professing ignorance of, and indifference to, the very fundamentals of generative grammar.

Reduction to neurology, at least "in principle," is often posited by the physicist and the biologist (and by many philosophers of language who ought to know better) as a preliminary, mandatory credential for generative grammar to be accepted as a natural science. Wisely, this dialogue faces head on the problem of reductionism and of the unification, by way of considerable new enlargements, of the more basic sciences. It very effectively refutes the assumption that either linguistics simply *is* advanced neurology in disguise or else it cannot even claim to be truly scientific. Nowhere have I seen this crucial and controversial problem discussed with such brilliance and thoroughness.

Strange as it may sound, generative grammar does not deal primarily and directly with languages as such (English, Chinese, Swahili, Tagalog, what have you), but, first and foremost, with naturally occurring individual computations of abstract structures that underlie the audible (or, in the case of sign languages, visible) expressions of those languages. These structures are specific to language, are part of human nature, and are instantiated in us effortlessly, incessantly, while we are intent on doing myriad other things. To most of these structures we have no conscious access, and it takes great subtlety, as well as a highly educated flair, to summon relevant linguistic evidence for or against a specific hypothesis. A point aptly made by the Linguist is that much of the traditional philosophy of mind and language is idle, because the most basic facts are drastically different from what they appear to be upon simple introspection or straight conceptual analysis. Thus, the systematic role that these abstract structures, by means of chains of internal computations (called derivations), play in determining the audible utterances and written expressions in the world's languages is of great concern to the generative grammarian. The central idea connecting what is hidden and what is manifest is that there is a *universal* set of principles, each of which leaves open a very narrow range of possibilities (literally to be counted on the fingers of one hand, or, in the limit, just one binary choice per principle), and that each particular language (or dialect, the distinction here being inessential) represents a specific set of choices, one for each of these possibilities, or parameters. Universal Grammar is thus instantiated in the mind/brain of the speaker of a given language or dialect by means of a complete set of specifications for (as it were) a panel of "switches" (this felicitous metaphor is due to James Higginbotham).

One might still think that the relation between the principles and parameters of Universal Grammar and actual spoken sentences is one of cause and effect, but this would be misleading. As Descartes warned, and as Chomsky has aptly reminded us all along, there is no reason to believe that there are, strictly speaking, causes at all in this domain, in any sense of the term "cause" that is even moderately well understood. We say what we say, when we say it, to whom we choose to say it, because we freely decide to do so. Linguistic expressions are *neither caused by external circumstances, nor independent of them*. This is the well-known Descartes-Chomsky paradox, exhaustively explained in this dialogue. Linguistic utterances are prompted, but not caused, by external circumstances, and are always subject to an act of free will. It is always possible, but never necessary, to say something appropriate in a form suitable to a given occasion. The actual form of the utterance, if and when the speaker freely decides to emit it, is then generated via the processes detailed in this dialogue. It would be a grave mistake, though, to consider such mental machinery the cause of what we say, or even "the" cause of how we say it. The study of grammar is not a study of causes in any meaningful sense. It is, in fact, a study of human knowledge of language, and it is far from straightforward that knowledge may literally count as a cause. I can think of no other place in the literature where these notions, and the reasons that give them substance, are better presented than in this dialogue.

"Oh, *now* I see!", our scientist is likely to say, in relief. "It's a mathematical analysis of languages." More bafflement ensues when one points out that the theory is not "mathematical" at all, although it has a formalism, a quasi-mathematical elegance, and a "formal logic" of derivations very much its own, and it definitely involves very abstract entities and operations. These are visualized with unparalleled effectiveness through the virtuoso graphic illustrations of this book.

Of special annoyance to the hard-nosed scientist, then, is the inevitable ensuing presentation of the typical data studied by the generative grammarian, namely, sentences from various languages and native speakers' intuitions about them: "These are your *data?!* Do you expect me to take sentences and *intuitions* as data for a natural science?!" The linguist can well point out that there exist by now large corpora of quite robust and perfectly replicable data, collected over a long period of time from many languages—and, if this were not enough, that native speakers' intuitions about grammaticality are in fact on a par with more standard perceptual judgments regarding, say, color vision, stereopsis, or motion perception, where the careful monitoring of these judgments (rightly) constitutes the foundation of most of the study of the psychology, physiology, and neurophysiology of perception. In fact, the linguist's experiments are no less reliable for being simple, natural, and inexpensive. When the data are not so clear, linguists indeed use other, less direct methods (EEGs, eye movements, reaction times, rates of nonnutritive sucking in infants, and so on), being symmetrically repaid with less direct and less conclusive results. Gathering data straight from performance is fine as far as it goes, but defeasibility increases, because of interference from other factors besides the structures of language (limited attention span, memory failures, acoustic noise, etc.). Since the internal structures are what one is really after, it is vastly more desirable to probe directly into linguistic competence, tapping intuitions as such, as is unproblematically done in, say, decision theory, probability theory, naturalistic moral philosophy, much of economics, and just about all of logic. It is an obvious constraint on a scientific domain that it should account for scientists' capacity to gather evidence for or against its theories. Physics and biology do not put it down to some inexplicable wizardry that we are able to perceive motion, visually scan tracks on a photographic plate, read dials, and see things in a microscope. It is no miracle either that we develop reliable "intuitions" about the significance of these observations for the relevant theories.

Alas, these considerations do not always manage to impress the hard scientist, and sometimes, at exactly this point, the patience of our interlocutor is irretrievably lost, and the real-life dialogue between the physicist, or the biologist, and the linguist terminates abruptly. In this expository sense, I think it is wise of Juan Uriagereka to have kept the presentation of linguistic data to the strict minimum.

This book was indeed badly needed, and I am confident that, at long last, a good number of natural scientists will listen longer and find greater patience in following the arguments and examining the data. They will thus ascertain that this brand of linguistics is well on its way to becoming a full-blown natural science, offering a serious promise of an advanced field of scientific inquiry whose idealizations, abstractions, and deductions will eventually match in depth and subtlety those of the most advanced domains of modern science. Generative grammar is turning into a natural science already, because of what it is now, not because of what it might one day turn into, when neural imaging and neurobiology will have provided dramatic new refinements. Juan Uriagereka's stratagem to motivate the scientific reader is a very early incursion into the vast scientific resonances of certain strategic choices. The big "whys" of contemporary linguistic theory are constantly interwoven with the "hows" and the "whats." I anticipate that his stratagem will work.

I confine myself here to offering immediate motivations to sit down and listen. These introductory reflections are especially aimed at my former colleagues: physicists and biologists—that is, readers who are, like the Other, perfectly conversant with the natural sciences of a more standard variety, and curious about the facts of language.

3

In retrospect, we often see clearly that the most difficult task for an incipient natural science is to identify the right level of analysis and idealization, the primary objects that are observable at that level, and the most basic patterns of variation and invariance characterizing those objects. This difficult phase of idealization and abstraction precedes the construction of any theory and any attempt at explanations, and often steers the development of suitable techniques of observation and model building. It is legitimate to say that the triumphs of modern biology all originally derived from the intuition that the recurring patterns of similarities and differences between individuals of successive generations offer a privileged key to understanding the organization of living systems, and that the proper level of analysis is ultimately the molecular one. Of immense importance was first the intuition, and then the discovery, that even viruses and the simplest unicellular organisms possess a genetics in the full sense of the term, and that most of what is true of them (I must insist, at the right level of idealization, not superficially) is also true of whales and people (here I am simply paraphrasing my former teachers, the French biologists and Nobelists Jacques Monod and François Jacob). The breakthroughs of modern biology, it is perhaps worth stressing, have been made possible by the systematic study of rather insignificant living creatures, such as the tobacco mosaic virus, the fruit fly, and intestinal bacteria, often grown in rather unusual and highly selective conditions. It is also worth stressing that millennia of casual observation of the most familiar and endearing animals had contributed next to nothing, from the scientific point of view, to our understanding of the basic underlying organization of living systems. I think that there are interesting conclusions for the scientific study of language to be drawn from these lessons of modern biology. They can help us understand some of the difficulties still encountered in vindicating the scientific status of the theories and the data presented in this book. I am old enough to remember a time when traditional biologists accused molecular biology of being contrived, myopic, based on artifacts and rare events. It rings a bell, therefore, when generative grammar is allegedly exposed for committing these very sins.

4

As this dialogue testifies, the study of syntax has by now accumulated excellent credentials for constituting a privileged window onto the organization of the human mind. Despite some forty years of healthy developments in linguistic theory, and the productive application of generative grammar to hundreds of languages and dialects of a typologically very broad range, this claim is considered highly debatable by many, and preposterous by some. In fact, our spontaneous casual fascination with language, the propensity for wonder and enjoyment to which I alluded above, is intrinsically unable to reveal that syntax is a primary, autonomous, and self-structured object of investigation. Indeed, our prescientific intuitions about language are bound to conceal that it is so. As the very opening of this dialogue aptly reminds us, if we approach syntax from top to bottom—that is, from the collective uses of language—we first encounter many layers of haphazard geopolitical contingencies and social conventions before we hit upon even the most generic systematicities of pragmatics and semantics. Syntax is often perceived as situated one level below this thin layer of pragmatic and semantic regularities, and subservient to them. (For expository purposes I am here deliberately using these terms according to the traditional classification: "syntax" as the study of systems of symbolic forms that are interpreted at a conceptual level; "semantics" as the study of the relations between expressions and things; "pragmatics" as the study of the use of linguistic expressions. But we will see shortly, and then much better in the dialogue, that it is far from granted that these standard demarcations can survive serious scientific scrutiny.) In such a traditional framework, then, the business of syntax is seen as one of freezing a set of "conventions" to string together contingent expressions for certain intentions to communicate. In this conception, what counts is the communicative intention itself, rather than the "contingent" form used to convey it. In this pragmatic and sociolinguistic perspective, syntax is a kind of adornment.

If, on the contrary, we move up from a utopianly "pure" physical characterization of the sounds of speech, we must ascend slowly, from amplitudes, frequencies, and temporal-spectral characteristics, to phonemes, from these to syllables, from syllables to words, and then from words to larger units. In this bottom-up perspective, the potential semantic ambiguities that arise in the attempt to combine words into larger units is what, allegedly, motivates syntax.

In the first approach (the top-down or pragmatic one), syntax is perceived as the mere "servant" of communicative aims. In the second (the bottom-up or physical one), it is perceived as a kind of peculiar "glue," useful in cementing lexical meanings into more elaborate and flexible units of expression. Characteristically, both perspectives present syntax as requiring some kind of special justification, whereas it is considered easy to explain why we need parsing and pragmatics. There would be no language worth the name if we could not segment the physically continuous stream of speech into meaning-bearing units (that is, words). That's why we need parsing. And even that would be worthless if we could not manage, somehow, to pin the individual words to relevant objects and events in the outside world. It thus appears obvious that we need parsing, and that we need to make use of words and their meanings. But then why are we endowed with all the intricacies and the complications of syntax? Why not stop at lexical semantics, perhaps adding some straightforward combinatorial rules on top? What is full-blown syntax for?

At this juncture, when the combination of word meanings is at stake, many think they can reply, "Syntax is there to reduce ambiguity." This is the most "plausible" explanation being offered in certain quarters. It is pointed out that, whereas *peanut butter* is a butter made from peanuts, *snow boots* are boots worn for walking in snow, not boots made from snow. Likewise, *stone traffic barrier* is some device made of stone and used to regulate traffic, not a protection against trafficking in stones, whereas *steel bar prices* are monetary values of steel molded in the shape of bars. One then proceeds to calculate that the string of words *Pennsylvania state highway department public relations director* could produce, in the abstract, 132 logically possible meanings. Predicaments like these are (revealingly) used to sanction the eminent reasonableness of possessing a syntactic device, very expedient for blocking unwelcome combinatorial ambiguities. Juan Uriagereka offers many precise and compelling counterarguments to this naive move, especially in chapters 2 and 6.

Clearly, in any such reconstruction, syntax is not acknowledged as primary; instead, it is viewed as derived from something else, both ontologically and epistemologically. To use a term that is central to this dialogue, these approaches present syntax as an *interface* between communicative intentions and the articulation of the sounds of speech, a filter that is useful in making these intentions unambiguously manifest. This conception is exactly the opposite of what the Minimalist theory maintains, and generative grammar has maintained all along: that syntactic structures are primary. What one deals with is the streamlining of speech sounds, all the way up to the selection of words from the lexicon, and the scaffolding of the logical form (i.e., the systematic constraints on interpretation) that arise at two distinct interfaces. The first interface lies between syntax and the articulatory organs, the other between syntax and the conceptual system, extending into the array of devices used to talk about the world, and express ideas, hopes, fears, desires. Syntactic computations, driven by powerful criteria of minimization, are truly universal, and it is they that determine various systematic constraints on sounds and meanings, not the other way around. As the dialogue makes clear, the specificity and the primacy of syntax do not mean that it stands in splendid isolation from everything else, in particular from all semantic questions. Yet they do mean that syntactic theory cannot be constructed from the demands of lexical recombinations plus some rules of thumb for clarity, usability, and mutual adjustment between speakers and hearers.

5

Curiously, right at this point evolutionary considerations come to the fore and constitute, in the eyes of many, a stumbling block. It is considered straightforward to justify semantics and pragmatics on adaptationist grounds, whereas it appears problematic to justify, on such neo-Darwinian grounds, the primacy of syntax. Many take it to be a necessary truth that syntax cannot be primary, because (so the story goes) survival pressures can only primarily shape the speed, accuracy, and representational power of *what* we say; they have no need to primarily shape *how* we say it. The how (syntax) must be derivative on more "basic" functional (communicative and simulative) needs. For reasons that are clearly laid out in this dialogue, generative grammar does clash with such impenitent adaptationism, and it therefore appears to collide with evolutionary theory. The crucial point, however, is that evolutionary theory must not be equated with strict adaptationism. It is one of the chief merits of this dialogue to offer perfectly convincing arguments reconciling generative grammar with evolutionary theory, while freeing it from the clamps of strict adaptationism.

In essence, the problem is, and always was, the following: no adaptationist approach to language (whether it is admitted or not) can select the right kind of syntactic organization on the basis of generic computation-optimizing constraints acting directly on sounds, interpretations, or uses. Indeed, these generic constraints cannot select any relevant type of syntactic organization over any other, and cannot even exclude some wildly implausible conjectures. The most elementary caricature invites us to imagine creatures that would form interrogatives, or negatives, by simply reversing the order of all words in a declarative sentence, creating its mirror image. No adaptationist consideration has managed to explain why we are not such creatures. More sophisticated fantasies of prima facie "possible," but actually impossible, human languages (as explained in the dialogue) cannot be excluded on the basis of adaptationist considerations. It is arguably the single most important global result of over forty years of progress in syntactic theory that there has been no way of deriving the syntactic principles actually governing human natural languages from any generic constraint issuing from functional designs pertaining to motor control, communicative efficiency, memory load, "logical" perspicuity, minimization of ambiguity, or the like. It is also an interesting and important fact, which could not have been predicted, that our most highly developed theories of language (and this extends as well to other domains of human cognition) are not computation-friendly and that conversely, much of what can be accomplished thanks to brute computational power sheds no light whatsoever on human capacities (even chess programs could not possibly achieve much if constrained to play with anything resembling human limitations on calculation). In the present technologically oriented climate this is a point worth stressing, to which I shall return shortly.

Some authors are persuaded that we have not tried hard enough, and that we should persist. They claim that an "explanation" of syntax by means of adaptationist criteria must, in the end, succeed, because otherwise the existence of language as we know it would be a "miracle." They allege that, in the absence of *generic* functional constraints on linguistic abilities shaped by a *specific* advantage in terms of survival value, the origins of syntax would be simply miraculous. Since serious science has no place for miracles, these authors deem it eminently plausible to try to derive syntax, at any price, from some optimization criterion *of an extralinguistic nature*. One encounters skepticism, if not downright hostility, when one invites these authors to examine considerable amounts of data from many languages and ascertain the remarkable success that quite specific syntactic hypotheses have already achieved in explaining these data. The adaptationists choose to disregard these data, and the impressive success of linguistic theory, unwilling to concede that a line of inquiry based on generic optimization criteria of a nonlinguistic nature cannot offer the faintest hope of success.

6

It may seem strange to criticize "optimization" strategies in presenting a "minimalist" program for linguistic theory. It is not. The notions of strict economy and minimization that are so central to the theory expounded in this dialogue are not generic and extralinguistic. These are deep, novel, extremely elegant and powerful concepts, full of deductive and empirical consequences (many of which are yet to be explored), but they are nonetheless strictly language-specific. This point is examined in great detail and with many novel insights in the dialogue, but it may deserve some immediate clarification.

In light of the comments in section 5, it should be noted that generative grammar departs sharply from the traditional avenues into the study of language, both the naive ones (among which I recommend including many of those currently advanced in certain milieux of artificial intelligence) and the scholarly ones (notably including many structuralist ancestors). We have to travel back in time and reach the point where Chomsky's approach to the study of language, ever since the mid-1950s, abruptly diverged from the long tradition that preceded it. In hindsight, it appears crucial to be able to share with him the commanding intuitions on *why* it was mandatory, and immensely productive, to single out a particular, in many ways unprecedented, level of analysis. In my experience, nonlinguists find it illuminating to learn that "meaning," if taken in the traditional sense, plays a very unusual role in characterizing this level. And here it is unavoidable to consider examples, in the form of sentences.

Some sentence pairs impose themselves on us as naturally "belonging together," others as (equally naturally) parting company:

(1) a. They saw that he was trying to escape.

     b. They saw him trying to escape.

(2) a. They suspected that he was trying to escape.

     b. *They suspected him trying to escape.

Plainly, to every fluent speaker of English, (1b) is very close (though not identical) in meaning to (1a), whereas (2b) is a most awkward rendition of a meaning similar to that expressed in (2a), and indeed sounds strange under any interpretation (whence the asterisk that precedes it). The important point is that this fact has much to do with "meaning," but not in the usual sense. The similarity between (1a) and (1b), on the one hand, and the dissimilarity between (2a) and (2b), on the other, are somehow determined by the meanings of the verbs *see* and *suspect*: witness the fact that *suspect* is naturally followed by a sentence (*suspect that . . .*), whereas *see* is naturally followed by the name of an object (*see a cat*), though it also admits a metaphorical interpretation involving whole sentences, as in (1). The contrast between (1b) and (2b) teases apart these two interpretations. Yet it would be pointless to sit down and think very hard about the *concepts* of seeing and suspecting, or about the social "use" of these concepts in our everyday life, in order to derive an explanation for these simple facts. By straightforwardly substituting verb for verb in (1b), we realize that *see* belongs to a group of verbs in which we also find, for instance, *catch, find,* and *spot*. Similar substitution shows that *suspect* bands together with, for instance, *know, denounce,* and *dissuade*. Within each group, the verbs have very different meanings. There is no deep unifying feature among them, at a purely conceptual level. In other words, if we examine the kinds of physical or psychological actions that correspond to each of these verbs in the objective world, we find no criterion that allows us to explain the asymmetry between (1b) and (2b). We cannot even begin to find a suitable systematic explanation for such elementary facts by examining "concepts" in isolation, or by examining situations, beliefs, actions, or behaviors. The difference between the two groups of verbs lies primarily in their ability to combine with, and select, other elements in a sentence. The relevant difference, in other words, is syntactic, not conceptual.

It stands to reason that myriad facts like these may belong to a specific level of linguistic analysis, neither divorced from that of full-blown meanings and concepts, nor assimilable to it. It also stands to reason that we want the structural complexity of this level of linguistic analysis to remain constant as more detail is added, as sentences grow longer and more elaborate, as we nest subordinates into main sentences, as we form interrogative or dubitative expressions. Moreover, it is eminently desirable that the core structures turn out to be invariant across different languages.

We already have a first intimation that such a level must be built on criteria of simplicity and non-ad-hocness and that, to some extent at least, it must be seen as autonomous with respect to other levels also belonging to the general domain of thinking and communicating.

We can also summon evidence, again of a rather elementary nature, that this level (somehow) spans a range intermediate between that of single words and that of full sentences. Its constitutive rules, whatever they turn out to be, must be sensitive to the form of words (i.e., to lexical morphology), but, once more, should not be assimilated to rules dealing purely with word forms. On the other hand, they are also, obviously, of a much finer grain than, say, a calculus based on the truth values of propositions as a whole and on their combinations by means of connectors (such as *and, or, if . . . then*).

For instance, we easily realize that deep commonalities in meaning exist between the expressions in (3),

(3) a. I know the man who is standing at the bar.
    b. I know the man standing at the bar.

but that this is much less the case (or not at all, on one reading) in (4):

(4) a. I found the man who was standing at the bar.
    b. I found the man standing at the bar.

Once more, we tease apart different possibilities of interpretation, we factor out different "valencies" for combination with, and selection of, other elements in sentences. When one explores the vast range of other similar cases, one finds it utterly implausible that an explanation could be based on the "concepts" involved (in this case, the "concepts" of knowing and finding). Generalizing the relevant data a bit, let us examine some deep commonalities among the following sentences:

(5) a. He saw the man standing at the bar.
    b. The man was seen by him standing at the bar.
    c. Where was the man he saw standing?
    d. Who did he see standing at the bar?
    e. He failed to see the man standing at the bar.
    f. He succeeded in seeing the man standing at the bar.

The important intuition here (ever since Chomsky's seminal work in the mid-1950s) is that in all of these expressions—and for the same reasons—*see* can be replaced with, say, *arrest,* but not with, say, *suspect* or *deny*. Notice that certain substitutions in fact preserve the interpretations and the roles, whereas others do not; and some may turn the sentence into nonsense, or even into gibberish. In spite of differences in word order, morphology (. . . *seeing,* . . . *to see*), and phrasal construction (active, passive, interrogative, subordinate, etc.), the rule that indifferently allows *see* and *arrest* in all these sentences, while disallowing *suspect* and *deny,* whatever it may be, applies uniformly. Therefore, no such rule can be stated in terms of the sequential ordering of the single words in the sentence—or in terms of infinitives versus gerunds, combinations of adjacent words, active versus passive, or anything of the sort. Traditional grammars, based as they are on the identification of characteristic "constructions" (such as passives and interrogatives) and the marking, as it were, of standard signposts in the sentence, prescribe piecemeal operations on words, or on fixed groups of words located at certain positions. They are therefore by their very nature inadequate to cope with the basic facts exemplified here. A class of intrinsically more powerful grammars is needed, in which the relevant rules apply uniformly even though certain elements in the sentence have undergone movement (i.e., despite "transformations").

This is a bare-bones reconstruction that I have found didactically expedient to suggest how Chomsky originally justified the need for a transition from "phrase structure grammars" to "transformational grammars." In the second, but not in the first, words and constituents (noun phrases, verb phrases, etc.) can be "moved" from one location to another, leaving some essential grammatical relations invariant (who is doing the seeing and who is being seen, who is standing, etc.).

Plainly, as we have just seen, there is no hope of constructing the rules of such more powerful grammars either on the basis of "pure logic" or on the basis of a standard "conceptual" analysis. Even less can we hope to explain these facts on the basis of regularities pertaining to the world of motor control, sensory perception, communicative efficacy, or social conventions. Form and meaning are both involved, but in a highly specific, context-independent admixture. We do have intimations, in other words, of the specificity and the autonomy of syntax.

It might have turned out, in the abstract, that this level of linguistic analysis, and its constitutive idealizations, were contrived, "unnatural," amorphous, arbitrary, and devoid of interesting crosslinguistic regularities. It might have turned out to be a haphazard "interface" of some sort. The all-important result has been that this level is, on the contrary, linguistically basic (one starts from here in explaining myriad linguistic facts), nonreducible (to extralinguistic considerations), autonomous (with respect to pragmatics and traditional semantics), and theoretically salient. It interacts systematically with other levels (notably morphology and lexical internal structures) in such a way that, so far, no other level of linguistic analysis has proven to be as productive as this one as the basis for a general theory of language, capturing profound commonalities across languages. Surely it does not constitute a mere "interface" between other levels.

Now, since the innermost organization of the mental faculty underlying this level cannot be adequately deduced only from truths of reason, and since it is not a consequence of generic design features for all viable symbolic systems of communication, it offers a unique and privileged window onto the nature of the human mind. This dialogue will in fact display a revealing picture of what has been learned so far about the human mind, and about the basic design of all human natural languages, by exploring, in great depth, this level and the mental computations that underlie it.

7

In contrast with these heartening results, I cannot avoid at least a passing mention of a certain "disillusionment" with generative grammar that I sense these days in certain quarters of linguistics and of cognitive science more generally. The whole approach is seen by some as overly abstract, overly mutable, and vastly underdetermined by data (as if all deep scientific theories were not, at least initially, vastly underdetermined by data). In the computer industry, I have heard the quip that every time a generative grammarian is fired, the efficacy of the machines increases by 5 percent. In those quarters we are in fact witnessing the triumph of brute computational force, admittedly without any claim that those machines indeed mimic what the human mind can do. There are also psycholinguists, child psychologists, cognitive psychologists, neurolinguists, and philosophers of mind and language who have grown impatient with the apparently endless changes in the theory. The news of another turn in generative grammar has not been well received in some quarters, and has confirmed some in their antecedent skepticism. There are linguists who are actively exploring other avenues in syntactic theory, staying closer to traditional models (notably exploring combinations of generativism with the older structuralist phrase structure grammars). Much will be said in this dialogue that is apt to dispel such skepticism and counter these conservative moves.

In my view, the central ideas of generative grammar that are especially chosen as targets for skepticism, and that are most persuasively defended in this book, are these:

1. Words, and groups of intimately associated words (constituents), can be moved from one place to another, generating closely related sentences and *preserving certain salient properties* (e.g., the power to select types of arguments; to refer to a particular entity; to be coreferring; to specify an agent, an object, etc.). Syntactic principles must be *invariant* with respect to these movements (or "transformations" in the terminology of the 1950s and 1960s). An obvious, but all-important, consequence is that syntactic principles in this theory, unlike the "rules" of traditional grammars, cannot be directly sensitive to word order as it is manifested at face value in linguistic expressions.

2. There are essential linguistic entities that have no physical manifestation (called by Chomsky "empty categories") but that are nonetheless present to the mind of the speaker and the hearer and can have manifest effects on the audible and visible elements. (Chomsky's first instances—in hindsight—were of the following kind: The sentence *He saw the man standing at the bar* somehow literally contains the declarative sentence *The man was standing at the bar,* and English speakers all intuitively understand that it does. Therefore, the words *the man was* are mentally present, though they have no physical—that is, phonological—manifestation. No traditional grammar ever paid attention to such facts.)

3. When one or more elements are moved from one place to another, a silent residue (e.g., a "trace," or a "chain" of such traces) is left behind. This is a crucial ingredient of the theory.

4. These silent elements (or chains thereof) cannot occur just anywhere in a sentence, nor are they linked arbitrarily to other manifest or silent elements. Systematic relations, expressed by specific principles, concerning the nature and proper management of silent elements, and the obligatory links within each chain, constitute an essential component of syntax, one that applies uniformly to all languages. It is not at all obvious why the basic design of natural languages should display such elegance and compactness.

This dialogue makes it clear that such central ideas of generative grammar, once suitably reinterpreted and generalized, are correct, revolutionary, and immensely productive for the scientific understanding of linguistic phenomena. Old and new critiques notwithstanding, they are in fact some of the central notions out of which, little by little, the Minimalist Program has arisen.

Nothing ensures that there will not be further important changes in the theory in the near future. In fact, everything suggests that, happily, there will be. That's how all natural sciences advance and grow. Chomsky revealingly insists that it is to be *hoped* that linguistic theory will change the next time a bright graduate student walks into the office to discuss his or her work. This book is ideally suited to explain *why* these revisions and redirections have been essential to the progress of linguistic theory. It may provoke rethinking of an attitude in some quarters of applied linguistics, that the changes in linguistic theory proper are to be deplored, that it may be a waste of time to "experiment" on the consequences of a theory that is destined to be basically revised in a few years—a troubling attitude that can only lead researchers (as Chomsky has mentioned in class lectures) to confine themselves to working on some peripheral and unimportant, and therefore unchanging, aspect of linguistics, or to remain stuck with hypotheses and predictions that have already proven wrong. Why should applied linguistics be exempt from the toil and trouble of doubts, revisions, and fresh starts? In my opinion, much of the new wave of disillusionment arises from sheer impatience, but impatience is hardly ever a reliable counsel in scientific matters. Many of the deep and fascinating questions (let alone the tentative answers to them) that are at the core of the field these days, and that are presented in this dialogue, would have been simply unthinkable ten or fifteen years ago. This is how progress "happens" to a scientific domain.

8

It is vital to recognize that syntactic objects and principles, as masterfully presented in this dialogue, are basic, not derived. (Chapter 4 outlines an interesting attempt to axiomatize "syntactic objects," further refined in an appendix by Jairo Nunes and Ellen Thompson.) In the eyes of the theoretician, these objects possess the same status as, say, particles and fields in physics, and genes in biology. These entities and principles do not in the least resemble those to be found in other cognitive domains, such as perception, motor control, or reasoning. In this sense, they are language-specific, even though they are universal (i.e., true of all human languages, present or past, actual or possible) and even though Minimalism vastly expands the bounds of "virtual conceptual necessity" (i.e., of what about the basic design of human languages must be as it is because it could not possibly, conceivably, be otherwise). This increased emphasis on "necessity" correspondingly restricts the options for possible varieties of languages and for linguistic explanation. It even restricts the latitude for linguistic description. In fact, trying to dispense with a particular technical apparatus makes the task of description much harder, and success in description yields much deeper explanation. Failure to understand cannot be papered over with technicalities that conceal real problems by way of elaborate nomenclature. Therefore, increased emphasis on necessity does not imply that syntax ceases to be autonomous and that the principles of Universal Grammar can now be deduced from general features of functional design, or from truths of reason alone. These principles in fact do have strong intrinsic plausibility and elegance, but they remain language-specific. They are also level-specific, because phonetics, phonology, and (at the opposite extreme) pragmatics are governed by other principles and countenance other basic entities. This is why it remains crucial to stress that syntax interfaces with sounds and meanings, but has a structure of its own. It is not an interface of some sort. Or rather, it is not an interface of *any* sort. There are computations at the syntactic level that are primary and not constrained by anything that is external to them, but that in turn constrain their realizations into sounds and meanings. This is a difficult, though vital, point, and this dialogue contributes significantly to the field by discussing it as clearly as could possibly be done, given the present state of our knowledge.

It is also important to stress that the Minimalist criteria advanced by the present theory, as well as the principles of Universal Grammar advanced by previous versions of the theory, are in an important sense uncaused. To be more precise, they are caused by human nature, presumably by the structure and functioning of our brain, via a quite long, presently unknown, chain of progressively ascending abstract invariants—but they are still, in the Minimalist framework, uncaused by the invariants characterizing other nonlinguistic components of the mind. The autonomy and the primacy of syntax, *pace* the adaptationists, appear to be amply vindicated. The dialogue argues for this position very convincingly.

Finally, having granted that details will continue to change, let us consider what would remain of the theory even if important aspects of it one day proved to be incorrect, or only very approximately correct. The permanent acquisitions are, in my opinion, clear-cut and decisive. Adopting just for the sake of argument a kind of ultraminimalist attitude on the Minimalist Program, the least that can be said is that a theory *like* this *might* be true. The dialogue will persuade us that it is rational to believe at least this much. Thus, one of the remarkable qualities of this field is that a system of considerable complexity, and clearly central to human life, appears to begin to yield, in part at least, "to something with the feel of scientific inquiry" (in Chomsky's own words). But if the central ideas expounded in this dialogue might be true, then syntax might really be autonomous, underived from other linguistic or generally cognitive levels, unconstrained by use or need, and not "learned" under any standard interpretation of this term. It might, therefore, be internally specified (up to the fixing of parameters). Then any attempt to show that it is *necessary* to explain the nature of language by means of forces and principles that are external to it cannot be right. Reductionist neurobiological assumptions are unwarranted, and it can be safely stated that the meandering evolutionary course that has led our species to possess the initial state of the language faculty that we do possess does not have to be steered by any direct selection. More likely, it is to be charted (as it is for so many other biological

organs and traits) following the lines of elaborate, internally constrained, and largely seren-
dipitous morphogenetic transformations. Making all this very clear is one of the signal
merits of the dialogue. These permanent gains are far from insubstantial, even if one were
to take a very prudent attitude toward particular aspects of the theory. But we need not
be, after all, so damn uptight. Let's rather see what the theory says, and why. Chances are
some aspect is, at least in the main, already correct.

I express my gratitude to Noam Chomsky, James Higginbotham, David Lightfoot, Andrea Moro, Daniel N. Osherson, and Juan Uriagereka for comments and criticism on a previous draft (and for much beyond). I am afraid that I
cannot express on their behalf, the usual waiver of responsibility, because they *are* responsible for much of what I say
here. Fairness dictates, however, that I claim exclusive responsibility for errors, omissions, or unclarities that may have
survived despite their invaluable help (this applies especially to Dan Osherson).

Preface

I find Noam Chomsky's Minimalist Program both healthily old and new at the same time—an homage to a long tradition and a legacy to future generations. Though I may of course be wrong about the future, I find it fair to say that, at the very least, past insights have survived and deserve to be heard. One central motivation in doing the present work was to search for the various sources that sustain Minimalism.

Another was to locate the Minimalist Program within current scientific concerns, particularly in terms of the ongoing debate between neo-Darwinians, and—as Massimo Piattelli-Palmarini calls them—neo-neo-Darwinians. At stake is whether language is an adaptation or an exaptation (a feature whose present function is not causally related to its evolution). The former is the traditional neo-Darwinian position; the latter, instead, views language as the accidental by-product of some unknown, unrelated mutation.

That lively debate is refueled by one of the basic premises of the Minimalist Program: that language is, in some sense, optimal. For the neo-Darwinian this might be good news, if the optimality in question could be shown to be functional. However, linguistic optimality is not functional at all, but only structural; in fact, functionally the linguistic system is definitely suboptimal—support, instead, for the neo-neo-Darwinian.

Of course, then the real question is "What justifies structural elegance?" At this point linguistic research becomes extremely interesting, not just as a branch of sociology, psychology, or biology, but in its own right: it gives us the remarkable opportunity to seriously explore the properties of a complex system, whose intricacies are not obviously reducible to standard evolution.

If only because language is so readily accessible and has been studied for so long, linguistic research should probably be seen as a guiding strategy in understanding complexity in various realms of nature. At the same time, linguistics can benefit from the methods and results of other sciences involved in complexity research. In this book I have tried to illustrate this desire for interdisciplinarity by way of an example that has fascinated such diverse people as Hofstadter, Penrose, Turing, and Chomsky himself (to mention only some recent examples): that features in such disparate domains as plant morphology, skin patterns, virus coats, and many others, should arrange themselves according to a famous series discovered in 1202 by a twenty-seven-year-old named Leonardo, the son of Bonacio, Pisan consul to Algeria (hence his nickname Fibonacci). The series is obtained by adding two successive numbers, starting with 0 and 1: 0, 1, 1, 2, 3, 5, 8 . . .

The questions that the example poses are obvious. Perhaps the most troubling ones are "What could possibly be biologically adaptive about this state of affairs?" and "How could such diverse entities as sunflowers, peacocks, and viruses have converged to it?" Complexity theorists thrive on this sort of example because it invites abandoning neo-Darwinian territory. But in fact, it suggests going even beyond the journey undertaken by neo-neo-Darwinians, for whom accidental history is the main factor in evolution. Why should history repeat itself in so many scenarios? And there's more, below and above individuals: for instance, microtubule structures in cells' cytoskeletons and (over time) certain elementary populations both arrange themselves à la Fibonacci. Ultimately, this is not directly inconsistent with either neo- or neo-neo-Darwinian perspectives; but what really accounts for it?

The general complexity approach is of this sort: something in the nature of "dull" reality—be it physical, chemical, or whatever, be it well reduced to known principles or not—is responsible for these transspecies and infra- and supraindividual regularities. I will not anticipate how any of this works, but I emphasize that there's nothing miraculous about it. At any rate, it is at least hard to deny that the Fibonacci phenomenon exists, and demands an explanation.

Chomsky was, in my opinion, justly moved by these patterns, and not only because they pose a problem for traditional biological theories (as D'Arcy Thompson had already noted half a century before), but also because—somewhat surprisingly—they share certain remarkable properties with the linguistic system, at least according to the Minimalist Program. I try to build this argument here and reflect on what it means.

Perhaps I should clarify what I do not think it means. The fact that certain very abstract properties are, as it were, shared by human minds and the form of sunflowers doesn't mean that our minds don't have much of a specific structure. At the level of abstraction I'm considering, even the double helix of DNA shares with the sunflower the abstract properties I have in mind for language. In particular, both structures can be shown to be *unboundedly discrete, economically underspecified,* and *morphologically optimal.* That is a notable fact, but it does not make us seek explanations for the structure of DNA in the properties of flowers.

This point cannot be sufficiently emphasized. The complexity literature occasionally reveals claims not far removed from the wild comparison I've just made. I want to believe that this is because most theorists are not fully familiar with linguistic structure. (I take the opportunity to welcome them to the enterprise through this book.) Of course, I also know that other theorists are intentionally making such wild connections; some of them are even linguists! My own position—like the Minimalist perspective—is one of (roughly Fodorian) modularity, strict innatism, and traditional Chomskyan naturalism.

Nonetheless, even the strictest syntacticians (and I take myself to be one) cannot help but wonder about the nature of their principles and representations. Such explorations are a third central motivation for this book. In this respect, I believe that Minimalist findings resemble similar discoveries in the natural world. I have even tried to suggest that Fibonacci patterns themselves can be attested in linguistic structures, just as they are in other mental representations touching on aesthetically pleasing (musical, plastic, architectural) structures. All of this, I take it, is interesting—but does not reduce linguistics to physics, or to aesthetic studies for that matter . . .

That said, the question remains what the findings mean for theories concerned with complexity. For the most part this is not my concern, although I can understand and expect that others might want to pursue such questions in the context of evolutionary studies, development, and perhaps other domains. The linguist, however, is justified in stopping about where this book does; in that sense, Minimalism can be seen as an exercise regarding boundaries. Of course, and as usual, these boundaries are to be taken as hypotheses, and (precisely because of that) very seriously.

It should be clear that, to me, these boundaries between linguistic systems and "outside" systems are sharply defined. I entirely agree with the neo-neo-Darwinians, who take the "outside" to be practically inaccessible—in direct ways—to individuals. So this book distances itself greatly from behaviorist, connectionist, or otherwise structuralist perspectives that do not come from *within* the mind. Even so, within the mind is also within reality—a point Chomsky has insisted on over the years—and in that sense we shouldn't be shocked if some of the principles that underlie the mind can (eventually) be unified with the laws of biology or physics. Crucially, though, the mind does not "pick up" the structure from its context—it just is how it is, instead.

I have presented matters in dialogue form; here's how the plot unravels. Chapters 1 and 2 are intended for a general audience. They put Chomskyan linguistics in a certain perspective and are designed to clarify Chomsky's overall views and goals. Chapters 3 and 4 give a reasonably detailed view of the Minimalist Program. I honestly believe that only a few times will the reader need a pencil to reflect on what's discussed. Chapter 5 does approach the demands of specialists. Nonetheless, it is written in such a way that the reader can skip the technical parts and proceed with an intuitive understanding. I invite everyone to read on, if only to reach chapter 6 with some useful, shared presuppositions. It is here that the most far-reaching ideas are discussed, but in order to appreciate that level of abstraction, the journey through previous chapters is advised.

Certain material has been prepared to aid the presentation: various illustrations; summaries that outline each chapter's basic ideas; a list of definitions and principles; a glossary (words boldfaced in the text are defined there); and an appendix that discusses formal matters more carefully than is possible in the main text.

To conclude, I wish to thank some individuals who helped me with the project, which was partially sponsored by NSF grant SBR9601559. The most detailed comments on this book were provided by Noam Chomsky; his generous advice and support simply cannot be adequately recognized. Many other colleagues' help was decisive in different chapters: Stephen Crain, Sam Epstein, Elena Herburger, Richard Kayne, Marcus Kracht, Linda Lombardi, Eduardo Raposo, Georges Rey, and Esther Torrego. I especially appreciated the contributions of Norbert Hornstein, David Lightfoot, and of course my teacher, Howard Lasnik, all of whom read and commented on the whole manuscript. Thanks also to the researchers credited in the notes. Jairo Nunes and Ellen Thompson produced the appendix and glossary and have been a constant help in editing the final piece. Phrase structure "bubbles" emerged from the wizardry of Chuck Goodrich and Dave McNally, at the Advanced Visualization Lab of the University of Maryland; they were able to design a crazy idea that I concocted over lunch with Joel Hoffman. Help from my many assistants has never gone unnoticed: thanks to my readers Ana Berlin, Rachel Crain, Lee Slack, and Viola Miglio (who worked on the Other's language), and to my editorial staff Juan Carlos

Castillo, John Drury, Keiko Muromatsu, and Dave Peugh. Finally, credit is due to Massimo Piattelli-Palmarini, whose very interest in the project is an honor; and to assistant editor Jerry Weinstein, and especially my editor Amy Brand—for patiently believing in this venture. Anne Mark, my copy editor, deserves a very warm, separate mention; she has understood the difficult nature of this book and has engaged in it beyond the call of duty (it has been an invaluable learning experience to work with her).

As Socrates put it, inviting us to converse, "Come then, let us examine our words."

The Linguist Meets the Other

The facts occurred at an uncertain time, in Cambridge. It was a magnificent afternoon when the linguist took a rare break from work. In the early spring, the gray waters of the lazy Charles carried large pieces of ice. Naturally, the river made him think of time.

He suddenly felt the sensation (psychologists relate it to fatigue) that someone else was there. He gazed at the air and thought he saw the other—he sensed his dim, ethereal shadow.

"Afternoon," said the shadow.

Startled, but always the perfect gentleman, the linguist responded. "Pleasure to meet you."

"We haven't met, or have we?" said the voice, which sounded as if coming from another world.

"The name is Such; Such-and-such. I'd shake your hand, but I can't really see you . . ."

In time, one's eyes grow accustomed to seeing in the dark of thought or through the densities of rain, fog, and mystery. So too, the linguist's eyes were literally figuring out the individual who slowly was taking shape. He didn't resemble his voice.

"Whatever I'm called, I can't say that's my name, because I believe I *am* what I'm called."

"And you're not a name . . ."

"I was merely testing you!"

"Oh?" replied the linguist, tickled by the childish joke. Then he admitted, "I too have read some of Lewis Carroll's riddles . . ."

"Good old Charlie, yes . . . For some mysterious reason, I always associated Charlie Dodgson with the river you're seeing . . ."

"Maybe it was their names."

"Ah, the obvious is rarely the true. Besides, I'm not seeing the Charles."

"Another philosophical prank . . . ?"

"Hardly. The river I see . . . I don't know its name. Maybe it is the Lethe—I can't remember."

"So you're not here?!"

"You're not here either . . ."

"Of course, but—"

"I don't mean to confuse you—I'm in Cambridge. And yet the Cambridge I see isn't the one you're in . . ."

"Well, there's a Cambridge in South Africa, another in Australia, a third in Canada, a fourth one in New Zealand, over a dozen in the US . . ."

"Yes, and then there's Cambridge . . ."

A silence punctuated the proud remark. The linguist reflected on the strange circumstance, and remembered having read a similar story once, in his youth; or was it not so long ago? He was very tired, and yet—a tireless conversationalist—he said, perhaps trying to provoke the other, "I hear this sort of phenomenon does occur in the vicinity of rivers. Two points in the space-time continuum connected through a wormhole that cuts the odd corner here and there. Borges described it rather accurately, I think in the early seventies. In his case, he got to visit his very self in the twenties, in Geneva."

"Surely you're joking, Mr. Such-and-such . . ."

"At any rate, physicists like to impress people with this sort of trick."

"Oh, well—it's a story. I like stories."

"Sometimes I wish I could work on those matters."

"Story telling? It's a tough life. I was in that business 'til I lost my memory. At least I think I was . . ."

"No, I mean wormholes and stuff. That sort of thing . . ."

"And what do you do, Mr. Such-and-such?"

And so it was that the two gentlemen began the minimalist dialogue that you are about to hear.

(The) L(inguist): Well . . . It's hard to impress people with what I do, actually. I study the human mind.

(The) O(ther): That *is* impressive . . .

L: It turns out to be quite difficult to study. I've been exploring the old idea that language—human language—is a window onto the human mind.

O: If I may ask, how many languages do you speak?

L: Me? Only one, I'm afraid.

O: Oh.

L: Sorry to disappoint you.

O: You don't. Knowing one language seems quite remarkable to me as it is. In all honesty, I've always been baffled by how many languages there are—not so much because of the diversity itself, but precisely because every human child knows at least one. Knowing Chinese is not the same as knowing English, and that always makes me wonder: in each instance, how is that knowledge obtained? As a matter of fact, children get their language very early, don't they? The little brats can't lift a spoon to their mouth without making a mess, and yet they produce these incredibly elaborate sentences . . . Is learning to speak easier than learning to clean up after oneself? I wonder . . .

L: I'm glad you ask. Certainly, the fact that children succeed in acquiring a given human language, in a pretty uniform way, at an incredibly fast pace, and with hardly any exposure to language, is one of the most serious matters that a scientific study of language has to address. To my mind, in fact, this is the central question, the "logical problem of language acquisition."

O: And what's the answer?

1.1 The Mystery of Language Acquisition
(which takes some notice of facts that people actually know, but do not know they know)

L: If you really want to know, you have to frame the question right. Let's start with the common view that children learn by instruction from their parents or caretakers, or by imitating them. That whole assumption is misleading in at least two ways. First, you must admit that some parents just don't spend a lot of time in the presence of their children.

——————————— even devoted caretakers are not geniuses—or linguists

O: That's true. It's a standard practice in many cultures not to address infants until they're seven or so, and they're considered "little adults."

L: By that time, though, they already speak like adults—so how did they acquire this knowledge? Teaching couldn't have anything to do with it.

Second, the fact that your mother had the patience to spend a lot of time with you, thinking that she was actually teaching you English, doesn't mean that she succeeded.

O: I beg your pardon?!

L: Oh, I meant "you" generically . . .

O: Still!

L: I have to stand by what I've said, really. To prove it, let's just review at random one of the sorts of arguments you can easily read about in the popular literature on linguistics. Do you think your mother might have thought about, say, what a *wh*-word is?

O: A what?

L: Precisely that! A question word, like *who, what, when,* or *why*—they all come with a *wh*-feature.

O: Why, most certainly! It's just elementary what those are!

L: And would you also say that she had thought about how the rule for question formation works in English?

O: She is a very witty one. As a matter of fact, I don't remember her teaching me that in English one places a word like *what* at the beginning of a sentence to ask, for example, *what are you driving at?*, but I wouldn't be startled if she had . . . And besides, one can't help but encounter this pattern when one listens to English questions. That must be the key.

L: So let's apply your explicit rule. You think that asking a question in English basically implies targeting some kind of sentence, like *you are talking to someone,* and then substituting *who* for *someone,* and then moving that to the beginning, to give *who are you talking to?* [see fig. 1.1].

O: I would think so, yes. And when I comprehend that, I can communicate, which presumably means I get positively reinforced by the community around me: I ask people this, that, or the other, and they answer back . . .

L: I see. So, consider targeting a sentence like *you are thinking that you are talking to someone.* What question do you get out of that?

—————————— *digression on the unbounded nature of linguistic structures*

O: I would just do what you said: substitute *who* for *someone,* and move it. That way I'd obtain *who are you thinking that you are talking to?* And . . . I say, look! The rule is as simple as it was before, although here it applies to a more elaborate structure: that is, the sentence *you are talking to someone* is embedded inside the sentence *you are thinking that.* Do you see? The embedding itself demonstrates that linguistic structures are *recursive,* as the mathematicians like to say. Speakers can apply the embedding process recursively, to structures of arbitrary complexity: *you are saying that you are thinking that you are talking to someone,* et cetera, et cetera. (And by the way, those also yield perfect results according to my question rule; to wit: *who are you saying that you are thinking that you are talking to?*) Needless to say, humans can't go on ad infinitum, because they get weary or they die, but as a matter of principle, they could utter a sentence or ask a question which is as long as they could possibly want. Which means that—abstracting away from inconsequential details about

Figure 1.1

Linguists base most of their analyses on data of the following sort:

(i)   you are talking to *someone*
(ii)   you are talking to *who*
(iii)   *who* are you talking to ____?

A grammatical sentence (of English, for instance) such as (iii) is analyzed as involving some sort of displacement: the element *who* is, in some sense to be made precise, the "logical object" of this expression, even though it is pronounced at the beginning of the clause. Situations of this sort are usually said to involve "movement," to be discussed throughout this book. Observe, also, that (i) and (ii) are hypothetical structures that are taken to be related to (iii). (For expository purposes, auxiliary fronting will be ignored here and in the text; it is discussed in figure 1.5.) The goal is to reduce the complex token in (iii) to something more elementary, of the sort in (ii) or even (i). This theoretical move is not unlike that which a physicist makes when trying to understand the present state of the universe from more elementary states of the early universe.

Figure 1.2

The first important point being made in this discussion is that linguistic expressions can be arbitrarily long, which entails that an infinite number of such expressions exist: to see that the process can go on forever, simply keep replacing the dots in (i)–(iii) with further expressions of the form *you are VERB-ing that.* The implied infinitude would be an important property of any system, but it is even more significant within an apparatus (knowledge of language) that must fit within the confines of the human mind, which is clearly finite.

(i)   you are saying that
              you are thinking that
                        ...
              you are talking to *someone*

(ii)   you are saying that
              you are thinking that
                        ...
              you are talking to *who*

(iii)   *who* are you saying that
              you are thinking that
                        ...
              you are talking to ____?

Note also that, despite the complexity of the examples, the rule implied in figure 1.1, whereby *who* is moved, is still operative (iii). As can easily be verified, further embedding of these expressions in similar ones has no effect on the workings of this general rule.

time, and human life, and matters of that ilk—there's no less than an *infinite* number of questions they can ask [see fig. 1.2]!

L: Thanks for the tip.

O: This is portentous, though, and it shows that language learning cannot be mere imitation. Were I—a language learner—to imitate you, I would say, "Thanks for the tip," or "Language is a window onto the human mind." But if I want to come up with any number of sentences of my own, then I need a way to go beyond the basic patterns I have discovered, to realise, for example, that I can embed a sentence within another sentence, as long as I wish.

L: So, according to you, first you imitate and next you generalize, and finally the cooperative community reinforces you in your guesses by way of communicating back and forth with you [1].

O: That's the least one would have to say . . .

_____   **how does one know what is impossible?**

L: So let's follow the argument where it leads. Let's take a trivial sentence, say, *you are talking to a man whom you just asked something.* Now target *something,* and apply your rule.

O: I told you. In this instance, we replace *something* with *what,* because *what* is the question word that we use for things, and *something* denotes a thing. And we get *what are you talking to a man whom you just asked?* Oops! Sorry. We get . . . we should get, well . . . *whom you just asked what are you talking to a man?* Blast it! That's not it either. Let me have another go. *What whom you just asked are you talking to a man?***!!

L: You said something?

O: No sir, I did not! I used a couple of asterisks and exclamation marks in place of a four-letter obscenity. I suppose I cannot ask the question you asked me to ask.

L: But I've imitated and then generalized. I thought . . .

O: Yes, yes: you beat the Devil. My rule doesn't work for this case; clearly it's an exception [see fig. 1.3].

L: But speakers *know* that it's an exception! They know that the sentence *what are you talking to a man whom you just asked?* plainly isn't part of English.

O: I suppose I'd have to accept that this is true.

L: But this is clearly where your imitation and generalization lead you. First, you find a pattern (move the question word, and so on). Next, you generalize it, and that gives you some grammatical questions. The problem is that it also gives you some ungrammatical questions—that is, some questions you know are bad. And how do you know that?

O: But you cannot ask that question in English—it simply doesn't make sense!

L: That judgment is too hasty. The question makes perfect sense, as your explanation of what you were doing explicitly indicated: you target a basic structure such as *you are talking to a man whom you just asked something,* and ask about what that something is. As it turns out, there's indeed a simple way of asking about this something, in perfect English: *what is the question such that you are talking to a man whom you just asked that very question?* Answer: "That question is, 'Do I know more than I am taught?'"

O: That doesn't follow my rule!

L: Oh, I know that. But you told me you couldn't ask that question in English—whereas in fact you can. What you can't do is use the explicit rule you stated to ask the sensible question I'm describing [see (iv) of fig. 1.3]. And then I ask: what's your mother going to tell you about the impossibility of using the standard rule of question formation in this particular instance?

O: Yes, well . . . She'll tell me that . . . the standard rule of question formation doesn't apply . . . well, across a relative clause. Needless to say, my mother is some kind of genius. It might be too much to expect that each child has a genius in the house to teach him language.

Figure 1.3

The second important point raised by this discussion can be illustrated with the examples below. Figure 1.2 shows that the sort of rule implied in figure 1.1 (movement of *who*) is really systematic. Nonetheless, not just any conceivable operation involving the movement of a *wh*-element is factually possible:

(i)   you are talking to a man
            whom you just asked *something*

(ii)   you are talking to a man
            whom you just asked *what*

(iii) *what* are you talking to a man
            whom you just asked ____?

What has moved out of the relative clause *whom you just asked (what)*. Needless to say, this relative clause is perfectly appropriate, and so is its association to the noun phrase *a man* (as (i) shows). Indeed, (iv) is a way of asking the question that (iii) is (unsuccessfully) attempting to convey:

(iv) what is the question such that you are talking to a man whom you just asked that question?

(iv) shows that (iii) cannot be dismissed as nonsensical. Rather, it seems that something is wrong with its linguistic form, whatever that might be. The fact that the unacceptability of (iii) does not follow from logic is very important, because native speakers know that it is impossible, but they cannot deduce this fact from mere reasoning. Something else is responsible for the status of (iii), and this is what linguists are trying to find out. Sentences like (iii) are described as "ungrammatical" and are usually marked with an asterisk or a question mark (depending on the degree of deviance that speakers assign to them; the question mark indicates a lesser degree of deviance than the asterisk).

Untitled. (Javier Uriagereka)

Figure 1.4

a. The following dialogue, reported by Cazden (1972), is a typical instance of child-adult interactions in which linguistic corrections are involved:

Child: My teacher holded the baby rabbits and we patted them.
Adult: Did you say your teacher held the baby rabbits?
Child: Yes.
Adult: What did you say she did?
Child: She holded the baby rabbits and we patted them.
Adult: Did you say she held them tightly?
Child: No, she holded them loosely.

When corrections are more direct, the results are often worse:

Child: Want other one spoon, Daddy.
Adult: You mean, you want THE OTHER SPOON.
Child: Yes, I want other one spoon, please, Daddy.
Adult: Can you say "the other spoon"?
Child: Other . . . one . . . spoon.
Adult: Say . . . "other."
Child: Other.
Adult: "Spoon."
Child: Spoon.
Adult: "Other . . . Spoon."
Child: Other . . . spoon. Now give me other one spoon?

(This dialogue is attributed by Pinker (1994, 281) to the psycholinguist Martin Braine and one of his daughters.)

b. Parents do not generally correct their children's grammatical mistakes, as the following dialogue illustrates (from Marcus et al. 1992):

Adult: Where is that big piece of paper I gave you yesterday?
Child: Remember? I writed on it.
Adult: Oh, that's right, don't you have any paper down here, buddy?

L: I won't comment on that. I'll only tell you what's been determined from real, carefully recorded conversations between normal parents and normal children. Plainly, children don't even understand the point of corrections [see fig. 1.4a]. And as for parents, they rarely challenge the grammatical mistakes their children make that they actually catch. What they do usually correct are violations of truth or propriety—not violations of **grammar.** This clearly makes things even worse from the point of view of instruction: The parent positively reinforces a sentence which, though truthful, may be ill formed according to the parent's grammar. Conversely, the parent "punishes" a sentence which may be perfect grammatically, even if it isn't truthful [see fig. 1.4b].

O: In actual fact, you're telling me that a model for learning language based on corrections by adults is virtually hopeless.

L: Exactly. And the difficulty is only compounded by a sociological fact that's patent in most societies: the enormous variety of input data for language acquisition. Just imagine kids growing up in preconquest California or in West Africa today. The community is linguistically diverse, and the parent (or, more generally, the sort of person that would be apt to engage in linguistic corrections) may not speak the same dialect as the child. In reality, the dialect children acquire is typically the one they hear on the street and on the playground, and not so much the one they hear at home. This is why most linguists assume something commonsensical, really: that children acquire a language on the basis of **positive data** from the environment, and not through corrections (that is, **direct negative data**) from instructors or responsible adults.

———————————————— imagine a LAD (language acquisition device)

O: In all honesty, sir, I do see everything you're saying. But I still have a real difficulty understanding how the rules of a language can be learnt, if my little theory is wrong. Try this thought experiment, if you will. Imagine an intelligent demon which is attempting to learn human language without any previous knowledge of this system.

L: Let's. But instead of using demons (who may pull miracles), let's assume a real extraterrestrial, or a mechanical, computational device, which we may call a "language acquisition device."

O: LAD for short—I like that! The key to my small experiment is that the LAD I am hypothesising only has the ability to imitate and generalise. Suppose it has processed six hundred and sixty-five sentences in which a question within a relative clause never appears. Can it conclude that this combination is unsuitable? Certainly not: the next sentence may contain precisely that sort of structure. After all, the LAD might never have encountered the sentences you've uttered today, and yet (if we want it to be modelling a complete knowledge of what we may call English), it must, as a matter of principle, be able to distinguish your perfectly adequate sentences from the perfectly inadequate (excuse my language) *what are you talking to a man whom you just asked?* That is to say, not having found an expression doesn't mean that this expression isn't possible in a given language, particularly because the pool of expressions is infinite. Now, how does the LAD know what counts as part of a language?

L: In fact, that's exactly where the *logical* problem of language acquisition lies. Given that the stimuli are so very poor (fragmented or even degenerate positive data presented in a random fashion, and no direct negative data), how can they result in such a complex behavior [2]?

O: Spot on, thank you. So?

L: I know of no answer to the question, given the LAD you've hypothesized.

O: Oh, how disappointing . . .

L: On the other hand, we could hypothesize a different LAD; namely, one that's somehow preprogrammed to know what's in a language—one that knows more than what you've implied, in terms of imitation and generalization.

O: A LAD that already knows what a relative clause is? Isn't that part of what it has to acquire?!

L: Maybe the LAD doesn't have to acquire that. Again, how would you acquire knowledge about relative clauses?

O: I don't know—you're the linguist!

The child in the dialogue gets positively reinforced by the adult, despite using a form that is incorrect in the adult grammar. In contrast, children of all times and cultures have experienced dialogues like this one (personal record of the author):

Child: Eat shit!
Adult: Go to your room.

Lies trigger a similar (if generally less aggressive) response, even if uttered in perfect English.

L: Up to now, linguists of my acquaintance haven't been able to provide an answer.

O: Well, do excuse my passion, but assuming knowledge which is prior to existence would commit us to the sorts of fantasies that Plato devised, about remembering long-forgotten spiritual information which is prior to material embodiment.

—————————————————— if Plato had only known about genes . . .

L: Essentially, I think Plato was right, if you replace the bit about "spiritual information" with something like "genetic information." Livers and hearts and eyes and so on are preprogrammed to process all sorts of information, and no one seriously proposes that the ability to deal with that information is something that children (or cubs, say) learn. I hope you're not suggesting that embryos are taught how to grow hair or feathers, how to quack or roar, how to point, and—

O: But all of those are genetic!

L: What makes you think the same isn't true of the basic behavior of human language? Personally, I don't even find it profound to claim that biological endowment is responsible for mental aspects of the natural world, whether these are human speech, or doves' systems of orientation, or bees' dances, or spiders' engineering of webs, or whatever. Why should one even imagine that what looks like the most complex object in the known universe—the human brain—lacks internal structure provided by the **genes?**

O: Needless to say, I've got no problems accepting that, for example, genetic instructions are in large part responsible for the way in which different species see; it would be irrational not to admit that core aspects of vision have accompanied the evolution of human ancestors as a species, and as a genus, and as a phylum, all the way back to millions of years ago. I'm even ready to grant the point for other aspects of human biology and even cognition. For example, I grant you that the notions involved in finding out that one quantity is more or less than another quantity, that one event is before or after another event, that certain causes lead to certain effects, and surely others, must preexist the task of comprehending the world. But this is true even for a variety of animals, who must recognise mate from predator, and sustenance from excrement, who must know that running towards something gets you there in due time, and running away from something else may be excellent in certain situations but certainly not in others. Without basic intuitions about objects, motions, causes, and notions of that ilk, the universe would be a senseless Hell for all the creatures! But relative clauses! My dear sir, you expect me to believe that humans carry innate knowledge about bloody relative clauses?!

———————————————————————————————— **a hopeless LAD**

L: Yes and no. I do expect you to believe that humans are born unconsciously knowing much about what a linguist may call a relative clause. Of course, most humans don't know the name "relative clause," and they wouldn't be able to tell a relative clause from a complement clause—just as most of them don't know the name "retina," or can't tell a retina from a cornea. How do I know that humans have knowledge about relative clauses which is prior to their acquisition of a particular language? Think of the logic behind it. Take the simplest token of what you think you may need to know in order to admit that you know a language like English. For instance, inverting an **auxiliary** verb over a subject to form a question, as in *are you talking about this?* You'll agree that if you don't know this English rule, you don't know something basic about English.

O: Certainly, of course. But the rule here is very simple. I suppose it's something like . . . Well, it can't just be "Front a verb," since **talking you are about this?* won't do at all. It must be something like "Front the auxiliary verb," as you suggested—but this isn't a transparently simple rule. (I can't use the same sorts of . . . subterfuge that you use, since how would a LAD know what an auxiliary verb is? That would pose the same conceptual difficulties I'm trying to avoid!) Therefore, I'd say the rule is much more unassuming: "Front the very first verb." Full stop. A LAD would simply encounter that simple pattern, using basic notions like "first element in a sequence."

L: So now let's test the rule. It obviously works in all the cases we've been discussing today, so that's good. Of course, it runs into trouble when it tries to form a question based on a structure like *you said something*—it would give **said you something?* That was possible in Elizabethan English, but not any more. But I don't want to derail your efforts so easily; so suppose this is a quirk of Modern English,

Figure 1.5

What is being explored is not so much the fact that certain examples being discussed are ungrammatical, but how this sort of pattern is to be described in linguistic terms. Decisions about what are possible linguistic rules carry not just a descriptive burden (the rules should describe the facts); more important, they have implications for the kind of theory of mind that needs to be assumed. For instance, on the basis of simple-minded cases, one may claim that the rule that fronts verbs in English questions is "Move the first verb." This is a very simple rule that uses presumably basic notions, such as "first in a sequence." However, "Move the first verb" yields the wrong results for (i), a straightforward sentence of English (see (ii)); instead, the proper question is (iii):

(i)   the man [who I am seeing] is asking something now

(ii)   *am the man [who I ____ seeing] is asking something now?

(iii)   is the man [who I am seeing] ____ asking something now?

What went wrong with (ii) is that the rule "Move the first verb" cannot "see into" a relative clause. If the rule were made more complicated, so as to refer to "the first verb after the subject," there would be a simpler way of referring to that verb: the auxiliary (a linguistic notion). The theory of mind implied by a rule like "Move the auxiliary" is very different from (much more intricate than) the one underlying "Move the first verb." A major argument for generative linguistics is based on the fact that no one has been able to show how such an intricate theory could be abstracted away from mere exposure to positive data.

and your rule is just predicting Hamlet's speech. Still, think about asking a question based on a sentence like *the man who I am seeing is asking something now.* Please try it.

O: *Is the man who I am seeing asking something now?* That's a perfect sentence—ah, rats! I haven't applied my rule; my rule actually produces this: **am the man who I seeing is asking something now?*

L: It does, doesn't it? You just fronted the first verb in the sentence and the result is terrible. Unfortunately, it was terrible in Elizabethan English, too [see fig. 1.5].

O: Right you are, so I must know that the first verb in this sentence is inside a . . . well, a relative clause, and this verb can't be the one to front.

L: . . .

O: But that only shows that the rules of language are more complex than, well, the simple patterns that even clever fellows can deduce on first try!

L: Oh, don't mind me—try as many times as you'd like. I've tried a few times myself, and I know others who've tried, too. So far we've reached the same conclusion as you: rules like auxiliary fronting are sensitive to the structural properties of the sentences where they operate. In plain English: you can't ignore a relative clause when doing auxiliary inversion. If the LAD didn't assume this **structural conservation** hypothesis about language acquisition, and furthermore, if the LAD didn't already know much of the structural makeup of what it's trying to acquire (realizing, say, that when something that we're calling a relative clause is involved, the auxiliary that fronts can't come from it), it's impossible to see how this LAD could acquire the simplest facts about English. And let me tell you: real children never make mistakes like the ones we've talked about. No child will ever just front the first verb in a sentence when asking a question, and end up with the word salad you got out of a relative clause. You can take that as a fact [3].

O: I believe you.

L: Don't get me wrong, though. I'm not saying that the child must necessarily know what a relative clause is, specifically. The sorts of structural patterns the child comes equipped with may be more abstract than that. But that's an analytic problem of finding out exactly what linguistic structures the human mind encodes prior to experience—how to preprogram a realistic LAD. The basic scientific and philosophical point stays the same, though: human beings are equipped with specifically linguistic knowledge as a matter of natural law. The linguist's task is, precisely, to find out the details of that knowledge.

O: . . .

L: Incidentally, this claim should hardly be surprising, given what we know about the universe. You seem ready to accept the innateness of, say, inborn fears (for instance, about snakes or darkness), or the desire to court and mate in certain ways, or more generally the means that all species have for figuring out the universe. And yet you want to place human language in a different sphere because it deals with structures like relative clauses? A chicken embryo in effect knows how to become a chicken—given its genetic code— and yet you don't want a human embryo to know how to become a person, in large part by acquiring a human language [4]?

O: I shall concede the point, for two reasons. Firstly, because in the sense of "know" that you are using, I would also concede that a tree "knows" that it is some kind of fractal structure [5]. That is to say, "know *x*" here has the sense of "is endowed with the (potential for) structural property *x*." But secondly, conceding the point doesn't affect my initial worry. The real issue is still one that, in some form, troubled Locke: If knowledge of something like language is, in some sense, instinctive or innate, how is it possible for small children to ignore it for a while (until they speak)? A more sophisticated version of the question would be this: If language is innate, how can children end up speaking *different* languages? I presume it is because children wait for a while that they end up picking a language spoken in their environment. Had they not waited thus, they would have come out of their mothers' wombs speaking the same language, without paying any attention to their environments—any more than children pay much attention to their surroundings when crawling or walking, seeing or digesting. All the behaviours involved in these phenomena appear to be largely identical across the species, as are crying, laughing, or even pointing a finger. I have no problems granting you both universality and even early emergence—two reasonable traits of innateness. However, I must wonder: are universality and very early emergence really what one sees in language?

1.2 The Mystery of Language Variation
(wherein the role of the environment is first examined, and the reader is first treated to very complex systems)

L: Yes, in large part that's exactly what one does see. But of course, there have to be aspects of human language that come from the environment; it's so obvious that it's almost a truism. In fact, it's utterly clear that all species have general properties that aren't genetically determined.

_____ genes and the environment

O: I'm certainly ready to grant you that, but it doesn't at all settle the question of why there are so many different languages. That is to say, surely some aspects of vision aren't genetically coded. But all humans appear to see the same way, however that is to be explained. Language is different, though, isn't it? I find this especially puzzling because, in stable environments, evolution alone favours a tendency for a learnt behaviour to become innate [6]. (An innate ability is of course safer for a creature to have than a learnt behaviour that depends on a fundamental experience, which may be wanting.) If so, why didn't linguistic options become fixed instructions for the species as a whole? The fact that they did not immediately suggests that genes are not involved in the linguistic process at all.

L: No; it shows that you're thinking about the problem the wrong way. In fact, learning a behavior has nothing to do with the core acquisition of language. Humans couldn't have fixed a learned behavior as innate, since there's no such learned behavior to fix, to start with. Learning is basically irrelevant.

O: ??!!

L: Let me put it this way: although you would normally say that an athlete learns how to throw a javelin, you wouldn't generally say that she learns how to grow her biceps. Language acquisition is a process more like biceps growing than javelin throwing. In fact, it's probably even more basic than biceps growing (which can happen after puberty)—say, along the lines of arm growing (which of course happens between ontogenesis and puberty) [7].

O: Hold on; now you're talking again about those aspects of language that you claim are innate, the presumably invariant ones . . .

L: No, no; in fact I'm talking about those aspects of the process that aren't there to start with—the clearly variable ones that seem to trouble you the most. I'm nonetheless claiming that they don't involve learning, any more than growing an arm does. The point is: there just isn't a one-to-one mapping between genes and characteristics, such as body parts, say [8]. The fact that genes contain just a basic program of instructions to specify, for instance, a process of cellular structuring is even more obvious for the trillions of neural connections that a baby brain brings to birth, which couldn't all be coded in the few thousand genes that correspond to the brain within the human genome. But a fetus is the product of both genes and early environment, which in the case of humans is stable for about nine months. I'm telling you this because the open program of language (the set of linguistic options that aren't innately specified and have to be fixed through environmental stimuli) can be thought of precisely in this light: it's a plastic, underspecified system [9].

O: Yes, I follow you there. It's an interesting thought, but it still doesn't solve my problem. Even if I were to agree that the "**triggering information**" for language to "grow" in this sense is in the blood or the amniotic fluid of the mother, or the first nourishment the child receives, how would this yield different languages? Surely you're not saying that all speakers of English come from genetically similar mothers, and so do all speakers of Chinese, and so forth. A child born to a Chinese mother can grow up to speak perfect English. Similarly, a child needn't be fed sushi to acquire Japanese!

L: Certainly. Which just tells you the obvious: triggering input for language isn't tied to a mother, or food.

O: What kind of input are you talking about, then?

L: Naturally, the input we want for language acquisition is linguistic data of some sort, before and after birth. Why shouldn't linguistic data count as input to fix biological creatures, as much as, say, light or sound does?

O: Hold on—before birth?!

L: Yes, children start hearing in utero, and certain very general information input—the sound of a particular voice, or even intonation patterns that allow the infant to separate speech from nonspeech—starts right there. And the process continues immediately after birth. Experimenters have in fact shown that within days infants can distinguish their mother's language (spoken by someone else) from another language [10].

O: Interesting . . . Yes, of course I grant you that birth itself isn't biologically central—although environmentally, it clearly is.

_____ **linguistic variation has little to do with learning**

L: From the perspective I'm taking, the existence of **linguistic variation** has nothing to do with learning—it's much more like variation in growing. Of course, that implies that the growing path in language isn't fully predetermined—but surely this isn't a unique situation. Small perturbations in the environment of a seaweed egg (due to an electrical current, or a sun ray) stimulate the appearance of the main axis for the cell [11]. Or take fish. Bonellia males are microorganisms that are parasitic on walnut-sized females. If a male doesn't manage to attach to a female, he himself becomes a free-living female. Researchers have found dozens of similar cases [12]. More to the point, perhaps, situations like this are very common in behavioral terms. Lots of animals have instinctive behaviors that crucially depend on environmental input—a good example is the white-crowned sparrow, which doesn't develop its territorial song unless it hears another sparrow sing it [13]. Some cases are especially interesting because they show that if the bird isn't exposed to the triggering experience during a **critical period,** later exposure is useless.

O: I could hardly disagree. It's absolutely clear, for example, that cats need visual experience to develop the neural structure of vision.

L: So the point is: to talk about learning in these behavioral instances would be like saying that a bonellia larva learns how to become a male, or a cat learns how to see.

O: Ah, but that's different. You see, nature is clever enough not to programme the shape of an organism into its genetic code, if the laws of physics or chemistry produce it anyway! Everyone agrees that bones needn't be programmed to be smaller than a skyscraper—simply because the cyclopean beings that would host such bulky structures would collapse under their very weight . . . Or think of the two distinct phases in the aquatic/aerial behaviour of the common salmon. The first phase, the impulse to jump out of a creek, is programmed into the fish's genes. But the second stage, its falling back to water, is a consequence of gravity [14]. Nature needn't specify that in the genes!

L: Physical laws certainly set up a channel for evolution to proceed. The shape of possible protein structures, for instance, is partly determined by how well aminoacids fit together: oil-loving ones cluster in the middle of the protein structure, while water-loving ones move to the surface [15].

O: Definitely yes. And the laws of physics determine the wiring of a brain; as a matter of fact, basically the same laws operate on optimising river junctions, and on electrical discharge patterns [16].

L: But we really don't know enough about genetics to determine how much in sync it is with physics or chemistry. Is there no natural behavior which is both determined by physics and (perhaps partly) coded in the genes? I don't know that we can answer that question [17]. More importantly, what we do know about development indicates that, for some reason, it sometimes involves diverse and rather plastic patterns, produced through very dynamic regulatory mechanisms that involve environmental information. In fact, organisms are apparently programmed to receive, record, and transmit unfolding developmental information, which may affect the ultimate shape of a **phenotype** [18]. I don't think we have any conclusive evidence to establish that this is merely in response to the overall environmental pressure of physics or chemistry at large. To begin with, physical laws are just too poorly understood to yield results which are usable in theories of evolution or development beyond fairly anecdotal or very general and speculative instances.

O: But ultimately everything is physics.

L: If you mean that in a terminological sense: what we understand is Physics. Otherwise, ultimately everything is what it is . . .

O: Yes, certainly . . .

Figure 1.6

[The following ideas, as well as the related ones in figures 1.8 and 1.21, can be found in any college biology textbook. Shapiro 1991 is very accessible, as is Burnie 1994.]

Mendel's experiments concerning sexual reproduction and the factors of heredity were carried out with garden-variety peas. The classical experiment involved artificial cross-pollination of flowers corresponding to plants that were uniform with respect to a specific characteristic, such as flower color. For instance, cross-pollination of purple and white flowers resulted in a first generation of plants with basically homogeneously purple flowers. Mendel let the second generation of offspring pollinate themselves and (with a bit of idealization on his part, as is now known) found the striking result that one-fourth of the offspring of purple parents were in fact white. He found similar results with other characteristics as well. A second striking result was that each factor (e.g., flower color and pea skin texture) exhibited the 3:1 ratio independently. Thus, all combinations of flower color and skin texture were found to be possible. Mendel summarized his results as abstract laws about heredity:

Law of segregation
Under parallel breeding conditions, the second generation yields an approximate 3:1 ratio of dominant characteristics to recessive characteristics.

Law of independent assortment
Factors segregate independently of one another, and thus all possible combinations arise.

This was the first scientific statement about the fact that certain characteristics inherited from two parents do not simply blend, and may reappear in later generations after having disappeared in earlier ones. This is possible because a given characteristic, in Mendel's view, is determined by two separate factors, one from each parent. In individuals that inherit one dominant factor and one recessive factor, the former masks the latter and manifests itself physically, but in individuals that inherit two recessive factors, the recessive factor manifests itself.

Mendel's work, published in 1865, was not fully appreciated until the twentieth century. Each of his "factors" is now known as an allele, one of two or more forms of the same gene. Most cells have one set of chromosomes from each parent, carrying alleles for a particular gene in identical positions on matching chromosomes. The same phenotypic characteristic may arise from different combinations of alleles; for instance, purple pea flowers involve a dominant allele for this color, but a given phenotype may result from a genotype with two dominant alleles, or from a genotype with two dissimilar alleles, one dominant and one recessive. Although genotypic differences do not necessarily entail phenotypic ones, the former will affect successive generations. This enhances the chance of transmitting recessive alleles; if two of these are inherited, one from each parent, the result may be an individual whose phenotype does not exhibit the dominant characteristic. Mendel's law of segregation is a subcase of this general situation. Since different alleles can be on different chromosomes, they assort separately in cell division, thus predicting Mendel's law of independent assortment.

---

digression about unification in the sciences

L: . . . and whether we succeed in unifying all the sciences tells us more about our limitations as human scientists than it does about reality and how it is shaped [19]. For instance, you have a science (standard biology) worried about essentially self-reproducing regions of physics which engage in evolution, and which make use of metabolism until they cease to exist. These properties raise an array of questions about the general form of the universe that standard physics hasn't been very successful, or perhaps even very interested so far, in dealing with. So then you expect that the science of biology is unified with the science of (standard) physics, and you hope that the principles of biology (whatever those turn out to be) and the principles of physics meaningfully relate. That would give you the sort of Physics that you're looking for, where a deeper understanding is reached. But if what you have in mind is a *reduction* of biology to physics, I think that's not something one can immediately grant.

O: But a smashing example of a real reduction has taken place in classical genetics. When Mendel made his claims about genetic regularities, they were purely abstract [see fig. 1.6]. Later on, chromosomes were found to embody genes, and in the last half century the embodiment has gone down to the DNA level.

L: That's a rare and partly misleading instance. First, the unification was to a large extent possible because Linus Pauling had shown how to unify chemistry with a broadly amended physics—so the more basic theory was ultimately extended, and not the other way around [20]. Second, it's really up for grabs whether Mendelian genetics is all there is to DNA evolution [see sec. 1.4]. In any case, extensions are far more common than reductions. Take for instance the way electromagnetism was related to the motion of particles. The former couldn't be reduced to the latter, so the theory of particle motion had to be extended. At the same time, early (contemporary) attempts at determining the structure of the atom were influenced by the periodic table (an explicit theory of the chemical elements). For instance, Thomson's influential model (the basis for Rutherford's) involved a set of circulating rings of electrons with a distributed positive charge filling the volume of the atom. The periodic table was taken to be derived from a restriction limiting the number of electrons involved: atoms of a given period in the table were all thought to have the same number of electrons in their outer ring, while differing in the number of electrons in their inner rings [21]. This is an extension of physical models to chemical ones, and not a reduction of any obvious sort (though a unification is indeed implied). At any rate, I don't see why a unification between physics and biology couldn't be possible; but it needn't be a reduction. It may be an extension, or it may go both ways.

--- *the emergence of order*

O: Let me tell you: these are old problems. One of the key issues in natural philosophy has always been the **emergence** of order from the irregular states of matter—the Greeks spent centuries wrestling with this beast. Until quite recently, the emergence of organic forms was taken to be basically miraculous, with morphogenesis a stubborn counterexample against a reduction of biology to physics. You know the old conundrum, I'm sure: in a universe that tends to inevitable disorder (in accordance with the second law of thermodynamics), why should life emerge as an ordering process [see fig. 1.7]?

L: In my view that question isn't totally well framed [22]. Thermodynamics works well in closed systems in thermal equilibrium.

O: True, true; therein one of the classic ways out: if life is an open system, subject to all sorts of outside influences, then the second law (as classically stated) doesn't really apply to it. The other way out is to "go macroscopic," as it were: life is but a transient state of a macrosystem which is indeed closed. In those terms, the normal state of the macrosystem is entropic; ultimately, the possibility for life within it will indeed disappear. Either way, life is taken to be an improbable event. It is either some kind of basically unpredictable oddity, or else an ultimately hopeless struggle for entropy, conveniently possible on planet Earth—a region of strongly changing entropy . . .

L: In a word, life is at the edge of this universe—which physics allows. Of course, this doesn't tell us anything about what life is, only that it's possible.

O: That's precisely what I'm driving at. Is it all a statistical miracle? How did all the various life forms emerge, even if life itself was totally accidental [23]?

Figure 1.7

[For a presentation of the following ideas, see Spielberg and Anderson 1987; for Boltzmann's proposals, see Meinzer 1994.]

The first law of thermodynamics is simply a statement about the conservation of energy. The second law can be thought of as a global statement about closed systems, asserting that there is no way to systematically reverse the flow of heat from higher to lower temperatures. The relevance of this law for physical evolution was recognized by Rudolph Clausius in the mid-1800s. It was he who introduced the concept of the entropy change of a system, which is traditionally defined as the heat addition to the system divided by its absolute temperature. The second law in effect demands that the rate at which entropy is produced inside a system is not negative, which basically means that natural processes cost energy. Simply put, a system that has reached thermodynamic equilibrium will inevitably tend to a state of lesser structural order and eventually will decay.

How can life emerge within those parameters? An answer was given by Ludwig Boltzmann, in his attempt to reduce biological evolution to the chemistry and thermodynamics of the late nineteenth century. It is important to emphasize that the classical laws of thermodynamics describe idealized closed system, whereas living systems are open, in constant exchange with their environment (living beings eat, breathe, excrete, etc.); in fact, if a living system is isolated, sooner or later it dies. To handle open systems, the second law must be amended to be sensitive to the environment. We may consider a metasystem (let us call it a "universe"), comprising the open system under discussion and the context where it exists. Then, where S is entropy:

(i) $S_{universe} = S_{system} + S_{context} \geq 0$

However, a useful formulation of the second law for open systems must eliminate any (impractical) reference to the system's context:

(ii) $T\Delta S_s - \Delta U_s - p\Delta V_s \geq 0$

(ii) is a function of the system's entropy (S) times the absolute temperature (which is common to system and context); the system's internal energy; and the system's volume times the pressure (which is also common to system and context). The point is that all these variables are system variables, whereas the contextual variables are eliminated (in part as a consequence of the first law of thermodynamics, which allows the context's heat to be determined from the system's heat). Basically, the second law for open systems (which is usually expressed in a more concise format than (ii)) entails that the system's entropy can indeed diminish so long as the context's, in turn, increases proportionately. This reasoning was used by Boltzmann to show how life is physically possible. The improbable state of affairs just described may arise in regions with strongly changing entropy; for instance, because of the sun's high temperature, Earth is a good spot to obtain energy with relatively low entropy. From this perspective, life may be thought of as a search for entropy. It is important to realize, however, that the present account says nothing about the complex internal structuring that is apparent in different living systems: it is allowed by (ii), but not explained by it.

Four of Darwin's finches. (From Darwin, *The voyage of the Beagle*)

Figure 1.8

[The ideas outlined here can be found, for instance, in Bruno 1987 or Goodwin 1994.]

As is well known, in 1831 Charles Darwin set sail as a naturalist aboard HMS *Beagle,* which was on a cartographic mission around the world. Crucial among his observations in the Pacific was the slight differentiation of species that he found in islands of the Galápagos Archipelago. For example, he studied fourteen different species of finches that did not exist elsewhere and that were very well adapted to the environment they inhabited. This sort of discovery posed a puzzle for the traditional creationist wisdom, which was static in character: each species would have to have been divinely created on each island, and nowhere else. The evolutionist alternative was more dynamic: different species of finches were the descendants of birds that had strayed from the mainland and had then evolved different beaks to better suit the environmental conditions on each island. This approach was more interesting, since it accounted for the structure of living beings in terms of history, instead of God's direct intervention.

Biological speculation had already given rise to the concepts of "adaptation to the environment" and "inheritance of characteristics" from parents to offspring. But even freethinkers of the time had not gone beyond connecting these two concepts, thus assuming the inheritance of characteristics that emerged from environmental pressures. Darwin was not particularly concerned with questioning this sort of explanation for the emergence of species; he was more interested in determining reasons for their extinction. He found an answer in the Malthusian concept of "competition" for limited resources (a population that grows exponentially will eventually outstrip its linearly growing food supply). The key to the survival of a species is how well adapted it is to the environment it inhabits; if its members are so well adapted that they manage to pass their characteristics on to their descendants, then those characteristics will persist. This state of affairs is commonly referred to as "natural selection." This key insight of Darwin's was shared by Alfred Russell Wallace, with whom he published the seminal work "On the Tendency of Species to Form Varieties; and on the Perpetuation of Varieties and Species by Natural Selection."

L: These days you have to be careful about even raising that question, or some people will accuse you of being a creationist . . .

O: To tell you the truth, I've been hearing that sort of nonsense for quite a while now. I think the year was 1614 when Walter Raleigh (can't recall whether he was a Sir then) had already concluded that the species found on the American continent hadn't been either directly created right over there (that replication of the creation in Eden was absurdly inelegant) or carried by Noah in his otherwise gargantuan ark (that was absurd, full stop) [24]. Raleigh took these species to evolve on the American soil, having all come from Old World survivors who managed to reach the New Continent. His was one of the first theories of evolution in some proper sense of the word.

L: Well, it was more than anything a theory of adaptation and inheritance.

O: True, since for him organisms were adapted to their environments and they managed to inherit acquired adaptive characteristics. This is a point that reaches all the way up to Lamarck, who was trying to make sense of the sort of diversity that Linnaeus had found [25]. But the ingenious Athanasius Kircher was fond of a rather more specific mechanism of differentiation over a century earlier than Lamarck: the old-time notion of promiscuous copulation. Notorious examples include the ostrich, a crossbreeding of a camel with some kind of bird . . . These were thought up on the basis of the mule, and needless to say, this sort of explanation got into deeper trouble as the morphology of more exotic animals was understood (the platypus was taken to be some kind of hoax!). Eventually, some authors concluded that The Old One had been clumsy enough to create species everywhere on the planet—the heretic line that creationists must still believe . . . Then Darwin came along, to account for extinction in terms of competition for limited resources, thus explaining away structure in terms of adaptive function [see fig. 1.8].

L: I'm certainly ready to ask, though, whether Darwin explained it all. He did provide us with a framework that makes it possible to even ask these questions, but there's a point where Darwinian explanations leave many of us unsatisfied. Of course, the classical skeptical question was formulated well before Darwin made a case for evolution (thus, when things looked considerably more miraculous). For instance, Kant was almost angry at Newton for not having much to say about the structure of a blade of grass. Goethe went further, worrying about simple life processes that defy a traditional materialistic treatment, such as the metamorphosis of a caterpillar [26]. It isn't immediately obvious that classical evolution has something ready-made to say about this, or in general about the various levels of organization and order, aggregation and convergence, and the mere impulse to fall into patterns that we find out there.

O: Now you be careful with those creationists!

L: Oh, life isn't the only issue . . . There are clearly various dimensions of complexity, with life being strangely gapped from standard matter, and mind from standard life, at least. At an even more basic level, obviously clouds of dust are formed, and stars, and galaxies, with elaborate arrangements and regular convergence across systems and scales. At each level, new properties clearly emerge, and ultimately new concepts are needed to describe the laws that hold for that level [27]. But rather than looking at this as a reason to despair, I see it as a time to be optimistic: just as physics moved into new dimensions partly by integrating chemistry, so too it may benefit from biology—or linguistics.

O: Have you ever puzzled over the whirlpools formed in rivers, or the silent forms of crystals . . . ?

L: I'm very busy these days—but as a child I distinctly remember asking about precisely those phenomena. Of course, those systems involve very remarkable **phase transitions**.

--------------------------------- *phase transitions can be conservative or dissipative*

O: Rather different ones, in actual fact, even if both are emergent phenomena within a system. Crystals arise from conservative transitions, and thus in closed systems near thermal equilibrium (a kitchen freezer performs ice crystallisation, which is easily reversed by unplugging the gadget). Whirlpools of turbulence, on the other hand, arise in open systems—down a creek, for example. Although the behaviour of turbulence isn't random, it happens to be incredibly complex and most difficult to predict in the general instance [see fig. 1.9]. Now, those dazzling whirlpools you saw as a child are central in

(Wallace and Darwin disagreed on a philosophically crucial consequence of their theory, which they conveniently set aside in their earlier works: whether the evolution of humankind was just another instance of natural selection, as Darwin believed.)

Note however that natural selection was based on the idea of fitness. Why should some individuals come to be fitter than others? If they could pass on those characteristics acquired through living in a given environment, all individuals in an environment should have the same traits, and hence survival of the fittest would make no sense: some individuals would survive, but this would be a matter of chance and not fitness. August Weismann noted this inconsistency a century ago and made a useful distinction between the "germ cells" and the "soma" of an individual, thus laying the foundations for modern genetics. Weismann held that hereditary information is confined (at least in some individuals) to the germ cells, which give rise to a new individual through a developmental process; his theory explicitly blocked the soma from affecting the germ cells. In effect, this view eliminated the possibility of inheriting acquired characteristics and reopened the problem of how changes in the germ cells could emerge. The classical answer to this new question became possible when evolutionary studies were coupled with Mendel's earlier results (see fig. 1.6).

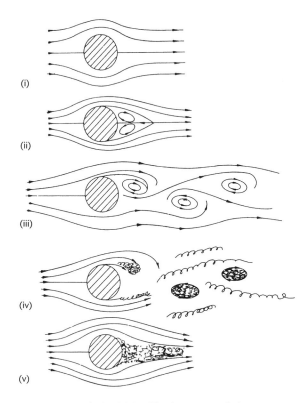

(i)

(ii)

(iii)

(iv)

(v)

Water hitting a cylinder. *(a)* Consider the structure of a homogeneous liquid, for instance, water flowing around a cylinder at slow velocity. *(b)* When fluid velocity is changed, the old structure becomes unstable and a new macroscopic, spatiotemporal structure emerges: two vortices form immediately behind the cylinder, with flows of water that collide behind the object and are directed backward, crashing against the "back" of the cylinder and then continuing to eddy around within the confines of the major flow. *(c)* At still higher water velocity, the vortices cannot maintain a balance, and they oscillate. *(d)* A final transition phase begins to emerge when velocity increases yet again. The vortices enter into quasi oscillations, and signs of turbulence form within and around the vortices, as well as in regions neighboring the points where the balanced whirlpools had first formed. *(e)* At very high water velocity, chaotic turbulence settles in the region where the vortices had been produced. (Adapted from Meinzer, *Thinking in complexity*)

Figure 1.9

[The following ideas are clearly presented in Meinzer 1994.]

Complex systems present emergent macroscopic behaviors that hold of the system as a whole but are not definable for its microscopic parts. For example, the whirlpools in *(b)*, or the turbulent region in *(e)*, are properties of the dynamic system of water flowing past a cylinder at higher and higher velocities. These features are not properties of H_2O, but properties of a collection of H_2O molecules when set in motion against a given obstacle, at specific velocities.

Certain forms of dynamic order exist in systems that are relatively close to equilibrium (conservative phase transitions), a typical example

determining the emergence of certain structural properties, as water flow increases, in the areas which converge towards the whirlpools. Very importantly, the emergent pattern in this instance is not linearly related to its source structure, and the global behaviour of the system cannot be reversed. This isn't easy to visualise with water turbulence, but think of the sort of turbulence created by the smoke from a cigarette [and see fig. 1.9]. Characteristically, smoke goes up in a straight line, which at some point starts to wobble, first producing smoke ripples, and eventually a diffuse flow. Now, given the flow, it would be rather hard to get the ripples back, and finally the straight line [see fig. 1.23].

L: Because the system is very sensitive to its initial conditions; a minor change can produce dramatic changes in the out-*haaachooo~!* excuse me—outcome.

O: To your health—and that's just what I mean. That small sneeze of yours could have devastating consequences in Yokohama and its surrounding hamlets. Given the appropriate weather conditions in your microclimate there, your gust could start a small breeze (a zephyr almost), which perchance might curl up and up into a draft, in due time twisting this blustery stuff upwards and upwards, developing into a most real gale which bashes those ignote tiers of the atmosphere to an upheaval of turbulence that, triggering a tremendous turmoil, storms down a mischievous blizzard, small at first, but . . .

L: I get the picture . . .

O: [. . . blah, blah, blah . . .] to finally roil down as a mammoth typhoon all along the Japanese coast.

L: I guess I'll have to watch the direction of my sneezes.

O: You do that, or the citizens of Yokohama will be seeking retribution! Now, what I'm trying to say is, although the typhoon in Japan can be causally linked to your sneeze, and whereas given a good enough computer we could even model the typhoon from a simulation of your sneeze, it would be a much prettier trick to model your sneeze given the typhoon—running the program backwards. Unfortunately, it seems that this isn't really doable, a situation which is typical in dissipative (that is, open) systems at points which are far from those of thermal equilibrium, and which makes their prior structure unrecoverable as it unfolds [28]. Now, you may think that it's a poor sort of universe that cannot run backwards, right?

L: Not particularly.

O: Right, the clockwork universe involves an idealisation which abstracts away from rocks finding themselves in the paths of water molecules (or molecules themselves interfering with one another) et cetera, et cetera. But the dynamic universe actually can be said to allow the common features of the other one, like stars and galaxies, et alia. How did these arise? The classical approach says that during the early inflationary period of the universe, minuscule deviations from early cosmic symmetry got amplified, to allow the density of matter to vary slightly from here to there. Through gravity, then, denser regions slowed down in their expansion, and began to contract, and the rest is the history of dust, stars, you, and so forth.

L: Wait, how did I get into the picture?

O: That is indeed the question: What are the details of the transition? On the one hand, we know that certain utterly simple rules can lead to so vastly complex a behaviour that it looks merely random (for example, the typhoon, and worse). But on the other hand, a sort of "antichaos" is at work, in which for some reason simple effects emerge from the utter complexity of **chaos** [29]. In the case that concerns us now, the emergence of dynamic order had the effect of sorting out the clutter. Ergo you come into the picture . . .

L: But aren't you jumping the gun? So far, we've talked about whirlpools and crystals, and then you mentioned star dust and typhoons. It's quite a different matter to establish that the forms of life emerge from these transitions.

O: I was thinking more along the lines of prebiological systems, but have it your way!

L: You seem stubbornly determined to have life (and I can hear you arguing the same for mind) reduced to physics.

O: Alas, our ways are metaphorical and vague! I grant you that. But nothing that I've said depends on a physical reduction; as you said, it could well be that we must extend physics to meet the demands of whatever science of complex systems we need to concoct, and

being crystallization. Conservative phase transitions involve reversible structures, such as those found in the various states of H_2O. In contrast, the particular sort of order illustrated by water flowing around a cylinder involves emergence at systemic states that are far from their thermal equilibrium (a dissipative phase transition). This (open) system is in constant interaction with the environment, and its phase transitions do not conserve structures: as new unstable collective motions (modes of the system) unfold, they influence and determine ("enslave") old, more stable modes, at a certain threshold. This slaving principle stated by Hermann Haken instantiates a mathematical procedure to eliminate fast-relaxing variables from a differential equation in a dynamic system, thus making it possible to reduce the degrees of freedom in the system: unstable modes (whose evolution is described by differential equations) serve as order parameters determining the global behavior of the system, and a macroscopic structure emerges there (see sec. 1.7).

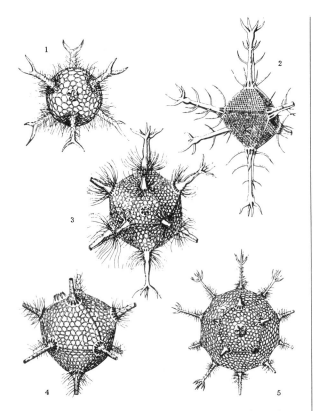

In 1917 D'Arcy Thompson adapted these skeletons of radiolarians from an 1862 taxonomy by Ernst Haeckel. Thompson emphasizes in his drawing the fact that these examples correspond to the five regular polyhedra known to classical geometers. (From Thompson, *On growth and form*)

Figure 1.10

D'Arcy Thompson's visionary *On Growth and Form* has been either ignored or misunderstood for decades, since its publication in 1917. Thompson partly dismissed Darwinian natural selection, assuming that it is relevant only in eliminating the unfit (still a crucial role, and Darwin's main contribution). More daringly, he took the progressive forces in evolution to be directly physical. In recent decades the use of mathematics to analyze development has become acceptable, and thus Thompson has been saluted by many scientists as a precursor. Moreover, evolutionary and developmental biology recognize nowadays that the genes interact with the (physicochemical) environment in determining the phenotype of given species, and take it as a major research program to determine how this interaction is to be specified.

It is instructive to glance over actual excerpts from the work of this pioneer of current studies on complexity.

Some seventy years ago much interest was aroused by Helmholtz's work (and also Kirchhoff's) on "discontinuous motions of a fluid. . . ."

[I]nstead of letting our drop rise or fall freely, we may use a hanging drop, which, while it sinks, remains suspended to the surface . . .

extend mathematics in a direction that will allow us to deal with whichever patterns we find [30]. But be that as it may, I find it worthwhile emphasising that this outlook is, well, new; nay, promising . . .

_____ form in life and its relation to physical laws

L: How is it new? Classically, it was noted—for example, by Boltzmann and by D'Arcy Thompson—that structure is the history of some particular process; that is, a succession of phase transitions leads to a hierarchy of more and more complex states.

O: The view that I'm sketching does agree with the general idea that structure is history, but there's an important difference as well. In the classical view, the relevant dynamic systems involve reversible structures near the point of thermal equilibrium. These are surely important in directly shaping organisms—setting the stage, as it were, for evolution to proceed.

L: D'Arcy Thompson explicitly invoked ice crystals (which arise from conservative phase transitions) as the sort of phenomenon whose physical basis is also the basis for various life forms [see fig. 1.10].

O: Right you are. But what I'm saying is different: while the current view hasn't been developed for actual living creatures, in computer simulations the idea has been that a significant number of phase transitions which would be relevant for life and form should arise in systems which are *far* from thermal equilibrium—and thus are more like turbulence than a crystal. My main point is that this implies not just some background for evolution to take place, but actually an ordering parameter to shape up, through successive curls and bursts, evolution's every path.

L: Those two views aren't incompatible, and in fact they're both also compatible with the fundamentals of classical evolution [31]. That is, as Darwin would have it, the initial self-reproduction step is perfectly accidental, although (to D'Arcy Thompson's satisfaction) physics constrains the pool of possible mutations that can take place, given a specific environment and specific properties of the creature that mutates (whether it's already small or large, for instance, and thus more sensitive to surface forces or to gravitational ones). And what you're suggesting, finally, is that a variety of evolutionary steps with a dynamic base optimize the system at points which are far from equilibrium.

O: Yes, conservative transitions are more basic than dissipative ones. What's central to the latter is that their dynamics load the dice of chance . . .

L: It's certainly an intriguing possibility, although of course the last step in the reasoning is the hardest one to accept. While it's easy to admit that certain kinds of organisms wouldn't stand a chance (say, on this planet or even in this universe), and that open dissipative systems may play a central role in the emergence of life and in constraining the workings of evolution, it's much harder to see exactly how the physical laws that predict the nonexistence of certain organisms, and roughly channel the overall shape of life, predict specific details of concrete organisms that do exist, and how they evolved or how they develop within the constrained spaces of kinetic systems [32].

O: That's a reasonable question, which I'm afraid only a fully developed theory of organisms will be able to answer; but I would point out in this respect some recent discoveries about corals, which exist in population reefs where interconnected races, subspecies, and species all live together and affect each other's evolutionary fate [33]. This happens to be specifically so because most of them are spawners, their gametes being released into the water for fertilisation. In situations of this sort, an entity which is larger than a conventional species—called a syngameon—is heavily dependent on a gene flow which is out there, swimming with the currents. My point is that this is now rather more than "roughly channelling the overall shape of life." The current dynamics in this instance (a standard physical process) has as much of a say in the evolutionary fate of a syngameon as sexual attraction (a standard biological process) has on the fate of a more conventional individual's descendants.

L: Well, maybe. One would have to come up with lots of those scenarios to give an accurate picture of development, morphology, and all the other biological mysteries. The point is, quite simply, that life and mind have always seemed miraculous to humans, much more so than illness and decay and death, which seem like normal states for matter of all forms to assume—and are fatefully described by the laws of thermodynamics. But contrary to what creationists do, we ultimately want to explain what we can about these hands

.[T]he figure so produced . . . is closely analogous to that of a medusa or jellyfish, with its bell or "umbrella," and its clapper or "manubrium" as well . . . .The living medusa has a geometrical symmetry so marked and regular as to suggest a physical or mechanical element in the little creature's growth and construction. (Thompson 1961, 73)

[T]he radiolarian skeletons are of quite extraordinary delicacy and complexity, in spite of their minuteness and the comparative simplicity of the "unicellular" organisms within which they grow; and these complex conformations have a wonderful and unusual appearance of geometric regularity. (Thompson 1961, 152)

[T]he little skeletons [of radiolaria] remind us of such things as snow crystals . . . , rather than of a collection of animals, constructed in accordance with functional needs and distributed in accordance with their fitness for particular situations. (Thompson 1961, 152)

This is only another proof (if proof be needed) that the peculiar form and character of these little skeletons are due not to the material of which they are composed, but to the moulding of that material upon an underlying vesicular structure. (Thompson 1961, 159)

and eyes, these smiles, and (what concerns me now the most) these simple words and sayings that all our children share. To just assert that these too must constitute emergent properties of dissipative systems is, at best, a crude metaphor; at worst, I must say, it may lead fanatics into seeing God's direct and ever-present hand at work.

O: Oh, but the general claim gives you a head start on the problem . . .

L: Yes, but it may be a wrong start—you have to be careful. In general, to understand how very concrete properties of organisms emerge (beyond those which result from the happenstances involved in evolutionary dialectics with a messy environment), one has to determine what the specific constraints are on possible organisms that evolution can try out (what the "mutation pool" is, so to speak). This itself is an abstract—and very tough—question, which as far as I know hasn't been answered or even systematically raised within biology [34]. After this is known, we can debate whether the relevant constraints are rooted in physics, or they may be established by yet to be discovered principles of biology (or some new science) . . . For instance, biologists are beginning to discover genetic pathways that are used over and over by nature—such as the one that guides the development of eyes in fruit flies. It turns out to be very much like the one that directs the development of certain worms' vulvas [35]. Similar connections show up in mice, frogs, cats, and surely in humans as well. If this is so, we have to be very careful when we talk about what nature is doing, and how. We're only beginning to understand these processes—how local or global they are, how simply or redundantly they're expressed [36] [see fig. 1.20]. What's the ultimate nature of general biological processes? How much do they affect evolution itself, limiting its workings? We don't know—at least not yet. We do know some basic details—for example, that nature displays a certain economy in choosing the molecular tools to shape the early embryos. So we find the same pathways forming both eyes and vulvas, for some reason. Moreover, we find out over and over that the molecules responsible for the early stages of embryogenesis (the ones that decide what the major axis of an animal is going to be) are reused for morphogenesis (deciding, for instance, on how a growing limb branches out from a trunk). In fact, genes themselves are commonly used again and again in the course of development, at different stages; and so we find that genes responsible for flies' segments are also responsible for brain segmentation in vertebrates. So nature gets to reuse successful patterns for purposes other than the ones they originally served [37]. But where does this economy (or different varieties of economy) originate? Does it (or they) stem from a physical (say, dynamic) reason, or is the reason more abstractly biological? Or even more traditionally: are these the result of standard evolution? I doubt that the latter is the case—even if many people believe so—but the question can't be decided a priori.

O: The concern is appropriate. Nevertheless, I'd worry about complex systems of the sort I'm mentioning, if only because the environment seems to be so fundamental to the acquisition of language [38].

1.3 Knowledge of Language

(wherein the amazing fact is noted that children do not listen to their parents and the Linguist argues for the amusing claim that English doesn't exist)

L: Oh, I don't believe that at all!

_____ **languages are very similar**

O: I beg your pardon? You don't think that the possible outputs of the LAD—Chinese, Swahili, Navajo, Basque, or Hebrew—are vastly different from English?

L: Of course they're different, but you'd be surprised how similar they are at a moderately abstract level. Not only do they all use words and **phrases**, and comparable phonological processes and basically identical semantic analyses, but in fact, once you get down to analyzing what's structurally possible and impossible in all of these languages, what you find are essentially the same processes. So much so that it's reasonable to conclude that we all speak Human language—just Human, for short—with mere dialectal variations among ourselves. But of course, first of all, without any triggering input, human LADs couldn't have acquired a language; and second, dialects of Human must be explained as much as Human must, and these, we must relate to the LAD's workings: since the input varies, the output varies.

O: Why does the input vary? In the case of the natural environment, a minor change in the initial conditions of a system can produce dramatic changes in the outcome. But what about the linguistic input?

L: It's a mess—among other things because it has to do with the Norman conquest, your family and societal background, who happens to have talked to you, and so on. Yet out of this mess an incredible order arises—to the point that the structure of language is almost identical from individual to individual, right away giving you an argument for the existence of a very strong unifying force in the acquisition process. Contrary to what happens in most messy systems out there, for which slight changes in a simple input produce drastic results in the output, here the input can be vastly different, yet the results in the output are minimally different in core structural aspects.

O: But you see, that's exactly what's found in systems arising at the edge of chaos, when it "collapses" into order! Processes like crystallisation actually somehow manage to ignore the chaotic details of how atoms vibrate when a crystal is formed. That's why order can emerge—otherwise, no two crystals would be alike. Hence, if what you're saying about language is true, its structuring process must be able to ignore the disarray it gets for input, and then of course we must ask what in the system allows that result [39].

L: We call it a human mind. Regardless of what does the trick for crystals, the human LAD has enough structure to sieve through the mess it takes as input, and it uses only some key information from that mess to pick out whatever it needs for its underlying, innate systems to become usable.

O: Right, but in all honesty, I still have trouble seeing how different languages could possibly emerge, given this picture. Two extreme cases are clear to me, assuming everything you've said. Case A— call it the "Esperanto scenario"—involves a fully universal language. Unlike actual Esperanto (which is invented), this virtual Esperanto would naturally emerge from the interaction of a LAD with linguistic data—any linguistic data. Virtual Esperanto would be a bit like human vision, where a large amount of structure is not determined by the genes, yet a universal structure emerges for other reasons, such as a very regular environment in terms of light sources. In contrast, think of case B, which I shall call the "Babel scenario." In the limit, a different language would emerge for each separate LAD. It would be a bit like human character itself, where every individual is in some sense fundamentally different from all the others, even if they share some basic, common structure. In the real world, language falls somewhere between the Esperanto and the Babel scenarios. There are clear pockets of regularity, English being spoken here, Swahili there . . . Needless to say, such pockets of regularity correspond to populations, but I don't see what in the picture you're painting would have this plain effect. Where on Earth does English fit?

L: Oh, English doesn't really exist [40].

O: . . .

L: . . .

O: Er . . . excuse me, but what are we speaking?

L: What exists right here are two individuals (let's hope that's true) performing certain behaviors. I babble, you babble, you hear, I hear; our minds are devices that impose some interpretation on all of that. Hopefully, that interpretation is reasonably accurate; and we aren't intending to lie; and we somehow figure out relations between the sounds we make and a certain reality we believe to obtain; and so on.

O: Aren't we communicating [41]?!

————— **independently of speakers, English is not even an abstraction**

L: What does that mean, to "communicate"?

O: Presumably, to transfer information—one of the fundamental functions of language, I should think.

L: Suppose we accept that as a definition. My dog is here, your dog is there, and information goes back and forth between them. What does that require?

O: My dog may visit your neighbourhood to deposit a pheromone, which your dog then interprets by using its olfactory abilities. Perhaps my dog can do the job from here, by barking or wagging its tail . . .

L: But what "does the job," as you put it? How do the two dogs interpret the scent as a territorial issue, or the tail wagging as, say, submissiveness or aggressiveness?

O: It's hard to go wrong. Urine clearly indicates a physical presence; as for visual signs, how many possibilities are there to start with? Surely it should be a trifling matter to match signal to interpretation, unless I'm missing something [42].

L: Let me first point out that, in terms of sheer phenomenology, it's way too abstract to talk about "signals" and "interpretation." It would be more accurate to talk about an "event of expression" concerning one dog, and an "event of interpretation" concerning the other dog. These may (but need not) appropriately match. Of course, inasmuch as there are only a few possibilities to match up, the likelihood that this will happen, and that effective learning will take place after a while, is probably large. (Note incidentally that I'm not saying by any means that this is how communication works between canines; rather, I'm saying that you could model a system this way, so long as you had only a few options.) That would be a standard behavioristic model.

O: Which won't work if there are an infinite number of intricate possible matchings. Very well, I see that—but there may be a finite set of *symbols* to articulate, in terms of certain rules.

L: That introduces new concepts that we have to justify and understand. What are those "symbols"? They're no longer mere chemicals like pheromones, or visual cues like tail wagging, that correspond to a certain kind of behavior. They're considerably more abstract, and the first obvious question to ask about them is how I know that my symbols are identical to yours.

O: You know because they work. Needless to say, that begs the question: to communicate is to transfer information by way of symbols that serve to communicate. Hence, I suppose you'd be forced to postulate some sort of code that you and I share, a public pronunciation, or a public meaning, let's say. Elements within this code must have certain properties, and we should have to agree on them. I believe that such a code is usually referred to as "the English language" [43].

L: What do you call a plump red fruit that you put in salads?

O: What? Er . . . a "tomato," I suppose.

L: You say "tomahto," but I actually say "tomayto."

O: But that's because we use different codes.

L: Yet we communicate!

O: All right, all right, but that's just a measly fact about pronunciation.

L: Take the word *disinterested*. What does that mean to you?

O: Why, 'unbiased', 'unselfish'; what else can it mean?

L: I'm sorry to disappoint you, but for most ignorant folk like myself, the word means 'uninterested'. And suppose I told you that the Queen is disinterested, meaning that she is uninterested. Have I communicated something to you? Well, you now take the Queen to be unbiased.

O: But that's not what you meant!

L: Yeah, but you didn't say anything about intentions before, when you defined communication [44]. You got something out of my set of symbols, just as your dog got something out of my dog's barking. Did my dog mean 'I hate you', or did it mean 'I sort of don't dislike you, but I fear you'? How can we really tell? When I go to Latin America, I try to chat as best I can in whatever Spanglish I speak. Do I communicate? Well, partly, I suppose—at least I hope so! In many situations in the world right now, this happens every day, with people only partially converging in their interpretations of each other's speech, but doing well enough to get by. And it happens even in much less extreme cases. How do you know that when I say, "I like music," for instance, I mean "music" in the same way you do? You may look in the dictionary to see what it says "music" means, but it certainly won't have much to say about what *I* take to be music, at least the kind I like. So what do you understand when I say, "I like music"? The task is hopelessly underspecified, really. To talk about communication here as a phenomenon that you can study scientifically is like talking about what it would mean to have a theory of "being near" something else. How near do you have to be, to be near? How do you answer a question like that with the usual scientific tools? In the case of dogs and their scents and barks, maybe there's something significant to say—I don't know. But in the case of human languages, I just don't see what we're talking about. What is that English language of yours? Abstracting it away from its speakers (which you had to do, in order to allow them to "communicate"), English just isn't a very serious scientific abstraction. Viewed that way, the English language has as much the status of a natural object as, say, the French liver does.

O: Hold on. I don't know much about the French liver, but I wouldn't be so cavalier about dismissing even madder constructs. To insist, systems spontaneously organise in this world into all sorts of intricate complex structures. All the phase transitions we discussed a while ago aren't properties of H_2O molecules, but emergent properties of a system of said molecules under certain, rather elaborate conditions. How do you know that there isn't an emergent sociological property which we may call the French language?

L: If positing the French liver explains something about natural reality, so be it; I haven't seen any explanation that depends on that, but someone can show me. To begin with, complex systems of the sort you mentioned as emergent must be local (thus need a locus), given their dependency on feedback. A storm hovers over Florida or Alaska, but not over Florida and Alaska (exclusively and at the same time). Life manifests itself in cells, individuals, and colonies, but not in entities that don't communicate chemically, and coexist in two different locations. Mind appears to be a property of some individuals, period.

O: I see your point, but think about emergent systems such as a certain kind of economy, with local relations in this instance being transactions of some abstract sort, instead of chemical reactions. You may be sceptical about the level of explanation of these constructs—or about their assumptions—but you should have no a priori reasons to disfavour this sort of study.

L: I don't. What I don't see is its connection to linguistics, at least in terms of the kinds of issues we were talking about. Maybe there *is* a sociologically particular way of speaking French, perhaps with a certain "je ne sais quoi." Maybe people speak faster, or louder, or with more gestures, there than here. I can see that. But what does that have to do with what we're discussing? Besides, when people talk about English—as depicted in the dictionary—they don't mean anything like what you're implying; rather, they're talking about an invention which doesn't seriously abstract from individuals (as when one talks about "the human genome," say). In fact, the dictionary is just a mixture of unsystematic abstraction and code of etiquette, in some crazy array [45].

O: But that's quite easy to remedy, really: posit a theoretical construct which is close to data. For example, you can think of English as a . . . a set of expressions . . .

L: That's a familiar proposal; I don't think it stands a chance [46]. There's no extensional construct without an indication of how this set is characterized. As Humboldt once stressed, knowing something like English can't mean knowing an infinite set of structures, since the human mind and brain are finite. So there must be a finite procedure (some set of rules, say) that generates this infinite set, and knowing English must mean knowing something like this procedure. But what are the rules? How do we find them? Rather than being "close to data," a set of expressions is, for the most part, totally removed from data for linguistics. The procedure that we need in order to generate the relevant structures is what constitutes our data. How to determine this procedure is no easy task, any more than how to determine the structure of atoms or genes is. Here we go back to where we started: if the rules that generate the set of relevant linguistic structures can't be learned, how do we know them? There's a question that's close to data! You're not observing languages in the abstract or as mathematical objects: these are constructs that human children acquire rapidly, efficiently, and uniformly, so whatever you propose as a generative procedure has to be consistent with this fact.

O: Hence you're looking for a set of rules . . .

—————————————————————————————— *digression about rules*

L: You're looking for whatever procedure humans use to generate the languages they speak. Maybe it's a set of rules, or maybe it's something more abstract than that; deciding on this is a purely empirical matter, and you have to deal with it through scientific reasoning (thus making use of the best theory you have available, which may of course change as research proceeds). In fact, early attempts at dealing with these matters followed a linguistic tradition that goes back to Pāṇini, twenty-five hundred years ago, in presuming that the **generative procedure** of human language is some set of construction-specific rules. But when you look at matters at a sufficient level of abstraction, you realize that there really aren't any construction-specific processes [see fig. 1.11]. This forces you to approach what at first appear to be construction-specific characteristics from an entirely different perspective [47]. For instance, the phenomena

Figure 1.11

Linguistic rules are construction-specific statements, along the lines of "Use a relative pronoun to make a relative clause" or "Move the logical object to subject position in order to make a passive." Rules can be language-specific; for instance, the English relative clause rule just mentioned does not apply in Japanese, and the passive rule does not apply in Basque. Likewise, there are rules that apply in Basque and Japanese, but not in English.

The existence of language-specific and construction-specific processes directly implies the possibility of language-universal and construction-universal processes, if the notion "specificity" makes sense. Clearly, there are several linguistic universals, some of which are obvious (all languages have words, verb phrases, noun phrases, sentences, and so on) and some of which are not so obvious (for instance, all linguistic processes are structure-dependent, as figure 1.5 illustrated for the inversion of auxiliaries). But are there processes that are universal to a construction, such as passive?

This does not seem to be the case. For instance, an auxiliary and a past participle are used to form the passive in English, but not in Spanish (where an auxiliary is used, but not a standard past participle) or Latin (where an auxiliary is not used at all in the present tense, and a separate verb form exists for this voice):

(i) a. Passive in English: the girl is loved
    b. Passive in Spanish: la chica es amad-a
       (cf. la chica ha amado 'the girl has loved')
    c. Passive in Latin: puella amatur

It is surprisingly difficult to find universal properties of a construction like the passive. Some do exist: typically, passivization involves the promotion of a logical object to subject position (iib); but then again, this general pattern is also shared by other constructions—for instance, the middle voice (iic).

(ii) a. Active voice: the butler   sliced   the cheese
     b. Passive voice: the cheese   was sliced ____ (by the butler)
     c. Middle voice: cheese   slices ____   easily

To the extent that there are no construction-universal processes, linguists are led to wonder whether specific constructions are anything but a taxonomic way of talking about specific properties of a given language, with no theoretical status in the system at large. This question has provided a major impetus for research in generative grammar over the last three decades, the conclusion being that constructions do not exist in any theoretical sense.

that were once thought to be specific to relative clauses and passives have been found to arise in other constructions as well, such as questions and the middle voice, respectively [see fig. 1.11 and chap. 5]. In turn, the mechanical work done by rules in expressing the patterns of human language has been assumed by other, more abstract devices. To put it bluntly, constructions were seen to be merely taxonomic artifacts of traditional grammar—once insightfully used to describe different languages and their dialects, but lacking in predictive scope. Similar issues have also arisen with Linnaean classifications. Biology used to distinguish the Linnaean plants and animals, plus fungi, bacteria, and a variety of single-celled organisms. Once geneticists entered the biological arena, though, they argued that organisms should be divided into nucleus-endowed eukaryotes and two superkingdoms of bacteria. These are the usual surprises you get when you look at the world scientifically, and commonsense and folk classifications are set aside. The same is true in linguistics; once you get abstract enough, you're no longer looking at passives or relative clauses, and more profound sorts of patterns become relevant. For these patterns, rules aren't of much significance, particularly because rules are by definition specific, while the abstract processes in question are universal.

O: And what have you to say about those rules one learns in school?

L: That's a different story altogether . . . There's probably nothing really wrong with schools teaching people to never split infinitives or to edit out the prepositions they end sentences with—as long as they recognize that they're essentially teaching the norms of a social group. Because that's what those particular rules are: social conventions. In fact, note that people have conscious access to these rules, just as they have conscious access to rules for driving in traffic . . . Teachers can test students on this, and the students pass or fail according to their skill, memory, and so on. With deep linguistic processes, all the knowledge a person has is totally unconscious. There's a sense in which no English speaker would fail the test of determining whether *left John* (as opposed to *John left*) is a sentence of English; at the same time, lots of people would fail the test of articulating what the rule is (the subject comes first), because people don't have immediate access to this tacit knowledge [48].

_____ could languages arise the same way species do?

O: Very well, suppose I grant you that English isn't—in the relevant, scientific sense—very real. As a consequence, you can deny a priori the reality of any possible principles of language variation or change, since these would have to operate on an object like English [49]. But is that a good result? Languages do change. It's even easy to think of linguistic change in basically the same way that one thinks of the evolution of the species. Why, even Darwin himself was familiar with the work of comparative philologists, who were trying to understand certain facts about linguistic change—such as the common origin of the Indo-European languages. He even used this metaphor for thinking about biological evolution, and to provide a paradigm for it.

L: But if you take the classical evolutionary paradigm, you can't make a convincing case that it extends to the linguistic instance, even if you put aside my argument that languages don't really exist.

O: Well, let me see. We need the following five claims [50] [see fig. 1.8]. Firstly, organisms transform in time; secondly, they all descend from a common ancestor; thirdly, species multiply, thus producing diverse organisms; fourthly, changes are gradual; and finally, "natural **selection**" operates. The first three claims are completely unobjectionable. As a matter of fact, the third claim, which was mysterious to Darwin, is now understood in its essentials [see figs. 1.21 and 1.22]. Claim four may or may not be accurate (the issue is the locus of much current debate).

L: But it's significant only inasmuch as it affects the details of claim five. Everyone who believes in evolution (i.e., is rational) would admit that natural selection plays a crucial role in causing inherited characteristics to disappear. But if a mutation made you into a phenotype which won't die out before transmitting its genetic code, are you necessarily evolution's gift to natural history [51]? That's not so clear, by any means. Maybe you're just okay, and whatever properties you have are perfectly reasonable for your environment—though not comparatively optimal, in some sense having to do with design optimality for your phenotype. In fact, maybe you even ended up with properties that are **maladaptive** in themselves but which, luckily, don't lead to your extinction because they serve useful purposes which have nothing to do with the selective reason for the mutation that gave you those properties. All of this is possible, and it would be rather compatible with evolution not being gradual, but bumpy; even considerably messy.

O: Of course, of course—so let us see. Firstly, languages do appear to transform in time; secondly, it is, I presume, arguable that they all descend from a common ancestor [52]; thirdly, languages possibly multiply, in the sense that a given language, like Latin, gave rise to various Romance languages. Indeed, a single Latin descendant, like Portuguese, gave rise to the languages spoken today in, for example, Brazil and Angola—which are different already. Fourthly, changes are . . . well, they may be gradual or not, I don't know, but we saw that this isn't all that central to the evolutionary paradigm [53]. Thus far, evolution and language change look rather similar. What about natural selection?

L: What about it? Are you prepared to say that the languages that exist in the world today are the fittest? That was certainly the position that people took in the nineteenth century; but from our present perspective, it sounds like nothing more than cultural chauvinism. Is there any meaning to the claim that English is fitter for survival on the American plains than the language of the Navajo? If English dominates the continent, it does so because of the strongest army in the world, whose finest attribute isn't precisely its verbal brilliance.

O: But can't one think of that as a natural disaster? For example, an asteroid crash, or a volcanic eruption, may create an irreparable environmental situation which a species can't survive. How does that differ from an invading army's creating an environmental situation which a language can't survive? Is that not what happened to thousands of languages throughout the course of human history?

L: Oh, don't use the past tense there; exactly the same thing is happening right now, and it's a political nightmare that most people haven't even begun to understand yet [54]. But I'm actually making a different point. First of all, if you were right that linguistic change reduces to human exploitation, and so on, then there wouldn't be a meaningful issue behind linguistic change—it would reduce to some factor of human sociology [55]. In other words, on this view, it's not a language that doesn't survive an invading army, but a society, either through direct annihilation (as has been happening on the American continents for five centuries) or through some equally effective means: for instance, linguistic measures of the sort that "English only" bigots want to impose in the US. On the other hand, you also have to consider that some language changes can't be explained away via "natural" disasters of this sort. Look at Latin, for instance, which played the invading role in the ancient world that English plays within the "new world order." Latin gave way to the Romance languages, some of which prevailed, and some of which didn't. There's no obvious correlation here with "linguistic might" or a "healthy adaptation to a linguistic environment."

_____   **an I-language is characterized from a set of principles and parameters**

O: May I point out that in arguing against my proposal, you've cheerfully admitted the existence of Latin, Navajo, English, and so forth. Now I seem to have cornered you! This is neither the Esperanto scenario nor the Babel scenario. I shall be ever so glad if you can tell me how the Real World scenario arises . . .

L: First of all, my specific argumentation doesn't presuppose the existence, in the appropriate sense, of all those languages. But to avoid a dreadful terminological issue, let's give a technical definition to the notion "language L."

O: Why, thank you! Let's!

L: Take it as a fact that on the one hand, languages have invariant properties which in some sense follow from natural law; on the other hand, given the plasticity of the linguistic phenomenon, individual languages also exhibit some degree of variation within the possibilities allowed by whatever laws apply within Human as a whole. It's obvious that actual learners somehow choose among these different options, by way of input data from the environment. Once you assume a set of linguistic **principles** to instantiate natural law, and a set of linguistic **parameters** along which languages can vary within the limits imposed by the principles, then you have a technical definition for a **language** L. (Note, incidentally, that the word "parameter" as used by a linguist has a technical import, which is different from—though related to—its import in other scientific disciplines [see fig. 1.12].) Our definition won't be an extensional, external-to-speakers definition of the kind you were looking for— a set of expressions or an **E(xternal/xtensional)-language.** Rather, language L will be characterized intensionally (through a generative procedure), and internal to speakers. We thus say this:

(1) *Definition of* **I(nternal/ntensional)-language**

Given a set of universal principles encoded as the initial state S_0 of an idealized language faculty, and a set of parameters of variation for S_0, an I-language L is a complete specification S_f of parametric options.

Crucially, an I-language is a natural object, corresponding (in an idealized way) to something going on in a child's mind after the parameters have been set in terms of input data. Technically, then, the final state of a LAD corresponds to an idealized I-language [see fig. 1.12]. The theory about the mental procedure implicit in (1) is what linguists call **Universal Grammar** (UG). (Somewhat sloppily, we also often call the procedure itself UG, although strictly speaking UG is just a theory about this procedure.) From this perspective, a language change involves fixing parametric options in different ways, in the course of history. That is, the mystery of language change reduces to the mystery of language acquisition [56].

——————————— language change involves resetting parametric options

O: Are you saying, then, that the logical problem of language acquisition is the logical problem of language change?

L: Basically, yes—but let's model an actual case. For instance, suppose that the linguistic system universally encodes the fact that to make a sentence, there must be a combinatorial relation between a symbol like *Fred* and a symbol like *called*. If nothing else is specified by the system, that will allow for two clear options: either *Fred called* (which is a normal sentence in a language like English) or else *called Fred* (which is a normal sentence in other languages of the world).

O: I suppose, in this actual case, the question becomes why a given I-language changes from one parametric setting to its mirror image.

L: It doesn't. I-languages don't directly relate to each other. Remember that we're assuming, first of all, the initial states of Jones's, Smith's, and my own language faculty (and so on), which are in fact a single, identical state S_0; given Jones's experience, I would have had her I-language, and vice versa. This initial state S_0 is as much an idealized natural object as molecules, fields, or visual systems are. The first task for the linguist is to figure out the properties of this state S_0, a system of knowledge which doesn't directly resemble anything like English or Italian, say, but is much more abstract. Of

Figure 1.12

To follow the debate in the text, observe the following basic schema:

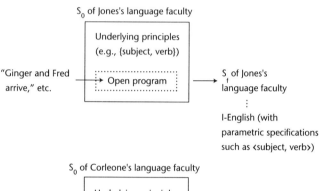

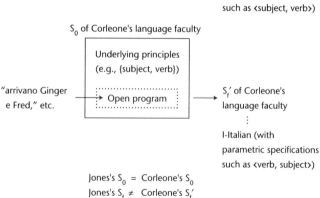

$$\text{Jones's } S_0 = \text{Corleone's } S_0$$
$$\text{Jones's } S_f \neq \text{Corleone's } S_f'$$

Bear in mind also that the notion "parameter" has different meanings in different disciplines. Perhaps its most general sense is "external variable": parameters encode variable quantities or properties that are relevant, but external to a system. For dynamic systems, an external variable is the (amount of) input that the system receives; for instance, more or less fluid velocity (hence, temperature) results in different states of fluid dynamics. For linguistic systems, parameters encode those aspects of the system of knowledge that are not directly specified by natural law—those that instead depend on input data from the environment. Where and why linguistic parameters arise is still an open question; the possibility even exists that the linguistic system encompasses different sorts of parameters (see sec. 2.7).

course, the most basic data used both by linguists analyzing a language and by children/LADs acquiring it (with whatever different tools they're using) comes from that language—say, English or Italian—or more precisely, from I-languages—in this case, I-English or I-Italian. Data like this allows the linguist to make certain hypotheses about a given S_f, and what's more important, about S_0. Crucially, S_0 is by hypothesis also the basis for S_f', the final state of someone—call her Corleone—who (contrary to what Jones does) accepts the equivalent of *arrive Ginger and Fred* as generated by her I-language, corresponding to her S_f'.

O: Actually, *arrivano Ginger e Fred* is what Corleone would say.

L: Well, whatever. The point is that Jones must say, instead, *Ginger and Fred arrived*. Then the linguist deduces that S_0 cannot impose the order <subject, verb>, in principle, or else it couldn't possibly be the basis for Corleone's S_f'. Here the linguist has to look at things more abstractly, hypothesizing something more basic for the initial program in S_0: namely, that S_0 doesn't specify a given linear order among basic constituents like subject and verb. In other words, linear order among these constituents is a property of S_f or S_f', but not of S_0 [see fig. 1.12].

O: Yes, I'm beginning to catch on . . . S_f and S_f' aren't independent states which turn into each other like water turns into steam or ice. Rather, S_f and S_f' are themselves states of S_0. A child/LAD trying to achieve S_f' starts from S_0—which nature provides—and not from S_f. Through the input data that S_f provides (assuming that S_f and its corresponding I-language are what occur in the environment) the child/LAD must reach S_f' [see fig. 1.13]. But how *can* a LAD reach S_f' from input data coming from S_f [57]? This is quite a puzzle.

L: On hearing a sentence like *Ginger and Fred call*, the child/LAD must make a hypothesis about how tokens organize. So let's distinguish *hypothesized* languages from *target* languages (again, thinking in terms of I-languages and not E-languages). It's a target I-language that occurs around the child/LAD, and we have to find out why (actually, in relatively rare instances) the child's/LAD's hypothesized I-language doesn't match this target I-language. Of course, certain **primary linguistic data** (henceforth, PLD) will lead to certain structural conclusions about a target I-language L_t, but only if the child/LAD actually processes the data, somehow figures out its significance, and then applies that significance toward determining the

Figure 1.13

The basic question about language change from the perspective of language acquisition is the following. Assuming the following schema, how is it possible for I-English input to yield two different sorts of output, after the acquisition process (namely, I-English and I-English')?

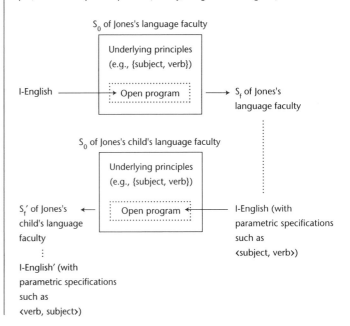

Figure 1.14

To see the complexity of acquiring a linguistic pattern, imagine a child/ LAD who has heard the token *Ginger and Fred call*. First of all, the child/ LAD must be able to realize that this is linguistic input (as opposed to some sort of nonlinguistic vocalization) and furthermore must be able to divide it into (four) relevant units of structure. The child/LAD does not know that this string of words is English (and hence whether to expect subjects before or after verbs, objects before or after verbs, etc.). This string could, for instance, be the way of expressing an imperative in a language that normally uses the order <object, verb>, instead of the English order <verb, object>. In such a language, imperatives would be of the form *Ginger and Fred call!* rather than *call Ginger and Fred!* In fact, many languages of the world systematically drop subjects; for instance, the Italian sentence *chiamano Ginger e Fred* is compatible with the mere *chiamano* which (if the context is clear) may have the same meaning. In principle, then, the child/LAD could hypothesize that the token *Ginger and Fred call* is the way to say something like *someone calls Ginger and Fred* (with a dropped subject and the object preceding the verb); in other words, the child/LAD would consider the language being learned to be like Italian.

Suppose one were to assume that the child/LAD needs to encounter tokens of a more complex sort (such as *Ginger and Fred called their agents*) to be able to set the parametric value <subject, verb>/ <verb, subject>. Note that this particular token could, in principle, be analyzed as containing the topicalization of *Ginger and Fred,* as in the English expression *Ginger and Fred, their agents called (them),* where the object is moved, as a topic, to the front of the expression. In languages like German, such a topicalization would involve not only moving the object to the front of the sentence, as in English, but also moving the verb to a position immediately after the topicalized object: S V O → O$_{top}$ S V → O$_{top}$ V S. In German, then, the equivalent of *Ginger and Fred called their agents (Ginger und Fred riefen ihre Agenten an)* corresponds both to the normal declarative English sentence *Ginger and Fred called their agents* and to the stylistically marked *Ginger and Fred, their agents called*—which entails that this particular token also is not conclusive to figuring out whether the language being learned is a <subject, verb> language or a <verb, subject> language.

Now suppose the child/LAD needs to encounter tokens of an even more complex sort in order to set the relevant parameters. For example, in German it is possible to tell whether a noun that takes a masculine article is being used as a subject or an object, because the article has a distinct form in each position: *der Fred* must be a subject, and *den Fred* must be an object. This would be of help in determining the order of subject, verb, and object in sentences like *die Ginger und der Fred riefen ihre Agenten an* 'Ginger and Fred called their agents' and *die Ginger und den Fred riefen ihre Agenten an* 'Ginger and Fred, their agents called'. Of course, a child/LAD learning English would never hear a sentence like this and hence would never get help from it in trying to set the parameter, because English articles do not display this morphological difference. Furthermore, data of this kind would not be helpful in German either in various circumstances—for example, if the sentence had been *die Ginger und die Marilyn riefen ihre Agenten an.* This is again ambiguous, because the article *die* is used for feminine nouns in both subject and object position. To conclude, note that data

properties of the I-language she's acquiring. If the child's/LAD's hypothesis H about L$_t$ corresponds to the way the tokens are organized in L$_t$ (leading toward a mental state S$_{ft}$), then no discernible consequence ensues: the child/LAD will indeed converge on S$_{ft}$ from PLD like this, in fact acquiring L$_t$. But in principle, the child/LAD could have analyzed the token data in a different way [see fig. 1.14].

O: That's what I can't seem to grasp! According to your proposal, every new child/LAD must start from scratch, going from S$_0$ to a given final state of his language faculty. Well, of course, I see that S$_0$ is not really "scratch," since the structures it allows are very constrained, which limits the pool of possible hypotheses that the child/LAD must entertain, given PLD. Fine. And I do also see that changes happen, as a matter of principle, if certain structures in L$_t$ (the target language of the community) can be analysed by the child/LAD as constituting PLD for L$_n$ (the changed, new language, resulting from the child's/LAD's hypothesis). But if the speakers who make up the community also grew up in an L$_t$ environment, why did they not analyse L$_t$ structures as PLD for L$_n$—as our hypothetical child/LAD does—rather than sticking to L$_t$?

L: Actually, whenever an actual linguistic change takes place, the input data is different.

O: But that begs the question! Needless to say, if—as I conjectured—a foreign army speaking L$_n$ invades a community speaking L$_t$, the structures of L$_n$ influence the way children born in this situation acquire L$_t$ . . .

L: And as I admitted, that situation has arisen time and again in human history. But even if languages also change without any sort of contact with other communities, you must conclude, as a point of logic, that the linguistic change emerges because of a difference in the input data, not a difference in the individuals' genes.

O: Then the data must be dynamic, in order to change.

L: I keep telling you: the data is a mess [see fig. 1.14].

1.4 Simple Learning Minds

(a discussion about the definite roles children play in organizing chaos, which goes on to suggest that what is most cherished about them may not have evolved, after all)

L: The only reason to think that the data is the *same* mess from one generation to the next is this fantasy we share that we call "English." In reality, children aren't exposed to English; they're exposed to whatever PLD sets they happen to encounter [58].

——————————————————————————— *some thoughts on PLD sets*

O: Certainly, sentence sets of this type could never be identical, even for identical twins living in the same circumstances. But what I'm trying to suggest is that they might be similar enough, converging into some sort of **attractor** that provides the kind of stability you're seeking, while being capable of drifting just enough to tumble into a **catastrophe** here and there [59].

L: Look, we don't even know that all sentences of I-English, say, are relevant within PLD sets [60]. In fact, perhaps only certain crucial parts of sentences, corresponding to linguistically significant domains of locality, are relevant to the acquisition process [see chaps. 5 and 6]. Only one thing is certain: the kinds of structures instantiated in different PLD sets within a given linguistic population must be, in the general instance, similar enough for learners to converge on very similar, if not identical, I-languages. But whether the data exhibits some sort of coherence, as in so-called complex systems, is entirely up for grabs.

O: But doesn't the very fact that languages exist and change demand such an assumption?

L: Not really, because the regularity in question might not be in the data, but in the population that produces the data—we just don't know [see fig. 1.15]. Linguists generally abstract away from all these issues, because they're truly cumbersome, and because linguistic change isn't by any means as robust a phenomenon as linguistic stability. In fact, many of us assume that the acquisition process is essentially instantaneous, with parametric options being trivially and directly fixed from input data [61].

O: By Jove, man! Are you seriously trying to suggest that children don't take time to acquire a language?!

L: Well, of course they do, but nobody's been able to tell why that is, although some serious conjectures are starting to be made. It could be because of limitations on memory, attention span, processing skills . . . Childhood is a complex state, if there is one . . .

of a rather exotic sort have been invoked in the present instance. In order to determine whether the language being learned is a <subject, verb> language or a <verb, subject> language, the child/LAD has to be sensitive enough to hear and pay attention to differences as slight as the one between *der* and *den*. Likewise, utterances that require articles (where they even help) are structurally more complex than utterances where articles do not appear; hence, the likelihood of their being part of the primary linguistic data that a child/LAD hears in finite time decreases. In general, the presence of primary linguistic data has to be robust enough (i.e., the child/LAD needs to be exposed to enough tokens) to allow for parametric settings in actual time (before age two or three in a child of normal cognitive abilities).

Figure 1.15

Given the logic of the situation, there are four different factors to consider with respect to language change from the point of view of the LAD:

1. The nature of the input data. These data are clearly not organized in any linear fashion (of the sort that might, in principle, be encountered in a classroom), although they could possibly be organized in some way that is yet to be determined.
2. The sensitivity of the LAD to amount of data (which is not proven). If the LAD is indeed sensitive to quantities of data, then what is the critical amount? Researchers are still debating whether this is important, but tacit assumptions often rely on accumulation of data patterns, thus presupposing a memory for given patterns and an essentially maturational decision procedure to set a parameter when a critical mass of data has accumulated.
3. The LAD's ability to determine "best hypotheses" to fit given data. This presupposes an evaluation procedure.
4. A wider population of learners. Such a population may pass through different acquisition states on the basis of differing input data, leading to intricate drifts of a sociolinguistic nature.

The last two factors are in all likelihood linearly dynamic; the first two are certainly more complex.

We know that children finish the job by a certain age (for core parameters, this is generally before age three, and even earlier than that for many children), and also that children start from S_0. But what happens in between is a typical "black box" puzzle: we only know the output, and we can hypothesize what the input should be like. The more we say the LAD is doing (for instance, positing sequential stages in the acquisition process), or the more structure we ascribe to the PLD set, the harder our task will be as theorists, because we still want to know how to go from the PLD input to the I-language output [62]. Of course, what you're concerned about now isn't the regularity in language, but the rare instances of variation. Then something's got to give: either LADs are more elaborate than most linguists have assumed, or else we need to say something about the patterns that the data presents, how they drift and why. Still, I insist: fundamental, what you may call "core" linguistic change appears to be rare and variable [63]. The syntax of French has changed significantly since the Middle Ages (though this works out to only a couple of major changes over the course of fifty generations of speakers); by contrast, Portuguese has remained fairly constant during that same amount of time [64]. I've purposely chosen two closely related Romance languages, each of which has been in contact with other languages. Whatever mechanism you posit for linguistic change, you want it to be insignificant enough not to mess up your analysis of Portuguese.

O: That's what I fancy about what I'm trying to say, assuming the LAD must suss out a data pattern. Even if S_0 is so constrained that the LAD only hypothesises a few possible patterns, there must be (as a matter of principle) at least enough manoeuvring room that it can come up with different data analyses—or languages wouldn't change without language contact. Is pattern recognition instantaneous?

L: I don't know, so I abstract away from the problem. That is, as far as the core linguistic system is concerned, it isn't crucial whether a LAD figures out a pattern all of a sudden or in various steps, slowly or rapidly, continuously or discontinuously, and so on, as long as it does figure it out and hence reaches its final state. Then you may as well say that the process is instantaneous, unless you have something else to say about it [see fig. 1.15]. But I do believe that the significance of all of this is fairly marginal, because what you don't want to fall into is the absurd situation of a child not picking out a language because the data is too messy.

O: That never happens?

L: Never—which is where theories should start. Even severely mentally retarded individuals have language, and can judge whether a linguistic expression is grammatical or not.

O: Oh, seriously!

L: No, seriously. There's a famous case in the literature of a woman who couldn't even understand *John loves Mary,* but would repeat the sentence if asked. And crucially, if somebody gave her the ungrammatical **John love Mary,* she would say it back *in a corrected form* [65].

O: Fascinating.

_____ *digression about creoles*

L: But look, take the most extreme case that we know of: the emergence of **creole** languages.

O: Indeed, those *are* interesting; in such cases language would seem to arise from scratch!

L: Again, not absolutely from scratch, if I'm right . . . In principle, a creole could arise wherever children are raised in an environment where their linguistic input is sufficient for the language faculty to develop, but not sufficient for it to lock onto a particular I-language [66]. In reality, creoles have arisen under tragic circumstances, on plantations. Historically, it happened that a community was enslaved and uprooted to another community that spoke a different language or even many different languages (on plantations, various languages were spoken by various groups). In such circumstances, it's not uncommon for an entire generation of people who aren't allowed to speak their native language, or who need to communicate with others who don't speak this language, to develop what's called a **pidgin.** This is a system of communication that in fact doesn't use all the standard procedures of human language; it just uses some deficient, rudimentary variant to get by with. (For instance, a pidgin speaker doesn't seem to have the sorts of recursive structures you noted earlier, and doesn't displace phrases.) However, what's interesting is that the children of speakers of a pidgin do develop a language which is as much a natural language as English is—we call this a creole. Of course, the children's problem is a deficient input of PLD, which isn't enough for them to converge on a given I-language. But even then, they manage to come up with an I-language, triggered from the rudimentary linguistic situation around them but unrelated to this situation in core respects.

O: You can't help but acquire a language . . .

L: If you're human . . . And note that you acquire a language even if the PLD you hear is deficient enough not to allow you to pick out the parametric specifications of a given I-language [67].

_____ LADs are elegant

O: If I'm following you properly, then, the PLD set must be clean enough to allow for a fairly stable answer to the acquisition puzzle. In fact, this is typical of open dynamic systems, whose instability is actually very, very stable within certain boundaries (think of the situation that exists in a small creek, for example, whereby the system is attracted into a handful of different patterns, but always the same ones [see fig. 1.9]). Likewise, thinking of language acquisition in terms of these systems would allow us to talk about the emergence of a pattern from a continuous data flow that the LAD receives as input (which resembles the flow of water that may lead to different whirlpool patterns). Notice also that which token the child/LAD hears when can't really be controlled (again, this resembles water molecules tumbling onto each other and onto pebbles in a creek). More technically, dynamic patterns of this sort (involving open systems) are the result of unstable modes of the system enslaving stable ones, a consequence of the system's feedback [see sec. 1.7 and fig. 1.28]. Perhaps something very much along these lines goes on in the acquisition process, whereby one of the possible patterns emerging from a system of data is sustained on the basis of feedback that confirms the pattern. To go from a harmonic flow of water to a turbulent one, nothing drastic needs to happen—the fluid velocity simply needs to increase. Once certain thresholds are surpassed, the system locks onto given patterns. It would seem to me that—in the recognition process—to lock onto given linguistic patterns, the LAD must accumulate data of a given sort, which keep feeding back until a stable state emerges. That is to say, if a sufficient number of data exist of the relevant sort. Situations of instability would be those in which data cannot be reliably used to lock onto a particular pattern, and the recognition process would then fluctuate between two different settings [68].

L: And how does a real child decide, then? Does she stay in limbo forever?

O: Hold on a moment—other factors may intervene. For example, it's populations of speakers that speak and acquire languages. This, I suppose, forces one to look at matters in an even more dynamic way: although a single child is acquiring a language, what he acquires it from depends on who else happens to be around, speaking within earshot—which may even be other LADs (as you said), trying as well to acquire the language. This may tilt undecided patterns in given directions, just because of the very dynamics of the group [69]. Besides—

L: Well, this is all very interesting, but clearly premature. Your suggestions crucially depend on the idea that a LAD doesn't immediately lock onto a parametric option as soon as it encounters a single token of data of a given kind. It waits until evidence mounts, in a feedback process whereby a pattern emerges; once it recognizes the pattern, the LAD is attracted to a particular parametric option. But then the first thing to do is figure out what kinds of data lead to what kinds of conclusions, which in turn implies having a clear picture of the kinds of conclusions the system needs to reach. To put it differently, without knowing what the parameters are that the LAD has to set, it's hard to know what specific evidence it can use to set them; and without a clear picture of what the evidence is, it's almost senseless to talk about the dynamics of the relevant system [70].

O: I can see that as a point of logic. Nevertheless, having a picture of how the learning process takes place, and how data fluctuate, given population drifts, may help in determining the very nature of the parametric options of the linguistic system.

L: At the present stage of our investigations, this is far from obvious. Quite frankly, we don't even know the basic facts. How large does the PLD set have to be? What constitutes a critical mass of data of a certain kind for a property to emerge? How is this property discerned by a realistic LAD? What changes have actually taken place historically?

O: Oh, you must know that at least!

L: Not really. First, we're dealing with an unreliable "fossil record": written texts. These correspond to the more or less formal performance of writers whose background and circumstances we generally don't know anything about. Good statistics only take care of part of this problem: we have to know what we're looking for. We might assert that in Latin things worked one way, and in Italian they work some other way. But that assertion is trivial, if Latin and Italian are irrelevant as such. We can't pretheoretically look at statistical regularities and then rest assured that they signify a linguistic change in parameters with some pretty linear properties. The function might correspond to anything—for instance, to the way the writers of the texts made systematic use of courtesy forms, which later ceased to be important for some reason. This would be a fact about sociology, not directly about linguistics. It could, very indirectly, have a bearing on possible PLD sets at one time or another; but that's very hard to establish. For the fact to be a truly linguistic observation, we clearly need a theory of linguistic parameters which tells us what to even look for.

O: I've granted that already, but I wouldn't dismiss the effect of population drifts on PLD sets; as a matter of fact, some of these drifts may be purely linguistic, in the sense that they aren't caused by politeness et cetera, but by the mere fact that the linguistic tokens that constitute PLD sets can vary.

L: But what are you saying beyond something programmatic? Yes, sure, PLD sets are population driven. So? What's next? As I've said, I for one don't really know what a PLD token is, let alone how such tokens organize into types! Thus, I find it a little too early to ask whether the nature of PLD sets permits a dynamic analysis of data, or whether in some instances the process is just messy, and it's simply the child/LAD that sorts out the mess by using its particular resources, which may even vary from individual to individual.

O: But why would all the children of a particular community generally converge on a particular language?

L: Maybe because there aren't so many parameter settings to change, to start with. Given few options, there won't be many ways to go wrong, even if the data is an absolute mess. Think of the creole instance, where the LAD must come out with an I-language from close to useless input. The most intriguing aspect of creoles is that they all share the same fundamental parameter values, regardless of what languages they were "built" from: verbs don't have overt endings, subjects can't be dropped, subjects precede verbs. And that's just for starters—they have many other constant properties [71] [see fig. 1.16 and sec. 6.5].

Figure 1.16

Tok Pisin developed in the Samoan plantations of New Guinea, from a Polynesian, Malay, German, and English substrate. Like all other creole languages, it went through a pidgin stage, when a group of native speakers of those languages spontaneously created a communication code, using bits and pieces of the heterogeneous linguistic stock. This was not a natural language. However, children who acquired a language on the basis of data from this pidgin code did converge on a whole new natural language. Having undergone this creolization process, Tok Pisin now has a large number of native speakers and in fact a lively literature. Here are ten basic expressions in Tok Pisin (data from Todd 1990):

O: I know, it's flabbergasting!

L: Not if, in the absence of reliable data, the child selects parametric values which for some reason are easily set. That's how you want to model your LAD.

O: And that was going to be precisely my next point: given situations of data instability, LADs go with the optimal analysis. That's a dynamic problem, finding an optimal solution . . .

L: Yeah, that's not unreasonable—but it doesn't have to be a problem in dynamics. Maybe certain structural analyses just involve (in some specific linguistic sense) a less cumbersome structure than others. Of course, to start with, a LAD that behaves like this has to be structured enough to pick out the most economic analysis among the possible ones, according to some metric of linguistic simplicity. Granting the LAD this sort of intricacy is certainly easier to accept than granting it a poorly understood pattern recognition ability, for all we have to assume is that the LAD has access to the initial state S_0 of the language faculty (an assumption that's needed independently), plus some ability to rank hypotheses according to how elegantly they fit the demands of S_0 [72]. In other words, it could be that when the LAD runs into a problem with the analysis (when the data happens to be too messy to yield unambiguous results), it simply goes with the cleanest hypothesis. In the case of creoles, this has to be a massive effort, because input data is of no help in setting any of the relevant parameters; but maybe, as you imply, in situations of normal linguistic change this same process takes place for one particular parameter, and not the entire system.

O: That would suit me.

_____ **order is restored by the LAD**

L: As I see it, the important point is simple, though: if complexity was all there is to language as we experience it, the linguistic system wouldn't be nearly as stable as it seems to be. In fact, we would expect it to be constantly drifting (think, for instance, of the mutations of species), to the point where it might even be completely unlearnable for (some) humans using only positive evidence.

O: Whereas just the opposite appears to be the case. But as I keep telling you, complex systems don't simply drift ad infinitum: they

(i) ol   i   wokim   haus
     they   auxiliary building house
     'they are building a house'

(ii) ol   i   no   go
      they   auxiliary   not   go
      'they didn't go'

(iii) haumas   taim ol   i   mekim?
       question-degree   time they auxiliary do-it
       'how many times did they do it?'

(iv) em   i   tok   yu   stap   hia
      he   auxiliary   said   you stop   here
      'he said you should stay here'

(v) wanpela   bikpela   man
     one-classifier   big-classifier   man
     'a big man'

(vi) haus   bilong   ol
      house genitive   they
      'their house'

(vii) dispela   tripela   liklik   pikinini   pik   man   bilong   Pita
       these-class   three-class   little   diminutive pig   male   genitive   Pita
       'these three little male piglets of Pita's'

Note the <subject, verb, object> pattern, and the fact that inflectional morphology is not strong. (The element *pela*, from *fellow*, is a derivational classifier.) For example, plurality is not marked on nouns, and verb forms do not encode temporal/aspectual distinctions. To the extent that the language marks these distinctions, it does so periphrastically, by means of separate items. For instance:

(viii) (ol)   pikinini   bilong   mi
        plural-mark   children genitive   me
        'my children'

This way of encoding functional dependencies can lead to elaborate systems for marking temporal (*bin* 'past', *laik* 'proximate future', *bai* 'indefinite future'), aspectual (*klosap* 'inceptive', *pinis* 'perfective', *stap* 'progressive', *save* 'habitual'), and modal (*inap* 'ability', *ken* 'permission', *mas* 'necessity') relations. This yields sentences like this one:

(ix) Wanipe   i   no   ken   kam
      Wanipe   auxiliary not   can   come
      'Wanipe cannot come'

It is also noteworthy that Tok Pisin has a variety of "serial" verbs (complex verbal forms produced by associating two more basic verb forms).

(x) bringim   i   go
     bring-it   auxiliary go
     'take it away from me'

Many of these properties of Tok Pisin—as well as its inability to drop subjects, its use of reduplication for aspectual, intensive, and semantic purposes (such as marking reciprocal actions), and several others—are rather typical of creole languages that have arisen in different places and under very different historical circumstances (see section 6.4 for further discussion).

stay within certain boundaries. Species mutate randomly, that's true; but, evidently, cats don't get to be as small as vorticellae or vorticellae as large as cats. Or if that sounds too patently physical—in a dull sense—think of social insect populations and how their organisation looks alike (though any two insect colonies have different numbers of individuals and exist in different environments); or how species converge on (slightly different, yet clearly comparable) organs for vision, locomotion, flight, and so forth; or how a given individual retains a certain integrity in spite of renewing most of its cells, or losing a whole limb (which in some species can be replaced by a similar one), or even part of its brain structure [73]! Granted, these are impressionistic details, but I'm attempting to suggest the presence of a unifying force there, as well.

L: I don't object to that, really—at least in principle. In the case of human language, the unifying force is obvious, at least in development: the human mind. Humans restore a very basic order to the linguistic phenomenon through the very process of language acquisition. There's a sense in which language, as a system "out there," is only relevant as PLD sets within given populations. Again, that's not an insignificant fact, because it gives rise to linguistic variation. However, the (in)stability of this data set is drastically affected every time a child enters the acquisition process. Now, think of it this way: if children didn't bring preprogrammed structure with them—if they came into the world only with mere analytic capacities (analogy, generalization, and so on)—then the importance of a socio/biological system of the kind you suggest may exist out there would be far greater, and its dynamics would drastically affect the way languages change, or even the way they're learned in individual instances. Some aspects of human behavior are probably of this kind, and thus obey very general tendencies that have been directly observed in other complex systems; culture, politics, and economics, for instance, are probably complex in the sense you want. And, of course, it could be (though this is all science fiction) that the evolution of language, or mind more generally, obeys the same sort of rationale. But the kind of language we experience through verbal behavior appears to be much less complex than all of this would imply—that's just a fact. If your hypothesis were right in its extreme version, you'd find out that Ancient Semitic, or any other language spoken thousands of years ago, or any two languages spoken on two different continents today, were as different from English as the hunting-gathering economy of our Paleolithic ancestors was from the consumer economy we live in today, or as a coral syngameon is from a flea or a fungus. There wouldn't be anything wrong with that picture, except that it just doesn't portray human language. In all fundamental respects, English is just as similar to Arabic as I am to an Arab. Almost identical, at a minimal level of abstraction. Give human history enough time, and—in structural respects—Latin or Ancient Greek will turn up again [74].

———————————————————————————— *innateness and universality*

O: Your point is well taken. Needless to say, I wouldn't be worried if Human (once an emergent phenomenon in evolution) were now so stable that it looked totally simple. But you've also suggested that, although a good chunk of Human is possibly genetically specified, some significant parts (at least the ones corresponding to parameters) are not. And if they're not, they'll be subject to the slings and arrows of outrageous fortune, luckily regulated by whatever dynamics directs systems out there.

L: Which is the case (in fact, even if dynamics are irrelevant, and only outrageous fortune is really at issue). But I have to clarify one other aspect of this matter. We often do (and certainly can) refer to the procedure that UG instantiates as "genetic," since we take it to be universal. That's a reasonable conjecture. Of course, I don't know that one (or a sequence) among the hundred thousand genes of the human genome is directly responsible for this procedure—nor do I think it matters. Suppose the procedure is (or is also) a consequence of how the brain develops, including some of those dynamic events you seem to be so fond of; in fact, to be deliberately precise and provocative, suppose Edelman's speculations about the brain were on target, and the establishment of given neural synapses were the result of Darwinian principles [75]. If the output of brain structuring in these terms is still essentially universal, then there's no reason not to expect UG to describe a relevant chunk of it, since UG isn't about genes, but about formal properties of human language. UG could equally well be true if human beings were made from musical notes instead of genes. Of course, problems start arising if your favorite theory of brain structuring (or for that matter, the human genome) predicts that Human shouldn't be universal. Then the brain theory has to be wrong, because Human is clearly universal.

O: You do admit the possibility—do you not?—that given the developmental view, a universal property that is developed **epigenetically** might not be able to develop under certain extreme circumstances.

Figure 1.17

Stephen Jay Gould (1991) introduces the notion of exaptation as follows:

Evolutionary theory lacks a term for a crucial concept—a feature, now useful to an organism, that did not arise as an adaptation for its present role, but was subsequently coopted for its current function. I call such features "exaptations" and show that they are neither rare nor arcane, but dominant features of evolution. . . . This article . . . revises the roles of structure and function in evolutionary theory, serves as a centerpiece for grasping the origin and meaning of brain size in human evolution, and thereby cries out for recognition as a key to evolutionary psychology. Historical origin and current utility are distinct concepts. (p. 43)

Concerning language, Gould says,

Those characteristics [such as vision] that we share with other closely related species are most likely to be conventional adaptations. But attributes unique to our species are likely to be exaptations. . . . As an obvious prime candidate, consider . . . human language. The adaptationist and Darwinian tradition has long advocated a gradualistic continuationism. . . . Noam Chomsky, on the other hand, has long advocated a position corresponding to the claim that language is an exaptation of brain structure. . . . Many adaptationists have so misunderstood Chomsky that they actually suspect him of being an odd sort of closet creationist. (p. 59)

Finally, consider the "spandrel" concept, introduced by Gould and Lewontin (1979):

Spandrels . . . are necessary architectural by-products of mounting a dome on rounded arches. Each spandrel contains a design admirably fitted into its tapering space. . . . The design is so elaborate, harmonious, and purposeful that we are tempted to view it as the starting point of any analysis, as the cause in some sense of the surrounding architecture. But this would invert the proper path of analysis. . . . Yet evolutionary biologists, in their tendency to focus exclusively on immediate adaptation to local conditions, do tend to ignore architectural constraints and perform just such an inversion of explanation. (p. 147)

Note that exaptations do have an immediate utility, although they are coopted for a different function. This is not the case for spandrels, which are "just there." Typical human activities, like music or sex-for-its-own-sake may well be spandrels, immediately raising the question of whether language is too.

L: Theoretically, although it's an outlandish enough possibility not to even worry about it. Imagine a child that developed without having access to a certain crucial protein inside the womb; the result would be some kind of natural monster, and you can't really study anything there. Obviously these aren't fruit flies or mice that we allow ourselves to torture, mutating this or that gene to see what happens. Normal children are the way they are, and it's hard to tease apart whether they are the way they are as a result of instructions that are entirely coded as genetic, or whether some of those instructions are a necessary (universal) consequence of the early environment. But, mind you, this case isn't any different from certain others: the visual system developing the capacity for binocular vision after a couple of months, the child undergoing puberty at a certain stage of maturation [76] . . . These are processes that aren't directly coded in the genes, and it isn't easy to establish the boundaries of what's genetic, and what's epigenetic, and what's totally environmental. Of course, if the organism doesn't get light at all, it's blind. And lacking the appropriate nutritional level can cause puberty to vary rather dramatically. But although lots of data exist in this respect, the mechanics aren't understood, as far as I know. Something must somehow involve genes—for language, for vision, and for puberty—since we as a species now have them all, and somewhere down the evolutionary line our ancestors (if we look far enough) plainly didn't talk, or see, or go through puberty. But whether that "something" is a change in the genetics of the brain or the thyroid gland, or a more basic change that, for instance, liberated some protein which is crucial to make the human brain (or thyroid) develop as it does—well, that's an open issue. It might always be an open issue, since it's just too tough a question.

O: But I hope you don't mean to say that it's not a real question!

————————————————— Universal Grammar may have been an exaptation

L: The truth is that it raises all sorts of problems that go even beyond the fact that observation at this level is basically hopeless. The only thing we know for sure is that these processes aren't something that humans *do*; rather, they're something that *happens to* humans. Language acquisition happens just as much as puberty happens. As to how they came about in the species . . . how can we really decide about that? I'm prepared to admit that the language faculty might have arisen in the human species as a result of properties of the brain that evolved for entirely different reasons, having nothing to do with the language faculty per se. That particular change would be the "real" genetic change that took place . . . In other words, language might be an evolutionary **exaptation**, which is a feature that may be useful for a given organism but didn't originate as an **adaptation** to fulfill its current function [77] [see fig. 1.17]. This is an alternative to the traditional adaptationist view, which posits a gradual process: language is something which grew out of somewhere to give us some evolutionary edge. (You fill in the "some"s.) Well, I don't have any reason to believe that this is right; to begin with, I haven't seen a plausible case being made for an evolutionary scenario, and I don't even see that there's any naturalistic connection between the principles of grammar and anything that plausibly determines evolution [78].

O: Hm . . . I see. So you take language to raise the traditional "wing puzzle" for Darwin: how does an organism go from nothing to an elaborate something (a wing), when evolution proceeds in a series of steps, each of which must be motivated by natural selection [see fig. 1.22]?

L: Yes, where does the impulse to "build" a wing come from, if you only have a rudimentary sort of structure that doesn't allow you to fly? What does your **genotype** gain from a mutation that will only have consequences a few million years down the road? In the case of language, adaptationists (have to) talk about things like communication being important to address this sort of problem, but I don't even understand what's meant by "communication" [see sec. 1.3]. And again, if you were serious about an evolutionary scenario for language, what you'd want to do is study language structure (just as you study wing structure), come up with a plausible proposal for why it evolved and what steps it took, and find a naturalistic explanation for each step in the environment humans inhabited at the time [79]. I can't even begin to imagine what to say here, if by "linguistic structure" we mean more than vague assertions like "Language has words." You could come up with some sort of evolutionary scenario for why words are good to have (and even there, I'm highly skeptical [see sec. 6.5]). But that's sort of like saying that wings are good to have—it doesn't tell you anything profound about wing structure. If you really look at the intricacies of the linguistic system, a naturalistic connection seems out of the question [80]. For instance, no language in the world allows a speaker to say things like *am the man who I seeing is asking something now?* This fact must follow from some principle P, whatever it is, which is somehow responsible for the conservation of a certain (in this instance, relative clause) structure [see sec. 1.1]. What could

The spandrels (striped, roughly triangular elements above the four columns) in the cathedral of Burgos, Spain, complement an octagonal support for the main cupola, a sixteenth-century masterpiece by Juan de Vallejo.

possibly be the evolutionary advantage of this principle? Or take an even more obvious example, our notorious *what are you talking to a man whom you just asked?*, which typifies another construction that's universally impossible. Say this follows from principle P′, and ask yourself, What's the evolutionary advantage of having P′, if it *disallows* the communication (in those terms) of a perfectly fine thought? If scientists could propose a sound explanation for why P and P′ (and all the others) evolved, then a gradualistic view could be reasonable. In fact, even if researchers were to find serious connections between what we do and what our cousin chimps or distant cousin dolphins are up to, maybe we could be reasonably patient with the gradualistic view. But every time someone has seriously tried to teach language to a chimp or a dolphin, they got very poor results, if success is measured in terms of how a three-year-old human talks [81]. Mind you, it could well be that these species are capable of some symbol manipulation, but that's beside the point. In fact, for what I mean by "language," the notion "symbol manipulation" is relatively unimportant; what counts is what kinds of manipulations are at issue. Take a look, in this respect, at what is allegedly the longest "utterance" that has been recorded from an ape using a signed language: *give orange me give eat orange me eat orange give me eat orange give me you* [82]. This may be an effective way of communicating the idea that "you should give me an orange to eat—or else" . . . but it isn't human language. To say otherwise is not to take human language very seriously—or animal communication, for that matter.

O: Your arguments against gradual adaptationism are suggestive, but mustn't you still explain why a certain cross-species continuity exists, for example, in the differing "strength" of conceptual powers? Aren't humans really brighter than the creatures they came from?

L: Are we? I for one doubt if I could figure out how to survive very long in the environment they used to live in! As far as I'm concerned, organisms are basically incommensurable [83] . . . Besides, conceptualization isn't as crucially related to core aspects of human language as it may seem at first [see chap. 2]. Even individuals who have serious difficulty carrying out simple conceptual tasks can make grammaticality judgments on very elaborate structures. In turn, language functions can be selectively impaired, or language can be spared altogether from brain damage, which indicates that language isn't just a trivial part of general cognition—whatever that means [84]. At any rate, recall the way Darwin dealt with the "wing puzzle" [85]. Mivart was trapped in the absurd position of claiming that a wing had to evolve suddenly—all of it, with all its intricacies of structural design. Darwin, while acknowledging the seriousness of Mivart's puzzle, solved it by eliminating an unmotivated assumption: why should "early wings" exist for flight? A wing that has only a small percentage of its current, flight-attuned surface is only an evolutionary oddity if we take it to be a flight implement. However, it may have been something else: a cooling system, a respiratory outgrowth, whatever—it doesn't matter for the argument. If so, then it may have been a perfectly legitimate evolutionary structure, although not a wing [see fig. 1.22].

O: Just so, and Darwin gave these structures a perfectly dreadful name: preadaptation. The idea is brilliant, but the name puts across entirely the wrong message. There couldn't be anything like a *pre*-adaptation—that was Mivart's whole point!

L: Which is exactly why Gould and his associates call the Darwinian preadaptation an "exaptation." But names aside, what matters is this: wings as we now know them in birds, for instance, didn't start out as wings; they couldn't have. (A different question altogether is to determine what wings did start out as, which people are still debating.) These issues are even more clear-cut with respect to language, possibly the best-understood instance of emergence within the natural world. Here we have an apparently unique, qualitatively different phenomenon, clearly correlating with a specific stage of organizational complexity in brain structure [86]. The adaptationist view is that this brain structure became what it is as language evolved—thus raising the question of what evolutionary purpose intermediate brain structures served as they were evolving. The exaptationist view is exactly the opposite: for some unknown reason, the brain became larger; in this process it somehow acquired a variety of features that became useful for innumerable purposes, including linguistic abilities.

O: The trick, of course, is to ferret out that "unknown reason" why the brain became larger.

L: Yeah, but that's neither an easy nor a crucial problem. A recent article that comes to mind, for instance, suggests that slender and heavy-boned australopithecines evolved different true adaptations for cranial blood flow. The slender folks developed a widespread network of veins, which over time became more and more elaborate. The adaptation might have been a response to something as trivial as their inhabiting savanna areas, with intense solar radiation. In other words, a larger brain was literally easier to cool [87]! Of course, good luck proving it—or any similar hypothesis.

O: If language has nothing to do, at least directly, with the adaptation that gave you the brain you have, then the possibility exists that language is like those **spandrels** of San Marco's Basilica where the four Evangelists sit, for us to contemplate. Given round arches at right angles, you get four spandrels. Once you have them, you may as well use their shape and magnificent location to produce a miracle of art [88].

L: Right, language is very possibly a "spandrel" of brain size. The real issue, then, is that trivial changes have tremendous consequences for a large brain, since they occur in the evolutionary context of whatever limitations exist on this sort of object. Starting with the different possibilities inherent in something with ten billion neurons, mushed into the size of a spaghetti entrée, what would physics do here? Plainly, we don't know. Maybe such a thing can only evolve in one way, and that's what we're seeing [89].

1.5 Simple Universal Minds
(three discourses on brain, Descartes, and matter, with other particulars of great interest and no lesser consequence)

O: That calls to mind the theoretical possibility of quantum computation in a neurophysiological object [90]. That is to say, in regular computers, all bits of information have definite states; in contrast, in quantum computers, the states of bits fluctuate. Such a computer exists in numerous states simultaneously, and can theoretically run phenomenally complex computations, and phenomenal numbers of them, all at the same time. Needless to say, no known computer is capable of this, but if the bits in actual computers were to shrink to atomic scale, then they might become so, as Feynman once observed. Now: what about neural computations? Could it not be the case that the spaghetti entrée you have in mind would allow parallel computations of phenomenal complexity [91]?

———————————————————————— *discourse about neurophysiology*

L: I don't know what that means—and I'm not sure I want to. The only reason I emphasized the scope of the problem is that it makes any serious talk about adaptation basically beside the point. If there are no alternatives in a brain like ours to the linguistic structures we actually see, what's the point of asking how their evolution may have proceeded? Given a single alternative, one can always come up with a reason for its existence, which makes the discussion unfalsifiable to start with [92]. But I believe it's even worse than that. The very belief that neurophysiology is even relevant to the functioning of the mind is just a hypothesis [93].

O: Oh, pray tell! I so much want to hear this one. If I recall, it was Alcmaenon of Croton who first thought of the brain as the locus of sensation and thought. Then of course, Aristotle lowered consciousness to its current folkloric resting place, inside the chest— thereby reserving the space of the brain for much cooler matters, like a ventilation system . . . More recent heretics—like Gall, to name the most notorious one—had the gall to contradict the mighty father, convincing the contemptuous scientific establishment that the brain is the organ of the mind. But perhaps you'd like to reestablish the credit of the old man, particularly after what you've said about cooling brains.

L: I didn't say "brain," did I? You're making a pretty quick transition from my "neurophysiology" to your "brain"! In fact, the brain per se isn't the only relevant thing to look at. Where does the brain end? Certainly it extends to the eyes, and all the way down to the nervous system throughout the body. And of course, in development all these things come from the same place: there's no way to tell whether a given cell is going to end up as a neuron or some totally different kind of cell. So at that point it's difficult to talk meaningfully about brains, and later on—in the developed individual—we get into all sorts of tricky questions like where the nervous system connects with the immune system, how it engages the locomotive system, and so on. Very subtle issues arise here. For instance, current research shows that by practicing a motion mentally (say, throwing a baseball), a person gets better at it physically. How does the nervous system communicate with the motor system in the absence of any actual movement [94]? Who really knows whether we're looking at the relevant aspects of the brain? Certainly there are parts of it that we don't even begin to comprehend. Look at glia, which outnumber neurons nine to one within the brain's body, occupying more than half its volume. What do neuroscientists really know about glial cells?

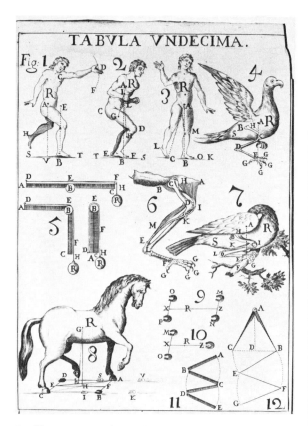

Borelli's conception of animal motion. (From Borelli, *De motu animalium*)

Figure 1.18

[Many of the following ideas can be found in Bruno 1987. On Newton's study of alchemy, see Dobbs 1975.]

Cartesian mechanics served as the basis for many attempts to elucidate animal motion, such as this early one by Borelli, who based muscle actions on the laws of statics and dynamics, within a universe that acts globally like a giant machine (the first principle). Descartes's machine represented a rationalist attempt to free the universe from traditional philosophical ghosts, and satisfied the Galilean desire to focus on mechanics as a fundamental source of motion, setting aside Aristotelian growth, change, and psychology as different sorts of processes. However, Descartes did systematically concern himself with human psychology, stressing that its creative aspect could not possibly be captured by mechanics. This forced him to postulate a second principle, proposing a substance to "host" the mind. This split has been the source of much debate and many intriguing proposals, including Leibniz's early attempts to explain the second principle in terms of global harmonies imposed on the first (material) substance. The fact is that Descartes's claims about mind were largely unchallenged (or ignored) until very recently, when a new scientific preoccupation with mind emerged. In contrast, Descartes's view of mechanics, itself a reaction against Aristotelian views, was challenged in his own time, by

O: Yes, of course—microtubules are a better instance. Paramecia and amoebae don't have neurons; why, they're single cells themselves! And yet they go about life swimming round merrily in search of food, escaping danger, avoiding obstacles and, alas, keeping a record of it all! How? Well, apparently the control system is part of the cytoskeleton, a structure of proteinlike molecules which glues the cell together, basically. In this cytoskeleton are the wonderful microtubules, the minuscule protein polymers that arrange themselves into the cell's centrosome; this "think tank" is fundamental to the process of mitosis, but in addition, it appears to be involved in the processing and transfer of cell-level information. Now, every neuron has its own cytoskeleton; what role do microtubules play within your mighty neurons? What is this micro–nervous system doing within the larger one? No one really knows [95]. But this sort of situation is typical in the history of science; what's shocking (among other things I've heard today) is that you may actually conceive of the mental as something other than the neurophysiological at some higher level.

L: We certainly do know a lot about the mental—from a scientific perspective. We know many things about how vision works, how language works; we have very good computational theories of these matters. But we don't know—we haven't established—that the body of principles we've unearthed in these regions of the universe has a neurological basis. All we know is that neurons exist, and they seem to be implicated somehow [96]. But that's like saying that atoms are implicated in the formation of life—it's a triviality. If you want to know what's going on in life, you can't just start by saying, "Atoms exist, and that's all there is to physics, so they must be responsible for life." What kind of reasoning is that?

O: But if mind isn't embodied in neurons and glial cells, et cetera, then where is it? Aren't you falling back into metaphysical dualism? You sound like Descartes, talking about a "second substance." Since a number of phenomena don't fall under mechanics (that is, causes and effects involving direct contact), you invoke a second substance, whose essence is "thought" [see fig. 1.18].

---

discourse on Cartesian dualism

L: Let's please be fair. Descartes did realize that the creative aspect of the human mind cannot be captured by mechanics. In fact, he was talking about language, and the idea that no device working according to mechanical principles could deal with the normal use of language. Properties like the unboundedness of human language, its independence from purely external stimuli (you don't need to say "Fire!" when you see fire, although you can) or internal states (you don't need to say "Ouch!" when your back aches, although you can), and its appropriateness to situations which are neither directly caused by, nor cause, the verbal behavior [97]. In other words, the usual properties that our language has, but the so-called language of bees, or the so-called language of computers, doesn't have. Plainly. So this is why Descartes needed a second substance; he followed standard scientific reasoning. And yes, then he had a typical unification problem: to show how mind (where the second substance operates) interacts with body (where the first substance operates). What Descartes did is standard in the sciences: sometimes you unify, sometimes you don't. His metaphysical dualism was essentially as naturalistic as, say, Galileo's decision to stick to only a few phenomena within the Aristotelian theory of motion (which included mechanics, perception, growth, and everything that changed). Galileo got modern science underway by isolating a set of phenomena among those that Aristotle sought to explain; deciding to understand that particular set rather well, he left the others for future research. It was business as usual.

O: But the fact of the matter is that Descartes's programme utterly collapsed within a generation. There was a ghost in his machine! And of course Newton demonstrated that the Cartesian theory of the material world was exactly inadequate. As a matter of fact, bodies do affect each other at a distance—a phenomenon that perplexed Newton and led the way to modern physics.

L: But notice: what Newton destroyed was Descartes's theory of body—not his theory of mind. Strange as Newton's results were, utterly defying common sense, it was hard to deny them, given their **internal coherence** and predictive power. But Newton had nothing to say about Descartes's conclusions about mind. What Newton wrecked was Descartes's machine, not his ghost! In fact, nobody has had anything to say about Descartes's conclusions for centuries [98]. Descartes's claim about automata was and still is absolutely correct, although for reasons he didn't really know. As Newton demonstrated, no mechanical principle can deal with anything in this universe—even basic motion. So although it was reasonable for Descartes to postulate a second substance, it was also wrong, given that Newton showed that there wasn't even a first substance. This completely changed the rules of the game, in new and much more interesting ways.

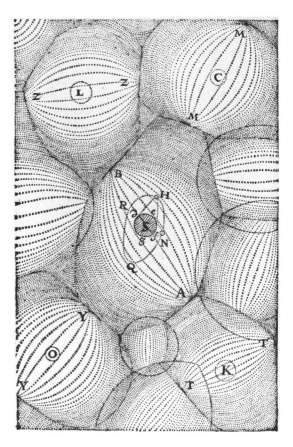

Descartes's conception of space. (From Descartes, *Principia philosophiae*)

Newton. Descartes (as well as Leibniz) rejected as inconceivable that action could occur at a distance (Newton's gravitation), and he tried to argue that space was not empty, but instead full of what he called the "plenum," a kind of ethereal stuff that allegedly swirled around in vortices. Thus, the motion of the heavenly bodies was taken to be in mechanical contact with the plenum. (In the illustration, the system of vortices is supposed to carry the planets around the sun.) It is this view that Newton's arguments destroyed. Newton's outlook was considerably less "materialist" than the mechanistic approach he was reacting against, and it in essence eliminated the received wisdom of what a body is. This may not be all that surprising, coming from someone who spent considerable time and effort speculating on theological matters and devoted half his life to rationalizing alchemy.

O: I'm smiling because I hear you questioning even the very material nature of this tired universe . . .

discourse about matter

L: What does "material" mean, though? Matter is what there is. It's interesting to see how leading scientists who were either Newton's contemporaries, or came right after him, regarded his conception of force—in effect, as a return to the dark ages of Scholasticism. Even Newton himself was uneasy about his conclusions—he conceded that he couldn't assign a cause to the power of gravity, and spent the rest of his days trying to figure out an explanation. This isn't uncommon in the sciences, although the repeated use of terms makes us forget about the gaps they name. What is the material, what are physical entities? While these terms had some sense within the mechanical philosophy, it's unclear that they mean anything in the Newtonian world—even more so in the universe of contemporary physics, with its notions of fields, one-dimensional strings in ten-dimensional space, and so on.

O: Well of course, from that perspective, similar issues arise about life. As a matter of fact, until the last century scientists thought of life as obeying a "vital force," and "organic substance" was thought to be produced exclusively by living things. It was—of all things—urea (an organic compound), which was experimentally produced from ammonium cyanate (an inorganic one), that proved that life's stuff was perfectly standard . . . This and similar experiments contributed to undermining the vitalist theses, so much so that living and nonliving matter were shown to obey the same basic chemistry.

L: Yes, so the question of "life" is actually similar to the question of "matter," in one sense. It's not very meaningful to ask at what level of complexity we have "life." A chemist, as you imply, would answer "nowhere"—in part a useful decision but not necessarily a matter of fact (if it is a matter of fact, that has to be established). For a biologist, in contrast, "life" starts with a genetic program—another useful decision, but maybe not a matter of fact either. For instance, is life possible without a genetic plan? What would it mean to have life in those circumstances? Would reproduction be possible? Would metabolism be possible—or necessary? Having these questions of course doesn't mean that you don't do chemistry or biology—quite the opposite. You make your useful decisions precisely to get useful answers, which hopefully cohere into a body of knowledge. All you have is the world, though, with its various aspects: chemical, optical, linguistic, and so on, these being more signs of our ignorance than ontological divides. A priori talk of boundaries here (whether they be "matter" or "life" or whatever) is senseless, and no serious scientist raises questions about what the "true criterion of the chemical" is, or "the mark of electricity," or "the boundaries of the optical," and so on. What does it mean for something to be material, or alive, then? Do you want to delimit the physical in such a way that it excludes, say, the mental? Suppose you did, and called it "matter"? Fine, now you have matter and it doesn't touch Cartesian thought. What is it that you have? I don't know what you'd have.

O: What you're getting at, then, is that the study of mind is merely another aspect of the study of the natural world . . . There's no sense, from your perspective, in calling it material or not, since we don't really know what matter is.

L: All we know is that there are certain phenomena out there and we try to account for them as best we can, by the usual procedures: observing them, describing them, incorporating them into a coherent theory that makes predictions, testing them, and so on. And I see no reason to separate the mental from all of this, just as there was no reason to separate the chemical, or the biological. Unifications should be sought—no doubt about that. But we can't afford to be dogmatic about where a given phenomenon falls and how we should account for it. If you chastise linguistics because it's separate from biology, or physics, or whatever, you'll lose a golden opportunity to understand the emergence of one of the most interesting types of cognition that life forms are capable of. I think that would be unfortunate.

———————————————————— the design of the grammar is elegant

O: It would, because if the picture you've been painting is correct, the form of cognition in question is very pretty indeed—which is nice, in a world full of oddities. It appeals to my sort of mind that you've turned my question about linguistic variation into an argument for elegance in design, first of all. The system is so well constructed, encoding only the essential, that variation results as a side effect. So I concede the point that linguistic variation is due to biological underspecification.

L: I didn't reach such a strong conclusion, although I'd be happy with it. To make that point conclusively, one would have to show that all linguistic parameters are instances of underspecification in the cognitive system or in a deep part of it, precisely because this (part of the) system doesn't need to determine aspects, such as word order, which are irrelevant for its workings. Then variation emerges within I-languages because these are the by-products of final states of the language faculty, which are fairly removed from its more abstract initial state S_0. As I say, this seems plausible, but it has to be demonstrated.

O: I perversely like the fact that the elegance we're alluding to is very dull, in a sense—very detached from linguistic functions [99] . . . When one first thinks of linguistic matters, as I have today, such things as English are very dear to one's heart. But you persuasively argued that, to the extent that the notion "the English language" makes any scientific sense, it does so only through the minds of English speakers. In these minds, the really well behaved state is S_0, the initial one—which is totally removed from anything humans directly experience. Then the acquisition process starts, and a much dirtier, ironically less concrete state is reached, which corresponds to an idealised I-English. The issue of what's "close to data" is thus turned round: English speakers' sentences are surprisingly far removed from data, whereas their much more abstract S_0 states are closer to real data for a scientific theory of language. In actual fact, this view that deep parts of the linguistic system essentially ignore what seem like fairly basic properties of languages (such as word order) invites the inference that, in the end, I-languages are epiphenomena of a deep cognitive system which, strictly speaking, may not have evolved at all.

L: Yeah, it could be that other species with large brains have access to S_0, but they haven't evolved the trivial means to translate these resources into anything like a human language, an epiphenomenon which makes possible this conversation, human history, civilization, and so on. Again, this would have to be demonstrated, though—and it hasn't been.

O: This ties in rather well with the fact that linguistic variation lives on, and thus a particular behavioural pattern ("subject first," for example) doesn't get genetically encoded. You see, I was initially troubled by your claim that language must be innate. Linguistic diversity makes one suspect that the language faculty is nothing but a general-purpose device, whether learnt from the outside world or corresponding to an inner world which is mostly unstructured. You offered some interesting arguments against both of these positions, which only compounded my question: if language is a rich, innate structure that arose through adaptation, why is it so plastic? For Heaven's sake, what possible adaptive pressure could there be to favour something which so patently hinders communication [100]?! To the extent that there should be any pressure, it should favour fixing a particular parametric option—I don't care which. But of course, the whole issue is moot if language is not adaptive, and variation simply a result of underspecification, in the system of knowledge that an exaptation bestowed on human beings.

L: Which means—I must say—that you were profoundly wrong in implying any connection between language acquisition and learning [see sec. 1.2].

O: In turn, there's one other domain where elegance is needed: in the analysis of input data. If what you said is true, then either the LAD is extremely elegant in its behaviour (encoding not just the principles that UG instantiates, as a sieve for what's possible, but also a metric to evaluate different alternatives in, perhaps rather common, cases of conflict) or else language acquisition may fail. This is a possibility, I presume.

L: Not for normal humans, as I've said before, but it is indeed for other species—which I suppose is what you mean. Having evolved some mechanism that allows us to acquire language isn't a necessary evolutionary turn (and not necessarily an adaptation [101]). You can imagine a creature with S_0 in place, and yet no ability to find parameter values to go from S_0 to a communicable S_f [see fig. 1.19].

O: But of course! Now you've noticed, I trust, that I've conceded many points today because . . . I may as well say it: your arguments are reasonable, and because they lead to considerable beauty in the overall conception you're beginning to develop of what you may call the mental universe—

L: I prefer to call it the universe, at a mental dimension.

O: But now I want to talk about UG (the linguist's theory) and its internal aspects. Would you also expect beauty internal to UG? How far into the system does simplicity go?

Figure 1.19

The following three elements of the human linguistic phenomenon are logically independent of one another:

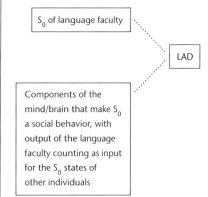

A species could evolve that had S_0, but no way of "making it public" (hence, individuals would generate no output that other individuals could use to set the parametric values of S_0). Likewise, a species could evolve that had no LAD and thus no way of connecting input data to S_0. These two evolutionary courses would result in behaviorally identical species: namely, ones that could not speak. Nonetheless, both species would have innate knowledge of language (assuming S_0 was intact).

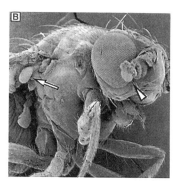

Fly with an ectopic eye under the wing *(arrow)* and on the antenna *(arrowhead)*. (From Halder, Callaerts, and Gehring, Induction of ectopic eyes by targeted expression of the *eyeless* gene in *Drosophila*)

Figure 1.20

The entire life plan of a cell, from its daily functioning to its programmed death, depends on proteins (see fig. 1.21). But arguably the most spectacular process that cells participate in is the growth and development of a multicellular organism, whereby a creature changes from a single-cell state to a complex state involving billions of cells and thousands of organs of different sizes and characteristics. In figuring out how an embryo grows and develops, the very behavior of each of its constituent cells has to be computed. This is no trivial task. Consider, for instance, what happens when the *eyeless* gene is turned on in parts of flies where it is normally not active.

As the photograph shows, the fly grows extra eyes under a wing and on an antenna. This behavior of the *eyeless* gene makes it a good candidate for a "master control gene," which is capable of triggering the formation of an organ by producing a protein that turns a cascade of genes on or off.

It is very likely that a model for the embryo must be context sensitive. For example, much of a frog's DNA is plausibly present to allow tadpoles to survive in different kinds of temperatures, a problem mammals do not face (Cohen and Stewart 1994). This illustrates that DNA does not correlate neatly with the morphology or the general structural complexity of an individual. If information about the environment in which the embryo develops must be integrated (in order to come up with a computational system to relate egg to individual), the hope of finding a traditional algorithm that models the process is fairly slim. A second possibility exists: this much detail is unnecessary, and the behavior of the embryo can be studied at a level where regularities can be established that do not depend on the behavior of specific cells (see fig. 1.28 and sec. 1.7). Under those circumstances it may be feasible to construct a theoretical model relating egg to individual, but the prospect appears to be far from imminent.

Note also that the present speculation presupposes a dimension of order that is not directly seen at the level being considered here (Goodwin 1994). This relates to a statistical fact that becomes apparent when one considers that each cell's plans are the contingent results of evolution. The process works by means of extremely rare mistakes in DNA copying (mutations). Many of these mistakes have structurally lethal consequences for the cell. Only in some instances is the resulting structure viable, and only in some of those is the mutation present in

L: The degree of elegance seems to be extraordinary. This is what I think makes linguistics closer to physics or chemistry than biology, somewhat mysteriously. The process of evolution, for instance, is very messy [see figs. 1.8 and 1.10].

O: There, now—you've already hinted at the puzzle I was concocting! You see, I was planning to trap you into accepting that the system of UG is elegant (which I knew you'd do, given your insistence on its simplicity). Then I thought I would corner you thus: life is not as elegant as you paint it! But the fact that you saw me coming doesn't entail that you shouldn't give me an answer . . . Life—particularly as we see it now after almost four thousand million years of evolution—is the result of fairly complex processes. I don't suppose I need remind you of this, but take a small cell, one of the principal "behaviours" of evolution. It's a bloody messy and diverse one, beautiful though it is. It could be that we find it so because we simply haven't discovered all the relevant principles; or it could be that there isn't much more to discover with conventional tools, and the universe at that level is just partly grotty—which doesn't mean it isn't interesting. The empirical answer to this question is far from settled for biology right now—as you insisted—and biologists walk with it, and similar questions, right into the twenty-first century. Needless to say, the question becomes particularly pertinent to our little exercise when you ask it at the species level: Given the genome of a species and a specific environment, can you predict how (or whether) it's going to mutate? Given a description of a fertilised egg (in actual fact, an entire DNA sequence, and the location of all proteins and RNA), can you predict how an embryo will develop? To put it differently, are these tasks computable [see fig. 1.20] [102]? Now suppose the situation in standard biology is this: these matters cannot obviously be predicted computationally, and to the extent that models are even found, they will be highly complex, not precisely of the $e = mc^2$ sort.

the language faculty exhibits discrete infinity, lack of overdeterminacy, and extreme economy

L: I see what you're getting at and, before you even raise the question, let me admit—gladly—that what we find in linguistics is very unusual for biological systems of the kind you're alluding to. Take discrete infinity, for instance. As you informally proved today, the output of UG is an infinite set of often intricate structures, each formed on the basis of discrete units like *what* and *is* and *science*.

Linguistic symbols are always discrete units; it doesn't make sense to talk about, say, half of a word or a bit more than a sentence.

O: Interesting . . . DNA appears to display something of the same property.

L: Well, although biochemists have cracked the DNA code, they haven't yet (by a long shot) figured out how the coding devices organize to encode development, morphology, and everything else [see fig. 1.21]. There are four nucleotide bases—not three and a half, not four and a third. So that's discrete; but exactly whether recursion occurs, and how many levels it involves, is precisely what has to be fully demonstrated. At any rate, even if discrete infinity did obtain at this level, it's not easy to find it at other, more articulated levels of the biological world. But there's more. A useful working hypothesis that linguists have entertained in the past few years is that the language faculty isn't overdetermined—in other words, the phenomena we want to explain don't follow from more than one principle. So suppose you wanted to explain why, when English speakers have the option of including a word like *went* in their lexicon, and also (in principle) a word like *goed*, they choose *went* and not **goed*. If one of your students proposed that this phenomenon follows both from, say, a principle that seeks the most specific structure (**goed* is less specific than *went*) and from a principle that seeks the least complex structure (**goed* has two parts, *go-* and *-ed*, and *went* has only one part), what would you say?

O: Were I a biologist, I don't know what I should say. A given form, like a wing, has resulted from rather different evolutionary paths. Bird wings developed from membranes whose possible purpose was cooling, and whose side effect was flight. But the origin of insect wings is arguably connected not to cooling but to aquatic behaviours [see fig. 1.22]. Many instances of overdetermination are found at the genetic level, within a given species—for example, the machinery that guides the growth of a neuronal axon. This "wiring of the nervous system" has lots and lots of redundancies built in—perhaps not surprisingly, given the importance of this system and the apparent complexity of the wiring [103]. Many instances of this sort occur, at many levels of the biological universe. But were I a physicist, my answer would be clear: the process should not follow from more than one principle. This is one of the most basic assumptions in physics.

a cell that is responsible for the next generation of individuals. Finally, only in some of those instances does the viable, transmittable structure correspond to a phenotype that is adaptive, given a specific environment, and only if a sufficient number of individuals find themselves in this circumstance, and are able to breed (thus transmitting their specific genotype), does a species emerge. The likelihood of this scenario is minuscule. Therefore, if scientists were to manage to meaningfully reduce the class of possible evolutionary scenarios by way of (perhaps as yet hidden) higher-order constraints, the likelihood of life as it now exists would be enhanced (Kauffman 1995). Other scientists, however, argue that likelihood is beside the point once the events that lead to present life and form have indeed taken place; other events would have had different but equally likely results. (Un)fortunately, the (life) experiment cannot be replicated, to see whether the same path is followed (as complexity theorists expect) or whether totally different life forms emerge (as historicists predict).

Figure 1.21

[For the ideas below, see the references mentioned in figure 1.6.]

It was not until the 1920s that ribonucleic acid (RNA, which contains the sugar ribose) was distinguished from deoxyribonucleic acid (DNA, which contains the sugar deoxyribose). The latter was found in chromosomes, and it carries the blueprint of living organisms.

Watson and Crick's 1953 model explicated the double helix structure of the DNA molecule. The spiral is made of millions of nucleotides (composed of deoxyribose, a molecule containing phosphorous, and a nitrogenous base) bound together by base pairs, whose sequence makes up the essential DNA code for a cell. (It is this information that instructs the cell how to make proteins.) Each nucleotide in the DNA strand contains one of four bases: adenine, thymine, cytosine, or guanine. Given their chemical structures, A pairs with T, and C with G, resulting in base pairs AT, TA, CG, and GC and consequently two complementary DNA strands. Before cell division, various enzymes help the two strands separate from each other, and they assemble free nucleotides from the cell to replicate the missing halves. Thus, when the process is complete, two copies remain of the specific genetic information that the cell carried. After cell division, each "daughter" cell keeps one of the DNA copies, which continues to serve its organizing function.

RNA is active in the manufacture of proteins. These are constructed by combining amino acids, in a specific order. A single DNA molecule usually holds the plans for thousands of proteins; a gene is, specifically, the length of DNA that codes (aspects of) a given protein. Proteins are assembled in two steps. The first is transcription: the DNA molecule partially unzips, with one strand again serving as a template. But this time it is m(essenger)-RNA that constitutes the corresponding strand, again through base pairing (though m-RNA contains the base uracil rather than thymine). After a gene is transcribed in this way, the m-RNA leaves the nucleus of the cell, and the DNA molecule closes up. The second step is translation. The code of the m-RNA is written in terms of codones, each consisting of three bases (which, given four bases, allows 4^3 combinations) and each coding a particular amino acid. The protein is assembled in the cell's ribosome, which reads the m-RNA's codones through a molecule of t(ransfer)-RNA.

Blue fly. (From Hooke, *Micrographia*)

Bat. (From Cuvier, *Le règne animal*)

L: Well, to the extent that the same working hypothesis has also been successful in linguistics, we can conjecture that it's more than an artifact of our mode of inquiry—a methodology, if you like—and that it in fact reflects something true about the language faculty that isn't obviously true about the world at a standard biological level. But there's more. Most peculiar of all peculiar properties is this. Over and over linguists keep seeing that the computations of the language faculty and the structural descriptions that they generate (phrases, processes of constituent displacement, phonological structures, and so on) obey some sort of economy: they're extremely parsimonious both in their shape and in the processes involved in obtaining that shape.

O: What does that mean, a process obtaining a shape?

1.6 Economy

(wherein it is averred that linguistic creatures "compete to survive," and the general assumptions behind this extraordinary circumstance are first unearthed)

L: The linguistic structure of every sentence is, in some very concrete sense, the history of a particular process. That means, essentially, that there is a logical ordering to that process, or that structures are derivative on the process: you logically start at some point X_0, and finish at some point X_f.

O: You mean, I start this sentence with the first word, *I*, and then I go on until I finish the sentence with the word *sentence* . . .

———————————————————— *digression about competence and performance*

L: Oh, no, no, no. No. No, put that aside for a moment: I'm not talking about how you produce that sentence at all, but rather about the internal structure of the sentence. Take, for instance, *I finish the sentence*. It has a clear hierarchical structure, right?—a subject, a verb, an object; a bunch of phrases; a sentence. We could obviously bracket the elements, as follows: [[I] [[finish] [[the] [sentence]]]]. Plainly, there's a logical ordering here, whereby the association between, say, [the] and [sentence] is more basic than the association between [finish] and [[the] [sentence]]; the former is logically prior to the latter.

O: Excellent, but how is that different from what I've said? I plan to say, "I finish the sentence" (so I think it). And then I say it—when I'm done, I have it. What's the secret?

L: The secret is that you have to separate the properties of the cognitive system that's encoded in the initial state S_0 of the language faculty, and whose parameter values are set through early experience, from the way that system is actually used. The investigative task, then, has to be viewed from two different perspectives, which linguists call **competence** and **performance.** Something's going on right now between us: we're using language. The complexity of this performance is phenomenal: it involves many variables and functions that aren't (even remotely) understood; many circumstances affect even the most basic processes; many systems are involved in the behavior (some of which might not even be linguistic). Linguists don't even know for a fact that different speakers use the same modes of performance, though they generally assume so. The question is, What do scientists usually do when they run across an overwhelmingly complex phenomenon?

O: Clearly, one must examine it at a higher level of abstraction—zoom out, as it were, to a higher dimension and see what regularities obtain there. A favourite example of mine is those maddening drips of water that leak out of old faucets. What—I ask myself as I'm lying awake hearing "drip-drop, drip-drop"—is the bloody frequency of a drop breaking, given a continuous flow of liquid [see fig. 1.23]? Given the complexity of the dynamics within the system, one can go right round the bend trying to decide whether there's any systematicity to when the next drop will drip by just looking at when each of them cares to break. But now watch what happens if we place the problem in a different dimension. Very specifically, suppose we record the time that elapses between one drop falling and the next, which produces a series of times. Suppose, then, that we make a two-dimensional graph, whose *x*-axis represents a time interval between two drops, and whose *y*-axis represents the next interval. Then what?

L: Regularities in the system are exposed that aren't obvious otherwise.

O: Actually, in all honesty nothing much happens with only two dimensions—the problem is still too complex. But . . . what you thought was the punch line does happen if we add a third dimension

Figure 1.22

The fascination with animal anatomy is prehistoric, but careful scientific observation did not take place until the Renaissance. In the seventeenth century, Robert Hooke, an expert in mechanics and optics who developed a compound microscope, provided the first accurate drawings of insects and some of their organs. But it was not until Linnaeus's taxonomic work on plant classes in the eighteenth century that natural history adopted the scientific method. In the nineteenth century, Cuvier (like Linnaeus, a staunch believer in the rigidity of species) extended the Linnaean system beyond plants, postulating phyla on the basis of the internal structure of animals. This fertile tradition (coupled with new philosophical and scientific notions) eventually led to the work of Wallace and Darwin on the origin of species. Wallace and Darwin did not device a completely novel theory of evolution; rather, they reinterpreted others' speculations in a revolutionary way, introducing the concept of natural selection (see fig. 1.8). After the initial theoretical outburst, questions immediately arose, many posed by Darwin himself. One of them concerned the functional and formal similarity among organs whose origins were manifestly diverse. For example, an insect wing and a bat wing have no obvious connection in terms of specific functional or structural origin.

As St. George Mivart demonstrated, the protowings that birds, insects, and mammals must have had would have been perfectly useless as flight devices; why, then, was their evolution favored? Mivart's solution to this problem—that organs evolved suddenly, as complete entities—was implausibly anti-Darwinian. Darwin's own proposal set the stage for Gould and Vrba's (1982) notion of "exaptation" (see fig. 1.17). He challenged the assumption of functional continuity: why must the protowings have been used for flight? But his revised proposal still leaves a question open: why do various organs with conceivably different origins all converge on the same useful function? The standard answer is that a useful design becomes streamlined as a result of accumulated successes (the failures dying out), each providing an evolutionary edge. Once a rudimentary flying implement is in place in a given species, convergent evolution through functionalism is supposed to cascade. Obviously, however, the larger the number of species that—starting from different sources—converge on similar functional solutions, the less likely it is that this convergence is the result of mere chance. Attributing it to "useful design" means little in the absence of a theory of useful design. In fact, some theorists of design (see, e.g., Petroski 1993) argue that there really is no such thing as usefulness, in an a priori sense, for at least technological design.

A storm on Jupiter. (*Voyager 2*)

Figure 1.23

[For the ideas below, see Gleick 1987 or Cohen and Stewart 1994.]

Chaotic regularity emerges, for example, in weather systems. In 1961 Edward Lorenz found empirical evidence, in weather systems, for an idea that goes back to Poincaré: errors and uncertainties accumulate, making predictions very difficult beyond a few systemic states. But although this system never finds a steady state in which to repeat itself, it almost does, particularly around certain pockets of regularity called "attractors." The photograph depicts a storm on Jupiter, large enough to encompass three Earths. The system whirls counterclockwise, as do the smaller systems below, producing the cloud patterns around them. Jupiter's atmosphere (like Earth's) changes constantly, never repeating a pattern, but systematically falling back into certain attractors. Chaos theory has found that this sort of regular irregularity in systems that are highly sensitive to initial conditions is predictably unpredictable, and that it arises from very simple functions involving few variables, contrary to traditional beliefs that complex behavior involves complex rules. Just as chaos involves complexity arising from simplicity, so some systems manifest a sort of simplicity within their known complexity (see fig. 1.9). This can be illustrated by water dripping from a faucet. If the flow of water is low, drops fall at regular intervals. As flow rate increases, the drops fall in an iambic, 2/4 rhythm (bah-bum-bah-bum) and then in 4/4 rhythm (with the iambic foot (two drops) echoing

to our graph, whose z-axis now captures yet another (the third) time interval in a sequence of four drops. It's then that fuzzy coalescences emerge in different regions of the graph, in which case we can begin to study the problem with something to hold on to: a chaotic pattern [104].

L: Linguists change viewpoints, too, from the dimension of performance to that of competence, abstracting away many variables and concentrating on new ones. Typically, the study of linguistic competence focuses on overall structural patterns, such as phrases; and it doesn't pay attention to things like the rate or intensity of speech, or the speaker's intentions in uttering a particular linguistic token—variables which are clearly very significant from the point of view of performance.

O: Very well, but don't forget that eventually we must return to the lower dimension, and predict when the next drop will fall.

L: We'd like to, but we may not succeed. It's possible that zooming out to higher dimensions allowed us to glance into the structure of the system (thus determining that it does have structure, in spite of appearances at lower dimensions), but maybe we can't do anything about the way the abstract structure manifests itself at the lower dimension, since things are just too complex down there [see fig. 1.23]. Again, this is more a matter of our limitations as scientists and human beings than a deep property of these complex systems. I'm particularly skeptical about solving the problem of linguistic performance, because it touches on some of humankind's deepest concerns—including, I should say, the nature of free will. At any rate, all we know for sure is that we can use significant parts of the system of knowledge that we call competence—otherwise I wouldn't be talking to you. But we don't know that we can use all the resources of the system of knowledge. In fact, it's worse than that: we know that we *can't* use large chunks of this knowledge.

O: Come again? What on earth is an unusable part of language?

L: Suppose I tell you that the cat the dog chased left. Suppose the dog had been kicked by a cow, so that it's a dog that the cow kicked. In other words, *the cat the dog the cow kicked chased left.*

O: Heavens! How do you ever process that?!

L: It can get worse: *the cat the dog the cow the man milked kicked chased left.* That sounds like word-salad, even though it's produced according to grammatical principles. And of course these instances are problematic only when the embedding occurs in the middle of an expression. Thus, it's easy to process a sentence like *I saw the man that milked the cow that kicked the dog that chased the cat.* Research on memory has given some pretty good insights into this particular puzzle. In essence the problem is that the speaker starts a sentence, and before she finishes it, she starts another one, and before she finishes that one, she starts another one, and so on. There's a threshold beyond which people can't keep up with so many sentences that haven't been finished, and processing crashes under sheer memory limitations [105].

O: Actually, Bach used that technique in writing some glorious canons [106] . . .

L: So I hear—which has nothing to do with knowledge of language, right? The bottom line is that matters of usability crosscut grammatical deviance. Take an ungrammatical sentence: say, **what* have you discovered the fact that English is?* This is deviant; it's not good English; but it's perfectly comprehensible. If a nonnative speaker of English asked you that question, you'd have no trouble understanding what she meant [see fig. 1.24]. So there's a usable but ungrammatical sentence to go along with the unusable but grammatical sentence I gave you before.

O: What you're now saying fits well with what we said about the acquisition of language a short while ago. It's surprising, at least to me, that human languages are both usable and learnable. It's perfectly reasonable to suppose that lots of logically possible languages that the human mind could in principle entertain are simply unusable or unlearnable.

L: Right. Somebody could of course perform a Nazi-type experiment, and try teaching, say, **predicate calculus** to a two-year-old, and see what happens. My guess is that this kind of "forbidden experiment" would tell us what common sense tells us anyway: children don't use or learn predicate calculus; if they did, some natural language out there would have turned out to be predicate calculus.

O: This situation is certainly not peculiar to language. Think of those lazy penguins—which don't themselves fly, but apparently

itself). This doubling of the previous rhythm continues as flow rate increases. The periodic doubling relates to the flow rate increase in a regular way: the amount of water that is needed to double the dripping rate is 4.669 times the amount of water in the previous state of the system. This is Feigenbaum's number, which generally describes any period-doubling cascade, regardless of how it is produced. Since it takes smaller and smaller changes in flow rate to double the rhythmic pattern, soon the pattern is indiscernible through simple observation; it becomes chaotic. Now, suppose the system comes to a halt at some arbitrary point immediately after a drop, and the exact rate of flow is known. Given the system's complexity, and given that understanding the breaking event requires understanding how continuous physical quantities (here involving a given surface tension that is partly a function of previous drops) become discontinuous in a finite time, predicting when the next drop will break seems impossible. However, something interesting happens: cascades of necks "grow" other necks near the breakup points. This scenario can be described by equations of fluid dynamics involving a "similarity solution," where structure repeats on a smaller scale after a while. Given appropriate liquid viscosities, the number of "neck growings" iterates, up to unknown limits. The elegance of this behavior suggests that there should be a simple way of predicting the next drop: if the laws of fluid dynamics predict the shape of the singularity, they may be able to predict its timing as well. Unfortunately, it is not known yet why these laws are involved, to start with. This is the sort of problem whose (potential) simple solution interests complexity theorists.

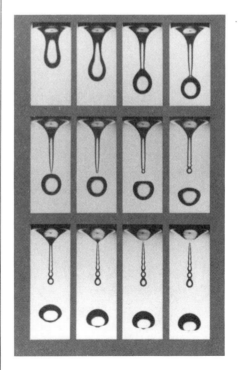

Sequence of the stages of fission that occur when a drop of water falls. (From Shi, Brenner, and Nagel, A cascade of structure in a drop falling from a faucet)

Figure 1.24

Me up at does
out of the floor
quietly Stare
a poisoned mouse
still who alive
is asking What
have i done that
You wouldn't have

Poem by e. e. cummings, cited by Chomsky (1965, 228 n. 5) to illustrate an ungrammatical sentence with clear, unambiguous meaning.

have evolved from a flying species. Given that this pre-penguin species could fly instinctively, either penguins have lost the instinct to fly or (obviously more likely) their body constants aren't very useful for flight on this planet. The former supposition would be hard to substantiate from an evolutionary point of view (it would have to be shown that there's an evolutionary advantage to not being able to *know* how to fly). The latter case, however, is trivial; whatever impelled the morphological changes that made penguins the way they are entailed, as a side effect, the inability to make use of an instinct to fly. From this perspective, the penguin in a very concrete sense knows (and even tries) flight just as any other bird does—but unfortunately penguins cannot make use of flight.

L: In the case of language, the partial (un)usability of regular languages shouldn't interfere with the way humans communicate, assuming they have reasonably similar systems; the same parts that are unusable for Jones will be unusable for Smith, and so neither of them will express any grammatical structures that involve those parts . . . They'll have to live with only being able to use the rest, which still allows them to produce an unbounded number of expressions.

O: Unless one of them who the other who doesn't deserve it will hate wants to be really funny.

 　　　　　　　　　　　　　　　　linguistic structures are optimally assembled

L: Precisely. You may recall, also, that there's a logical point X_0 where we have an unordered bunch of words, and a logical point X_f where the entire sentence is assembled. A priori, there could be a variety of different ways to get from X_0 to X_f, right? But this is what happens: the shortest path wins [see chap. 5].

O: I say, is that so?! That's delightful . . .

L: That's apparently what's happening. Of all the ways the structures of human language could be assembled, they're apparently assembled in the one that's most economical [107].

O: Needless to say, I should like it if you could substantiate your claims in an explicit manner—but I hasten to add that I find them very interesting. It's particularly noteworthy that this kind of economy should exist within your specific framework of assumptions.

L: The framework is definitely very specific. In fact, this is an important point to keep in mind, particularly when lots of scientists are working on the mind, and a variety of metaphors, tools, and even theoretical constructs are borrowed back and forth. Note that alongside the highly publicized "cognitive science," there's no such thing as a comparable "body science," and at this point it would be remarkable to develop a theoretical framework that's valid for different body organs—hearts, livers, lungs, and the others. The mind is also composed of various "mental organs"—the linguistic system, the visual system, and so on [108]. They may be as different from one another as the circulatory system is from the digestive system. For instance, the visual organs constitute an **input–output** system, in the sense that vision involves a retinal stimulation mapped to some internal image. The core cognitive system of human language (now putting aside the processes that allow us to use that cognitive system) doesn't involve this kind of input–output process. Instead, it's a **combinatorial** system that's responsible for assembling linguistic structures in a given way [109]. Why should these different systems share the same architecture? In fact it would be surprising if they did, in any detailed way, and at any rate this would have to be established empirically, and not just assumed.

O: That's true, but the more you divide the mind into various modules, the deeper the following mystery becomes: Suppose I grant you the internal beauty of this system of yours. What, in the theory, predicts this beauty? And suppose you answer that question appropriately—whatever reason you give, it won't extend to a theory of vision, given your assumption that vision and language are different kinds of systems. And then, if the visual system is also elegant, you must predict its elegance from a totally different angle.

——— **the elegant aspects of human language may not have evolved**

L: I don't see that at all. Underlying your question is a presupposition which I actually do share: surprise over the fact that a system like human language could evolve in a biological creature. How can something which I'm claiming is structurally so elegant be said to arise in the organic world, where other systems with anything like the basic properties of human language don't seem to exist? But you could turn that presupposition into an answer to your mystery, by assuming that human language hasn't really evolved. You see, I don't think that language is functionally elegant, and in that sense I don't think it's a plausible result of a chain of adaptations. But I do think

Sunflower. (Alejandro Berlín)

Figure 1.25

[Most of the following ideas are summarized in Jean 1994.]

D'Arcy Thompson (see fig. 1.10) argued that ideal geometry provides optimal solutions to problems of morphology, a classic example being phyllotaxis ("[t]he regular arrangement of [a plant's] lateral organs (leaves on a stem, scales on a cone axis, florets in a composite flower head)"; Prusinkiewicz and Lindenmayer 1990, 99)). The basic phenomenon involves growth of a central point or apex away from specific primordial lumps of structure (e.g., florets). (Visually, it would seem as if the florets grow, but in fact new "plant stuff" comes out of the apex.) The problem is how to (efficiently) pack this structure within a given area, in a regular, mechanical fashion. Addressing this problem, Vogel (1979) devises a formula (discussed in Prusinkiewicz and Lindenmayer 1990) to describe the patterns of florets in a daisy's capitulum, which is built on the following explicit assumptions: (i) all florets are the same size; (ii) florets are densely and regularly packed within the flower; (iii) the ordering number n of florets in a plant (counting outward from the center) is inversely proportional to the age of the plant; (iv) each new floret issues at a fixed angle with respect to the preceding floret; (v) the position vector of each new floret fits into the largest existing gap between position vectors of the older florets. From (i) and (ii) it follows that the total number of florets that fit inside a disk of radius r is proportional to the disk area. From this result, coupled with (iii), it follows in turn that the particular proportion is a squaring function of the number of florets; $r = c\sqrt{n}$, for c a constant scaling parameter. In turn, (iv) and (v) are intended to derive the divergence angle, between a reference direction and the position vector of the nth floret, in a polar coordinate system originating at the center of the capitulum. This angle is approximately 137.5°, the noble angle that can be obtained by subtracting

that structurally it's very elegant—and in that sense it doesn't relate to any obvious adaptation either. As an exaptation, however, it can certainly emerge (as a singular epiphenomenon of a brain that got large enough for some obscure and/or trivial reason). In turn, if the phenomenon is physicochemical in its essentials, or perhaps dynamically complex in the sense you like to talk about, one would expect it to be as well behaved as other phenomena of that nature are. Then its extraordinary elegance is somewhat less peculiar.

O: If that's true, mightn't humans someday find another species with essentially the same system of knowledge, but no brain like theirs?

L: Or another species might find us, yes. Or if the processes of evolution are the same in other regions of the universe, we might find aliens who have basically the same system of knowledge in fundamental respects—maybe without even having the same general chemistry. That would be because, in large part, universal principles of UG would reflect rather directly core options of the larger universe—whatever that universe is. At any rate, from this perspective, the fact that the language organ and the visual systems converge (somewhat) in being elegant doesn't pose any new problems. More obvious instances of convergence have been known for quite some time.

————— digression on daisies, peacocks, and other wonderful creatures

Take, for instance, the arrangement of florets in the capitulum of a daisy's or sunflower's corolla. It's an exquisite spiral pattern with well-known mathematical properties [see fig. 1.25]. The number of spirals is in the Fibonacci sequence.

O: Remarkable, isn't it? For instance, the capitulum of a small daisy typically has twenty-one or thirty-four spirals, and that of a large one, eighty-nine or a hundred and forty-four spirals. The same sort of pattern can be found in the "eyespots" of a peacock's tail.

L: That's the point. There's obviously no evolutionary or functional connection between a plant's reproductive organ and a peacock's display, yet there *is* obviously a formal connection [110]. In both cases these patterns emerge as the result of a growth function; but why should it be the same function? Also, why should it be a function whose value can be mapped onto the Fibonacci series?

Whatever the locus of this formal regularity is, it's not anything trivial about the specific material realization of the daisy or the peacock . . .

O: Needless to say, biologically what matters isn't the daisy or the peacock proper, but the specification of their primordial growth. The key to these sorts of spirals is that features (like florets or "eyespots") migrate from a center pole by repelling each other, an idea that goes back to Church's work in the twenties [111]. To get the picture, imagine four bugs, two males and two females, each in a different corner of a room. Male A in the north corner wants to mate with female B in the east corner, who wants to mate with male C in the south corner, who wants to mate with female D in the west corner, who wants to mate with male A.

L: They've got a problem.

O: But they don't know it! Suppose they get the irresistible urge to move towards each other, all at the same time. What paths will they follow and where will they meet [112]?

L: Assuming they all follow optimal paths, each will trace a curve whose endpoint will be the center of the room.

O: Those curves are logarithmic—the same ones we find in the daisy capitulum and the peacock tail. With respect to the bugs, what's relevant is an attracting force, with the bugs starting in distant corners of the room and converging towards the center, a bit like water running out of a sink. But of course we can run the experiment backwards: imagine that the four bugs haven't resolved their four-body problem, and each simply decides to hate its would-be mate. Now what?

L: Obviously, they'll fly away from each other, following the same paths they took before, except in the opposite direction.

O: Splendid. Now consider a different version of the problem. Imagine a hive full of bees in the midst of a meadow. The bees hate each other and want to fly away—but there's only a small crack to let them come out, one at a time. What direction must each bee take in order to keep moving as far as possible from all the other bees? If bee B flies at a 180° angle from bee A, then when bee C emerges from the hive, it will necessarily fly, at best, at a 90° angle

Peacock's tail in display.

360° times the famous Greek noble number (that is, $(\sqrt{5} - 1)/2$; see fig. 1.27) from 360°. Any other angle is less efficient at solving the packaging problem; for instance, rational multiples of 360° would result in florets' arranging themselves along radial lines (four for 90°; six for 60°; nine for 40°; and so on). Among irrational multiples of 360°, the noble angle provides an optimal solution (springing from the fact that the noble number is badly approximable by rational numbers). This model correctly describes the arrangements of florets, whose salient feature (to the human eye) is two sets of spirals composed of nearest neighboring florets, each set's cardinality being a member of the Fibonacci sequence (which is built by approximation to the noble number; see fig. 1.27). The spirals, however, are epiphenomenological: they delineate a pattern of florets that actually grew at different times.

What explains the state of affairs described by Vogel's formula? Douady and Couder (1992) attempt to explain it by obtaining the noble angle from system dynamics. The key to Douady and Couder's proposal (which is discussed in the text and goes back to early ideas by A. H. Church) is the assumption that when elements like florets "migrate radially" at a specified velocity, they are actually repelling each other, as if they were magnets with the same polarity. This hypothesis was experimentally demonstrated with silicone oil placed in a vertical magnetic field. Polarized drops repelled each other; when they were given a magnetic boost outward, the "daisy" pattern appeared, with the required 137.5° angle between spirals. Although promising, this experimental result is however still far from providing a real solution; what needs to be established is the nature of the repelling forces. These forces are obvious in the experiment, but not in actual phyllotaxis (see Jean 1994).

from each of the other two bees—so that's not an optimal solution. Indeed, no rational division of 360° gives a good result. Say bee B flies at 120° from bee A, and bee C flies at 120° from bee B—when bee D comes out, it will have to fly at an angle of less than 120° from two of the other bees. The optimal solution would be that as bees spiral their way out of the hive, each one keeps a regular distance from all possible bees it will encounter on its way out, including bees that have taken its same path much earlier. One can easily show that the ideal angle for this scenario is the Fibonacci angle, approximately 137.5° [see fig. 1.25]. It's only at this angle that, no matter how large the system grows, all bees will be proportionally far from one another.

L: So the spirals that we see aren't really primitive.

O: Spot on. Two bees in the same spiral (or two features in the same region of the daisy, et cetera) haven't left the hive (the apex of the capitulum, et cetera) one immediately after the other. In actual fact, our bees A, B, C, and D will all be flying different spiral paths, until the pattern comes full circle (depending on bee size and the actual space between bees), and some bee X traces the path of bee A—bee A having by then flown far enough not to be too close to bee X. Now given a sufficiently tightly packed bee-space, an observer will gain the impression that a second spiral path has been formed. This one, though, is simply a mirage resulting from the packaging [113].

L: If this is all correct, the peacock's display must be just a reflex of skin patterns.

O: Spot on again—the same sorts of patterns that we see in human hair growth. Simply imagine a collection of peacock skin-bumps, each the origin of a feather with one "eyespot." If the primordial bumps are appropriately arranged, the feathers will follow. Now what's ultimately relevant in the daisy's and peacock's growth functions isn't so much the actual features we see (florets or feathers) as their more basic constituent parts, whatever those are [114]. To see what I mean, consider this new thought experiment: a hypothetical daisy with a single petal, which we may ask Georgia O'Keefe to paint for us—it would look like a calla. This continuous feature would coil itself around the capitulum, given that its particles obey the relevant repelling forces; however, although the material integrity of the petal would be stretched, perhaps to some limit, it wouldn't break into smaller units. Now go back to daisies. Apparently, the "material integrity" (now speaking metaphorically) of what grows to form florets, petals, and other features, does break in successive lumps, which are a bit like water drops.

L: That implies another force that keeps these lumps together, within the general repulsion pattern.

O: Actually, it's really the same force that, as it were, "resists" growth. You see, three sorts of forces appear to be involved. The first keeps the entire system together. The second is the growth function. The third is what results in the discrete units—that's what you're talking about now [115]. But the first and third forces are the same at different levels. Here the issue is how a dynamic singularity emerges [see figs. 1.23 and 1.26]: a discrete lump out of a continuous mass of stuff, given opposing forces. The system is impelled to grow, but its fabric resists this. This tension is resolved in terms of several lumps in which the different forces become locally stable, in a sort of dynamic equilibrium of opposites. In any case, I'm by no means attempting to imply that all is known about why these pretty and rather common patterns ultimately exist; my only point is that, although they are manifested in fully developed individuals, the key to their existence lies in the early plans for their development, or perhaps their evolution.

a messy brain, a fearful tiger: how do complex systems with continuous input settle into fixed discrete outputs?

L: That's all very interesting; of course, the same kind of story can be told about different, convergent mental organs, without invoking a "unitary" theory of mind—with the same caveats I raised before about whether physics, in the narrow sense, is the way to encode the relevant regularities we may find [116].

O: I certainly grant you that if the mind has organs, it poses, as a matter of principle, the same sorts of questions of morphology that more common organs do in the "body" world that we're more accustomed to dealing with. But you must grant me one other property that's common (very specifically) to visual and linguistic systems: ultimately (and no matter how indirectly), a brain which appears to be quite unkempt is employed to produce something which, apparently, has got computational properties.

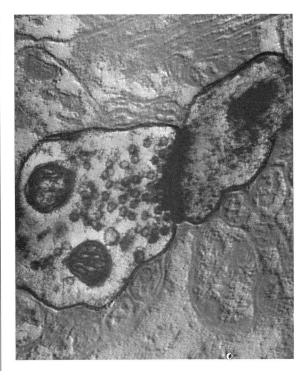

Neuron. (From Klivington, *The science of mind*)

Figure 1.26

Turing (1952) captured in general mathematical terms the idea that periodic patterns are the result of short-range activating and long-range inhibiting chemical reactions. Very little is known about the molecular and cellular bases for such processes, although it seems that they always involve this synchronized pattern of activation and inhibition. Using coupled nonlinear, differential equations, Meinhardt (1995) offers interesting computer models (for seashells). To the extent that these computational models are modeling something real, researchers may be closer to answering Blake's question in "The Tyger":

What immortal hand or eye
Could frame thy fearful symmetry?

Of course, tiger stripes and seashell patterns are only two of many cases where continuous processes yield discrete results in living creatures. Another well-known (though unrelated) case is neural firing, a remarkable instance of which is shown in this microphotograph: The photograph depicts the axon of one neuron (left), the dendrite of another (right), and the synapse (cleft) between them. It was taken at the instant when the axon fired an electrical signal into the dendrite, transferring a chemical neurotransmitter to it. For this event to take place, the transmitting neuron must be stimulated up to a threshold; if the threshold is not reached, the axon will not fire. At the same time, as long as the threshold is reached, the actual strength of the stimulus does not matter. The frequency of neural impulses can be increased (that is how "more pain," for instance, is distinguished from "less pain"), but their amplitude cannot.

Figure 1.27

The ratio of successive terms of the Fibonacci sequence approximates $(1 + \sqrt{5})/2$ (the noble number, expressed backward in figure 1.25). For the first few terms of the series, the ratio of each term to its immediate predecessor is rather far from this 1.6180339 . . . limit ($1/1 = 1$; $2/1 = 2$; $3/2 = 1.5$), but as the series progresses, it converges exponentially (e.g., $55/34 = 1.61765 . . .$, $987/610 = 1.618033 . . .$). (Interestingly, the noble proportion appears to be pleasing to various cultures with no obvious direct connection; in addition to clear, deliberate instances in classical and neoclassical art, the pattern is found in at least Pharaonic, Mesoamerican, and pre-Celtic architectural design and in various crafts (see Doczi 1994).) The formula for calculating the nth term of the sequence (from Land 1960) is

$$T_n = \frac{1}{\sqrt{5}} \left\{ \frac{1 + \sqrt{5}}{2} \right\}^n - \frac{1}{\sqrt{5}} \left\{ \frac{1 - \sqrt{5}}{2} \right\}^n.$$

Consider the first half separately. Since $1/\sqrt{5} = 0.4472136 . . .$ (and $(1 + \sqrt{5})/2 = 1.618034 . . .$), we obtain the following approximate values for the continuous product $C = 1/\sqrt{5}\{(1 + \sqrt{5})/2\}_n$: $C_1 = 0.7236 . . .$; $C_2 = 1.1708 . . .$; $C_3 = 1.8944 . . .$; $C_4 = 3.0652 . . .$; $C_5 = 4.9597 . . .$; $C_6 = 8.0249 . . .$; $C_7 = 12.9846 . . .$; and so on. This gives an exponential curve. As it proceeds, the curve goes through real values that are hard to distinguish from the whole values 1, 1, 2, 3, 5, 8, 13 (the Fibonacci series).

The second half of the formula for calculating T_n corrects the difference between the real approximation and the whole value. Note that $(1 - \sqrt{5})/2$ is a negative number, $-0.6180339 . . .$, which is relevant in calculating the correction (for C_n to approximate T_n) $E_n = 1/\sqrt{5}\{(1 - \sqrt{5})/2\}^n$. For instance, the square of $(1 - \sqrt{5})/2$ is 0.3819659 . . . , a positive number; its cube, $-0.2360678 . . .$, a negative number; and so on. This results in positive/negative increments:

$$T_1 = \underset{C_1}{0.7236068 . . .} - \underset{E_1}{(-0.2763931 . . .)} = 0.99 . . .$$

$$T_2 = \underset{C_2}{1.1708204 . . .} - \underset{E_2}{0.1708203 . . .} = 1.0000001 . . .$$

$$T_3 = \underset{C_3}{1.8944272 . . .} - \underset{E_3}{(-0.1055727 . . .)} = 1.99 . . .$$

etc.

L: Remarkable ones indeed. Which raises a very general, not new, and extremely interesting question about the nature of complexity: how can messy inputs result in simple outputs? This is the kind of problem Alan Turing addressed, at a more basic level, when he tried to show how basically continuous systems can settle into systems with fixed digital properties (how a tiger's stripes, for instance, arise from the growth of its fur) [see fig. 1.26] [117].

O: In the case that interests us, the ultimate theory of mental phenomena that are discrete in nature will have to wrestle with the continuity found in neural maps [118] . . .

L: But I insist that there's no problem of principle here, since various systems exist that map continuous input to discrete output. The phenomenon is general, too—just look at the leaky faucet you were talking about earlier. Dripping water is a dynamic singularity, involving the formation of simple, discrete units of water from a flowing mass of liquid [see fig. 1.23]. Abstractly, neural firing itself is a phenomenon of roughly the same kind: only when a neuron is stimulated to its critical threshold does its axon fire [see fig. 1.26].

O: Right you are. But you see—it's one thing to say that systems (should) exist which map continuous input to discrete output; showing how they do it is a different matter altogether, particularly when the discreteness you're concerned with is unbounded in character. Note, in this respect, one aspect of the flower-peacock phenomenon that we haven't discussed yet: why does the number of spirals match up with the Fibonacci series? We now know the spirals aren't primitive—but an equivalent question emerges: why do the primordial features of daisies and peacock tails correspond precisely to that series? Now, the Fibonacci series is nothing but an ordered set of whole numbers, satisfying almost exactly (as it grows) an exponential function. For example, the fourth term of the sequence can be calculated continuously as 3.0652 . . . , or discretely as 3. The fifth term, as 4.9597 . . . , or 5. The sixth term, as 8.0249 . . . , or 8. And so forth [see fig. 1.27]. Recall that the exponential function in question originates because of the way in which primordial features "escape" from each other, at an angle calculated in terms of the noble number, 1.618034 . . . The Fibonacci numbers are the best approximation there is, in terms of whole numbers, to the noble series. What I'm trying to say is that continuous, measurable, and potentially unlimited quantities (of the sort involved in lengths, velocities, et cetera, which are the stock of all growth processes) relate to discrete, organised, yet theoretically unlimited features of plants, peacocks, and so forth [119]. To insist, this is an issue that O'Keefe's hypothetical daisy (or real calla) wouldn't have to face, with its single continuous petal. On the other hand, real daisies do have to wrestle with it, as their primordial features are being formed from a central apex. Then, whatever the attracting forces are that result in these primordial lumps, they must correct the irrational output of the noble growth function to some approximation in the set of natural numbers. As a matter of fact, it isn't totally clear that the approximation is accomplished **algorithmically,** for the solutions that actual plants produce are often merely approximate. If the ideal answer is the Fibonacci number fifty-five, they grow fifty-four or fifty-three petals, often fewer (and very rarely more) [120].

L: That fact is probably important. Obviously, if some algorithm executes the approximation, it would have to lie outside the particular system we're now exploring—the one accounting for the continuous function, say in evolution. That is, the growth patterns may follow from the limitations that physics (in the broadest sense) imposes on possible evolutionary steps. But then we're left with the problem of explaining how the meta-algorithm works that maps the optimally dynamic solution to a discrete, workable whole quantity of features: how did its algorithmic nature emerge in a world of continuities [121]? We've just pushed the problem one step back. Of course, maybe that's what we need to do, and we may in fact discover the nature of the meta-algorithm. Eventually, though, we'll have to wrestle with some level of continuity that arranges itself discretely, in the course of evolution. That's the tough question, particularly in these cases involving unlimited possibilities. If in fact there is no such meta-algorithm, but only some approximation, then there's no further question to ask. Given conflicting demands for a solution, an approximation is as good as it gets, which is good enough for a workable universe.

O: I entirely agree, but matters may be even more drastic than you're implying. What if the trick works basically every time development takes place, without its details even being expressed in the genes? The facts strongly suggest that a given plant doesn't have a genetic instruction to "spiral" rightwards or leftwards, or to instantiate a particular integer of the Fibonacci series. These are formal details that arise in epigenesis [122]. Apparently, something like "kind of growth" is all that's genetically coded.

More precisely:

$$T_0 = \frac{1}{\sqrt{5}} - \frac{1}{\sqrt{5}} = 0$$

$$T_1 = \frac{1}{\sqrt{5}} \left\{ \frac{1 + \sqrt{5} - 1 + \sqrt{5}}{2} \right\} = \frac{2\sqrt{5}}{2\sqrt{5}} = 1$$

$$T_2 = \frac{1}{\sqrt{5}} \left\{ \frac{1 + 2\sqrt{5} + 5 - 1 + 2\sqrt{5} - 5}{4} \right\} = \frac{4\sqrt{5}}{4\sqrt{5}} = 1$$

$$T_3 = \frac{1}{\sqrt{5}} \left\{ \frac{1 + 3\sqrt{5} + 3.5 + 5\sqrt{5} - 1 + 3\sqrt{5} - 3.5 + 5\sqrt{5}}{8} \right\} = \frac{16\sqrt{5}}{8\sqrt{5}} = 2$$

etc.

The terms with $\sqrt{5}$ cancel, leaving the Fibonacci whole numbers.

Apparently, nature uses this growth function for reasons having to do with repelling forces acting among growing elements of certain life forms (see fig. 1.25). But apart from the repelling forces that result in the spiral patterns, attracting forces (akin to surface tension in water) seem to result in the formation of feature lumps. Since the noble number is irrational (cannot be expressed by a fraction), a correcting factor is needed to approximate the continuous and the discrete values of the growth function. An interesting question is whether, just as repelling forces derive the noble angle, the attracting forces that result in feature lumps could derive the correcting factor.

L: Well, maybe—I don't know anything about these matters. It seems to me, though, that in addition to the genetic "kind of growth" message, you'd need something about "when to stop"; I say this because a sunflower obviously has more features than a daisy.

O: Quite right—so yes, that too would be genetic. What I mean, though, is that "kind of growth" and "when to stop" are very general genetic codings. Consider in this respect the function of genes that tell cells how rapidly and in which axis to grow. A minor adjustment in one of these genes may result in structures as drastically different as a fin and a paw. Run the developing clock a little more slowly in a dog than in a fish, and the **controlling gene** will stick longer at its task of telling skeletal cells to structure. Although the gene is ready to stop after achieving a fin in fish development, it carries on in dog development, creating "wrist" and "finger" structures [123]. Needless to say, then, what we want to find out is how the "clock" works that times these events—this is the elementary genetic coding that you expect to discover, and not something as obvious as a coding for "paw" or "55 petals." Differently put, this is an interesting case of underdeterminacy in the natural world, of the sort you pointed out in linguistics. The genetic code for flowers needn't really say anything about fifty-five petals, if approximately that kind of solution will emerge every time a particular flower develops.

L: I understand what you're saying, but I can't conclude much from it, even if it's true. Of course, I can conclude that the sorts of properties found in human language (say, discrete infinity and underdeterminacy) are present at some level in the biological world, if we look abstractly enough. And that certainly takes away part of the mystery behind the fact that language exhibits these properties.

O: But you could do more than that: you could take the tools that are needed to describe these Fibonacci examples and apply them to linguistics.

L: That would probably be a mistake.

1.7 Language and Form

(wherein the Other speculates wildly on the origins of life and form, with other ruminations pertaining to dynamic linguistic principles that partake more of truth than of discretion)

O: Suppose I don't follow you there . . .

L: Well, in effect, you've shown one particular way a continuous input is mapped to a discrete, theoretically recursive output, as a result of the dynamics of a system that at the same time involves growth and featural convergence. Right?

———————————————— *we understand linguistics; do we understand the rest?*

O: In the meantime achieving a unification, if I may say so, between whatever theory is responsible for the dynamic description of the input (for example, the tension between repelling and attracting forces) and the theory that's ultimately responsible for the computational description of the output (a mapping of features to the Fibonacci series).

L: What permits that would-be unification is the fact that you understood the computational output—which has been essentially known since the eighteen hundreds [124]. It would have been very hard indeed to even ask the right questions if you proceeded from the dynamic description alone. For instance, you may have known that a certain repelling force is operative, as it is in magnetic fields, say. Fine. But would it occur to you to ask whether there is also an attracting force which gives rise to singular features, and is ultimately responsible for making the continuous function discrete? Not obvious. On the other hand, having a computational model of the output, you know that something must be responsible for the discrete units, even if the input is continuous. So you go back to the drawing board and ask: is there anything else going on in the system? Or as you put it: what's the difference between the hypothetical O'Keefe calla-daisy and an actual daisy? Then you may or may not be in business, but at least you have a real question. Similarly (though, admittedly, at a more complex level), linguistics provides a variety of well-established conclusions about language, most of them of an algorithmic sort. Of course, biology and the brain sciences aren't yet able to provide any solid bases for these conclusions, at least in any generality. But whose fault is that? To conclude that linguistics is at fault because it's partly figured out how the algorithms work, and that linguists should go look for metaphors from botany to redo their algorithms and make them fit with "material stuff" is . . . well, insane; it would be equally insane to have concluded, a century ago, that chemistry was wrong because it couldn't be unified with the physics of the time, since nineteenth-century scientists couldn't square continuous physical energy with discrete chemical matter—would you have asked Mendeleyev to redo his periodic table on the basis of plant growth?

O: That's essentially what happened: for the longest time, the chemist's atoms were taken to be metaphysical entities, and chemistry was given an instrumental, operationalist interpretation, full stop [125]. Thomson's model, which you mentioned earlier, was rather exceptional in this respect . . . I'm trying to say that these are notoriously old debates, with as much sociology to them as pure science, I'm afraid.

L: Well, now it's even worse than that. In the case you're talking about, chemists and physicists—each with highly elaborate theories—were trying to hold on to their conclusions. The present case isn't really comparable, because science only has rudimentary ideas about how the brain works. So what do we do with any experimental results we might get? For instance, linguistic violations of a syntactic nature (like *called Fred in English) trigger different electrophysiological responses than violations of a semantic nature do (for instance, a sentence that sounds perfect but makes no sense at all, like *more people speak in riddles than I do*). However, since there is, to my knowledge at least, no appropriate theory of the electrical activity of the brain, there's only so much we can do with that kind of result. (I suppose we can reinforce what we already knew: that syntax isn't semantics.)

O: You don't know why the actually occurring results were found, and not, let's say, the opposite ones—is that the concern?

L: Of course—we should be concerned with that. All that we have is an observation, but no explanation for why things happen that way. In contrast, computational theories of the mind are much more established; for instance, linguists have things to say about why a sentence is deviant or not, within the scope of a theory that goes beyond specific instances.

O: You mean: linguists have developed laws of UG that predict certain structures to be possible, while others are deviant . . .

L: Not only that, actually. Certainly, for the last few decades we've had theories of that kind, which have had a considerable degree of descriptive and explanatory adequacy. But we're trying to go beyond that. Very concretely, we're trying to develop what we call the "Minimalist Program," or "Minimalism," that addresses the sort of perfectly elegant theory that intrigues you. From this point of view, not only are we concerned with predicting linguistic structures—we're in fact trying to determine why certain classes of structures are (in)adequate. The question is still somewhat vague, but extremely interesting: given the contingent fact that language is used, which yields some conditions that are external to the system, is there a perfect (if you will), conceptually necessary, and optimally economic way of meeting those external conditions? You think this question is similar to the question of whether, given some contingent facts about peacock skins or flower corollas, there's an optimal way of meeting those conditions. And I agree that it's the same sort of question—but how much would you learn about the daisy phenomenon if I told you something about relative clauses, or even something about neurology?

O: Possibly not very much—and I do see that. Nevertheless, the linguistic issues you've raised do remind me, in rather intricate ways, of the dynamic conditions which living organisms face, given certain assumptions. Notice, first, that whereas physicochemical dynamic systems lose their structure when their energy source is cut off (stop a flow of water, and there goes your turbulence), biological systems conserve much of their structure in the absence of energy, for quite some time. This suggests that these systems combine both approximately conservative and dissipative structures [126]. In a sense, this isn't very surprising, if life emerges between stability and chaos. The approximately conservative structures, to start with, are responsible for overall formal features, such as skeletons. As we've said, these kinds of structures are the way they are, to a large extent, because of basic physical forces. Hence, the biological structure depends on where it is located. A large animal living in a terrestrial environment has to have a bone skeleton, because the force it must wrestle with is gravity; in contrast, a small animal living in an aquatic environment must deal with the surface tension of water, and thus its skeleton will be shaped along the lines of a drop of water [see fig. 1.10]. One might even think of formal criteria of structurally possible life forms to express this convergence of approximately conservative structures and the environments where they occur [127].

L: I'm not sure we know enough about, say, body plans to decide whether—except as a metaphor—your analogy is ultimately meaningful.

_____   economy considerations are representational or computational

O: The reason I suggest it is this. You've talked about four kinds of economy within the linguistic system. Firstly, overall economy in the design of the language faculty, with such properties as parametric options arising as a side effect. Secondly, economy in the device responsible for the acquisition of parametric settings, the LAD. About these two, you've talked at length. Mostly in passing, you've also alluded to a third and fourth. The third is implicit in your wondering whether there's an ideal way of meeting contingent conditions on language. To the extent that you're thinking about meeting a set of conditions optimally, you must have in mind, I presume, that those conditions display a certain harmony or symmetry (otherwise it's unlikely that the question about "optimal solutions" could be meaningfully posed). And then of course a fourth kind of economy is implicit in your questioning whether these harmonious conditions, whatever they are, can indeed be met through optimal assembly paths (the fact that conditions are pretty doesn't in and of itself guarantee that they can be met nicely).

L: Yes, that taxonomy's essentially correct. We can think of the third kind of economy as **representational,** because it arises in the representational interactions of the linguistic system with other mental systems [and see sec. 2.1]. The fourth kind can be called **computational,** and it should arise from the inner workings of the linguistic system.

O: Lovely! And I discern some groupings here as well, if I may say so. Overall economy may correlate with representational economy: to the extent that linguistic representations are harmonious in some sense, the harmony might be attributed to the very structural design of language. Acquisition and computational economy are also plausibly related.

L: Yes: the sort of LAD I discussed—which is capable of picking out the simplest analysis of messy data, according to a linguistic metric—may have the problem-solving capacity that UG implies, for the computational system. This is assuming the LAD adopts given structural analyses because they involve a hypothesized linguistic computation of the shortest kind (that is, of the shortest kind that's compatible with input data). I might add that this isn't a necessary assumption, but it's a natural one: provided that the LAD is programmed with all the information that UG carries, it's also capable, in principle, of using that information to analyze the messy data that it gets.

———————————————————— *speculations about the conservation of structures*

O: Excellent. Now, I'd like to suggest that the first subgroup of economy considerations is conservative, whereas the second sub-group is dissipative. Let me explain, starting with conservative economy considerations. You insisted that the LAD must assume some sort of structure conservation when postulating hypotheses about possible linguistic structures [see sec. 1.1]—it doesn't acquire processes based on nonlinguistic notions such as "first item in a se-quence," for example. Is the LAD's behaviour not a consequence of its being preprogrammed with the principles of UG, in which case it cannot even attempt a learning strategy that would involve units which aren't recognisable by the linguistic system? That recalls the notion that life forms don't attempt body plans that wouldn't be structurally possible for biological systems. Could it not then be the case that these two facts about life and grammar are but two instanti-ations of the same fact: what underlies living creatures involves, in part, approximately conservative dynamic structures?

L: But—

O: Hold on, hold on. Before you say anything, let me make a sec-ond point, which is actually more radical than the first. To insist on this, living creatures are, in part, approximately dissipative dynamic structures, and I should like to relate this to computational economy.

L: I could have predicted that . . .

O: Current work in complex systems has tried to interpret some of the classical, Aristotelian views in a new light, which I suspect is in the spirit of your programme. I'm thinking of the concern with the migration of form—the essence of life—as opposed to life's partial stability—which it directly shares with nonliving structures.

———————————————————— *speculations about dissipative order and the emergence of life*

The research programme suggests this: dissipative phase transitions, corresponding to **symmetry breaking of equilibrium states,** are

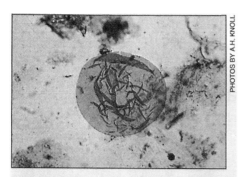

PHOTOS BY A.H. KNOLL

Life gets complicated. Earlier than 1 billion years ago, most planktonic algae were simple and similar *(top)*. But after that time, complexity and diversity set in *(bottom)*. (From Kerr, Timing evolution's early bursts)

Figure 1.28

[The ideas that follow can be found, for instance, in Meinzer 1994 and Goodwin 1994.]

Notions like those presented in figure 1.21 may lead to the wrong impression that the DNA of an organism is a self-replicating mechanism; in truth, DNA replicates only within the specific context of a dividing cell. If there is no cellular organization around them, even if replicating nucleic acid templates are given an appropriate context that includes an energy source and the necessary building blocks (nucleotide bases and the relevant enzymes), their behavior is uncharacteristic. As expected, they produce both new copies of the initial templates and the occasional mistake. Interestingly, though, the system evolves toward a greater frequency of shorter templates: that is, DNA replicating on its own drifts toward structurally simpler structures, unlike what often happens in nature. The photograph illustrates the common tendency for species to become more elaborate in structure; this tendency to-

behind the origin of form in life. In this respect, there's been a significant shift from Boltzmann's type of approach to life's raison d'être [see fig. 1.7] to a view of life as a rather natural property of this universe. The key point is that order emerges within the sort of highly dynamic systems that we've discussed today because of a fundamental feedback property that they exhibit, which allows them to develop stability and a hierarchy of complex structures within themselves. In essence, macroscopic structures emerge when "strong" unstable modes eliminate "weak" stable ones, thus limiting the ways in which the system can behave. In a manner of speaking, different modes "compete," and given modes are "selected"—which reduces the complexity of the system [128]. This makes me raise two conjectural correlates. The first is that, in order to evolve through successive instabilities of dissipative systems, living systems must have developed procedures to increase their distance from thermal equilibrium, given the fact that unstable modes take over stable ones, and less stable modes are further from thermal equilibrium than more stable ones [see fig. 1.9].

L: So a system has to increase its entropy production [see fig. 1.7], vis-à-vis a previous stage in its evolution.

O: In direct satisfaction of the laws of physics. (That is to say, when these laws are applied to kinetic systems that are far from equilibrium.) Yes indeed. Notice also that every time these systems are changed in the direction of greater distance from equilibrium, new dominant instabilities arise through fluctuations in the system, which stabilise beyond given thresholds. This causes increased dissipation, which influences the threshold for yet a new phase to emerge . . .

L: Your point is that life hasn't emerged in a single unlikely burst, but from a cascade of narrower and narrower entropic events [see fig. 1.28].

O: Well, that's the punch line, yes. Boltzmann's answer to the entropy riddle must involve a dissipative structure [see fig. 1.9], whose probability is rather minuscule in equilibrium statistical mechanics; yet the probability of such structures is total in these far-from-equilibrium conditions that we're now discussing [129]. Which may actually mean that (if life ultimately stems from these sorts of basic processes), living creatures should be found wherever the physical and chemical conditions are favourable—

L: And they might not even involve DNA structures at all, or any molecular structures of the kind we're familiar with.

O: Spot on! This may have a bearing, too, on the debate between "punctuated equilibrium" and the traditional "gradualism" in evolution [130]. If evolution is bumpy rather than smooth, then something must be explained. Chance can have much to do with lack of linearity, but what explains the points of equilibrium amidst an ever-changing environment? To answer this, you may wish to get something like dynamics into the picture.

L: But to be fair to the traditional view, possibilities internal to the logic of evolution include "adaptive gridlocks": the impasse produced by a situation where a selective pressure of some sort exists, but evolving in one direction would have certain lethal consequences for an organism in its particular environment, and evolving in another direction would have other lethal consequences. In circumstances like this, a species remains stable until a small population is isolated in a new environment, where the gridlock disappears [131].

O: To be sure—but that still leaves open the question of how large-scale shifts in morphology can take place [see fig. 1.28]. Up to a thousand million years ago, life was extremely simple (and had been for the three thousand million years before that—where "simplicity," mind you, means "bacteria"). Then, suddenly, evolution seemed to put on its seven-league boots: its pace quickened among algae, DNA found its way into cell nuclei, and the creatures that later gave rise to animals appeared.

L: But I guess we have to ask whether a genetic change took place then—say, to just pick one, the emergence of sex.

O: The fact is that no environmental change has been detected which could have driven this burst, and hence the possibility arises that the transition took place for internal reasons. "Soon" after, multicellular beings jumped into the picture, and about five hundred million years ago the Cambrian revolution took place. Then species emergence went up by a factor of ten, and even more complex creatures (of the sort more familiar to you) appeared [132]. Three factors are arguably present: (i) the transitions are sudden, not gradual; (ii) the pace of the transitions increases; and (iii) each transition produces, in general, structurally more complex species.

ward greater complexity is only possible within the context of a cell, and the question is what that context adds.

Biologists fall into various camps on these matters. Mainstream (neo-Darwinian) researchers are not particularly troubled by them, and take genes (not cells, individuals, or any higher-order entities) to be the crucial units for evolution and development. Among those who are interested in the possibility that the genes' immediate context is as important as genes themselves, two tendencies emerge. The larger group is composed of historicist scientists; they attribute complexity to accumulated oddities. A smaller group is composed of researchers who believe that predictable processes take place within the immediate context of DNA's evolution, whose basis is not specifically biological; from this perspective, complexity has a basis in physics.

There is nothing much to explain about either the neo-Darwinian or the historicist tendencies; one expects gradualism in evolution, and the other does not, but no deep cause lies behind either possibility. In contrast, the complexity view faces a major challenge: to specify how physical constraints reduce the evolution space. Most attempted explanations go back to early work by physicists and mathematicians, which reached a solid peak in Ilya Prigogine's demonstration in the mid-1940s that, under certain conditions, there are stationary states of systems whose entropy is minimal. This was an important conclusion, which opened the way to considering entropy production as the central variable in systems that are far from thermodynamic equilibrium and allowed the study of stability within generally unstable systems. Classical stationary states arise as a consequence of a system's output being fed back into it, which may result in a phase transition at a new level of stability for the system (see fig. 1.9). Corresponding to these transitions, which are induced when unstable modes eliminate stable ones, new macroscopic structures emerge. All other things being equal, the second law of thermodynamics for open systems requires that new modes in the system must be further from thermal equilibrium than previous ones were (see fig. 1.7). And indeed, unstable modes (the ones taking over) are further from equilibrium than stable ones, as desired.

Complexity theorists hope that states of affairs like the one just outlined correspond in meaningful ways to the evolution of organisms and the complexity that evolution can induce in a cellular context. Evidently, the evolution of a species is a sort of broad thermodynamic event, encompassing a physical time/space within which it occurs, and a variety of local interactions involving both gene transmission and connections among entities. (Sexual reproduction illustrates the latter, but so do many other processes, including direct genetic transmission and "horizontal" transmission of genetic information through viruses.) This macroevent may find points of stability in terms of the minimal entropy of given stationary states (within given individuals, cells, or whatever relevant space). For this to be the case, biological systems should generally evolve procedures that increase their distance from thermal equilibrium; this would give rise to new dominant instabilities through fluctuations in the system, which stabilize beyond given thresholds. If so, the accumulation of structural complexity, although in principle compatible with historical accidents, has less to do with them than with the demands imposed by the laws of thermodynamics.

This is very reminiscent of one of the recurring situations in complexity milieux: apparently chaotic behaviour at one level gives rise to a certain form of order at the next. If you look at it in very basic terms, a cell endowed with a nucleus and mitochondria is decidedly less chaotic than the separate, free-living cells of a prokaryotic sort that end up joining forces to form the eukaryotic cell. But what is lost in chaos for the overall system of cells in a symbiotic relation is gained in structural complexity for the new cell with a nucleus and organelles. Complexity somehow emerges out of chaos [see fig. 1.28].

L: At the same time, consistency with a model doesn't prove the model's validity. For instance, we talked a while ago about convergence of organs like the eye, which surprisingly enough appears in dozens of apparently unrelated evolutionary scenarios, with significant differences in precise functioning and morphology. Well, as it turns out, recent findings show that eyes as different as the fruit fly's and the mouse's share an ancestral regulating gene, dating back half a billion years [see fig. 1.20] [133]. Given a common ancestral cluster of light-sensitive cells, plus the recently discovered, shared control gene, different eyes could have independently evolved in relatively dull ways. The point is: what looked like an interesting problem for traditional views—how can so many species be so lucky as to reinvent very similar eyes so many times?—may have just been a case of scientists' not having found the simplest answer; sometimes things are as simple as they look.

O: Rarely, but I do take your point. Nevertheless, it would be reasonably nice, within the large picture, to find out that certain patterns in our complex universe—which otherwise appear to defy thermodynamics—can be explained by known physical models. That's the main point, not whether the eye is a good or a bad example to illustrate the claim. The sunflower/peacock convergence is perhaps a more plausible example of nongenetic morphogenesis. Just as one may describe life's emergence in terms of an event cascade, so too one may describe Fibonacci patterns in this dynamic fashion. There's a very real sense in which morphological units in these patterns involve both growth up to a critical point and a subsequent bifurcation [134]. This produces self-similarity of successively smaller structures, in a fractal manner. The morphological arrangement entails the creation of form in the historical process of growth; it is growth dynamics that change a given form, but then that form is fed back into the dynamic process—thereby affecting it in ways that stabilise given systemic modes. Triumphant modes determine the conditions for the next bifurcation in the system, and so forth. Dynamics determines shape, which determines dynamics . . . All the way down!

L: Look, I'm also skeptical that the general properties of organisms are the sole result of gene activity [135]. What I don't see, however, is that the sort of answer you suggest is an all-purpose account of morphology—let alone systematic behavior. As far as I'm concerned, a variety of serious challenges remain for the so-called "sciences of complex systems," not the least of which is what's meant by a "complex system." Definitions pile up, ranging from relating complexity and entropy, to constraining it to grammatical complexity (the degree of universality of the formal language required to describe a system) [136].

———— *speculations about the calculus of variations and related optimizations*

O: Granted; nevertheless, and more to the point of our concerns today, let me suggest a second, slightly more speculative conclusion.

L: More speculative?!

O: Yes, indeed. This concerns the way in which variations are calculated within dynamic problems [137]. Needless to say, when systems reach the level of complexity that turbulence involves, little is known even now about their exact behaviour. But in less complex phases, variations are easier to calculate. The classic instance goes back to the earliest studies on the propagation of light through air: light in this circumstance appears to travel along a straight line, which was assumed to be the shortest path between two points. But this observation was challenged by Fermat: when crossing two media, light takes a detour from the shortest path, and bends into characteristic diffractory angles whose value depends on the medium being traversed.

L: The classical argument had two parts. The substantive claim was that light chooses the shortest path; the formal claim, that the shortest path is a straight line. This common wisdom does run into experimental difficulties of the kind you raise. But physics didn't give up on the idea that a law of economy drives the substantive behavior of light. Instead of distance, light's course was taken to optimize "action," to use Maupertuis's notion.

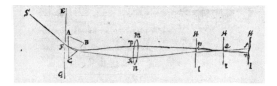

Newton's early experiment with prisms. (From Newton, *Philosophical transactions*)

Figure 1.29

[The following ideas can be found in college textbooks, for instance, Radin and Folk 1982. Stevens 1995, 27–39 and 59–68 (from which the following is adapted) is illuminating yet demanding.]

An intuitive example of Feynman's gives a hint of classical treatments of light's behavior (see Fukui 1996). Imagine a lifeguard surveying a beach, suddenly realizing that a person is about to drown. The lifeguard is at point *0*, the person in danger is at point *f*, and water and sand lie between the two. The lifeguard's problem is not how to get from *0* to *f* by the shortest path, but how to get there by the fastest one. Were there only one medium—sand *or* water—and no other complicating factors, the straight line would be both the shortest and the most efficient route to take. But in Feynman's scenario, at least one other factor is significant: people usually run faster than they swim. So the problem becomes that of maximizing the running path, vis-à-vis the swimming path, in which case the lifeguard should not run in a straight line toward the drowning person.

　　Various classical mechanical problems raise similar issues—for instance, a roller coaster moving along a track. Newton's second law (force equals mass times acceleration) can determine, in principle, the basic behavior of the moving car—but only if at all points the forces that obtain in all of the relevant circumstances are known. Down a roller-coaster track, these forces are not easy to determine. However, one thing is known about them: they must keep the car on the track. Therefore, they can be deduced from their effect on the car. To do this, though, Newton's law must be generalized in such a way that it can incorporate the various forces of constraint that act on the roller coaster, keeping it on track; the problem must be viewed dynamically, invoking such notions as the potential energy of the car (some function of its position and possibly of time, if the car is in motion) and its kinetic energy (some function of its velocity). The initial and final states of the system are known: at first (when the ride is about to start) the car's potential energy is maximal and its kinetic energy is zero, and at last it reaches a point where it will descend no further and hence go no faster (although this is also when it goes fastest), at which point its kinetic energy is maximal and its potential energy is zero. At all points in the ride, the sum of kinetic energy and potential energy is constant. More interestingly, the difference between kinetic energy and potential energy says something useful about the system's dynamics. It is possible to define a quantity, called a Lagrangian (*L*), which ranges over velocity and position, and which equals the kinetic energy minus the potential energy. This quantity can be used to rewrite Newton's law, by way of the Euler-Lagrange equation that describes a particle's motion in one dimension (an idealized version of the roller-coaster problem, which involves more than one particle):

O: Just so—and this general solution had to be coupled with corresponding formal conditions to explain why given paths are more economical (in terms of "action") than others. Then the overall answer stays the same: light finds the optimal path to go from here to there [see fig. 1.29]. To understand what light is doing in a system of this sort, we must find the values of a function that optimises its range of variations within the system.

L: But what's that got to do with—

O: Let there be a relation between different possible ways a given linguistic structure can be assembled and the structure itself. If the grammar of human language actually chooses the least costly manner of assembling the structure, what you're facing is an optimisation problem, which must assume a cost function and find its minimum value.

L: Well, that's a nice analogy, but unfortunately, after you set up the general problem, one question remains: how do you find a given solution to it? Solutions for the physical systems you've mentioned certainly exist. But the formulation of the physical problem won't help you solve the linguistic one. In effect, you're suggesting that the fact that the linguistic system chooses the most economical way of relating assembled structure to computational ordering may be an abstract instantiation of Hamilton's variational principle [see fig. 1.29]; just as this principle describes a mechanical path and, say, electricity, a deeper version of it may also describe a successful linguistic computation. But this reasoning is meaningful in the case of electricity because the appropriate variational quantity has indeed been determined. However, to go from the realm of the metaphorical to something concrete, one would have to determine the "linguistic Lagrangian," which doesn't make a whole lot of sense, inasmuch as we're dealing with discrete systems here, and not with measurable quantities [see fig. 1.29].

O: Surely, which only means yours is a discrete optimisation problem—those are common in computer science.

L: They may be, but the claim isn't very helpful unless one really understands the relevant variables that come into play (how exactly structure is assembled, and what counts as a valid assembled structure), how these variables relate, and what criteria one bases the optimization of the system on. These are very difficult questions, and it would take me quite a while to address them for you, even tentatively.

O: Oh, I've got plenty of time!

L: If you'd like, I can tell you, because this is where the real linguistic investigation gets interesting. But you shouldn't lose sight of one other important thing. When systems are too highly dissipative, they get too complex and start behaving in unpredictable ways. I mean this literally: propositions concerning open systems can't be verified, and our knowledge about them is only approximate. For many such systems, we're forced to replace the deterministic description of single elements by probabilistic distributions, and how they evolve. A typical example is the evolution of economic trends, for instance, where the flick of a butterfly's wing can make a market fall and scientific theorizing is a nightmare. In contrast, core aspects of linguistic systems are a simple, direct function of their parts. Crazy patterns might turn up in peripheral regions of language, perhaps having to do with anthropological variables affecting the meaning of words within populations, or the social implications of accents, and so on—the parts of language that seem basically unpredictable (or at least, that linguists can't predict yet). Or as I said earlier, maybe the structure of abstract PLD sets is of that complex sort as well, for some reason. To the extent that this is the case, this complexity does affect the acquisition process, at least somewhat. But the crucial fact remains that the principles that UG tries to encode are regulators of this mess; it would be a serious mistake to take UG to be a mere "pattern finder" of intricate environmental structures. Plainly, the environment isn't structured, or if it is, organisms can't directly assimilate this structure [138]. In sum, then, dynamic as the core UG system is, I don't really see its "complexity," at least in its present state. Another matter is whether its emergence in the species (in evolution) or even in the individual (in development) obeys a rationale that can ultimately be traced to the mysterious workings of "complexity." I've admitted that a plausible case might be made for the evolutionary scenario, once we set adaptations aside—and because otherwise we have a deeper mystery to account for: why language is elegant. But of course, good luck tracing the details of something that happened over fifty thousand years ago and doesn't show up in any fossil record . . .

O: Granted, granted, but it may show up elsewhere.

(i) $\dfrac{d}{dt}\dfrac{\partial L(x,\dot{x})}{\partial \dot{x}} - \dfrac{\partial L(x,\dot{x})}{\partial x} = 0$

Crucially, the particle path that satisfies the Euler-Lagrange equation makes the function A (the action) a minimum:

(ii) $A\,[x(t)] = \displaystyle\int_{t_i}^{t_f} L(x,\dot{x})dt$

Intuitively, the action is just a function related to the momentum and position of a body. The traditional principle of least action (ii) asserts that this action, when taken over a particular path, must be a minimum—which is independently determined in terms of the equation in (i). Many classical problems have this mathematical format, where a function $x(t)$ depending on time t is given with a derivative $\dot{x} = dx/dt$, and the goal is to find the function $x(t)$ that makes $A[x]$ a minimum for some given function L (in the present case, kinetic energy minus potential energy, and thus a function ranging over position (x) and velocity ($\dot{x}$), the derivative of position over time). The criterion for the actual path of a particle $x(t)$ (which in the concrete roller-coaster case would have to be generalized to a collection of particles in the relevant number of dimensions) is for the action associated with that path to be minimum (Hamilton's principle):

(iii) $\partial A = \partial \displaystyle\int_{t_i}^{t_f} L(x,\dot{x})dt = 0$

The roller coaster will stay on track so long as the design of the track is consistent with the least action path. Hamilton's variational principle (with an appropriate Lagrangian) also predicts classical electricity and magnetism, and an extended version of it is used in quantum mechanics.

L: Where, though? Comparative studies with other species aren't very helpful either, since we're talking about a system underlying specifically human behavior. Maybe someday morphogenetics and/or molecular biology will offer a solution, but that's not going to happen in my lifetime [139].

O: On the other hand, is it a mere accident that what you think of as a formal linguistic universal has got the characteristic flavour of a traditional dynamic problem? To insist, numerous physicochemical problems involve the calculus of variations, and I can think of a couple of biological problems that have that flavour too. For example, the structure of the microvascular network in such a poetic organ as the human heart is defined by the cardiac muscles' cells, with capillaries arrayed parallel to them. Apparently, the system's growth is guided by the need for the vascular system to follow the lines of least resistance [140]. Or think of neural wiring, which (as I mentioned before) is optimal, with neuron arbors acting like flowing water, both at a local and at a global level [141]. And of course, to say all these things isn't necessarily to say that nature "knows" what's best, or if it does in some sense, that it employs some perfect compromises in whichever multidimensional problem-space is relevant. As a matter of fact, it could well be that nature is using some rough-and-ready heuristic that happens to work miracles—or that simply works the way it does, though that way may seem miraculous to you. As you observed, nature seems to "find" optimal solutions when choosing the same molecular tools to shape early embryos, reusing successful patterns over and over (for example, the same pathways for different organs) [142]. And think of protein folding. Every protein chain seeks a given coil which puts it in an optimal energy state—that's its natural form [143]. Now are these accidents, or is this an indication that, at some level, something basic is going on (even if just a rough, but deep heuristic), which humans only partially grasp when describing it mathematically?

L: But . . .

O: Please, if I may—the Fibonacci examples [see figs. 1.25 and 1.27]; the dynamics of the system result in a pretty pattern, which has, as a side effect, the nice consequence of providing an optimal space-filling solution for features like florets and skin bumps. I call this a side effect because I very much doubt that the pattern itself is genetic (even if its basic growth function might be), and because I quite fail to see how optimal skin-bump distributions, and optimal primordial growth in plant features, could be meaningfully related. Perhaps they are, but it's so mad an idea that we may as well dismiss it; to start with, the same sort of packing distribution arises in a variety of other biological systems (snake skins, jellyfish tentacles, virus coats) [144]. It's probably more illuminating to think of the pattern as a property of any system with the relevant "forces," like the bee scenario I concocted [and see fig. 1.25]. But once the space is optimally filled with features, flower and peacock alike may use them as extraordinary spandrels. For instance, the peacock, apart from a natty attire, has developed (in conjunction with an eye-spot arising for some other reason on each of its tail feathers) a most fashionable sexual gadget. What I'm trying to say is that these useful phenomena piggyback on a more elementary dynamic economy [145]. Even if some aspects of that economy are genetically coded, and emerged in the usual gradual way (or not; that's irrelevant), the new macroscopic properties of these creatures are emphatically not a mere modification of existing structure. They constitute an instance of true emergence, a new phenomenon that corresponds to some specific level of organisation and has the properties of discrete infinity, underdeterminacy, and some sort of economy [146].

At this point the Other's shadow became so tenuous that one could scarcely make out his features, and his voice grew fainter and fainter . . .

"I entirely agree," said the Linguist, still ready to go at it, "that we should concern ourselves with economy in different aspects of the natural world. But I disagree with the way you've set up your question. If you're serious about understanding how the linguistic system works and how it might compare with other systems, you have to start by studying some linguistics."

"I'm afraid the wormhole is closing off for today. Look me up tomorrow!"

"Wait!"

"What?!" the Other was able to say.

"You haven't told me who you are!"

Then there was silence. For a moment the Linguist wondered whether the cruel universe didn't care to represent the ebullient fellow any longer. But it was getting late and cold—and he could feel it. So he just chose an optimal path to walk on, by the dark river.

Needless to say, the next day the Linguist did again take his walk by the Charles, if only because otherwise this story could not continue. He also wanted to check for himself whether he had dreamed the whole thing the day before, and otherwise ask the Other what his name was. But before he could even speak . . .

"I must warn you to look sharp," hissed the Other under his breath.

"What do you mean?"

"Mum's the word," whispered the Other. "We're being watched . . . "

"Oh?" the Linguist whispered back.

"I think this conversation is being recorded . . . "

"You mean . . . by a spy?"

"Next time the wormhole opens, watch closely in the distant background . . . "

"Are you having visions of Divinity?"

"Possibly worse. If you imagine the wormhole opening as a book does, and picture yourself inside it, look right through the pages—you'll see a dim image of—"

"Maybe the FBI or the CIA are watching."

"We're not saying anything subversive, are we?"

"They're always after research on the mind, to try and control it. In fact, they used to fund behaviorists of all sorts to see if they could come up with a technique to erase people's minds. They still try, actually."

"Don't say such things . . . "

"It's all right. They did understand behaviorism, but they won't follow the kinds of questions you're raising. We're fine."

(The best thing to do is to ignore the incident, and keep talking in the past tense, as if nothing happened.)

After a long, pregnant silence . . . (What a terrible sentence.) After a long, awkward silence, the Other finally spoke, nervously at first.

O: I'd say I've got a few more questions.

L: Shoot.

O: Would you please tone down your metaphors?!

L: Sure, look, the worst that can happen is they classify our proposals . . .

2.1 Levels of Representation

(an agreeable presentation of various topics, ranging from representation to the nature of linguistic data, and touching on the curious procedure of computation for human language, which is briefly characterized)

O: Well, er . . . let's . . . get cracking, shall we? Yesterday you . . . vaguely talked about "external conditions" on language. I've been curious—what do you take that to mean?

L: If an extraterrestrial asked you what the essential parts of human language are, what its basic makeup is, what would you say?

O: I? No, no, please. I don't really feel like talking . . .

L: In fact, the external condi—

O: Although, after what you told me yesterday, I'd simply say that the essentials of human language are just like the essentials of alien language.

———————————   **internal properties arise to meet external conditions**

L: Certainly, if the assumptions are right, and if the aliens had similar performative conditions to meet, the hypothesis would be that they have a cognitive system similar to ours, as an optimal solution to the same constructive problem. Of course, their system might be optimal in a slightly different way, perhaps for environmental reasons.

O: These abstract ideas . . . Well, they seem to accord with the old intuition that knowledge of language combines knowledge of some substance and knowledge of some form. Yes. The form is, I suppose, structure; and the substance is . . . well, whatever some specific performance conditions on sound and meaning express . . .

L: Yeah, from this perspective, external conditions on language result from the simple facts that language is uttered and that in the course of being used, it conveys some sort of message. What Minimalism suggests is that the internal properties of the language faculty exist precisely in order to meet external conditions, which is what imposes the heaviest empirical burden on the theory [1]. To start with, the structure of an expression must tell the speaker how to say it, which means it has to include instructions for the **articulatory** systems and for **perceptual** mechanisms. At the same time, by way of saying something, we question, we assert, we command, and so on . . . So the structure has to include a set of instructions for those systems as well.

O: Don't they ever get mixed up?

L: Linguists have to make strong assumptions in this respect, which in fact, being assumptions, may be wrong. For starters, we assume that articulation and perception share a single set of instructions. Following the important work of Trubetzkoy and Jakobson early this century, we postulate a single type of structure that's generated by the linguistic system and interfaces with—that is, sends a given structure to—the part of the mind that's responsible for motor articulation of speech sounds, their auditory perception, and so on. We call that particular structure **Phonetic Form,** or PF, and we think of it as a **level of linguistic representation.** This notion is very important. In essence, linguistics is about levels of representation like PF, and how they're constructed, and what properties they have.

O: I see.

L: You may, but here some people start worrying about the word "representation."

O: What is there to worry about?

_____ *digressions about representation and about mathematics*

L: This may be partly our fault. We chose the term "level of representation" for a totally technical notion, and intellectuals started taking the name literally [2]. It's as if somebody took the term "work" from physics and applied it to account for labor relations. The problem here is that a tradition exists according to which a linguistic **sign** is said to select an object in the world (its **referent**), in a manner determined by its **sense** [see sec. 2.3]. In this view, the sign is supposed to "represent" the referent by way of its sense [3].

O: I'm afraid I tend to get rather lost in these abstract ideas. Consider a linguistic symbol, an element from that PF level you've proposed; I presume that a stress symbol, let's say, might be a good example. Are you implying that this symbol picks out an object of some sort?

L: You're right on the mark in bringing the discussion down to that level. Obviously these issues are language specific—even speaker specific. There's no reason to believe that the way I pronounce the stress in the word *bingo* has exactly the same physical properties, in terms of the frequency of the sound wave, its amplitude, and so on, as the way you pronounce it.

O: Nor do separate utterances of that word by the same speaker necessarily lead to the same motions of particles, et cetera. The speaker may have a cold, or be *screaming*—ahem, excuse me—or whispering, . . .

L: So if there is indeed some connection between the linguistic system and, in some vague sense, the world, it's extremely indirect and should be studied empirically.

O: I should think that what is remarkable—more than the relation between a phonetic symbol and the world—is the very existence of the symbol itself. To start with, as we saw yesterday, symbols are discrete entities in a world which is generally made up of continuities [see sec. 1.6]. Next, if I understand you correctly, an [r], for instance, must be a very complex, very abstract entity, encoding instructions for both the perception of the object [r] and the production of this object [4]. This is totally bewildering to me.

L: Yes, the perception of an [r] involves the hearing system, and a certain wave pattern with rather concrete physical properties; in contrast, the production of an [r] involves an awesome coordination of muscles. So you're justified in worrying about how the way people produce an [r] can relate to the way they hear an [r] [5]. Yet there are reasons to believe that the human mind/brain is capable of doing the trick. But indeed, this is much more intriguing than what an [r] relates to outside of PF. To tell you the truth, I don't even see that [r] relates to anything meaningful out there; but let me continue raising the question because, although the matter is self-evident at the level of PF, similar issues arise—and aren't so self-evident—in what we can call the level of **Logical Form,** or LF.

This is another level of representation that linguists postulate, whose purpose is to interface linguistic expressions with the cognitive systems where concepts and intentions are determined—the components which are taken to be responsible for the way we represent beliefs, attitudes, volitions, decisions, and so on. Since linguistic expressions are used to assert, command, question, and the like, these **intentional/conceptual** matters are obviously relevant [see fig. 2.1].

O: Well, sir, I can see that your intentions and what you know about the world are somehow involved in the way in which you've built up that sentence. But, once again, how do you know that a single level of linguistic representation interfaces all the components that are responsible for semantics, pragmatics, and all that?

L: Linguists may well be wrong in this new assumption, and thus we have to be fully aware that we're making it. If future research proves that we should abandon it, we will—just as we could in the case of PF, although there at least it appears to be correct. What you have to keep in mind is that both articulation–perception and intention–conceptualization are matters of performance and thus may be fairly idiosyncratic, to the point that they may even be speaker specific. For an individual's way of pronouncing an [r], way of stressing words, or tone of voice, this is obvious; but the null hypothesis is that the same is true for an individual's way of referring, or judging—

O: Oh, much more so! What scientific evidence is there that those tasks are uniform, universal—the stuff of scientific enquiry?

L: Well . . .

O: My question isn't innocent: on the one hand, you want external conditions, of the sort indirectly seen in semantics and phonetics, to determine the properties of expressions; but on the other hand, you don't know what those external conditions are.

L: In the case of phonetics, we have a reasonably clear picture, perhaps because the evidence is more accessible and people have been looking at it (scientifically) for quite some time [6]. But I do admit that in the case of semantics little is known for sure [7]. However, this isn't to say that we don't have any evidence about what expressions mean. Quite the contrary: so much is known about meaning

Figure 2.1

For the first time, we are now considering a specific model of linguistic knowledge. This model goes back, in some form, to Aristotle, although in some respects it is simply obvious: linguistic expressions involve sound and meaning. (A caveat must be added: signed languages appear to be like all other natural languages, and yet they do not use sound. See, however, figure 2.28.)

PF is taken to interface, in some unclear sense, with the "outside" world, in that it is the part of the system that is responsible for making language public. LF interfaces, in some even more unclear sense, with the "inside" world of beliefs, attitudes, volitions, decisions, and whatever else affects linguistic meanings. It should be emphasized that PF is not just the form of the LF substance. PF and LF each involve their own specific substance, and these two substances appear to be rather different in nature (as is expected, since PF has to do with the motor-perceptual system, and LF has to do with the intentional-conceptual system). Part of the linguist's job is to figure out the substantive details of PF and LF. At the same time, the linguist must establish what determines the form of these substances. All refinements to be discussed in this book are ultimately based on the elementary and (virtually) conceptually necessary model sketched above.

that empirical research can readily proceed on the computational system, working from the point of view of the internal coherence of this system. Of course, it would help a great deal if we had a real theoretical understanding of that side, but we don't—we just have what we have. Many systems of logic have been devised—but these are mostly mathematical. You wouldn't want, say, calculus or statistics per se to directly tell you the actual properties of the universe at some scale.

O: Ah, well, this is a very tough bird! In the recent past, those were thought of simply as methods that were devised in order to understand properties of the systems that scientists investigate.

L: And then we have to look at reality (in whatever large sense we care to characterize it) and check whether the formal method fits the data, and the other established parts of the theory, and so on.

O: But surely not everyone advocates this view. In physics, for example, the field clearly divides: some hold physical models as prior to mathematical ones, and some do not. The latter view is very traditional. For instance, the Pythagoreans believed that the universe was an equation that could be expressed through natural numbers.

L: But that belief was demolished the minute they could prove the famous theorem. The hypotenuse of a right triangle whose legs measure 1 is the square root of 2. It's easy to prove that this number isn't a ratio of a natural number. In fact, Pythagoras proved it.

O: Then he jumped off a cliff . . .

L: The point is, a mathematical model is just that: a model. If you don't then place it within a model of reality, what's the point of the game? The reason Kepler leveled the Aristotelian a priori apparatus is that he bothered to look—or asked Tycho Brahe about the facts—and then he was able to establish that the motions of planets are neither circular nor constant, thus are "imperfect."

O: Kepler postulated his most notable law within the context of his harmonic studies. As you know, he ascribed a musical scale to each planet, which he calculated on the basis of its velocity as it approached and moved away from the sun. Then his mathematical impetus led him to conjecture that the tones of "our terrestrial domicile," Mi-Fa-Mi in his system, stand for Misery, Famine, and Misery [8] . . .

L: He must have been joking.

O: It's hard to know—he was a mystic . . . Then again, mathematics is necessary if one wants to do, say, physics precisely. And since reliable observations in physics are so hard to obtain, sometimes all physicists have got is a mathematical model to speculate with, on the basis of its internal beauty.

L: Linguists have exactly the opposite problem: too many reliable observations to make sense of.

——————————————— *discourse on the nature of linguistic data*

O: Oh, do you really? Doesn't it worry you that linguists seem to work with judgements by native speakers about the acceptability of given sentences? How reliable is that?!

L: I'm not worried at all, actually. First of all, many times linguists are concerned not with the acceptability of a sentence, but with what it means, what kind of structure it plausibly has, and so forth. How unreliable is it to say that *Ginger and Fred call* means the same as *chiamano Ginger e Fred,* in two systems that use slightly different parametric options and lexicons [9]? How unreliable is it to say that *Ginger and Fred* performs the same grammatical function (subject) in both instances? And so on—totally basic. Second, most acceptability judgments are completely uncontroversial. If I tell you that in English it's possible to say *John left* but not **left John,* you can obviously trust my intuition. Of course, you can also send me and two hundred other native speakers to a lab, give us both of those sentences, and monitor our brain reactions. Then you run the statistics, and you find out that, always according to our reactions, *John left* is a good sentence of English for ninety-nine percent of us, and **left John* isn't. You'll get some noise (a couple of us might be sleepy), and that's why you may not get a hundred percent accuracy, but by and large you've wasted thousands of dollars and a lot of time in running the experiment. Third, if better evidence comes along, fine; we use whatever evidence we have, and search for better experiments just as we search for better theories.

Figure 2.2

In the production and processing of sentences, real time is of the essence. It would be rather unnatural for the human language processor to wait until the end of a sentence to assign it a particular structure, since it would have to store potentially unlimited amounts of unstructured information (in the sentence that has just finished, thirty-six words; try memorizing thirty simple natural numbers). Instead, the processor assigns a hypothetical structure as the real one unfolds, making changes if necessary. For example, the parser may have heard (i),

(i) I know that . . . ,

assigning it the hypothetical, partial structure (ii)

(ii) [I know [that . . . ,

and expecting an embedded sentence (e.g., *the earth is round*) to follow. But suppose that the next word is not the first word of an embedded sentence, but a noun, which can indeed associate to *that* (in other words, in this case *that* is construed as a demonstrative element, not as a complementizer introducing a sentence). For instance, the sentence could have been (iii):

(iii) I know that friend of yours

Then the processor has to revise the hypothesized structure, assigning the sentence a noun phrase complement structure instead of a sentential complement structure. Interestingly, in some instances the parser cannot recover from its first hypothesis; it is said to have been "led down the garden path." For example, try processing the following sentence:

(iv) the dog just walked down the path barked

Most people have difficulty processing (iv), and they think at first that it is not a good sentence of English. But it is. In English, reduced relative clauses are common; one can say "I own the dog which was just walked down the path" or (more colloquially) "I own the dog just walked down the path." The unprocessable sentence has as its subject the noun-phrase-with-reduced-relative-clause *the dog just walked down the path* and as its predicate the verb *barked*. But the processor, receiving the incoming string *the dog just walked down the path,* cannot help hypothesizing a standard sentential structure for it, taking it to be a full sentence and not a subject with a reduced relative clause; then the processor receives the verb *barked* and is uncertain what to do with it. Normal speakers take quite some time to recover from this garden path effect and may not be able to accept such a sentence until it is pointed out to them that the peculiar processing is also grammatical, given the properties of English. Under what circumstances the processor does and does not go into garden path states when given sentences whose processing may be ambiguous is currently a topic of lively debate.

O: But hold on. All the standard judgements you obtain from speakers are necessarily mediated by a performance factor: their actual processing of the sentence they're hearing. I presume sentence processing must deal with . . . , well, an actual speech signal that a speaker has access to, from which the entire linguistic structure (syntax and meaning, at least) is to be reconstructed.

L: Yes, the speaker/hearer's task is to somehow come up with the structure of a sentence that she hears (or sees); and this processing obeys its own mental rules—whatever those are [see fig. 2.2] [10].

O: Right. How, then, do linguists know that the very real effect they're getting from the speakers is actually related to their grammatical knowledge, and not a performance effect relating to the processing of the sentence? If I've understood, this processing can be affected by the way the speaker is feeling, or by general limitations on memory, or presumably by any number of other irrelevant factors . . .

L: Well, of course. But in just about any science, the creative experimental work consists of separating noise from data, through reasoning. Experiments have to face the same empirical tests as theories, and just like theories, experiments are evaluated by how well they contribute to understanding (there's no other metric that we know of). At any rate, the mere existence of thousands of languages with involved structures, all of which hypothetically obey UG and exhibit certain parametric options which a child can easily fix, is as rich an observational pool as any natural science would want . . .

O: I suppose so.

L: No question. To put things in perspective, keep in mind that linguists distinguish, on conceptual grounds, between **usability** and **feasibility.** We say that a linguistic theory is feasible if it allows us to solve the problem of how children can acquire those thousands of different languages, the first question that we talked about yesterday. Any theory about linguistic competence must be feasible—or it's worthless. As linguists, we like to restrict the format of UG because the fewer options there are, the more feasible that linguistic theory is, and the closer we are to answering the acquisition question. Usability, on the other hand, is a much more complex issue. Of course, we know that language is to some extent usable; but we just use the parts we use, and that doesn't tell us much about the general problem of what is and isn't usable in principle [and see sec. 1.5]. Data exists on usability as well, and lots of people are working on it; but, admittedly, questions posed about it are extremely hard, and some of them possibly unsolvable. This doesn't entail, though, that feasibility questions are unsolvable, since they don't depend on usability questions for their solution.

O: But you don't think that mathematical constructs, such as formal languages and computational models, will also tell you much about feasible and usable theories?

L: It's not a matter of principle. Maybe they will, maybe they won't. A priori, a computer language has as much in common with human language as the DNA code does. Would you want DNA to tell you how to solve your next linguistics problem?

O: Curiously, when Gamow figured out how chemical bases specify amino acids, he thought of DNA as a string of words, each made up of three letters.

L: Yeah, and Einstein cooked up relativity by imagining an elevator falling—but you don't call the elevator guy to unify the forces, or a physicist to fix the elevator! This is a matter of how people get their metaphors—maybe from computer science, from mathematics, from biology, from art, from sports . . . There's no limit here. I don't see why mathematical or computational tools should be granted any special status. Certainly those models work according to certain formal principles and have internal beauty and so on. But what does that tell us about reality? Maybe something, maybe nothing, just as art or sports might. In fact, the computer metaphor has misled us into thinking that language is efficient, allowing humans not only to convey information, but in fact to do it very fast, almost instantaneously. However, I don't even think that the systems of language are particularly well designed for communication (whatever that is)—nor do I see any reason why they should be [see sec. 6.6].

O: . . .

-------------------- **Full Interpretation of legitimate objects at a level**

L: In any case, you may start with a scientific metaphor or a given model, but then you have to get down to business, doing science by the usual means and with the usual caution. It could be that Intro to Baby Logic tells you how, say, LF is designed; but it would be as remarkable an accident as finding out that the digestive system has a musical base. Scientific findings rarely happen that way, and unfortunately you have to do a lot of dirty work before structures emerge, usually with properties that are to some extent peculiar to the system that you're studying.

O: In actual fact, then, you must still determine what are legitimate LF objects, and I suppose the same is true for PF objects.

L: Which is one of the reasons I'd rather call what we're working on a "program," not a model—because we're not even sure about our vocabulary. At PF, this is the problem of universal phonetics. But a similar question arises for LF, perhaps even more so there. To take an a priori view here, stipulating that the objects of LF deal with "representations" of some sort (now in the nontechnical sense)—that's pulling a fast one. This is why I really insist that when I talk about "levels of linguistic representation" I'm using the term technically. We should have called these "levels," period—or perhaps "levels at which linguistic entities relate to one another." It's hard to find good names.

O: I say, is there some sort of criterion for validating legitimate PF and LF representations, if they indeed have their expected properties?

L: We call that the principle of **Full Interpretation.** We say that a representation λ satisfies Full Interpretation at LF if it consists entirely of legitimate LF objects. At the same time, a representation π satisfies Full Interpretation at PF if it consists entirely of legitimate PF objects. And the assumption is that the conditions that hold of LF and PF—of course, once they're empirically determined—will entirely reflect purely substantive properties of the interfaces.

O: The plan looks Aristotelian . . .

L: In a sense. However, for Aristotle the relation between substance and form was ontologically necessary, the very definition of reality. In contrast, we assume that the relation has to be established scientifically. Very specifically, we can't simply explain it away a priori, by saying, for instance: well, this is logic, which is eternal, and this is sound or some other physical support (which you can make eternal by turning the human voice into something divine, or invoking music), and they match . . . On the contrary, we're talking about a capacity which is dedicated to language, something which may have little to do with logic. This capacity is what allows for a structuring procedure of a specific kind, which we're taking (by empirical hypothesis) to implicate levels of linguistic representation. Certainly, each of these levels is thought of as a reflection of performative components that the linguistic capacity interfaces with, and in that sense (and only that sense) sound and/or some relevant physical support relates to something like logic (or a similar construct). I expect the relevant relation to be very remote—and very hard to establish.

O: Hmm . . .

L: Note also that, assuming a dedicated language faculty, the issue about linguistic substance should be understood as one about **natural interactions:** what linguistic properties follow from (the context) where the language faculty is found? In turn, the issue about linguistic form is simply one about the **internal coherence** of the system: what linguistic properties follow from the (kind of) mechanism the language faculty is?

O: But if Minimalism is right in that the internal coherence of the system relates to its natural interactions—as a computationally optimal solution to an ideal coding—then properties of both sorts should go hand in hand.

---

linguistic universals are substantive or formal

L: Yes, and to the extent that this is the case, Minimalism gets strengthened as a hypothesis. But of course, in order to determine this meaningfully, we need to empirically investigate the sorts of (different) principles of language that arise because of substantive (interactive) and formal (internal) reasons. Substantive universals determine primitive items of PF and LF. For instance, all languages make use of some small number of fixed, universal, PF **features,** each of which can be characterized in a way that's independent of any particular language. The same can be said, in principle, about LF features, with the usual caveat about knowing little here.

O: I presume, also, that the substantive properties of whole expressions are a function of the properties of their parts . . .

L: Yes, we take relations between expressions and their parts to be **systematic** [11]; for example, an expression like *Socrates is mortal* involves a subject *Socrates,* a predicate *is mortal,* and some sort of specified relation between this subject and this predicate—which doesn't all of a sudden change if the subject or the predicate changes. In turn, there's no such thing as a global, substantive property of this expression which arises even though the parts don't carry the relevant information for this property.

O: That contrasts with the holistic character of competing computations that you mentioned yesterday. Whether a computational process is an optimal candidate isn't clearly a direct property of its parts: one must consider alternative computations that can be achieved with those parts, and among the possible alternatives, choose the one that's optimal.

L: That's right; the property of "being optimal among a set of competing computations" is reached very indirectly, and through complex procedures whose calculation is far from obvious, and is currently being investigated. This is actually a perfect instance of a formal universal, arising because of the internal coherence of the system, which is trying to optimally meet some externally specified conditions.

—————————————————— computations start in an array of lexical items

O: Yes . . . I do see that PF and LF vocabularies are necessary, and how the principle of Full Interpretation requires expressions that combine PF or LF features to be of a certain sort. Then again, you also imply a computation whose output determines the form of PF and LF expressions. What is its input?

L: The computational system of human language (C_{HL}, for short) operates on familiar bundles of primitive features: garden-variety words. The old idea that a language consists of a grammar and a dictionary is essentially right. Generative grammar—my field of study—holds that the grammar is an instance of a more general, innately specified procedure. But the dictionary is still that: a repository of sound-meaning associations that people use to form sentences. Technically, linguists call this a **lexicon.** C_{HL} operates on items from this lexicon to yield the structural description (SD) of an expression; it's this assembled object that has to meet the criterion of

Full Interpretation. Again technically, an SD is built from an array A of **lexical items.**

O: What is A?

L: An **array** of lexical items—

O: I quite see that, but is this array a set, or a sequence, or . . . ?

L: Yes [see sec. 4.5].

O: Having me on, are you? A set, or a sequence, or any other such construct has got properties of its own; that's how we know they're different from one another. From that perspective, don't you need to say that the array A is itself a level of linguistic representation, encoding some properties?

L: We could, but there are reasons not to [see sec. 2.6]. In any case, those properties you're alluding to—whatever they are—aren't really substantive properties of the lexical array.

O: I suppose that's where I don't follow you: how the fact that, let's say, the array is a sequence isn't every bit as substantive as saying that LF has . . . what? . . . phrases or PF has . . . syllables . . . That sort of thing.

L: I'm not saying you couldn't claim that this is a substantive fact of the linguistic system, and then have a principle like Full Interpretation determine the legitimacy of arrays [12]. All I'm saying is that Minimalism has a different take on this. The properties of A, or for that matter any other properties we may observe in whatever structure is subject to C_{HL}, should eventually follow from one of two things: either virtual conceptual necessity, or else external conditions that arise through the substantive, interface levels of PF and LF. Saying that A has substantive properties goes against this expectation, since the lexical array doesn't arise in the interface levels.

O: What on Earth do you mean by "virtual" conceptual necessity?

digression on necessity

L: Yes, well—the "virtual" part is important. Consider for instance the fact that we assume set theory to express our notions.

O: I see. Needless to say, this isn't a necessary assumption to make, although basically all modern sciences are expressed in terms of constructs which are either set-theoretic or can be reduced to set theory.

L: So when I say that certain formal properties of the system may follow from *virtual* conceptual necessity, it's because there's no *actual* conceptual necessity to assume something like set theory. But I'm not just saying this to avoid trouble. Remember late yesterday, when you were arguing for the naturalness of understanding representational economy as a structural problem (what are the possible arrangements of the system?) and for understanding computational economy as a dynamical, open problem (how does the system obtain those possible structures?). Suppose you were right in your wild Hamiltonian speculations; would this be a necessary property of the linguistic system, or even the universe at large?

O: I don't suppose so, no. One can perfectly well imagine a pagan universe of the sort Greek mythology (unlike Greek philosophy) conceived, with gods performing all sorts of pranks to amuse themselves at the expense of mortals.

L: I often think that view is correct, though I still insist on the universe making sense, following causes, having origins, and so on. Maybe we're fooling ourselves here, but to the extent that we bother to look, there appears to be a lot of order out there. But to call this state of affairs necessary is to be doing theology.

O: Very well, so the intended reasoning is: the array A presents whichever properties it's got either because it basically couldn't have any others within the assumptions we're making (in other words, because they're virtually conceptually necessary), or else because PF or LF demands that it have precisely those properties.

———————————————————————— a computational system building structures

L: Yes. The system is designed to meet elegant PF and (especially) LF substantive representations in the most elegant way. In the past, researchers have proposed a variety of principles that hold of linguistic representations and computations [13], but the current program suggests that all linguistic principles have this elegant character to them. Nothing is superfluous about the way they work. This is what Full Interpretation is saying: the symbols of LF and PF are exactly the ones that are structurally necessary and sufficient to meet the defining characteristics of those levels (particularly LF). In turn, the workings of C_{HL} itself are elegant: its operations seem to be designed in such a way that not only are the PF and (especially) LF results elegant, but furthermore they are built elegantly.

O: What do you mean by "built"?

L: We've been exploring a **strongly constructive** way in which C_{HL} operates on the array A. Intuitively, think of it in terms of a Cartesian homunculus doing the dirty work in your brain.

O: Ah, the ghost! . . . The ultimate theory of these matters should— one would hope—get rid of homunculi . . . unless you're ready to explain how their brain works [14]!

L: Be careful with the metaphor. Remember: we're modeling linguistic knowledge, not linguistic performance. So don't think that the homunculus does the dirty work as you speak; we have virtually no idea what goes on as you speak. When I use the metaphor of— as you call it—the ghost, I'm concentrating on what procedure is involved in *knowing* what speakers know about language, which is much more abstract (and more predictable) than whatever goes on in performance. For instance, we don't care about which particular words a speaker chooses in order to express a thought. That would be like caring about which particular numbers somebody chooses to balance their checkbook—which has nothing to do with a theory of addition or multiplication.

O: Fine; now, this "competent homunculus" (or procedure) takes some item from A—whatever that may be—does something with it, then takes the next item and does something with it, and so forth. Is that it?

L: Right. When the procedure's finished, you have a linguistic expression whose structure you know. That's a strongly constructive system, which we take to be essentially universal [see fig. 2.3].

O: So there may be hope of Brits' and Yanks' someday communicating!

Figure 2.3

Although the reductionist tendency of the Minimalist Program has pared the hypothesized model of grammar to its essentials, its basic, technical design can be traced back to Chomsky and Lasnik 1977 (see also fig. 2.1). In the present model an I-language L is taken to be a set of idiosyncrasies (or parameter settings). The universal computational system, C_{HL}, is strongly constructive, in that it starts with a (variable) array A from the lexicon and at some point maps the assembled structure to PF and LF branches:

Given: A = {a, b, c,...}, where *a, b, c,...* are lexicon items
$C_{HL}(A) = (\pi, \lambda)$ for π, a PF representation, and λ, an LF representation
$\Sigma = \{K_0,...,K_n\}$ for $K_0,...,K_n$ phrasal representations by C_{HL} from a given A in a given computation

Then:
$$K_0$$
$$\vdots$$
$$K_n$$
$$\pi \qquad \lambda$$

By way of operations of various sorts, in a series of steps $K_0, \ldots, K_n$, C_{HL} builds a phrasal representation K from an array A. A final, "splitting" operation sends the set of phrasal representations $\Sigma = \{K_0, \ldots, K_n\}$ to the PF and LF components. In the PF component, PF rules apply to Σ, yielding representation π, and in the LF component, LF rules apply to Σ, yielding representation λ. So the well-formed formulas of a linguistic computation by C_{HL} are the expressions that satisfy Full Interpretation.

2.2 Words [REPEAT THRICE]

(or what if Shakespeare did not exist? a mostly pleasant conversation that passed between our characters when thinking about other characters)

L: There's a great deal of idealization to all of this. That C_{HL} is universal certainly isn't a necessary conclusion, to start with.

——————————————————————— variation is a matter of PF

O: What might the alternative be?

L: That's the right question. We established yesterday that variability within the linguistic system doesn't imply genetic differences among speakers; the system's design allows certain possibilities for variation (perhaps as a side effect). But variation, as we saw, also implies acquisition by a language learner, and you simply can't acquire something which isn't accessible to you.

O: Right?

L: So variation must be determined by what's "visible" or "audible" to the child acquiring language, that is, by primary linguistic data.

O: Your point being that this pretty much restricts variation to PF . . .

L: In principle, variations could exist at LF as well, but that possibility's outlandish enough that we can forget about it in this context. I mean, we can't "hear" LF; it's all just mental computation. Any variation there would imply that the LAD can somehow pick things out of the context of usage, and fix computational properties in terms of contextual cues. But children are terrible at figuring out contextual rules, whatever that means.

O: Children? I'm terrible at those rules myself . . . When to say "thank you," when not to interrupt a conversation, which people to speak to . . . Rules! They've always gotten me into trouble.

L: Yeah, well, it's hard to see how any of this contextual stuff could be used to acquire anything systematic and productive about LF. Of course, we humans do acquire the meaning of concrete words, which is pretty mysterious in itself (and to some extent, probably contextual [see secs. 6.3–6.4]). But LF deals with whole sentences, scores of them. Words associate to contexts in fairly transparent ways, but most sentences don't—so I just don't see what kinds of evidence could be used to learn specific information about sentences which isn't either preprogrammed or a consequence of PF differences. The point is that if nothing about LF can be acquired on the basis of positive input data, then we really expect LF not to tolerate any parametric variation. Which of course means that all human languages should be abstractly alike, given comparable lexical arrays.

O: Assuming the invariance of C_{HL}, what do you take to be the actual range of variation that can be acquired from PF cues?

——————————————————————— **linguistic symbols are arbitrary**

L: Plainly, adding items to the lexicon doesn't change the computational system. So with regard to C_{HL} it's perfectly irrelevant how many words a language has for, say, snow or colors [15]. I mean, I don't know of any language that allows its speakers to use some grammatical process just because it has a word for some variety of lemming, or where some strange construction exists for asking questions because the language has a verb for not succeeding in sneezing. This is again all rather trivial. The lexicon is as large as speakers need it to be, and the part of the lexicon that supports their conceptual structure has nothing to say about the syntax they use to relate their concepts.

O: Then there's variation here, but it has no consequence—which suggests that lexical knowledge and grammatical knowledge are quite different. Very intriguing . . . And by the way, I presume it's also true that, even if two speakers both have a word for sneezing, they may of course pronounce it differently. You say *sneeze,* and Spanish speakers say *estornudar;* and indeed Russian speakers say something that sounds remarkably like *hachoo,* and it means 'I want'.

L: It's totally arbitrary.

O: It is, isn't it?—the connection of sound and meaning. 'Tis amusing, though! Not only can one laugh—one can cackle and chuckle and guffaw and howl. One can roar and snicker and titter and—

L: I get the point. This is actually one of Saussure's major contributions to the study of human language [16].

O: Really . . .

————————————————————————————— *digression on reference*

L: Well, the arbitrariness isn't obvious if you want to seek a direct connection between word and object. Naive ideas along these lines are probably at the core of the mystical character of naming: when you know something's name, you can summon it, and it almost seems as if you have power to control it; you can sort of do that trick with dogs, anyway . . .

O: Oh, I love calling matters! Did you know, for instance, that in some communities a cow's got both a public name and a private name, known only to her owner? In public she's called "Brownie," for instance; but her name is actually "Matilda." That way, if the animal is cursed, the spell will have no effect, because it was cast on Brownie, not Matilda [17].

L: Charming . . .

O: Quite the opposite!

L: Well, for a long time one of the hot topics in philosophy was whether names are in fact essential to things, and the story went that in Paradise name and thing were indistinguishable, and part of God's curse was the separation . . .

O: Ah, but things aren't so simple as that. True enough, Yahweh bestowed on Adam the monumental task of naming all the animals—plants weren't mentioned [18]. This episode might be viewed as a sign that naming is conceived by the book's Author as prior to sinning. Nevertheless, it's best interpreted otherwise: Yahweh presents (only) the beasts unto Adam, who is hence to recognise himself as being different (which he does, subsequently feeling lonely). And this interpretation may in turn be taken as a metaphor for cognitive development: Adam (a growing, innocent child) develops the ability to recognise that other creatures have an existence independent of his, thereby making the desire to name them a bit more reasonable. Then again, why would Adam need names? When Eve was created, well-known events dramatically ensued.

After the Fall, Adam explicitly named Eve, for a particular reason: she was to be mother to all humans (as you know, *eve* in Hebrew has the import of 'life'). Theologically, this is the first genuine naming [19].

L: A descriptive theory of names . . .

O: Indeed—but is this justified?

L: Who am I to challenge it . . . ?!

O: I thought you didn't like authority arguments.

L: Modern philosophical speculation into these matters assumes that a symbol—as in the case of "Matilda" and the cow this name in fact names—expresses a rather direct referential relation between some sign and some object in the world. But matters are certainly more complex. If you ask me, a linguistic expression offers a very intricate **perspective,** which humans somehow use to refer to what they take to be the actual world (which, incidentally, needn't be the actual world, and almost certainly isn't) [20].

O: Mind you, I'm only a dilettante where these matters are concerned, but I've heard something about the philosophical labours that treat the meaning of symbols. Needless to say, if word and object were the same, the relation between the two would be insignificant. However, what happens when we assume (as is obvious) that objects are not words? Evidently we need a connection between the two, perhaps mediated through concepts of some sort, hence raising quite absorbing questions about individuation, categorisation, et cetera. For instance, philosophers distinguish **descriptive** nouns like *man* from **rigid** names like *Shakespeare*. Although one can use *Shakespeare* to refer to Shakespeare, in order to use *man* to refer to Shakespeare one must have recourse to rather more ornate expressions called descriptions, such as *the man who wrote Hamlet*. The noun *man* itself can be used to refer to the *kind* of man, much as a name refers to a given individual [21]. But *man* does not directly refer to Shakespeare—rather, it describes him [see fig. 2.4].

This view of descriptions, parenthetically, develops a logical analysis for a classic ontological riddle [22]. Russell took a description to be an expression of designation, by way of a property. The traditional puzzle that these expressions posed, I believe, is this. Suppose I say, "The Perfect Being does not exist," and suppose you

(i) *William Shakespeare signature*

(ii) *the man who wrote* Hamlet

William Shakespeare. (Benjamin Holl, from a print by Arnold Houbraken)

Figure 2.4

(i) is a name, used to refer to Shakespeare in all possible counterfactual situations (i.e., the name is rigid).

(ii) is a description, used to refer to Shakespeare in the actual world (but had the world been different, it might have applied to someone else).

(iii) man → ABSTRACT KIND

(iii), a description, is used to refer to a kind in all possible counterfactual situations (i.e., a description rigidly designates an abstract kind).

Berty educates his precocious child. (Same Choice)

Figure 2.5

ask, "What is it that does not exist?" One would think that, if I say, "It is The Perfect Being," I am attributing some sort of existence to It—which, if true, entails I contradict myself. Do I, however? In truth, ordinary people perceive no contradiction. Consequently, Russell just set about purging philosophy of errors about existence. Whereas traditional accounts would analyse *The Perfect Being* as directly referring to The Old One, Russell argued that the expression is quantificational, indirectly picking out the unique perfect being. In that way, when someone says that "The Perfect Being does not exist," he may mean one of two things: either that there is a unique x which is a Perfect Being and it is not the case that x exists, or else that it is not the case that there is a unique x which is a Perfect Being and x exists. The first reading of the sentence is still contradictory; but the second one is not [see fig. 2.5]!

L: But philosophers also take a position on the issue of names. Someone can say, "The author of *Hamlet* doesn't exist," without falling into a contradiction; but according to Russell, to say, "Shakespeare doesn't exist," is quite literally bad grammar. This, I don't understand.

O: If Shakespeare isn't a description of something, Russell's theory predicts that one can't really say, "x is a shakespeare." Hence, when someone says, "Shakespeare doesn't exist," that sentence can't be analysed as saying that it isn't the case that there is a unique x which is a shakespeare and x exists; and the sentence should be declared bad grammar.

L: Oh, I understand the reasoning. But just what do you (or Russell) mean by declaring something bad grammar? Grammaticality isn't for anyone to declare; what linguists try to do is figure out whether native speakers take an expression to be grammatical or not. It's a purely empirical matter. I don't know about you, but I don't have the slightest problem saying that Shakespeare didn't exist. So I don't see that your claim is factually correct.

_____ *names as predicates*

O: That wasn't my claim, but Russell's. And to be accurate, the Russell you're talking about is Russell in his mature years. The early Russell did on many occasions take the view that names stand for definite descriptions [23].

L: This Russell always has an answer!

O: . . .

L: . . .

O: I see! You wish me to tell you what the name *Russell* is doing in these phrases you and I have uttered, referring to the one and only Bertrand Russell, after articles such as *the* or demonstratives such as *this* . . . Very nasty. But as I say, there's certainly a Russell who could argue that names stand for descriptions. For instance, the name *Shakespeare* stands for *the author of Hamlet.* If so, to say, "Shakespeare did not exist," is akin to saying, "The author of *Hamlet* did not exist." Which is taken to be perfect grammar, I might add. Then again, I may have no descriptive knowledge about Shakespeare (hence not know that he wrote *Hamlet*), and yet I may claim (perhaps wrongly, perhaps rightly) that he did not exist [24].

L: If you know that Shakespeare had the name *Shakespeare,* then you do know something about Shakespeare.

O: True, an observation raised by Quine [25].

L: A truism.

O: Nonetheless. I then avail myself of the predicate *is Shakespeare,* or *shakespearises,* or some such creature. The name *Shakespeare* is then derivative on the expression *the thing that shakespearises,* thereby allowing me to argue that my sentence *Shakespeare does not exist* expresses this thought: it is not the case that there is a unique x which shakespearises and x exists.

L: That's not accurate. What you're saying is that the name stands for a descriptive expression (thus being a substitute for something of the form *the such-and-such*). If that were so, what would you say about the obvious grammatical fact that you can say *the Shakespeare I like* or *this Shakespeare* or *a Shakespeare* (as we just saw for Russell). If *Shakespeare* stood for the entire expression *the thing that shakespearizes,* then the expression *the Shakespeare I like* would stand for **the the thing that shakespearizes I like,* with two determiners, which is straightforwardly ungrammatical. Unless of course you were to argue that the determiners which may appear in front of names are

Adam naming the creatures.

Figure 2.6

The fact that determiners can appear in front of names is one of the most serious reasons not to treat names differently from nouns, at least from a linguistic standpoint. According to the standard view of quantificational determiners (e.g., Barwise and Cooper 1981), an element like *most* is a relation between what is denoted by its associated nominal and what is denoted by its associated verb phrase:

(i) a. *Syntactically*
     [[most [people]] [like children]]
   b. *Semantically*

Now consider the examples in (ii):

(ii) a. most/all/few . . . Johns are geniuses
    b. *the John is a genius
    c. der Johann ist ein Genie
        the Johann is a genius
    d. the Bertrand Russell that discussed these issues was a genius
    e. the new John is a genius

In English all quantificational determiners can take names as their first argument (iia), except for definite articles (iib). However, this seems like a quirk of English, since the exception does not exist in other languages (see the colloquial German (iic)) and disappears when the name is accompanied by a restrictive relative clause (iid) or a restrictive adjective (iie). Therefore, it is sound to say that the determiners found in (ii) are the standard determiners described in (i). This conclusion immediately entails one of two things: either whatever *John* and other proper names denote is of the same type as whatever *people* and other common nouns denote, or the theory of quantification implicit in (i) is wrong. The latter is not a welcome result at this point, since the linguistic theory of quantifiers is considerably more elaborate and solid than any linguistic theory of names is. Consequently, it seems safe to follow the former path, which leads to a theory of names of the sort hinted at in the text.

entirely different from the determiners which appear in front of nouns; as far as I know, though, they're the same in both instances [see fig. 2.6] [26].

O: . . .

L: It's very possible that all human names are just predicates. They don't stand for descriptions; rather, they *are* descriptions. If one's accepted, in some form, the proposal that the predicate *shakespearize* exists (that's the key), then how to encode this linguistically is a purely grammatical issue. Encoding it as a predicate like *writer* or *man* is plainly what the facts dictate, which basically suggests that what one may call "logically proper names" don't really exist in natural language. The closest we come are contextual expressions like *this* (and the speaker points at something like this river). Indeed, if I point at the river and assert, "This doesn't exist," I'm using very poor reasoning—although (I would argue) still perfect grammar. (That is, the expression is grammatically adequate, though without a logical interpretation.) But setting aside those ostensive demonstrations, human language seems to be built around more standard descriptive names for artifacts, states, people, and so on.

O: I don't suppose you're saying that a description like *man* has the same status as (in your sense) a description like *Shakespeare*. The noun *man* need not apply to Shakespeare in a **counterfactual** situation. If I say to you, "Shakespeare could have been a computer, although he was a man," then I'm making sense. (Think of Hal in that movie *2001;* it would have been quite appropriate to say, "If Hal had been a man, I wouldn't have destroyed it; but it was just a computer.") But if I say, "Shakespeare could have been Marlowe, although he was Shakespeare," then I'm making very little sense [27].

L: So names aren't the same as nouns . . . What's the big deal?

――――――――――――――――――――――― *rigid matters*

O: I don't wish to bore either of us with the details of this, but it can be shown that if one assumes that names are predicates, then it's awfully hard to capture the distinction you admit: that names are rigid but nouns are not.

L: I guess I don't really see that. If I say, "This city could have been that city," I seem to be making as little or as much sense as if I say, "This city of Cambridge could have been that city of Cambridge," or even, "Cambridge, Massachusetts, could have been Cambridge, England." The expressions with the predicate *city (of Cambridge)* seem to me to be just as rigid, in this context, as the expressions with the bare name *Cambridge*—so rigidity can't be a property of names per se.

O: Ah, but the context is fundamental: you've said, "*this* city (of Cambridge)"; it's via the demonstrative that you introduce rigidity this time [28]. Indeed, as Russell observed, demonstratives are the purest logically proper names.

L: Fine, so then you can say that names acquire their rigidity via a grammatical element, like a demonstrative [29]. Every time you say, "Shakespeare," you're in effect saying, "this/that Shakespeare," and so on [30].

O: But then rigidity is in the eyes of the beholder . . .

L: Which I think is right. Farmer Smith knows that at home the cow is Matilda, while in the fields she's Brownie—each name applies in an entirely different "world," even if the cow exists in both. What unifies Matilda and Brownie is only Farmer Smith's knowledge of the facts. If the devil knew about this connection, any curse on Brownie would damn Matilda!

O: I wish you were right, but what philosophers would say is that, at the level of semantic reference, the cow is really Matilda. When Farmer Smith calls her Brownie, he's just trying to beat the Devil, or at least the neighbour who may wish to curse the cow. The key is rotten misinformation—that's all [31].

L: I don't think so, really. *Clark Kent* is a name that applies to some individual in exactly those moments when *Superman* doesn't [see fig. 2.7].

O: Only because Lois Lane is supremely obtuse . . . We all know that Kent is Superman!

L: And then what? Do we get a prize for knowing? What's the status of that knowledge we all (think) we have? What if Kent gets re-

Whenever Clark Kent is Superman, the city is safe. (Same Choice)

Figure 2.7

placed by another alien every time he goes into a phone booth, and Lois Lane is right after all? Is that what semantic reference is then supposed to capture, a kind of knowledge which isn't in anybody's head and just by some lucky accident happens to be in Lois's head? Or look, take a more natural example. Suppose a child calls her pet caterpillar "Gregor," and the butterfly it turns into, "Sylvia." One day she realizes that Gregor is (or became) Sylvia, just as she knows that she is (or was before) the person who looked like a baby in the photo album. I'd want my theory of reference to capture the fact that, for a relevant slice of universe, Gregor is rigidly Gregor, just as Sylvia is rigidly Sylvia. What does rigidity mean here? Presumably it has to do with the fact that humans can regard some aspects of the world as both permanent and mutable at the same time [32]. If I call this river "Charles," I'm taking it to be lasting in my experience. If I call it "river," I'm focusing on its transient nature: today it's a river, tomorrow it may dry out and become a playing field; in this world it's a river, but had that hill over there happened to emerge somewhere else (in another world), the river might have been a creek, or a mere valley. All of this depends on my perspective on the world, or the child's perspective on hers, and so on. For the child, Gregor and Sylvia, while they remain what they are, are roughly as permanent, and perhaps as salient in her experience, as anything else that she can name. Of course, I'm suggesting all of these ideas as a hypothesis about cognition, which then has to be verified through the usual means, to see where it fits in with the rest of our stories about the mind, and so on. In any case, I know how to argue for minds taking things to be more or less salient or familiar, and permanent, and assigning them name predicates when they are. But what would be the real-world alternative, setting minds aside? What is the reference of *Shakespeare* "out there"? From a physical perspective, there's no thing-in-the-world with the properties of the intricate modes of reference that a name like *Shakespeare* encodes [33]. We can regard Shakespeare with or without regard to his works. From one perspective, he'd be the same person even if he hadn't written a single line; from another, it's perfectly irrelevant that the person we refer to as *Shakespeare* (and who actually calls himself, in print, *Hallam* or *Collier*) may have been the man of wit that actors, and drunkards, hung around with in Elizabethan brothels and taverns. Shakespeare may have been the Earl of Southampton, and he'd still be Shakespeare. In fact, a given **occurrence** of the term *Shakespeare* can invoke both functions simultaneously. Thus, I can say that "Shakespeare was such an illiterate con artist that we must rethink his identity and assign it to Bacon" [34].

O: Right. Objects in the world don't obviously have these properties, but mental objects may have them, and then people spend time debating what they mean. But you see, here is where philosophers would say that there are *abstract* objects with the relevant properties [35] . . .

——————————— *digression on prototypes and fuzziness, with a response*

L: I don't really understand what that means. What are these mysterious relevant properties of something that we designate rigidly, like Shakespeare? Psychologically, this question might have some answer, difficult as it may be. We'd need to look into how humans individuate relevant entities, how they categorize kinds which only manifest themselves through entities, how they succeed and when they don't, and so on. But what does all of this mean mathematically? Suppose we're not interested in the tough question of how humans determine whether something is a fish, or a mammal, or Shakespeare, and instead we want to ask "deeper" questions such as what these are in some abstract, speaker-independent sense . . . What do we do then? What kind of research do we engage in?

O: I suppose we see how much we can do with standard mathematical definitions (very little) and then push our logic beyond. A simplistic (and classical) approach would tell us that mammals, for example, have got essential properties. Nevertheless, it's basically impossible to devise a standard procedure to determine the set of properties that something must have in order to be categorised as a mammal [36]. A DNA structure would seem to do the trick, but one may be empirically wrong about DNA—and a definition seeks a necessary and sufficient set of properties, one which is not dependent on contingent findings. These sorts of difficulties lead philosophers into developing new theoretical notions—for example, **prototypes**, which provide a more fine-grained distinction than the question "Is this a mammal?" allows.

Under a prototype view, you'd ask, "Does this fit the prototype for a mammal?" [37]. Needless to say, even prototypes are tricky. Suppose we treat them in terms of probabilities. Now, is Jones an X? This is now a question about how well Jones matches (what probability he has of fitting) a central member of the category X— central members being prototypical. Thus, for example, if X had been "bachelor," we'd be asking ourselves whether Jones is like Henry Higgins, or some such prototypical bachelor. But now suppose that X is "horse rider"—technically, someone like your

Figure 2.8

[For the issues that follow, see Lakoff 1986.]

Prototype effects emerge whenever members of a category can be distinguished as central or noncentral. The former are exemplary and seem to help in understanding a category as a whole. They are recognized faster and used more frequently by adults, acquired earlier by children, and typically used in instances of example-based reasoning. It turns out, however, that determining how a prototypical system works is no easy task—and prototype theory is more problematic than implied in the text. Prototypical categories in human language are more often than not related to purely psychological associations that resist any simple-minded mathematical characterization. For example, entities that are experienced together tend to be categorized in the same class. Thus, Dyirbal (spoken in Queensland, Australia) uses the same classifier for fish and for fishing implements (in spite of having a separate classifier for inanimate, inedible objects). Both mythical beliefs and contextually dependent properties like harmfulness determine classifications more readily than experienced characteristics do. In Dyirbal, for example, birds are classified as male or female depending on mythical associations; and fire is classified together with other dangerous things (Dixon 1972).

In sum, then, although human categorization could be based on the centrality of the basic members of a category (whose core is structured in terms of common properties), categories also appear to be structured through processes of causal association, involving culture-specific experiential domains, systems of beliefs, and "elsewhere" cases. However, this is no a priori obstacle to finding regularities of a different nature (not arising from the prototypicality of structures) in systems of classification, as the later section on classifiers suggests.

Fuzziness typically arises in scalar situations, where degree-to-which is important. Nevertheless, more human concepts are fuzzy than the few adjectival instances mentioned in the text, even when it is unclear what the dimension is within which degrees are relevant. Is a trailer or a tepee or a cave a house? Is a mat or a tatami a bed? Answers are unclear, and they are specific to speakers and situations. A tatami may be a bed for someone who uses it to sleep on, or it may be a bed if compared to a tepee. Analytic instances, like grandmother or bachelor, would seem to resist fuzziness; for instance, prototypical or not in his deeds, Don Quixote may be said to be a bachelor, for he is an unmarried adult male. However, that conclusion presupposes a given frame of reference, where marriage exists, is monogamous, heterosexual, for life, and so forth. Once this frame of reference is questioned, fuzziness also rears its head and intuitions fail as to whether unmarried or homosexual partners, celibate individuals, ex-priests, and others are bachelors (Lakoff 1986).

Buffalo Bill. Well, first of all, Jones eats, drinks, sleeps, et cetera—activities which most people who aren't cowboys or Huns don't engage in with their horses. A probabilistic account will be of precious little help in determining how much like Buffalo Bill Jones is if we're considering Jones as a whole, for most of the time he doesn't ride horses! Then we have to limit the contexts where the prototypical issue arises. In relevant situations of horse riding, Jones rides horses (in other words, he is like Buffalo Bill). That still leaves certain questions open: What situations of horse riding should be considered relevant? And how many times does someone need to be in one of those to be considered a rider? But suppose we find out. Next, we have to allow for the real possibility that Jones is a horse rider, but he broke his neck, and so it happens that—horse rider though he is—during the time of the neck ordeal he doesn't look like Buffalo Bill at all! So now we must build in something like the "inertia" of the situation: had things proceeded in their normal way, Jones would have been appropriately riding horses. And of course, then the question is, how do we calculate that inertia? . . .

We could also try to develop an alternative to set theory. Instead of starting with elements which are within sets, and identity relations, and all the usual operations, we make similarity a basic notion and define fuzzy sets, where the question is not whether an element does or does not belong to a set—but *to what degree* it belongs [38]. This will help when having a property is a matter of degree, which arises with graded concepts like "poor," "clever," "old," "angry," "hungry." We can say that a person is some of these things to some degree; that's fuzzy [see fig. 2.8].

L: If you want to study that in the abstract, that's fine—it'll be like asking about what surreal numbers are, for instance (and I mean this literally).

O: But is that different from what happens in any other science? Mathematicians, computer scientists, complexity theorists—they all study models in the abstract that may then apply to concrete empirical investigations.

L: Which may be useful if we really know what those empirical investigations are all about—not otherwise. Remember the Fibonacci patterns we talked about yesterday [see sec. 1.6]—in fact, let's go back to even simpler instances that Henry Moseley studied a century and a half ago: the section of a nautilus shell. The growth of the shell proceeds outward, and an equiangular spiral emerges as a result. This shell can be described mathematically, as you said: it's the graph of a logarithmic function [see fig. 2.9]. But it's much harder to determine whether this function is telling us something about the nautilus's DNA or about what's involved in its epigenesis. To just claim that this is an informational fact, whereby some computational code gives an organized output, is missing the point about how subtly the equiangular spiral emerges.

O: You sound like a reductionist now . . .

L: Not in the least. I'm not saying the nautilus fact should reduce to physics, or even biology. All I'm saying is we have to do more than propose a computational model that resembles the nautilus shape. That's a descriptive step, but if we want to understand what's going on, we need a feasibility criterion [see sec. 2.1]; that is, we have to grasp what the empirical issue is. For instance, we have to distinguish a cognized spiral from a phenomenon in nature which, as scientists, we may describe as a spiral. In both instances there's a serious empirical matter to determine, and ultimately we want both systems to involve something very much like a logarithmic function; but how do we reach that logarithmic answer in each case?

O: Well, I take it that reference to a spiral through the concept of a spiral cannot be an extraordinary coincidence!

L: It is what it is—an interesting fact. All we know is: (i) there's some phenomenon out there; (ii) there's some phenomenon in here (in the head of anyone who's thought about a spiral); (iii) what's out there and what's in here may be connected, more or less successfully, by creatures of our sort. That's the scenario. The really difficult and interesting question is, how do (i) and (ii) relate?

_____ *digression on language and scientific reasoning*

O: Fair enough, but there's a catch that worries the philosopher [39]. In doing scientific research about the ((i), (ii)) relation—or any empirical relation, really—humans are using the notions that (ii) involves. Thus, it matters, for example, whether the space where these relations occur is Euclidean or whether the relations are set-theoretic. And suppose your empirical study of cognition somehow proves that humans conceptualise in Euclidean terms. What does that tell you about human scientific research on space?

The constant growth of shells.

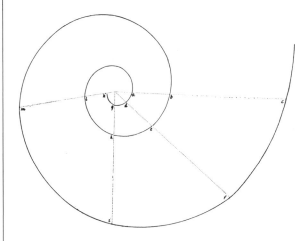

Moseley's calculations regarding the nautilus shell. (From Owen, *Memoir on the pearly nautilus*)

Figure 2.9

The nautilus, first studied scientifically by Richard Owen, provided an important piece of evidence for nineteenth-century philosophers of nature, who used its shell as evidence for the contention that nature's aim is the perfection of form. Henry Moseley studied the nautilus form mathematically in 1838. Moseley argued that the distance *ab* in his diagram is roughly one-third of the distance *bc;* the same ratio holds between *de* and *ef, gh* and *hi, kl* and *lm,* and so on. That is, a mollusc shell's spiral grows, but as the photograph illustrates, its shape remains constant. Moseley went on to propose an important generalization: that the growth energy required by living organisms is proportional to their mass.

L: It tells me nothing! Human research on space is a matter for physics to determine. The fact that somebody conceptualizes the matter in English or in German is an accident. As far as I'm concerned, logicians could develop an Esperanto version of logic to talk among themselves about these philosophical matters, one where the very notions they use are non-Euclidean when they talk about physical space, and quantum when they talk about little parts of objects. Just do it: it won't be natural language or regular cognition.

O: But how can you split cognition that way, between regular thoughts and the mind of angels? If humans conceive that would-be language of scientific research, it will be some sort of human language . . . By definition.

L: We're not communicating. The "scientific language" notions that you're talking about, if they existed, would have been cooked up by humans, that's true. But the means they'd use for that constructive task aren't the means involved in regular knowledge of language. For ordinary language, humans use their ordinary linguistic module, just as they use their ordinary visual module for vision. For what you might call extraordinary reasoning, scientific theorizing, artistic performance, and a variety of supercreative activities that humans can perform, evidently more than one mental module is involved, and coordination from a central mental system appears to be necessary. At this point, we're talking about a whole new ballgame, where conscious effort is required, training, skill, talent . . . People are better or worse at these tasks, depending on a variety of factors, whereas it doesn't make any sense to say that people are better or worse at how they construct a grammatical example or how they understand that a spiral they see is indeed a spiral. Everybody can see or talk about a spiral, but not everybody immediately understands what's involved in the spiral shape, or the different ways that shape can be achieved [40].

O: How, then, does one establish the validity of scientific conclusions? That's what troubles the philosopher.

L: I don't know, but I don't see how postulating this "scientific language" of yours would address the question. For instance, knowing what *atom* or *molecule* "really" means in the "scientific language" won't be any help in determining whether these are the right notions. Just look at what happened in real life, when scientists used those notions in their theories. Nineteenth-century physicists talked about atoms and molecules interchangeably (meaning corpuscles); your "scientific language" would lead us to believe they were talking about two different things—a conclusion that attributes remarkable irrationality or downright stupidity to those scientists [41].

O: I don't quite see how one does make sense of what someone else, with different assumptions, is saying; but I do see that you don't concern yourself with this problem.

L: I'm not sure you do see—in two different ways. First of all, I'm just trying to figure out the properties of actual natural languages, and thereby peek into those aspects of the human mind that seem to me reasonably within grasp, such as its modularity or its organization in terms of levels of representation. Is that all there is to a mind? Surely not; scientific reasoning, among other achievements, seems considerably more complex—so be it. Does that complexity mean that human research is shaky and we should either stop doing science (however it is we do it) or develop a language to express it in unequivocal terms? As a scientist, I think that's nonsense—no scientist I know of worries about such a "validation." But even more to the point, there's a second problem with your comment: we can't conclude from that alleged problem with scientific validation that natural languages are somehow deceptive or deviant versions of some better logic-for-science. Quite frankly, it's only for people with an intellectual background that language seems deceptive—it isn't for most humans. People talk in ways that make them understood by others, since both speakers and listeners happen to have the same, say, Euclidean notion of space, and thus communication proceeds without much trouble.

O: But what is it that's communicated?

—————————————————————————— perspectives on lexical meaning

L: That's a meaningless question, really. Suppose you wanted to determine what it is that you communicate when you say "spiral." Physically there's no unified thing out there that has an independent existence as a spiral. The spiral that leads to a black hole is very different in nature from the spiral you see in your bathtub, not to mention the one in a shell.

O: That alleged difference may disappear when the forces get to be unified. But I see the point; in the case of the snail, the "forces" involved are presumably biological—growth and resistance to it, one might say. There's also an obvious genetic component in this case, since—unlike plants—snail shells are right-handed, their chirality being genetic. Then again, one could argue that a "system" does exist out there that manifests itself in different levels of reality.

L: I don't see what evidence there is for the "system" in question, unless one argues that it has a cognitive basis: humans become aware of a handful of given phenomena and mentally unify them because they all, somehow, match the mental representation of a spiral that the human mind produces. That seems much more reasonable, and doesn't force us to relate snails and black holes, or to postulate Platonic levels of reality where "systems" exist independently of a mind that generates them.

O: That leaves you with the task of determining how that grammar of mental constructs works. How humans generate given patterns that they may match with phenomena they become aware of. To determine this procedure, I'd say you need to resort to such tools as prototypes, fuzzy sets, complex topologies—

L: It could be that the grammar of concepts does have mechanisms that coincide with those found by mathematicians. I've argued that this isn't necessary, but I admit that it's possible—though I'm even doubtful about that. For instance, people seem to take "having moles" to be accidental property of humans, yet they take "having thoughts" to be prototypical. Would a mathematical analysis give us that result? How do we predict that humans should take moles or freckles or hair growths to be inessential? And conversely: why is it important for thoughts to be prototypical of humans? A different sort of intelligence—say, that of dogs—might conceive this differently. Maybe, to my dog, what's essential about humans is a given scent, while the matter of thoughts is just a capricious twist of nature, leading me to pat dogs, or scream at them, without rhyme or reason—just like storms, or the vagaries of love and death, appear to me.

O: Actually, a mathematical analysis could say something about that, in particular. To be concrete, suppose the grammar of concepts is a **genetic algorithm,** which randomly generates hypotheses to match the sort of reality humans can be aware of. Suppose these hypotheses are concepts and that for each hypothesis, one finds something "out there" which matches, with its properties, the different symbolic aspects of the hypothesis. If this is the case, the hypothesis will be useful for reference, communication, or expresiveness and will thus "survive" as a concept [42]. This genetic algorithm could indeed have generated a hypothesis for the notion "human" according to which having moles is essential; however, this particular hypothesis wouldn't be as successful as the one according to which having thoughts is essential, assuming that having thoughts is central to the human experience.

L: I don't see it. To make a plausible scenario for why the concepts humans have, with all their characteristics and oddities, are the way they are, you'd have to devise alternative sets of concepts and show that humans wouldn't have been able to refer, communicate, have internal thoughts, and all the rest, with those alternatives. To say that humans have the concepts they have because it was good to have them is to say that the concepts are what they are because they are. It's not a scientific theory. I can equally well say the opposite: taking the notion "having moles" to be essential to the concept "human" would perhaps allow us, say, to get some insight into cell growth. It would have been very useful for the grammar of concepts to come up with that result, but it didn't [43].

2.3 Systems of Features

   (wherein it is concluded that Middle English is actually not
   Modern English)

O: Well, I hope at least you admit the regularity of the symbolic system our discussion implies—or when I say, "Lovers at first bite," you would be able to understand, "Bite at lovers first."

_____ this is how a *t* is pronounced

L: Yes, but that's not where the emphasis should be placed; as I've already said [see sec. 2.1], the systematicity is so strong that people share intuitions about it. While communication is, to some extent, a complex happenstance, knowledge isn't. But otherwise, yes: we have to characterize this systematicity, and right away we can say two things about it. First, systematicity should be taken literally, presupposing a shared system which is nonetheless introduced from a speaker's (relatively) idiosyncratic perspective. This is obvious for a

Figure 2.10

Consonant chart, with [t] highlighted. (From Halle and Clements, *Problem book in phonology*)

	Bilabial	Labio-dental	Inter-dental	Dental, Alveolar	Palato-alveolar	Palatal	Velar	Uvular	Pharyn-geal	Glottal
Stop voiceless	p			(t)	č	c	k	q		
voiced	b			d	ǰ	ɟ	g	ɢ		ʔ
voiced implosive	ɓ			ɗ			ɠ			
Fricative voiceless	ɸ	f	θ	s	š	ç	x	χ	ħ	
voiced	β	v	ð	z	ž	!!	γ	ʁ	ʕ	
Nasal (Stop)	m	ɱ		n	ň	ɲ	ŋ	N		
Lateral Approximant				l	l̆	ʎ				
Central Approximant				r		y	w			h

symbol like [t], say. What does [t] stand for? It takes a whole system of knowledge to answer that question. We don't need to go into this in any detail, but [t] is consonantal and not vocalic, and within the system of consonants it has a number of features that distinguish it from other consonants (it's a stop, it's voiceless), and so on. Take that system away, and we don't have a [t] [see fig. 2.10]. Conversely, within that system it's not crucial whether somebody pronounces the [t] with the whole tip of the tongue or just part of it, or with the tongue against the front teeth or touching the alveolar ridge. Individual variations clearly exist, giving peculiar shades to everyone's speech—this is what I mean by a "perspective": in this case, my pronunciation of [t]. Of course, speakers have to stay within certain parameters, or else they produce a different consonant (for instance, if someone voices a [t], it comes out as a [d]). These parameters have to be empirically established, just as the value of given constants has to be empirically established in physics. Similar issues arise for the meaning of *man* or any other such term, although this is harder to determine. First, the systems involved here are less clearly understood, and may be more complex in nature, encoding extremely elaborate perspectives. But second, although determining these matters fully would be interesting, it doesn't matter for our purposes, if we're trying to understand the range of variation of C_{HL}. I really want to emphasize this: whatever complete answer we give to this intriguing question, it lies beyond anything that could possibly affect the computational system of human language.

_____ **lexical variations do not affect syntactic computations**

O: That's certainly consistent with everything else we've said about this system, and about how it relates to the acquisition device, the use components that PF and LF interface with, and so forth. What you're now saying, in actual fact, is that variations in conceptualisation (be they within semantic units or within phonological units) have nothing to do with variation in the formal properties of the computational system. Hence I-language L may differ from I-language L′ in, for example, how each one orders the basic relations {subject, object, verb}, in the semantic space each one devotes to family relations or colour terms, and in the phonological space, if you will, that each one occupies (for instance, L may have three vowels and L′ may have thirteen). But these properties aren't correlated, are they? No implication exists such that if L has three vowels, then objects must precede verbs in L, for example.

L: Exactly. Of course, the general properties of the substantive system (where variation doesn't arise) do affect the formal, computational system, reducing the space where it can even operate. For example, it's because of the existence of general cognitive processes that all human languages manifest systems of reference, and invoke notions like Shakespeare through expressions like *Shakespeare*. That no doubt affects the sorts of computations that C_{HL} can even try. And similar issues can be raised about the properties which are relevant for PF, like the linearization of syntactic constituents in terms of "preceding" and "following."

_____ epistemologically prior linguistic knowledge

O: What about the other way round? Does the formal system affect the substantive one?

L: Right away I can tell you this: children acquire lexical items at an extraordinary rate, almost a dozen a day in the explosive stages. This immediately tells us that whatever concepts are assigned lexical labels during the explosive stages of acquisition don't just constitute a random list, but are extremely well articulated into a system. In part, this system may be structured in terms of resources of the mind which aren't linguistic, but which nonetheless present similar properties, in that the initial state of these other mental capacities is innately rich [44]. (I say this because, when anyone has seriously bothered to study the lexicon of Human, the issues about **poverty of the stimulus** that I raised yesterday, when I was talking about grammatical knowledge of syntactic constructions, arise again very clearly [45]). But it's also clear that a great many of these lexical structurings relate to the sorts of processes that C_{HL} allows, although to make a convincing case, I first have to show you how this system works [see chap. 6]. In any case, one can talk about substantive linguistic notions, and how they relate to each other, independently of whether the ultimate origins of these notions are clear, or even how exactly they fit into the formal system. I'm thinking of substantive features that arise when sentences are viewed as descriptions of events, which thus encode notions, for instance, of event participation (**agent, patient, instrument**), event location (**goal, source, theme**), and, often, intricate matters of causation, intention, and others [see sec. 6.4 for a partial presentation] [46]. Apparently, these semantic connections in lexical structure have the same sort of status for LF that phonetic connections have for PF, and both of these appear to be epistemologically prior.

O: . . . ?

L: Abstract the problem away from semantics, to take away its mysticism. A child acquiring Arabic faces words with the vowels [a], [i], and [u]. A child acquiring Dutch faces words with vowels like those, plus [e], [o], and many others, including a variety of round vowels that sound strange to me, as a speaker of English [see fig. 2.11].

O: Oh, but that's banal! The child just has to hear whichever vowels he hears!

L: It's not as simple as that; otherwise, all adults learning Dutch or Chinese would be able to pronounce these languages perfectly—by hearing them correctly—just like they learn, say, how to drive. Yet adults are pretty terrible at this, even if they have perfect hearing. But this is what actually happens. At a very early age—within days of being born—infants can identify all sorts of sounds, even those that aren't part of their linguistic environment. If a normal adult speaker of English hears two **click** sounds from a Bantu language [not represented in fig. 2.10], she won't be able to tell the difference between them, just as many adults learning English as a second language have a hard time telling a long vowel like the [ii] in *these* from a short vowel like the [i] in *this*. But although an adult English speaker won't be able to tell one click sound from another, a newborn will. In fact, infants in the babbling stages may spontaneously produce two or three different clicking sounds—no matter what their linguistic environment is [47]. Furthermore, unless the language spoken around them has clicks, they lose that ability very early on. At less than one year of age, as children pick up the rudiments of their first language, their general capacity to figure out all

Vowel chart. (From Halle and Clements, *Problem book in phonology*)

Figure 2.11

Although this chart illustrates the general space of possibilities, different languages use more or fewer vowels.

Unrounded			**Rounded**		
Front	Central	Back	Front	Central	Back
i	ɨ		ü		u
		HIGH			
ɪ					ʊ
e	ɜ		ö		o
		MID			
ɛ	ʌ		ɔ̈		ɔ
æ	ɐ				
		LOW			
	a	ɑ			ɒ

sorts of elements from the vocabulary of universal phonetics fades dramatically—and by puberty of course it's gone altogether.

O: Brilliant. The child is equipped with the essential vocabulary of universal phonetics prior to learning what specific vowels and consonants his language has!

L: The same is also true for the vocabulary of universal semantics, where the notions to test are individuation, agenthood, causation, and the like. I'm no experimentalist, but I do realize that such testing may prove very difficult with children who don't yet actually produce language. I think, though, that the ingenuity of experimental researchers will go on making the same point over and over: only the necessary limitations of our experiments (for ethical and practical reasons) stand between the innate specifications of the mind and our research as scientists [see fig. 2.12].

---

general conjectures on functional items

O: I wonder: have children with deficits been tested for these sorts of things?

L: Obvious ethical considerations call for extreme caution in cases like that. But look at the few so-called wild children (who for one tragic reason or another were raised with no exposure to language). These children (who appear to be normal in other respects) are successful in picking out words, even after the critical age of puberty when the ability to figure out grammatical structures disappears. That's what's most interesting, actually: these children acquire lexical structures, but they can't combine them [48].

O: Hm . . . Is it not true that a child who learns a word must, of necessity, be picking out its phonetic and semantic features, whichever those are?

L: It is.

O: Is it not also true that linguistic phenomena are characterised in terms of elegant combinations of phonetic/semantic symbols, what you call PF and LF?

L: That's also true, yes.

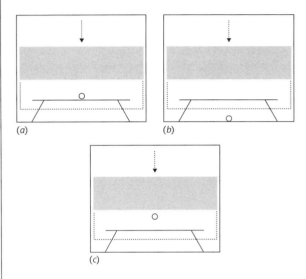

Figure 2.12

If experiments to determine how much babies know prior to experience are not to be intrusive, they have to be extremely ingenious. In the one alluded to in the text, babies are given a pacifier; various phonetic units are presented to them; and the sucking patterns that they exhibit are recorded (Eimas et al. 1971). The experimental technique is based on the finding that when babies are startled, they stop sucking; when they are bored, they resume sucking. The experimenter plays a tape that repeats, for instance, a [p]; after several repetitions the baby gets bored and starts sucking. Then the experimenter suddenly changes the [p] to a [b], and the baby stops sucking—an indication that she has recognized it as being different from [p]. As the chart in figure 2.10 shows, [p]'s and [b]'s are almost identical, differing chiefly in terms of voicing. Techniques of this sort can be used successfully within weeks of birth (days, for some tasks); the critical age for this type of discrimination experiment (after which children are no longer capable of distinguishing elements that do not occur in their linguistic surroundings) is often considerably less than twelve months (see Mehler and Dupoux 1994 on the general topic).

In principle, similar tests can be carried out for semantic terms—for instance, to determine the baby's innate ability to conceive of an object as a unified whole (i.e., as being individuated in some way). Spelke et al. (1991) present a series of careful experiments that come close to showing this. The general setting for the experiment is a puppet theater. A ball is dropped from above and briefly disappears behind a screen; the screen is then lifted to show the ball in its new location. The child watches what goes on, and his reactions are carefully observed (through techniques similar in spirit to the sucking paradigm). The key situations can be summarized as follows: After the ball is dropped, it reappears *(a)* on top of a surface (e.g., a table) that is in its path of descent; *(b)* below the table; *(c)* above the table, hovering over it. Graphically: Obviously, scenarios *(b)* and *(c)* are surprising for adults. We expect objects to preserve their material continuity and to move in continuous paths, and scenario *(b)* violates the first of these expectations. Scenario *(c)* violates our conceptions of gravity. In contrast, three- and four-month-old children tested in the experiment readily accepted scenarios like *(c)*. However, they did find scenarios like *(b)* surprising, suggesting that at this early age children are already endowed with the notions of continuity that are a prerequisite to conceptualizing objects. Because the children tested are so young, the experiment disproves theories about object conceptualization that are based on developing sensorimotor capacities or mere communication.

O: Then what is the child missing? Why, if he has acquired the words, can he not combine them appropriately in order to reach the desired PF and LF output?

L: The particular child I'm thinking about (an adolescent who'd passed the critical age for language acquisition) could say "pink," and "pretty," and "go," and hundreds of other words, but when she tried to form sentences, she'd say things like, "I like elephant eat peanut."

O: . . . !

L: I do understand your puzzlement, and it's justified. But in order to suggest an answer, we have to look at a very important and traditional notion (which was first theoretically considered, at least, by the Persian grammarian Alfarabi around the year 900 [49]). Language presents two sorts of quite different lexical elements: those that encode standard lexical representation, like *white,* and *book,* and *read;* and those that are purely **grammatical formatives.** While the members of the former class are varied, and new members are added to the class all the time, the members of the latter class are very few in number, always short, and often weak—to the point that sometimes they're not even pronounced. Up to now, we've been basically talking about members of the first class, and we've seen that they're separate from the syntax, part of a different module. But this isn't the case for the second class, the so-called **functional** (or grammatical) **items:** they constitute a sort of interface between the lexical and the syntactic modules. In fact, functional items can be separate words, like English *shall,* or just **inflectional morphemes** which are attached to words, like the past tense morpheme *-ed.* Actually, diachronically these elements change a great deal: words like *ha* in earlier stages of many Romance languages, which had the future import of *shall* in Modern English, have become **bound morphemes** in the present-day variants [50].

O: Right, Spanish speakers say *amar-a* (verbatim, 'love-will-s/he') to express what English and mediaeval Spanish expressed as 's/he shall love' [see secs. 6.4–6.5].

L: Very good! And apart from the fact that these functional items change from words to morphemes, their having a phonetic **matrix** or not—as linguists put it, their being *strong* or *weak*—is in fact syntactically crucial.

O: I don't understand. You're trying to tell me that what wild children don't seem to be able to pick out are these few, small, semantically peculiar, functional items . . . whereas they appropriately build up their lexicon, with its thousands of subtleties . . .

L: Puzzling as that may seem, yes. Functional items are central in determining syntactic computations. If you don't acquire them, you may as well kiss language good-bye.

O: Well . . . If these formal items are somehow driving C_{HL}, shouldn't they critically relate to the exaptive mutation that, according to you, gave humans access to language [51]?

L: That's a possibility. Certainly, pidgin languages (which, you may recall, aren't standard natural languages) make full use of conceptual structure by way of lexical items of various sorts; and people who try to acquire language after the critical age do have perfectly articulated lexical capacities. But neither of these protoforms of language involves obvious functional expressions; clearly, *I like elephant eat peanut* contains no *that*'s, no *the*'s, no tense **morphemes,** no plural markers [52] . . .

O: What we're in effect implying is that, for example, the slender australopithecines whose brain grew larger (for cooling reasons or what have you [see sec. 1.4]) got access to these functional chappies . . .

L: Of course, to make a scientific case, we need more than a good guess.

O: And do we have the slightest notion what these creatures are?

L: In short, no. We know that they exist, that there's a handful of them—perhaps only **determiners** ((in)definite articles and the like), **tense markers** (perhaps with possible extra specifications for the internal timing of events), and markers of expressive **force** (signaling assertions, questions, and so on) [see fig. 2.13]. But we don't really know how these items relate to one another, or even whether the substantive interpretations that we attach to them ("**propositional** force," "tense structuring," "referential articulation," or whatever) are appropriate in full generality. And of course, we don't have any idea how they relate to other cognitive capacities that are very possibly associated with them, such as the ability to enumerate,

Figure 2.13

[The following ideas are reported in Covington 1984.]

By the eleventh century, grammarians studying Latin had distinguished two rather different forms of grammatical dependency: *regere, gubernare,* or *poscere* 'to require a noun to be in a particular case' (e.g., verbs usually "govern" an accusative object, nouns "govern" a genitive element); and *concors* 'agreement' (e.g., in a given Latin noun phrase, such as *homo albus* '(lit.) man (nominative case) white (nominative case)', the adjective and the noun must agree in (among other things) case, whatever this case may be). Both case and agreement were identified as grammatical or inflectional items, and the grammarians asked (as indeed Arab and Jewish grammarians already had) how inflectional elements relate to lexical ones. They did not intend this question trivially or mechanically, but with rather modern philosophical and scientific concerns: What are the rules for relating case or agreement in nouns and verbs? Do those structural properties follow from general cognitive and real-world structures, or are they specific to language?

Fourteenth-century grammarians proposed a rather elaborate and insightful theory of grammatical dependencies, which offered hypothetical answers to these sorts of questions. Thomas of Erfurt developed a theory whereby grammatical constructions could arise only through very specific dependencies involving agreement. Noting that verb and adverb exhibit no obvious agreement relation (hence no obvious dependency, according to his theory), he nonetheless posited the dependency for theoretical reasons, assuming it to be abstract. This was thus, perhaps, the first instance in which an abstract null inflectional item was proposed.

In modern research, functional items have gradually been assumed to be separate syntactic units. In the early 1950s, an abstract inflectional element (later dubbed *Infl* or *I*) was assumed to occur in every sentence, encoding subject-verb agreement and tense specifications (Chomsky 1955). By the late 1960s, it became apparent that clauses in general (not just embedded clauses) are introduced by complementizers (*Comp* or *C*) (Bresnan 1972). In the 1980s, it was argued that the main constituent of a noun phrase is not the noun, as had previously been assumed, but a determiner (*Det* or *D*) (Abney 1987). These are the principal functional elements assumed by most researchers (though in the past decade numerous other particles with possible functional import have been proposed). Needless to say, determining the inventory of functional items is a purely empirical matter.

Patently, languages differ in whether they pronounce these sorts of elements. Current theories assume that major functional items are universally present, but the way in which they are accessed by the part of C_{HL} that provides instructions to articulatory and perceptual organs may differ from language to language. This is in fact the main source of linguistic variation, as discussed below in the text.

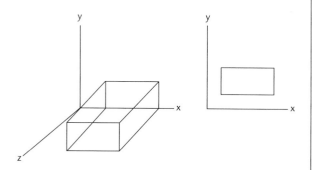

Figure 2.14

R may be (or at least relate to) the ability to understand how *n* dimensions relate to *n*+1 dimensions. For example, humans are capable of understanding how a three-dimensional object looks in two dimensions, and vice versa: Functional elements may relate to one another in this way as well. For example, Det may encode a typological operation for *n* dimensions; Infl (carrying Tense), one for *n*+*m* dimensions; and so on. From this point of view, functional items would be the result of a "warping" operation W, such that, for P a presentation of a mental space with dimensions D, and P' a presentation of a mental space with dimensions D',

W(P, D) = (P', D').

If this view is correct in some form, R is the ability to innately, unconsciously understand W. R may be related to the human capacity to enumerate, and it is essentially present in the relation between natural numbers and integers, integers and rational numbers, and so on. Notice also that by hypothesis, systematic variation emerges in human languages in terms of functional elements—basic dimensions, in present terms. Parameters of variation are essentially variables that the system does not specify. Variables are naturally expressed in terms of dimensions, each variable corresponding to a scale in a given axis.

and other mathematical capabilities of humans that presuppose recursive operations. It's in fact entirely possible that a single general ability is at issue here, call it R. R may allow us to unconsciously comprehend recursion [53]. R may allow humans to count, and also to understand that it's possible to escape from the dimension of integers to a dimension of rational numbers (or more generally, from *n* dimensions to *n*+1 dimensions). It may well be that a Determiner marker (such as a definite article, which is intuitively associated with individual reference) and a Tense marker (such as a present/past marker associated with an action) are just two similar bounding devices of particular mental spaces, which R relates in some way. Perhaps the notion Tense is dimensionally more complex than the notion Determiner [see fig. 2.14]. These are all possibilities we should seriously explore, if we want to understand what these functional items ultimately are, why language possibly develops like an organ that's programmed to do so, and why a critical period for triggering experiences is involved in this development, which somehow involves functional structure.

O: I can see how exciting it must be to ask such questions. But I must point out that there seems to be a gaping hole in your theory . . .

_____ **how functional items affect syntax**

L: We don't need to have a full understanding of what functional items are in order to proceed with our inquiry, any more than classical physics needed to understand what matter or energy ultimately are in order to study mechanics.

O: Right. Besides, what's wrong with having holes in one's theory? Gödel built a career on that premise . . . Now, in all honesty, I'm still finding it hard to relate these functional items to regular syntax . . .

L: Let me give you an example. Take the parametric change that occurred between Early Middle English and Modern English. Unfortunately, I don't know any actual data.

O: Not to worry. What sort of sentence are you looking for?

L: Just a fragment from Early Middle English—say, the equivalent of *you don't see her.* Why?

O: What about *thou seis noght hir* 'you see not her'? Would that do the trick?

L: I thought you had no memory!

O: When I truly start to think about it . . . what a muddle! You said that variation is always insignificant; yet it would seem to me that in this instance the two languages (Middle English and Modern English) differ quite notably—so much so that what is a possible verb phrase in Middle English isn't a possible verb phrase in Modern English. That is to say, in Modern English *you see not her* is ungrammatical with the meaning of 'you don't see her'. I take that to be quite different from the Middle English sentence that I gave you!

L: But that's the point: we don't have to say that the difference lies in the computational systems of Early Middle English and Modern English [54]. If there's an obvious difference between these two stages of English, it's that the verbal morphology of Middle English includes strong inflectional elements, as we can see by simply comparing the Middle English *se-is* to the Modern English *see*. Think about the structure involved in both cases. Better yet, I'll draw it on the ground.

[And as though he were writing on a messy blackboard, the Linguist picked up a stick and scribbled on the dirt the stuff of human language. The Other peeped from his end of the wormhole, intrigued by the pretty doodles that began to emerge, like a bush that grows in springtime.]

L: Can you see what I'm drawing?

O: As if you'd faxed it to me!

L: Here are the relevant structures:

(1)
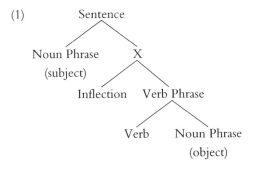

Modern English

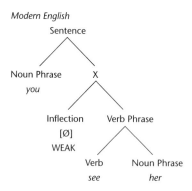

Middle English

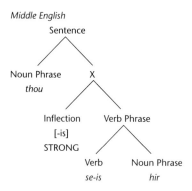

Figure 2.15

In the diagrams, lexical items are represented with letters, using standard writing conventions. However, in a grammatical sense lexical items are symbolic units carrying phonetic, semantic, and formal information. Each lexical item could have been represented instead with, say, a number, to be associated to a particular set of symbolic instructions. Normally linguists either use the convention shown here (writing out the lexical items) or—when detail is necessary—give an explicit listing of relevant phonological, semantic, and formal features. Note also that the Inflection nodes in the examples are both purely abstract. The Modern English Inflection node is said to be weak, in that it carries no featural specifications. In contrast, the Middle English Inflection node is said to be strong, in that it carries featural specifications that have to be matched up against compatible features carried by the verb. This matching process is referred to as checking.

I realize I haven't explicitly told you what phrases are, or what subjects and objects are, or what the X in (1) means [55], but let's proceed with the intuitive understanding that in *you see her* the subject is *you,* the verb phrase is *see her,* the object is *her,* and the Inflection node encodes tense and similar specifications, which can be expressed through elements like *shall* (as in *you shall see her*). All these words are connected as the lines indicate.

O: I like this game! Now, this Inflection node can be pronounced, as in *you shall see her,* but it needn't be, right? After all, *you see her* is present tense, but one needn't say *you do see her.* That's emphatic.

L: In fact, even in *you see her* there's a sort of abstract Inflection node, which I'll come back to immediately. But first let me go back to Modern English *see* and Early Middle English *se-is,* which encodes present tense and **agreement** with second person singular. Although *se-is* has two parts (*se-* and *-is*), it's a single unit of lexical representation that's stored in the lexicon as such, as *seis* (actually, as some abstract, phonological representation of this). My assumption is that in both Middle and Modern English, sentences are represented by way of structures like (1), with a separate phrase for the verb, another for an inflectional element, and so on [see fig. 2.15]. Then the question is how each language treats the node encoding inflection. In the case of Modern English, this is sometimes obvious: it's lexically represented by words like *shall.* But sometimes it's not obvious, and I postulate, if you will, a partially null Inflection (say, for present tense), which in most (Modern) English dialects is realized as null morpheme which isn't pronounced, for all persons other than third singular. However, in the case of Middle English, what goes on is slightly more subtle. The verb itself has a morpheme expressing tense and agreement, and this morpheme must appropriately relate to the node expressing inflection in terms of a separate syntactic formative. What happens then is that the Middle English verb literally associates to the Inflection node, thereby **checking** the features of its tense and agreement morphemes against those of the Inflection node [56].

morphology involves syntax

O: The verb *seis* "merges" with the Inflection node . . . It's very curious—do you know what this reminds me of? I've always wondered why the word *happiest* and the phrase *most happy* mean the same and—as far as I can see—can be used in very similar contexts.

Now, in my naïve theorising, I always thought that *happiest* was a shortened version of *happy-most,* that *happier* was short for *happy-more,* et cetera. Differently put, just as *field of dreams* and *dream field* look somehow related, so *most happy* and *happy most* or *more happy* and *happy more* (which for some reason are pronounced *happiest* and *happier*) should also be appropriately related . . .

L: That's a very acute observation [57]. We're not yet ready to discuss how accurate your conclusions are, but I do want to emphasize that you're indeed on the right track. So I'll grant you this much: your examples show that a word like *happiest* has nontrivial parts to it that relate it to a phrase like *most happy.* The word *happy* doesn't actually hop onto a word like *most,* though. It's tempting to think about things that way, but in most cases it leads to complications, not the least of which is how to actually get *happiest* from *happy-most.* (Although what you've said might be true in a small number of instances [see sec. 2.7 and chap. 6].) So what we assume instead is that the word *happiest*—or rather, to go back to the Middle English example, the word *seis*—is listed as such, a full item, in the lexicon. Nonetheless it has to "merge" with another symbol which has very much the import of *most* in your example, or is something like a present tense element in mine. Okay? And now there's only two straightforward ways of executing what you've just described in plain (Modern) English.

O: You mean the actual "merger" of the word and the abstract element it welds to? Well, one would have to either "lower" the Tense to the verb, or "raise" the verb to the Tense. I am, somewhat metaphorically, thinking in terms of the picture you drew for me in (1).

L: Exactly right. And for reasons that are irrelevant now [but see chap. 4], the "lowering" operation has some serious problems, so linguists have found themselves forced to adopt the "raising" solution.

O: That is, for Middle English.

L: Correct. For Modern English the problem doesn't arise, because *shall* is a separate word, so we don't have to worry about "merging" it with anything, and the comparable null inflectional morpheme is a weak element (weak elements don't need to be morphologically checked). If things proceed in this intuitive way, consider what position the adverb *not* (*noght* in Middle English) occupies in a structure like (1). It modifies the state of "seeing her," so let's say that it's attached as in (2), forgetting now about what Y means:

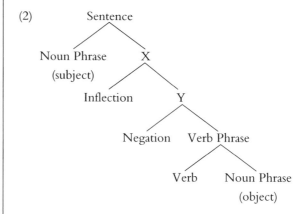

(2)

O: Let me see if I understand this new graph.

L: It's not a new one, really. It's the old diagram in (1), with a negative adverb added—that's all.

O: Hold on! I want to try my hand at it . . . So in Middle English the adverb appears between the verb and the object—*thou seis noght hir*—simply because somewhere in the syntactic computation this process takes place—et voilà!

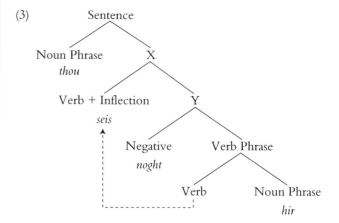

(3)

Here the verb "merges" with the inflectional morpheme, right?

L: You've got it. That's why the difference that we observe between the two stages of English, which on the face of it seems to be massive, actually reduces to a trivial difference. Children acquiring

Middle English only had to realize (however they did it) that Middle English had a strong inflectional element that had to be checked with a verb that raised to "merge" with it, while children acquiring Modern English don't have to realize any such thing.

O: Would you care to clarify what you mean by "checking a feature"?

L: We'll have to discuss this notion in rather more detail as we go along. For now, though, think of a **strong** functional **feature** (like the one in Middle English) as a sort of "virus." When the system detects one of these, it has to act immediately, in order to eliminate it. That is, in these circumstances C_{HL} behaves like the immune system, dispatching a relevant antibody to take care of the "virus." That's the intuition behind the operation you drew in (3).

O: Very intriguing. And the variation between Middle and Modern English is in terms of this viral feature . . . Modern English lacks it, so the immunisation operation in (3) isn't really necessary . . .

L: That's right [58].

O: From this perspective, an I-language is a choice of options in the formal system of the lexicon (which may be viral or not—technically, strong or not). Plus of course a certain lexical arbitrariness. This entails that there exists only a finite array of languages which differ structurally . . .

L: Possibly a very tight array, in fact, which is good news from the point of view of the feasibility criterion we were talking about earlier: the smaller the set of possible languages the child/LAD has to acquire, the easier the task will be, and the closer we'll be to explaining the acquisition riddle.

O: Brilliant.

L: . . .

2.4 The Inclusive Nature of LF

(featuring features and introducing at last just what's in a word, with an entertaining discussion of how it might shape LF)

Figure 2.16

Obstruents: [−syl, +cons, −son]

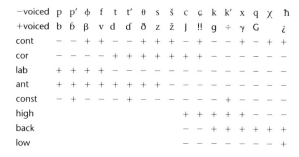

	p	p'	φ	f	t	t'	θ	s	š	c	ç	k	k'	x	q	χ	ħ
−voiced	p	p'	φ	f	t	t'	θ	s	š	c	ç	k	k'	x	q	χ	ħ
+voiced	b	ɓ	β	v	d	ɗ	ð	z	ž	ʝ	ǃǃ	g	÷	ɣ	G		ʢ
cont	−	−	+	+	−	−	+	+	+	−	+	−	−	+	−	+	+
cor	−	−	−	−	+	+	+	+	+	+	+	−	−	−	−	−	−
lab	+	+	+	+	−	−	−	−	−	−	−	−	−	−	−	−	−
ant	+	+	+	+	+	+	+	+	−	−	−	−	−	−	−	−	−
const	−	+	−	−	−	+	−	−	−	−	−	+	−	−	−	−	−
high									+	+	+	+	+	−	−	−	−
back									−	−	+	+	+	+	+	+	+
low									−	−	−	−	−	−	−	−	+

Notice certain implicational relations: all the labial (*lab*) obstruents are anterior (*ant*), and all the nonanterior ones are nonlabial. Note also that features like *high, low*, and *back* are relevant only for a certain class of obstruents.

O: You may take that as a compliment . . . But now let me return to lexical structures. A word like *snow* is used to refer to snow (the word itself doesn't stand in any direct relation to snow) and implicates a system of knowledge with intricate properties, similar to the system that obtains for phonetic symbols [see fig. 2.16]. Right. So *snow* is a mass term, unlike *flake,* or some such term, which is not. What does this mean, though?

——————— **the features of lexical items must be determined empirically**

L: It means that, among the features that you ascribe to the lexical entry *snow,* one of them is [+mass], perhaps.

O: But how does one determine that?

L: Empirically. The linguist has to find out what the relevant constants are within lexical spaces. The mass versus count distinction is one of them, and others are obvious: whether something is abstract, artifactual, animate . . . In principle, the task shouldn't be different from that of determining what the phonological constants are. To think otherwise is to ascribe to LF constants a mystical reality that we don't ascribe to other constants.

O: Well, again I think I need to look at a concrete example. Please imagine a complex expression such as *my dog*. Were I to say to you that my dog bites, you would be justified in concluding—would you not?—that I have a dog.

L: Yes, given the form of the expression *my dog*. So you want your system of features to be able to determine this kind of fact.

O: But what if I say to you that my dog doesn't bite? Can you then conclude that I have a dog?

L: I can well imagine that you (being the fan of Lewis Carroll that you are) might say to me that your dog doesn't bite—because you don't have a dog [59]!

O: I can do, can't I?—yes, I can indeed . . . Now, we can use this little game to test whether a presupposed feature of an expression is indeed part of its lexical meaning. Hence, the expression *my dog* encodes the **presupposition** that I own a dog: when denying that my dog bites, I can be denying just that presupposition. I know that *my dog* encodes the relevant presupposition because the sentence *my dog doesn't bite* can be true if I don't own a dog (even if another dog which might be in the vicinity, and is definitely not my dog, does bite) [see fig. 2.17].

L: I'd say you're not being very cooperative; but people pretty often do say the kind of thing you're saying. For instance, when filling out applications, people frequently have to answer questions like, "Do your children live at home?" They can answer, "I don't have any children," or they can actually answer, "No" (if they don't have any children), which many people do if they don't want to bother going into long explanations.

O: Right, but the whole point is to test whether a given expression encodes information for further computation at LF. Apparently, *my dog* does encode (in some abstract form) the information "I have a dog," which can be negated [see fig. 2.17]. Now, how about an expression like *snow?* Does it equally encode a presupposition that it is, for example, a mass term? That's what you would predict!

L: Look, before we even go into any of this, let me stop and make a disclaimer. I don't think that anything you and I can conclude right now will be of help in determining the relevant constants of LF.

O: But why ever not? My logic is perfect!

L: It's too complex a task to do it like this, and in this instance the evidence is indeed very subtle. We have to be serious, do the experiments right, test speaker reactions carefully, and so on. In fact, the experiment should be done with children—the younger the better.

O: Sir, you and I have plenty of concepts . . .

L: Yeah, but our adult minds are already too messy [60] . . . We know too much! What linguists are interested in are the constants at S_0, the initial stage—and only indirectly in whatever goes on right now. That is, if we can ever hope to distinguish innate features from information people pick up from the environment.

O: Right, which is the point I'm trying to raise—as, I might point out, Quine did also [61]. It will be excruciatingly difficult to make the right distinction between knowledge of the world around us and innate semantic knowledge.

Figure 2.17

Consider (i):

(i) my dog doesn't bite

According to some speakers of English, (i) is true either if the person who utters it has a dog and the dog does not bite, or if that person has no dog. The latter judgment can be explained if the expression *my dog* encodes, in some form, the expression in (ii):

(ii) I have a dog

Thus, (i) has roughly the same import as (iii),

(iii) it is not true that biting obtains of something I own which is a dog

which has roughly the semantics shown in (iv):

(iv) it is not the case that there is a biting event e for a possession relation R, where R is the subject of e and *I* and *a dog* are the terms of R

The negative operator can deny either the existence of the biting event or the existence of the possessive relation.

L: That it's difficult is a truism. That it can't be done, we have no evidence for. These aren't a priori matters, so we should take the trouble to look.

O: But what in Hell are we looking for?!

_____ LF features and meaning postulates

L: Suppose you conjecture that the mass-count distinction is one of the LF constants (you could be right or wrong about this, but you make the claim as an empirical hypothesis). In fact, for practical reasons, linguists make this kind of conjecture on the basis of what they see overtly in some language of the world: a separate morpheme encoding some abstract notion, or perhaps an agreement feature of the kind that triggers a syntactic process, as in (3). The simple fact that some inflectional morpheme triggered the operation in (3) proves that this particular morpheme involves a feature which is relevant for syntactic computation and is therefore a possible (though not necessary) candidate for an LF constant [62]. So say we find something like that as well for the mass-count distinction, and we bet on its being one of the LF constants. How do we test the conjecture? Consider the word *coffee,* for instance. People use this word with a mass interpretation, as in "We don't keep our coffee in the fridge," and with a count interpretation, as in "Could you please give us two coffees?" But here's what we want to know: When I say something like, "A coffee was given to us," is there a presupposition that we were given something which is [+count]? And when I say, "Coffee was given to us," is there a presupposition that we were given something which is [−count] (= [+mass])? And now the crucial example: what if I say, "A coffee wasn't given to us, because it wasn't poured in a cup; we had to drink it from the coffeepot"?

O: Oh, dear me . . . I suppose I'd have to agree that "a coffee" is something that must be properly poured into a cup. If someone said to me, "There, have some coffee," pointing at a coffeepot for me to drink from, I'd excuse his rudeness on the grounds that he was, well, expressing himself quite accurately. But if he said to me instead, "Here, have *a* coffee," I should probably ask, "Where's the cup?" Right, I do see your point. The expression *a coffee* denotes something which is [+count], therefore something which must come in some measure or other—usually a cup [see fig. 2.18].

Figure 2.18

Consider (i):

(i) a coffee wasn't given to us

In the same vein as the examples discussed in figure 2.17, (i) may be judged to be true if the speaker was not given any coffee, or if the speaker was given coffee, but it was not poured in a cup. The latter judgment can be explained if the expression *a coffee* encodes, in some form, the expression in (ii):

(ii) an amount of coffee is measured in a cup

Thus, (i) has roughly the same import as (iii):

(iii) it is not true that giving obtains of something we were presented with which is an appropriately measured amount of coffee

The negative operator can deny either the existence of the giving event or the existence of the measure expression.

L: But I insist: to reach that conclusion meaningfully, you'd have to do the test with children.

O: Using something other than coffee, I should hope! To sum up, then: by the mere fact that I use the expression *a coffee,* I know that I invoke the presupposition that something countable is being used. But I know more than that, I submit, when I use that word. I know, for instance, that coffee is roasted, grows somewhere in tropical areas, is handpicked by underpaid chaps, et cetera. There are numerous statements that anyone can associate with coffee, ranging from the most general to the most ad hoc (I can imagine someone associating coffee with restlessness, say, or a row with a particular waiter). Shouldn't these too be part of the lexical meaning of *coffee* [63]?

L: There are no "shoulds" here. We're trying to determine these matters empirically, not settle them on the basis of posturing. Undoubtedly, the kinds of **meaning postulates** you've just raised are very unlikely to be **intrinsic** lexical features of *coffee*.

O: You're confusing matters now, I must say. I haven't used the term "meaning postulate," have I? Had I done so, I would have said that the intrinsic lexical features of *coffee* are precisely what meaning postulates should express. These kinds of postulates were proposed by Carnap to deal with analytically true sentences which are not true as a consequence of their form. For example, all instances of *a coffee* must involve a proper *measure* of "coffeehood." More formally: All$x$[coffee(x) → measured (x)] [64]. The possibly analytic truth of the sentence *a coffee is measured* follows only if the postulate is assumed; in contrast, the truth of the sentence *the author of Hamlet exists* follows from its very form.

L: I do understand—and I don't think I'm confusing anything. Meaning postulates seem fine as a way to observe the phenomenology of certain correlations; for example, the postulate Most$x$-[coffee(x) → grown-in-the-tropics(x)] gives us a fancy way of operating with the usual assumptions about coffee. But what I have in mind for the measure of coffee is actually quite different; plainly, there's something more fundamental about the relation between *a coffee* and its measure than there is about the relation between it and the tropics [65].

O: How d'you know?

Figure 2.19

Consider (i):

(i) a coffee wasn't given to us

The truth or falsity of (i) is hard to judge if the speaker was given coffee appropriately poured in a cup, but the coffee had not been handpicked by underpaid fellows. This judgment can be explained if the expression *a coffee* does not encode in any direct form (at LF) the expression in (ii):

(ii) coffee is handpicked by underpaid fellows

Since (ii) is not encoded within (i) at any level, the negative operator in (i) cannot be negating (ii).

L: Because I ask. Logically, we can't show any of this. But when we test it with speakers, different effects show up. To start with, what I want to continue calling a meaning postulate never triggers a grammatical process in any language of the world, and never shows up as a grammatical morpheme—as a measure phrase, for instance, can. That's empirical. At the same time, consider the **implications** that a sentence like "A coffee wasn't given to us" allows. Can I utter that and then add: " . . . because it hadn't been handpicked by underpaid fellows"?

O: That seems an unreasonable thing to say [see fig. 2.19].

L: Which, again, we should test. But suppose we do determine that it's a necessarily lexical property of *coffee* that it be either a mass or a count term, but not that the substance it denotes be handpicked. Then these sorts of necessary properties of lexical items are taken to be their intrinsic features, the constant vocabulary of LF. Intuitively, these will be things like mass and count, singular and plural, animate and inanimate, masculine and feminine; not many others. The rest is what I'd call meaning postulates, for lack of a better term.

classifiers and lexical implications

O: Well, hold on! It so happens that speakers of Dyirbal—an aboriginal language of Australia—use the grammatical classifier *bayi* when they refer to men, kangaroos, the moon, storms, rainbows, boomerangs, and so forth (. . . !); *balan* to classify women, echidna, crickets, water, fire, the sun, the stars, et cetera (. . . !); *balam* for edible fruits and the plants they grow on; and *bala* for everything else [66]. This is far from peculiar. Languages can grammatically classify according to geometrical shape (Burmese distinguishes round, long, and flat objects), natural attributes (Chinese distinguishes fauna, flora, and marine creatures), social and cultural attributes (again, Chinese distinguishes domesticated, vehicular, mechanical, constructional, instrumental, even literary items . . .) [67].

L: So?

O: What I'm trying to suggest is that these sorts of conceptual systems seem to fall beyond the computational view of mind that we're assuming. They follow their own tendencies, which depend heavily on contextual experience [68] . . .

L: Any sort of phenomenon looks messy if you just stare at it the way you have. You could make similar lists of animals, say, and then conclude that there's no such thing as body plans in nature. Well, that appears to be false, but it has to be established empirically how chordates relate, how arthropods relate, and so on. The same is true for grammatical classifiers [69]. If you think about them for a while, clear generalizations emerge, and symmetries and harmonies of various sorts readily appear.

O: So?

L: Well, there's no reason to believe that the relevant constants of LF that we're looking for (since that's what we're exploring) couldn't extend to the sorts of generalizations found in classifier languages—or that they should be limited, specifically, to a classification in terms of masculine and feminine.

O: And?

L: It's highly probable that the sort of device that human language employs to classify in grammatical terms is (as may be the case for functional items) more akin to a mathematical dimension than to a plus or minus parameter.

O: Then?

L: What major classes of noun forms exist can be predicted. Suppose that, upon investigating the matter, you were to come up with three binary parameters for encoding nouns—general ones like a substance parameter, a form parameter, and perhaps a change parameter. (You'll notice I'm trying to invoke these Aristotelian notions in order to go deeper than "animate" or "masculine.") Parameters allow combinations, which clearly exist. For instance, factually a classifier for animacy presupposes the ability to change, a certain form, and a certain substance. In contrast, a classifier for a count term presupposes a form and a substance, but not the ability to change. And a measure item presupposes a substance, but nothing else. On the other hand, this parameter system predicts certain combinations that, in fact, don't exist. For instance, no grammatical morpheme that I'm aware of encodes something which changes, has substance, yet has no form. The ocean would count as the right sort of object to be linguistically encoded this way—but lexical items which specify just this sort of entity don't seem to exist in

Figure 2.20

The discussion in the text involves the dimensions illustrated here:

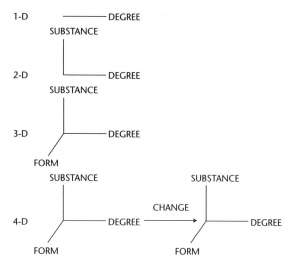

The implied formal apparatus is not unlike the one relating numerical categories. For example, natural numbers can be thought of as one-dimensional objects generated by taking a trivial (zero-dimensional) base and applying a successor or summation function; integers can be generated by taking natural numbers as base and applying a subtraction function; rational numbers can be generated by taking integers as base and applying a fractionary operation; and so on. Infinite application of these "type-lifting" operations to successively more articulated bases would yield the transfinite class of real numbers. This infinitely complex structure has a fractal shape; no matter what scale of complexity one examines, one can always find it in some sort of base that allows numerical categories of a certain type to be generated. The size of each class of categories is infinite, but there is a definable sense in which successive categories are progressively more complex in type. This progression can be demonstrated implicationally: each natural number is an integer, but not vice versa (-2 is not a natural number); each integer is a rational number, but not vice versa (2/3 is not an integer); and so on.

The conjecture explored in the text is that this sort of implicational structure is present in the conceptual system of humans, as manifested in the linguistic system. Note that the dimensional labels "degree," "substance," "form," "change," and so on, are intended to be Aristotelian in character, but in no sense ontologically real (as in the Aristotelian system). Physicists certainly make substantive use of dimensions, and their particular dimensional arrangement may be seen as ontologically real. In contrast, the substantive use of the dimensions discussed here, whether they have an Aristotelian arrangement or any other, is cognitive.

Basically, what the dimensions say about nouns is that the structure, for instance, of mass expressions like *a pound of chicken* is essentially two-dimensional (cf. the structure of integers), whereas the structure of count expressions like *many chickens* is essentially three-dimensional (cf. the structure of rational numbers), and so on. Similar

natural languages. Similarly, there's no classification for formal but not substantive items; for example, numbers and alphabet symbols don't get a special classifier [70]. These restrictions suggest that the noun system displays a sort of underlying harmony, and basically that the way to organize these mental spaces is in terms of progressively articulated dimensions of some sort. We can start with a basic dimension 1-D, taking 1-D items to be abstract. Adding a second dimension for substance, we get concrete 2-D items (e.g., mass terms). Adding a third dimension for form, we get countable 3-D items. Adding a fourth dimension for change, we get animate classifiers, at 4-D [see fig. 2.20] [71].

O: I see; so you believe that a mass term is to a measuring item like "gallon" just as a count term is to a classifying item like "masculine."

L: That's the intuition, and more complex relations are possible too; if we move up to the dimension of change, we find items which are presented as capable of mutating (animacy is the core instance of this), and we need a more elaborate classification in order to be able to refer to them. Then we can ascribe transient properties to these items. For instance, we'll be able to say that, when taken in four dimensions (including change), Noah can be qualified as being "drunk." This is a predicate that applies to a stage of Noah. At the same time, we can say that, taken in three dimensions (up to having some form, and thus counting as an individual), Noah can be qualified as being "Jewish." This is a standing property of Noah [72].

O: One that applies to him while he exists . . . ?

L: Noah's existence is beside the point. What counts is my notion of him. I don't even know whether Noah existed, and even if he did exist and died a long time ago, he's still Jewish. It doesn't make a whole lot of sense to think that he stopped being Jewish because he doesn't exist any longer. In my mental representation of Noah, I can (linguistically) conceive of him as an entity in three dimensions (something more articulated than a mass term), and within those dimensions "when" isn't defined—for that we need a dimension of change.

O: But then how can we ever talk about the fact that Noah existed in the past?

L: His existence is past with respect to my frame of reference, which is now, at this very speech act. In that sense, the entire event of

Noah's existence is prior to this conversation [73]. But internal to that event, when Noah is presented in three dimensions, no further change potential can be encoded, and all properties expressed at that level will be standing properties of Noah; that is, properties that hold irrespective of the event he's a part of [74]. This is regardless of whether the entire event itself takes place before now, now, or after now. The minute we introduce a dimension of change, though, then we can talk, within the specific time-frame of the event we're referentially invoking, about transient properties that last only during a given event. For example, say that Noah's drunkenness lasted from the moment that he found some fermented grapes until the moment he woke up from his siesta. That delimits a particular event, which sets up a context for us to be able to invoke reference to a "slice of Noah," so to speak: a fourth-dimensional presentation of the three-dimensional (unchanging) Noah.

O: Do you, then, take these dimensions to encode reference?

L: I don't know how reference is encoded. The dimensions just delimit a space of referential possibilities. Within those confines, clear variations emerge which affect ultimate reference, whatever that may be. For instance, within the dimension of change many Indo-European languages distinguish male-like things from female-like things; but other languages may use different sorting techniques—and if that's social, so be it. There has to be something social here. Whether or not a given language uses kilos or pounds (or a similar morpheme encoding such measures) is a trivial historical fact. The point is, nothing we've seen so far leads us to believe that we have to give up the computational theory of mind—even in these messier lexical domains . . . Quite the opposite: something very systematic is going on, and we hope to explain it in a principled way. For instance, take an expression like this: *expensive hardcover books that weigh more than five pounds are boring* [75]. The predicate *boring* applies to an abstract entity; the predicate *weigh,* to a concrete entity; the predicate *hardcover,* essentially to an individual entity; and the predicate *expensive,* contingently to an individual entity (individual books tend to become cheaper with time). How can *books* be the subject of all these predicates? If we had to classify *book* as [+concrete] (to take *weigh*) or [−concrete] (to take *boring*), we'd fall into an obvious paradox; likewise if we had to classify *book* as, say, [+stage-of-individual] (to take *expensive*) or [−stage-of-individual] (to take *hardcover*). If instead we say that *book* is a 4-D expression whose change potential is encoded and which therefore also involves a 3-

considerations apply to aspectual classifications of verbs, which sometimes go by the name "Aktionsart." In and of themselves, these sorts of claims are no more or less troubling than asserting that the spin of bosons can essentially be expressed as an integer, whereas the spin of fermions can essentially be expressed as a noninteger rational number. These are factual matters that may be right or wrong, but are not senseless; they simply depend on empirical verification. (Note that what is relevant here is the *structure* of integers, rational numbers, and so on, not scalar values, which are irrelevant at this level of abstraction.)

Needless to say, at this stage the factual claim about the conceptual arrangement shown above is entirely tentative and not even descriptively obvious. More importantly, though, a successful theory should be able to go beyond a particular description. In ascending order of methodological significance, the theory should first be able to account for the actual (sequence of) acquisition of concepts by children (see chap. 6). Second, it should be able to account for mental states in individuals with linguistic or other cognitive deficits, as well as various disorders and breakdowns. Third, it should have a bearing on the fact of performance that concepts relate to their referents; why, for instance, is a two-dimensional expression used to refer to a mass phenomenon, and not some other, more complex type? In the limit, the theorist would want to know why certain quantum fields need a formal expression of the sort that certain human concepts arguably do. Even in the event that this congruence existed, it might well be a coincidence; then again, it might be a deep fact about how cognition relates to other aspects of the known universe.

D encoding of form, a 2-D encoding of mass, and a 1-D encoding of an abstract concept, then we're in business: the predicate *boring* applies within the 1-D dimension; the predicate *weighs,* within the 2-D dimension; the predicate *hardcover,* within the 3-D dimension; and the predicate *expensive,* within the highest, 4-D dimension.

O: And you want this structuring of events to give you, as well, the structure of lexical presupposition . . .

L: Of course. Now presuppositions are just a matter of how the dimensions are added; a 4-D, animate item has to have form, substance, and so on. The other way around, no implication holds: an abstract 1-D item encodes no substance, form, and so on. Our *coffee* example is a simple subcase among others we could discuss (for instance, in a language where a given gadget is classified as animate, and thus 4-D, we know we can assume valid, solid implications in terms of the gadget's having a form, a substance, and so on—we know, for instance, that it won't be, say, a mass of liquid).

O: Photons don't really have substance (at least, they have zero rest mass). Here, then, is a concrete item (a photon whose effect has shown up in some reaction), presumably one with some specific form, which nevertheless has no mass. Isn't that a counterexample: in your terms, a 3-D item whose 2-D specification is missing?

L: No, because the dimensions are an empirical claim about *mental* organization. My suggestions aren't about a theory of (basic) physical reality; they're about a theory of how the mind frames concepts. Then it's a totally empirical matter whether, when faced with the term *photon,* humans are capable of linguistically understanding it as having form, but no substance.

O: You don't understand that a photon may not have mass?!

L: That's beside the point, since it involves my science-forming capacity. The question is different: we're not talking about scientific understanding, but about linguistic structuring. Apparently, linguistic structures can't encode form without also encoding substance. If it's true, this says something about the conceptual system of humans in its linguistic guise, even if it doesn't necessarily say anything about the scientific or artistic capacities of humans, our problem-solving capacity, our capacity for love and virtue, or whatever it is we use in order to conceive of photons as massless.

O: And are you claiming that the sorts of associated statements I postulated for an expression like *coffee* (my knowing it's handpicked, and so forth), although quite real to me, do not directly fit into this basic system?

L: In principle, an infinite number of meaning postulates can be associated to any particular expression, like *coffee* (I know it's not milk, it's not a hamburger, it's not the city of Cambridge . . .). Yet that doesn't tell us anything useful about the kinds of properties the expression in question exhibits at the syntactic level of LF. Unlike the ones that follow from the basic dimensions we've just outlined, those aren't intrinsic lexical features. Consequently, a purely lexical **inference** based on the presence of one of these postulates at LF won't be justified (although the presence of meaning postulates encoding world knowledge may allow certain contextual **implicatures,** assuming that speakers are cooperative [76]).

_____ *rhyme and reason*

O: I shall have to think about this.

L: As I see it, there's nothing even very profound about anything I'm saying. The matters we've been talking about may not be so common for noun systems, but they're just obvious for the **aspectual** properties of verbs. These clearly divide (at least) into **states** like *love,* **processes** like *run,* **achievements** like *climb,* and **accomplishments** like *build* [77]. When I say, "Jack built a house," I'm presupposing something about a process of house building; so implications go from accomplishments to processes. The opposite clearly isn't the case: when I say, "Jack ran," there's no obvious accomplishment of Jack's, nothing to show as a result of the run. This is all simple stuff that we want to distinguish from the fact that there are a zillion meaning postulates to associate to *build* or *run.* Incidentally, similar issues clearly arise in phonology. Formally, the implication relations of the kind we're considering for LF are very much like **rhyme** or **alliteration** is for PF. Here too some features create a successful poetic pattern, while others don't. These can be quite abstract . . .

O: Why, I never thought of presuppositions or implications in that light! But I suppose you might be right; there's nothing formally different about these with respect to LF, and rhyme or alliteration with respect to PF. And I do see the abstractness of both . . . For instance, Shakespearean rhyme forces many pairs like *increase* and *memory, field* and *held, husbandry* and *posterity, glass* and *was, usury* and *thee, noon* and *son.*

L: It seems that Shakespeare, like many poets before and after him, was well aware (even if unconsciously) of the abstractness of linguistic representations, and could produce beautifully profound rhymes on the basis of these representations. Such techniques were well known to traditional bards, whose apparently "irregular" patterns show deep, nonobvious regularities which common aesthetic sense finds very pleasing [see fig. 2.21] [78]. This is all to say that whatever shapes up PF is a complex issue whose reflex is shown in processes of this poetic sort. To determine whether a rhyme or an implication is successful isn't easy, and it·requires thinking about what sorts of features shape up PF and LF.

—————————————————————————————————— *analytical terms*

O: I follow the general thrust of your argument, but I still have difficulty accepting that an inference like "my paternal (natural) uncle hasn't visited you because I have no paternal uncle," is perfect for you, whereas one like "my paternal (natural) uncle hasn't visited you because my grandmother only had one boy" isn't . . . Logic dictates that—

L: That's the wrong approach. I'm not making a point of logic, and I couldn't care less about inferences per se. We're using inferences to see what the properties of LF elements are. Note that you've introduced a very complex, relational term—*uncle*—with clear analytic meaning. We can even think of the whole term as a classifier, to accompany names—as in *Uncle Sam*, which is a way of presenting Sam as an uncle, or in an "uncle dimension." Like knowing other classificatory items, knowing the meaning of *uncle* implies a whole network of cumbersome family relations, including the fact that X's uncle is one of X's parents' siblings, therefore one of X's grandmother's children. But again it's a purely empirical matter whether these complex networks are robustly established as intrinsic lexical features beyond the general dimensional setting. Your question seems to imply that they should be, because you seem to find the inference appropriate. Interestingly enough, there's one circumstance under which the reason you gave for the claim that it wasn't your uncle who visited me is totally invalid.

Figure 2.21

Consider the Shakespearean rhyming pair *glass/was,* found in sonnet 5:

Then, were not summer's distillation left,
A liquid prisoner pent in walls of *glass,*
Beauty's effect with beauty were bereft,
Nor it, nor no remembrance what it *was:*
But flowers distill'd, though they with winter meet,
Leese but their show; their substance still lives sweet.

Recall the chart of distinctive features in figure 2.16. If these syllables are pronounced [glas] and [waz], all of the features in their rhyme are identical, except for one: [s] is voiceless, and [z] is voiced. The single mismatch adds an effect of tension to the pair, breaking the monotony of a rhyming pattern while keeping it intact. Poets often make use of these sorts of effects, whose success depends on relations analogous to those involved in implications and entailments, on the semantic side. In fact, excellent poets also make use of less obvious semantic dependencies in their poems, through parallelisms and subtle associations that are based on lexical and semantic implications. A famous example from Andrew Marvell illustrates the point:

Had we but world enough and time,
This coyness, lady, were no crime.

The words *time* and *crime* are paired phonologically, which focuses the reader's attention on comparing them semantically as well. Both of them are used as abstract terms, abstractness being a feature that is very possibly part of their LF representation. In turn, a variety of meaning postulates can be associated with both *time* and *crime* that relate them pragmatically; in the present context; the most obvious one is that the main crime of humanity is knowledge, for which a fatal punishment is given: time. In Paradise, time is nonexistent, and coyness therefore should be trivial; in fact, no crime (other than knowledge) is possible. Outside Paradise, though, time runs out, and everything that obstructs knowledge is criminal. Coyness prevents (carnal) knowledge and is therefore to be resisted. The poet knows this, and quickly makes the point in only two lines.

O: . . . Why, bless me, you're right! If my mother and my father were in fact brother and sister . . . Right, it isn't patent at all, prima facie. So the inference I used was, in actual fact, not really appropriate!

L: I have to insist: that's the wrong focus. All we can say is that certain structural properties of expressions are fixed and intrinsic to lexical items, a result of human beings' natural endowment; but choices clearly exist within these natural dimensions, which are very general spaces for thought. We have to acquire those specifications, and in the case of lexical knowledge, we in fact keep doing so until we die; there don't appear to be critical ages for lexical learning, though the pace of acquisition is faster before puberty. People have relatively conscious access to this sort of acquired knowledge, thus being able to say, for example, what an uncle is; in fact, people often disagree about the use of classifiers, and their meanings easily shift (for instance, you probably know lots of folks who use the word *uncle* to refer to any elderly male friend of the family). By contrast, people don't really have conscious knowledge about the fixed, intrinsic features of lexical items, and thus the linguist must unearth, say, that uncles are animate, countable, or whatever, through the usual experiments; these aren't the features people think about when they define what *uncle* means. Just keep in mind that the internal conditions on the meaning of words are extremely rich—totally unsuspected. And barely understood, if you ask me.

——————————————————————— *on featural systematicity*

O: If what you're saying is true, a given proposition might license certain lexical implications in a particular language which aren't licensed in another . . .

L: I think that's quite possible (just as a given phonetic form may license certain rhyming patterns in one language, but not in others [79]). Take, for instance, a language which marks gender as a grammatical feature, so that the word for *spouse* has different forms depending on the gender-marking morpheme that accompanies it. Then imagine the following sentence: *Pat's spouse couldn't have visited us because Pat is a nun.* In English this sounds rather cryptic (compare: *Pat's husband couldn't have visited us because Pat is a nun*). But a language like Spanish encodes gender into the morphology of the word for *spouse*. Spanish speakers say *esposo* or *esposa,* I believe, depending on whether the spouse is male or female. There the implication should be fairly transparent, without having to invoke world knowledge about people named Pat and the kinds of spouses they're likely to be married to.

O: I see the point. Well, I'm personally not particularly bothered by concepts per se, so long as we conceive of them as psychological notions (of course, the world itself isn't labelled, and it's rather phenomenological [80]). But if we take this step, we should ask questions beyond the assumption that, let's say, a child is something I can point to. I'm saying this because I've often read or heard philosophers say, "That [and they point] is a table, and I know it's a table because I can point to it." How did my pointing get to be successful, to start with [81]?!

L: Of course, you could point to all sorts of weird things; for instance, you could point to the four legs of a cow and call that entity *muuuu,* and then you could say, "Muuuu goes from the cow's trunk to the ground." Fine, but then (as psychologists and linguists) we have to go out and see if any actual language encodes concepts like that. The **truth-conditional** semantics of this expression would be trivial: the sentence is true if and only if muuuu goes from the cow's trunk to the ground—as in the real world. But is it a human sentence?

O: I recall Bertrand Russell raising similar points. He also noticed that if you've got a herd of cows, and one breaks a leg, you can't say that the herd broke a leg.

L: That appears to be true in all the languages we know of, regardless of their classificatory systems. Logically there's no reason why languages couldn't have words that mean things like 'four legs of a cow' or 'scattered object with cow parts as parts', but in fact they're linguistically impossible notions [82].

O: What does their linguistic impossibility follow from, though?

L: That's an analytical question. Intuitively, naming requires spatial contiguity. Then, depending on the dimensions of any given expression, different conditions may apply. Most multidimensional expressions won't tolerate funny namings of noncontiguous objects or events, like calling the four legs of a cow *muuuu* (compare *back, head, tail,* and so on), or giving a single name, say, *care,* to a combination of the two extremes of human existence, childhood and old

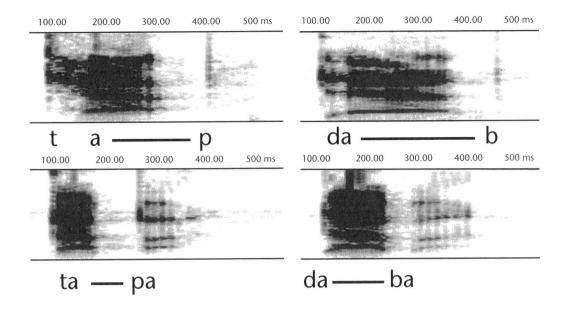

| 100.00 | 200.00 | 300.00 | 400.00 | 500 ms |

t   a ——————— p

| 100.00 | 200.00 | 300.00 | 400.00 | 500 ms |

da ——————— b

| 100.00 | 200.00 | 300.00 | 400.00 | 500 ms |

ta —— pa

| 100.00 | 200.00 | 300.00 | 400.00 | 500 ms |

da —— ba

age. Of course, abstract, unidimensional expressions do allow some such tricks, perhaps because spatial contiguity means little at this level. For instance, *beauty* is something we can find in many places; or less poetically, what we call the US is something that, apart from the mainland, includes Alaska, Hawaii—and large chunks of the rest of the world . . .

O: Then an intricate Gestalt theory is needed, addressing all sorts of issues having to do with conceptualisation from a human perspective . . .

L: Gestalt is too narrow a term. Children also categorize in terms of event participation, causality, intentionality, and whatnot . . . So we need to develop systems to understand these categorizations, whatever it takes [see fig. 2.22]. But for our purposes, we only need to worry about those lexical features that affect the syntactic computation—or that in any case are syntactically encoded and make it into LF. It's a purely empirical matter whether, say, questions of event participation (whether a given referring expression is taken to be a crucial actor within an event) are to be expressed in LF terms, or whether they become significant in the post-LF semantic components. Current research is looking into these important matters, but although (at least in the case of intrinsic lexical features of categories) syntactic systematicity is strongly suspected, it's also still largely undemonstrated [but see chap. 4].

Spectrograms of English *tap, dab* and Spanish *tapa, daba*. In these spectrograms, vowel formants show two clear regularities. First, the English vowel in the words *tap* and *dab* is longer than the corresponding (first) Spanish vowel in the words *tapa* and *daba*. Second, in both languages the vowel is longer in front of a voiced consonant (like [d]) than it is in front of a voiceless consonant (like [t]). Also compare the English initial stop consonant [t] with its Spanish counterpart. The English consonant involves a stronger air release (aspiration) than the Spanish consonant.

Figure 2.22

Very intricate relations, both universal and language-particular, emerge within phonological, semantic, and formal systems of features. For example, it is a universal phonetic property that vowels are longer in front of voiced consonants than they are in front of voiceless ones (the vowel in *tap* is shorter than the vowel in *dab*). But it is a language-particular property of English that the [p] in *pat* is pronounced with a characteristic air release, whereas the [p] in *tap* is not. Between these two rather extreme cases are others whose status is harder to determine. For instance, whether vowels are long in certain environments may be related to whether a given language allows syllables that are closed by a consonant (as in English) or not (as in Japanese).

In syntactic terms, the fundamental categorial features $[+/-N]$ and $[+/-V]$ (see fig. 2.23) seem to be universal. Intrinsic features involving abstractness, the mass/count distinction, number, and gender (perhaps expressed in terms of dimensions of the sort outlined in figure 2.20) are possibly also universal, in the sense that the vocabulary of phonetic features is universal. Some languages do not make use of all of these (just as some languages have only three vowels, whereas others have several). However, here too matters must be viewed sufficiently abstractly. This is exemplified by a simple scenario discussed by Noam Chomsky in various places (e.g., 1993): The ball is as far from

(a)   *(b)*

the walls of the box in situation *(a)* as it is in situation *(b)*. However, if asked whether the ball is near the box, people (including small children) answer "yes" in the first instance, but not in the second (where the ball is *in*—not *near*—the box). This reveals considerable intricacy in the meaning of a word apparently as trivial as the preposition *near;* in particular, it encodes the notion of boundary. This unsuspected richness inherent in apparently simple lexical concepts should be kept in mind when analyzing the structure of concepts in a language, like English, that appears not to avail itself of the cumbersome dimensions that, for example, East Asian languages explicitly exhibit through the use of classifiers.

O: Are there really any features whose systematicity is demonstrated?

L: Definitely, categorial ones. These correspond to one of the oldest observations about language—namely, that it divides into parts of speech. The major categories noun, verb, adjective, and preposition are analyzed as corresponding to two basic binary parameters, V and N. Another old chestnut involves intrinsic features of some sort, although these are relational ones (rather than categorial). This was known to linguists as early as the fourteenth century, when serious questions were asked about why natural language should have the parts of speech it does, and how different syntactic items are in construction with one another. It was pointed out that items combine according to certain relational modes, which ultimately depend on their categorial status: for instance, tense relates to verbs, while articles relate to nouns. This is very systematic across languages, so that certain logical possibilities simply aren't found—for example, there's no language where tense is related to nouns, or where nouns or verbs are completely absent [see fig. 2.23]. At any rate, there isn't anything metaphysically profound about these features. Whatever depth there is to these matters, it appears to be psychological.

2.5 The Invariant Parts of the Computational System
    (the first thing you wanted to know about convergent computations but were afraid to ask)

O: Right. These sorts of linguistic universals offer a very decisive challenge to the philosophical claim that concepts are merely abstractions, which humans reach on the basis of experience. Then again, an even greater challenge is posed by the syntactic aspects of S_0, the initial state of the language faculty . . .

—————————————————————— **the basic architecture**

L: Yes, of course. Consider the kinds of questions that arise when we think about the computational system. Putting external conditions into the picture, we came up with the formula $C_{HL}(A) = (PF, LF)$.

O: I hate bloody formulae.

L: Actually, I do too. What this says in plain English is that the expression **mapped** by C_{HL} from the array has a PF π and an LF λ

for a given structural description SD. This in turn implies that the homunculus, remember, takes the array from the lexicon to form an object which is accessible to the computational system. In essence, this is the procedure for forming phrases out of words. We can talk about this procedure later on; for now let's just say that phrases are **projected** from lexical items, and plan to define projection as we move along [see sec. 3.1]. The homunculus then does its work, for instance moving the verb as you did in (3) and carrying out similar processes which we should also consider in detail later on. A computation of this sort is usually called a **derivation** [83]. In essence, a derivation is like a single construction worker who builds structural elements and manipulates them one step at a time (instead of a whole crew that has the ability to work on several tasks at once). In the case that concerns us, the structural element is called a **phrase marker** [84]. At one point in the derivation, an operation called **Spell-Out** sends the phrase marker K to PF, where morphophonological rules readjust it to the demands of articulation/perception. What remains of K is sent to LF where it gets appropriately readjusted to meet the demands of intention/conceptualization. We say that these computations (now, technically, a derivation) **converge** at LF or PF only if they produce an object which meets the outside conditions of these levels—whatever those turn out to be. Otherwise, the derivation **crashes** [see fig. 2.3].

O: A set of invariant principles determines what counts as . . . what? A possible computation and a linguistic expression?

L: Yes, which is nothing but a possible "derived" (i.e., computed) object. Within a given language, these principles determine a specific set of derivations and SDs that they generate, each a simple pair (π, λ) . . . And recall that this is a step in the direction of characterizing the internal coherence of the system and the natural interactions that it engages in with respect to other components of the mind/ brain. That is, *how* you are able to access PF and LF is a consequence of the internal mechanisms of the system. In turn, *that* you are accessing PF and LF (and not something else) is a consequence of the interactions between this system and other cognitive components.

O: Let me see if I've grasped the technicalia . . . A derivation D converges at LF if λ is legitimate, and it converges at PF if π is legitimate. Differently put, only derivations that meet Full Interpretation converge, right?

Figure 2.23

A verb is [+V, −N] (has verbal features, but not nominal features).
A noun is [−V, +N] (has nominal features, but not verbal features).
An adjective is [+V, +N] (has both kinds of features).
A preposition is [−V, −N] (has neither).

This system of features shares much with Aristotle's manner of deducing the four classical elements from a heat parameter and a humidity parameter. Aristotelian classifications were taken up by Scholastic philosophers and grammarians. For Modistic grammarians, the relevant classificatory notion was the *modus significandi,* by which they sought to explain why language assumes categories, and how these categories combine. They distinguished *essential* modes of signifying (those by virtue of which a part of speech is what it is with regard to class, e.g., "noun") from *accidental* modes of signifying (what is added to a part of speech after it has all its essential features; what modern linguists would think of as inflectional features), which were taken to be relational (see Covington 1984, which is also the source of the quotations that follow). Then, to "establish *construction* is to join constructibles by means of their modes of signifying in such a way that together they can express a single concept [i.e., linguistic sign]" (Thomas of Hancya). Furthermore: "Construction is formed out of two and only two elements" (Radulphus Brito). It should be emphasized that this rather contemporary view of syntactic construction is dramatically different from what is commonly referred to, in modern terms, as "a construction"—that is, a specific type of construction such as the relative clause or the passive. The Modistic grammarians were looking for the general principles of syntactic constructibility and viewed specific types of constructions as mere data with which to test their scientific hypotheses about language. These hypotheses were as abstract as many of the notions discussed in the text: for example, the "dependent constructible is potential, since it plays the role of matter, and the terminant constructible is actual, since it plays the role of form" (Simon Dacus Modista). This notion of asymmetry between the elements that enter in construction has survived, in some form, to modern times. Modistic grammarians in fact first noted that sentences are constructed in a certain grammatical order. In these diagrams, the "secundum" is shown to enter into construction with the "primum," previously established; this procedure allowed grammarians to distinguish different levels of phrasal complexity:

(i) videt Platonem

   sees   Plato

(ii) Socrates videt Platonem

   Socrates sees   Plato

(iii) Socrates videt Platonem qui disputat

   Socrates sees   Plato   who is debating

Importantly, grammaticality *(congruitas)* is "caused by the compatibility . . . of modes of signifying, which are intrinsically the concern of the grammarian. But the semantic well-formedness *(proprietas)* . . . is caused by the compatibility of the meanings of the words . . . [which] is not the concern of the grammarian, but rather of the logician" (Thomas of Erfurt). Grammaticality conditions were stated in terms of requirements imposed on the *terminans* by the *dependens*.

L: Exactly. Otherwise D crashes either at PF or at LF. What this means is that the interface levels have the property of **interpretability.** UG ensures that every linguistic symbol is somehow accessed by systems that interact with the language faculty. So for instance, take dolphins, which apparently can articulate through both sides of their blowhole, a trick we humans can't manage with our nose; the condition on interpretability of PF tells us that no human linguistic representation can have a feature, say, [+split] (for articulating sounds through one nostril or the other). Similar instances could be constructed for LF, although here we have no idea what the possible range is. But in any case, when (or if) we say that the symbols of LF are things like **predicates, arguments,** and so on, we're saying that there's something natural about those symbols, in terms of their interpretability in relation to some cognitive component.

---

convergence is determined by independent inspection of interface levels

O: Can π and λ each be legitimate representations, and yet not be able to be paired for some UG reasons?

L: No. By assumption, it's a property of language that (π, λ) are always paired. If π and λ are both legitimate (and only if this is the case), the entire expression is legitimate. The conjecture here is that convergence is determined solely by independent inspection of interface levels, PF and LF. We have the substances of phonetics and meaning, and we have specific forms for these substances, which seek convergence into what we call PF and LF. Those particular levels are mapped in terms of processes of C_{HL}. But what establishes whether the phonetic and logical forms are acceptable is inspection of the substances whose form they determine. A legitimate substance makes a derivation converge; an illegitimate substance makes a derivation crash. That's all. The sole work that C_{HL} does is to give form to these substances. If π and λ are in fact legitimate, not being able to pair them for UG reasons would be adding unmotivated power to UG.

O: Then it must be meaningless to ask whether a derivation converges or crashes other than at the levels of PF or LF.

L: That's right—which isn't to say, though, that a derivation can't "go wrong" somewhere else. In principle there can be derivations which don't even crash, because they're **canceled** along the way.

O: How?

L: By producing an illegitimate derivational object, as opposed to an illegitimate representational object at LF or PF. Crashed derivations (as well as, of course, convergent ones) are derivations. On the other hand, it's possible that a given derivation literally ceases to be one. For example, I told you when we were discussing (3) that for some reason, downward movement is impossible. That process would be an instance in which a derivation falls into some sort of trap along the way, and it just can't get out of it [see sec. 4.5]. In that case, we don't say that the bad derivation crashes at PF or LF; rather, we say that it's canceled (ceases to be a derivation). Only complete derivations that reach PF and LF converge or crash, depending on whether the objects formed in the derivation meet PF and LF demands: a derivation forming λ converges at LF if λ satisfies Full Interpretation (FI), and otherwise it crashes; and the same is true for PF, with respect to π. And be careful, too, with the confusing terminology here: in principle it's possible to have a convergent derivation (meeting FI) which nonetheless doesn't get a valid interpretation after LF or PF, in the interpretive components proper.

─────────────────── convergent derivations may not be interpretable after all

O: Do you mean something that reaches these levels by meeting FI, but then cannot be dealt with by the articulatory/perceptual or intentional/conceptual devices?

L: That's right. Consider for instance the way English speakers pronounce the past tense morpheme in *canned* or *asked*. In the first of these words it's pronounced [d]. Interestingly, though, in the second word it's pronounced [t]. There's an obvious sense in which a [t] is a [d] without voicing. But why should the [d] be devoiced after a [k] sound? In other words, what's wrong with pronouncing *asked* [askd] [85]? Well, it's not obvious that this sort of string should crash at PF; after all, it's formed by perfectly legitimate objects in a perfectly legitimate fashion. However, one may argue that although [askd] converges as a PF string, it has no interpretation in the articulatory/perceptual components [see fig. 2.24]. In fact, a convergent derivation may produce utter gibberish, if it converges at LF but then fails to obtain a semantic interpretation. So take something like *which guy did you meet Mary and Sue?*

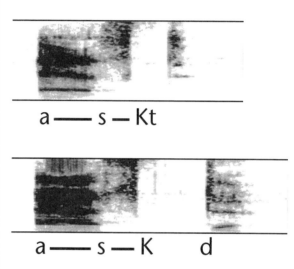

Spectrograms of [askt] and [askd].

Figure 2.24

Observe the gap near the end of the two items, before the last area of shading. This blank area corresponds to the closure of air release for the stop clusters [kt] and [kd]. It is clearly longer in the case of [askd], as a result of a rather forced pronunciation. The shorter time span for the gap in [askt] corresponds to a more natural pronunciation. Notice also that, at the end of [askd], the formants of a parasitic vowel emerge (two almost parallel horizontal lines at the bottom). This vowel "wants" to be the nucleus of a new syllable, forced by the abrupt violation of the sonority hierarchy. Syllables may be thought of as obeying a sequence, whereby the most sonorous peak corresponds to the syllabic nucleus, with sonority valleys on either side. This sonority hierarchy is clearly respected in [askt], but not in [askd]. Essentially, then, [askd] ends up being pronounced as [ask-də], with two syllables, so that it will respect the sonority hierarchy. (See, however, figure 2.28 for a strong indication that the hierarchy in question is of a more abstract nature than is implied here.)

O: What's that supposed to mean?

L: That's the point. It's not obvious what it means, but it's not obvious either that there's anything really wrong with its syntax.

O: But the sentence is just rubbish—it's unprocessable, it's completely ungrammatical!

L: Well, all we know for sure is that it's unacceptable (in other words, I agree that it's rubbish). But we don't know a priori whether it's unprocessable, ungrammatical, or uninterpretable. I doubt that it's unprocessable, because of the very similar *which guy did you meet Mary and his girlfriend?* This might not be a very eloquent question, but it's not particularly difficult to process (its answer being something like "I met Mary and *Bill's* girlfriend" or simply "Bill"). If anything, the unacceptable sentence has fewer words (and essentially the same structure), so it should be easier to process. As for its grammaticality, what could be wrong with it? To make things clearer, suppose that Sue is the guy's girlfriend, so that whatever role *his girlfriend* is playing in the good sentence, *Sue* could be playing in the bad one. Of course, the intuition is that the sentence is unacceptable because while *Sue* is just a name, *his girlfriend* includes a pronoun that can relate to *who;* after all, *who* and *his* seem to be invoking reference to the same individual. In the bad sentence, there's no *his,* and *who* is left without any objects to **bind,** which for some reason linguistic **quantifiers** don't like [see sec. 3.7].

O: Well, there you go: vacuous quantification is ungrammatical.

L: But what in the grammar does that follow from? It's not obvious at all. Instead, a ban against vacuous quantification looks like a semantic constraint of some (nontrivial) sort [86]. Violating that constraint results in an uninterpretable sentence, but not in an ungrammatical sentence, for the sentence does converge at LF: its parts are perfectly well formed LF parts. In sum, a *convergent derivation* doesn't need to yield an **interpretable representation.** Convergence is a competence property of derivations—whether or not they meet FI—whereas interpretability is a performance property of representations resulting from these derivations. And it's not at all clear what interpretability means, because linguistic expressions can be deviant along all sorts of incommensurable dimensions. All that competence can tell us is, "The form of this substance (be it at PF or LF) is okay"; it can't tell us, "It means such-and-such." That's performance.

—————————————— interface levels are comprehensive and complete

O: . . .

L: Incidentally, I've mentioned interpretability—but I'm also assuming other properties of interface levels. Take for instance what might be called **comprehensiveness,** which means that any expression of human language is representable at these levels.

O: Surely you don't mean that any human thought can be represented thus . . .

L: No. I don't know much about thoughts, and the little I do know tells me that people can have nonlinguistic thoughts [87]. So all I'm saying is that PF and LF are the only levels for representing *linguistic* expressions. Finally, I'm assuming that the levels are **complete,** which basically means that they're interface levels. That is, in principle it's possible to have levels of representation that aren't interface levels, but interface levels have the property that they contain all the information that's needed for a given kind of (performative) interpretation. So for instance π is an output representation for a given lexical array A which enters C_{HL} and which obeys certain natural output conditions motivated in terms of the A/P component. If C_{HL} had to go on operating on π to reach the A/P component, then π wouldn't be an interface. So what I'm saying is that π has all (and only, given FI) the information that's needed to reach A/P. And to insist, that doesn't mean that the workings of C_{HL} will produce a successful result; they may produce a syntactically valid result which ends up having no coherent or useful interpretation.

O: It occurs to me that if all of this is correct, then you have nothing whatever to say about, for example, the fact that American English has a nasal twang, or that French has a peculiar intonation that—

L: To the extent that those are matters which lie beyond the sorts of PF cues that phonologists study, the answer is "I don't." In fact, to emphasize your point even more dramatically, think of the way we talk to babies, rather generally: the high pitch, the somewhat simplified syllables, and so on [88]. This has no grammatical significance in terms of the internal coherence of the system: no principle of grammar is sensitive to whether I'm talking to you or to a small baby. In fact I can choose to speak to you as if you were a baby or vice versa. It would be inappropriate, but it wouldn't be

Figure 2.25

Interesting evidence that vowels and consonants may fall into different representational tiers comes from Classical Arabic (see McCarthy 1979). In this language, verbs are formed from consonantal roots like *ktb* 'write', and grammatical information is encoded in vowel patterns (e.g., *a − a* 'perfective active causative'). This is naturally represented in terms of two separate tiers:

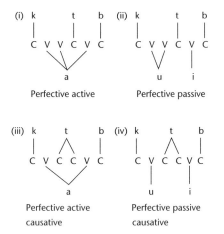

Perfective active   Perfective passive

Perfective active   Perfective passive
causative   causative

Note that the actual, pronounced form of a given word depends on how well the consonant and vowel tiers adjust to a basic template. For example, whereas in (ii) the underlying vowels link up to the vowel slots in the template to produce /kuutib/, in (i) the underlying grammatical formative [a] spreads to occupy an extra vowel position in the output form, pronounced /kaatab/. The same thing happens in (iii), pronounced /kattab/, as opposed to (iv), pronounced /kuttib/; in this instance, the linkage of the underlying consonant [t] to two consonant slots has an additional grammatical effect. These sorts of patterns are common in Semitic languages and have been found in other languages as well. In some instances in Germanic languages, grammatical information is encoded in vowel changes (residues in English are found in "irregular" tense and plural patterns: *drink/drank/drunk, mouse/ mice*). Various languages exhibit phenomena like "vowel harmony," whereby all the vowels in a word have the same vocalic character (exotic instances like *teeny-weeny* in English give the flavor of this phenomenon).

ungrammatical in any obvious sense. So the fact that some property of language is systematic to some degree doesn't necessarily entail that it has to be grammatical—it may have a different basis. We can think of similar examples for LF. For instance, *coffee* probably has the grammatical feature of being a mass term, but it doesn't have the grammatical feature of being the kind of thing that grows in tropical regions. It's a deep mistake to assign the same status to those two properties, just because they're properties: the mass characteristic very likely shapes up (in part) the level of LF (and allows very intricate **selections,** like the one that distinguishes *much/little* and *many/ few*), while I have no reason to believe that the meaning postulate about the tropical regions enters the LF computation at all. Some properties like meaning postulates or baby talk are simply matters of performance, and not represented either at LF or at PF.

────────────────────────── **PF and LF have different properties**

O: So both PF and LF are **interpretable,** comprehensive, and complete. Right. But apart from the fact that they use different primitive symbols, do these systems differ in any essential properties?

L: In fact, quite radically. Every LF feature has its origin in some sort of lexical structure, and ultimately the LF level itself is nothing but an arrangement of lexical features. We can think of this as the **inclusiveness** of LF (a defining property of the level). This property doesn't hold of PF, though. Here the most obvious example that comes to mind is stress assignment in a language like English, where the stress of the whole expression isn't a trivial function of the stress of the parts. Take for instance the word *accident,* pronounced [ˈak-sə-dᵊent] with main stress on [ak], and add the **suffix** *-al* to it; what do you get? Certainly not *[ˈak-sə-den-tᵊl]; instead, you get [ak-sə-ˈden-tᵊl], where [ak] now only carries a secondary stress. Or take the famous case of the word *torment,* which is pronounced [ˈtȯr-ment] as a noun and [tȯr-ˈment] as a verb. Not to mention compounds, where the first element gets the main stress; thus, the difference between a black board and a blackboard is that the name of the latter is pronounced with main stress on *black,* and the name of the former with main stress on *board.* In fact, secondary stress in words is even more contextually dependent than primary; all sorts of complex metrical rules are responsible for its various adjustments [89]. And of course, similar issues can be raised about intonational patterns, **liaison** phenomena, and even the ultimate shape of words, which is heavily dependent on a variety of contextual cues, and involves all sorts of features that aren't in any sense obvious properties of the constituent parts of the PF expression. I'd go even further: it's not even clear that there's any such thing as "the constituent parts of a PF expression," at the very least in the way this is meant for syntactic structures, which are rather obvious combinations of words into phrases, and phrases into larger phrases, and so on. PF structures possibly involve different structures: for instance, they may have separate dimensions for all the vowels and consonants in a given expression [see fig. 2.25]. So the bottom line is that PF is something very concrete, and LF is something very concrete, but they're birds of a different feather.

———————————————————————————— derivational properties

O: Fair enough. Let me ask you also about C_{HL}'s guts. You've mentioned that a derivation may be cancelled if it violates some specification of the constructive algorithm. This is different—is it not?—from the other sort of property of derivations that we've discussed: they are optimal.

L: Very different. The point about cancellation is similar to what would happen to a chess game if one of the players cheated—took a knight off the chessboard, say, or hopped over five squares with it. That would be the end of the game, right? But compare that with studying what's the most efficient closing from a given stage in the game, or what's a good opening, and so on. While a rule-breaking move ends the game, an inelegant move doesn't, in itself. In language we seem to find both sorts of derivational properties. Downward movement illustrates a derivational cancellation. As for derivational elegance, or economy, consider an array like {there, seems, a, man, to, be, here}. This can yield both the perfect *there seems to be a man here* and the impossible **there seems a man to be here.* In a sense this is puzzling, because the chunks of this ungrammatical sentence are all well formed: *there seems . . .* appears in *there seems to be a man here,* and *. . . a man to be here* appears in *I believe a man to be here.* So something is a bit peculiar, at first sight, about the impossibility of **there seems a man to be here.* One way of looking at this impossibility is to note that there actually exists a more economical way of getting this derivation to converge—namely, *there seems to be a man here* [see fig. 2.26]. Of course, then we have to explain *why* this alternative is more economical; but you can see the general point. And remember, there can be perfectly convergent and even optimal derivations that have no interpretation whatsoever [see fig.

Figure 2.26

Consider the array in (i):

(i) {there, seems, a, man, to, be, here}

One possible nonconvergent combination using the elements in this array (among others) is (ii) (and see sec. 6.1):

(ii) *seems there to be a man here

Two possible convergent combinations are (iii) and (iv):

(iii) there seems to be a man here

(iv) *there seems a man to be here
      (cf. *there seems to be a man here* and *I believe a man to be here*)

Crucially, however, only (iii) is grammatical. The conclusion (to be established in section 5.5) is that although (iv) converges (unlike (ii)), the derivation that results in (iii) is more economical and therefore the grammatical choice. Keep in mind, also, that (ii) does not even compete in the optimality race.

Figure 2.27

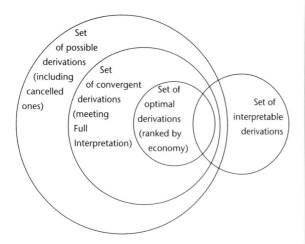

2.27]. At the same time, since derivational economy isn't just an all-purpose device, but is rather specific to the competence system, it must have no bearing on interpretability.

2.6 Representational Alternatives

(and nonalternatives, with a brief description of chains, amazing objects later to be used at great length and with vast consequences)

O: This is becoming a technical festival! There's no use piling up definitions if we don't ask how much in all this computational machinery you've been introducing is mere notation—hence something which hasn't got any reality of its own and could be expressed differently.

L: That's a very important question.

O: Right you are. What are the theoretically possible alternatives to a strongly constructive system—and are they **notational variants** of it?

——————————— *what are possible relations among the array A, PF, and LF?*

L: Let's think about that. The question we started with is, how much special structure does the language faculty have beyond inevitable conditions? The question has two aspects: what conditions are imposed by virtue of (i) the place that the language faculty occupies within the cognitive systems of the mind/brain, and (ii) familiar general considerations of simplicity and the like.

O: And Minimalism hypothesises that the language faculty is a **dedicated capacity** which is a "perfect" (conceptually necessary and optimally economical) way of meeting external conditions on language.

L: Yes, but keep in mind that, since grammatical derivations are a subset of the convergent derivations (which are a subset of the logically possible derivations) [see fig. 2.27], we have to encode a procedure to tell us how to select, among alternative possibilities, the one that's the least costly. For this purpose, I suggested before a derivational system, starting in an array A from the lexicon, and somewhere splitting the structure to PF and LF branches. Could we look at things differently, "representationally" so to speak, and still have a Minimalist system? The components that seem to be involved are clear:

(4) Articulation   Lexicon   Conception

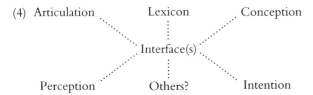

Perception   Others?   Intention

Simplifying the picture, by narrowing down possibilities in a more familiar way:

(5)

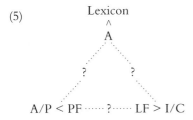

A/P < PF ······?······ LF > I/C

Here we grant that, for any linguistic expression, there is no more than a PF, an LF, and a lexical array A. But note that we're now not committing to a derivational system whereby PF and LF are obtained from computations on A. Rather, we're now being deliberately naive about this, asking what the possible relations are among A, PF, and LF in (5). Are there conditions that hold of just any pairings in the triplet (A, PF, LF)? In the past, linguists thought there were, for instance, conditions on (A, LF), some kind of **homomorphism** according to which A was thought to be very similar to LF.

O: I thought A was an inconsequential list of words drawn from the lexicon. How could that have the same form as the, presumably, highly elaborate structures of LF?

L: Largely for historical reasons, linguists tended to think about A as a very elaborate structure that went by the name of "deep structure" [90]. At one time, we thought this structure had real substantive properties, not just the formal, trivial properties that the array may have if it is a set or a sequence or something like that. Deep structures were thought of as phrasal representations encoding basic lexical **dependencies** and constraining a class of possible derivations. Curiously, people from many disciplines totally confused

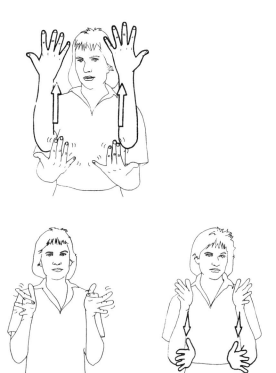

A possible sign (GO-UP-IN-FLAMES) *(top)* and an impossible sign *(bottom)* in American Sign Language. (Carol Padden)

this idea and started talking about the "deep" structures of dreams, phenotypes, the universe, and even the morning cartoons. Early on, several linguists realized that these ethereal "deep" structures, if they existed at all, would have very little justification and would be doing very little work [91] . . . A number of researchers tried to entirely eliminate them, but this wasn't easy, for empirical reasons we needn't be concerned with now [see chap. 6]. But even if we think about it just conceptually, it's not that easy to see reasons to assume any linguistic levels other than LF and PF, given the Minimalist picture. We're thinking of a linguistic expression as the optimal realization of conditions that interface with the A/P and I/C components. While the A/P and I/C components are conceptually undeniable for what we call human language, any additional structure or assumptions would obviously require further empirical justification. Otherwise, we'd be departing quite significantly from the reductionist spirit of the program.

O: Granted, but what about conditions between PF and LF in (5)?

L: Wouldn't you expect these two levels to use different kinds of symbols?

O: You haven't really told me what the symbols of LF are. But you did say that PF is ultimately some speech signal . . .

L: Well, be careful—think about signed languages. Strictly, those don't involve a speech signal in the traditional sense; people don't pronounce or hear them. Yet researchers have found that signed languages aren't collections of rudimentary gestures trying to mimic the expressions of spoken languages [92]. Quite the opposite: signed languages have a syntax which is pretty much the same as the syntax of spoken languages, and—surprisingly—they also have a phonology which displays properties not unlike those of spoken languages. Of course, these phonological properties aren't based on any sound signal; instead, they're visually expressed. But just as the tongue, teeth, lips, and so on, are the major points of articulation that modify the speech signal to produce all sorts of vowels and consonants in spoken languages, so too there are clear "articulators" in signed languages: the hands, the eyes, the eyebrows, and so on. The hands, for instance, modify a visual signal to produce phonological units that carry the syntactic structure [see fig. 2.28].

O: Fascinating . . . Phonology isn't about sounds! Then PF must be something quite abstract, I suppose. Furthermore, I have no reason to believe that PF is chunked up in the way that words and phrases are. At least to my ear, it would seem that one word merges into the next, with no great respect for word boundaries or phrasal groupings. Right. I shall posit this, then: PF has no word boundaries; it is some sort of continuum [93]. Regarding LF, I have no clear idea yet as to what its constructs are. You were sceptical that they may be the typical elements of logic, but it doesn't really matter. Whatever LF is, I fancy that its constructs are different from those of PF. Which is enough for me to claim that, well, it would be peculiar to have a condition on the pair (PF, LF)—although I can see that if linguists were able to argue for such a condition, it would be excruciatingly difficult to express it derivationally, given our assumptions.

L: Yes. If the model in (5) encodes derivational relations, the answer to the question marks has to be the arrows I'm drawing here in (6), indicating some sort of derivational mapping:

(6)

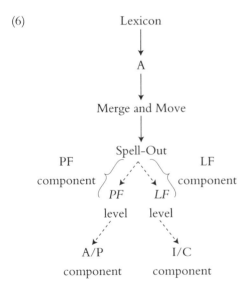

In this system the derivation goes forward from an object built with the elements in A to a point where (i) the object spells out a PF representation and (ii) an LF representation is built with the object as it exists at the point of Spell-Out. In fact, note that the model includes—in addition to PF and LF *levels*—PF and LF *components*, which represent the sets of derivational steps that map the relevant levels. As a consequence of this architecture, there can be no direct connection between the levels of PF and LF.

Figure 2.28

Klima and Bellugi (1979) argued persuasively that signed and spoken languages are syntactically homologous. Recently a similar claim has been made for phonology, where the affirmation may seem more surprising. Perlmutter (1992) argues that American Sign Language (ASL) has a syllabic structure, whose basic segments are movement (M) and position (P). One of his arguments is based on the existence of secondary hand movements such as finger wiggling and circling. Although secondary movements can occur either on an M or on a P, they can always occur on an M but cannot occur on a P if it is adjacent to an M. For example, the sign in the first illustration, which involves finger wiggling throughout M, is well formed, but the sign in the second illustration, involving finger wiggling on P, followed by M, is impossible.

By looking at matters abstractly, Perlmutter (pp. 416–417) invites the following comparison (where *OK* designates a valid occurrence of a secondary movement; *P* and *M* again designate position and movement elements in ASL; and *C* and *V* designate the consonants and vowels of spoken syllables):

(i) a. $[*]_P$ $[OK]_M$ $[*]_P$ (ii) a. $[*]_C$ $[OK]_V$ $[*p]_C$
     b. $[OK]_M$ $[*]_P$ b. $[OK]_V$ $[*]_C$
     c. $[*]_P$ $[OK]_M$ c. $[*]_C$ $[OK]_V$
     d. $[OK]_M$ d. $[OK]_V$
     e. $[OK]_P$ e. $[OK]_C$

If this isomorphism is viable, the situation could be described as in (iii):

(iii) a. A V (M) is always a syllable nucleus.
      b. A C (P) can be the nucleus of a syllable only if it is not adjacent to a V (M).
      c. Secondary movement features can occur only on the syllable nucleus.

Then Perlmutter inquires why (iiic) should hold. He accounts for this fact in terms of the sort of sonority hierarchy discussed in figure 2.24. Explicitly put (Perlmutter 1992, 418):

(iv) a. Classes of segments are ranked in a "sonority hierarchy."
     b. Sonority peaks are the nuclei of syllables.
     c. Vs (Ms) are more "sonorous" than Cs (Ps).

Essentially, Perlmutter suggests this: the fact that a P can be a syllable nucleus only if not adjacent to an M in ASL is explained in the same way as the fact that a C can be a syllable nucleus only if not adjacent to a V in oral languages. Of course, ASL syllables are soundless, so syllabic peaks and whatever valleys accompany them must be expressed in terms more abstract than those assumed when only sound is at stake. The exact nature of those terms is an issue for future research (see sec. 6.6 on related matters).

O: Nevertheless, suppose that (6) were not correct, and no derivation carried us from A onwards, but PF and LF existed as separate entities in their own right. Would it then be possible to relate PF and LF meaningfully—that is to say, directly?

_____ **matters of production and perception do not determine relations among levels**

L: Well, first of all, no trivial mapping is going to carry you from a speech signal at PF like "I'mo prove that" (actually, something with the shape in, roughly, [äm-ə-ˈprüv-dä]) to an LF with the import of something that may translate as: for some time in the future there is an event of proving, such that the speaker is the subject of that event and the object of that event is some contextually determined object referred to by *'that'* [94].

O: Hold on, hold on! Don't I do precisely that when I hear the PF you've just pronounced—which I can't repeat with my proper English—and I manage to assign an interpretation to it . . . ?

L: No! That's a matter of performance, how you get from a PF signal to a full-blown structure. (Just as it would be a matter of performance how a PF signal comes out of my mouth when I think up something, want to say it, plan to say it, attempt to say it, and say it.) The competence question is different: we're trying to come up with the properties of the expression, its PF and LF properties, the words it involves and how they relate. When I say it would be hopeless to do this from the point of view of a function from PF to LF, what I mean is that in trying to do it, we would be taking PF, with its reductions, contractions, liaisons, intonational nightmares, and all, as the basic storehouse of linguistic knowledge. It would be possible, but bizarre—not even worth considering. On the other hand, the reverse—a function from LF to PF—may not be so hard, and linguists have thought about that possibility in the past [95]. Nonetheless, it isn't easy to make that proposal work either, because it's just a fact about human language that its logical relations are more messy than its grammatical relations, not less [96]. So for instance, when an English speaker says *the father told the child about himself,* that can have two interpretations. The father can be telling the child about the father's youth, say; or he can be telling the child about the child's infancy. This tells us that, plausibly at least, two different LFs are involved, one for each interpretation. But if that's true, then it's not so easy to see how different LFs would yield the same PF. Similar issues may arise for ambiguous expressions like *some problem underlies every complex theory,* which can be true in two obvious circumstances [see fig. 2.29] [97].

O: Yes, yes . . .

L: Again, no simple-minded mapping carries us from those two interpretations to the PF involved in both structures. It's not that doing things that way would be impossible, but it wouldn't be trivial either.

---

a single interface level

O: Well, then. I shall just say it more cautiously: it's unreasonable to expect anything other than what we've established, with one possible exception—and this is the one that concerns me. Why couldn't there be conditions on the entire triplet (A, PF, LF)? To have something to talk about, let's imagine a single structural representation as in (4), and call it S(ingular)-structure. Now suppose that from this S-structure we read off PF and LF, and find out what the lexical array is [98]. The way we've designed the model (as in (6)), there shouldn't be conditions on the entire triplet (A, PF, LF), because there's no derivational way of expressing such conditions. Now, I've told you that I'm distrustful about assuming just two interface levels, PF and LF, that connect directly to the rest of the mental universe—so you can imagine how I feel about assuming just a single one! Nevertheless, I should like to consider this possibility because to my mind it's a conceivable one, given the issues that we've raised, and as a matter of principle [99].

L: Okay, so the alternatives we've explored (and rejected) so far would still be essentially derivational, in the sense that PF is (directionally) mapped as a definite output from LF, or something like that. But the one you're now asking about would be a radically nonderivational theory, one that imposes rich filtering conditions as an alternative to **internal computational steps.** To see how each system would work, imagine you encounter the structure *Plato, I like.* From the derivational point of view, *Plato, I like* clearly shows that movement has taken place—being deliberately naive about it.

O: Indeed *Plato* is the object, and it does appear to have been moved to the beginning of the sentence. When I think about it, this little fact is remarkable in and of itself: that the object should appear in the sensory output literally displaced from its plausible site of interpretation . . . !

Figure 2.29

Compare the two (informal) readings of (i) in (ii) and (iii):

(i)   some problem underlies every complex theory

(ii) there is one problem that underlies every (relevant) complex theory, for instance, Gödel's

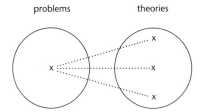

(iii) for every (relevant) complex theory, there is a problem underlying it: in physics, it may be loss of information into black holes; in linguistics, it may be the properties of the performance systems; in biology, it may be the protein-folding problem; and so on

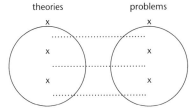

L: As the Port-Royal grammarians first emphasized, it's a universal property of Human that it involves displacement—any theory has to capture that basic fact. The way we do that in a strongly constructive system is by postulating an initial array which includes the actual lexical items of the sentence, building a given phrase marker, and then literally displacing the phrase *Plato* to the front. (That is, more technically, we relate a phrase marker where *Plato* is the direct object of *like* to another phrase marker where *Plato* is at the left periphery of the sentence.) Then what we get via movement, ultimately we ship to LF and PF, where we hope it satisfies FI. If it does, the derivation converges. But now, how would you do all of this from a representational point of view?

O: I certainly couldn't do the computation as you've outlined it. I should need to start with *Plato, I like* and recover from that whatever structure tells me that *Plato* is actually the object of *like*. In a word, I should have to think of the problem statically, with no beginning; the structure simply exists according to some linguistic axioms. But then I suppose I need to conceive a complex object, a relation between the displaced *Plato* and the position that it "should" occupy in the phrase marker.

L: That's essentially how it's done, and in the process what we call a **chain** gets created. From a derivational point of view, a chain is just the history of movement—thus, the history of a mapping from some phrasal object to some other phrasal object [100]. But from the representational perspective, such displacements have to be captured in terms of primitive objects that are made up of some sorts of elements, arranged in a given fashion. In our example, the first element is or has to do with *Plato,* and we need another element that occupies the object position and is somehow associated to *like*—some abstract element that we don't hear—which links to *Plato*. And now the chain has to be a primitive element of the theory, not something that we obtain computationally by relating A to LF via derivational steps; we've denied ourselves that possibility [see fig. 2.30].

O: But how are we to tell something that is a chain from something that isn't?

Figure 2.30

The structure in (i) can be treated in different ways, depending on whether the system is derivational or representational:

(i) Plato, I like

(ii) *Derivational approach*
Phrase marker I: [I like Plato]
Phrase marker II: [Plato [I like]]

Movement is a relation (I, II):

(iii) *Representational approach*
A relation must be established between *Plato* and *like*.

This can be done by crossing branches, if the formal theory (like the graph theory proposed in Blevins 1990) allows it,

or by invoking a copy of *Plato* and treating the pair (Plato, Plato) as a single object (Brody 1995):

L: We have to build that into the system, introducing constraints that rule out representations which don't conform to whatever we decide a chain is [101]. Of course, the complex object that we're calling a chain is intended to have an articulated internal structure, with very particular properties. So for instance, I told you that movement never takes place "downward" in a phrase marker. For reasons that don't concern us yet, this is true; and it's a fact that any system, derivational or representational, has to capture.

O: But the two systems would capture it rather differently, out of necessity. A derivational system says that it's a property of the derivation (downward movement leading to cancellation), whereas a representational system would have to say, I suppose, that it's a property of the chain per se (unwanted chains being discarded) [102].

L: Yes. Note that the representational system doesn't rely on combinatorial, constructive devices that map the relevant symbolic representations, but on output conditions that filter the bad ones out. Combinatorially, a representational system may be totally trivial; it may just axiomatically define some basic set-theoretic objects. What sorts of objects these are, though, is what matters—and this is what representational filters determine. In contrast, in a constructivist system we want to get the right objects through constructive procedures for assembling the parts.

O: Do you know what this reminds me of? The two different views of the universe—the dynamic view and the stationary one . . . These are very old perspectives, going back to Heraclitus and Parmenides; their contemporary instantiations are, of course, the big bang model (cosmic evolution starts in an initial singularity) and the steady state model (the universe simply exists, according to the principles of physics [103]). Now the arguments for one model or the other should be empirical; for instance, in physics the issue is which sort of model best allows for unified forces. I should like to ask, then, what's the issue in linguistics?

L: It's not always clear, even if there may ultimately be some serious differences. But—as in physics—the differences will never be obvious, since in one instance we're literally constructing our formal object piece by piece, and in the other instance we're looking for some set-theoretic definition to **recursively** characterize the formal object. Of course, under the dynamic model, in the ideal case information is literally erased as processes unravel. For instance, the

English

	Onset	Fill-Nuc	Parse-Seg	*Coda/Liquid	*Coda/"n"
☞ /berlin/				•	•
be<r>lin			*!		•
be☐lin		*!			•
berli<n>			*!	•	
berlin☐		*!		•	
be<r>lin<n>			*!*		
ber☐li<n>		*!			
be<r>lin☐		*!			
ber☐lin☐		*!*			

Japanese

	Onset	*Coda/Liquid	Parse-Seg	Fill-Nuc	*Coda/"n"
/berlin/		*!			•
be<r>lin			*!	•	•
☞ ber☐lin					••
berli<n>		*!	•		
berlin☐				•	
be<r>lin<n>			*!*		
ber☐li<n>			*!	•	
be<r>lin☐			*!	•	
ber☐lin☐				**!	

Kikuyu

	Onset	*Coda/Liquid	Fill-Nuc	Parse-Seg	*Coda/"n"
/berlin/		*!			•
☞ be<r>lin				•	•
be☐lin			*!		•
berli<n>		*!			
berlin☐		*!		•	
be<r>lin<n>				**!	
ber☐li<n>			*!	•	
be<r>lin☐			*!	•	
ber☐lin☐			*!*		

Definitions

Onset:	Start syllable with a consonant.
Fill-Nuc:	Do not add a nucleus.
Parse-Seg:	Do not delete a segment.
*Coda/Liquid:	Do not associate a liquid with a coda.
*Coda/"n":	Do not associate the segment "n" with a coda.

Technical apparatus

Constraints are shown across the top of the tableaux in order of dominance. The highest-ranked constraint is leftmost. Competing candidates are arrayed in the leftmost column. The candidate that corresponds to the input form is enclosed in / /. A single solid line between two constraint columns indicates that the constraints that head those columns are ranked with respect to each other. A single dotted line between two constraint columns indicates that there is no

linguistic computation typically involves simple steps expressible in terms of fairly natural relations and properties. But the very context that makes them natural is partially wiped out by later operations and isn't so easy to discern in the ultimate representations—those to which the derivation converges [see sec. 4.6]. So the derivationalist says that the point is to look at processes as they unravel, where we expect them to obey conditions which are quite elementary, the primordial stages before complexity takes over. In turn, the representationalist argues that there's always enough information left in the context to be able to determine the relevant structures involved.

O: And then they play ping-pong.

L: That's right. What can be done derivationally can also be done representationally, and vice versa. Occasionally, notational arguments are also given that one or the other model is more efficient in representing matters—but I rarely understand those arguments.

O: Hm . . . it seems to me that a strong case for a nonderivational theory could be constructed if one were to motivate radical filtering conditions—to be specific, conditions that simply could not be expressed as internally motivated derivational steps [104].

2.7 Optimality Theory

(a real alternative, introducing the controversial possibility that this intriguing proposal could be incorporated into the model at large)

L: There's an interesting proposal going around these days, so far mostly within phonology, that has the right form [105]. Let me illustrate the basic line of thought with an intuitive example. The way people say the word *Berlin* differs from language to language. English speakers say [bər-'lin]; speakers of other languages don't.

O: Japanese speakers say something which sounds like [be-dü-'dēn], Kikuyu speakers say [be-'lēn], and—

L: Yes, so why do languages differ this way? (Let me assume for the sake of argument that the underlying representation for these words in different languages is the same.)

———————————　　*violating a soft constraint does not entail ungrammaticality, but a ranking of grammaticality*

Optimality Theory suggests that phonology provides the learner with a variety of output conditions which basically serve to rank possible representations: conditions like not representing certain vowels in order to meet syllabification restrictions, syllabifying dummy (epenthetic) vowels, giving syllables a particular format . . . So for instance, a representation such as [brln] for *Berlin* may violate some of these output conditions (intuitively, a syllable without any vowels shouldn't be a great syllable). Interestingly, though, the output conditions don't automatically filter out representations that violate them. Rather, they basically assign each of them a *degree* of grammaticality. All in all, the one representation whose degree of grammaticality is highest (i.e., violates the fewest output conditions) wins the race for grammaticality.

O: I see, so this proposal has a . . . well, a spirit of economy about it as well.

L: Certainly. But here, economy doesn't come from a derivation at all—rather, it comes from the interaction of different representations with **soft constraints** (as opposed to **rigid conditions** of the sort encoded under FI in the derivational system). If representation α violates constraint C, the result isn't necessarily ungrammatical, so long as alternative representations to α violate a larger number of constraints. In fact, the claim is that there's variation in the way different languages value different constraints provided by UG. So that's the general picture: a bunch of output conditions ranked in different ways. For *n* such conditions, in principle there are *n!* rankings—which poses an interesting question for learnability [see fig. 2.31] [106].

O: It looks like a system that a connectionist would dream of!

L: It's the sort of problem that connectionist networks are designed to solve, though other systems can do the job as well. Besides, some contentful aspects of the theory aren't derivable from connectionism [see fig. 2.32] [107].

---

why all words aren't pronounced [ta]

O: I'm sure I haven't understood all that you've said, so perhaps this question will be utterly naïve—but what prevents all words in a language from being pronounced . . . oh dear, what would the optimal syllable be? Well, I shall plump for [ta]. Why are all words not

evidence to rank the constraints that head those columns with respect to each other. An empty cell indicates that no constraint violation has occurred. Shaded cells do not participate in deciding between candidates, because higher-ranked constraints have already made the crucial decision. The symbol * marks constraint violations; there is one * per violation. The symbol ! marks the fatal constraint violation that causes each suboptimal candidate to lose to other candidates. The symbol ☞ indicates the winning candidate. Unparsed segments are enclosed in < >. Epenthesized segments are represented by the symbol □.

Figure 2.31

Consider the treatment of syllabic codas in English, Japanese, and Kikuyu. Each of these languages chooses a different resolution of the tension between the coda condition on liquids (whether consonants of this sort (e.g., [r]) are allowed in syllable-final position) and the Parse and Fill constraints. The Parse constraint aims at integrating as much underlying representation (generated by the function Gen) as possible within the final grammatical form. In other words, Parse avoids "deleting" segments (although this notion is inappropriately derivational, even if intuitive). In turn, the Fill-Nucleus constraint aims at not postulating extra syllabic nuclei; the fewer syllables per word, the better. (In the tableaux below, a constraint preventing the association of a nasal segment to a coda is also added, and always ranked lowest.) Notice that English allows liquids in coda position by ranking Fill and Parse rather high. Japanese does not allow liquids in coda position, and repairs the structure by epenthesis (the addition of a default vowel segment—here, *u*—again in metaphorical derivational terms), ranking Fill low. Kikuyu does not allow liquids in coda position either, but repairs the structure by ranking Parse low. (In the tableaux that follow, vowel and consonant quality have been ignored for ease of exposition. Kikuyu and Japanese do not distinguish between [l] and [r], so these are represented as the class of liquids (English makes the distinction, but this is irrelevant for the case in point).)

Figure 2.32

Suppose that a value v_i is associated to a given violation, and that in language L, violation V has value v_n and violation V′, value v_{n-m} (in other words, V′ violates a constraint that is ranked lower on the grammaticality hierarchy than V). Suppose furthermore that V′ is combined in a given linguistic form with V″, whose value is v_{m+k}, where k<n but k>n−m. Put differently: the combined value of V′ and V″ is larger than the value of V. If the system were a standard connectionist one, a form that undergoes V′ and V″ would be predicted to be outranked by a form that undergoes V, all other things being equal. But in fact empirical results show that this is never the case. For instance, no phonological form that violates a highly ranked constraint is grammatical, if an alternative exists that violates less highly ranked constraints (even if it violates many of them) (see Smolensky 1994).

pronounced [ta]? Or if there's only one optimal word, why isn't the next word the second-most optimal, so that the language ends up with a vocabulary like [tata], [baba], [mama], et cetera [108]? Why should a lexicon ever contain, ahem . . . *emasculate* and other such nightmares?

L: We have to keep in perspective the fact that phonology is an intricate input-output system, whereas what we've been looking at so far are combinatorial systems. For instance, today we've talked about phrases built up from lexical items. In that system we start out with a variety of elements that don't look at all like what we end up with. We might start out with, say, *hir* and *seis* and *noght* and *thou* and some functional items like Tense, and we combine all of that in order to get a structure like [*thou* [*seis* + T [*noght* [. . . *hir*]]]], or some such thing. But in phonology things are different: we start out with an underlying representation like, say, /berlin/, and we have to end up with a derived form like [be-dü-'dēn]. The lexicon and the syntax already hand us a representation as an input, and we have to adjust it to produce a grammatical output within the particular language we're looking at. Virtually by definition, then, we have to obtain an optimal PF matrix as our encoding of the PF representation. Nobody doubts that, since Pāṇini first looked at these issues twenty-five hundred years ago. Where differences between theories emerge is in terms of how we get the optimal encoding. The traditional, Pāṇinian approach is based on computational rules that work on the input to produce the output—rules that say things like "Add an **epenthetic vowel** in the context of blah-blah-blah" or "Harmonize vowels when these particular conditions are met." The notation is fancier, but that's what the computational approach boils down to [109]. What optimality theorists are pointing out is that these rules don't explain the facts adequately, even if they can describe them. Then they propose the rankings of constraints that I mentioned, as an alternative to a rule-based system. But it's true for Optimality Theory also that an input-output relation has to be established, since—virtually by definition—phonology is about the optimal input-output relation for lexical material in a syntactic context. Well, then, every system needs to indicate an explicit relation between, say, *emasculate* and a crazy output like [ta]. In a rule-based system, there's obviously no way any sound rule will relate a pair like that. In an optimality system, in fact nothing prevents this mapping, but the idea is to make the mapping less preferable than the mapping between whatever the underlying form of *emasculate* is and the actual output [i-'mas-kyə-lāt]. Basically, then, the (relative) faithfulness between the output form and the input form has to be ranked highly above whatever optimality constraint makes us go in the direction of [ta] and the like.

O: I see . . . one simply says that the output must be, for instance, contained in the input, is that right?

L: That's one way, although other functions could be invoked, in principle. In fact, traditional Pāninian theories are about these sorts of functions. Of course, optimality theorists are saying that these functions are the wrong ones, so we now have to look at their alternative—a matter I won't go into [110].

O: But I don't suppose we can say the output is identical to the input . . . if it were, how would all those forms of pronouncing *Berlin* ever be possible?

L: Of course—everybody agrees on that. Precisely where the interesting empirical work lies is in finding out the details of the faithful mapping.

O: Well, then: so the details of the theory remain to be puzzled out. But if it proves a workable theory, it will be one in which **output conditions** could not be mimicked in a derivational way.

L: At least not trivially, for instance with a system like C_{HL} that uses only serial movement operations and the like. The alternative system is a lot more flexible: constraints can be ranked in various ways, and in fact can be violated. This is a rather different architecture, which is why I'm saying that it's not a notational variant. No trivial derivation has the effects we've been discussing in terms of the ranking of output constraints.

O: It's an intriguing sort of approach; has it resolved any knotty problems so far?

L: In phonology, lots [111]. Optimality Theory research in syntax is just getting underway, but it's already produced some results, and it will undoubtedly produce others, particularly in very specific, nontrivial input-output domains, such as morphological patterns, and certain syntactic patterns that are a nuisance for the standard syntactic system [112]. I'm thinking of paradigms that appear to be hopeless from the standard perspective.

Figure 2.33

The distribution of auxiliary selection in Standard Italian is as follows:

(i)   *Standard Italian*

a.   Maria ha comprato i   libri
     Maria has bought   the books
     'Maria has bought the books'

a'. *Maria è comprato/a   i   libri
     Maria is bought/agreement the books

b.   Maria ha dormito
     Maria has slept
     'Maria has slept'

b'. *Maria è dormito/a
     Maria is slept/agreement

c.   Maria è arrivata
     Maria is arrived.agreement
     'Maria has arrived'

d.   Maria si   è comprata   un libro
     Maria reflexive is bought.agreement a book
     'Maria has bought herself a book'

Auxiliary *have* is always used, except with intransitive verbs where the single argument of the verb is the logical object (ic) (see sec. 6.1 on this class of verbs) and with transitive structures involving reflexive pronouns (id). This pattern is common in other Romance languages and is also found elsewhere—for instance, in Germanic languages (see Grewendorf 1989). However, Kayne (1993) shows that matters are more complex elsewhere, even within closely related dialects. For instance, in Central Italian dialects it is possible to use *be* with all intransitive verbs and even with transitive verbs:

(ii) *Central Italian dialects*

a.   Maria è mangiato
     Maria is eaten
     'Maria has eaten'

b.   Ntonio è rotta   la brocca
     Ntonio is broken the jug
     'Ntonio has broken the jug'

In the Novara dialect, *be* is selected for transitives and pure intransitives (whose single argument is a logical subject; again, see sec. 6.1), but only when the verb is inflected for first and second person. When the verb is inflected for third person, *have* must be used instead. Furthermore, although the auxiliary verb is *be* rather generally, when the object is a clitic, the auxiliary verb must again be *have*:

(iii) *Novara dialect*

a.   mi i son mia parla
     me I am not spoken
     'me, I have not spoken'

b.   mi i t'o   mai parla
     me I you-have never spoken
     'me, I haven't spoken to you'

O: And those might be . . . ?

───────────────────────────────────── *speculations on auxiliary selection*

L: Take a look at auxiliary selection. As you probably know, in some languages certain intransitive verbs get the auxiliary verb *be* (and speakers say things like *The king is arrived*), whereas most transitive verbs take *have* (*The king has visited the town*). It looks like we have a nice little pattern going here, until we find out that many languages use the equivalent of *The King is visited himself* when the transitive expression invokes a reflexive. So we complicate our pattern, adding reflexives: "Select *be* with intransitives and reflexive transitives" . . .

O: Not to be difficult, but I would add that speakers in Padua can use both *be* and *have* with reflexive transitives. And if the reflexive is used impersonally, then the auxiliary must be *have: se ga bala tuta la note* (verbatim, 'there has dancing all the night'), and surely not *se ze bala . . .* ('there be dancing')!

L: Except, I'm told, if yet another reflexive clitic is added with a reflexive reading. Then the auxiliary can be *have* [see fig. 2.33] [113] . . .

O: I understand! Patterns of this sort must be perfect for optimality approaches. Nevertheless, do you take this particular instance to be an input–output system? That's not at all clear to me.

L: It turns out that auxiliary forms like *be* and *have* are possibly derived [114]. That is, many languages don't pronounce *be* at all, particularly in its present tense form. Others appear to use a pronoun to encode **predication.**

O: A pronoun, yes! As in that introduction to Conrad's book, spoken in creole: *Mr. Kurtz, he dead,* which meant that Kurtz was dead. Then of course, the same construction turns up in standard Aramaic: *'anaḥnā himmō 'abdōhī dī- 'elāh-šmayyā w'ar'ā* 'we are the servants of the god of heaven and earth'. Verbatim: 'we *they* his servants of god . . .'

L: I am impressed.

O: About my memory for these trivialities? It's no blessing, really. I wish I could remember, instead, what it was that I was supposed to—

L: I'm actually impressed that you didn't use the pronoun *we*, but *they*, which exhibits plural agreement!

O: Ah, that too, yes. Had the subject been singular, I should have used *hu* 'he' instead.

L: The point is, of course, that *be* isn't really an obvious, sacred form in the English lexicon, and is perhaps some sort of functional item. Descriptively linguists have found a great variety of possibilities here. The same thing happens with possession relations. Again, not many languages have a counterpart to *have*; rather, possession is often expressed through whatever form the language has for *be*, plus a **dative** element. So in many languages speakers say *money is to me* to mean 'I have money' [see fig. 2.34].

O: That's right, that's what happens in Ewe: *ga le asi-nye* 'money is in my hand=I have money'.

L: Actually, there's something of this alternation in plain old English as well. *NYC has five boroughs* and *there are five boroughs in NYC*, for example, mean basically the same thing, yet their structures are rather different [115].

O: But isn't that because you're using different words?

L: Yeah: in one instance I used *there* and in the other I didn't. Fine. But the question is about the auxiliary selection: it's not totally obvious that the items *are* and *have* are listed as such in the lexicon. It could well be that the lexicon contains a single element Aux(iliary), and if Aux appears in some concrete context, let's say the context *there . . . five boroughs in NYC*, then it's pronounced *are* (a form of *be*). In contrast, if Aux appears in the context *NYC . . . five boroughs*, it's pronounced *has* (a form of *have*). Perhaps *have* is itself *be+in*, the locative corresponding to the *in* of *in NYC*. In fact, colloquial English has contractions for *be* and *have* which are really identical, as in *it ain't my fault, I ain't gonna take it,* and *you ain't seen nothing yet,* or *he's a fool* and *he's got no money.* This suggests that the contractions work on the same lexical root. The point is, it wouldn't totally surprise me if auxiliary selection weren't so much a matter of selecting an

---

Finally, in the Paduan dialect, reflexive clitics may appear with either *be* (iva) or *have* (iva') auxiliaries. However, when the reflexive clitic takes on an impersonal use (ivb), then the auxiliary must be *have*—unless another reflexive clitic is added with a reflexive reading, in which case some speakers can use auxiliary *have*:

(iv) *Paduan dialect*
    a. la Maria se   ze vestia
       the Maria reflexive is dressed.agreement
       'Maria has dressed herself'
    a'. la Maria se   ga vestio
       the Maria reflexive has dressed
       'Maria has dressed herself'
    b. se   ga/*ze bala tuta la note
       reflexive has/is danced all the night
       'there was dancing all night long'
    c. se   se   gera visti
       reflexive reflexive will.be seen
       'one will see oneself'

Figure 2.34

What follows is an excerpt from Benveniste's (1971) insightful discussion on the nature of *be* (pp. 164ff.) and *have* (pp. 168ff.):

"[T]o be" . . . was not a linguistic inevitability. In a number of languages at different periods of history, the junctive function, usually established by a pause between the terms, as in Russian [, Hungarian, and ancient Semitic], has tended to be realized . . . in a morpheme. But the function of predication [in Aramaic] can be given a definite sign: it is the so-called pronoun of the third singular that serves as the "copula"; it is then inserted between the subject and the predicate: *'elāhkon hu 'elāh 'elāhin* 'your god, he (=is) the god of gods.' . . . The same schema is found in Arabic[,] . . . Turkish, . . . [and three] Iranian languages. . . .

That "to have" is an auxiliary with the same status as "to be" is a very strange thing. . . . ["To have"] has the construction of a transitive verb, but it is not. . . . In fact, "to have" as a lexeme is a rarity in the world; most languages do not have it. . . . For instance, in Arabic, *kāna l-* 'to be-to' represents the only possible equivalent of "to have." Such is the situation in the majority of languages. . . . [I]n Turkish a predicate of existence, *var*, or of nonexistence, *yoq*, is constructed with a pronoun suffix: hence *bir ev-im var* 'a *(bir)* house-mine *(ev-im)* is: I have a house'; in Mongol (classical), the dative-locative of the pronoun or of the noun of the possessor is constructed with "to be": *nadur morin buy* 'to me *(nadur)* a horse *(morin)* is *(buy)*: I have a horse.' . . . [I]t is the same in Kurdish[.]

Classical Georgian has the same construction, "to be-to," which coincides with that of Greek models in translations. . . . In the African domain one could cite from Ewe (Togo) the expression of "to have" by "to be in the hand" with the verb *le,* 'to be, to exist' and *asi* 'in the hand': *ga le asi-nye* 'money *(ga)* is in my *(-nye)* hand: I have money.' [Likewise] in Vai (Liberia) . . . [and] Kanuri. . . . We shall not continue to accumulate proofs which would rapidly turn into a catalogue since it is so easy to verify the predominance . . . of the "mihi est" type over the "habeo" type. And even with little knowledge of the history of the language being considered, one will frequently observe that the development is from "mihi est" to "habeo" and not the reverse.

auxiliary, as a matter of producing one according to some morpho-phonological procedures. If so, this would be an input-output system: *be+in* (more abstractly, *pronoun+agreement+in*) goes in and *have* comes out, and so on. And if it's indeed such a system, an optimality approach perhaps isn't inappropriate—assuming one accepts the overall architecture of the theory. (Of course, other, more traditional rule-based morphophonological systems can also, in principle, produce the desired output form; whether they're more or less adequate than an optimality alternative is something that has to be determined empirically.)

O: Should all verbs undergo these processes?

L: I seriously doubt it; this is the worst-case scenario. At any rate, the bottom line is that, together with these peripheral facts (which are, no doubt, extremely pervasive), Human also exhibits core combinatorial facts like the merger of phrases that we've talked about today, and core movements, and many others that we should talk about. For those, I haven't seen a real alternative.

O: Why couldn't optimality theorists assume that architecture as their input, and then have soft constraints rank the outputs?

———————————————————— *understanding the generative procedure*

L: They could, and some have. For instance, they posit a function *Gen* that produces structures like the one I showed you in (1), and then they rank possible movements, of the kind we looked at [116]. But this is why I'm saying that an optimality approach isn't particularly useful for combinatorial systems: what we want to understand is why Gen gives the structures that it does, a matter I hope we'll have a chance to discuss and which follows on trivial grounds in the terms I've been assuming. Note that if the structure that you have to rank according to soft constraints is given to you by some other system (e.g., syntax in the case of morphology or phonology), then you don't have to pose the question of how whatever structure you start with for ranking purposes is generated. The optimality system doesn't have to generate it at all: it receives it from a different system. But the buck stops in the syntax. Nothing generates syntactic structures other than syntax proper, so we need a function to do this. A hard condition, not a soft output constraint—a genesis for the structures. We can debate what happens to structures generated by C_{HL}, whether the final form they take in different languages is a matter of such-and-such parametric choices. But the bottom line is that something has to give us those structures, whether it's called C_{HL}, Gen, or God. Personally, I'm interested in understanding the nature of the combinatorial function.

O: And you don't see how an optimality system will tell you anything useful about that . . . Is that it?

L: Even if it had anything useful to say about the rest of the architecture. Of course, one should keep an open mind about any new approach that may clean up the act, in particular, of peripheral aspects of language. (And I mean "peripheral" technically, as opposed to core aspects—each being important in its own way.) Otherwise we'd be forced to postulate several parameters for the little picture of auxiliary selection that I painted earlier, one of which would separate a couple of Italian dialects from the rest of the languages of the world . . .

———————————————— *the mapping to PF departs from the mapping to LF*

O: There's something about what you're now saying, this duplicity in the language faculty, which I find slightly surprising. The system as you sketched it in (6) seems to exhibit both a reasonably clean mapping between the array A and LF, of a combinatorial sort, and at the same time—you seem prepared to admit this—the possibility that the mapping to PF is less clean, obeying an architectural design that looks quite different.

L: I haven't said that! All I've said is that an Optimality Theory approach isn't inconceivable for input-output systems, such as those involved in the representations of words at PF.

O: Very well, but you do admit a difference between the mapping to LF and the mapping to PF, whatever its nature . . .

L: That's just a fact, and I've told you already: phonology is different [117].

O: But is it not a departure from the elegance of the system at large, that this difference may exist?

L: Things would be cleaner if PF didn't exist—but we wouldn't be talking about Human. PF does exist, and with it come all sorts of

A B C

Skull, vertebral column, and larynx of Newborn *(a)* and adult Man *(c)*, and reconstruction of Neanderthal *(b)*. G—geniohyoid muscle, H—hyoid bone, S—stylohyoid ligament, M—thyrohyoid membrane, T—thyroid cartilage, CC—cricoid cartilage. Note that the inclination of the styloid process away from the vertical plane in Newborn and Neanderthal results in a corresponding inclination in the stylohyoid ligament. The intersection of the stylohyoid ligament and geniohyoid muscle with the hyoid bone of the larynx occurs at a higher position in Newborn and Neanderthal. The high position of the larynx in the Neanderthal reconstruction follows, in part, from this intersection. (From Lieberman and Crelin, On the speech of Neanderthal man)

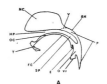

A B C

Supralaryngeal air passages of Newborn *(a)*, Neanderthal reconstruction *(b)*, and adult Man *(c)*. NC—nasal cavity, V—vomer bone, RN—roof of nasopharynx, P—pharynx, HP—hard palate, SP—soft palate, OC—oral cavity, T—tip of tongue, FC—foramen cecum of tongue, E—epiglottis, O—opening of larynx into pharynx, VF—level of vocal folds. (From Lieberman and Crelin, On the speech of Neanderthal man)

Figure 2.35

Lieberman and Crelin (1971) argue that Neanderthals did not have the anatomical prerequisites for producing the full range of human speech and may have lacked the neural detectors involved in its perception/production. Nevertheless, they also argue that Neanderthals did have more phonetic abilities than present-day nonhuman apes and thus may have had a form of protolanguage. They even explicitly suggest that Neanderthals may have represented an intermediate stage in the evolution of language, for which they resurrect Haeckel's 1907 "law" that ontogeny recapitulates phylogeny; thus, they suggest that newborn humans resemble Neanderthals (see Lieberman 1984). As for the force of the phonetic argument per se, the question is what is meant by "a larynx that is suited for speech." Very probably, Neanderthals could only have produced nasal versions of the vowels in words like *bit, bet, but,* and *bat,* in addition to reduced vowels without any partic-

interesting things, peripheral as they may be. Linguistic variation, movement, maybe the very nature of morphemes—who knows? That's just the way things turn out to be. I'm actually happy that PF is there, forcing us to face a departure from a perfect system. The link with the A/P components might have been what exposed the clean A → LF mapping to the outside world.

O: Hah! This reminds me . . . In the early universe, there were ten billion and one protons for every ten billion antiprotons. What would have happened if total symmetry had obtained instead? Nothing, absolutely nothing; not a proton would have escaped its antiparticle, and each would have annihilated the other. Total symmetry equals no dynamic imbalance; a minuscule difference instead, almost too modest to mention, is in fact the cause of . . . well, all forms of existence [118].

L: In our case, the difference between PF and LF is quite significant—at least so it appears. At any rate, without PF humans might never have found out that they have this system of knowledge—at least, it might have been considerably harder to figure this out.

O: I wonder: do you suppose that Homo sapiens differed from his precursors in that the latter lacked PF? Why, Neanderthals, for instance, had an elaborate system of thought and even communication—one need only observe their rudimentary crafts, their use of fire, their ritual burial sites . . . Then again, whatever linguistic system they employed wasn't elaborate enough to trigger objectual art, for instance.

L: I don't know about any of this . . . Conjectures to that effect exist, mind you; the argument being that Neanderthals had apelike larynxes that were incapable of producing speech as we know it [see fig. 2.35]. Obviously, if the sort of anatomical apparatus that allows a creature to produce lots of consonants and the usual vowels is central to PF, then PF couldn't have appeared prior to the laryngeal lowering. However, I'm doubtful that PF is about speech, since signed languages don't have speech, but do seem to have PF [see sec. 2.5]; then that argument about larynxes seems considerably less forceful. In principle, of course, I have no problem admitting that some mutation gave us PF, and before that we may have had the rest of the system as a result of some other exaptation (or a series of them). But demonstrating this is a tougher business.

O: . . .

L: Are you by any chance bothered by this?

O: Actually, I think not.

As he spoke these words, the Other disappeared abruptly, much more so than the day before, and the Linguist was left musing over Cartesian questions that he liked to ponder, particularly in the presence of wormholes. And the FBI. Almost instinctively, he erased what he had been drafting on the ground.

ular vowel quality. They could also have produced dental and labial consonants ([t], [d], [p], [b], [s], [z], [f], and [v]), although they could not have distinguished the nasal [m] from the nonnasal [p] or [b] (all of their consonants would have had a nasal character). How good or bad that is, is hard to tell; certainly, an arbitrarily large complement of words would be possible with such a powerful apparatus. The facts discussed in figure 2.28 are relevant here, though: present-day humans who lack the ability to produce speech are nonetheless capable of normal uses of human language. If Perlmutter's (1992) arguments about syllables in ASL are correct, why could Neanderthals not have used their hands and facial expressions to do what present-day deaf individuals do? The answer is perhaps that modern humans have the neural structure to do what they do, which is only (relatively) marginally related to actual speech; speech is certainly a good way of expressing language, but so are signs. Then the reason Neanderthals did not have human language (if this is true) could not have been that they were unable to produce speech; it must have been more that they lacked the requisite mental abilities. Contrary to what Lieberman and Crelin suggest, then, modern humans are such not because they can say so, but because they can think the way they do.

This day the wormhole opened earlier than before, and by the time the Linguist arrived, the Other had been waiting for a while.

"I think I've got some answers!" he screamed as the Linguist approached. "The mysterious stranger, remember?"

"Still thinking about that?"

"Have you read *Don Quixote?*"

"A long time ago."

"What does Don Quixote read?"

"Chivalry books, or something."

"That's irrelevant. What else does he read?"

"I guess I forgot, I'm too busy."

"*Don Quixote!*"

"Yes?"

"That's what he reads!"

"What does he read?"

"*Don Quixote!*"

"Yes, Don Quixote, what does he read?"

"But I'm telling you!"

"*Don Quixote?!*"

"Yes, who else? You understand?"

"No, that's what *he* reads?"

"That's what *who* reads?! Don Quixote reads *Don Quixote!*"

" . . . "

"We've got no extension: we're characters in a piece!"

"Have you been getting enough rest lately?"

"A dialogue, actually."

"I see. And how can you tell?"

"I've got some evidence. It looks as if we're constructed."

"Isn't everything?"

"Our every word seems to merge with some other word, as if to meet a purpose. Only rarely do we digress, and when we do, we don't talk about politics or the weather, but about the nature of science or the role of mathematics . . . "

"We're digressing right now."

"We're reflecting on our existence!"

"Isn't that a good sign?"

"It's not conclusive. And instead of examining those grand matters, which are basically beyond our grasp, I'd worry about specifics. For example, my idioms are off here and there, and I'm coming up with jokes I'd normally never make!"

"I'm happy to hear that."

"And wormholes like this are the stuff of science fiction comics . . . "

"That's disappointing."

"I think I should like to call my solicitor."

"If we really do inhabit some mere abstract space, this peculiar exchange should go on for some time, and the plot should unravel with us searching for clues, as if in a bad detective story . . . "

Everybody hold your breath.

O: . . .

L: You're too paranoid. These questions about existence were basically left (un)settled in the seventeenth century, and they're ultimately boring. It may be that we're indeed constructed in a mental space of some sort; but we can't tell. Besides, mental spaces are considerably tidier than what's out there.

3.1 (Virtually) Necessary Properties
  (wherein some extraordinary conjectures on alien languages
  are skillfully provided by the daring Linguist)

O: Very well; but I've alerted you (primarily because you ascribe no theoretical consequence to mere characters). So let me move on to indispensable stuff, such as those parts of the symbolic system that come, as you'd say, "for free," because they are (virtually) conceptually necessary . . .

L: Yes, we have to very carefully distinguish properties that don't need to be stipulated as properties of UG from properties that are specific to Human and that maybe Martian wouldn't have.

O: Ah, so I'm finally going to grasp some alien languages!

---

assumptions about Merge

L: These aren't easy matters to determine. First, there's a theoretical issue in judging what "simplest" or "conceptually necessary" means. Whenever I say, "This is optimal," I really mean, "This is an optimal solution." There may be others. In fact, if things weren't that way, we'd just go to the Math Department and ask them to give us the solution to the grammar of Human—but we don't do that with empirical research. Second, there's a practical issue: specific properties of language aren't necessarily observable in behavior. So let's recap. To construct what linguists call phrase markers (a representation of phrases), we need an operation of **merger** (let's in fact call it *Merge*) at the core of C$_{\text{HL}}$.

O: Otherwise, presumably we'd crash, at PF or LF.

L: Which means, first, that Merge is externally determined, in terms of properties of those interfaces. Second, consider the assumptions we make about Merge. We take it to be a **binary operation** on phrase markers.

O: Which isn't conceptually necessary.

L: In turn, we have to separate lexical and functional items from the lexicon that enter into the merger.

O: Which again isn't "for free" . . .

L: Yeah, but we should return to this issue when we understand the system better [see chap. 6]. As for the objects in the array A, we assume they're collections of features, part of universal vocabularies for PF and LF which should be mentally represented.

O: And whose nature presumably derives from that of the A/P and I/C components.

L: Yes—here we may be getting to what you want. Suppose that Martian symbols are also collections of features. (It's hard to see what else they could be, but keep in mind that this is also an assumption.) Take for instance any two symbols, and consider the options we have of merging them. That is, for any α and β, what is the nature of the object γ that we get by applying Merge to (α, β) [see fig. 3.1]?

<hr>

constituents and labels

O: I presume that interpreting conditions would detail that, somehow, γ must include α and β. I took you to be assuming that language has got phrases, which is like saying that an expression is not interpreted as a mere sequence of lexical items.

Dangerous Liasons. (Same Choice)

Figure 3.1

The fact that sequences of words arrange themselves into phrases is possibly the oldest observation of linguistics. Medieval grammarians went so far as to describe specific modes of dependency that create phrasal constructions and argued that these relations are always binary (Covington 1984). Phrases are determined by way of "constituency tests" of the sort developed by structuralist linguists. Intuitively, phrases are units of an order higher than that of lexical items, and specific combinations of these items produce specific sorts of phrases.

Figure 3.2

Keep in mind the following assumptions about categories that must be true in order for the Linguist's argument to be valid:

(i) a. Syntactic categories are sets of features.
     b. Features are just properties with some given value (determining whether a given category has that feature).
     c. The properties of phrases are drawn exclusively from the properties of the elements that constitute them.
     d. Phrases are built from their parts in a uniform way.

(ia) and (ib) follow from virtual conceptual necessity, given an elementary set theory and obvious assumptions about simplicity (e.g., "all-or-nothing" values as in (ib) are more basic than scalar values). (ic) and (id) follow from substantive properties of LF, such as its inclusiveness and its uniformity.

Even more basic assumptions about syntactic objects are also required:

(ii) a. To construct phrase markers (phrasal constructs), C_{HL} includes a Merge operation.
     b. Merge is a binary operation.

(iia) arguably follows from substantive properties of LF, and (iib) is deduced below (see figs. 3.17 and 3.24).

L: Yeah, and lots of strings of words are ambiguous, which makes sense if the phrasal arrangement of these words is different for each interpretation [see fig. 3.2]. In general, given how we interpret the simplest relations between, say, predicates like *appear* or *read* or *intelligent* and their arguments (elements like *this idea,* or *the reader,* or *Socrates*), we must know the differences among different kinds of phrases that enter into these relations. So the object we're dealing with when we're merging α and β has to at least be the set {α, β}, the simplest object we can construct assuming that α and β are the **constituents** of γ [1]:

(1)   {α, β}

O: Is that all? Mustn't we say something about the type of object that (1) is?

L: For empirical reasons, apparently we do; for instance, verb phrases behave differently from noun phrases, at both PF and LF. So you're right: we have to determine the type γ of the object {α, β} (which we may represent as {γ, {α, β}}, calling the underlined γ the **label** of the phrasal object).

O: So the syntactic objects you're considering thus far are, first, lexical items, and second, combinations like that in (1), with a certain label whose properties we must determine.

L: Yes, in the simplest instance, α and β come right out of the lexicon, which is just a list of items of some sort. But of course γ doesn't come out of that list, and so we have to figure out what it is. In the ideal world, it shouldn't be anything but a set of properties which ultimately come down to the properties that are encoded in lexical items, so that γ doesn't have any reality of its own, apart from what it gets from being a relation between α and β.

O: Because, otherwise, your representations wouldn't have the property of what you've termed "inclusiveness" [see sec. 2.5], and you'd be departing from an "inflationary" syntactic model, adding extraneous elements as you go along . . .

L: Furthermore, γ should be determined from (α, β) in a **uniform** way—the procedure doesn't depend on a given choice of α or β.

O: That's sensible; if we're looking for universal laws, that is.

L: So the question is, given our assumptions [see fig. 3.2], what subset of features of α and β is γ going to be?

_____ projection is the only valid set-theoretic option for Merge

O: Assuming set theory and an optimal world, surely you must admit that the most basic options are (i) γ is the **union** of α and β; (ii) γ is the **intersection** of α and β; (iii) γ is identical to α or to β. Other possibilities exist, but they don't follow from conceptual necessity. If I take your assumptions earnestly, these are the first options that should be ventured.

L: Agreed; so let's consider them. Do you see any problems with (ii)?

O: The only problem I perceive is that if α and β haven't any features in common, their intersection is the null set, which means γ would have no properties at all! I don't see how this option can be general for Human, though I suppose it could be true about a fictitious language where given phrases haven't any properties, and speakers don't produce these phrases and don't give them any particularly structured meanings. Conceivably, that's telepathy!

L: There . . . That's the first thing you've learned about alien languages: they could be using your option (ii).

O: I love it. We've got Betazoid sussed out . . .

L: Seriously, though, general merger shouldn't proceed this way.

O: What about (i)? You said that verbs are thought of as $[+V, -N]$, correct? And nouns are thought of as, what? $[-V, +N]$ [see fig. 2.23]. Now, if I want to merge, for example, *dig* and *this* (I love American slang), then I'm relating a $[-V, +N]$ element and a $[+V, -N]$ element. That should yield an indeterminate object. Should it not?

L: Yes, if the system of features is binary (all or nothing), and the values are opposite (something does or doesn't have a property), there shouldn't be a value for something which is both $[+V]$ and $[-V]$, or $[+N]$ and $[-N]$. The union of the features of *dig* and *this* results in an object which has no definite characterization.

O: Hah! So aliens that use option (i) have got a quantum language! Oh, I do love this game . . . This must be the way shapeshifters talk!

L: Another one of your alien creatures . . .

O: They're unstable at the particle level . . . Really wonderful. But the rest of the universe must be using some version of (iii), which should include Klingons, Vulcans, et cetera, et cetera. Most humanoids.

two projection options?

L: Let's call these the class of languages that *project*. So far, there are two projection options, as you said: α can project or β can project, which means that $\underline{\gamma}$ has either the features of α or the features of β. So in our example, either *dig* projects, or *this* does.

O: Yes, but intuitively, I'd like to say that *dig this* is a "dig" and not a "this" . . . Then it would seem as though we want *dig* to project, do we not?

L: I think that's generally true, yes. So then the plan is to show that "dumb" mergers fail.

O: On conceptual grounds alone, wouldn't we want every merger to be unambiguous—that is, to allow only one projection? That would be a more elegant theory!

L: Not only that; it would be very much in the spirit of the whole program. Remember: PF and LF are where substantive properties are expressed, and the rest is formal. If you think about it, to say that there are two possible ways of merging two objects suggests that there's something substantive about Merge: if we do it this way, we get one thing; if we do it that way, we get something else. That looks like the wrong approach. There should be an explicit, formal way of doing Merge, and then if we failed to do it that way, the derivation should be canceled, because we did something impossible. So let's just assert (2):

(2) *Definition of Merge*

Given a term $\tau_i = \alpha$ that is targeted for merger, and a term $\tau_j = \beta$ that is to merge with τ_i, τ_j *merges* with τ_i if and only if a new term $\{\underline{l}, \{\tau_i, \tau_j\}\}$ is obtained, such that $\{\underline{l}, \{\tau_i, \tau_j\}\}$ immediately dominates τ_i and τ_j and $\underline{l} = \alpha$.

O: I told you I'm not impressed by formulae! I think I've understood nothing beyond the *the*'s and the *and*'s . . . **Terms? Target?** Even the notion **dominates** isn't clear in this context . . . What are you on about, sir?!

L: Look, "terms" are just objects that the formal system recognizes: the elements in the system that enter into and result from various constructive operations. When you do arithmetic, *2* and *3* are the terms of the "plus" operation in 2 + 3. Well, in the same way, α and β can be terms of the linguistic operation Merge. This can be defined precisely, but I didn't want to alarm you even more, so I was trying to just go with your intuitive understanding [see chap. 4, (17)]. "Target" is used to encode the basic **asymmetry** of the linguistic operations that build structure. That is, if what we're saying is right, α and β don't merge; rather, β merges *with* α, the element that projects. So to be able to talk about this, we call α the "target" of merger. As for "dominates," all I can say is that the notion is easier to describe than to define explicitly at this stage [see app.]. Intuitively, though, whenever we have a hierarchical structure, we obviously have domination relations, right?

O: What you mean by "dominates," then, must be what people mean by this notion when they talk about, for example, the structure of trees. The trunk dominates the branches, and the branches dominate the leaves, and the trunk dominates the leaves as well (because it dominates the branches), et cetera. If that's right, then, let's see . . . immediate domination would be the direct relation between the trunk and the branches, but not the relation between the trunk and the leaves, because only the branches immediately dominate the leaves.

L: I couldn't have said it better.

O: Then, fancy words aside, (2) is saying that a linguistic phrase marker is a way of encoding the asymmetry of Merge.

L: That's a fair interpretation of a phrase marker, yes. You can see the effects of this asymmetry in the following graph [2]:

(3)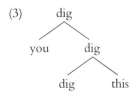

O: And how did the system know that, in this instance, *dig* is targeted for merger, instead of *this* or *you?*

L: We'll obviously have to encode into the system something to the effect that it's because of *dig's* properties that it, and not *this* or *you,* is targeted for merger. The intuition is that *dig* is "missing something" which *you* and *this* provide, but that intuition is going to have to be fleshed out as we go along: we'll have to come up with a feature of *dig* that's somehow satisfied by having *this* merged with it, and so on. For now, we should leave it at that [see chap. 6]. However, I should point out an obvious difference that you can already see between *dig* and *you* or *this:* the latter don't project any further, while the former does—twice. This fact is important for a variety of linguistic subsystems, and so linguists distinguish what we call **maximal projections** (X^{max}), and **heads** (X^{min}) [see fig. 3.3]. A #head# is basically a lexical item, and a |maximal projection| is a category which isn't immediately dominated by any other category with the same label [3]:

(4) a.

$$| \text{dig} |$$

|#you#| dig

#dig# |#this#|

b. |{dig, {{dig, {#dig#, |#this#|}}, |#you#|}}|

|#you#| ←*MERGE*→ |{dig, {#dig#, |#this#|}}|

|#dig#| ←*MERGE*→ |#this#|

Note that elements like the intermediate *dig,* which aren't inside any sort of brackets (either "#" or "|" in the notation I'm now using), have no theoretical status from the point of view of the subsystems of UG that make use of maximal projections and heads.

O: I see; but their structure is nevertheless there . . .

L: Yeah, the intermediate projections are computationally present: they're terms which result from some merger and engage in further merger. In fact, if you look at (4b), which is nothing but (4a) as it proceeds derivationally, observe that first |#this#| merges with the maximal projection |#dig#|. *Dig* is a maximal projection at this point, because it's not yet immediately dominated by anything. Of course, after the merger, *dig* is dominated by the resulting, more complex object, whose label is *dig*. Precisely because of this, *dig* ceases to be a maximal projection. Now the intermediate projection is the maximal projection, since prior to its merger with *you* it isn't dominated by anything. In sum, what counts as a maximal projection is relative to what element dominates what other element, and it changes as the derivation proceeds. At the point of merger, the two terms of the Merge operation are maximal projections, although later on one of them gets "buried" inside its own projection. From that point on, although the "buried" element is still a term, it won't lead to a formal object which in itself determines a convergent derivation, as a head or a maximal projection does.

O: So this is like the relation between a physiological process and its corresponding anatomical structure [4]. Although the structure is there, whether it has an effect on the process depends on the specific details of the system. For example, skin tissue has a superficial layer of dead cells (the stratum corneum) on top of an inner layer of live cells. Eventually, dead cells fall off, and others replace them. Of course, dead cells play no role in the process of tactile sensation; nevertheless, they're structurally there, and have consequences—they create a protective film over the sensitive, inner dermis.

L: As usual, be careful with analogies. (In our example, only external layers of structure are relevant for linguistic processes—so this is more like your skin example backward . . .) Note, also, that *you* and *this* are simultaneously both heads and maximal projections [5]. So the properties of the projection phenomenon are quite specific to it.

O: But these distinctions you're now making between levels of projection aren't part of a theory of how Merge works; they seem to be entirely outside this system.

L: Yes, but keep in mind that the phenomenon we're investigating is projection, not Merge. As a phenomenon, projection has proper-

Figure 3.3

Some traditional observations suggest that only heads or maximal projections move to different positions within a phrase marker:

(i) a. *Head movement*

   was it ____ too good to be true?

b. *Maximal projection movement*

   [*too* [*good to be true*]] though it was [____], he nonetheless believed it

c. *Intermediate projection movement*

   *[*good to be true*] though it was [too [____]], he nonetheless believed it

Similar facts obtain for gapping/ellipsis phenomena:

(ii) a. *Head gapping*

   this *is* too good to be true, and that ____ too true to be good

   (is)

b. *Maximal projection ellipsis*

   this is [*too* [*good to be true*]], and so is that [_____]

   (too good to be true)

c. *Intermediate projection ellipsis*

   *this is [*too* [*good to be true*]], and so is that [nearly too [_____]]

   (good to be true)

Figure 3.4

General terms for the X-bar schema:

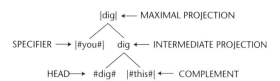

Specifiers and complements must be maximal projections; however, they can be heads as well (though they need not be—thus, consider replacing *you* in the diagram by *your aunt*).

ties that result from the operation of Merge, and properties that result from the structures obtained. In particular, notions like head or maximal projection are necessary for various subsystems of grammar that specifically operate on these structures, and intermediate projections aren't. It just seems to be a property of Human that its subsystems operate on lexical items or maximal phrases, and nothing else [see fig. 3.3]. Why this is, is a very interesting substantive issue in itself, and it should relate to properties of PF and LF. Intuitively, it seems that PF cares (among other things) about **words,** perhaps taking them as accentual units for articulatory/perceptual reasons. In turn, LF seems to be concerned with phrases encoding relations of projection between a head and some element it merges with. So for instance we call *this* in (4) the **complement** of *dig,* and *you* the **specifier** (or "spec") of *dig,* and LF seems to be extremely sensitive to these sorts of dependencies. (Excuse the terminological shower, but I'm afraid you'll need to familiarize yourself with these specific terms.) [See fig. 3.4.]

——————— *on why the system deals only with heads and maximal projections*

O: Now presumably when the child acquiring a language encounters tokens such as *dig this,* he immediately assigns them a structure like the one in (4) [6].

L: That's the hope. Of course, the theoretical desire is to allow very few options—none, ideally, except perhaps for PF variations in terms of the morphological strength of functional items. The child's task is then very highly constrained by the fact that linguistic structures must be projected this way.

O: I see that as a step towards a feasible theory. However, these . . . heads, complements, specifiers, maximal projections . . . How much of all that jabber is conceptually necessary? Let's not lose sight of that!

L: In the simplest possible world we expect all subsystems of language to be looking at the same structures, hopefully those that come for free at interface levels and thus don't have to be motivated formally for C_{HL} but instead follow from substantive or necessary properties of the system. So here we have an interesting situation. Empirically, linguists have found that C_{HL} works on heads and maximal projections. That's just a fact [see fig. 3.3]. But why should it be? Once again, if we say this is just how C_{HL} works, we're ascribing a pretty substantive property to the computational system (it makes a real difference whether a projection is maximal or not). If C_{HL} only encodes formal properties, the empirical fact we've found should follow from the properties of the interfaces.

O: You mentioned that LF is sensitive to phrases—it's enchanting to see you comfortable with that assumption. Finally, an LF property!

L: I'm generally cautious about what the properties of LF are because we don't have much evidence about what bare output conditions on that side of the grammar really are. But inasmuch as phrases are real in Human (and few things seem to be as real as that) and their nature doesn't seem to stem from PF, which is about phonological contours and (perhaps) word-level units, then it would seem that phrases and their dependencies really are LF stuff. Of course, this all depends on certain assumptions, but the assumptions don't seem to be particularly unreasonable. So then one hopes that LF is the kind of system that's capable of seeing heads and maximal projections, for some reason. The intuition is, in part, that LF is a purely inclusive level, and all its information must be specified in the lexical items that enter the derivation. So it's hardly surprising that LF should be sensitive to lexical items (i.e., "heads," in our technical sense).

O: Hold on. I thought you were taking words to be PF stuff.

L: Words are words, and you shouldn't confuse them with either heads or phrases. Heads are items from a lexicon—technically, trivial phrases with no dependents. Some lexical items never make it as PF units, because they have no phonological weight. Inflectional morphemes, for instance, typically aren't separate words, even though they're heads [see sec. 2.3]. In contrast, words are units of a more complex sort than heads, with both a PF reflex and an LF reflex [see chap. 6]. PF-wise, a word is, roughly speaking, a collection of phonetic symbols that arranges itself around a stress peak. So there's no confusion here if we keep things clear [see fig. 3.5]. Now LF appears to be about phrases, trivial (heads) or not—in which case they appear to need to be maximal. This itself is interesting. It would seem that maximal projections are domains where lexical dependencies are established. For instance, a verb phrase seems to be the domain where the verb establishes its lexical connections with its arguments, roughly as in (4) [see chap. 6] [7]. It seems that LF isn't really happy with projections whose lexical relations aren't

Figure 3.5

Word-level units may not directly correspond to units in the lexicon. This is obvious for compounds, which are treated as PF blocks of some sort and yet are made up of different lexical items *(box delivery, check payment, first class)*.

Word-level units may also have internal structure that is clearly syntactic. For instance, a verb like *walked* or a noun like *friends* has both a lexical part *(walk, friend)* and a grammatical part (the morpheme *-ed* or *-s*). How to analyze these sorts of elements has traditionally been a much-discussed topic. In principle, three possibilities exist. The first alternative goes back to Chomsky 1955. It basically asserts that the lexicon lists the morphemes and the lexical items separately, and they are joined into single words in the course of the derivation. However, in many languages important morphophonemic readjustments are necessary; the so-called irregular patterns of English tense and plural morphology offer a glimpse of this sort of difficulty. Thus, if one were to hypothesize *-ed* as a marker of past tense (in order to obtain *walked, canned,* etc.), what would one have to say about past forms like *knew* and *stood*? In view of difficulties like this one, a second theory proposes that lexical items come fully inflected from the lexicon. A third alternative is that lexicon items start their derivational history in extremely abstract guises. Lasnik, forthcoming, suggests that, in fact, languages may vary along these lines. If correct, this view entails that the previous two are not theoretical alternatives, but parametric options.

fully determined, and so intermediate projections are objects which LF may not be "seeing," in some sense. In fact, we hope that in the end it's this property of LF that predicts why Merge should be defined in the asymmetric way expressed in (2). In any case, it's important to note that we've reached this conclusion about LF just in terms of the internal coherence of the system (by exploring, for instance, the kinds of elements that move—heads and maximal projections), without having to examine the properties of the poorly understood I/C components. So it's possible to make progress on what LF should look like if we take our assumptions and our research program seriously.

O: The way you put it—that because of LF, C_{HL} only sees heads and phrases—it would seem that those operations that take place after Spell-Out, on the phonetic side of the model [see chap. 2, (6)], may not be limited to heads and maximal projections.

L: You're right, in principle—which relates to the claim I made yesterday that the mapping to PF is neither inclusive nor uniform [see sec. 2.5]. In fact, it's rather clear that the phonological component needs to see all the internal structure of a projected phrase, if only to assign a phonetic representation to its parts and determine its general prosodic properties [see fig. 3.6].

O: And is it not fair to say that there's nothing necessary about the mapping to LF being limited to heads and maximal projections?

L: Yes, of course; the claim is factual, and it could well be that these properties of C_{HL} aren't found in Martian. Perhaps Martian is doing more complicated tricks, looking at intermediate structures in its LF mapping . . .

3.2 Phrasal Representations

  (wherein these are discussed, and a mysterious yet true case
  is artfully exposed)

O: I say—how do we know that a given condition is internal to C_{HL}; or how do we know that it's an outside interface condition?

L: Well, of course we don't know that a priori. All we have is a phenomenon of grammar, and we make a hypothesis that plausibly accounts for it; then we go out there and test the hypothesis against different sorts of data, and see what kinds of predictions the proposal makes for the rest of the theory.

Figure 3.6

The PF component needs to see the internal structure of a projected phrase in order to assign some phonetic representation to its parts and delete all phrasal structure (of the sort in (4)), to reach objects of a prosodic and purely phonetic nature. Thus, consider the stress pattern of *blackbird* versus *black bird,* or of the different compounds that can be obtained by stressing words differently: *(he's my favorite) Mississlppi pretzel seller (but I like pretzel sellers from other states more than I like him)* versus *(he's my favorite) Mississippi prEtzel seller (but I like Mississippi bagel sellers even more).* Note also that stress may itself be a feature of the output form that was not obviously part of the lexical entry, which entails that PF cannot be an inclusive level of representation (see also the pronunciation of *Berlin* in different languages, sec. 2.7). Likewise, the mapping to PF is not uniform; it yields different sorts of outputs depending on contextual specifications (e.g., pronouncing an [s] in *electricity* [i-lek-ˈtri-sə-tē] when *electric* [i-ˈlek-trik] is in the immediate context of a suffix like *-ity*). The mapping is not uniform, either, with respect to whatever specific operations occur prior to Spell-Out (e.g., those illustrated in figure 3.3), which look very different from these phonological operations.

O: Ah, yes, the usual . . .

L: But this doesn't mean that just anything goes, and we can advance any proposal we like. As things stand now, we assume on the one hand representational elegance, and on the other hand computational elegance [see sec. 1.7]. Whatever theoretical decision we make had better be adapted to one of these two kinds of parsimony, which makes us hope that the properties we've found this way aren't ghost properties that reflect more on our mode of inquiry than on reality; but of course this isn't a guarantee for discovery.

O: Nothing is. But look here, suppose you've got this nice little phenomenon, and you've persuaded everyone with flawless arguments that it's got nothing to do with the direct workings of C_{HL}, and hence what underlies the phenomenon isn't operational economy, but convergence at the interfaces.

L: Well, I already disagree with that assumption.

O: But, please, do let me go on . . . for the sake of argument. Now, convergence can still fail in two unlike ways, at PF and at LF, and I don't even see that—a priori—one would know whether the problem that our phenomenon may illustrate needs to be a matter of PF or LF convergence. For instance, tell me whether this example is fitting. I've been thinking: consider the Latin sentence *Brutus Caesar occidit.*

———————————————————————— **Brutus Caesa<u>rem</u> occidit!**

L: I believe you mean *Caesa<u>rem</u>.*

O: I meant what I said, I'm afraid—that's the point. You say *Caesarem,* with accusative case, instead of *Caesar,* with nominative case, because you want to put this name in object position—you want Brutus to have killed Caesar . . . so trite! Had it been in subject position, you'd have said *Caesar;* believe me, I had to study Latin—ad nauseum; nay, ad infinitum! In any event, this is what you lot call **case,** isn't it? It is, indeed—well, then. Either English also has this sort of process, or else . . . well, we're dealing with a major linguistic variation here, correct?

L: It's easy to argue that English also has what can be called abstract **Case,** with a capital C [see fig. 3.7] [8].

Figure 3.7

Arguments that English has abstract Case start, first of all, with the rather concrete morphological distinctions existing among pronouns (*he, him, his, I, me, my,* etc.), as well as that between genitively marked phrases (e.g., *John's*) and all other nominal forms. However, more abstract (plausibility) arguments can be produced as well. Consider the following paradigm:

(i) [for him/John to talk to me like that] was not such a great idea

(ii) *[him/he/John to talk to me like that] was not such a great idea

(iii) [for John/*he to talk to me like that] was not such a great idea

(iv) [(the fact) that he/*him talked to me like that] was not such a great idea

The complementizer *for* is required when an infinitival sentence starts with an overt subject (compare (i) and (ii)). In languages where case is overtly marked (e.g., Latin), infinitival sentences like (i) are independently known not to involve the assignment of nominative (subject) case, unlike regular tensed sentences (iv). This suggests that *for* is somehow responsible for the (abstract) Case of the subject in (i). The idea is that nothing other than *for* could determine Case in an infinitival context, hence the ungrammaticality of (ii) when *for* is absent. The proposal is confirmed by the fact that *for* determines accusative (object) Case, and not nominative (*I did it for him/*he*), which predicts the ungrammaticality of (iii) with pronoun *he.* Of course, (iii) is grammatical with *John,* but this name is assumed to be receiving abstract accusative Case, even if it does not show up in its morphology. (Note the terminological difference: abstract <u>C</u>ase versus morphological <u>c</u>ase. A morphological case is a phonetic instantiation of abstract Case, but some abstract Cases have no morphological realization.)

O: Oh, I believe you—that's not my concern now. Here's my query. It's not clear to me how Case could be a property of the computational system. I realise I still know little about this system, but suppose for the sake of argument that I've already convinced you that it has nothing to say about Case . . .

L: So what's the point?

O: Right, well, then suppose that, in the ungrammatical *Brutus Caesar occidit,* the derivation is failing to converge at LF or PF. How do we know which of these possibilities is the correct one?

_____ Case as an interface feature

L: Maybe Case is an LF feature of some sort, ensuring that a given element that depends on a head is "there" in some sense; if a dependent of a head doesn't have Case, it's invisible to that head. From this point of view, if an element doesn't have Case, it's not a legitimate LF nominal structure and since it doesn't meet the requirements of Full Interpretation, the whole derivation crashes [9].

O: Oh, but frankly, I can come up with a plot for a PF condition as well.

L: Sure, but then you'll have to battle it out!

O: Well, let's do. I shall start with a question. When you draw phrase markers on the ground, they of course are linearised from left to right, so that for any binary relation, one element is to the right of (or, rather, comes after) the other. Now, on the one hand it's evident that most linguistic objects can't be freely scrambled; but on the other hand, the fact that we must linearise all phrasal elements might follow from the more basic fact that human speech is embedded within biological (entropic) time. Then my question is, when you draw the phrase markers, do you intend them to have the **linear order** they end up in, or is that merely an artefact of mapping a more abstract mathematical object onto a bidimensional plane?

L: Yes.

O: Most amusing. Which?

L: Well, of course this is also an empirical question . . . I think the most interesting answer is that the phrase marker is like a Calder mobile in the air—actually, some abstract space [10]. Like this:

(5)　　　|dig|

|#you#|　　dig

#dig#　|#this#|

[Unfortunately, the object the Linguist created in the air can't be reproduced on a page (but see fig. 3.8). Maybe when the film of this dialogue is shot, the moving pictures will do justice to his mobile. For now, simply imagine the object, keeping in mind that dotted lines represent relations that aren't temporally specified.]

O: Excellent; that's a rather more intriguing prospect! Very well, then—I'd say that, perhaps . . . perhaps Case is there to contribute to the linearisation of two items [11]. It is indisputable that at some point humans do linearise in biological time, is it not? Otherwise sometimes I would say *dig this* and sometimes I would say *this dig*.

L: To put your speculation in perspective, let's just remember that phrase markers are objects that we need to use in linguistics; as I've said, if anything is an established fact, it's that Human has phrases. But the phrase marker is clearly a complex object with certain formal properties, and, again, merely formal properties (setting aside those that trivially follow from conceptual necessity) should be a consequence of the external interfaces. Ideally, this is how things should work. So we should ask this very question about phrase markers: what properties do phrase markers have, and why do they have those properties and not others? Intuitively, phrase markers encode two very basic notions. On the one hand, they encode the relation between two lexical items, one of which **precedes** the other—or rather, among any number of lexical items that stand in some such relation. On the other hand, they encode the basic dependency between two (or any number of) items which relate to each other to form some kind of phrase which dominates all of its constituent parts [see app.].

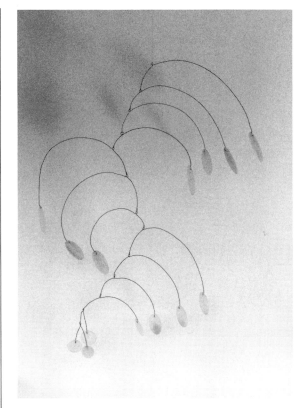

Mobile. (William B. Wade)

Figure 3.8

It does not make sense to ask whether some of the hanging shapes in this mobile are to the left or to the right of others. At any given point in time and from a given viewer perspective, a certain ordering emerges as a consequence of the mobile's structure. However, the ordering changes with time; that is the whole point of a mobile. Kayne (1994) has argued that linguists should view phrasal relations in essentially this light. The linear sequence of lexical items at PF is mapped into real time according to whatever hierarchical structure phrases have. An interesting mental exercise is to fix the order of the pieces in this mobile according to Kayne's procedure discussed in the text. (The resulting object will look roughly like half of a fish's spine.)

O: Yes, I'm glad you mention this, because I'm dead keen on raising the following point. I've had some experience with computer languages over the years, and got relatively accustomed to representing ideas like the ones you're talking about in terms of instructions of the form in (6a), taken from the work of logicomathematicians like Thue and Post, which encode rules like those in (6b):

(6) a. $M^\frown X^\frown N \rightarrow M^\frown Y^\frown N$

     for X a symbol, and M, N, Y strings of symbols

  b. Starting axiom: $S \rightarrow A\ B$

    Rewrite rules: [1] $B \rightarrow C\ D$

                 [2] $D \rightarrow E\ F$

                 [3] $F \rightarrow E$

                 [4] $A \rightarrow i$

                 [5] $C \rightarrow s$

                 [6] $E \rightarrow e$

It's easy to see that the grammar in (6b) allows one to produce derivations like this:

(7) S

    AB   (by starting axiom)

    ACD   (by [1])

    ACEF   (by [2])

    ACEE   (by [3])

    ACEe   (by [6])

    ACee   (by [6])

    Asee   (by [5])

    isee   (by [4])

This particular grammar always generates the string *isee*.

L: I'm quite familiar with these systems myself, though I think it's slightly misleading to call them grammars, and to think they generate languages, without further qualifications [12].

O: Why, though?

L: Consider a familiar phrasal representation of the string *isee* as generated by your grammar [and see fig. 3.9]:

(8)
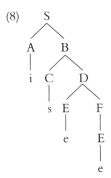

You have to admit that, while this structure corresponds to the string *isee*, it has little to do with the structure of the Human sentence *I see.* Linguists soon realized that they needed to limit the kinds of structures that rule systems like the one in (6a) allow. The rules in (6b), for example, are in accord with the schema in (6a); but nobody wants to say that these are linguistic rules! We can construct even crazier rules that respect the schema in (6a), but yield structures that don't resemble anything like what we see in Human. For instance, an obvious variant of (6) yields (9):

(9)
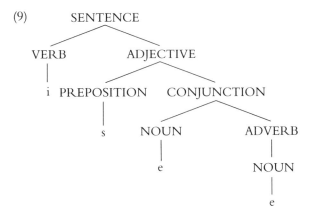

We can say that hypothetical grammar weakly generates the string *isee*, but it doesn't strongly generate the *structure* that humans assigns to the sentence *I see.*

O: These rules merely encode hierarchical relations; they encode nothing about the specific phrasal relations allowed in Human.

Figure 3.9

The grammars presupposed in these examples (of the sort discussed in Chomsky 1957) are trivial algorithms that manipulate items from a given vocabulary (such as A, B, C, D, E, and F in (6)). They start with some arbitrary symbol S and rewrite it as some string of symbols from the vocabulary. This is done until vocabulary items are reached that carry instructions for not being rewritten any more (these are *i*, *s*, and *e* in (6)). (Whereas lowercase symbols cannot be rewritten any further, capital symbols must.) (6a) explicitly states that, in the context of strings M . . . N, the string containing the single symbol X must be rewritten as string Y, which may contain one or more concatenated symbols. Concatenation is commonly signaled by the symbol ⌢, although it is usually omitted in informal writing (i.e., M⌢Y⌢N is expressed as MYN). In this way, sets of strings are generated that usually go by the name of elements of a **formal language**. An object with the familiar form in (8) can be thought of as an informal characterization of the following set:

(i) PM = {S, AB, ACD, ACEF, ACeF, ACeE, ACEE, ACEe, ACee, AsD, AsEF, AsEE, AsEe, AseF, AseE, Asee, iB, iCD, iCEF, iCEE, iCEe, iCeF, iCeE, iCee, isD, isEF, isEE, isEe, iseF, iseE, isee}

To understand how this set is generated, note that one need not follow the derivation of *isee* outlined in (7); it can also proceed as in (ii) (assuming, as the derivation in (7) shows, that the rules being used are not ordered):

(ii) S
    AB   (by starting axiom)
    iB   (by [4])
    iCD (by [1])
    isD (by [5])
    isEF (by [2])
    iseF (by [6])
    iseE (by [3])
    isee (by [6])

In fact, consider *all* possible equivalent derivations of the string *isee* (i.e., all possible ways in which the grammar in (6) can generate *isee*, including (7) and (ii)). All of the derivational lines in each of the equivalent derivations can be lumped into a set of strings; that set is PM in (i), a phrase marker—by definition a set of strings for the equivalent derivations of a given terminal string like *i* ⌢*s*⌢*e*⌢*e.*

L: That's precisely the point. Human only allows structures of a very particular kind. For instance, it only allows phrases XP of an X type if they immediately dominate a category of an X type. Thus, say, a verb phrase must have as its immediate constituent either a smaller verb phrase or a verb; a noun phrase must have as its immediate constituent either a smaller noun phrase or a noun; and so on. This is what we called projection earlier today; traditionally, it was called the headedness of structures [13].

O: Very well, so we must restrict our rules from those in (6a) to only those which have the format in (10):

(10) $M^\frown X^\frown N \rightarrow M^\frown \ldots ^\frown X^\frown \ldots ^\frown N$

L: You can do that, but you should start wondering whether we need the rules at all, for the description of Human. The rules go top-down in generating phrasal structures, and you may wonder why not go bottom-up, as we did a while ago [see sec. 3.1]—in other words, start with a lexical item and derive the structure that dominates it [14].

O: I believe I can prove to you that the structures obtained that way are mathematically identical to the structures obtained with my system [15].

advantages of projection rules

L: No need to; you're right again. But remember, we're not doing mathematics; we're trying to find out what's true. We now have two ways of achieving the same results, so one of those two ways isn't correct (perhaps neither is), in the sense that it doesn't correspond to the mental representation of the relevant structures. We always have to remember that we're trying to model the human mind, the actual tacit knowledge that speakers of Human have in their mind when thinking Human. Well, then, what has to go? The top-down rule or the bottom-up projection?

O: That's a tough question, if both devices capture the same information . . .

L: A tough question it is, but we have to (at least try to) figure out the answer to it [16]. Again, it may be that neither of the procedures we've considered is correct, and they're just superficial expressions of a more profound process that future investigations will unearth. Meanwhile, though, we have to proceed with what we've got, trying to decide between the two competing hypotheses. So then the question I put to you is this. Assume that as a result of your linguistic research you've convinced yourself that only a few sorts of structures exist in Human. First, you already know that all Human phrases are headed. Second, suppose you also admit that all Human phrases are binary branching. Now, isn't it true that nothing in the format in (6a) predicts these two facts?

O: Certainly. That's why I narrowed (6a) down to (10). We could restrict the format in (10) even further, in an appropriate way. For example, suppose I devise a **metarule** that says something like "Only rules which exhibit binary branching are ever possible" [17]. What then?

L: You've added *two* stipulations to your theory. (10) is of course more stipulative than (6a), and now you're proposing to add more stipulations, to allow only for rules obeying the format in (11):

(11) M⌢X⌢N → M⌢X⌢Y⌢N
      for X and Y symbols, and M and N strings of symbols

In order to compare the elegance of the two theories (the one implicit in (11) and the one I introduced before [in sec. 3.1]), we have to note that the bottom-up theory doesn't need to assume any such restrictions. Remember, the Merge operation builds in a certain asymmetry which results in a binary projection.

O: Steady on! I accepted without argument that Merge is binary. That too is a stipulation.

L: But that can be conceptually justified on the basis that binary relations are the simplest kind of all [18]. More importantly, I can show you later on that nonbinary mergers can be ruled out independently [see sec. 3.5]. In turn, the rewrite rules have to be constrained both in terms of their being binary and in terms of their yielding headed structures.

———————   *phrase structure rules do not say much about linguistic structures*

O: Your second point at least is justified. And to show you that I'm an honourable arguer, I shall even give you another conceptual

Figure 3.10

One interesting illustration of the useful work of rewrite rules involves the Fibonacci series (1, 1, 2, 3, 5, . . .), which is manifested innumerable times and in innumerable ways in the natural world. As it turns out, this series can be elegantly generated by two simple rewrite rules:

(i) a. $0 \rightarrow 1$
     b. $1 \rightarrow 0\,1$

As figure 3.9 indicates, standard rewrite systems involve the random rewriting of given symbols as particular strings, according to the rules. However, Aristid Lindenmayer extended this Chomskyan system in a curious way (see Rozenberg and Salomaa 1986): by requiring that all relevant rewrite rules be applied to an entire derivational line. In this L-system, as it is known, the first step is to rewrite 0 as 1, as per (ia), and the second is to rewrite 1 as 0 1, as per (ib) (this much is uninteresting). But at this point the Chomskyan system allows two different derivational alternatives: either to rewrite 0 as 1, or to rewrite 1 as 0 1. An L-system offers no such option: both operations must be undertaken simultaneously:

(ii)

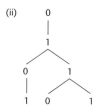

The same is true of the next derivational line, which must be rewritten as follows:

(iii)

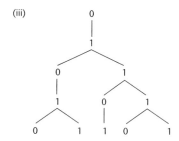

And so on. Now count the number of symbols per line; obviously, the Fibonacci series emerges. From this perspective, the series is elegantly encoded as the result of applying, in an L-system, the basic rules in (i).

argument for the theory you seem to sympathise with. Structures generated bottom-up by Merge are more specific than structures generated top-down by rewrite rules. Rewrite rules generate (i.e., describe) plants (leaves and roots), river networks, vein/artery/ nerve networks, genetic structures . . .

L: Oh, and many, many others. The structures you've mentioned all have a single root, but nothing about rewrite rules per se forces this either (that is, there's no theoretical reason why the X between the strings M and N in all versions of (6a) should be a single symbol, instead of a string of symbols—the latter assumption is the simplest of all!). Removing stipulations about single-rootedness, rewrite rules can generate snowflakes, animal paths, growth functions, all sorts of mathematical curves, fractal structures . . . you name it! These are very basic devices [see fig. 3.10].

O: That's what I'm getting at. They're so frightfully general that they tell us nothing specific to linguistics. To say that linguistic structures are characterised by rewrite rules has the same sort of theoretical status as saying that traditional physical forces are scalar. It's true, but it doesn't tell us much. So we have to get cracking and see what specific functions are operating and why. To say that physics uses number theory is a banality nowadays (although the assumption could of course be wrong). And I now see that saying that linguistics uses the rewrite rules that are used to describe formal languages may well be a banality—another truism (which again is made on the basis of a very general assumption that could itself be wrong).

L: It's not that the structures (or rather, some structures) described by rewrite rules don't obtain in linguistics. They do. (As you say, unless the entire business is deeply wrong.) But that's not the end of the story. It could be that these structures exist because of devices that generate them which have nothing to do with whatever devices generate genetic codes, river networks, nerve branchings, snowflakes, or fractals. Unless we're prepared to find out at this point in time what underlies all of these. That's a tough one, though [19].

O: Indeed. For now, we should perhaps go on doing hydrodynamics and topology and neurobiology . . . separately . . .

L: And of course linguistics. Which shows you—as we've seen— that phrase structures are trivially and naturally generated in terms of Merge.

O: And Merge is part of UG—a grammar in the appropriate sense of the word.

knowing rules and knowing principles

L: That's the intention. Incidentally, it's possible to add several nails to the coffin of rewrite rules as primitive linguistic devices. First, there's a very important conceptual distinction between the two sorts of theories. The rule theory is claiming that, apart from lexical items, humans know lists of rules like the ones we've looked at; the Merge theory, instead, claims that humans only know lexical items—the general procedure we're calling Merge follows from virtual conceptual necessity, assuming LF is about phrases and lexical items are sets of features. Knowledge about lexical items is unavoidable and trivial. That's what human children spend years attaining and modifying—it's not even controversial that they need to learn (and thus end up knowing) that. Then the real distinction between the two theories is this: one says that humans know sets of rules, the other says nothing of the kind. The second theory is obviously simpler, and poses fewer problems in determining how it is that the human species evolved to know what it does. So, for instance, philosophers often raise the question of what it means for humans to know rules. Well, the question doesn't even arise if humans don't know such rules, at least in the case of language.

O: Needless to say, philosophers will still worry about knowing whatever principles underlie Merge. But at the very least there are fewer of those to worry about!

L: Still, there's more to be said—and this relates to your questions about linearity in Human expressions. We obviously don't want rewrite rules to linearize all sorts of structures out there in the universe. Some might be linearized; for instance, one of the main distinctions among different genetic codes is precisely in terms of how they're linearized, whatever that follows from. But other structures that rewrite rules generate are nonlinear. Take a look at most plants in your garden: their branches are rarely mapped into any linear sequence, and they bundle into various floral arrangements. So the formalism itself shouldn't (and doesn't, in the absence of further stipulations) give the appropriate result for Human structures. The question, then, is how to linearize these.

O: Nothing in the mechanism of Merge gives us linearity either!

Furthermore, once a sufficiently complex object is generated, clear regularities emerge. For example, the string of symbols 0 1 could be compiled as a single, complex symbol 0-1, since 0 and 1 are always adjacent:

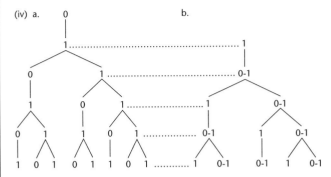

(iv) a.   b.

Now note that the object in (ivb) is generated with the rules in (v):

(v) a. $1 \rightarrow$ 0-1
    b. 0-1 $\rightarrow$ 1 0-1

It is easy to see the similarity between the rule systems in (i) and (v). This similarity results in an object with so-called fractal characteristics; that is, (iva) is similar to itself (or self-similar), in that its very basic structure appears indefinitely at different levels of complexity (e.g., (ivb)). Intuitively, even a huge version of the Fibonacci object (expanded to an nth derivational line of arbitrarily large size)—so huge that an observer could no longer keep track of the minuscule Fibonacci structure that went into the basic building of the object—would still manifest a Fibonacci structure, albeit at a different scale. The beautiful sunflower on the jacket of this book involves this basic property of L-systems.

Note finally that the systems of rules in (i) and (v) crucially do not involve the "headedness" stipulation in (10), which is central to linguistic systems. That is, in order for the Fibonacci series to be described as above, it must be possible to rewrite a symbol of type X (e.g., 0) as a symbol of type Y (e.g., 1).

3.3 Precedence by Hierarchy

(wherein the Linguist introduces the intriguing command relation, of great use throughout this dialogue, and the Other takes him on a most amusing trip)

L: Hear me out. Remember that projection itself doesn't encode anything but the basic asymmetry of Merge, and Merge is ultimately imposed on the system because it needs to end up with a single object, not a wild collection of objects, to ship to the interpretive components.

O: Then that part of the phrase marker is actually deduced. It's not that the phrase marker doesn't encode this information (via domination of phrases over their constituent parts) . . .

L: The phrase marker does capture this, but it's not a substantive property of the system. It's a formal property that actually follows from requirements on the interpretive interfaces. Then, after having asked whether we can deduce dominance relations, we can ask the same question for precedence relations. And this is where your speculation may come into play: at PF, since this system is embedded in real time through concrete articulatory/perceptual mechanisms that appear to demand a strict sequential concatenation of symbols, we need to map the abstract relations represented in the "mobile" in (5) into some kind of sequence that corresponds rather directly with a possible time sequence.

———————————   *methodological considerations on the locus of explanation of a phenomenon*

O: That was expressly the point I was trying to make. For any two constituents that are related in a binary fashion in (5), you must decide on one taking linear precedence. And my thought was that this is what (abstract) Case does for noun phrases. The element with Case might be linearly ordered with respect to an element without Case, in such a way that the system maps one directly in front of the other, and then that result can be shipped to PF, where the derivation won't crash. Were things not organised this way, the derivation wouldn't meet Full Interpretation at PF. *Quod erat demonstrandum!*

L: Quite easily done! But that was just a speculation, remember?

O: So was yours.

L: Which is why I have no problem admitting that Case features may not be interpretable features of either PF or LF.

O: But then they must be properties that the computational system cares about!

L: So? Case is whatever it is, and the possibilities are: either an interpretable property of PF or LF, or an uninterpretable property of the system. The answer lies there somewhere.

O: Oh, come, come: where?!

L: What does it matter, a priori? The answer to your initial question (whether there's a procedure for knowing if a given phenomenon is to be accounted for in terms of PF or LF convergence, or for that matter somehow directly by the computational system) is clearly "no."

O: It took you that long to confess it?!

L: I was trying to illustrate to you that these are—

O: —empirical questions . . . !

L: But this is important. I know of no empirical way of persuading myself that a phenomenon could not have anything to do with the direct workings of C_{HL}, say (your starting assumption). Mind you, I don't even think the matter is a priori established for whether a phenomenon is driven by PF or LF! Of course, if it's about sound, then it's PF, and if it's about meaning, then it's LF. But things are rarely that clean. Is Case about sound? Well, sometimes it has a sound, and sometimes it doesn't. Is it about meaning, then? Maybe, but this isn't obvious [20]. To start with, languages don't all have the same Case system [see fig. 3.11]. Then we have to worry about why this should be so, if Case were a feature interpretable at LF—and given that we expect parameters of variation to arise only for PF reasons. That's the factual base, anyway. Could Case then be some sort of uninterpretable feature that affects only the system's computation, and in some languages may be strong enough to induce variations? If so, then that's what you have to show, with empirical arguments.

O: I suppose there's no way around that . . .

Figure 3.11

Compare the Case systems of German and Basque:

(i) a. ...daß der Johann den Peter geschickt hat
   that the-subject Johann the-object Peter sent has
   '...that Johann has sent Peter'

   b. Jonek Pello igorri du
   Jon-subject Pello-object sent has
   'Jon has sent Pello'

(ii) a. ...daß der Johann gekommen ist
   that the-subject Johann come is
   '...that Johann has come'

   b. Jon etorri da
   Jon-object come is
   'Jon has come'

(The German sentence is placed after a complementizer in order to avoid main clause movements involving the verb and one of its dependents.) German and Basque are fairly similar in that they both exhibit a basic <subject, object, verb> order, they both select the same sorts of auxiliaries for transitive (*haben/ukan* 'have') and intransitive (*sein/izan* 'be') structures, and they both mark Case overtly in noun phrases. However, they differ in what particular morphological case is chosen in each instance. The distinction is not obvious in regular transitive structures, where both German and Basque exhibit subject and object case markers. However, when there is only one verbal dependent, German marks it with subject case morphology, and Basque marks it with object case morphology. (See Grewendorf 1989 for German and Ortiz de Urbina 1989 for Basque.) Each of these types of case distribution is common among the world's languages.

L: Not if you're doing empirical science.

_____ deducing precedence relations

O: Let me return to the linearisation idea that arose in our discussion about Case, which I find most absorbing. Doesn't the linearisation view predict that only certain phrase markers—namely, those which can be linearised according to some concrete procedure—are possible Human phrase markers?

L: Yeah, that's right—and independent of your specific ideas about Case, which we don't need to (and won't) assume. The important issue, of course, is that a conjecture about a procedure for linearization limits the class of possible structures that human children even have to consider when learning a language.

O: To make the discussion concrete, can we discuss an actual condition on linearisation that you would assume?

L: Sure. But to do that, I have to introduce some auxiliary notions. As I said, a phrase marker has an obvious hierarchical structure, whereby certain phrases dominate certain others. So recall the structure in (5). You can see that |dig| dominates everything else, and *dig* dominates #dig# and |#this#|. Given these domination relations, we can define an interesting relation of grammar that linguists call **command** [21]. Recall also that the computational system C_{HL} can only see X^{max}s and X^{min}s, so command has to be defined for these categories alone, assuming it's a relation of UG.

O: Are you implying that domination is a relation intrinsic to phrase markers (any phrase markers [but see app.]), whereas what you now want to define as command is a relation which is specific to UG, and hence to linguistic phrase markers?

_____ a definition of command

L: The command relation could be defined for any phrase marker, but I don't know of any domain of natural science where it plays a role, other than linguistics. Suppose that's true. (Arguments exist that something very much like command is important in the structure of proofs and other mathematical constructs [22], but I haven't seen a clear application in any natural domain.) If so, we want command to be not just another trivial property of phrase markers, but a property that's highly significant for linguistic phrase markers alone. I know you hate formulas, but I have to go into them again so you can follow my point. This particular formula is trivial, though. Let's define the command relation as a relation of C_{HL}, the computational system, holding between any two elements α and β in a phrase marker, as follows [see app. for more precise definition]:

(12) *Definition of command*
    Where α and β are accessible to C_{HL}, α *commands* β if and only if (a) α does not dominate β, and (b) the first category dominating α also dominates β.

Consider these definitions with regard to (5).

O: May I have a bash at it? I shall draw my intuition first, because I'm much better with pictures than with words. As a matter of fact, do let me pretty up your ugly phrase markers, with my graphics programme here on this side of the universe . . .

———————————————————— *a voyage toward the center of categories*

L: Oh, how you like tricks!

O: This will allow us to see (12) at work, and will give us a snapshot of phrase markers, where we can see their very guts. To get the idea of my pictures, consider a real-life example: the merger of multinational corporations [23]. Say Pepsi wants to merge with Kentucky Fried Chicken. In the mathematical representation we can think of each company as a set of features, and in the visual representation we can assign each one a bubble.

L: A bubble?!

O: Yes—a soap bubble or a balloon. Bear with me for a moment. Now, after the merger, we have a larger company. But the name of the new company isn't Pepsi/Kentucky-Fried-Chicken (a further merger would yield a disastrous name—say, Pepsi/Kentucky-Fried-Chicken/Pizza-Hut). Instead, the conglomerate takes the name of the stronger company, basically unchanged: Pepsico. The point is, α merges with β, and the name of the result is α. Mathematically, this corresponds to what we saw for syntactic categories. Visually, we can represent it thus: bubble β and bubble α gravitate round each other, and they're enclosed in the space of a larger bub-

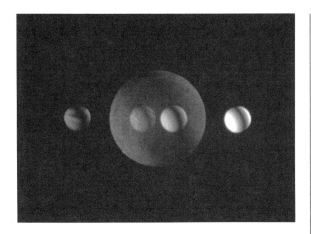

Figure 3.12

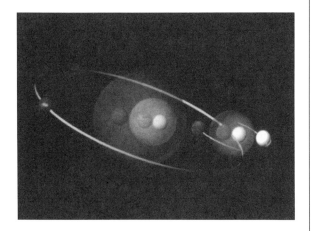

Figure 3.13

Schema of object

    [[dark] [[marble] [ivory]]]

       ↑ *you*   ↑ *dig*   *this*

Projection   Projection
  of *dig*   of *dig*

ble. Let's use colours to distinguish bubble β (ivory white) from bubble α (marble grey); then we can use grey for the larger bubble that encloses α and β. In the company example, marble grey would be the colour of Pepsico, whereas the structure of the inner, merged companies remains intact—Pepsi is still marble grey and Kentucky Fried Chicken is still ivory white [see fig. 3.12].

L: I hope all of this is taking us somewhere . . .

O: Do be patient. Now, using this technique, we can map your ugly (5) into a much more amusing object [see fig. 3.13]. The basic structure of this object is the same one I've just described for Pepsico, except that it presents one further level. To be exact, I map the word *this* to an ivory bubble and the word *dig* to a marble grey bubble, which is the one that projects. In its turn, this larger, projected bubble relates to the dark bubble on the left, which corresponds to the specifier *you*. You see the relation between the *you* bubble and the *dig this* bubble in the innermost, rather big bubble which encodes all structural relations. You can think of the outer rings as the derivational history of the inside object, which is what exists at any given point in derivational time. That is to say, the outer rings are a bit of an afterimage of what once was the central bubble, which encodes the currently existing structure, the colour of the bubble being its label—that is, its syntactic type [see fig. 3.13].

L: Very ingenious.

O: I like games. Well, then; now that we've got a picture of our phrase marker (5), I can proceed with my analysis of the command relations in a more intuitive fashion. Since command is a relation of C_{HL}, and this system sees only certain categories—which you marked with # and | signs—I shall turn the bubbles that C_{HL} does not see into polyhedra. Let's do this in a new picture, and since we no longer really care about the derivational history of the central bubble, let's get closer to this bubble, ignoring the rest of the structure. Now—and this is most important—I've changed the intermediate marble grey bubble in the previous picture [fig. 3.13] for a polyhedron of roughly the same size and structural location. The intuition is that whereas the intermediate projection is still part of the structure, C_{HL} doesn't recognise it as a syntactic object—those are only bubbles (that is, heads and maximal projections) [see fig. 3.14]. To emphasize the point: all objects that Merge creates (bubbles or polyhedra) are part of the structure. Nevertheless, only bubbles are actually accessed by C_{HL}. And once again, these definitions are not part of the Merge operation, but they are acceptable hypotheses about how C_{HL} works, so we must encode them in order to determine command relations. To talk about objects within object-spaces, and so forth, I shall use some familiar mnemonics. Let's say that when a category α dominates a category β, α is the **mother** of β; and if α and β have the same mother, then they are of course **sisters,** et cetera. Then I believe that your definition of command is intended to convey the formal intuition that an object in a phrase marker which is accessible to C_{HL} (a bubble, and not a polyhedron in my pictures) commands its sister and the descendants of its sister. Bubble-wise, even if you are a bubble, you don't command the bubbles that you enclose or that enclose you, but you do command those bubbles that live in the same object-space as you do, and the bubbles that these enclose. For example, [fig. 3.14, left] the dark bubble commands both the marble grey and the ivory white bubble, which are enclosed in the polyhedron, an object which lives in the same object-space as the dark bubble does. Needless to say, since this polyhedron isn't a bubble, it isn't seen by the computational system, and although it is part of the structure (hence, for example, delimiting the object-space where the ivory white and marble grey bubbles live), it itself commands nothing, and nothing commands it either. Is that basically correct?

L: Exactly right, yes: only those "aunt" relations in a phrase marker that correspond to elements which are heads and maximal projections (the elements that C_{HL} recognizes) are valid command relations [see app. and fig. 3.15]. So that's command, okay? That, plus of course the trivial relation between a category and its sister, what we can call "mutual" command—which turns out to be quite an intriguing instance.

O: But where on Earth is all this going? I thought we were interested in linearisation . . .

precedence results from command

L: We are. First, let's set aside the relation between α and its sister β, where symmetric command holds (α commands β and vice versa). This is an interesting case that complicates matters, and we should return to it. As I say, leaving it aside, and given the intuition that (asymmetric) command is an "extended aunt" relation, we can easily prove that it's a **transitive** relation.

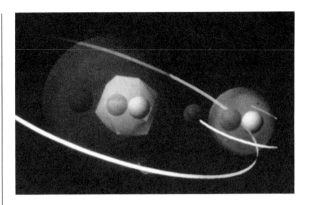

Figure 3.14

The basic structure of this object (a closer view of the inner bubble) is the same as that of the object in figure 3.13. However, it now contains a polyhedron, corresponding to the object that at some point in the derivational history (seen at the right of the picture) was a regular projected bubble. This means that although derivationally the object in question is at some point a maximal projection (hence a bubble enclosing other bubbles), it is eventually taken by the system not to be a maximal projection, but only an inaccessible, intermediate projection. This turns out to be central in determining appropriate command relations. Keep in mind that derivationally the object was a genuine maximal projection, prior to its further merger with a specifier (which is still represented by the dark bubble at the left of the picture). In fact, had the object not been a maximal projection (and thus accessible to the system), it could not have even merged with its specifier (which is an accessible element).

Figure 3.15

To intuitively grasp the notion of command, first observe that the "command horizon" of a category is determined by what its sister dominates. For instance, in the graph in (i) the "domination horizon" of α determines the "command horizon" of its sister, β:

(i)
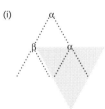

Yet not all categories in a phrase marker have a command horizon; in fact, only those categories that C_{HL} recognizes do. In (i) the shaded area is an appropriate command horizon *only if* β is, for example, a maximal projection (as will be the case if α has projected). Below, it will also be important to determine whether given categories stand in a mutual command relation; however, this is important for matters of linearization, and not for command relations themselves (which obviously hold in situations of mutual command).

O: Right: If a category α (asymmetrically) commands a category β, and β commands another category γ, then α commands γ.

L: And again, setting aside the sister relation, all other instances of command are not symmetric. If α (asymmetrically) commands β, then β doesn't command α.

O: Why, of course—since you're setting aside the only instance where symmetric command would hold! Notice, by the way, that this gives you what mathematicians call a linear ordering of the elements that the "visible-extended-aunt" (asymmetric command) relation holds of [see app.]. That simply means that all the elements thus ordered can be placed in a single row, which is amusing!

L: It may actually be more than that. Think of what we've done: we've characterized a linear ordering within syntactic structures in terms of the asymmetric command relation. Couldn't it be the case that it's precisely this ordering that, if mapped to time, is responsible for the actual string of words that comes out of a speaker's mouth [24]?

O: You mean, you want command to dictate which words should precede which other words in a PF representation?!

L: It's fairly natural, actually. Here, let's be as explicit as possible; assume (13)—the LCA, for short—as a procedure for linearizing linguistic phrase markers:

(13) *Linear Correspondence Axiom*
      A category α precedes a category β if and only if (a) α asymmetrically commands β, or (b) γ precedes β and γ dominates α.

Given (13), there are actually two ways in which α can precede β. One is basic—it's just the intuition that α precedes β when α asymmetrically commands β. The other one—

_____ testing the LCA

O: Hold on, let's make sure that this base step works. We're now making predictions about possible phrase markers in Human. Generally speaking, would you wish to say that the subject of a sentence commands the verb?

L: Sure—that's one of the intuitive ideas behind command.

O: Well, then, if I understand the base step of the LCA in (13), you expect that the subject always precedes the verb.

L: That's right; by and large I think that's true.

O: I shall return to some manifest exceptions in a moment. In any case, now that we see that, for example, *you* in (5) precedes *dig,* because *you* commands *dig,* I can also see why a recursive step is needed in (13) . . . Suppose that, instead of *you,* (5) had *your aunt,* as in (14). It's easy to prove, I believe, that whereas the whole phrase *your aunt* (whose label is |your|) commands *dig,* the daughters of this phrase do not. As a matter of fact, it's undeniable that whereas |your| is the "extended aunt" of *dig, your* is in no direct family relation with *digs,* as the bubbles in my version of (14) clearly show [see fig. 3.16].

(14)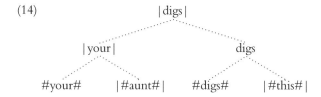

L: That's correct. But of course we still want to say that *your* precedes *digs;* it obviously does. So how do we manage that?

O: Through the recursive step in (13b). We can say that *your* precedes *dig* because the base step in (13a) allows us to conclude that the dominating phrase |your| precedes *dig.* And since |your| dominates *your,* then via (13b) we conclude that *your* precedes *dig* [25].

L: So now we've got a way of determining the precedence relations in a phrase marker.

--- *why command should matter*

O: But I've got two sorts of questions—one conceptual and one empirical. Conceptually, why should command matter? Here's what you've done: you removed a property from Human phrase markers, and you stipulated it as an axiom. This looks pretty formal to me! Weren't we supposed to deduce this from economy or virtual conceptual necessity?

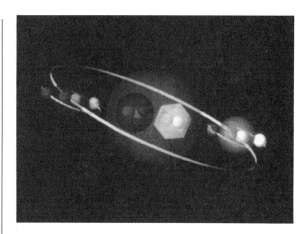

Figure 3.16

This picture presents both the derivational history (in the outer rings) and the actual structure (in the inner bubble) of *your aunt digs this,* according to the following schema:

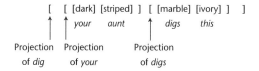

Focusing on the large, central bubble, it is clear that the whole specifier *your aunt* (the medium-sized dark bubble containing the small dark and striped bubbles) commands the bubbles inside the polyhedron occupying the same object-space. However, the bubbles inside the dark specifier bubble do not command outside the domain of the specifier bubble that encloses them, nor are they commanded by anything (the polyhedron is the only structure that might do so, but it is not recognized by the computational system). In sum, *your* (the small dark bubble) and *aunt* (the striped bubble) stand in no relation to *digs* (the marble gray bubble) and *this* (the ivory white bubble). This is intuitively clear from the large, central bubble: each pair of small bubbles inside it occupies its own object-space. This fact corresponds to a deeper derivational phenomenon: as the separate outer rings in the picture show, there is no point in the derivational history at which the dark and striped bubbles to the left are assembled with the rest of the bubbles in the object; the bubbles to the left constitute their own structural subdomain, both in the course of the derivation and in the resulting representation.

L: First, it may well be the case that we can't deduce the axiom. So it stays an axiom of C_{HL}—so be it. There's no point in deducing it trivially.

O: But—

L: Just a moment! Second, there are ways of deducing the axiom—at least its base step—thus turning it into a theorem [26]. Note that the axiom basically instantiates three separate postulates: (i) hierarchical structures of the kind that Merge produces have to be linearized; (ii) this is done (basically) according to command relations; (iii) the resulting linearized object maps to a characteristic PF sequence of time slots for articulatory/perception purposes. Let's say that (i) follows from bare output conditions [27], whatever those are [see sec. 3.5]. In turn, let's examine (ii), by considering the command relations that obtain in another variant of (3), *you dig this stuff.* We can think of command as a canonical (perhaps, the only) syntactic relation that arises through closing the Merge relation in a given domain [28]. Specifically, α commands the elements of β when α merges with β [see fig. 3.17]:

(15) a. Relations in which |#y#| is the commander:
        <|#y#|, {d, {#d#, | {t, {#t#, |#s#|}}|}}> [by Merge of |#y#| and {d, {#d#, | {t, {#t#, |#s#|}}|}}]
        <|#y#|, #d#> [transitively, given the top line in (a)]
        <|#y#|, | {t, {#t#, |#s#|}}|> [transitively, given the top line in (a)]
        <|#y#|, #t#> [transitively, given the top line in (a)]
        <|#y#|, |#s#|> [transitively, given the top line in (a)]
     b. Relations in which #d# is the commander:
        <#d#, | {t, {#t#, |#s#|}}|> [by Merge of #d# and |{t, {#t#, |#s#|}}|]
        <#d#, #t#> [transitively, given the top line in (b)]
        <#d#, |#s#|> [transitively, given the top line in (b)]
     c. Relations in which |{t, {#t#, |#s#|}}| is the commander:
        <| {t, |{#t#, |#s#|}}|, #d#|> [by Merge of |{t, {#t#, |#s#|}}| and #d#]
     d. Relations in which #t# is the commander:
        <#t#, |#s#|> [by Merge of #t# and |#s#|]
     e. Relations in which |#s#| is the commander:
        <|#s#|, #t#> [by Merge of |#s#| and #t#]

Setting aside symmetric command relations [as in (d)/(e) and the top line of (b)/(c)], the asymmetric command relation defines a linear ordering <y, d, . . . >.

O: What you're saying is that if we're looking for a linear order in a structure like (15), we've got no problem: it's there under our noses, given the way in which we've *built* (15) through Merge.

L: That's right, and since the properties of Merge follow from bare output conditions—plus virtual conceptual necessity—we're on our way to a deduction. But we're not there yet; we still have to deal with postulate (iii). Suppose we've managed to determine the sequence <you, dig, this, stuff> for the instance we're discussing now (rigorously speaking, we've only determined <you, dig, . . . >, but we'll let that go for the time being). We still have to map that onto a given PF sequence, with *you* immediately preceding *dig* and not *this,* and so on. Let the mapping be instantiated through a concrete procedure, call it L. What alternatives exist to the "smart" version of L (the one that does give the PF sequence that you hear when I say this sentence)?

O: I suppose many come to mind. For example, PF could map <you, dig, this, stuff> into a sequence of times <t_1, t_2, t_3, . . . , t_n>, where *you* is mapped into t_1, and *dig* is mapped to, for example, a t value which is twice as large as t_1 (namely, t_2), and *this* is mapped to a t value which is twice as large as t_2 (namely, t_4), and so forth. That would furnish a sort of stuttering PF: *you-dig-silence-this-silence-silence-silence-stuff.* We could venture a polka rhythm too, and a waltz would always be elegant; then again, the lambada tempo would be a wee bit inappropriate, but most alluring. Or we could raise the stakes, by mapping words to times through some nonlinear function. A simply glorious function comes to mind which—

L: All right, all right. The point is, anything's possible, if we don't constrain the mapping [see fig. 3.18] [29]. Somehow procedure L has to ensure the mapping of the linear sequence of linguistic symbols onto the trivial sequence of time instants in a one-to-one fashion (that is, the relation is **isomorphic**). And of course the question then arises, is this an axiom?

O: I hope not, if we're trying to deduce the LCA. Why, it would seem as if operation L affects the structure, just as other operations do, determining a concrete mapping from structured phrasal objects

Figure 3.17

More technically, but equivalently to the statements in (15), the command relations for |{<u>d</u>, {|#y#|, {d, {#d#, | {t, {#t#, |#s# |}}|}}|}}| can be expressed as follows:

(i) a. How |#y#| commands:
   {{|#y#|}, {|#y#|, {d, {#d#, |{t, {#t#, |#s#|}}|}}}}
   {{|#y#|}, {|#y#|, #d#}}
   {{|#y#|}, {|#y#|, | {t, {#t#, |#s#|}}|}}
   {{|#y#|}, {|#y#|, #t#}}
   {{|#y#|}, {|#y#|, |#s#|}}
   b. How #d# commands:
   {{#d#}, {#d#, |{t, {#t#, |#s#|}}|}}
   {{#d#}, {#d#, #t#}}
   {{#d#}, {#d#, |#s#|}}
   c. How |{t, {#t#, |#s#|}}| commands:
   {{|{t, {#t#, |#s#|}}|}, {|{t, {#t#, |#s#|}}|, #d#}}
   d. How #t# commands:
   {{#t#}, {#t#, |#s#|}}
   e. How |#s#| commands:
   {{|#s#|}, {|#s#|, #t#}}

The objects in (i) are not phrase markers, but sets expressing command relations. These sets are mapped from phrase markers. For example, given the phrase marker |{<u>d</u>, {|#y#|, {d, {#d#, |{t, {#t#, |#s#|}}|}}|}}|, the relation {{|#y#|}, {|#y#|, {d, {#d#, {t, {#t#, |#s#|}}}}}} can immediately be determined: |#y#| must have merged with {d, {#d#, |{t, {#t#, |#s#|}}|}}, since these two are sister constituents in the phrase marker. Then {{|#y#|}, {|#y#|, {d, {#d#, {t, {#t#, |#s#|}}}}}} says that |#y#| is ordered with respect to {d, {#d#, {t, {#t#, |#s#|}}}}, which is more intuitively expressed as in the text, by way of the angle bracket notation: <|#y#|, {d, {#d#, {t, {#t#, |#s#|}}}}>. Rather crucially, standard set-theoretic notation (brackets) is being mixed with new notation to encode whether something is a head (#) or a maximal projection (|). This is important because command is defined only for categories that are accessible to C_{HL}, which is a specifically linguistic notion. If command were not defined only for accessible categories, it would be necessary to conclude, for instance, that the inaccessible {d, {#d#, |{t, {#t#, |#s#|}}|}} commands its sister |#y#|, in which case there would not be an asymmetric command relation between these two, and it would not be possible to order |#y#| before its sister. In the particular phrase marker under discussion, this is not necessarily a bad result, so long as |#y#| still commands the elements of its sister, which it does. However, consider a slightly more complex phrase marker, for instance, (14), whose official representation is as follows:

(ii) |{<u>d</u>, {|{y, {#y#, |#a#|}}|, {d, {#d#, |{t, {#t#, |#s#|}}|}}|}}|

If {d, {#d#, |{t, {#t#, |#s#|}}|}} is allowed to (asymmetrically) command the elements of its sister |{y, {#y#, |#a#|}}|, then, by the induction step in (13b), the elements that {d, {#d#, |{t, {#t#, |#s#|}}|}} dominates should precede the elements that |{y, {#y#, |#a#|}}| dominates. And since |{y, {#y#, |#a#|}}| also (asymmetrically) commands the elements of {d, {#d#, |{t, {#t#, |#s#|}}|}}, the elements that |{y, {#y#, |#a#|}}| dominates should precede the elements that {d, {#d#, |{t, {#t#, |#s#|}}|}} dominates—which creates a paradox.

onto a concrete sequence of phonological units at PF [30] . . . If this is so, could we not argue that the isomorphic mapping is the simplest of all?

L: Oh, we could. The question is whether we'd be right—these matters are too poorly understood. In any case, if your suggestion is correct, you'd be deriving postulate (iii) from economy considerations [31]. That is, a derivation using the isomorphic relation is simpler than its (equally convergent) competitors, and is thus preferred [see fig. 3.18]. Does this make you happier?

O: At least I see a way to proceed. In any event, now I do comprehend the importance of the command relation.

L: That's right. Whether we take linearization to be axiomatic or theorematic, it's arguably accomplished via the command relation.

3.4 Some Interesting Predictions

(about phrasal rearrangements, which allow the Other to exhibit his prodigious memory)

O: But don't think that I've forgotten my empirical question! Your approach predicts that subjects must always precede verbs at PF. But the little I know about Irish tells me that in this language the verb may come before the subject. Let me see: *bhuail siad Conlon (arist),* that is, literally 'beat they Conlon (again)', which means 'they beat Conlon (again)' [32].

—————————————————————————————— *various movements, in Irish . . .*

L: I must admit that anyone who can pronounce Irish really impresses me!

O: Thanks, but I'm afraid I caught you in a wrong prediction . . .

L: I don't see that. Given the LCA, it must be the case that those instances you've mentioned involve some sort of verb movement past the subject, to a higher, commanding position, so that the verb commands the subject.

O: What a grotesque thing to say!!

L: Any more than predicting that ninety percent of the matter in the universe is really there, but invisible?

Figure 3.18

Place a sequence A = <1, 2, 3, 4, . . . > of timing PF slots on an *x*-axis of coordinates, and place the sequence B = <α, β, γ, δ, . . . > of linearized objects on a *y*-axis. Now consider the following mappings:

$y = x$

$y = 2x$ (more generally, $y = nx$), for *n* any positive whole value

$y = x^2$ (more generally, $y = x^n$), for *n* any positive whole value

$y = f(x)$ (where *f* is an infinite number of procedures) For example, y_1 is mapped to the *x* value three times removed from 0; y_2 is mapped to the *x* value prior to x_1; y_3 is mapped to the *x* value three times removed from x_2; and so on.

O: . . .

L: The relevant structure is (16).

(16)

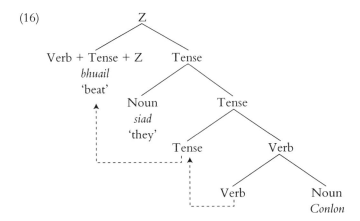

Here Z is a category outside the sentence proper, whose details are irrelevant right now. And note that since we've argued that lexical items project, we don't have to use notations like "sentence" or "verb phrase," as we did yesterday. A "noun phrase" is a projection of a noun, and a "verb phrase" is a projection of a verb, and a "sentence" is a projection of Tense, and so on [33].

O: Please don't try to divert my attention from what really intrigues me! I think I should like to build another puzzle for you. Consider Japanese, which is like English backwards, as it were. Let's see . . . take *Morihiroga Kazuoga Inokio aisiteiru to itta* (literally 'Morihiro Kazuo Inoki loves that said')—'Morihiro said that Kazuo loves Inoki'.

——————————————————————————————— *. . . and in Japanese . . .*

L: Once again, I'm impressed with your abilities, and insist on a simple point: you know what the LCA tells you. Under the assumption that the complement of the verb 'say' in your example is structurally lower than the subject of the main clause—since the subject clearly commands the complement—you know that the structures in question have to be the result of some movement [34]. This is complicated to draw. First, to keep track of the various movements, I'll leave a copy of the moved element in parentheses in the position where the movement originates, okay? So if I want *Socrates* to move in a sentence like *I like Socrates,* I'll normally signal that by moving *Socrates* and leaving a parenthesized copy behind: *Socrates, I like (Socrates),* where the parentheses indicate that that occurrence of *Socrates*

All these functions map a linear sequence A onto a linear sequence B, but only the first class of solutions is empirically correct. Now suppose all four solutions, and perhaps others, converge at PF. Presumably, the system must find the particular solution that is optimal among the convergent ones. Assuming that something like symbol count is relevant in determining the simplicity of an equation, the first procedure shown here is simpler than the other three.

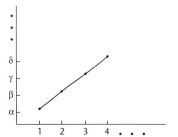

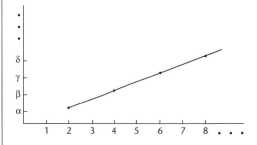

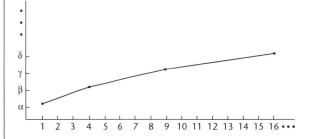

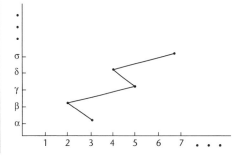

isn't pronounced, but the word actually started there, in object position. Second, let me break the Japanese sentence into two parts. On the one hand, there's the embedded clause—what was it?

O: Kazuoga Inokio aisiteiru to 'Kazuo Inoki loves that'.

L: Right. I'll represent that in (17a). On the other hand, there's the matrix clause, er . . . *Morihiroga . . . itta* 'Morihiro . . . said', which I'll represent in (17b). In (17a) the object *Inokio* moves upward internal to the embedded sentence, to a position P which needn't worry us yet [see sec. 4.6]; and the entire sentence itself moves upward to the periphery of it all, to a position commanding the complementizer (Comp) *to* 'that'. Next, in (17b), the entire embedded clause moves upward, this time internal to the matrix sentence, just as the object *Inokio* did in (17a) (of course, the embedded clause is itself the object of the matrix clause):

(17) a.

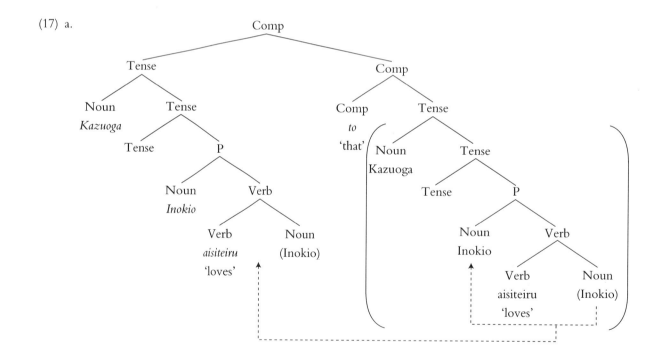

b.

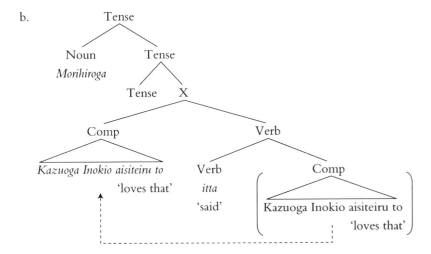

O: Dear me, now you're giving me a headache. These are complicated pictures to understand . . .

L: I'll walk you through them. First, the verb probably doesn't raise to Tense in Japanese, which means it's unlike the verb in, say, Middle English. We saw that Middle English Tense was strong, "pulling" the verb upward to "check" Tense morphology. (Meaning that the "viral" Tense morpheme had to be eliminated by means of the moved verb.) So we have to assume the opposite for the Japanese Tense, so that it doesn't attract the verb [35].

O: And what you're calling a "complementiser" is presumably what you were calling "Z" in the Irish example in (16) [36].

L: That's right, yes. I'm just being a bit more precise with the labels in (17) than I was in (16). But let's not worry about labels now.

O: And for some reason, complements in Japanese raise to some position that you're now labelling "P."

L: Yes. Again, let's set the reason aside so we don't make the story too complicated. But the logic of the system shows you that the movement in question has to be postulated . . .

O: And so the initial phrasal relations are altered as a result of all this, just as we saw in (16) for Irish, or as we saw yesterday for Middle English. Damn!

L: . . .

O: I'm capable of embracing rather abstract ideas if they make beautiful predictions consistent with the rest of the theory. And I can see how the LCA (which should be called the LCT(heorem) if my conjecture was appropriate) restricts the possible hypotheses that a child learning languages would need to entertain, for it says essentially that in terms of very basic structures all languages are the same—Modern English, Middle English, Irish, Japanese, and, I suppose, all other Human dialects as well. They all start with the same basic structural plan and for some reason (call it a virus, I don't care) in some of them certain phrases undergo movement and different output orders result.

L: That's right.

O: And that's reasonably beautiful and simple and learnable by children (because they can hear the output of movement to learn any of the relevant languages). But suppose I'm trying to convince someone at a party that all of this is not just some esoteric illusion . . . All these viruses and movement and . . . you know . . .

_____   *. . . which have important consequences*

L: Strategy one. You get an apple, take a bite, and lecture them, as I heard someone do once. "If we are satisfied that an apple falls to the ground because that is its natural place, there will be no serious science of mechanics. The same is true if one is satisfied with traditional descriptions about why phrases appear in the order they do. However, recognition of the unsuspected richness and complexity of the phenomena of language creates a tension between the goals of descriptive and explanatory adequacy" [37].

O: Oh, I love that tone! But there are some gatherings where it would be frankly suicidal to take such an approach . . .

L: Strategy two. You serve yourself (or them) some wine. Then you set the stage by asking, "Is there a way I could convince you that the movement analysis I postulated for the Japanese sentence in (17) makes some predictions that an analysis without movement wouldn't be able to make?"

O: If you don't mind my saying so, you must give it some mystique. Pretend you're Orson Welles, and say, "Here's where our conjecture becomes exceptionally suggestive. As a matter of fact, there is such an argument to be made, ladies and gentlemen!"

L: Are you making fun of me or did you get the picture?

O: Yes.

L: So anyway, you need a napkin or something to scribble on, and you say, "Consider these English examples":

(18) a.   Bill loves himself
     b.   *Bill said that [himself loves Hill]

Anaphoric elements like *himself,* for some reason that we don't have to worry about [see sec. 4.3], need to be very close to their antecedent. Thus, (18a), where *Bill* and *himself* are **clausemates,** is perfect, but (18b), where *Bill* and *himself* are in different clauses, isn't.

O: Here, I suppose you get some "oooh"s . . .

L: Some, though there's always the wiseacre who claims that (18b) is perfect for him. Which you dismiss by saying, "We'll be predicting facts about the English spoken by everyone other than this gentleman!"

O: And people clap . . .

L: Well, you hope they do. But so far the only thing you've done is set the stage.

O: Absolutely—you haven't told me a bloody thing yet!

L: Here comes the punch line: "Now, watch what happens in Japanese." Here it helps if you know some Japanese (which is never my case) or if there's a cooperative Japanese speaker, like yourself, in the audience. You give them the sentences, emphasizing that both are good in Japanese. Actually, do you have the sentences in your data bank?

O: Actually, I do—it's a curious variant to the others I've shown you:

(19) a. Morihiroga zibuno   aisiteiru

      Morihiro   himself loves

      'Morihiro loves himself'

  b. Morihiroga [zibunga Inokio aisiteiru to]   itta

      Morihiro   self   Inoki   loves   that said

      'Morihiro said that himself loves Inoki'

Blimey! I understand!

L: Thank you. At this point you proceed to explain, "What you've just seen is a powerful demonstration of the wonders of Human. You're probably wondering why our Japanese friends can say (19b), while we cannot . . . The answer is . . . "

O: In our conjecture. I see it, I really do. I can even explain it myself, I believe. Compare the two structures:

(20) a.

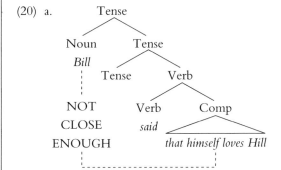

  b.

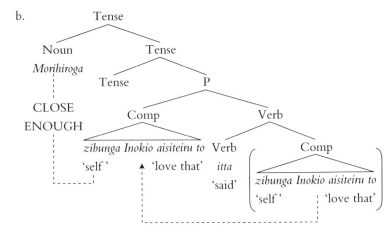

What our analysis does for Japanese is hoist the embedded clause up, as you tried to show me in your (17) and is patent in my (20b). Now, that unquestionably alters the structure, does it not? And as a consequence of this transformation, the anaphor is now structurally much closer to its antecedent than it is in English. Now, given that it can be independently proven that anaphors must be close to their antecedent (I do presume you've got a concrete way of making the notion "close" precise . . .) [see chap. 5], the Japanese (20b) can achieve this result simply by way of the massive realignment that our conjecture predicts. This results in the anaphor *zibunga* 'self' being much closer to its antecedent *Morihiroga* than the comparable anaphor *himself* in English is to its antecedent *Bill*. Needless to say, if you hadn't provided this realignment, you'd be left with no explanation for why Japanese and English differ in the proper licensing of their anaphoric elements.

L: That's it. Linguists actually have given other arguments of this sort [38].

_____ the system procrastinates

O: I'm rather impr—Hold on! Why couldn't English pull the same stunt that Japanese did? Here's a mad experiment. Suppose I move the embedded sentence as we did for Japanese. (21a) is still a dreadful English sentence. Why hasn't this movement licensed the anaphor *himself,* just as it did in Japanese for *zibunga?*

(21) a. *Bill [himself loves Hill that] said

b.

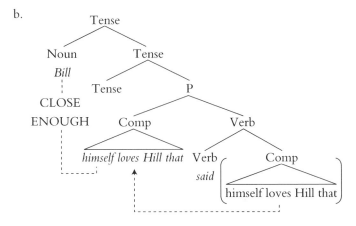

L: Just the right question. It should, shouldn't it? Your structure in (21b) also gets the anaphor *himself* close to *Bill,* as the structure in (20b) gets *zibunga* close to *Morihiroga.* But now notice a crucial difference between English and Japanese. Remember I told you that movement is always motivated by the need to satisfy some morphological requirement (the immunization character of checking)?

O: Which means that the Japanese movement we've been contemplating must have some cause, some virus that the structure needs to be immunised against by moving the embedded sentence, or something of that ilk.

L: I won't bother you with the details, but in Japanese there are overt case markers to check, and similar little (but strong) creatures that don't appear in the overt syntax of (Modern) English [39]. Now, here's the question: why should an element move if it doesn't have to in order to "check" morphemes? Japanese needs the movement (independent of the licensing of anaphors), given the morphological properties of this language; but English doesn't. That is, you've now considered two alternative derivations starting with the same initial array of lexical items: (21b) and (20a). More economical derivations rule out less economical derivations. In fact, both (21b) and (20a) converge at LF and at PF, but (20a) clearly does it with fewer movement steps than (21b). So if this sort of **procrastination** that English seems to be exhibiting is thought of as part of the formal characterization of what economy means for C_{HL}, then (20a) will eliminate (21b) as a possibility—for (20a) is more optimal [see fig. 3.19].

_____ the need to express something never drives a derivation

O: I see. But you're making a subtle assumption here that I want to comment on, since I find it very provocative—thought-provoking, that is . . . The derivation in (20a) converges without the extra movement, and therefore this movement isn't undertaken, even if a grammatical structure that would allow for the anaphoric interpretation would emerge as a result of the extra movement.

L: That's indeed my assumption. The English derivation has no purely grammatical justification for the extra movement. In the Japanese instance, the movement is justified in terms of checking some morphology, which English doesn't need to check. The important point is that "expressiveness" or "communicative purposes," or even "speaker/addressee intentions," play no role in grammatical processes [40].

Figure 3.19

The basic schema for both English and Japanese:

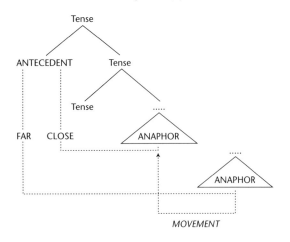

MOVEMENT

The only difference between the two languages is that the relevant movement of the embedded clause is arguably justified in Japanese, but not in English. Since the movement is not necessary in English, for it to occur would not be economical—even though, if it were possible, an interpretation for the English sentence (similar to the Japanese one) would be available.

O: But now let me, once more, play advocatus diaboli. Consider an intellectual responding to you thus: "You are so naïve and simpleminded, Mr. Linguist! You've entirely disregarded interpretation! Why couldn't you have chosen to move the embedded clause as in (21b) precisely in order to avoid the nonsense that you've so eagerly produced? (21b) would have an interpretation if *himself* could move to a position which is close to its antecedent *Bill* (something like 'Bill said that: he himself loves Hill'). In other words, your analysis is *wrong,* Mr. Linguist, and a corrected, sound version of it—one worthy of its proponent—would give a result which is absolutely contrary to fact, for the sentence in question is utterly ungrammatical in English, even with the well-intended interpretation. In still other words, the analysis that predicts the data is loopy, and the sound analysis doesn't predict the data—and so your whole theory's a nonsense."

L: That's a curious instance of refutation by denigration! I've suffered that sort of argument more than once, but it still amuses me. Of course, as you've twice admitted, my crazy theory does yield the data, and it was your sound alternative that didn't. This may not be a trivial fact, since I take it that there's indeed a naive, even simpleminded claim to be made with respect to your deep proposal. Humans plainly prefer a shorter derivation to a longer one, regardless of what meaning each derivation entails. If a shorter derivation converges without the extra movement, then the longer derivation that requires this operation is disallowed. In (21b) the movement of the embedded clause isn't permitted because (in English) the derivation converges without that extra step. Derivations are driven by the mechanical requirement of feature checking only, and not by a "search for intelligibility," whatever that might possibly mean. And that's that.

O: Now that I think of it, the immune system also works (or actually, procrastinates!) that way. It gets activated in the presence of an intruder, full stop. As a consequence of the activation, many things happen: the patient gets a fever, sweats, et cetera. Suppose that for some demented reason you wanted to get those effects. (For example, you want to dodge a wedding ceremony by pretending that you have some beastly viral infection.) You cannot, I'm afraid, tell your leukocytes, "Time to do some exercise!" These fellows have a "mind" of their own, and work only when they estimate that work is necessary. And what you're saying is this: the workings of C_{HL} are as mechanical as those of the immune system, or any other system in this beautifully dense universe of ours.

L: Well, as long as you remember that metaphors are (just!) for understanding, yes: that's basically what I'm saying.

3.5 Further Intriguing Predictions
(featuring amazing clitic elements, deducing why phrasal relations should be binary, and getting our characters into their first heated dustup)

O: Now, let us return to (3), the phrase marker we've carefully studied. I've granted you that the linearisation conjecture is correct, and this means that the specifier (for example, |#you#| in (3)) always commands the head, regardless of the structure; therefore, the specifier always precedes the head.

————————————— specifiers precede whatever else is in the structure

L: Right again. Let me illustrate this before you go on with your challenge. A subject is a type of specifier, and I already told you that the subject precedes the verb. But if we look inside a noun phrase, we find a very similar situation. For instance, alongside the sentence *Nero destroyed Rome* we have the noun phrase *Nero's destruction of Rome,* and here again the specifier *Nero* commands and therefore precedes the head *destruction*. Or take for instance question formation. How do people make information questions in English?

O: Haven't we discussed this already? The speaker chooses *what, who, why,* and so forth, and moves it to the beginning of the sentence . . .

L: More specifically, linguists propose that *wh-*words like *what, who,* and *why* move to the specifier position of the Complementizer (which from now on I'll call Comp or C); in English main clauses the auxiliary *will* also moves, for some reason [41]:

(22)

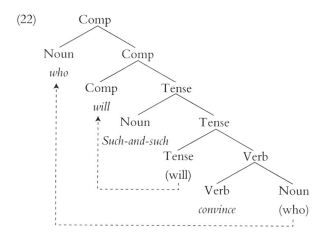

Of course, (22) is a rather general way of making questions in other languages as well.

O: Though it occurs to me that whereas some languages, like English, do move an overt *wh*-word, others don't obviously move anything—Chinese comes to mind [42].

L: You're right about the facts. But what's really interesting is that all languages that move regular *wh*-elements always move them to the left, as in (22), and never to the right [43].

O: Hm! That's true. Then the true mirror image of English doesn't exist, really.

L: Right. And if you think about it, that's exactly what the LCA predicts, since as you said a specifier always commands its head, and that means that the specifier will always precede the head.

_____ *but do heads always precede their complements?*

O: I must say that this is completely true only in an entropic universe, where time goes forwards.

L: What?

O: If gravitational attraction eventually stops the universe's expansion and makes it start to contract again, our inevitable fate will be to collapse back into a Big Crunch. Which means Humpty Dumpty will recompose himself, and every place we now find a precedence relation, we'll then find the reverse. (So for (22), we'll say *ʔecnivnoc hcus-dna-hcuS lliw ohw*.)

L: . . .

O: But although I now understand that specifiers command and therefore precede heads, what about the relation between a head and its complement? I've patiently left this important question pending—until now. I do see how a head can precede a complex complement—say, in the relation between *that* and *love* in (21). Which I shall formally draw for us in (23) (sticking only to the relevant parts):

(23)   {said,{|{that, {|{Tense, {... #love#...}}|, #that#}}|, #said#}}

   #said#,←↑→ |{that, {|{Tense, {... #love#...}}|, #that#}}|

                  #that# ←↑→ |{Tense, {...#love#...}}|

                                       . . .

Given the object |{that, {|{Tense, { ... #love# ... }}|, #that#}}|, we can assume the linear sequence <#that# < . . . #love# . . . >>, with the desired effects: eventually, *that* is mapped as preceding *love,* et cetera. But consider a simpler case, something like *I like it.* I commands both *like* and *it.* But what about these two sisters? If the structure is as I'm drawing now, either *like* commands *it* or vice versa; they clearly enter into a relation of mutual command [44]:

(24)   Verb

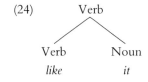

        Verb   Noun
        like   *it*

L: Which again—assuming the LCA—means . . .

O: That (24) is an impossible phrase of Human.

L: To be very precise, (24) is a phrase marker that can't be linearized: we can't tell whether *like* precedes *it* or vice versa, since (as you noted) neither one commands the other. This is why I emphasized earlier that situations of mutual command are interesting.

O: Now we're stuck!

_____   *an interesting wrinkle for the LCA, given a bare phrase structure*

L: Well, first we could weaken the LCA so that nontotal orderings are admissible under certain conditions.

O: Hold on, hold on! Axioms can be weakened, but what does it mean to weaken a theorem?! There's nothing to weaken: the theorem follows from something else . . . Are you going to weaken that something else? Are you going to weaken economy, in the case of the LCT (for that's how I deduced the LCA)?

L: You keep bugging me with this theorem business, when to me it's perfectly okay if we take the LCA to be an axiom! If it were an axiom, we could weaken it in situations where two heads stand in a mutual command relation. That particular subpart of the phrase marker wouldn't be ordered.

O: Non mi piace. If you leave that part of the phrase marker unordered, how in Hell do you order the heads that enter into a mutual command relation, firstly; and secondly, precisely how is the LCT to be weakened to allow for objects which the natural LCT (which is a theorem) bars anyway?

For an eternal instant, there was silence. Had an intruder witnessed the impasse, he or she (or it, if it were a dog, say) would have sensed a sharp air of frustration on the Linguist's side of the wormhole, and a calm yet perfectly irate attitude on the Other's side. (The sort that scientists—being humans and not dogs, say—do not like to admit they experience, particularly when they share a strong difference of opinion.)

L: All right, so first suppose we find a way of making a phrase marker like (24) survive the LCA—otherwise this sort of phrase marker would be predicted never to occur, contrary to fact.

O: And that way, sir, would be . . . ?

L: We could for instance follow the suggestion you made earlier today, and make the LCA relevant only at—or rather, after—Spell-Out.

O: Oh, all of a sudden you like my idea . . .

L: It would be saying that after Spell-Out is where linearity really matters. There's no clear evidence that this sort of linear ordering plays any role at LF or in the computation from the initial array to LF. In fact, all of that is "inside the speaker's head," as it were, and it isn't obvious that things have to be linear there—at least in any trivial fashion. What do we know about the internal computations of the mind/brain? At that level, things could easily happen, say, simultaneously, or in various dimensions. Who knows? So let's say we have no reason to believe they need to be mapped into the exact time sequence that we seem to be mapping PF forms to. There the mapping to time is obvious. The difference among *pat, apt,* and *tap* is basically their sequential ordering in time. So the mapping into time for PF structures is crucial—in this universe . . .

O: Then you need to say that it's PF that wants linearised phrase markers, and it acquires them through the LCA/T. That is to say, the linearisation we're studying is *not* a property of phrase markers in general, but only of those phrase markers that feed PF. I'm beginning to fancy that.

L: Ordering applies to the output of Morphology, assigning a linear temporal order to the elements it forms, all of them heads.

O: But that still doesn't answer my first question: how do we linearise a structure like (24)? I'll grant you that at LF or during the computation to LF this phrase marker isn't linearised. Still, at PF you've just told me that it must be linearised . . .

―――――――――――――――――――――― *cliticization . . .*

L: Okay, so now that we've constrained the LCA (or the LCT, really, because the crucial point holds for both: PF demands linearization, period), let's accept that the derivation crashes unless the "offending" structure has changed by the time it reaches Spell-Out, so that the structure in question is rendered irrelevant. The idea I have in mind is that, somehow, Morphology can convert the offending structure into a "phonological word" which isn't internally subject to the LCA/T, assuming that the LCA/T encodes a procedure which is examined after Morphology does whatever work it does with words.

O: Are you having me on again?

L: . . . (!!!!!)

O: . . . (?????)

L: Not really. Note that the way we usually pronounce *I like it* is actually something like *I like't.* The *it* becomes dependent on the previous word. This is what linguists call a *clitic:* a weak element that exists as a parasite on a word such as *like,* in our example [45]. Suppose the structure we obtain as a result of this "cliticization" is something like (25):

(25)

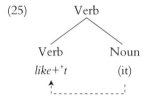

Suppose, furthermore, that clitics are part of "phonological words"; they're almost like morphemes in the sense that they're not separate words, with their own stress and autonomy. Then it's likely that their linearization inside the word obeys a morphological condition, something that the syntactic computational system we're describing has nothing to say about [see fig. 3.20].

O: Is a clitic a head?

L: Yes, it's just a lexical item that ends up being part of another head.

O: Then a head with a cliticised element will have two heads: itself and the clitic! Must be a hydra that we're dealing with . . .

L: No—it just depends on how we define "head." Obviously, to allow for all sorts of head movements (not just cliticization), we have to say that when various heads end up forming a single syntactic unit, they constitute a single head, and not multiple heads. So then we say that a head is a lexical item which isn't contained inside any other head—some trivial recursive procedure of that sort [see app.] [46]. The important thing, though, is that when we're working inside heads, we're dealing with morphology, so the LCA has no bearing on this issue. In turn, the copy that's left behind when *it* gets cliticized, which I'm writing as the parenthesized (it), isn't pronounced at PF. If this is correct, then PF doesn't have to worry about its linearization. That is, the element in question is nothing but an image of the element that has moved, a "**trace**" if you will [47]. (I'll often use the symbol *t*, instead of the parenthesized copy of the moved element, to represent these traces of movement.)

Figure 3.20

The nature, structure, position, and displacement of clitics has been one of the most widely studied phenomena in linguistics. Modern scientific proposals go back to the work of Jacob Wackernagel, who argued for a special placement rule for clitic elements within Germanic languages (the famous "verb-second" position of clitic verbs). To this date little is known about why clitics behave the way they do (and even less about why this behavior differs so widely across languages), even though the literature is full of interesting proposals. In essence, two major lines of research have developed: (i) clitics are "affixes of phrases" and are placed within phrasal boundaries as a result of morphophonological requirements (Anderson 1992); (ii) clitics are syntactic heads that must move to a site like Comp, for undetermined reasons (Kayne 1991). Of course, it is possible that (ii) explains the overall syntax of clitic dependencies and (i) provides the overall morphophonology; however, such a unification has not yet been achieved. It is important to note that the Minimalist system forces its proponents to find solutions for this puzzle, for so far it has nothing to say about the linearization of objects like those in (25), precisely involving clitics. To say that a clitic's linearization "inside" a word obeys a morphological condition presupposes understanding (i) and possibly also (ii).

Figure 3.21

Focused structures present a very interesting problem: their interpretation seems to be crucially related to a given phonetic representation. For instance, consider (i):

(i) a. John hasn't seen Mary; in fact, he hasn't seen anyone today
    b. John hasn't seen MARY; #in fact, he hasn't seen anyone today

The continuation of (ib) is less appropriate (#) than the continuation of (ia). Intuitively, it seems that by focusing *Mary,* the speaker introduces the presupposition that John has seen somebody other than Mary. But how did LF know that *MARY* was emphasized? The model being assumed here is derivational and bifurcated, which entails that PF does not communicate with LF, or vice versa. Note also that it must be determined whether the focus effect in (i) reaches LF; it may not—and could instead be a purely interpretive fact of performance. Here linguists differ. For some, the effect is semantic (post-LF) or pragmatic, hence performance-related in present terms; for others, it is syntactic, even if it has semantic consequences. The latter is a priori more troubling for the present model, inasmuch as it must face the fact that a sentence like (ib) has a clear PF reflex (emphasis on *MARY*) somehow associated with its LF (on that view). Undeniably, though, in many languages focus has a specific syntax. For instance, consider the Basque example in (ii):

(ii) a. ez   du   Jonek   Miren   ikusi
        not   has   Jon-subject Miren-object   seen
        'Jon hasn't seen Miren'
     b. MIREN   ez   du   Jonek   ikusi
        MIREN-object   not   has   Jon-subject   seen
        'Jon hasn't seen MIREN'

To the extent that the displacement of *MIREN* in (iib) is to be syntactically justified, there must be an F feature that *MIREN* checks in the site to which it is displaced. This may provide a clue about why a particular structure can have both PF- and LF-associated properties. In particular, apart from its syntactic consequence in triggering movement as in (iib), feature F may have a particular PF reflex (emphasis) and some kind of LF reflex (whatever it is that licenses the presuppositions in these instances). This view makes a prediction: the PF realization of F as emphasis may vary from language to language—and indeed it does. Spoken languages use at least stress, intonation, and reduplication to highlight focused items, and iconic cues are possible in signed languages. This suggests that F simply indicates "emphasis" to the PF component, which then executes this order in a variety of ways. In contrast, F should have universal import where LF structures are concerned, given present assumptions (although this is harder to establish conclusively). Finally, if F has the categorial correlate in (26), it also provides a solution to the linearization problem sketched in the text.

O: Why, that's very clever, but . . . Frankly, I should like to see some evidence that this is more than a trick to keep the show rolling. For example, although people do pronounce *I like him* and *I like her* as *I like'im* and *I like'er,* as you said, they also pronounce them as *I like HIM* and *I like HER.*

L: That's right, but note that those involve focusing. That is, the interpretation of *I like HER* is something like 'it is her that I like', or 'as opposed to him, I like her'. It's very likely that the focusing has to be marked in the structure, so that both PF and LF recognize the appropriate structure for interpretive purposes (thus, for instance, leading to a characteristic stress/intonation). This is arguably done by way of an abstract F category that's associated to an element like *her,* thereby producing a branching structure where F and *her* are sisters, as follows [48]:

(26)

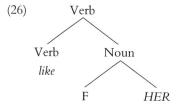

This of course breaks the mutual command between *HER* and *like,* and the LCA/T can then linearize the elements. Then at LF we get the right focused interpretation, and at PF we get the characteristic emphasis associated with this kind of structure [see fig. 3.21].

. . . and other difficult linearizations

O: All right, but look: you'll have to pull the same stunt for every single right branch. At the bottom of the structure, you'll necessarily find a situation of mutual command.

L: Obviously the conclusions the system forces on us are very strong, which is what makes them interesting [49]. Basically, under these assumptions, every right-branching structure has to end in a "trace." In fact, there are a number of phenomena that point precisely in this direction. I'm thinking of processes that depend on the "heaviness" of a right branch. For instance, we can't say that a proton which has split is a **proton split;* rather, we have to say that it's a *split proton.* But in English a proton which has split into quarks is indeed a *proton split into quarks,* and not a **split into quarks proton.*

O: That's rather curious—it never dawned on me before!

L: A one-word adjectival expression like *split* has to appear in pre-nominal position. But when the adjectival phrase consists of several words, like *split into quarks,* it has to appear after the noun. Now these facts can be naturally explained if we think that in fact *proton split into quarks* tells us pretty much what the basic underlying structure is, where *proton* and *split into quarks* are sisters, and of course the category *proton* commands everything inside the adjectival phrase. It's just like what you said about the sentence in (21). However, when the adjectival phrase consists of just one word—which is the case in *split proton*—the sort of problem turns up that you noted for (24), where *proton* doesn't asymmetrically command (thus precede) *split*. What happens then? Apparently, *split* moves upward, perhaps to some specifier from which it asymmetrically commands (thus precedes) *proton*. Why doesn't *split into quarks* do the same thing in the other instance, yielding **split into quarks proton?*

O: Because it needn't; it would rather procrastinate. That's extremely clever. All right; I see the general point.

L: Actually, it's more general than you might think. What we can call "light phrase shift"—leftward movement of a short expression—is quite common, whereas similar leftward "heavy shifts" are much harder to find. So English speakers constantly say things like *I turned on my Marconi radio that my father left me* as opposed to **I turned my Marconi radio that my father left me on,* but on the other hand, with the light pronoun *it* the result is the opposite: *I turned it on* versus **I turned on it* [50].

O: What about structures like *I like Ike,* where *Ike* is a name, and not a clitic? Those aren't focussed . . .

L: Well, here we get into the complex question of the structure of names. In many languages, names are systematically introduced by a determiner—so in colloquial German, people would say *der Ike,* literally 'the Ike' [51]. In effect, then, we're dealing with more structure here than in the case of *it.* The same thing happens with demonstratives like *that,* which probably have internal structure including a determiner and something else, maybe a locative adverbial part. So the general rule is always the same: linearization problems in right branches disappear the moment we posit more structure. Of course, at the very end of the right branch we hit rock bottom, and we have to cliticize.

O: So this view of yours again raises questions about morphological outputs and whether these should be treated in terms of Optimality Theory [see sec. 2.7].

L: It raises questions about morphology, period. For instance, *this, that, these, those* have rather different forms. If they all involve a determiner and some kind of adverbial, what are those? Even if one were to suggest that the common determiner is *the,* how about the adverbial? Whatever it is, it has to yield outputs such as *-is, -at, -ese,* and *-ose.* I know of no trivial, obvious candidate for this. Which suggests that the final outputs of the demonstratives are achieved in terms of some morphological processes. In general, instances of systematic regularities across a morphological paradigm behave this way, raising the question of what a paradigm is [see sec. 6.4] [52].

_____ the place for a linearization procedure

O: But in a nutshell, we needn't weaken the LCT, although we now understand it as enforcing some procedure L, which is aimed at obtaining a linearised object at PF—and not before. Differently put, it is still the case that if by PF two regular heads stand in a mutual command relation, the derivation crashes—at PF. In this sense the LCT is as strong as it was before. But it now has a precise place within the architecture of the derivation, by ensuring that procedure L applies. Since L is the procedure by which phrase markers are linearised, we must ask when it is relevant (that is, a procedure applies at a concrete stage in the derivation). It must apply prior to PF, or the phrase marker won't be linearised. To put it yet another way: the last point at which the LCT is relevant (and therefore at which procedure L can and must apply) is immediately after Morphology does its job. This means, if I've followed you, that structures like (25) must be created prior to the application of L: in that way, the trace left by an element like *it* will not pose a linearisation problem at PF (perhaps, though I want to return to this as well). And concerning the *it* cliticised onto the verb *like:* it gets ordered according to morphological procedures, hence independently of L, or even C$_{HL}$, for that matter [see fig. 3.22].

L: I might add that this sequence of events doesn't have to be stipulated. In the ideal world, operations should be able to apply anywhere, but the stupid orderings would give wrong results. For instance, if procedure L applied to a structure prior to the cliticization of *it* or prior to Morphology that orders *it* with respect to *like,*

Figure 3.22

The bifurcated model of the grammar with Morphology and the linearization procedure:

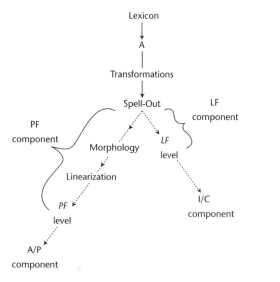

(24) would be ruled out in that particular derivation; it would never reach the desired structure in (25) and thus would never compete with alternative derivations for optimality purposes. Luckily, an alternative derivation exists in which things proceed the way we've sketched them, with (25) appropriately resulting in a convergent PF derivation.

O: Because only convergent derivations compete with one another. But you've also told me that derivations don't proceed merely in order to obtain a convergent result. Movement, for instance, seems to be triggered by the need to satisfy some requirement . . .

L: Yes, so we have to say that elements like *'im* and *'er* are clitics in the lexical array, so that they're allowed to cliticize. They have a feature in their lexical makeup that allows them to enter into a morphological relation with elements like the verb *like* and others. So consider all the possibilities. First, suppose the array contains *her,* the strong pronominal form. If it's a sister to *like,* one derivation will crash at PF because the phrase marker can't be linearized. In the alternative derivation, *her* cliticizes to *like,* which isn't justified morphologically. So these two are no good. Does that mean that there are no convergent structures that involve the verb *like* and the pronoun *her?* Not at all: we can derive (26), which is perfectly fine from the point of view of the LCA/T (with *her* presumably merging with F for focus reasons). Furthermore, there are no simpler alternatives to (26). In turn, suppose the derivation had started with *like* and the weak pronominal *'er.* Then the cliticization of *'er* to *like* would be justified, assuming that clitic elements are in some sense lexically **affixal** entries—so that they're allowed to cliticize [see sec. 6.3]. This derivation is totally different from the one in (26) and also from the ungrammatical derivations involving *like* and *her* without an F category. It's comparable to a derivation in which *'er* doesn't cliticize; but that one will clearly crash for linearization reasons [53].

O: Meaning that *I like 'er* (where *'er* isn't cliticised at all) is ungrammatical—which is true. Similarly, *I like her,* with no focus on *her* (and no cliticisation, since *her* isn't a clitic), is also ungrammatical. That seems right, for *I like her* appears to require an emphatic interpretation, just as *I like'er* can't have that interpretation [see fig. 3.23]. Doesn't it pay to be precise?

L: I've never denied that. But please don't get too caught up in notational or formal issues [54].

Figure 3.23

For Valentine's Day, you can try writing your own phrase markers for your secret Valentine. The passionate style: Array: {love, you}. Moves: none. Linearization: none. Result: complete crash.

The cheating style: Array: {love, you}. Moves: you (by cliticization). Linearization: fine. Result: illicit move and crash.

The emphatic style: Array: {love, you, F}. Moves: none. Linearization: fine. Result: convergence (but raises an interpretive doubt: 'love YOU, not someone else . . . ')

The subtle style: Array: {love, 'ya}. Moves: 'ya (by cliticization). Linearization: fine. Result: perfect convergence.

The shy style: Array: {love, 'ya}. Moves: none. Linearization: none. Result: complete crash.

Tell him/her (/or it!) that you have a total crash on 'em.

O: In this instance taking the LCA to be a theorem has had some smashing consequences, I believe. It has forced us not to weaken it, as you were inclined to do, initially.

_____ deducing binary branching

L: These are empirical matters. You were ready to say that the theory was wrong because it didn't predict *I like it,* and that was a case of jumping the gun—falsificationism, pure and simple. Now, don't think I have any problems with deductions; of course I don't. Take for instance the absence of ternary (or *n*-ary) relations that we mentioned earlier, and you seemed to be distressed about. Note that ternary branchings would complicate the linearization picture considerably, as (27) shows [55]:

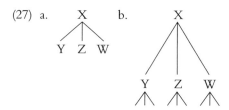

(27) a.   b.

In cases of multiple mutual command of heads (27a), we'd basically need to resort to multiple cliticization [56]. In turn, in situations of multiple mutual command of phrases (27b), it's unclear how to organize the nonprojecting phrases among themselves, given what we've said so far. That is, crucial to our command relation is the fact that (in binary relations) only one structure projects, and thus the other structure is accessible to the computational system, defining a unique command relation that determines linearization. If we had two (or more) structures that don't project (and are thus both (or all) accessible to the computational system), how would we get one to command (and thus determine precedence over) the other(s)? We wouldn't be able to linearize those projected phrases [see fig. 3.24]. So we can actually deduce why Human phrases are binary.

O: Very nice indeed. Which proves again that one must be precise and coherent.

L: But this should never be pursued at the expense of giving up insight.

O: Even if it leads to internal contradictions?

Figure 3.24

Consider the case of multiple mutual command of phrases sketched in (27b), making X a projection of W (hence, Z and Y are maximal projections):

X = |W|

|Y| |Z| W

What is the linear relation between, in particular, |Y| and |Z|? Since these elements stand in a mutual command relation, it is impossible to determine whether the elements that |Z| dominates should come before the elements that |Y| dominates, or vice versa.

L: Progress is always based on resolving internal contradictions.

O: But they must be recognised.

L: Which isn't always easy.

O: Are you quite determined to have the last word?

L: Well, it's always nice.

3.6 Empty Categories Are Not Empty

(a primer on traces of movement, with some more discussion on relations among features)

O: Now, let me change gears here (although I'm still pursuing my pending questions!). You seem to be talking about what you called the "trace" of moving something as though it were real. I thought you were leaving a copy of the moved element just to keep track of what has moved. But in discussing (25) you were asking how to linearise the trace element (it)! This, my dear sir, seems reprehensible, coming from someone who—by pursuing a minimalist programme—wants to ensure that we're not sneaking in improper concepts, entities, relations, conventions, or similar ghosts. What are traces?!

_____ **traces are real**

L: But traces are as real a category as there can be! If I hadn't postulated the trace in question, I'd be in trouble conceptually and empirically. Take (22). An element like *who* starts out as the complement of *convince,* okay? And the question we're now asking is, what happens after *who* moves? Does *convince* still have a complement? The answer must be yes, both from the point of view of the LF component and from the point of view of the PF component.

O: I hope that's true, because earlier I meant to ask you this question: If the trace *t* of moving, for example, *him,* in *him, I think I understand t,* has some syntactic existence (and is more than mere notation), it certainly stands in no linear relation to the verb (since mutual command obtains in this instance). That's just a modest, elementary fact. If phrase markers must be totally ordered after Spell-Out, one in which a verb and a trace of an element like *him* are

Although understanding of question formation has vastly improved over the millennia, people are still struggling with the role of auxiliaries and the place of negation.

sisters (such as (25), I'm afraid) simply cannot be a Human phrase marker. This is quite aside from the fact that the trace is not pronounced.

L: Perhaps it isn't, actually. We're the ones to decide, and it's indeed possible that the fact that speakers don't pronounce the trace of a moved *him* (including a cliticized version) suffices to satisfy the LCA, which may only be relevant for elements with a PF matrix [57]. After all, we're justifying the LCA precisely in terms of PF linearity. So here, then, is a consequence of the reality of traces for the computational system: they allow us to linearize structures like (25), as we saw.

O: Well, all right, but this is still within the boundaries of the particular example that concerned us a while back. Let's move on, since that sort of example has left me knackered. Could we discuss your LF and PF arguments for the existence of traces?

semantic arguments

L: The LF argument is this. The semantic import of a question can be thought of as a quantification over a set of propositions. So if the question was something like *who has the Linguist convinced?,* we can think of it as a quantification over propositions like "the Linguist has convinced Such-and-such," "the Linguist has convinced his mother," "the Linguist has convinced Dick Nixon," and so on . . . until we exhaust the **range** of the relevant set. Then the question is asking which of those propositions is true. Something like that, in any event [see fig. 3.23]. Then, in our semantic representation, we probably want to have some quantifier—let's say that's what *who* is when it moves to the specifier of Comp—and we also want to have some **variable** inside an **open expression,** something like 'the Linguist has convinced *x*'. Very roughly, we can then think of the variable as the element that's being assigned the role of the fellow who's convinced.

O: Yes, yes—these are things one can find in any introduction to linear algebra, or logic [58].

L: All right, but we're now asking about their syntactic reflex—if there is any. The way I've set up the question, we need an element in the typical position receiving the role of the convinced individual [see fig. 3.25].

O: In the complement of *convinced*, yes. That's an argument that a structural element is needed in the position of complement of *convinced*, even if a quantifier like *who* is displaced from the position of the variable. And I suppose *who* and its trace enter into a chain relation.

L: That's right. We can look at several of those later [see chap. 5].

O: Super! So the trace may perhaps map to a semantic variable. The translation doesn't seem to be totally clear, particularly because you want LFs to be inclusive, thus not adding any material that wasn't lexically represented in the initial array. One might then ask you, where do these variables come from? Aren't you adding them? But that's probably an unfair question . . .

L: The variable is part of the semantic representation, not the syntax. The syntax just provides a structure that can be mapped into the relevant semantics, after LF. Of course, LF is still perfectly inclusive: the trace is just a copy of whatever has moved—so there's no new lexical material [see fig. 3.25].

O: I thought you'd say that. (Basically, that *somehow* the relevant traces are mapped to some semantics to be determined [59].) Look here, I do see the general point, and am willing to grant it—even if the details seem extremely unclear to me, as yet. But what about PF? What argument could one possibly make that traces exist at PF? Did you not say the trace is gone by the PF component?!

---

phonetic arguments

L: No; it must be gone by the PF *level* [on this distinction, see chap. 2, (6)], since it isn't pronounced; which presupposes some sort of **deletion.** Now consider the deletion. This transformation works by targeting a phrase marker and making some of its features invisible to one of the interfaces. The structure that's left behind after the deletion is still accessible for further computations, though—it hasn't been wiped out. It's just that it doesn't have PF or LF properties, depending on what's been deleted. Babbling, for instance, has a PF matrix, but presumably no LF. I can show you more interesting examples later on, also, of objects with a very articulated PF structure that don't correspond to an LF structure [see sec. 3.7]. In turn, traces are typical objects that may be there (must be there, if the

Figure 3.25

Traces have often been used to syntactically represent a semantic variable, with a displaced element like *who* acting as its binding quantifier, to yield a rough semantics of the sort in the cartoon. If considered in full generality, this raises nontrivial questions about LF inclusiveness. Thus, compare (i) and (ii):

(i) a. who has he convinced t
   b. for which *x*, he has convinced *x*

(ii) a. he has convinced everyone
    b. for every *x*, he has convinced *x*

Suppose the (rough) semantic representations in (ib) and (iib) directly correspond to the LFs of (ia) and (iia). In order for these LFs to be inclusive, it must be shown that variable *x* corresponds to a lexical feature of some sort. This can be done by assuming that an expression like *who* carries within it at least two different features: a quantificational one ([wh]) and a referential one ([R]). When *who* is copied (via movement), the following representation results:

(iii)   who [he convinced (who)]
      [+wh]   [+wh]
      [+R]   [+R]

Then the key is to interpret the [wh] feature in the position to which *who* has been moved, while still interpreting the [R] feature in the lower occurrence (see sec. 3.7). This LF is now totally inclusive (thus corresponding to lexical features). In turn, it maps to a straightforward semantics, the [wh] feature receiving an operator interpretation, and the [R] feature receiving a variable interpretation. Obviously, though, whereas (ia) involves movement, (iia) does not—so how can a quantifier and an *x* variable be mapped for (ii)? In the past, linguists argued for raising of an element like *everyone* in (iia) in the LF component (see May 1985); but how would this movement be justified within the current framework? (Recall that raising cannot take place simply in order to obtain a given interpretation.) Various proposals exist in the literature on quantifiers: for example, generalized movement (to specific positions; Beghelli 1993); piggybacking on already existing movements (Kitahara 1992); and restricting movement to marked instances, providing in-situ interpretations for quantifier and variable in most instances (Fox 1995). See Hornstein 1995a and Reinhart 1995 for references and discussion of these and related matters.

argument about LF that I made a moment ago is a valid one), yet carry no sensorimotor instructions for PF. With this in mind, consider (28):

(28) a. I want to convince Such-and-such
     b. I wanna convince Such-and-such

In most dialects of American English, speakers say (28a) as shown in (28b).

O: We do that here as well, except perhaps in certain areas of Cambridge.

L: Same thing here. But now look at this:

(29) a.   I want Such-and-such to convince the queen
     b. *who do you wanna convince the queen?
     c.   who do you wanna convince?

When the speaker contracts *want to* as in (29b), she can't be asking a question whose answer could be something like (29a) [60].

O: That's very true, actually . . . But (29c) is again perfect. Hm . . . In a structure like the one underlying (29a) the element before *to* can't be extracted; but the element after the verb certainly can be. That's bloody bizarre!

L: If you think about it, it's exactly what you'd expect if traces are real and their structural presence can affect a morphological process. (30a) is the structure underlying (29b), and (30b) is the structure underlying (29c):

(30) a. who do you want (who) to convince the queen
     b. who do you want to convince (who)

You see, in (30a) the trace (who) interferes in the morphological formation of the contraction between *want* and *to*—that is, the formation of the word *wanna* at the onset of the PF component, which is nothing but *want* with a cliticized *to*—whereas in (30b) this obviously isn't the case [see fig. 3.26 for more arguments for the existence of traces].

consequences for the ordering of components

O: Help me understand the order of things here. What happens when? I'm finding it a fair old job, to keep track of every step . . .

L: Apparently, Morphology has to be ordered prior to the L procedure for linearization. Otherwise, elements cliticized onto heads would be ruled out before even having a chance to exist as word-level units, linearized by morphological processes [see fig. 3.22]. Because Morphology affects lexical material, the results don't directly match up pristine lexical structures, and all sorts of readjustments may be necessary to meet PF demands.

O: Readjustments of what, pray tell?

L: Of feature matrices. See, in principle, features can be or become part of a word in three ways [see fig. 3.5]: (i) they're fully coded in a lexical item in the lexicon; (ii) they're added to a lexical item as it becomes part of an array for derivational purposes; (iii) they're added in the course of the derivation. Of these, (ii) makes the fewest assumptions. To see this, assume that the lexicon is just a list of idiosyncrasies, a view first explicitly advocated by Leonard Bloomfield [61]. If a feature is systematically associated with a class of lexical items, that feature shouldn't be listed in the lexicon, but should be added to the item by way of a rule-governed process. (ii) provides one: when the array is formed that will determine the derivation, all the necessary features have to be associated with the lexical items (agreement features, Case features, tense features, whatever . . .). (iii) provides the other one: the features aren't part of the lexical item in the initial array (they may even be an entirely separate lexical item of a functional sort); they get added when certain relations are established through the computational process. While possible, this process needs additional empirical justification, since it adds an assumption about lexical forms.

—————————————————————————— morphological questions

O: I've often been impressed by the contortions that some of my Portuguese friends can get into with pronouns. In Portuguese, speakers can stick a pronoun between a verbal root and its future morpheme: for example, *falar-lhe-ha,* literally 'talk-to.him/her-will'.

L: I know. And of course your point is that here elements seem to gain morphological dependents in the course of the derivation [see

Figure 3.26

An ingenious experiment by Swinney et al. (1988) shows that human language processing is sensitive to traces. In their experiment, the researchers used a previously well-established technique for studying lexical access, called *cross-modal priming.* To try a very rough version of this technique, ask someone to repeat the word *top* twenty times, rapidly, and indicate that you will be asking a question that should be answered quickly and without much reflection, since it is trivial. While the person is repeating *top,* interrupt with "What do you do in front of a green light?" You will find that people invariably answer, "Stop" (which of course is not what they do in front of a green light). By saying the word *top,* the person has activated the phonological class that includes the word *stop,* which is also semantically related as the opposite of the correct answer to the question. The point is that words activate other related words, which makes access to them somewhat automatic. Most carefully executed experiments involve lexical decision tasks, asking subjects to determine whether a given token is a word or not. Interestingly, subjects can perform this task more rapidly and efficiently if they have previously processed a related word. For example, the subject may have been asked to process a sentence like *they accused the boy.* Upon processing the word *boy,* the subject is asked to decide whether a different token is a word. This is the key: if the word is lexically related to *boy* (e.g., *girl*), the subject makes the decision more quickly than if the word is not lexically related (e.g., *thief*). (Decision times in these experiments are extremely rapid, results differing only by milliseconds.) Swinney et al. used this technique in a novel situation. Suppose *the boy* is moved as in (i):

(i) the policeman saw *the boy* that the crowd at the party accused *t* of the crime

In this instance, *the boy* is no longer present after *accused,* although it is somehow "understood" there. Theoretically, this is explained in terms of a trace (*t*) in object position, as discussed in the text. But is this element anything other than a hypothetical, abstract object? Swinney et al. showed that it plausibly is. When given a lexical decision task after *accused* (note, not after the displaced *the boy*), subjects showed the same priming effects that they show when *the boy* has not moved; in other words, they can decide more easily that *girl* is a word than they can decide that *thief* is. This would be unexplained if there were no symbolic representation of *the boy* after *accused.* But if there is indeed a syntactically and semantically active trace of *the boy* (even if it has no phonological realization), the priming effect is straightforwardly explained. (The general priming effect disappears after new words are processed; that is, it could not have been the actual occurrence of the word *boy* seven words earlier that triggered the relevant effect.) In the last few years, several researchers have replicated Swinney et al.'s results with other, more sophisticated techniques.

Figure 3.27

Clitic interpolation, of the sort mentioned in the text, is a pervasive phenomenon that again highlights the mysterious nature of clitics. No matter how the phenomenon is analyzed, it poses very demanding questions. Consider, for instance, the (substandard) Spanish form *sient-e-se-n* 'seat-you(formal)-self-plural'. How can the clitic become part of the word? In this instance, the clitic is not just "leaning" on the word periphery but is actually inside the word, leaving the agreement marker to its right. A radically lexicalist analysis could argue that the *se* element in this Spanish dialect is simply part of the lexical item *siente-sen,* which is precompiled as such in the initial array. This would commit the theorist to the view that separate lexical items (like *se,* which appears in various contexts in isolation) can nonetheless be part of a word.

fig. 3.27] [62]. But to evaluate the full spectrum of cases in Human, we have to look at the other extreme, Arabic, which literally spreads morphemes into verbal roots, such as *ktb* 'write' [see fig. 2.25].

O: Yes: Arabic speakers say *katab* to encode a perfective active form, *kutib* to encode a passive version, *aktub* and *uktab* to encode imperfective active and passive, respectively, and so forth. There are dozens of forms . . .

L: All of which use the root *ktb* and differ only in their morphological shape depending on what morphemic element gets **infixed.** Well, it isn't easy to see how these forms could be obtained in a derivation. If *ktb* merges with *a,* let's say, the result should be **ktba,* or some such thing. But how does the *a* get inside the word? It seems more reasonable to expect a form like *katab* to be lexically formed, with subsequent checking in the syntax. So the matter might even be parametric, with languages differing in how they set the parameter (e.g., Portuguese vs. Arabic).

O: When you assert that the Arabic forms are lexically combined, are you not assigning some constructive power to the lexicon?

L: Again: I'm assuming that the grammatical part of the lexicon is nothing but a repository of exceptions. Whatever isn't predictable (including arbitrary pairings of sound and meaning) goes right into the lexicon. (Of course, the lexicon also interfaces with other cognitive domains responsible for concept formation; regularities surely exist in those, but they're not obviously grammatical [see sec. 2.4].) But remember option (ii) from a moment ago: if we say that features are assembled upon entering the initial array, we're not invoking a combinatorial lexicon.

O: But since the verbal paradigm of Arabic is predictable, surely some combinatorial function is needed.

L: Yeah, something has to relate lexical information to the syntax proper, which is why option (ii) says that elements are assembled in the initial array . . .

O: Doesn't that grant the array the status of a level?

L: Not a syntactic level, no. The array is a collection of lexical items, and these admittedly have properties. But this collection isn't syntactically structured. If it were, and if principles of grammar applied to determine the structures, then it would be a syntactic level of representation. But I'm not changing our basic assumptions when I say that items in the array are constructively assembled according to lexical rules (in fact, universal—perhaps cognitive—ones, or language-specific ones).

O: My, my . . . I do seem to be making heavy weather of filling in each of the steps. I thought you told me that the level responsible for words—namely, Morphology—operates much later, immediately prior to procedure L for linearisation.

L: Yeah, that's where Morphology needs to be, and whether or not some lexical process needs to happen early on is a purely empirical matter [63]. From a syntactic point of view, it doesn't really matter if, instead of a fully specified lexical matrix in the initial array— something like *book* with the semantic features of *book* ("artifact/ abstract-entity," etc.) and its phonological features ("begins with a [b]," etc.)—we simply had a set of purely formal features ([+N], [−V], etc.) with a code—say, the number 14—which says that at the point of Spell-Out all the featural information will be encoded. Maybe that's when all the morphological adjustments happen. Of course, we need something that allows us to address the lexicon— for instance, this 14 code—so that before the point where PF and LF split, the phonological form of *book* is appropriately related to [búk] and not to [fút] or [kat], and the semantic form of *book* is related to something which has the properties of a book, and not a cat. The obvious. So the point is, for all the syntactician cares, we could be doing things this way, without even encoding full lexical features in the initial array, which would then be a collection of matrices of formal features, each paired with a set of codes addressing these matrices to specific lexical information. It's just that for the purposes of discussion and presentation that's a very opaque system, and it's not obviously the simplest hypothesis either—but we don't know for sure what "simplest" means in these domains.

O: The way you've painted the picture, Morphology has a dramatic role in the actual form of expressions, including certain linear orderings at the word level.

L: Correct. In fact, I suspect Morphology is directly involved in the peculiarity of the mapping to PF, which is radically different—in terms of inclusiveness and uniformity—from the mapping to LF. As

Figure 3.28

The key to deducing the LCA is finding an ordering within syntactic objects that trivially maps to a linear PF relation. The command relation is one such natural relation within given phrase markers:

Within a basic element of this sort, command (which arguably follows from Merge) is in fact the only relation holding among terminal items; it is thus natural to expect command to be the ordering relation for PF purposes. However, this clearly does not work with more complex phrase markers:

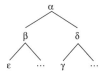

In this instance, although one would want to say that ε precedes γ, there is no command relation between these elements. The induction step of the LCA encodes an extra relation, which crucially includes domination. However, this extra relation does not follow from any obvious building operation and is thus formally stipulated.

Otto Jespersen once noted, morphology is the repository for all the quirks and oddities of history that make it into the linguistic system. The way he put it: nobody ever dreamed of a universal morphology. No doubt it's a truism to say that languages are historical, but sometimes we have to remind ourselves of this [64].

3.7 Further Consequences of Linearization

(with arguments about Spell-Out, the nature of traces, and other matters of great curiosity, including the notorious "reconstruction effects")

O: The plot you're now unravelling relates to two more of my increasingly infamous pending questions . . . The first concerns the induction step of the LCA/T, which is not so easy to deduce, I'm afraid. A structure like that corresponding to *you dig this* directly encodes a sequence equivalent to <you, {dig, this}>, which makes its mapping to PF rather effortless. (Once again, that doesn't linearise {dig, this}, but we've already dealt with this matter.) Nevertheless, consider *your aunt digs this.* The LCA linearises the object by invoking the induction step for *your* and *aunt.* But if we want to deduce this too (making the relevant sequence <your, aunt, digs, this> follow from an LCT), then we must say something about how this particular sequence is encoded within the phrasal structure of *your aunt digs this.* And . . . I do not know how to do this!

L: This is one of the reasons I didn't want to make a big deal about deducing the LCA. It seems as if the induction step is very hard to deduce; it just doesn't follow from anything obvious [see fig. 3.28].

——————————————————————— *multiple Spell-Out*

O: Unless . . . this is telling us that procedure L for linearisation isn't even attempting to linearise the wholly formed phrase marker, but only skeletal parts.

L: Are we communicating [65]?

O: Pray, tell me this: precisely how did you assemble the phrase marker corresponding to *your aunt digs this?*

L: I gave you an explicit procedure for doing it.

O: Very well, let's get on with it, then. We start with the array {your, aunt, digs, this}, and we merge two items—say, *digs* and *this*—projecting *digs*. That's grand, and it gives us [digs, this]. Now what? Suppose we next choose *aunt* from the array, and we merge it with [digs, this]. That gives us [aunt [digs this]], with (we hope) *digs* projecting. But now look: were we now to add *your,* we'd evidently obtain [your [aunt [digs this]]], and not [[your aunt] [digs this]]. So we're in trouble.

L: But that's trivial. Another derivation is possible in which two different phrase markers, [your aunt] and [digs this], are assembled separately; after they've been built in parallel, they can be merged straightforwardly [66].

O: I was hoping you'd say that. Fine, so at some point in the derivation we've got two skeletal phrase markers: [your aunt] and [digs this]. Give me a phrase marker of arbitrary complexity, and I can always reduce it to a set of phrase markers all of whose branches are linearly ordered by a command relation—let's call those "command units" [67]. So suppose you give me a jumble of a phrase marker, with several levels of embedding and all sorts of nasty combinations of paths. Consider (31), where the objects in (c) are the command units needed to assemble (b) (I shall simplify irrelevant details): (31) a. that this cumbersome sentence will prove my point of view affects the Linguist's theory about phrases

(31) a. that this cumbersome sentence will prove my point of view affects the Linguist's theory about phrases

    b.

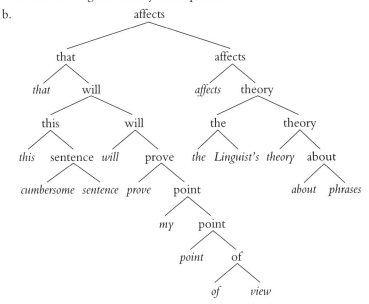

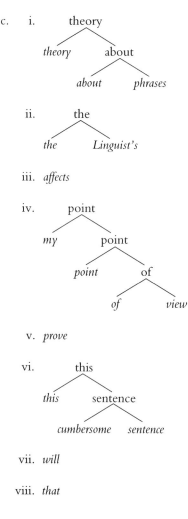

c. i. theory
        theory   about
                  about   phrases

    ii.   the
           the   Linguist's

    iii. *affects*

    iv.   point
          my   point
                  point   of
                            of   *view*

    v. *prove*

    vi.   this
          this   sentence
               cumbersome   *sentence*

    vii. *will*

    viii. *that*

No matter how complex the object in (31b) is, in (31c) it has been reduced to either words or phrase markers whose structure follows from trivial projection. If we follow steps (i) through (viii), applying Merge every time a new word comes into the derivation, we easily obtain (31b).

L: What's the point?

O: Suppose we were trying to linearise the successive objects merged in (31c), instead of the large object in (31b). Then the procedure could be executed simply on the basis of the base step of the LCA. Or to put it in my own terms, then the linearisation of each phrase marker would be a direct consequence of its command structure, without having to invoke an induction step for the LCA. In essence, the LCA would be directly reduced to a rather elegant LCT: α *precedes* β *if and only if* α *commands* β. Full stop.

L: At the cost of introducing multiple Spell-Outs, one per object in (31c).

O: But you told me that Spell-Out is just a rule, nothing remotely close to a level! There's no reason, then, why Spell-Out must wait until the entire phrase marker is fully assembled. What I'm saying is very much in the spirit of your own conception of Spell-Out.

L: Maybe, but now Morphology's going to have to apply at all those points, and phonological rules are going to have to target each of the objects that undergo Spell-Out, and—

O: Hold on, wasn't that true all along? How did you conceive of Spell-Out, explicitly?

—————————————————————————————— *single Spell-Out*

L: As I see it, Spell-Out applies to the entirely formed phrase marker, stripping away those elements which are relevant only to the PF computation and leaving behind a residue that makes it to LF, through syntactic processes of exactly the same kind as those that apply prior to Spell-Out. Furthermore, as I said before, I take Spell-Out to deliver the phrase marker to Morphology, which is responsible for the construction of word-level units.

O: Exactly—that's what I thought. Then Spell-Out is targeting in-dividual nodes within the phrase marker where featural information is encoded. After all, the operation "strips away" certain features and leaves behind certain others. But features are encoded in categorial objects: presumably all categories have features (at least heads must), and hence the procedure is targeting those chunks where features lie. What I'm trying to say is that one can't simply target the root of a phrase marker, and be done with it; one must proceed node by node, cleaning up one's act. Do you follow me?

L: That's easy to do.

O: Why, of course! But I'm trying to generalise this idea of "pro-ceeding node by node" to the simplest scenario:

(32) Given a structure $\{\underline{\alpha} \ \{\alpha, \beta\}\}$, α may be spelled out.

That is to say, if we find a category α which projects, we spell out the part that does not enter any further projection, routing its phonetic information to PF and the rest of its information to LF. Then, in some instances, we'll come upon two categories which are both projected and hence not spelled out. These are points in the phrase marker where two already formed structures are being combined. But again, one of them will project, which means we only spell out the other one (to be exact, those parts of the other one which haven't yet been spelled out; that is, the category corresponding to the label). And we keep doing this until we're done, spelling out the root node. That's all.

L: That can't be all, or we'd never have a chance to move anything: when we hit a category, we spell it out. But if this is the case, how could we possibly move *Socrates* in *Socrates, I like?*

O: Which is why I'm saying in (32) that Spell-Out may apply, not that it must do. If Spell-Out applies too early in a language that requires viral immunisation, forcing some displacement, the derivation will crash at PF. But we can follow the other route: not to spell out this part of the structure (*Socrates* in your example) until it has moved, in which case the derivation won't crash. That is to say, Spell-Out applies up to convergence.

L: But now why should Spell-Out ever apply early—in which case it would have to apply several times, instead of once and for all? That should be the most economical alternative.

O: You're probably right about that. So if possible, Spell-Out would apply once and for all, according to my view. Nevertheless, it can't if we've got a complex object, like the one in (31)—that's the intuition. If we wait too long, we don't know how to spell out such a complex object, if the LCT reduces to an if-and-only-if requirement between command and precedence—the base step in our (13a). In that case, we're forced to spell out more than once.

L: Then your proposal couldn't possibly work. Consider the phrase marker corresponding to *his students, I believe were fond of Plato,* which obviously involves movement:

(33) [his students [I believe [(his students) were fond of Plato]]]

Presumably, *his students* is moving for PF reasons (to be concrete, let's say that there's a topic feature that's being checked this way). But if *his students* hadn't moved, this would be one of those situations in which, according to your approach, Spell-Out would have to apply early, since neither *his* nor *students* commands the other heads within the sentence. Now look what's happened: because *his students* has moved, leaving a copy behind, there's no possibility of linearizing the embedded copy, and thus this perfectly grammatical sentence should never be possible. In fact, your theory predicts that movement should never take place from subject position, since moving a subject as we did in (33) will leave a copy behind which can't be linearized, according to your elegant LCT.

O: Au contraire! My theory predicts, as you said, that the embedded copy of *his students* in (33) cannot be linearised. That much, I thoroughly agree with. Therefore, I submit the following proposal: the copy of a category which has moved must be deleted. Since—as you suggested—elements with no PF matrix aren't subject to the LCT (that is, linearisation doesn't matter for them), then the fact that my system cannot linearise the embedded copy directly predicts why copies of moved elements cannot be pronounced. That is to say, my system predicts why English speakers say *his students, I believe were fond of Plato,* and not *his students, I believe his students were fond of Plato.*

L: Yeah, that would be a nice result, except that it now predicts that English speakers should be able to say *his students, I like his students,* since there's no obvious problem in linearizing the trace of the complement *his students* [see fig. 3.29].

O: You're right about that too . . . 'Tis a pity, though, for it would be nice to deduce from this puzzle the fact that traces are never pronounced . . . Nevertheless, grant me this much: my Spell-Out-Anywhere proposal doesn't run into trouble with (33), given that, for some reason, traces aren't pronounced.

L: I still think your proposal is going to be extremely messy. In effect, one would have to compute which way of spelling out a phrase marker is the most economical, which would be a nightmare. But anyway, I don't fully understand the consequences of what you're saying. You'd be predicting, for instance, that each of those skeletal command units you produced in (31c) should have its own prosodic reality, which isn't obvious [68]. That's the first empirical

Figure 3.29

The basic movement in (33) (*his students, I believe t were fond of Plato*) is as in (i), where F is some topic feature:

(i)

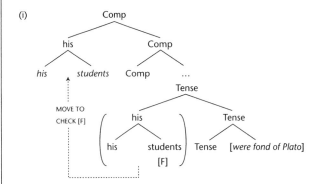

(ii)

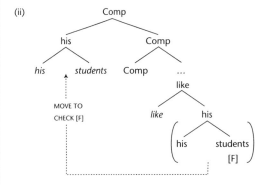

Note that at no point does either *his* or *students* command the rest of the structure above the projection of *his*. In this respect, (i) contrasts with (ii) (*his students, I like t*): In this instance, *his* and *students* are commanded by *like*, and by various other elements within the structure, as desired. The question then is how to linearize *his* and *students* in (i) with respect to the remaining structure, in particular if *his students* needs to move (and hence cannot be partially spelled out). The induction step in (13) does achieve the appropriate linearization, but it seems stipulative.

consequence that comes to mind. Conceptually, aside from your attempt at simplifying the LCA (which doesn't particularly move me), your reasoning does remove even the slightest temptation to think about the point of Spell-Out as a structural level, since plainly there's no structural object corresponding to a point of Spell-Out in your terms: you just have chunks of an object which is fully assembled only at PF and LF, with Morphology (and Prosody, etc.) affecting the chunks in whichever ways these nonsyntactic processes operate. That's a result, but I just don't know whether the change you propose can be maintained on other grounds. To begin with, you're in effect denying the existence of LF and PF as separate levels.

O: Er . . . Yes, that's true—but I still have the corresponding components!

L: I know, but the fact is that you access the A/P and I/C components dynamically, as the derivation proceeds [69]. It's hard to know whether that will create other problems, or even exactly what it means.

—————————————————————————————— *spelling out traces*

O: Fair enough. Now, since we've raised the issue of why traces shouldn't be pronounced, allow me to raise one other point about simplifications within the system. Nothing that you've said predicts that the phonological features of traces should delete. Why don't they stay as regular copies? I was anticipating that my suggestion would have this effect, but you've shown that it doesn't.

L: That's how Human works. Maybe in Martian traces don't have to delete; but in Human they do.

O: But can't we deduce that?

L: If we could, it would be true of Martian as well.

O: That depends on how we deduce it. For instance, perhaps it follows from properties which are themselves not conceptually necessary, and hence Martian wouldn't have to exhibit them.

L: Yeah, but Venusian might. We have to stop somewhere.

O: There are no rules regulating where we should stop!

L: There aren't, but I don't see the point in getting bogged down with something like that, if we don't have anything to say about why Human is the particular way it happens to be. It's just a fact, and that's that.

O: But we're in the business of explaining facts.

L: Some of them—the ones we have an explanation for.

O: Very well, then, here's an explanation [70]. Suppose we've got an object like *you dug this,* whose topmost category's got, as we've established, the formal structure |{d̲, {{d, {#d#, |#t#|}}, |#y#|}}|, mapping to the PF sequence <y, {d, t}>. Now suppose I move *this* to form *this, you dug this.* I'm not parenthesising the copy of *this* because I'm actually trying to deduce the parenthesis (also known as "deletion of phonological features"); so let's look at the structure prior to the deletion of these features within the trace of *this.* The structure should be a projection of some X, which merges with the moved *this.* The form of the new object is {X̲, {{ . . . |{d, {{d, {#d#, |#t#|}}, |#y#|}}| . . . }, t}}, which maps to the PF sequence <t, y, {d, t}>. D'you follow?

L: No.

O: Look what we've got: *t(his)* both precedes and follows *y(ou).*

L: But that's trivial. All you have to say is that each copy is a different *occurrence* of *t(his),* and the puzzle disappears.

O: Of course I know I can do that; but I don't want the puzzle to disappear. Thus, suppose I don't introduce that stipulation about occurrences, or I make it irrelevant for PF purposes. Something more interesting happens: C_{HL} must eliminate either the first or the second *t(his),* in order to linearise the chain. Assuming there was a reason for *t(his)* to move in the first place, it should be the lower copy whose phonological features are deleted. Deletion—so you've told me—means not having something like a PF set of features. Then the representation of the relevant PF sequence after deletion is this: <t, y, {d}>. No problem emerges for linearising *t(his):* it precedes *y(ou).* Full stop. Now the need for copy deletion is deduced.

L: That's possible, but it doesn't seem to be general enough.

O: Why?

L: Quite simply because your approach predicts that the top **link** of a chain is what counts for interpretive purposes, while the rest of the chain doesn't. But that can't be true. It's arguably true for chains at PF, but it's certainly false for their interpretation at LF. In this respect let's look at (34), which goes by the name of a "reconstruction" effect [71]:

(34) *which portrait of himself* did you say that I believe Rivera likes?

O: Oh, come now! I thought you said earlier that anaphors must be dreadfully close to their antecedent! Look at (34): the anaphor can be miles away from the antecedent! You've cheated before . . .

L: I don't think so. Remember that a copy theory of movement predicts that the relevant structure should be something like (35):

(35) which portrait of himself did you say that I believe Rivera likes (which portrait of himself)

That is, *which portrait of himself* moves to Comp, leaving behind a copy.

O: I see, and if the copy contains the anaphor at LF, then it's actually relatively close to the antecedent *Rivera* [72]. Nice . . . Parenthetically, this is a very powerful argument for the existence of traces: if the trace (that is, the copy) didn't exist, the anaphor wouldn't have an antecedent.

L: Precisely—but now look at this. Obviously, at LF (35) has to be reduced to something like (36), the essential structure that feeds interpretation:

(36) which (portrait of himself)
                  ↑
            NOT INTERPRETED AT LF

      did you say that I believe

      Rivera likes (which) portrait of himself
                          ↑
                NOT INTERPRETED AT LF

The structure that feeds the I/C components is this:

(37) which . . . Rivera likes portrait of himself
[= for which *x* [Rivera likes *x*, a portrait of himself]]

Nothing in your proposal could possibly predict these facts, if your reasoning for why moved elements leave traces (i.e., why the PF features of their matrices must be deleted) is a consequence of linearization *at PF*. We're at LF now, where—by hypothesis—linearization isn't relevant.

O: We could make it relevant.

L: We could, of course, but then go back to (24): if phrase markers have to be linearized at LF as well as at PF, how is that object involving mutually commanding heads going to survive the linearization? That's why we resorted to restricting linearization matters to PF, to begin with. And look, even if you were to linearize both at PF and at LF, the bottom line is this: at PF you would be linearizing *which portrait of himself* in the matrix clause, and at LF you would be linearizing *portrait of himself* in the embedded clause. There's no way around that: the LF interpretation of the reconstructed phrase doesn't correspond to its PF interpretation, no matter how many tricks you have up your sleeve. So you're going to have to try harder to deduce the fact that movement leaves traces. Strictly, that's only true at PF, where the matrix copy is pronounced and the embedded copy isn't. At LF, the results of movement allow you to look into the copies, and (at least part of) the moved element has to be deleted. In (36), for instance, only *which* is interpreted in the matrix clause, while *portrait of himself* has to be interpreted in the embedded clause. And that's a fact your speculation had nothing to say about [73].

At this very moment, communication between the Linguist and the Other became even more distorted, and all the Linguist could hear was:

"I get—"

And then the Other was gone. The Linguist was left wondering what he could have possibly meant . . . "I get tired of these sorts of arguments after a while"? Or "I need to get up early tomorrow and therefore I must leave now"? The Linguist even thought that perhaps the Other meant to say, "I'd better go now," but he said [ge-tar] instead of [be-tar] because performance can often produce bizarre, scrambled results like "I getter bow now." It really didn't occur to him that the Other might have been using a cliticized version of *it,* because otherwise he wouldn't have been able to linearize the relevant phrase marker. But very smart people are like that sometimes; they don't get it!

After his abrupt disappearance the previous day, the Other was edgy on the fourth afternoon, and when he emerged at the meeting point, he was both late and angry. Without even saying "Hello," he launched right into what concerned him.

"There's something very fishy about the whole bloody thing!"

The Linguist stared back, a bit shocked by the remark, and had no clue what the Other might be talking about.

"The blooming dialogue!" he insisted. "Our character status, what we're saying, et cetera, et cetera, et cetera!"

". . ." reflected the Linguist. "I thought we'd settled that yesterday . . ."

"How could we? We're still here!"

"We might go back in time and check—if we're characters . . ."

"But that would change our entire history."

"Look, we can spend the rest of our existence doubting ourselves."

"That's metaphysics, and what we're suffering from is garden-variety rip-off."

"That's what's worrying you?"

"I should like to call my solicitor . . ."

"This is very probably an FBI conspiracy. But there's nothing we can do."

". . ."

"Other than talk."

". . ."

"At least we won't get bored . . ."

"It's all a fiction."

"I'm a busy person—I've no time for fictions!"

"You're just a busy character."

Like a feature that doesn't make it all the way up to the interface levels, a misguided seagull blasted into the wormhole. The Linguist gravely stared at the bird's invisible path, and sighed melancholically.

L: Let's play the part as best we can.

O: . . .

L: . . .

O: Well, you left me very puzzled yesterday. I've been worrying about this question all night.

L: Yes?

O: If I understood you correctly, there really must be virtual movement.

4.1 Movement in Languages "without Movement"
(wherein mysterious ellipses are shown at work and features are argued to be the source of amazing transformations)

L: What do you mean by "virtual movement"?

O: Movement that one doesn't see or hear—but is there! For instance, whereas Irish has verb movement (one hears it in PF) English doesn't (one hears no such thing in PF). We've made the not unreasonable assumption that at LF languages are alike: given the same array of lexical items in English and Irish (putting aside the arbitrary fact that English speakers say *man* whereas Irish speakers say *fhear,* et cetera), after the computational procedure applies, we reach equivalent LF configurations. We thought this was reasonable because we didn't think there would be much evidence for the language learner to set a parameter that made English one way and Irish the other *at LF.* And the rest follows.

――――――――――――――――――――――――――――――――― covert movements

L: Matters aren't quite as trivial as you imply.

O: But it's elementary! The structure that's fed to the LF component in English is *they beat Conlon,* whereas the structure that's fed to the LF component in Irish is *beat they Conlon.* If at the LF level the two structures must be equivalent, then either the verb lowers in Irish in the LF component, or the verb raises in English in the LF component. Either way, this is **covert** movement.

L: There's indeed some LF movement in Human, and the system that allows this is the one we already have [1]. I wouldn't call the movement "virtual," though, because the movement is as real as it gets; in fact, we could argue that it's even more basic than standard **overt** movement. At any rate, all we need to assume is that, af-

Figure 4.1

Overt and covert syntax:

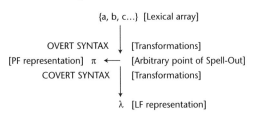

ter Spell-Out, the computational process continues, working with whatever phrase marker had been assembled prior to that point in the computation. Of course, it's this prior-to-Spell-Out phrase marker that gets shipped to PF, and thus pronounced. So whatever operations happen in the LF branch after Spell-Out aren't part of the overt syntax, and as you said are covert. In principle, they're equally real; it's just that they don't have a reflex in terms of what people hear or pronounce [see fig. 4.1]. In fact we can't say that something particular—say, movement—is restricted to the overt component of the grammar. That would be like saying the mapping between the array A and LF isn't uniform, when in fact it is. The intuition we're pursuing, however, is that rules of grammar can't refer to a specific part of the grammar, like the overt (or for that matter the covert) part. Needless to say, all sorts of covert operations are going on—that's life. Ellipsis, for instance.

———————————————————————————————— *ellipsis*

O: I like my elliptical sentences; they're short.

L: Oh, I do too!

O: Which?

L: What?

O: My elliptical sentences or yours?

L: Ah—well, both, in fact! Yes, so as you can see these are in fact complex structures, with nontrivial interpretive properties, which allow us to encode different referential dependencies among elided noun phrases . . .

O: I'd say the human mind is rather generous in dealing with covert information. Why, just now you don't see all the angles of my grimace, and yet you do reconstruct my features—do you not? And were I to draw a cube in two dimensions, you could reconstruct its missing parts, and identify it as a three-dimensional object [see fig. 4.2].

L: Oh, no doubt about it—ellipsis has all kinds of extraordinary properties that indicate a very intricate structure. Witness:

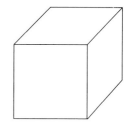

Although this image could represent three faces of a cube, it could also represent three faces of a variety of other polyhedra, among others:

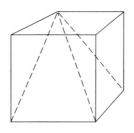 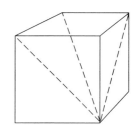

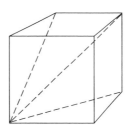 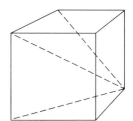

Figure 4.2

Interestingly, among the interpretations for which missing information has to be postulated, the cube interpretation is the first to be considered. However, once the other possibilities are pointed out, viewers have no trouble reconstructing their missing sides, either.

(1) a. Phil walked by the bank, and so did Lou [walk by the bank]
    b. Phil kicked the bucket, and so did Lou [kick the bucket]
    c. Phil saw an old friend, and so did Lou [see an old friend]
    d. the window was shattered, and so was his dream [shattered]
    e. Phil finished his first novel, and so did Lou [finish his first
       novel]

_____ *parallel interpretations*

The interpretation of all these examples displays a certain parallelism. I've carefully chosen them so you can always interpret the first sentence in two different ways. (For instance, walking by the riverbank versus a financial institution.) Remarkably, the second sentence—the elided one—in all these examples has to be interpreted the same way as the "antecedent" sentence. Thus, it's very odd to say something like, "On a sunny afternoon Hammett finished *The Maltese Falcon,* and so shall I on this sunny afternoon" [2].

O: Unless of course you're writing it again! But if you don't mind my saying so, the second sentences needn't be elided. The parenthesised material on the right-hand side of your examples can actually be pronounced. To my ear, when I say something like, "Marlowe will mumble a lie and so will Archer mumble a lie," I give a high pitch to the first part of the second sentence, and then the tone falls with a long good-bye [see fig. 4.3] . . . And is it not true that here too the observed "parallelism" obtains? Consider the oddness of saying, "On a sunny afternoon Hammett finished *The Maltese Falcon,* and so shall I finish *The Maltese Falcon* on this sunny afternoon." I don't suppose you'd say this sentence is felicitous, any more than the one involving ellipsis is.

L: Yes, the "parallelism" seems to be necessary here as well, which suggests something quite remarkable. Elliptical sentences are normal sentences which aren't seen by the PF component.

Figure 4.3

Observe the phonetic contour of *Marlowe will mumble a lie and so will Archer mumble a lie*. Note, in particular, that the contour drops after the first, stressed syllable of the subject *Archer*.

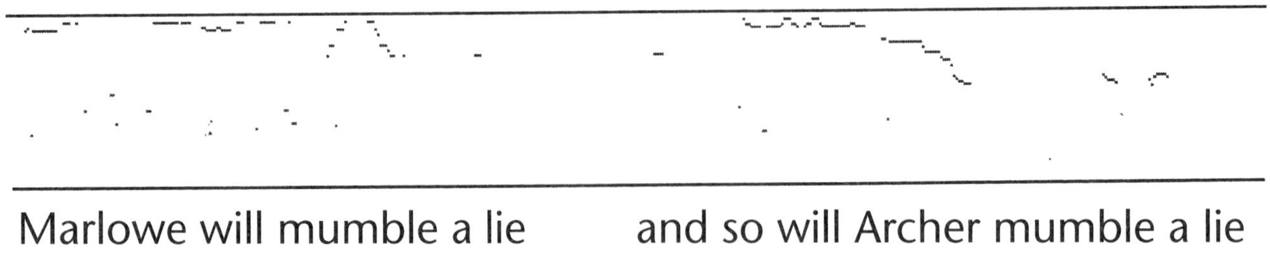

Marlowe will mumble a lie   and so will Archer mumble a lie

O: You mean the elided material is there in the structure, but its PF features have been deleted . . .

L: That's right. The basic structure is always something like *John read a book and so will Bill read a book,* with the relevant "parallelism." Then one of two things can happen to the second occurrence of *. . . read a book.* First, it can get the special intonation that you mentioned, which linguists call a **copy intonation.** Second, the PF features of material that's marked with this copy intonation can get deleted, resulting in true ellipsis.

O: And the grammar truly has these two options? Surely one wouldn't expect that!

L: Yeah, well, it depends on whether they're equally costly or not [3]; besides, there may be differences in emphasis between the two kinds of structures, which may involve focal features of some sort. But to tell you the truth, the phenomenon is very poorly understood.

————————————————————— *interpretive parallelism anywhere?*

O: I say, doesn't "observational parallelism" also obtain if one stares at two Necker cubes, one next to the other [see fig. 4.4]? That is, if the right cube is interpreted in a given position in space, the left cube must be interpreted the same way—mustn't it?

L: Well, that may or may not be the same sort of "parallelism." The good news is, there are linguistic cases that support your observation [4]. Take for instance (2):

(2) a. Phil always walks by whichever bank Lou does
     b. Phil likes to see whichever old friend Lou does
     c. Phil always finishes whichever novel Lou does

Here the structures aren't quite "parallel," but it seems as if they're "inclusive" in some unspecified sense. Certainly, the phrase where the ellipsis obtains is embedded inside the matrix sentence. Still, these examples have to display a certain homomorphism: in general, the interpretations in the elided sentence and its "antecedent" can't be chosen randomly. And this looks like one of the situations that arises with Necker cubes. In particular, when one Necker cube is inside another, the viewer is also pretty much forced to interpret

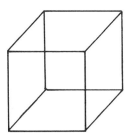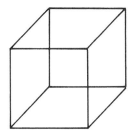

Necker cubes. (From Kuno, *Functional syntax*)

Figure 4.4

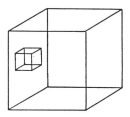

Embedding and embedded Necker cubes. (From Kuno, *Functional syntax*)

Figure 4.5

their projections in the same direction [see fig. 4.5]. The bad news for your observation, though, is that the kind of visual games we can play with Necker cubes is rather different from the kind of interpretive differences we find in sentences. Thus, for instance, a viewer's interpretation of a Necker cube constantly shifts back and forth. Sentential ambiguity hardly ever works that way, and can be considerably fuzzier. At the same time, with a bit of trickery, the visual effect with Necker cubes can easily be destroyed [see fig. 4.6].

O: The appropriate context can also force nonhomomorphic reading—in cases of ellipsis. I submit:

(3) a. the beggar walked by the bank, and so did the executive—ironically, they each walked by a different sort of bank
     b. once again, the damn cow kicked the bucket, and tragically so did the farmer who was milking her, when the bucket hit him in the head

L: The data is pretty murky, but people have argued that the **implicatures** we're dealing with can be **defeased,** precisely by loading the context one way or the other [5]. Which suggests that in fact the homomorphism constraint we're discussing is some sort of pragmatic condition. Whether it's also present in the visual system, as you've suggested—that's harder to establish. But regardless of this, I agree that we're looking at a condition that isn't part of the grammar: the homomorphism bit.

O: But you still want to say that the "deletion under identity" part of the analysis does follow from the syntax.

L: Yes, that's independent of how the ultimate interpretation is obtained. Once again, we have to separate the derivation from its interpretation. In the kind of derivations we've been discussing, the peculiar property is a certain identity of lexical material which leads to a given PF effect—whether a "copy intonation" or a deletion of PF features. Under these circumstances of lexical identity, we also note a certain parallelism of interpretation. That's the part that falls outside UG, interesting as it is [see fig. 4.7].

O: In a nutshell, then, rich structures exist at LF which have no PF reflex. And I suggest to you that this should be general, and should extend to movement operations as well—hence preserving the uniformity of the syntactic mapping.

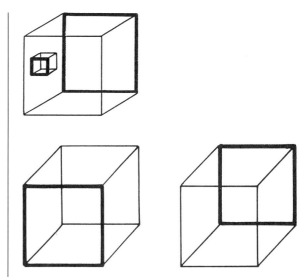

Modified Necker cubes. (From Kuno, *Functional syntax*)

Figure 4.6

---

it is features that enjoy moving

L: I agree with the claim that the mapping to LF is in many crucial respects just like the mapping prior to Spell-Out. But now we have to be extremely careful, because there are also some differences.

O: But if the mapping is uniform, how can it show differences?!

L: The mapping itself is uniform. But it's a plain fact that, at some arbitrary point, the derivation branches off to PF [see fig. 4.1]—and that will have interesting consequences. To see this, we have to ask a fundamental question that we keep avoiding. What is movement?

O: Why do you persist in pulling the rug from under my feet?! I took your word when you talked about elements moving to an inflectional node, et cetera et cetera, because the results of such an assumption are beautiful and I was quite taken with the analysis. As a matter of fact, I started thinking that movement should also extend to the LF mapping. And now you ask such a basic question: why movement! It's daunting.

L: I don't want to discuss this in pseudophilosophical terms—don't worry. The question is simpler, although I agree that the general question of why movement should exist, departing from the optimality of the system, is very tough indeed. But let's be more modest. What do categories achieve by movement?

O: You told me that features of categories are checked when the categories move . . . If so, I don't see that phrases themselves receive any special gifts upon movement, although their features certainly may . . .

L: Precisely. It's features that need to undergo checking in given positions, often far away from where they start in the derivation. For instance, in the Middle English example we discussed a couple of days ago, the verb has to move to the inflectional node where Tense resides, so that the tense feature of the verb checks the functional head Tense, remember [see chaps. 2 and 3]?

O: I'm very glad you put it that way, because I've been meaning to ask what might sound like an obtuse question. Why don't the features themselves move? Aren't categories mere collections of features? Why can't something like feature F leave the bundle of

Figure 4.7

Conditions for ellipsis (or "copy intonation"):

Antecedent for ellipsis	Target for ellipsis
... [X]	[Y] ...

(i) *Formally*
   X = Y

(ii) *Substantively*
   a. At PF the target is assigned a status that is interpreted by the A/P components as "not pronounced" or as "assigned a copy intonation."
   b. At LF the target is assigned a status that is interpreted by the I/C components as "identical in interpretation to the antecedent."

features B and move to bundle of features B′—to join feature F′? What's wrong with that?

L: Nothing's wrong with that. I think this is the way things should work.

O: But they don't—that's my problem . . .

L: But they do—that's my point . . . Precisely at LF things should work exactly the way you've suggested. It's features that move, not phrases [6].

O: But then why do phrases move in the overt component?!

L: Let me first qualify the general point about features entering into syntactic processes. Recall that features are just properties of matrices: a phonological matrix, a semantic matrix, and a formal matrix. A feature is to one of these matrices what mass or spin or color is to a subatomic particle.

O: I see . . . Various physical processes target, for example, the mass of a particle, but one cannot say that the mass of a particle moves from here to there; rather, because of its mass, a particle with mass may move from here to there, and a particle without mass, will not.

L: That's a valid analogy. The elementary particles we're dealing with are matrices: the phonological feature matrix (PFM), the semantic feature matrix (SFM), and the formal feature matrix (FFM). These three are bundled up into lexical items (atomic elements of some sort). The A/P interface cares about PFMs encoding sensorimotor instructions; the I/C interface cares about SFMs encoding God knows what sorts of instructions; and FFMs are relevant only to the syntax proper [see fig. 4.8]. If you're wondering why FFMs can't move by themselves in the overt components, remember: prior to Spell-Out you just have lexical items. Of course, why feature bundles don't exist separately from lexical items is a topic in itself: what it means to have words. But let's set that aside [and see sec. 6.4], assuming that for some reason the system of movement has to involve features which are part of lexical items, and not features which are somehow hanging around in free space. Then it's clear that prior to Spell-Out there's nothing to do other than, at least, move lexical items. However, the process of Spell-Out "splits the

Figure 4.8

Schematic lexical entry for *book*. The details of the internal matrices are deliberately rough (for more accurate possibilities, see the discussion in section 2.4).

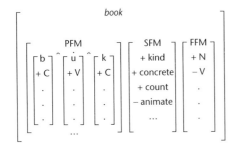

atom" of words into their PF and LF components, stripping the PFMs away from the rest [7]. In a sense, Spell-Out affects the structural balance of feature matrices that holds within a lexical entry, by literally stripping away the phonological features. Now phonology isn't relevant any more, and the question arises of how much structural integrity is left behind. When a given transformation now targets, for instance, the FFM, there's no reason why the entire set of matrices—the lexical item—which has now been "unglued," should react as a unit. That's the basic intuition [see fig. 4.9].

_____ so why should phrases ever move?

O: Hold on. Although what you're saying squarely predicts that in the covert components only feature matrices should move, it doesn't predict that anything other than lexical items should move in the overt components. But phrases move all the time!

L: Which must mean that some property of the PF component forces constituents larger than lexical items to move around. For instance, consider phrases like *Chandler's book,* and suppose we analyze them as in (4) (a structure for genitive dependencies which is slightly more precise than the one you proposed yesterday [see chap. 3, (31)]):

(4)

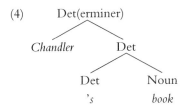

Suppose also that we want to replace *Chandler* with *who,* as follows:

(5)

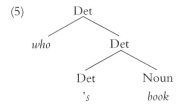

Finally, suppose we're trying to target *who* for movement (or rather, some feature within *who*), to wherever it has to go. If we just move *who,* the result will be (6) (where *t* is the trace of *who*):

Figure 4.9

The object in figure 4.8 after Spell-Out:

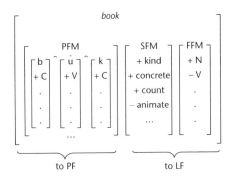

Prior to Spell-Out, these matrices cannot move separately, since they are not separate objects. Spell-Out splits the structure of the lexical item in figure 4.8, shipping the phonetic part to PF and keeping the rest on the syntactic path to LF. From this point on, it is possible to move (covertly) just the matrix of formal features, which is its own integral formal object.

(6) *who*   ...   Det

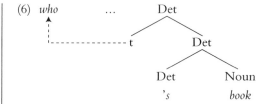

Whereas the elements *who* and *'s* in (5), and *Chandler* and *'s* in (4), can trivially associate to form words like *whose* and *Chandler's* (presumably, *'s* cliticizes upward to form a PF unit with *Chandler* or *who*), it's not so easy to see how that could happen once *who* has taken off on its own. In fact, the result should be something bad, like **who have you read 's book?* [8]. So that's not an option.

O: Because the *'s* element is left stranded . . .

L: Correct. PF doesn't like these stranded affixes [9]. In fact, let's make that explicit:

(7) *Wording Requirement*
    At PF all morphemes with phonological content are hosted within phonological words.

O: I've heard folk say things like, "Who have you read his book?"

L: Yeah, but then see what they're doing: the *'s* is supported with a pronoun like *he,* so they're actually saying *he's* (which for some crazy reason is spelled *his*). The point is, once we control for relevant factors, the syntax is behaving in a perfectly uniform way. (In both instances—*his* and *whose*—(7) is satisfied.) Note also that *whose* can't move (that is, *who* and *'s,* which again is illogically spelled *whose* and not *who's*), because in that case two parts of a phrase marker—that is, not a proper constituent—would be moving simultaneously:

(8) *who* *'s*   ...   Det

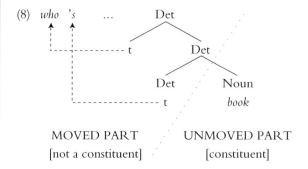

MOVED PART   UNMOVED PART
[not a constituent]   [constituent]

This predicts that *whose have you read book?* is always ungrammatical, as it is. Which means we're left with having to move the whole constituent *whose book,* if we want to target the *wh*-feature of *who.*

O: What if instead of dealing with elements like *'s,* which obviously have got some phonological content, we were dealing with null morphemes? According to (7), those should be able to survive PF without the aid of a generous word . . .

――――――――――――――――――――――――――――――――――― pied-piping

L: Which makes a prediction. Consider question words. They all have this funny shape—they start with a sort of *wh*-element. And not just in English, either. In lots of Indo-European languages the question words start with this kind of element, which suggests it's a separate, determiner-like lexicon unit (in the Romance languages, for instance, it's usually spelled *qu-*). So let it be true that the form of questions is [wh- + something], where we don't need to worry yet about what "something" is. Now imagine a language with a null *wh*-element. What would happen?

O: So far as I can see, the null *wh*-element would be able to move by itself, leaving the [something] behind. (7) says nothing about null elements. Are you trying to tell me that some languages overtly move just a *wh*-morpheme?!

L: Japanese, for instance, behaves exactly like that.

O: Well, hold on. Consider (9):

(9) a. Morihirowa darega Inokio aisiteiru to itta no
       Morihiro who Inoki loves that said question
       'Morihiro said that who loves Inoki'
       (i.e., 'who did Morihiro say loves Inoki?')
    b. Morihirowa Kazuoga dareo aisiteiru to itta no
       Morihiro Kazuo who loves that said question
       'Morihiro said that Kazuo loves who'
       (i.e., 'who did Morihiro say Kazuo loves?')

The words *darega* 'who-subject' and *dareo* 'who-object' haven't really moved, I shouldn't think! For example, 'Kazuo loves Inoki' is *Kazuoga Inokio aisiteiru;* and 'who does Kazuo love?' is *Kazuowa dareo aisiteiru no.*

Figure 4.10

Japanese and Portuguese are historically unrelated languages; however, the correlations between question words and indefinites observed in the text for Japanese can be observed for Portuguese as well. For example, 'who' is *quem*, 'someone' is *alguem,* and 'no one' is *ninguem.* The *qu-* part is the *wh*-feature, which in Portuguese (unlike in Japanese) is overt. The 'some' part is *algu-,* the 'no' part is *ningu-,* and the 'one' part is *-em*. Now consider a Japanese question side by side with the corresponding (Continental) Portuguese question:

(i) [[∅] [Morihirowa [[[t darega Inokio aisiteiru] to] itta]]
    wh- Morihiro   one Inoki loves   that said
    'Morihiro said that who loves Inoki'
    (i.e., 'who did Morihiro say loves Inoki?')

(ii) a. *[o Zé diz [que quem quere o Sá]]
        the Zé says that *wh*-one loves the Sá
     b. *[*qu-* diz [o Zé [que -em quere o Sá]]
        wh- says the Zé that one loves the Sá
     c. [quem diz [o Zé [que t quere o Sá]]]
        wh-one says the Zé that   loves the Sá
        'who does Zé say loves Sá?'

In Japanese the 'one' part is left in situ, after movement of the null *wh*- (i). The same situation leads to a PF crash in Portuguese (iia). (iib) involves a derivational cancellation if what forces movement to Comp is a strong feature in this category. (iic) is the grammatical derivation, involving pied-piping of the entire *wh*-phrase.

L: But you can't test what I'm saying by simply looking at the position of *dareo,* which you're somewhat misleadingly glossing as 'who'. What I'm saying, actually, is that you have to think of a *wh*-expression as being made up of a *wh*-feature and something else. By hypothesis, the *wh*-feature is null in Japanese; if so, and if it can move all by itself, you can't tell me where it is by pointing to the stuff that was left behind . . . Look, start by considering the Japanese translation of 'someone', 'something', 'somewhere', and so on.

O: 'Someone' is *dare-ka;* 'something' is *nani-ka;* 'somewhere' is *doko-ka;* 'sometime' is *itu-ka;* 'for some reason' is *naze-ka;* shall I go on? Oh! The *wh*-words in Japanese are *dare* 'who'; *nani* 'what'; *doko* 'where'; *itsu* 'when'; *naze* 'why'. Surely these two paradigms have something in common . . .

L: Let's say that the *-ka* part of the quantificational elements ('someone', 'something', and so on) has the import of a quantifier, and the rest is some indeterminate *restriction,* invoking people *(dare),* things *(nani),* times *(itu),* and so on [10]. *Wh*-phrases in Japanese involve these sorts of items plus some kind of abstract question element. So in effect 'who' isn't *dare,* but *wh-* + *dare;* and 'what' isn't *nani,* but *wh-* + *nani,* where *wh-* is a null question element. This seems to be a pretty general state of affairs in other languages as well: words for 'who', 'what', and so on, consist of a *wh*-element (which can be null or overt) and essentially an existential category roughly meaning 'one' or 'something'. If the *wh*-morpheme has no PF realization, it can move autonomously, leaving behind the 'one' fragment. Thus, a Japanese question word appears to have been left in situ, but this is only a mirage: what was left in situ isn't the *wh*-part, but the indeterminate 'one' part *darega* [11]. In other languages—English and Portuguese, for example—this option doesn't exist, because the *wh*-part separated from the 'one' part can't survive PF, given the Wording Requirement. In turn, the option where the entire *wh*-phrase is left in situ presumably leads to a PF crash, if Comp has to be checked in questions (i.e., assuming Comp involves a strong feature in questions). Thus, the only option left is for the 'one' part of the *wh*-element to take a "free ride" with the moved *wh*-morpheme [see fig. 4.10]. Linguists often refer to such free rides as "pied-piping," by analogy with the piper who took the Hamelin rats and children along after him [12].

O: Though he charged for rats, and took the children because the burghers wanted a free ride . . .

L: You've got the picture . . .

O: And the reason why Japanese doesn't allow this sort of . . . "pied-piping" is that there's no need to invoke any pied-piping here, really . . . The 'one' part is left in Hamelin!

L: Exactly right. So anyway, it may actually be quite accurate to say that the form of a *wh*-word is [wh- + something], after all . . .

O: I'm speechless.

L: . . .

O: I'm not joking.

L: It's all in your LF. At any rate, now you see that differences between the overt and covert mappings reduce to trivial morphological facts, and are therefore expected [13]. Intuitively put, if humans had telepathy instead of regular speech, which has to use vocal cords and tongues and so on, we'd be moving just features. And the main point is this: the mapping to LF itself is totally uniform. Do you see it?

4.2 Extending Structures

(attempting a definition of movement, and pushing it through trying tests, which include traveling back in time)

O: I do: it's features that trigger movement, and the minimal syntactic element containing them is what must move, *ceteris paribus*. In the covert component, this means movement of feature matrices alone; but in the overt component, since Spell-Out hasn't yet split up lexical items—and PF demands interfere—larger chunks of structure must get a free ride. These could be matrices of matrices of features (lexical items), or larger, organised sets of these (phrases), depending on various factors. In any case, the movement process itself is indeed uniform.

L: That's the picture.

---

transformational operations

O: Now, Move as you've tendered it looks very similar to Merge—and yet you've defined Merge for categories (matrices of matrices of features, or larger set-theoretic combinations of these), and not features or feature matrices. Am I missing something?

L: When I characterized merger [see sec. 3.1], I wasn't being as precise as you want me to be now. But in principle, Merge should be able to use any lexical material, ranging from feature matrices to complete phrases. Then we have to explore each instance in turn, to see whether it runs into any problems, either in the merger itself or at the interface levels. You're right in implying that Move and Merge are closely related—though Move has a number of peculiar limitations that we should discuss in some detail [14]. But these are all combinatorial operations that build structures, which linguists call **transformations.** Merge is **binary,** while Move is **singular.** Merge takes two objects K and L, and combines them, as we saw, so that one of them projects.

O: As a matter of principle, objects that merge can be feature matrices, lexical heads (atomic collections of feature matrices), or more complex phrase markers . . .

L: Yes, although I insist that independent limitations might rule out some combinations in particular contexts—but let's set that aside for now. The initial set of features C_{HL} works with is given by UG, from a universal vocabulary of phonetic, semantic, and formal features. Lexical heads are composed of such features, and may be associated with any other sound and meaning postulates that one can relate to them. Given features of heads determine their syntactic history. For instance, apart from its major N and V formal features, whether a term is a count or a mass term, animate or inanimate, singular or plural, and so on, may have a very important reflex in the sorts of structures where it can appear, the morphological shape of other elements that it determines through agreement, the structures of lexical entailment that it licenses, or even the movements it needs to engage in to check some features—the case that interests us here. Of course, not all features are relevant in this way. For example, whether a term refers to an entity which reflects light of a given wavelength, or is handpicked by underpaid workers in a tropical area, . . . that appears to be syntactically irrelevant. It could have been otherwise, but it isn't in Human [see sec. 2.4].

O: Perhaps those are inherent features in Venusian . . .

L: There wouldn't be anything incoherent about that, since these are substantive features of Human LFs, which don't follow from conceptual necessity or any sort of a priority.

O: I presume also that the entries in one's lexicon must be listed, since these vary from speaker to speaker.

L: Of course; and this is a list that has to be learned—there's no way around that. Finally, phrases are always derived through Merge, a binary transformation in that it holds of pairs of objects. But singulary transformations are also possible. That's what we intuitively call Move. Move takes a phrase marker K, and within that, it takes a subpart τ. The subpart can be a projection, a head, or a feature matrix, in principle. Finally, it copies τ in such a way that it can merge with K:

(10) Step 1:

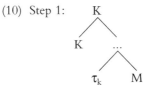

Target structure

Step 2:

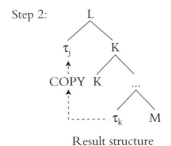

Result structure

––––––––––––––––––––––––––––––––––––––– a working definition of movement

To have something concrete to refer to by way of a definition—even if it's just a working definition—let's say that movement is characterized as in (11):

(11) *Movement chain (working definition)*
    Given a term $\tau_i = K$ that is targeted for merger, such that $K = \{\underline{\alpha}, \{ \ldots \{\tau_k, M\} \ldots \}\}$, and a term τ_j that merges with τ_i, such that $L = \{\underline{\alpha}, \{\tau_j, K\}\}$, the pair (K, M) is a *movement chain* if and only if τ_j and τ_k are identical.

Figure 4.11

Gloss of (11) (use (10) to follow it):

(i) "Given a term τ_i = K that is targeted for merger, . . ."

This part of the definition indicates that Move involves Merge.

(ii) ". . . such that K = {α, { . . . {τ_k, M} . . . }}, . . ."

Note that τ_k is intended as a term of K, and that the definition assigns label α to K (which is not obvious in (10), where K is simply shown as projecting without its label being specified).

(iii) ". . . and a term τ_j that merges with $\tau_{k'}$ . . ."

Again, Move clearly involves Merge.

(iv) ". . . such that L = {α, {τ_j, K}}, . . ."

τ_j is intended as a term of L; the definition also assigns label α to L, an important point. This means that the result of movement will be a structure projected from the target of movement. Notice also that τ_j is the sister (i.e., {τ_j, K}) of K; in other words, movement creates a structure that is sister to the target.

(v) ". . . the pair (K, M) is a *movement chain* . . ."

That is, a chain is a pair of phrase markers.

(vi) ". . . if and only if τ_j and τ_k are identical."

Finally, this is the key to the definition. The indices *j* and *k* assigned to τ may be confusing at first, but they are intended as distinct, precisely so that the definition can determine that they must be identical.

O: There you go again!

L: Wait: (11) is just a formal description of the visual representation in (10)—nothing more mystical than that. The phrase marker in (10a) (i.e., τ_i = K) is targeted for movement, and the phrase marker in (10b) (i.e., L) is the result of the movement. These two differ only in the fact that L contains a copy of the moved term τ_k, which is merged with K to yield L. The movement succeeds precisely because τ_k and τ_j are exactly the same element. We can then formally define a chain as the history of this movement [see fig. 4.11].

O: What, then, is the ontological status of the chain?

L: A chain is called that because it literally "chains" two phrase markers that share certain properties; this is why (11) says that a chain is a pair (K, M) [15].

O: But . . . I thought a chain linked the element that moves to its trace.

L: Yeah, that's certainly true too; and if we want to, we can express that. In essence, Move creates a term τ_j which is identical to an already existing term τ_k (in fact, this is the only case where two terms can be identical). But we of course want to distinguish the two elements that are formed through this movement operation, and we do this by inspecting the context in which each term appears. The sister of τ_k, namely M, is clearly different from the sister of τ_j, namely K, allowing us to keep track of occurrences. We can thus identify the initial position of τ_k as the pair <τ_k, M>, and the raised position of τ_j as the pair <τ_j, K>. Then the pair of pairs <<τ_j, K>, <τ_k, M>> is a completely specified chain, now understood as a pair of positions. Of course, that notation doesn't really add much to the simpler (K, M) notation, so we may as well stick to the latter [16].

O: I find it interesting that the result of movement {α, {τ_j, K}} should contain the target K. It seems as though the phrase marker that one obtains by movement *extends* the target phrase marker, which your definition in (11) seems to explicitly dictate (hence, L is obtained by merging τ_j with K) [see fig. 4.12].

the extension condition

L: Yeah, well, Merge generally obeys this **extension** condition too [17]. Just as the lowering operation in (12b) isn't a valid movement (descriptively, it doesn't extend the structure of the source of movement), so too the result in (12d) isn't a valid merger. By contrast, the merger in (12e) (which extends the phrase marker from β to X, the projection of β or γ) is perfect:

(12) a. Step 1:

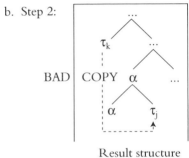

Target structure

b. Step 2:

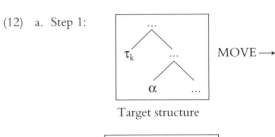

Result structure

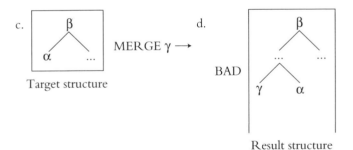

e.

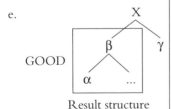

Result structure

O: So it's not only Move that never goes "downwards." Both Merge and Move are, in actual fact, sensitive to the command relation: τ merges/moves to K only if τ commands K. This command relation pops up everywhere!

Figure 4.12

The "extension condition" is encoded in (11) (see, in particular, stage (iv) of the gloss in figure 4.11, which determines the form of the target of movement). This can easily be shown by highlighting within the structure in step 2 of (10) the very structure that is involved in step 1:

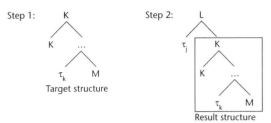

Movement always has this character: it never goes "backward"; rather, it extends the structure of whatever phrase marker was assembled prior to movement.

L: That's true, and certainly important. Descriptively, you can think of the extension property of transformational processes in terms of their having a **cyclic** nature. That is, there seems to be a "cycle" of operations: some apply before others, and the first to apply must correspond to "inner" structures, while "outer" structures come next, and so on. Of course, a lowering operation would go against this cyclic nature.

O: I wonder, though . . . Yesterday we were on our way to deducing why command may be relevant for linearisation. Perhaps we can also deduce the fact that command is relevant for these building operations, because of properties of the structures formed when Merge and Move apply. Now the notion "downwards" has a much more tangible meaning. Firstly, I see how movement going upwards works; that's just what you sketched in (10). But how would the movement going downwards work in (12b), given our official notation? Let's instantiate (12b) in a slightly more concrete example:

(13)   Step 1: $\{\underline{\alpha}, \{\{\alpha, \{\alpha, \beta\}\}, \gamma\}\}$

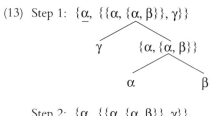

Step 2: $\{\underline{\alpha} \ \{\{\alpha, \{\alpha, \beta\}\}, \gamma\}\}$

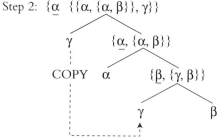

L: But that's only because your graphs in (13) are very misleading—in fact, wrong. You've related the official notation to a node in a tree, when you should have related it to an *entire tree* [18]. Put differently, when you merge α and β, not only do you get the new object $\{\underline{\alpha}, \{\alpha, \beta\}\}$—furthermore, the older objects are history. Gone. A more accurate representation of your objects in (13) would be (14):

(14) Step -1:　　$\{\underline{\alpha}, \quad \{\alpha, \beta\}\}$　　$=$　　α

$$\alpha \leftarrow \text{MERGE} \rightarrow \beta \qquad \alpha \qquad \beta$$

Step 1:　　$\{\underline{\alpha}, \quad \{\{\alpha, \{\alpha, \beta\}\}, \gamma\}\}$　　$=$　　α

$$\gamma \leftarrow \text{MERGE} \rightarrow \{\underline{\alpha}, \{\alpha, \beta\}\} \qquad \gamma \qquad \alpha$$

$$\alpha \qquad \beta$$

Step 1½:　　COPY γ

Step 2:　　$\{\underline{\beta}, \quad \{\gamma, \beta\}\}$　　$=$　　β

$$\gamma \leftarrow \text{MERGE} \rightarrow \beta \qquad \gamma \qquad \beta$$

O: All right—I wasn't being precise enough. But my question still stands. First of all: how does the γ copied in your step 1½ know how to locate the object β with which it wishes to merge?

L: Turning that very question into an instruction: "Find the phrase-theoretic object β within the only existing structure at this point, the larger phrase-theoretic object $\{\underline{\alpha}, \{\{\alpha, \{\alpha, \beta\}\}, \gamma\}\}$." That in itself is trivial.

O: And then how does the newly formed term $\{\underline{\beta}, \{\gamma, \beta\}\}$ relate to the larger object $\{\underline{\alpha}, \{\{\alpha, \{\alpha, \beta\}\}, \gamma\}\}$?

L: That's a more interesting and important question [19]. Of course, we can't answer it a priori, either. It could be that the two objects don't need to relate. Then again, the intuition is that they must re-late—but if so, we have to show what that relation is, why it has to hold, and so on. To show you that matters can't be handled on an a priori basis, consider the following straightforward possibility. Suppose that after merging the lowered γ to β, thus obtaining $\{\underline{\beta}, \{\beta, \gamma\}\}$, you substitute this object for β in the larger $\{\underline{\alpha}, \{\{\alpha, \{\alpha, \beta\}\}, \gamma\}\}$, thereby creating an even larger, but perfectly appropriate $\{\underline{\alpha}, \{\{\alpha, \{\beta, \{\beta, \gamma\}\}\}\}, \gamma\}\}$.

O: In (15), I haven't done the replacement; it could be done as follows (where, not to fall into the sloppiness you accused me of a moment ago, I use arrows to indicate mergers, instead of tree branches):

(15) Step 1: $\{\underline{\alpha}, \{\{\alpha, \{\alpha, \beta\}\}, \gamma\}\}$

$$\gamma \leftarrow \mid \rightarrow \{\underline{\alpha}, \{\alpha, \beta\}\}$$

$$\alpha \leftarrow \mid \rightarrow \beta$$

Step 2: $\{\underline{\alpha}, \ \{\{\alpha, \{\alpha, \{\beta, \{\beta, \gamma\}\}\}\}, \gamma\}\}$ "overwrite"

$$\{\underline{\alpha}, \quad \{\{\alpha, \{\alpha, \mid \beta\}\}, \gamma\}\}$$

COPY+MERGE

By lowering γ to merge with β, we get a new element, as in step 2. Let's say that this new element is a projection of β. But now note: prior to the lowering, α was merged with β; after the lowering, α cannot be merged with β because we're making β merge with the lowered γ, so α must merge with the result of merging γ with β, which is $\{\underline{\beta}, \{\beta, \gamma\}\}$ if β is the head. Well, now we've got spaghetti, right? Because we've got a different object from the one we had before. For example, the copy of γ which hasn't lowered should relate to $\{\underline{\alpha}, \{\alpha, \{\beta, \{\beta, \gamma\}\}\}\}$ after step 2, but that same copy of γ relates to $\{\underline{\alpha}, \{\alpha, \beta\}\}$ before step 2.

(16) $\{\underline{\alpha}, \{\{\alpha, \{\alpha, \{\beta, \{\beta, \gamma\}\}\}\}, \gamma\}\}$

$$\mid \{\underline{\alpha}, \{\alpha, \{\beta, \{\beta, \gamma\}\}\}\}$$

COPY+MERGE

$$\alpha \leftarrow \mid \rightarrow \{\underline{\beta}, \{\beta, \gamma\}\}$$

$$\beta \leftarrow \mid \rightarrow \gamma$$

To accept this sort of process is simply to accept parallel universes which may converge on the same state of affairs. In physics, this goes by the name of the "grandmother paradox." You go back in time and murder your grandmother—and then what? Do you vanish? Were you to do so, how could you have killed Granny? You have to overwrite the entire course of history (which is like leaving the universe you were in and proceeding as though nothing had happened in a parallel universe).

L: There certainly is an internal logical timing to the derivation, which tells us that the merger of α and β is logically prior to the result $\{\underline{\alpha}, \{\alpha, \beta\}\}$ of that merger. When we consider this logical, derivational time, standard movement carries us forward in it, building structure outside of what has been built up to that point. In contrast, lowering does carry us, in a sense, backward—forcing us to go inside the already existing structure. And yes, as a result of that, we get objects whose representational shape is ambiguous, in that they could have come from two derivational paths. However, to conclude—from that alone—that lowering is impossible . . . well, it just doesn't wash. It depends on subtle issues of the kind we've talked about already, like whether the system at large is derivational or representational [see sec. 2.6], and whether the derivational history of a representation has to be unique, or a given representation has to be recursively characterized in a single way.

O: Granted, matters concerning alternative histories are subtle in other sciences as well. Yet I think there's somewhat of an insight behind what I'm saying. The official notation appears to capture the fact that this rather huge and rather ugly object $\{\underline{\alpha}, \{\{\alpha, \{\alpha, \{\beta, \{\beta, \gamma\}\}\}\}, \gamma\}\}$ carries along the history of its structure. It's not just the label $\underline{\alpha}$ of the term that's decisive; how this label was obtained is important as well, which is expressed by keeping track of all the constituent elements.

L: I don't really think this particular notation does what you're claiming. **Syntactic objects** would be coherent even under a purely representational system, with no derivational procedures to construct them, but some simple set-theoretic rules to describe them instead [20]. Which is to say: brackets per se don't annotate derivational history, though one can change the notation so this history is in fact built in.

O: Well, as I'm beginning to see it, these convoluted terms are like trunks of trees. Whatever growth function is going on in trees works outwards; that's why you count rings to determine how old they are. Viewed dynamically, the structure of an organism at any given point equals the effects of its development over time. Creatures don't really like to grow inwards. Merge also instantiates a particular growth function: that by which the phrase marker extends.

Figure 4.13

Gloss of (17) (the definition of "term"):

(i) "Where (a), (b), and (c) are syntactic objects— . . ."

This gives a list of possible objects for C_{HL} to operate on.

(ii) ". . . (a) an FFM; . . ."

As is seen throughout this chapter, C_{HL} must operate on objects that are part of lexical items [see fig. 4.9].

(iii) ". . . (b) a labeled lexical item; (c) a phrase marker K = {L, {α, β}}, where α, β are syntactic objects and L is the label of K . . ."

These two are obvious: C_{HL} operates on lexical items and phrases.

(iv) ". . . and where K is a root phrase marker— . . ."

That is, (17) defines "term" for topmost objects within a derivation.

(v) ". . . then (i) K is a term, . . ."

This is the base step of the definition.

(vi) ". . . or (ii) if P is a term, the members of the members of P are terms."

This is the important, induction step of the definition. It looks at an object of the form { . . . { . . . }} and determines that the members *of the members* of this set are terms. That is, given something like {α, {α, β}}, the constituent elements (α and β) in the set (not the label $\overline{α}$) are terms. For further discussion of these matters, see the appendix.

L: Yes, but (if you want to keep your metaphors straight) you have to ask why such an extension property should hold of either of those growth functions. In order to make your "deduction" for the cyclic nature of syntactic transformations, you have to assume that something like what you called the "overwriting" of the phrase marker is banned for some reason. In the case of a tree trunk, you're not dealing with "overwriting" at all, but with the impossibility of expanding against some rigid structure that's already been assembled around the core; or maybe inward growth has been naturally selected out of a given species because it leads to the destruction of its individuals—whatever. But what does the ban against "overwriting" follow from? Why should I not be able to change any given part of a phrase marker, as in step 2 of (15)? Of course, if I do that, I have to make sure the object I end up with obeys the defining properties of Merge. Otherwise, not only am I "overwriting" the phrase marker—I'm creating an object which isn't a phrase marker at all. To use your grandmother analogy, it would be like going back in time, killing the poor lady, and then changing the laws of physics to accommodate the event. That, we don't want—obviously. However, going back in time, doing your thing—in our case, merging downward—and then correctly "overwriting" the phrase marker . . . that may be appropriate, in principle. Here, "in principle" just means "in accordance with (17)," where I explicitly define the notion "term" that we've been using all along [see app. and fig. 4.13]:

(17) Where (a), (b), and (c) are syntactic objects—(a) an FFM; (b) a labeled lexical item; (c) a phrase marker K = {L, {α, β}}, where α, β are syntactic objects and L is the label of K and where K is a root phrase marker—then (i) K is a *term*, or (ii) if P is a term, the members of the members of P are *terms*.

This presents, first, an explicit axiomatization of syntactic objects. (17a) and (17b) say that feature bundles and lexical items are syntactic objects; (17c) describes the recursive procedure of projection, whereby labels from lexical items are assigned to whole projected categories (note that the notion "label" is intrinsic to lexical items, not to feature matrices). Second, (17) offers a recursive definition of terms of syntactic operations, whereby root phrase markers are terms, and essentially all subcomponents of terms are also terms (this prevents labels, which are direct components—and not *sub*components—of terms, from being terms themselves). What you have to ask yourself, then, is whether the overwritten object in (15) obeys (17).

O: Of course it does. But my emphasis is not on that aspect of the issue (which I do not take to be a problem). What I'm trying to say is that whereas derivational history is clear and unambiguous in structures which are extended, it isn't clear and unambiguous if one goes backwards, raising tricky "loss of information" issues.

L: But even if you can establish empirically that these sorts of issues are unwanted (so in fact operations that have this backward character are themselves unwanted), that still has to follow from something. Otherwise, you'll have a new axiom: "Derivational information can't be lost." But how is that more profound than saying, "Structure can't be built downward (or backward, or however you want to put it)"? The fancy term "loss of information" doesn't make the axiom any deeper.

_____ what does our phrasal notation capture?

O: What about this, then? If overwriting of a phrase marker is allowed, then the process of building phrase markers isn't **monotonic:** we must change the structure assembled up to point t when embarking on an operation that takes place at point $t+n$.

L: That's even worse, even if the term is fancier still: you're now confusing a notational device with something that's real within the linguistic system. The notation is just a way of encoding certain properties of phrases. For instance, the statement "Write brackets around α and β if they are elements that merge" is just a way of saying that a relation exists between α and β. Writing the brackets has no theoretical cost, any more than writing the symbol "+" has a particular cost when you're doing addition. If somebody said that addition is a more costly arithmetical operation than subtraction because addition involves two pencil strokes to create "+," while subtraction involves only one stroke to create "−," you'd say they were crazy—of course, these two names for relations could have been encoded in terms of colors . . . black and white, or whatever. The notation itself is of no particular interest, and how costly it is to produce is theoretically meaningless. Therefore, whether we build the brackets in the object {α̲, {{α, {α, {β, {β, γ}}}}, γ}} monotonically or nonmonotonically is neither good nor bad.

Figure 4.14

The "new coding C" may be command, as argued in Epstein, forthcoming. Thus, consider the command relations in step 1 of (13), repeated in (i):

(i) $\{\underline{\alpha}, \ \{\{\alpha, \ \{\alpha, \beta\}\}, \gamma\}\}$

$$\gamma \leftarrow | \rightarrow \{\underline{\alpha}, \ \{\alpha, \beta\}\}$$

$$\alpha \leftarrow | \rightarrow \beta$$

a. Relations in which γ is the commander:
$\langle\gamma, \{\alpha, \{\alpha, \beta\}\}\rangle$ [by Merge of γ and $\{\underline{\alpha}, \{\alpha, \beta\}\}$]
$\langle\gamma, \alpha\rangle$ [transitively]
$\langle\gamma, \beta\rangle$ [transitively]
b. Relations in which α is the commander:
$\langle\alpha, \beta\rangle$ [by Merge of α and β]
c. Relations in which β is the commander:
$\langle\beta, \alpha\rangle$ [by Merge of β and α]

Suppose that β moves, as in (ii), adding the command relations in (d):

(ii) $\{\underline{\alpha}, \ \{\beta, \ \{\alpha, \ \{\{\alpha, \ \{\alpha, \beta\}\}, \gamma\}\}\}\}$

$$\beta \leftarrow | \rightarrow \{\alpha, \ \{\{\alpha, \ \{\alpha, \beta\}\}, \gamma\}\}$$

$$\gamma \leftarrow | \rightarrow \{\underline{\alpha}, \ \{\alpha, \beta\}\}$$

$$\alpha \leftarrow | \rightarrow \beta$$

O: I gather that much . . . But consider, for example, a theory of formal arithmetic that introduces the operation "multiply" and states its properties; then a programmer decides to implement it one way or another with some particular sequence of steps.

L: That's the right analogy. The algorithmic steps that the programmer uses aren't part of the theory of arithmetic. She could write 6 × 6 = 36 starting from the left, or from right, or from the symbol "×," and so on. What matters is whether when she's done, the expression is mathematically coherent, according to the laws of arithmetic (6 × = 36 6, for instance, would be incoherent). In turn, your laws are expressed in (17); if the object obeys them, that's all that matters.

O: But there could be something significant about the suboperations the programmer has been forced to use.

L: Or she's chosen to use, or her computer allows her to use, or she happens to know about (there could be others she's simply not aware of) . . . I can't even imagine how many uncertainties there are—so many that they make this line of reasoning pointless. The same with your notational "deduction" of the absence of lowering. Could be significant, but I'm skeptical. As far as I'm concerned, if we want to prevent generating an object that obeys (17) according to some sort of lowering process (as indeed we do), we have to achieve this by some other means—an axiom like "Don't move down," or whatever.

O: Why, of course, that particular axiom won't be general enough, for we've agreed that merger going downwards won't do, either. And certainly, if we allow merger going downwards, of the sort in (18b), the notation won't tell us that $\{\underline{\alpha}, \{\{\alpha, \{\alpha, \beta\}\}, \gamma\}\}$ is generated according to the cyclic derivation in (18a), and not according to the noncyclic one in (18c):

(18) a. $\{\underline{\alpha}, \ \{\{\alpha, \{\alpha, \beta\}\}, \gamma\}\}$

$$\gamma \leftarrow | \rightarrow \{\underline{\alpha}, \ \{\alpha, \beta\}\}$$

b. $\{\underline{\alpha}, \ \{\{\alpha, \{\alpha, \gamma\}\}, \beta\}\}$

$$\{\underline{\alpha}, \ \{\alpha, \beta\}\}$$

$$\gamma \leftarrow | \cdots \cdots \cdots \cdots$$

c. $\{\underline{\alpha}, \ \{\{\alpha, \{\alpha, \beta\}\}, \gamma\}\}$

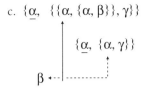

$\{\underline{\alpha}, \ \{\alpha, \gamma\}\}$

β

L: If what you're giving me is a reason for why we should have a formal axiom preventing lowering, that's fine. I have other reasons I think are more plausible (in fact, I believe the reasons for preventing merger as in (18b) aren't the same as those for preventing lowering). At any rate, the axiom plainly isn't deduced.

O: What I'm trying to say is that it would be deduced, were we to take the notation as encoding the derivational history of Merge or Move. As you said: brackets don't do that, but we can invent some new coding C to do it [see fig. 4.14].

L: Even so: it's still a different (and if you ask me, open) question whether derivational histories can in fact be changed. That they can't may in fact be true; but if so, you have to show what this follows from. Alternatively, you have to show that something bad ensues from your "new coding C," when the derivation proceeds noncyclically. Either way, a complex prospect [see sec. 4.7].

O: I say, are we quite certain that all syntactic operations are cyclic?

4.3 Noncyclic Mergers?

(wherein binding theory is sketched and the rare behavior of adjuncts is bluntly shown)

L: That's an important empirical question—in fact, the first one we should have asked about these matters. As it turns out, merger appears to be cyclic in general, but there are some intriguing instances that appear to defy this generalization. In order to illustrate them, I have to solidify some comments I made yesterday about binding [see sec. 3.7].

———————————————————————— referential dependencies

O: Please do. That very process has been troubling me, I must say.

L: Let me start by giving you a couple of principles that will be significant in this respect, and which you should take as tentative [21]:

d. Relations in which β is the commander:

$\langle\beta, \{\underline{\alpha}, \{\{\alpha, \{\alpha, \beta\}\}, \gamma\}\}\rangle$ [by Merge of β and $\{\underline{\alpha}, \{\{\alpha, \{\alpha, \beta\}\}, \gamma\}\}$]

$\langle\beta, \{\underline{\alpha}, \{\alpha, \beta\}\}\rangle$ [transitively]

$\langle\beta, \gamma\rangle$ [transitively]

$\langle\beta, \alpha\rangle$ [transitively]

$\langle\beta, \beta\rangle$ [transitively]

This defines a linear order $\langle\beta, \gamma, \{\alpha, \beta\}\rangle$, as desired (see sec. 3.3).

In contrast, suppose that γ moves down, as in step 2 of (13), repeated in (iii).

(iii) $\{\underline{\alpha}, \ \{\{\alpha, \ \{\alpha, \ \beta\}\}, \ \gamma\}\}$

$\gamma \leftarrow \quad \rightarrow \{\underline{\alpha}, \ \{\alpha, \ \beta\}\}$

$\alpha \leftarrow \quad \rightarrow \beta \quad \{\underline{\beta}, \ \{\gamma, \ \beta\}\}$

$\rightarrow \gamma$

This would not add any command relations (lowering cannot produce command relations that were not defined prior to the movement). Furthermore, the relation between α and γ is not defined, if command holds transitively only between a given element α and the elements within the term β that has merged with α. Importantly, α has never merged with $\{\underline{\beta}, \{\gamma, \beta\}\}$ in the derivation outlined in (iii), so there is no way for α to command γ from this strictly derivational perspective. This means that there is no linear order between α and γ; thus, these two elements cannot be linearized at PF, and the derivation crashes.

Portrait of Diego Rivera behind his portrait of Paulette Godard, by Frida Kahlo (apocryphal).

Figure 4.15

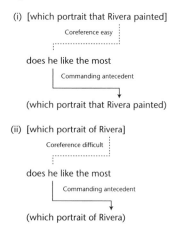

(19) *Binding theory (working hypothesis)*
At LF:
   a. an anaphor is commanded by its antecedent;
   b. a name may not have a commanding antecedent.

These are conditions on the relation between noun phrases in a sentence. For some reason, noun phrases are sensitive to other noun phrases in their command domain. An anaphor has to have a commanding antecedent, whereas a name can't have one. So you can think of (19a), in particular, as a step in the direction of understanding what's meant by the statement "An anaphor is close to its antecedent." This isn't the whole picture, but it reduces the class of possible antecedents for an anaphor.

O: But you see, sir, this is what troubles me: why should I assume (19)—or anything like it?

L: Because I'm telling you to; it's a working hypothesis.

O: Ah, but now it makes little sense to me. What sorts of principles are those? Why do they hold of UG? What kind of economy are they supposed to be encoding [see fig. 4.17]?

L: (19) is just a descriptive tool. Your questions are valid, but for all we know (19) may be a consequence of I/C conditions, which are manifested in this way at LF [22]. Note also that (19b) has the flavor of being the reverse of (19a), and is intended to describe the basic, intuitive fact that, for instance, the two instances of *Bacon* in (20a) can't corefer, whereas in (20b) they can:

(20) a. Bacon puzzled Bacon
      b. Bacon's friend puzzled Bacon

O: Hm . . . And that's directly what (19) describes, since *Bacon's* doesn't command *Bacon* in (20b), whereas the first *Bacon* clearly commands the second in (20a). I declare—this bloody command relation is truly central!

L: But this is all a set-up for my real point, which is to demonstrate that certain syntactic relations aren't obviously cyclic. Consider these contrasts [and see fig. 4.15] [23].

(21) a. which portrait that Rivera painted does he like the most?
      b. which portrait of Rivera does he like the most?

O: (21a) is straightforward. The pronoun *he* can refer to anyone in the world, including Rivera. I could, hence, answer that question by saying, "The portrait of Paulette Godard," and that would refer to a portrait that Rivera painted. (21b), I find more problematic. Whereas *he* can refer to people other than Rivera, I find it hard to believe that *he* can be intended to refer to Rivera himself in this instance. Am I missing something?

L: I doubt it; I agree with that intuition, anyway. And if things are indeed as you say, we have a rather serious puzzle.

O: Right you are. The representations of the sentences in (21) involving traces should basically be as in (22) [see sec. 3.7]:

(22) a. which portrait that Rivera painted does he like (which portrait that Rivera painted)
 b. which portrait of Rivera does he like (which portrait of Rivera)

I'm simply copying in parentheses the same element that's been extracted. And there's the rub. So far as I can see, both representations in (22) violate (19b). If we look at the copy of the moved element, we see that in fact *Rivera* is commanded by *he* in both instances. That's a flat violation of (19b), and both sentences should be ungrammatical if coreference is intended. Quite a surprising result, if you ask me! Thinking about it naïvely, I should have said a priori that (21b)'s interpretation (where coreference is difficult) is puzzling, whereas (21a)'s isn't particularly surprising. But the very opposite is true. (21b)'s interpretation is described by (19b), if it's got the representation in (22b). Since the configuration needed for (19b) to apply is met, *he* cannot be interpreted as being the antecedent of *Rivera*. Therefore, *he* and *Rivera* must refer to different individuals in (21b), which accords precisely with my claim. But then by that same reasoning, *he* and *Rivera* should not be allowed to corefer in (21a) either, inasmuch as the relevant structure is (22a), and hence the configuration needed for (19b) to apply is met [see fig. 4.15].

Now, here I've got a couple of questions. This binding theory in (19), does it encode some convergence conditions, or is it a post–LF theory?

L: Yes.

O: I hate it when you do that!

L: But I'm serious, it probably has aspects of both, convergence and post-LF interpretability . . . At any rate, I certainly don't know for a fact that one option holds to the exclusion of the other.

O: Very well, but apart from affecting possible interpretations, the sorts of structures outlined in (22) must also obey syntactic requirements, must they not?

L: I don't have definite expectations, but I don't see a problem with that either, at least in principle; what do you have in mind?

O: I could certainly circumvent the devastating effects of (19b) in a structure like (22) as follows: suppose I simply delete the lower copy of *which portrait . . . ?*

L: You mean instead of deleting the upper copy?

O: Just so. I can be quite devious and say, were I to interpret *portrait et cetera* in its lower site, I should be in trouble with the law (as per (19b)). So then, what about deleting that copy, and using the upper one instead, where (19b) would be entirely irrelevant?

L: There are only two problems with that: it's exactly the wrong theoretical solution, and it doesn't work empirically. First, it's wrong for derivations to be that smart, knowing when to sneak out of trouble. The procedure for deleting parts of the copies at LF should be totally mechanical, whatever it is. Something as dumb as "All other things being equal, interpret all the lexical material in the *wh*-phrase in its original position, except for the *wh*-operator" [24]. Once this is the case, you won't have as much leeway as your reasoning implied. But second, even if you allowed yourself these gambits, your solution wouldn't work.

O: I know: because although it predicts that (22a) is good, we can pull the same rabbit out of the hat with (22b), and then we predict the structure should be grammatical—contrary to fact [see fig. 4.16]. But this is expressly what I had in mind: since allowing such freedom in the structural position at which we interpret *wh*-material

Figure 4.16

If the copy of the moved element is not interpreted in its original position, both (i) and (ii) are predicted to be grammatical under coreference. This is correct for (i) but incorrect for (ii).

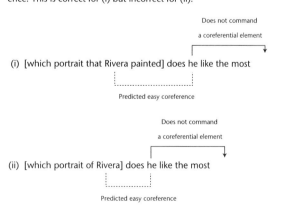

works out so poorly, it would seem that UG instead tells us when to interpret each copy (telling us, for example, that we must go with the lower one at LF, as you suggested). But that's a syntactic requirement.

L: Yes, although it's not part of the binding theory in (19). It could still be that the theory in question applies after LF, and whatever condition forces the *wh*-material to appear "low" within a structure at LF blindly feeds the semantic interpretation.

O: I see. Yes, so it could be that LF forces a given structure for syntactic reasons, and the structure doesn't change on its way into the interpretive components (if no operation can affect it after it abandons the syntax), and then when it comes to the point of being interpreted, it gets in trouble with the law—namely, (19) or whatever interpretive law we may think of.

L: A perfectly reasonable possibility; I'm not necessarily advocating it, but I don't see a problem with it, either. Nor, as I said, do I see any problem with the alternative view, whereby (19) rules out a structure like (22b) at LF. It's just an empirical matter, determining whether (22b) converges at LF but doesn't get interpreted because it violates (19b), or whether it doesn't even converge because it violates (19b) at LF [see fig. 4.17].

O: Very well, but in either event we have no way of distinguishing (22a) and (22b).

L: We'd have to argue that the structure of (21a) isn't (22a) . . .

O: Who on Earth would wish to do that?!

-- *where are modifiers attached?*

L: There's a real difference between *which portrait that Rivera painted* and *which portrait of Rivera.* As you can see, *that Rivera painted* is a relative clause, while *of Rivera* is a prepositional object of *portrait.* Consider a construction like *the portrait of Rivera which Frida Kahlo painted,* where I introduce the term **adjunct** to refer to the sort of dependency that the relative clause establishes with *portrait.* Could its structure be as follows [25]?

Figure 4.17

The status of binding conditions like those in (19) is somewhat unclear. They involve at least one structural relation (sensitivity to command) and one interpretive relation (a referential implication). The interpretive condition must be a matter for the I/C components, after LF. However, whether the command restriction is part of the competence system, or is also a matter of performance, is an open question. A theory arguing for a performance-based account of command relations for binding has to demonstrate that this structural relation is natural in the I/C component, which immediately entails that I/C structures are either phrasal or homomorphic with phrasal structures (command being a phrasal relation). Whether this is true has not been established.

On the other hand, it may seem that the overall task of explaining command within binding is easier for a standard grammatical account of the command requirement, but this is not obviously so either. To see this, compare (19a) and (19b). Whereas the former is a licensing requirement (stating the form of possible structures), the latter is a filter (stating the form of impossible structures). A licensing condition of the type in (19a) may actually follow if, for some reason, the features of the anaphoric element must, at LF, associate with those of its antecedent (Lebeaux 1983, Cole and Sung 1994). Provided that this association process is an instance of movement, it should adhere to command conditions—as any other instance of movement would. But why should the same be true of (19b)? Unless a powerful reason is provided, it is theoretically suspect to propose that a name cannot have a commanding antecedent because of the name's association (through movement) with that impossible antecedent. Why should the name relate thus? And if it does not, why should the relation (antecedent, name) be sensitive to command restrictions? Then an explanation that does not depend on movement is necessary; but none is forthcoming. Stipulating (19b) may be descriptively adequate, but it does not constitute an explanation (see Reinhart and Reuland 1993 for important background and discussion).

Finally, the examples in (22) compound the problem even further. The ungrammatical status of (22b) crucially depends on the moved *wh*-phrase's reconstructing back to its original position. (Another way of saying this is that the original occurrence of the moved *wh*-phrase is interpreted, perhaps with the exception of the operator itself (see sec. 3.7), in the prior-to-movement site.) Why that should be the case is not clear either (and see Barss 1986 for recalcitrant data).

(23)
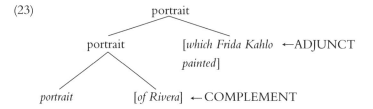

O: I doubt it. If the structure is (23), the LCT predicts its linearisation to be the ungrammatical **which Frida Kahlo painted portrait of Rivera*, since *which Frida Kahlo painted* asymmetrically commands *portrait* [see fig. 4.18].

L: The first question should be, how exactly are adjuncts related to the heads they modify? The second question should be, across languages, how are (say) relative clauses ordered with respect to the heads they modify?

O: I presume you're asking the second question because you want to know whether relative clauses always follow their head, as in English. If this isn't always the case, then you don't know for a fact that heads must command the relative clauses they take. Well, ad rem: Chinese speakers say *meige ren dou mai-le* [*yiben* [*Mao xie de*] *shu*], literally 'every man all bought [one [Mao write relative-marker] book]'—that is to say, 'everyone bought a book that Mao wrote' [26]. And this isn't peculiar to Chinese: other languages work the same way.

L: One of these days you're going to have to tell me how many languages you speak . . . So empirically we have to determine, first, what should be the basic order of the relative clause vis-à-vis its head. Being deliberatively naive about it, I'll say: Chinese suggests the relative clause should command the head noun, whereas English suggests the noun should command the relative clause. One of those is very possibly wrong; maybe both are.

O: I might have a way to decide that. Any given head can have more than one adjunct; for example, relative clauses can in some instances be added to a structure ad infinitum. Thus: *the portrait of Rivera which Frida Kahlo painted which shows him side by side with Godard's portrait . . .* And now look: the head—let's say—*portrait* could command all those relative clauses only if the structure were (24):

Figure 4.18

Note the simple reasoning:

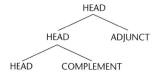

ADJUNCT commands HEAD and COMPLEMENT. Therefore, ADJUNCT should precede HEAD and COMPLEMENT.

(24) a.

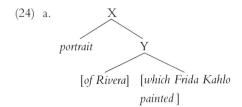

b.

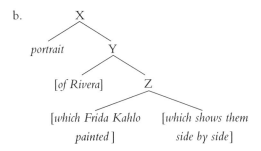

But that's rather hopeless, since the structure of the head's dependents must change every time a new one's added (regardless of what the actual labels happen to be).

L: Not only that, but mapping the object in (24) into an appropriate semantics seems difficult [27]. This is because, when adjuncts are stacked as you're stacking them, they typically invoke particular interpretations. You can easily see this by comparing the phrases *a small large reptile* and *a large small reptile.*

O: That's very clear. Camarasaurus was a small large reptile (as compared with, for example, Ultrasaurus). Dryosaurus was a large small reptile (as compared with Pterodactylus) [see fig. 4.19].

L: Thanks for the tip.

O: In my reading on predicate logic, this goes by the name of **modification scope** [28].

L: Correct. Descriptively speaking, we know that the modifier that takes "wide" scope sits outside the modifier that takes "narrow" scope. So if *small* is combined with a phrase with the import of 'large X', we know that the resulting object is interpreted as a 'large X which is small'. Conversely, if *large* is combined with a phrase with the import of 'small X', the resulting object is interpreted as a 'small X which is large' [29].

An afternoon in Colorado, Jurassic time (fragment). (Doris Tischler, with the advice of Wade E. Miller)

Figure 4.19

1. Camarasaurus supremus (40–50 feet, 18–20 tons)
2. Ultrasaurus macintoshi (80–90 feet, 100 tons)
3. Dryosaurus altus (12–14 feet, 250–300 pounds)
4. Pterodactylus antiquus (2-foot wingspan)

O: Then I shall venture a mad guess: the structure that Chinese displays is more basic, and the adjunct relative clause should command the head, as in (25):

(25)

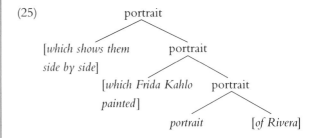

That gives the correct scopal facts. Although of course now the question is what to do with English, where the PF ordering isn't anywhere near what (25) indicates. Might we get the right order by raising *portrait* somewhere?

L: We might get the right PF order—though even that's far from clear. But we certainly won't get the right scope for the relative clauses. To see this, consider the relative clauses (i) and (ii) (I know they don't sound all that natural, compared with the adjectival versions, but let's abstract away from that): (i) *a dinosaur which is large which is small;* (ii) *a dinosaur which is small which is large.* Clearly, these invoke different descriptions. But watch what happens if we raise the head noun, as you suggest:

(26) a. ...

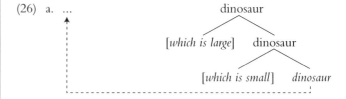

PF: *dinosaur which is large which is small (dinosaur)*

b. ...

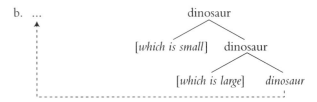

PF: *dinosaur which is small which is large (dinosaur)*

O: Hm! That's exactly the wrong result. (26a), for example, forces us to associate the PF *dinosaur which is large which is small* with an interpretation whereby this is a small dinosaur which is large for a small dinosaur. But intuition says it means the reverse!

L: Also, to get the PF *portrait of Rivera which Frida Kahlo painted which shows them . . .* you have to raise not only the head *portrait,* but also the complement *of Rivera.* That is, you have to raise the intermediate projection of *portrait* that dominates the head *portrait* and the complement *of Rivera.*

O: But you've told me that C_{HL} doesn't even see intermediate projections . . .

L: Correct: they're inaccessible to C_{HL}. So your hypothesis can't be right, and we have to say something quite different for the linearization of adjuncts, or the very structure of relative clauses.

———————————————————— *late adjunctions do not reconstruct*

O: Well, it does seem as though—to put it mildly—adjuncts don't directly obey the LCT. Which, if true, seems problematic. Shall we go home now?

L: Not until we know exactly how it is that adjuncts relate to their heads. It could well be that there are good, principled reasons why the (head, adjunct) relation shouldn't obey the LCA. In fact, let me raise a further point, which I think is directly related to these surprising linearization facts. Suppose that while a complement has to be related cyclically to the head that takes it, an adjunct doesn't. Let me draw it [30]:

(27) a.

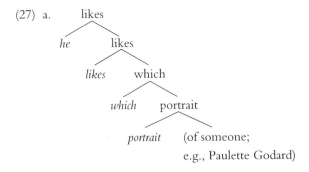

b.
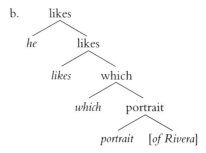

(27b) is clearly doomed with respect to binding condition (19b). However, suppose (22a) starts out as in (27a). After you move *which portrait,* you get a structure like (28a). It's at this point, after the movement of *which portrait,* that you may decide to merge the phrase *that Rivera painted,* as in (28b):

(28) a. *Move* wh-*phrase*

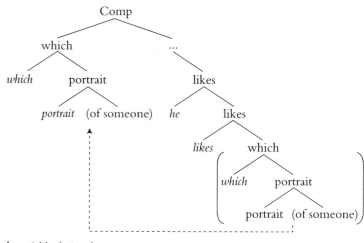

      b. *Add relative clause*

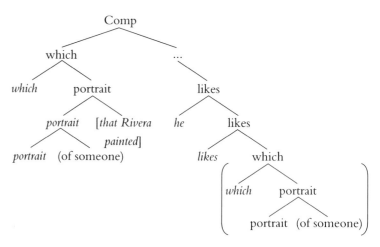

In this structure *he* doesn't command *Rivera,* simply because no copy of the relative clause containing *Rivera* is left in the command domain of *he*. This would explain the contrasts that we saw in (21) with respect to binding.

O: That's clever, but you've got considerable explaining to do now . . . Firstly, either I'm missing something, or else the chain in (28b) is positively improper, since its links clearly aren't identical after you add the relative clause [see fig. 4.20] [31].

L: That depends on how exactly the adjunct relative clause is added to the highest *portrait*. It could well be that it's added in a dimension that doesn't affect the structural relation between the two links of the chain (which portrait, (which portrait)). This in fact could be a general property of adjuncts.

O: That may be true, but you won't be astounded when I tell you that I'd like to grasp exactly why adjuncts behave this way, so that they're added at any point in the derivation, or—you're now speculating—perhaps even in a different dimension . . . Honestly! . . . Just as I'd like to grasp exactly how adjuncts are to be linearised. Or what adjuncts are to begin with . . . !

4.4 Adjunction

(which is necessary for head movements, as well as not too rare instances of parataxis, or so it seems)

L: Before I satisfy your curiosity, let me emphasize this. Your intuition, remember, was that extending the phrasal structure inward requires changing the structure of what's been assembled up to that point. But in (28b) we're adding an adjunct inside an already assembled phrase marker, in a noncyclic fashion which leads to a nice analysis of a surprising binding fact. So that looks like a serious counterexample to the idea that syntactic history is always a record of syntactic "growth"—or, to be technical, is always cyclic.

O: It is indeed.

a notation for adjunction

L: The fact is that we've run out of notational options for adjunction, so let me try something different. Normally, merging α

Figure 4.20

Compare:

(i) *Chain before adding the adjunct relative clause*
[[which portrait] does he like [which portrait]]
(Identical links)

(ii) *Chain after adding the adjunct relative clause*
[that Rivera painted]
[[which portrait] does he like [which portrait]]
(Identical links?)

with β results in γ, a category with the features of β. If things were just like this, syntactic combinations would be totally trivial, with familiar arithmetic properties [32]. But things are slightly more interesting. Apparently, we can also relate α and β to get a new object built from β which is itself not a category, but part of one.

O: Sir, you've utterly confounded me.

L: Let's be concrete. Suppose you make a dummy copy of β upon merging it with an adjunct α, yielding the pair ["β," β]. This pair is still a single category, and you can think of each element in the pair as a **segment** of the category. Note that I'm putting the dummy copy of β in scare quotes, to suggest that it hasn't any reality of its own—it's not a term.

O: Hold on; β (which was there before this funny merger) is real, and α (which is what moved) is also real—but you mean to tell me that "β" is merely an artefact of this particular process?

L: That's right; linguists call this sort of operation *adjunction,* and we say for concreteness that the label of an adjunction is a pair built from the element to which something adjoins [33]. So, for instance, the label of the created structure ["β," β] is <u><β, β></u>; the constituent construct is of course $\{\alpha, \beta\}$ (that hasn't changed, for α is relating to β); and thus the entire set-theoretic object that results from the adjunction is $\{$<u><β, β></u>, $\{\alpha, \beta\}\}$. (Compare this with a merger of α with β, whose label would be <u>β</u>.)

---

terms of adjunction

O: We are assuming the definitions in (17) for terms. Then whether the object $\{$<u><β, β></u>, $\{\alpha, \beta\}\}$ is a term depends, to start with, on whether it is itself a root phrase marker K—in which case it is a basic term, as per (17i).

L: That's a rare instance, but it's one to keep in mind, yes.

O: Needless to say, most terms will be embedded inside other terms, in which case—as per (17ii)—the embedded objects will be terms if and only if they are members of members of a term K.

L: What we want, remember, is that in cases involving an adjunction site ["β," β], "β" isn't a term, but β still is, as well as the whole ["β," β].

O: Of course—but now let me be fastidiously explicit, will you?

The Linguist was not allowed to answer. As if possessed by a desire to demonstrate that he too could handle formulas, the Other engaged in a tireless attempt to formulate adjunction. Readers whose interests are more general may wish to gloss over this passage (which has been preserved for accuracy in reporting) and move directly to the next subsection; those whose interests are more specialized may wish to delve into these matters even further in the appendix.

O: Allow me to represent the structure we've been discussing with the adjunction notation you've just introduced. Two possibilities arise, I believe (once again, I shall use initials instead of full words for ease of exposition):

(29) a.

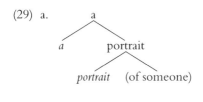

   b.

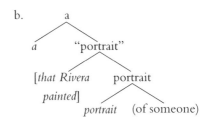

(30) a.

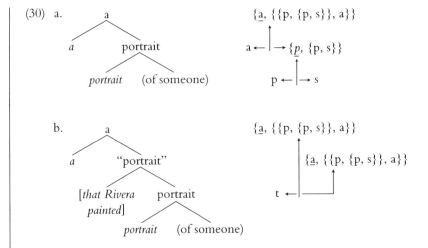

b.

In (29), the result of the adjunction—["portrait," portrait]—is a term. In (30), the result of the adjunction is not a term. This is because there is no object $\{<\underline{p}, p>, \{\{p, \{p, s\}\}, t\}\}$ in (30) which is the member of the member of any term, since the top category isn't overwritten when the adjunct is merged noncyclically. In contrast, in (29) I've overwritten the object $\{\underline{a}, \{\{p, \{p, s\}\}, a\}\}$ after the result of the adjunction process—namely, $\{<\underline{p}, p>, \{\{p, \{p, s\}\}, t\}\}$—is created. In the overwritten $\{\underline{a}, \{\{<p, p> \{\{p, \{p, s\}\}, t\}\}, a\}\}$, it's easy to see that the structure that **Adjoin** creates (which I've boxed in (29)) is indeed a term, since it's a member of a member of a term. Then the question should be, which is the correct model for Adjoin: the one expressed in (29) or the one expressed in (30)?

L: You know the answer: provided that we want the result of the adjunction to be a term ["portrait," portrait], (29) is the correct structure.

O: But is it? I thought we wanted the adjunct not to affect the structure already formed—don't we want something like (30)?

L: No; in (30) absolutely no relation exists between the adjunct *that* . . . and whatever it adjoins to. You may as well not have generated *that . . .*, because it hasn't affected the structure. That seems wrong, since obviously *a portrait of someone* really isn't the same thing as *a portrait of someone that Rivera painted*. We want to encode that difference in the structure, even if we don't do it by the means that standard Merge allows—but (30) provides no means whatsoever.

label adjunction

O: Oh, I very much agree with that conclusion. But you see, I had a modification of (30) in mind, if you'll allow me to show it. It's (31), where the adjunction to {p, {p, s}} is simplified not to produce a category with a new label <u><p, p></u>; it merely produces a relation {{p, {p, s}}, t}, with no label:

(31) a.

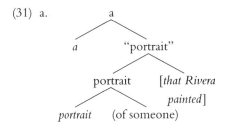

b. {<u>a</u>, {{p, {p, s}}, a}}

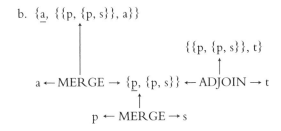

Needless to say, (31b) is not a tree, but why should it be [34]?

L: Yeah, there's no a priori reason to believe that syntactic representations should be trees. All that we've defined and motivated so far are very simple-minded objects—trivial sets. The fact that their set-theoretic relations can be mapped to graphs of a certain kind is anecdotal, and just a good way of drawing the objects on the ground or a piece of paper.

O: What I'm trying to say is that (31b) is very perspicuous. Importantly, <u>a</u> relates to {p, {p, s}}, as it did before the adjunction, and no overwriting ensues. Adjunction simply has no consequences for the already assembled structure: the overall structures with and without the adjunction of the relative clause are identical. Nevertheless, it's not the case that the adjunct produces nothing whatever; it does: the relation between it and a part of the merged structure. The intuition, however, is that this relation is expressed, as you'd put it, "in a different dimension." This, parenthetically, would also address the uniformity problem that I raised with respect to (28b). Within its own dimension, the chain (which portrait, which portrait) is perfectly uniform.

L: Yeah, that might be right [35]. However, how do you characterize the new relation as a syntactic term? Even if it's in another dimension, in order for it to be recognized by the system, it has to be a term. Your object {{p, {p, s}}, t} isn't a term, because it's neither a member of a member of a term (17ii), nor a root phrase marker. Why? Because it's not even a phrase marker, since it has no label (it doesn't meet the defining conditions for syntactic objects in (17a–c)). This means you need to complicate your (31) to something at least as complex as (32):

(32) a.

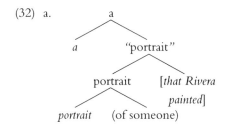

    b. {*a*, {{p, {p, s}}, a}}

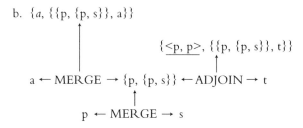

Now the object {<u><p, p></u>, {p, {p, s}}, t}} is at least a term. It isn't a term in relation to the rest of the structure, but it's indeed a term in and of itself. (By saying this, I don't necessarily want to commit to saying that (32) is the correct structure of adjuncts—that's much more complex to establish.)

O: Well, we could redefine the notion "term," so that the adjunct in my (31) is a term even if it has no label.

L: You can always do something else. But then you have to show what that is—the usual. Look, no matter how you express these matters notationally, the factual and theoretical issues are reasonably clear. The price you don't want to pay for your notation is entirely disconnected structures, like your (31), where the adjunct just doesn't bear any relation to what it adjoins to. We know that the adjunct is indeed related to something in the structure, even if loosely. Besides, we can see the need for real labels (whether pairs or something else) even more clearly the minute we move to more familiar instances of adjunction. We've talked about this all along: we have a Tense node, for instance, and we move a Verb to merge with it. The merger in this case has to be an adjunction.

_____ why adjunction is needed

(33)

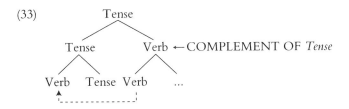

Prior to the movement the verb phrase is the complement of Tense. If the relation between the verb and Tense weren't adjunction, we'd be forced to conclude that the raised verb is the complement of Tense (the sister to the head #Tense#) [see fig. 4.21].

O: I see . . . And needless to say, as a consequence, the element which was a complement prior to the movement of the verb to Tense (the verb phrase) would then have to be reinterpreted as a specifier. This is assuming that a specifier is a sister of a nonhead. In the would-be scenario, merging the head #Tense# and the raised verb clearly gives rise to a nonhead, and this nonhead would be the sister of the verb phrase.

L: Right, so we take the other obvious option, and we say that the verb movement results in an adjunction. Of course, we want to say that the raised verb and Tense are connected—so much so that in the languages where the verb adjoins to Tense (e.g., Middle English), these two form an object with morphological status, whereby the Tense features are checked for some morphological reason, and presumably also an appropriate unit of interpretation is formed for LF purposes [see sec. 6.2].

O: I follow what you're saying, but I must confess that my emphasis in trying to push the sort of structure in (30), or its more elaborate variants in (31) and (32), was to avoid the grandmother paradox— hence allowing me to stick to cyclic mergers, which I hope will follow from something.

L: I don't want to go back to that boring formal stuff . . . Let's look at some empirical cases, and see how your ideas about adjunction

Figure 4.21

Consider the movement in (33) if adjunction operations did not exist:

(i) *Prior to movement*

(ii) *After movement*

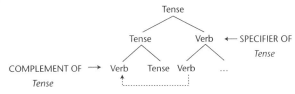

The relational status of the verb phrase changes from (i) (complement) to (ii) (specifier). Among other things, this unwanted step would destroy the command relations between Tense and the verb phrase (after movement, Tense would no longer command the verb phrase, since it would not be a sister to it). Presumably, this sort of derivation crashes or is uninterpretable at LF. The alternative in terms of adjunction faces no such difficulties; but see the text below for complications that adjunctions introduce.

fare when they meet reality. I guess that you'd analyze (33) as in (34), assuming you accept the slight modification I suggested in (32), to make it coherent:

(34) $\{\underline{T}, \{T, \{V, \{V, ...\}\}\}\}$

$\{<\underline{T}, T>, V, T\}$ ⌐—⎟→ $\{\underline{V}, \{V, ...\}\}$

V ←⎟→ T ——⎟—— V ←⎟→ ...

Now: how are we to establish command relations in these structures?

O: True. If we don't succeed in that task, the LCT may well rule out all of our attempts.

―――――――――――――――――――――――― *linearizing adjuncts*

L: There's both an empirical and a theoretical issue. Suppose our conclusions about the hierarchy of modifiers were correct: the hierarchically superior adjunct takes widest scope, and so on, until we reach the head. Intriguingly, the string of words in (26), which involves relative clauses, is essentially a mirror image of the string of words involving adjectives. That is, *a dinosaur which is large which is small* is a small large dinosaur, and not a large small dinosaur; conversely, *a dinosaur which is small which is large* is a large small dinosaur, and not a small large dinosaur. Think about it [see fig. 4.22]. This already indicates that the PF ordering of these adjuncts can't be a matter for the LCA to determine (the postnominal orderings clearly aren't predicted by the LCA). But a stronger conclusion would be this: for some reason the LCA doesn't even apply to these adjunction structures. If that were true, the LCA couldn't rule the structures out, any more than a fundamental principle of biology has anything to say about a rock; it just doesn't apply [36].

O: But that's squarely what my structures would predict! In my terms, the adjunct isn't connected to the term it adjoins to. At bottom, it's not even in the same plane. If command relations are established among connected terms in a phrase marker, it's not unreasonable for me to say that a head does not command the object that adjoins to it, and hence the LCT cannot rule this object out. Of course, we still need a procedure for linearising the head and the adjunct—but that's another story.

Figure 4.22

(i) a. a dinosaur large in size, small in size ≠ a large (in size), small (in size) dinosaur (e.g., Dryosaurus)
   b. a dinosaur large in size, small in size = a small (in size), large (in size) dinosaur (e.g., Camarasaurus)

Judgments of grammaticality in these examples are somewhat degraded, even though in terms of interpretation, the phrases seem fairly clear. Crosslinguistic variation is also notable in these instances (see, e.g., Webelhuth 1989). Apparently, the schematic relations in (ii) describe the facts accurately:

(ii) a.

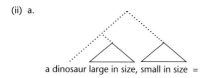

a dinosaur large in size, small in size =

b.

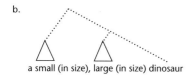

a small (in size), large (in size) dinosaur

However, it is clear that the LCA cannot predict both sorts of order, (iia) and (iib), while remaining consistent with semantic interpretation (see Crain and Hamburger 1992 for relevant discussion). In fact, whatever predicts the ordering facts in (ii) must be sensitive to "height" of dependency, in such a way that *dinosaur* relates to *large* before it relates to *small*. This virtually requires treating the ordering in question as a stylistic matter with no bearing on the structures that feed LF; in other words, it is very likely that whatever orders the constituents in (ii) applies in the PF component. It must be emphasized that basic adjuncts are to be distinguished from adjuncts of movement. Only in instances of movement must a chain be formed; hence, only in these instances are there strong reasons to say that the adjunct is connected to the rest

L: Not a trivial one, though, for although *a dinosaur large in size* is good, *a large dinosaur* is okay but **a dinosaur large* isn't, at least in English. And then there's the fact that relative clauses are prenominal in Chinese, but not in English; and so on. You still need to say a lot about linearization, although in principle I agree with you that this might not be predicted by the LCA, for adjuncts. At any rate, though, I see a tougher challenge for your kinds of structures. (33) is the core instance of adjunction. We can make up all sorts of stories to deal with peripheral relative clauses and modifiers, but head movement is central to this system. Of course, your approach predicts that an adjoined head isn't connected to the trace it leaves behind. So take a verb that moves to adjoin to Tense, leaving a copy in its original site. In my terms, this should result in a movement chain, one whose lower link is a trace commanded by the moved head. In your terms, though, the moved head isn't even connected to the rest of the phrase marker, so you have no way of defining a movement chain, for instance as in (11).

O: I could have a different definition of chain.

L: Yeah, you'd have to say what that is. It won't be easy. For instance, I don't see what in your approach predicts that head movement should go upward.

O: And how do you explain that fact?

────────────────────────────────────── movement and base adjunctions

L: It doesn't matter how I do it; I can [see sec. 4.7]. This is because in my terms the head that moves is connected to the rest of the phrase marker, as a result of which I can establish any formal relation I please, even if I can't deduce it as elegantly as you'd like me to— although I think I can do that too. But you can't even try. For you, the objects are totally unrelated. This might not be crazy for sentential adjuncts, relative clauses, and so on. I don't totally dislike your speculations there, since those structures all seem to be in a league of their own, and they probably involve a whole separate sentence that somehow gets attached to the head. So suppose I even grant you that this disconnectedness that you're seeking works fine for those instances, and similar ones. These mirror images we've discussed may well be a consequence of disconnectedness, with some other linearization requirement determining the handedness, left or right, of these nonsyntactic dependencies (following traditional ter-

of the phrase marker (the chain ranges over positions across a phrase marker). It is thus in principle possible that basic adjuncts (as opposed to adjuncts of movement) stand in a relation of parataxis (literally, "parallel syntax") to the rest of the phrase marker. From this perspective, the ultimate reason behind the linearizing of their various PF manifestations might be related to discourse matters. Importantly, although the basic adjunct is somehow related to a nominal head (perhaps through some kind of anaphoric dependency), this relation might not materialize into a term, as a result of which command relations may not be determinable (thus making the LCA inapplicable). This contrasts with the situation emerging for adjuncts of movement, where standard phrasal connectedness must hold and it is therefore necessary to determine whether the head commands the adjunct or vice versa. Even so, the LCA may still be inapplicable if head-adjunct relations essentially hold at the word level and thus are determined by morphological considerations.

minology, this phenomenon may be referred to as **parataxis**) [37]. But nothing like this will be of much use for garden-variety head movements, where we plainly need the formation of a chain, and thus a given, characteristic connectedness. This is a crucial difference, actually. Relative clauses and other large adjuncts don't move: where you see them is where you get them. In contrast, heads have to move to check whatever morphology they associate with, in a given functional projection; thus, heads crucially involve a chain. If you can be patient, I'll show you lots of properties of these chains that need to be explained in terms of connectedness [see chap. 5]. I do realize that by sticking to my sorts of structures, we have to depart from an optimal system of labeling, and the general form of merged objects. So be it; when we're ready to deduce these stipulations, we will. Or maybe they don't follow from anything, and this is just the way things are, for some accidental reason, perhaps having to do with morphological principles of the kind in (7). (Alternatively, we'll find a more elegant notation where these issues become trivial.)

O: I didn't mean to lead you astray.

L: You haven't; this discussion is illuminating. But I think that at the very least we have to conclude that head chains demand (34) or a similar variant, even if your (34) were useful for adjunctions which aren't the result of movement. Consequently, as things stand right now we haven't yet deduced the cyclic nature of all transformations. We have to keep looking, to see if we understand things better, and then we can match intuitions with results.

O: . . .

4.5 The Array as a Numeration

(together with some economy considerations of so much interest that the entire derivational system might well rest on them)

L: I'd like to show you some other domains of UG where things work cyclically, somewhat unexpectedly. Let's look again at the matter of uniformity prior to and after Spell-Out. Before this point, C_{HL} has access to the lexical elements in the array A, whereas after Spell-Out, it doesn't. Why?

how do PF and LF structures manage to be compatible?

O: Empirically, I suppose this is to ensure that, for example, what's pronounced as *Socrates died in prison* doesn't get interpreted as—I don't know—'I wonder whether Socrates died in prison', or something of that ilk [38] . . .

L: That, of course, is a perfectly legitimate interpretation, but not one you'd want to sanction in relation to the PF of *Socrates died in prison*.

O: And what about ellipsis?

L: Ellipsis is totally different, as we saw. That case starts out with a full structure built from the lexical array, which then gets marked for deletion at PF under conditions of parallelism. The case you've brought up starts out with some structure—say, *Socrates died in prison*—and then lexical structure gets added to that after Spell-Out, but in the LF component (thus, without any consequences for the PF component). We have to prevent that. In general, this point is straightforward, and a way to ensure the appropriate correspondence would be to exhaust the lexical items in the array prior to Spell-Out.

O: Although we still have the question pending from a couple of days ago: exactly what is the array?

how do we determine the set of candidate derivations?

L: Yes, so there are two related issues here. One is relatively straightforward: the matter of **compatibility** between PF and LF . . . we want to make sure that everything doesn't mean just anything. The second is nontrivial, and it's the matter of **optimality** [39]. The assumption we're making is that when derivations converge, they're always the optimal ones. But what's the **reference set** of equivalent candidate derivations, from which we pick out the optimal one(s)? That's a difficult question.

O: We're assuming that the reference set of candidates is a set of derivations built exclusively from the elements in the array.

L: Correct. And the hope is that answering this optimality question also provides an answer to the compatibility question.

O: That's reasonable. Well, then—is the array a set?

L: It can't be. For two reasons. First, a lexical item can appear more than once in the array.

O: Oh, of course—that's a bloody killer.

L: So if an element occurs more than once in the structure, which in fact happens all the time, then it must be that the structure in question is more complex than a set.

O: And I can see the second reason why the array can't be a set. Given the same initial array, we can end up with the structures *Socrates thinks Plato likes arguments* and *Plato thinks Socrates likes arguments*. Presumably the derivations of these two entirely different sentences are never compared for optimality reasons [40].

L: Presumably, yes.

O: Then whatever the array is, it must be something more complex than a set, for otherwise it's hard to see why we couldn't just say that the derivations of those two sentences could legitimately be compared, inasmuch as they use the same elements.

L: If the array were a set, it would have to be legitimate to compare the derivations of those different sentences, as coming from the same array. This captures the wrong notion: we shouldn't be allowed to compare entirely different sentences like these.

O: Is the array a sequence?

L: That should be the next obvious possibility; but it fails too. Consider the sequence <there, seems, a, man, to, be, here>. Two convergent derivations are possible: *there seems to be a man here* and **there seems a man to be here*. Remember, these both converge, but the idea is that the first one is more economical, in some sense to be made precise. But now look: in order to reach that conclusion, we must have allowed the two structures to pick up the elements from the initial array in rather different orders. So the array can't be a sequence, because a sequence is an ordered set, and if we're allowed to pick up elements from the array in two different orders, we're in effect dealing with two different sequences. But we don't want to say that there are two different arrays for our sentences, because we want the two alternative derivations to be candidates in the same reference set. So the array has to be the same for both derivations, but it's not a sequence and it's not a set.

O: Well, then, what is it?!

L: Just to express the desired compatibility between LF and PF, we need an object that exhausts the lexical items to be used up in each structure. Let's call that a **numeration.** Let's give a number *n* to every lexical item *x* that we use in a structure, such that *n* tells us the number of occurrences of *x* in the structure, okay? So for instance *Socrates*-2 would mean two occurrences of the word *Socrates,* as in *that Socrates was a philosopher did not particularly impress Socrates.*

O: The enumeration is a function over the lexicon . . .

L: Nu-meration, not *e*-numeration! I don't want to use a concept with a meaning in standard mathematical terms; I'm making this up. But anyway, yes to your assertion. Let's say that C_{HL} pulls something out of the lexicon, assigns it an occurrence value (one occurrence per structure is one, two occurrences is two, and so on), and then reduces the numeration by one every time the lexical item is placed into a structure. So for instance, as soon as *Socrates* merges with *impress,* to produce the structure *impress Socrates, Socrates*-2 becomes *Socrates*-1. And let's say that the derivation isn't done until the numeration is zero and all occurrences of all lexical items are used up.

───────────────────────────── **answering the compatibility question**

O: But how does this solve the compatibility question? Why does C_{HL} not access lexical stuff (the numeration) after Spell-Out?

L: The simplest assumption is that Spell-Out can apply anywhere [see sec. 3.7], with the derivation going wrong under a variety of circumstances. For instance, if the elements in the numeration haven't been used up, or if—

O: Hold on! I thought crashing a derivation meant "not satisfying FI." What if the representation that results from a partially used-up numeration does satisfy FI? How does that crash, even if all the elements haven't been used up?

Details of execution. (Same Choice)

L: We don't need to say that the derivation crashes, actually. It may be canceled—it's not a valid derivation. At any rate, it seems that we have a real mapping from the numeration onto the interpretive levels, a *complete* mapping. We have to assume that.

O: I can assume that, but my question is why a derivation that doesn't comply with that proviso should crash, as opposed to being cancelled.

L: As I say, it may well be that the derivation is canceled, in general. It may also be the case that it crashes, though, if—as a consequence of not using up the items in the numeration—some crucial feature in a selected item doesn't get checked; so various possibilities emerge. But the bottom line is that we simply have to exhaust the items in the numeration. Derivations also crash or get canceled if they've left items dangling around without attaching them into a phrase marker; that sort of thing (presumably) can't obtain a valid interpretation at LF, or again certain strong features which aren't checked would induce a derivational cancellation [see fig. 4.23]. And hopefully the derivation also crashes if it continues accessing the numeration after Spell-Out.

O: Why?

L: Suppose an element selected from the lexicon can't be embedded. If this is the way C_{HL} works, then the issue of adding extraneous material after Spell-Out only arises at the **root** of the phrase marker [see fig. 4.24]. But now note: if an entire lexical item is selected in the covert component at the root of the phrase marker, this item will be introduced as a whole lexical unit, with semantic, phonological, and formal features. And thus this derivation will crash at LF because the material being added is illegal at that level: LF has no way of handling phonological features. In turn, this sort of option may not even be available in the PF component, if the process of lexical selection is part of the uniform mapping from the array to LF, and has nothing to do with the phonological mapping.

O: What about selecting an item in the LF component, at the root of the phrase marker, and with no phonological features?

L: That's certainly a possibility: if the selected item has no phonological features, selecting it covertly wouldn't lead to an LF crash. And maybe this particular process is indeed instantiated. For instance, an intriguing asymmetry between main and embedded clauses is that the latter are typically introduced by a complementizer like *that, for, if,* or *whether,* but the former aren't [41]. Thus, we say *I like Ike,* but not **that I like Ike* (as a matrix clause). In all other respects, main and embedded clauses are extremely similar, phonologically, semantically, and syntactically. But this particular asymmetry can be explained away if matrix clauses in fact do have complementizers, except that they're not overt. This would follow if such complementizers are selected in the covert components, which is simpler than selecting them overtly, and then subjecting them to Spell-Out. Of course, this sort of null element can appear only once per clause: at the root [see fig. 4.24]. At any rate, if this is indeed what happens, then it's not totally accurate to say that Spell-Out happens (or must happen) only when the numeration is fully reduced to zero. The root complementizer selection would be an instance of Spell-Out happening prior to the numeration being fully reduced. The point is: we don't need to say anything about when to spell out; if we do it too late, we'll crash in most instances. So the description about compatibility now follows: PF and LF have to match up, except at the root and in a handful of cases.

O: Very well. What about the optimality question?

_____ **answering the optimality question**

L: We want the derivation in (35a) to rule out the derivation in (35b), because (35a) is more economical:

(35) a.   [there seems [(there) to be a man here]]

      b.   *[there seems [a man to be (a man) here]]

(I realize I haven't motivated the movements in (35), but just assume them for the sake of discussion [see chap. 5].) Both derivations have the same number of mergers, and a single movement. In (35a), *there* moves from the position of subject of the embedded clause to the position of subject of the matrix clause. (The assumption is that in English all sentences need a subject.) *A man* doesn't move in (35a). In (35b), *there* never moves, but *a man* does get to move, to occupy the subject position of the embedded clause (again, all clauses need a subject in English). So we can't just say that (35a) has fewer derivational steps than (35b), because they have the same number. How

Figure 4.23

The matter of having to exhaust the items in a numeration raises interesting questions about what this formal object is. In pre-Minimalist models, the issue did not arise, because derivations started by producing "deep" structures. The items in "deep" structure had to be "used up" when LF was reached, or else derivations would not be mappings from "deep" structures at all. Derivations are now said to be mappings from the numeration to LF; but is this substantive or formal? If the former, it is necessary to determine exactly what goes wrong in a derivation that does not exhaust the items in a numeration. Such a derivation may directly terminate, much as a spelling bee may not be won by someone who spells only part of a word. This case is arguably different from that of leaving items unattached to a phrase marker, after they have been selected from the numeration. Presumably, this raises Full Interpretation problems for, at least, LF (where a single object is not produced), and thus a derivation in these circumstances would fail to converge.

Figure 4.24

Lexical selection after Spell-Out:

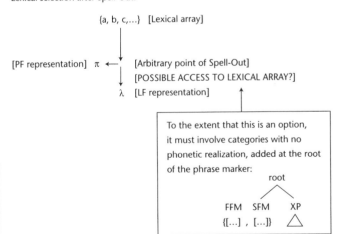

about procrastination? Although in (35b) *a man* doesn't procrastinate—it moves to subject position overtly—it's also true that in (35a) *there* doesn't procrastinate.

O: You've made me believe that (35a) is more economical than (35b), but as a matter of fact—

L: Just a minute! What I've made you believe is true, but now I have to demonstrate it. Economy has to be precisely defined, and I think I can show you a natural way in which (35a) is indeed more economical than (35b) [42]. The intuition I'd like to pursue is that economy is evaluated cyclically, so that (35b) is less economical than (35a) because already in the embedded clause C_{HL} chose not to procrastinate, while in (35a) it waits until the last minute, and then it has no choice other than not procrastinating because otherwise it'd get no subject for the matrix clause. So the idea is to try and use up the elements in the initial array as fast as possible, instead of moving things around as the derivation proceeds. Another way of asking the crucial question is this: as C_{HL} took a derivational step, did it have a more optimal derivation without overt movement? If it did, it shouldn't have taken that step. And obviously, looking at the phrase markers in (35), it's clear that *a man* and *here* merge, and *be* and *a man here,* and *to* and *be a man here* (up to that point the two derivations are identical). Then C_{HL} has a choice: either it merges *there* with *to be a man here* (that is, it uses another element from the array), or it moves *a man* to subject position. So in the first instance we get *there to be a man here,* and in the second we get *a man to be (a man) here* [see steps (iii) and (iv), fig. 4.25].

O: And that's where the second one buys a ticket to Hell, because it didn't procrastinate there and then. Very interesting.

L: Of course later on *there to be a man here* must out of necessity not procrastinate—otherwise we won't get a subject in the matrix subject position, right? But then is then and now is now. The other one moved up too early. The crucial derivational point is *to be a man here* [see step (iii), fig. 4.25]. The one "bad" step that (35b) takes—namely, not procrastinating by moving *a man*—is a fine step in other instances. (For example, *I believe a man to be here* is a perfect sentence of English, and its derivation includes what turned out to be the "killer step" in (35b)—namely, *a man to be (a man) here.*) So there's absolutely nothing wrong with the step per se; it's only when we compare it with other possible routes the derivation may have taken

Figure 4.25

Determining optimality as a derivation proceeds:

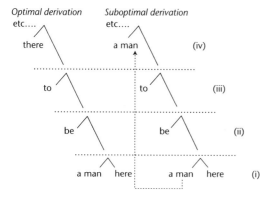

Lexical array common to both derivations:

{there-1, seems-1, a-1, man-1, to-1, be-1, here-1, Tense-2, Comp-2, . . . }

that a potential problem turns up. In the case of *I believe a man to be here,* there's nothing else the derivation can do, and everything's just fine.

O: Sorry to ask such a basic question, but you appear to be comparing *a man to be here*—as in *I believe a man to be here*—with the sort of structure that you obtain in *there seems to be a man here.* Isn't *a man,* though, a complement of *believe* in one instance, and a subject of sorts—or some such thing—in the other?

L: There's something to that observation, but you have to be very careful with the implementation [43]. In terms of its semantic import, *a man* clearly isn't the object of *believe,* in the sense you get when you say something like "I believe the government." Thus, note that you can say, without falling into a contradiction or an absurdity, "I believe the members of our government to be pathological liars." That has the same semantic import, roughly speaking, as saying that you believe this: the members of our government are pathological liars. Clearly, the phrase *the members of our government* is a subject in the embedded clause. Now, having said this, I'll readily admit that this phrase is somehow "promoted" to what we can descriptively call "grammatical object" position in the main clause. Thus, for instance, the understood subject of the embedded clause receives accusative Case, which is typically assigned by a verb like *believe: I believe him to be a pathological liar.* We can return shortly to how this result is mechanically achieved [see sec. 4.6].

O: Very well; now, if I follow you correctly, there are two main parts to your proposal. Firstly, the reference set is determined by however far we've gotten into the derivation; secondly, lexical selection of the elements from the initial array isn't costly.

L: You're correct on the first count, but not entirely on the second. We can't really say that Select is costless, because it doesn't just happen alone: we select and we merge, and Merge is a transformational operation—so it does have cost.

O: Is Select a transformational operation?

L: No. A transformational operation is a mapping between phrase markers, and Select is just a mapping between the numeration and a phrase marker. It's really like setting your pieces on the chessboard. Cost starts being computed after you move your first pawn, not before. The first transformational operation you engage in is an instance of Merge, and that has cost [44]. The real question, though, is whether at any given point Merge is more or less costly than Move. If Move is more costly, then my argument of a minute ago goes through.

O: When I come to think of it, the complete Move operation really includes Merge within it . . .

L: At least when it's performed prior to Spell-Out, that's right. Of course, after Spell-Out you can say that Move just involves the copying of a feature from a given head somewhere else, and that's the end of the story. So an instance of covert movement shouldn't be, all other things being equal, any more or less costly than an instance of merger. However, as we saw today, movement prior to Spell-Out involves an ancillary operation, which the Wording Requirement in (7) demands; we can't just move features around prior to Spell-Out, so when a feature F engages in movement at this stage of the derivation, it has to take a bunch of free-riders with it. Those free-riders have to be merged, as our working definition in (11) indicates. So strictly speaking, there are two operations going on: the movement of feature F, and the ancillary operation of merging the free-riders that go with F. That's obviously more costly than either just moving F, or just moving the free-riders.

O: I say, from this point of view, isn't the strategy of procrastination simply telling us that if Move is delayed until LF, less work is done [45]?

L: In effect, yes. The intuition is that overt movement is too much trouble, and you do it only if you have to for some other reason; but then you have to merge the free-riders as well, which you don't have to in covert movement.

O: That's nice. Hm . . . the split between PF and LF is quite decisive!

L: Language the way we see it is very much a reflex of this split. This is one of the main reasons I'm trying to be cautious about what might exist on the LF side of the grammar; we really are deeply clueless, much more so than we often realize. When philosophers talk about LF-related matters, they're doing philosophy of language. But what is the root of philosophy of language if language really is different, at some moderately deep level, from the way we perceive it? For instance, if I'm correct, a sentence like *who did John see?* comes out the way it does, with *who* displaced forward, not because of a profound property of questions, but actually because of a low-level fact about English. To start with, the minute we look at other languages, we see that *who* isn't displaced, and to the extent that a *wh*-feature is indeed displaced, it moves by itself, leaving behind an essentially indefinite predicate. In other words, if we want to analyze the semantics of this question, we're probably better off saying that it means something like '*wh-x* John see something *x*'. But the point is: this semantic analysis isn't obvious. We have to do some serious linguistic analysis, and look at different languages, and trust our theoretical model that tells us something about what moves why, and so on.

O: I certainly see that logic doesn't dictate that analysis of questions! But apart from the clear impact that Spell-Out has on the important theoretical point that you raise, I'm intrigued by the fact that the really constructive part of the derivation takes place prior to Spell-Out. That's when C_{HL} actively merges and moves (with Merge as an ancillary operation). The post-Spell-Out part of the derivation seems to be merely the realm of featural readjustment, with perhaps a single merger at the root, where C_{HL} adds a very silent complementiser . . .

L: Yeah. This is important, too, for comparative issues arising among alternative derivations, which are going to be decided mostly in terms of prior-to-Spell-Out operations. Think about it. First of all, after Spell-Out, Procrastinate is irrelevant, so we can't use it to decide what's optimal. Second, after Spell-Out the lexical array only gets accessed in exotic instances, like adding null complementizers. This means that all possible derivational steps taken after Spell-Out are going to be in the same competitive arena; an important point, provided that competition arises only among derivations which share a common structural core. That is, there's what we can call a "derivational horizon" beyond which no comparison is possible. Early on, when only a few items from the numeration have been selected, the derivational horizon is wide. As structural commitments are made (in part, as a result of random choices of lexical items; in part, because of the formal workings of C_{HL}), the derivational horizon narrows down, and fewer alternatives exist . . . until

Figure 4.26

Determining optimality as a derivation proceeds:

Two equally costly derivations
etc....   etc....

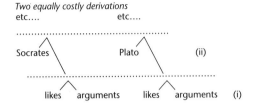

Lexical array common to both derivations:

{Plato-1, Socrates-1, *thinks*-1, likes-1, arguments-1, Tense-2, Comp-2, ...}

Reduced arrays after step (ii):

{Plato-1, *thinks*-1, Tense-2, Comp-2, ...}
{Socrates-1, *thinks*-1, Tense-2, Comp-2, ...}

Figure 4.27

The intuition behind dynamic economy (formally expressed in (37)) is easily seen in terms of derivational horizons. Suppose that derivation D, coming from the initial numeration N, has reached stage S. Then the reference set for comparative purposes is determined both by the reduced numeration N_D (the part of N that D could still access) and by D at S: it is a set of convergent extensions of the partial mapping of N → S, using the remains of N_D (a partial numeration). Given this set, operation O is blocked if operation O' yields a more economical derivation.

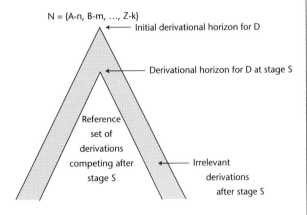

the numeration is exhausted and the derivational horizon practically disappears, since the derivation is almost complete [see fig. 4.27]. It's from this perspective that we never have to worry about comparing *Socrates thinks Plato likes arguments* and *Plato thinks Socrates likes arguments*: although these two use up exactly the same initial array, the reference set of competing derivations in each case is quite different [see fig. 4.26]. In one derivation we merge *Socrates* and *likes arguments*. This means that the partial numeration we're left with gives us access to the derivational horizon made up, in effect, of the set of derivations that began with this derivation and have access to the partial numeration (the reduced numeration at this point, which includes *Socrates*-0, because we used up *Socrates*; and *Plato*-1, because we haven't yet used *Plato*). If we'd proceeded differently (for instance, selecting *Plato* instead of *Socrates* to generate *Plato likes arguments*), then we'd be left with a partial numeration that includes *Plato*-0 and *Socrates*-1. Of course, that's a different reduced numeration, and thus the reference set, which is a fixed function of the derivation and the partial numeration, would be a different reference set from the one we had before; from that point on, comparison between the two derivations involves two different derivational horizons, and is thus illicit.

_____ further reflections on the numeration

O: I understand, and I find it hard to see how a representational alternative to this computational system would capture these results [see sec. 2.7].

L: That's very true, but I won't have time to go into it. At any rate, note that when the numeration has been reduced to zero, and the derivation has reached LF, if any further transformational operations are necessary (by hypothesis, only featural movement), then it would seem that all these covert operations are, at least to a first approximation, equally costly. That is, we may still want to prevent idle movement with no syntactic purpose, or at least leave it as some sort of last resort operation [46]; but the bottom line is that we won't have an easy measure of comparison like we did before Spell-Out, where Move clearly ends up costing more than Merge, and Procrastinate is clearly advantageous. After Spell-Out, not only is it very hard to observe what's going on, but even if we could determine what the facts are, it would be hard to decide what's optimal, once we set aside outrageously uneconomical moves [47].

O: Derivational horizons narrow down as the derivational cycle proceeds, literally with every new instance of Merge. Hence, haven't you now built a given derivational cyclicity into the optimality checking?

L: That's the punch line I was trying to reach. The point is, of course, that without this cyclicity, we would have no way of determining an appropriate (empirically correct) reference set of alternative derivations for the tricky (35), given the sort of dynamic economy that obtains in these areas. To put matters explicitly:

(36) *Numeration (definition)*
Given a lexicon L, a **multiset** N is a *numeration* if and only if all of the elements of N are members of L.

(37) *Dynamic economy*
Given a set of derivations R all starting in numeration N, and where D is a partial derivation of any member of R and N_D is the sub-multiset that corresponds to D, the *reference set* Δ for all the derivational continuations of D is a *fixed function* $F(D, N_D)$.

O: Are you trying to tell me that this cyclicity is not a consequence of a notational system representing the derivational history of merger . . .

L: That's right: it has nothing to do with your grandmother paradox. This abstract cyclicity is a very general property, relating to the very dynamics of the system [see fig. 4.27]. How it relates to the phrasal notation we're using is only marginally interesting—if at all.

4.6 Clockwork
(containing a further account of movements, and featuring motives for them to happen, based on agreement in Case and presenting the case of agreement)

O: You know? I'm still a wee bit perplexed about the differences among languages—why Irish or Spanish should do something overtly, whereas English does it covertly, et cetera. Procrastinate simply means "If you can get away without moving overtly, don't move."

—————————————————————   it is not deadly not to procrastinate

L: Procrastinate isn't an absolute constraint, though. C_{HL} doesn't violate something if it doesn't procrastinate. It only violates something if it doesn't procrastinate when it could have. If it waits until LF, however, the only thing that moves is feature matrices, going wherever they need to check something or other.

O: There! For some reason some movement must take place by LF anyway—why? Why doesn't everything just stay put?

L: Yeah, well . . . Okay, so movement has to happen prior to Spell-Out if strong morphology needs to be checked. But there must be a requirement that makes movement happen by LF, and that we haven't established yet. So let's look again at that Japanese example we discussed yesterday. What was it?

O: Morihiroga Kazuoga Inokio aisiteiru to itta: 'Morihiro Kazuo Inoki loves that said'.

L: What's probably crucial are those Case markers appearing to the right of all the names: *-ga* and *-o*. It's usually features like this that drive the movement. If relevant features are strong in a given language—like Japanese—movement has to happen prior to Spell-Out in order to check them. That's the "virus" line [48].

---

agreement and verb shells

O: How and where is Case checked?

L: Let's go on with our survey of the world's languages. Take Basque. I suppose you know how to say in Basque: "Kazuo loves Inoki."

O: "Kepak maite du Iñaki." Had to change the names, though—for accuracy.

L: So just as in Japanese the morpheme *-ga* marks the subject and the morpheme *-o* marks the object, in Basque the morpheme *-(e)k* marks the subject and a null morpheme marks the object. But there's one obvious difference . . .

O: Basque has got that odd little *du* dangling round.

L: Yes, that's sort of the equivalent of English *shall*. An auxiliary marker which in Basque always has to be there, and always has to be a clitic.

O: Usually on the verb, but not always [49]. Curiously, this clitic changes depending first of all on who the subject of the sentence is. For example, *du* is used to mean that the one who does the loving is third person. If the subject is first or second person, then the auxiliary is respectively *dut* or *duzu*.

L: Yes, well, here's what's really curious: not only does the auxiliary change with respect to the subject's person—it also changes with respect to the *object's*. That's what's usually called "object agreement" [50].

O: That's very true. Whereas *dut* is used for I-she/he/it, *zaitut* is used for I-you. So Basque-speaking lovers tell each other, "Maite zaitut."

L: You've already impressed me. But here's what's important: suppose that the Case features in our third person example, *-(e)k* and zero in the case of Basque, are in fact checked in the object agreement marker and the subject agreement marker.

O: I'm afraid I'm getting confused again.

L: Recall the structures we talked about yesterday [see chap. 3, (17)], where I drew a mysterious P for Japanese. Let me repeat them now as in (38a), next to the Basque facts in (38b) (and note that I'm now being more precise than yesterday, since I'm making P project):

(38) a. *Japanese*   b. *Basque*

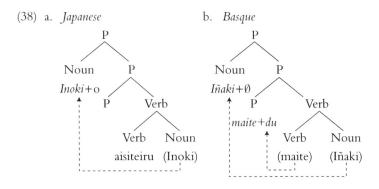

The architecture here is obviously very similar, and we might wonder what this P is. Maybe the simplest hypothesis would be to say that P is just an abstract manifestation of an **extended projection** of the verb, what we can think of as a verb **shell** [51].

O: Oh dear, more and more confusing. Verb shell? What are you on about now?

L: Look closely at the Basque element *du*. It's a verbal auxiliary. Basque speakers can't really say, "Kepa loves Iñaki"; rather, they say something like, "Kepa has loved Iñaki."

O: English speakers can say that too!

L: No, no, you see: in English we say that when we're talking in the present perfect form; for present tense of course we say, "Kepa loves Iñaki," with no auxiliary. But in present tense in Basque the auxiliary is required, which suggests that in English we don't hear it, but it's there nonetheless.

O: What's there? An auxiliary?

L: What's an auxiliary?

O: You tell me!

L: I am: it would seem to be a lexicalization of an abstract, schematic verb shell, which is always there, but receives a PF matrix only in certain languages—for instance, Basque [see sec. 6.1 for further justification of these sorts of categories]. Actually, in English we lexicalize *do* in certain instances (e.g., when a negative particle is attached to it, as in *I don't speak Basque*).

O: I see that, but I'm still not grasping the relevance of these abstract verb shells vis-à-vis the matter of Case.

---

checking Case

L: Here's where the fact that the abstract verb exhibits agreement in Basque becomes relevant. Agreement is a two-place relation of checking, between something like a noun phrase (or rather, some relevant features) and something like a verb (again, the relevant features). For instance, in Basque the name *Iñaki* agrees with the auxiliary *dut* in person (third) and number (singular). So how do we establish this relation? A natural way would be to claim that relations like this have to be established in terms of basic dependencies of the sort we looked at yesterday [see sec. 3.1]: heads and specifiers. Suppose that's the right notion [see sec. 5.4]. Then (39b) shows what's going on in the Basque verb phrase (abstracting away from verb movement), and (more abstractly) (39a) shows what's going on in the Japanese verb phrase:

(39) a. *Japanese*

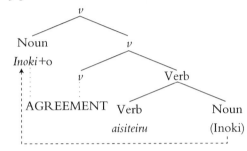

b. *Basque*

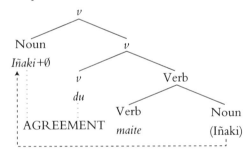

O: I presume your intention is to have these utterly mysterious verbal shells serve as placeholders for a relation between the moved noun phrases and (indirectly) the verb, since I don't suppose you're calling *v* what you called *P* in (38) purely on a notational whim . . .

L: That's right; but for the moment please set aside the substantive question about the meaning of the shell. What you should focus on is precisely the "support" nature of these auxiliary shells, and how they apparently serve as coders for agreement—as addresses, if you will, marking the relevant dependents by way of some crucial features, like number or person.

O: Suppose I accept that. If I follow what you're saying, you're trying to design a very delicate system here, where items move round

Figure 4.28

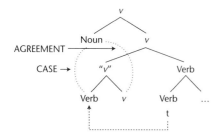

with clockwork precision to enter into rather dynamic relations. Quite specifically, you seem to be proposing that standard person/number agreement and Case are manifestations of a specifier-head relation involving the verb.

L: To be very precise: I want to propose that standard agreement is determined with respect to what I'm calling a "*v* shell" *v*. As for Case, it's also checked in the specifier of *v*, but not with respect to properties of *v* per se [52]; rather, it's the verb that determines Case properties [see fig. 4.28].

O: Steady on! Whereas I could accept that for the Case of objects, what do you intend to say about the Case of subjects?

_____ **predicting the Case of subjects**

L: The notions have to be extended appropriately. In fact, it's very reasonable to say that, in general, the Case properties of the subject depend on the Tense of the sentence. Thus, while a tensed clause allows nominative (subject) Case on the element in its subject position (*he* understands this), a nontensed clause doesn't allow the direct checking of Case on the element in its subject position. So **he to understand this* isn't a possible infinitive, and instead it's necessary to invoke a Case marker like *for,* yielding *for him to understand this* [see fig. 3.7]. We thus say that nominative Case is a function of a *tensed* verb, not just any old verb. At the same time, accusative (object) Case is a property of the verb itself, and so on. The point is that Case properties depend on characteristics of Tense and the verb and the like, and we must therefore also assume that these properties are checked in the Tense projection.

O: Does that mean that when subjects are selected, they're directly inserted into the Tense projection?

L: Not quite. In general, something *moves* to a **checking domain** [see sec. 6.1] [53]; it doesn't start its derivational life out there. Consequently, the subject couldn't have started in the Tense projection; rather, it comes from lower within the structure—from a domain where its basic semantic relations are encoded [54]. It's through movement that the subject reaches the position where it checks Case and agreement.

O: I see, so the subject comes from the verb phrase, as in your illustration of how command works in *you dig this* [see sec. 3.3].

L: That illustration, in fact, was a bit simplified. For reasons that aren't very relevant now, the position where the subject starts is taken to be a specifier of the *v* shell that I've just introduced [see secs. 5.1 and 6.1].

O: I thought the moved object was what occupied the specifier of the *v* shell!

L: In fact, a category can in principle host as many specifiers as it has sisters to its nonhead projections [see fig. 4.29]. Thus, the fact that the moved object is indeed a specifier of the *v* shell doesn't preclude the subject from starting its life as a specifier of this very same head, since the complement of the head is the VP—and the rest of the dependents of *v* which produce categorial mergers (as opposed to mere adjunctions) are all specifiers. But the focus now shouldn't really be on where subjects and objects start, but where they end up: the place where they check their Case and agreement properties. (40) shows the sorts of structures I have in mind, in a somewhat simplified form [see sec. 6.1]. Crucially, subject agreement and Case are checked within the Tense projection, and object agreement and Case are checked within the *v* projection:

(40) a. *Japanese*

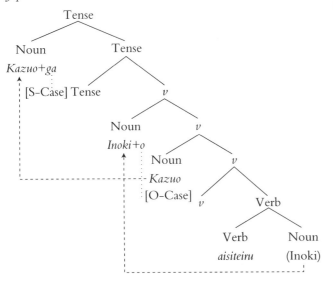

Figure 4.29

Since a specifier is defined as the sister to a nonhead, there can be as many specifiers as there are sisters to nonheads; in contrast, there can be only one sister to a head (a complement):

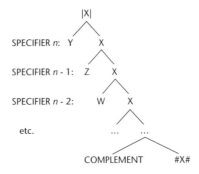

b. *Basque*

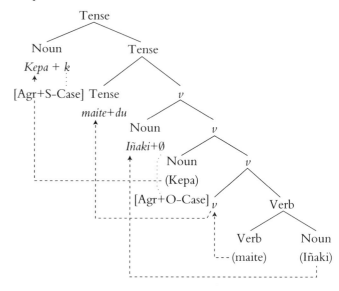

O: The assumption, then, is that there is total symmetry between the subject and the object inflectional dependencies.

L: Yes; simply put, the relation of the noun phrase object to the verb is mediated by *v*, while the relation of the noun phrase subject to the verb is mediated by Tense. (In turn, the verb ends up overtly incorporating, or its features end up covertly relating, to *v* and Tense.) "Subject" and "object" are now merely taxonomic labels: what counts are appropriate structural relations of the kind in (40).

O: And I presume this is also what you have in mind for the promotion of subject to object in *I believe a man to be here* . . .

L: Exactly right [55]. At some point in the derivation, *a man* occupies the specifier of Tense in the embedded clause; at another point, *a man* (or rather the relevant features from this element, if the movement is covert) associates to the checking domain of the matrix *v*:

(41) a. [I [*v* [believe [[a man] Tense [to be here]]]]]
    b. [I [F [*v* [believe [[a man] Tense [to be here]]]]]]

Provided that the embedded clause is infinitival, Tense can't check the Case features of *a man*. Nonetheless, the matrix *v* has an accusative feature available that does the trick, if the appropriate feature from *a man* raises to the domain of *v*. Consequently, the Case of the embedded-clause subject isn't the regular nominative, but rather an exceptional accusative.

O: Most intriguing.

─────────────────────────────── agreement as a strong feature

L: In both abstract positions, also, agreement and Case are determined by the features of the functional categories *v* and Tense, which may be of different sorts. The key is that a noun phrase in the specifier-head relation to these heads must bear the appropriate Case and agreement features, which get checked in the specifier-head configuration—at least, when movement is overt, as it is in Basque and Japanese [56].

O: And all these movements are overt in Basque and Japanese because the abstract shells in these languages contain a strong feature.

L: Correct [57]. In fact, you can think of the whole phenomenon of agreement precisely in this light: agreement is a strong feature that forces raising. Languages would then differ on whether they must introduce these features associated to a given item in the numeration, or may do so, or can't even try to [see fig. 4.30].

O: There's still something I don't grasp. Suppose that *v* has got a strong feature in Japanese and Basque; that viral agreement feature will force the raising of the objects in (40a) and (40b), correct?

L: That's what I'm assuming now.

O: But how are we then to distinguish the fact that the Basque verb also raises to *v*, whereas the Japanese verb does not?

L: There has to be more than one strong feature at stake. As we saw in (40), Basque has the kind of feature that a verb checks, thus forcing verb movement, but Japanese doesn't. However, as you said, both languages have the kind of feature that requires a noun (or maybe determiner) to check it, thus forcing the movement of noun phrases; and this isn't the case, say, in English.

O: You mean for English objects . . .

Figure 4.30

(i) represents a language with a strong feature in *v*, forcing movement:

(i)

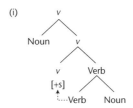

(ii) represents a language without a strong feature in *v*, where movement is costly:

(ii)

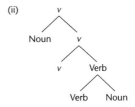

L: English subjects do have to raise, that's true. But let's set the matter aside now, since it doesn't seem to be related to Case [58].

O: Very well, but I'm still confused about my initial question. Let's return to English, where objects do not move overtly. How exactly do they get their Case checked? Alternatively: why does their Case need to be checked?

---

uninterpretable features

L: Those are different, but related questions. To start with, remember that two things are happening. First, there's the checking of strong morphological features, which has to take place prior to Spell-Out. A functional item with a strong feature carries a "viral" element which, if not eliminated, will lead to a canceled derivation; this directly triggers overt movement, as fast as possible. Second, there's the question of LF interpretation. Some features can't be interpreted by LF—call them **uninterpretable features.** For instance, Case features are this type, unlike, say, number features in nominals. That is, the plural feature that distinguishes *mice* from *mouse* is clearly relevant to the interpretation of this expression, but the genitive Case marker that follows *mice* to yield *mice's* (as in *the mice's cheese*) seems basically uninterpretable, and the intuition is that it has to disappear by LF—or the derivation will crash at this level.

O: But if an uninterpretable feature isn't a strong feature (i.e., a viral intruder), then it needn't disappear quickly.

L: Right. So the direct object in English, say, has no need to raise overtly, since the relevant abstract shell in this language doesn't appear to have a "viral" feature that needs to be checked. Therefore, direct objects procrastinate. They still have to move by LF, though, if they carry uninterpretable Case features.

O: And at LF only the **bag** of features carrying Case must move, not the entire phrase . . .

L: All other things being equal, pure and simple procrastination is always the favorite option. But in the covert mappings, certain movements may be inevitable in order to lead to a convergent LF.

O: If an element needs to move to check a strong feature, can it also check an uninterpretable feature which cannot survive LF—early on, as it were?

L: Sure, assuming the uninterpretable feature is part of the matrix that moved to check the strong feature (even if the particular element that's responsible for the checking of the strong feature isn't the uninterpretable feature that needs to be eliminated for LF purposes) [59]. Remember: the operation of moving features is totally uniform. Whatever differences there are follow from the nature of PF and LF. But there's no way of stating something like "Target F *after* Spell-Out." That makes no sense in this system. All we can assume is "Target F." If we do things right, entirely wiping out those features that LF or the derivation itself can't deal with, then the derivation won't be canceled, and it'll converge at PF and LF. If we Target F too late, the derivation may be canceled if a strong feature hasn't been checked. If we Target F too early, although the derivation may converge at PF and LF, there'll be a simpler derivation that procrastinates. So either we time things right, or we're in trouble [see fig. 4.31].

But now: what exactly happens in the covert component? The theory suggests that only features, and not full phrases, move to the checking sites. The question, then, is how does feature movement differ from the kinds of head and phrasal movements we've been discussing all along? I'd like to come back to these kinds of questions in the next couple of days, but this is the reason why I said we can't trivially assume identical LFs for all languages. Equivalent LFs, yes; but not identical. Thus, while verbs overtly moved to Tense in Middle English, what moves to Tense in Modern English (if indeed anything does) are formal *features* of the verb, not the entire verb [60]. So far, the only fairly established conclusion with respect to these matters is that a reason must exist for movement along the lines of what we just saw for Case, or before for *wh*-movement, whereby a given feature is checked.

O: I understand. Now, you'll detest this, I know, but I shan't be able to go in peace today if I don't return to this matter. Let's come back to English, where the object doesn't raise to the specifier of the *v* shell (unlike in Basque). In the covert mapping after Spell-Out, the object needs to move, though—more accurately, the FFM (a matrix of formal features) containing the Case feature of this object needs to move [61]. Now, assuming that covert and overt movement are uniform, is it not the case that the English movement will force overwriting, again raising the grandmother paradox?

Figure 4.31

When the fundamental processes apply:

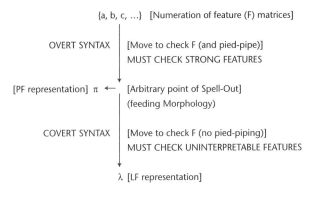

4.7 Some Open Questions to Exercise With

(of the battle fought between the worthy Linguist and the valiant Other on behalf of some ideas that, although tentative, nonetheless merit the reader's attention)

L: That's the second thing I was trying to prove to you: noncyclic movements appear to be possible in the covert component. This suggests that cyclic mergers are a result of checking strong features, period. When a functional category with a strong feature is selected, the system identifies some kind of problem; something has to be done, since the structure can't deal with strong features. In fact, there's a very small window in derivational time that structures have for doing something. Suppose, for instance, that you're going up a Basque phrase marker, and you find this v shell with two strong features (mark them *!* and ***), as in (42):

erase strong features

(42)

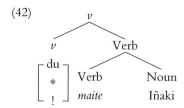

So the structure has to be "immunized," or the derivation will be canceled. Say that * is literally **erased** by the action of moving a verb like *maite* to the domain of *du,* and *!* is erased by the action of moving a noun like *Iñaki* to the domain of *du.* This, of course, would produce (43), where the strong features are now checked (I indicate this with a check mark, which I translate as "C_{HL} has no further access to me; I'm gone"):

(43)

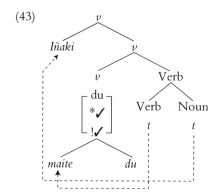

The idea is to prevent the "viral" features from spreading beyond the category containing them. That is, we don't want to continue the derivation as in (44) without checking * and !:

(44)

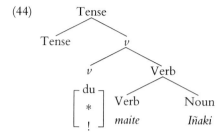

This sort of derivation should be immediately canceled, since the infection hasn't been stopped at the root. Of course, none of these issues arise in the LF component, if LF movement is needed to check uninterpretable features, but not strong ones. Uninterpretable features don't have to be erased as fast as strong features (since the former aren't "viral")—so that kind of checking can wait 'til LF, at which stage C_{HL} proceeds noncyclically.

O: Why are uninterpretable features not also viral?

L: Maybe they are, in Martian; not in Human, though.

O: Why can't the infection wait a while—why must it be dealt with immediately?

L: That's how the system reacts—maybe Martian—

O: Not always, if I've followed you correctly! Consider a Japanese version of (42), as in (45). Here the viral feature ! within v is checked by Inoki, which entails that the category v must combine with the verb phrase, despite being infected. Yet you don't wish to allow this in (44).

(45)

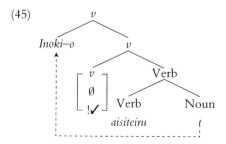

L: These are very different cases. A category like *v* with a strong feature has to be allowed to combine with its complement, or it won't ever be possible to check the strong feature—for the simple reason that the checker comes from inside the complement. That said, (45) is trivial: *v* combines with the verb phrase, and then *Inoki-o* moves to check the strong feature in *v*. The checking process happens without even abandoning the projection where the problem (the "viral" feature) occurs. In contrast, in (44) C_{HL} abandons the projection of *v*, going on with the merger of Tense without taking care of the problem when it arises [62].

_____ head movements enlarge heads

O: In any event, at LF the phrase marker will have to be overwritten, because I presume that you're allowing the noncyclic adjunction of features at that level, given what you're now telling me just about strong features.

L: I'm allowing these adjunctions, yes.

O: Even if the resulting operations aren't monotonic . . .

L: This is getting to be very monotonous! First, I don't think that "overwriting" is an issue at all. Besides, the matter of head movement is really very simple. You target a phrase marker—say, Tense Phrase (TP)—and you modify its head: you just make it a bit larger. For concreteness, you can think of the mechanics this way: the FFM that moves by itself at LF is simply added to the FFM that it targets. This is really the only way in which features enter the recursive procedure of the grammar: by ending up making a larger lexical item. Of course, categorical objects of the form $\{\underline{\alpha}, \{\alpha, \beta\}\}$ aren't sets of feature matrices, but sets of sets of feature matrices (i.e., lexical items). Then, by affecting the head of a construction (simply enlarging it), the categorial structure of the projected phrase marker is itself unaffected. Thus, suppose the FFM of the verb *aisiteiru* is moving at LF in the Japanese (46) (remember that the PF matrix is already not part of this object, having been shifted to PF). Here the LF phrase marker doesn't need to be "overwritten," since all that's involved is an internal change in one of the matrices within one of the categories: the *v* shell.

(46)

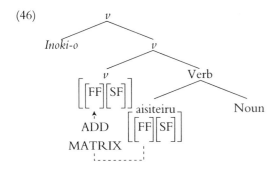

O: Well, that might work for adjunction at LF, but I still fail to see how it helps you deal with the labelling issues we've talked about today, involving $\underline{<v, v>}$. That is to say, I do realise that the label of the adjunct in (46) is simply *v*. Nevertheless, when movement takes place prior to Spell-Out, a free-riding structure gets carried along which creates a new categorial object, and we must decide whether that object is a term of the dominating structure or not, which basically means—in your own terms—that we must decide whether or not to overwrite the dominating structure. Suppose we were to decide that the adjunct is a term of the higher structure; are we then committed to overwriting? I think not.

L: I really don't see that this is an issue. Really.

_____ *parallel movements*

O: Please yourself, but I think what I have to say is interesting in and of itself. Suppose that movement transformations needn't be singular, as you said today (hence staying within a given phrase marker), but instead can be either singular or binary (as Merge is, involving two different phrase markers). To put it differently, perhaps the singulary/binary distinction isn't all that important: the transformation simply uses whichever terms it can use, and in the process it produces copies as it needs to, when it needs to. As a matter of fact, I'm assuming also that these copies can dangle, unattached, just as full phrases combined from items selected from the numeration can do [63]. We noted earlier that *a man* must be assembled separately from *saw a woman,* to generate *a man saw a woman* [see sec. 3.7]. That is to say, we need to build separate phrase markers in parallel also; hence, we need to be able to take items out of the numeration without merging them into a given phrase marker, storing them in "memory," as it were. And I'm now suggesting that we may do that not merely with items that we select from the numeration, but also with items that we copy from some phrase marker. I presume that this too is the null hypothesis, once we allow for "hanging structures" (I'm simply saying that they can also be derivational copies). Now, this liberalisation of the system has a nice consequence: adjunction need not extend the phrase marker, even when it is done overtly. Given my liberal options, the derivation can proceed as in (47) and (48). First, adjoin across phrase markers:

(47) $\{<\underline{T, T}>, \{V, T\}\}$ $\{\underline{V}, \{V, ...\}\}$

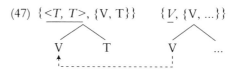

Second, merge:

(48) $\{<T, T>, \{\{<T,T>, \{V, T\}\}, \{V, \{V, ...\}\}\}\}$

$$\{<\underline{T,T}>, \{V, T\}\} \longleftrightarrow \{\underline{V}, \{V, ...\}\}$$

$$V \qquad T \qquad V \qquad ...$$

Now no overwriting of the projection of T is necessary—as a matter of fact, this is the projection of $\underline{<T, T>}$ all along.

L: Head movements look like a problem for the extension condition on phrase markers (whatever motivates the cyclicity of phrasal building) only if the head movement operation isn't seen in the right perspective. The operation is simply a way of making a head larger, period. This means that when C_{HL} moves a head, it targets XP and makes its head X larger—so it's still extending XP, really.

O: I've already conceded that point; the question, though, is what happens to the free-riders that tag along with the movement. To start with, what happens in an instance where the free-riders move to a specifier?

L: We have to separate the movement of the feature proper from the ancillary operation that sends the free-riders along, as a repair strategy to satisfy the Wording Requirement. To be explicit:

(49) a.   *Actual movement*   b.   *Ancillary Merger*

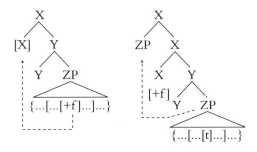

   c.   *Repair strategy completed*

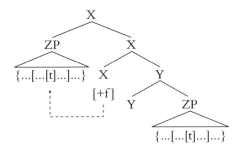

Feature [+f] moves to X; in other words, the target structure is X (49a). Nevertheless, because [+f] carries as a free-rider an entire maximal projection (that is, ZP), the entire ZP pied-pipes to merge with X, as its specifier (49b). Finally, the step in (49c) is essentially morphological: it covers the gap left by the moved feature.

O: Very well. Clearly, the syntactic movement in (49b) is cyclic. (49c) isn't, but you tell me that this is a morphological repair, which I can accept. In any event, this last move obviously doesn't affect the overall syntactic structure, and hence no overwriting is needed. Now consider an instance in which the free-rider moves to a head, as in (50):

(50) a.   *Actual movement*   b.   *Ancillary adjunction*

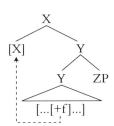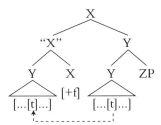

c.   *Repair strategy completed*

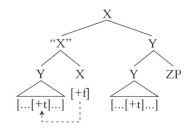

I'm prepared to admit that (50a) is neither more nor less cyclic than (49a), or your (46) for that matter. Let us say the movement is cyclic, in that it targets X, making its head larger and not really touching the syntactic structure above it. But next take (50b). If this movement really creates a new piece of syntactic structure, which we may dub "X," or ["X," X], or whatever you care to call it, it won't be added cyclically [64]. We can choose to disregard this, saying that in any event we are only affecting the head of X, or that adjunction is special in some sense or another. Alternatively, it would seem to me that we could proceed as in (47), without resorting to further stipulations.

L: But that's what's not accurate. If you think about what (47) implies, you do need further stipulations. Strictly speaking, (47) is not cyclic, given that cyclicity has to do with single phrase markers, and you're now extending matters well beyond that. In fact, the derivation in (47) is *para*cyclic, in the sense that no particular structure is targeted for movement, and a mere copy is projected. Given the way our tentative definition of movement in (11) works, we can't really target no structure, can we? But suppose we were to change that definition, to allow for your parallel displacements. Then the next obvious question is why the second step should be as well behaved as you've made it. Why not go on merging the phrase marker headed by T with some other element selected from the numeration, instead of merging it with the phrase marker headed by V?

O: Yes, well, perhaps C_{HL} is forced to merge as fast as it can to produce a convergent derivation. The second step in (48) is granted, given this assumption: I adjoined V to T in order to produce a convergent derivation (assuming that overwriting or noncyclicity leads to a cancelled derivation), and then I proceeded to merge as fast as I could. The derivation you suggest, where you keep merging the projection of $\leq$T, T$>$ (which you obtain by adjoining V to T) with some other element selected from the numeration, would not involve an early merger.

L: And what does that earliness requirement follow from?

O: Following a line of reasoning that you seem to fancy, I could say that this is how things happen to be in Human. Do observe that this does not directly contradict Procrastinate, which is now derived from the amount of work required if movement happens after Spell-Out. Here we're talking about movements which all happen before Spell-Out anyway, and hence are equally costly. In those circumstances, it may be that the grammar simply gets it over with as fast as possible. In actual fact, there may be a way of deducing the earliness requirement as well: the derivational alternatives to early merger are more costly. Let's say that the derivation always minimises operations, up to convergence. We saw earlier that derivations avoid movement if they can get away with merger. What "early merger" might mean is, "Avoid selecting and merging a further element from the numeration if you can merge the ones you've already selected." That is to say, "Maximise the results of your derivational effort, once you've undertaken it" . . .

L: Yeah, but that's like saying that Select has cost, when it isn't even a transformational operation.

O: Well, we could say that operational cost is sensitive to any operation, whether transformational or not.

L: I don't see how that's going to work, given that we want Merge to be cheaper than Move. Now every time C_{HL} merges, it applies Select and Merge, both with cost if you're right. Every time it moves, it applies Move F and Merge. Where's the difference in cost?

O: Perhaps in the repair strategy; Move encompasses Move F, and Merge, and Repair, as in (49) and (50). I suppose what I'm saying is, "If possible, merge what's already selected, since Select itself is costly; if not, then merge what you can select from the numeration which involves no repair strategies; and when every other possibility has been exhausted, then move."

L: Perhaps.

O: Well, don't just "perhaps" me! I've tried to suggest a way to predict cyclicity in derivations from the absence of overwriting. Axiomatic or not—as you'd say—that appears to derive the facts, by and large. All operations involving Merge (including overt Move) are cyclic if overwriting is disallowed. Apparent counterexamples are explained away: covert LF movement doesn't involve Merge; relations with basic adjuncts may be different altogether; and the core instance of adjunction, head movement, could be achieved without invoking overwriting, were we to simplify the system to allow parallel movements. That's my picture. Thus far you haven't described yours. Why should Merge be cyclic, in your terms, if the fact that Move is cyclic follows from the nature of viral features?

—————————————————————— cyclicity and the definition of Merge

L: The smart merger has the form in (51a), and involves the definitional cost of relating α to β. Period. The stupid merger has the form in (51b), and involves the definitional cost of relating α to β, and then targeting γ within β [see fig. 4.32]:

(51) a.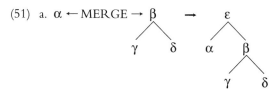

      b.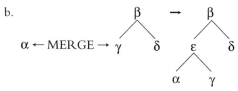

Since the merger in (51a) is easier to define, we go with that one.

O: But why should we care about the difficulty of a definition?! What concept of economy is that? That has nothing to do with derivational economy, and I fail to see that it has anything to do with representational economy either!

L: The suggestion involves a deeper kind of economy, and I don't see why, in principle, we should rule out the need to invoke economy in various dimensions. (The first day we saw economy in the learning procedure, and possibly in the very fabric of parametric variation [see sec. 1.5].) So it could well be that the cyclic property we're now witnessing both in the extension condition and in the idea of a numeration follows from economy in the very design of the grammar.

Figure 4.32

Defining cyclic mergers requires expressing relations between two root nodes, α and β. Any relevant definition must state, "For root nodes α and β, α merges with β if and only if . . ."—followed by some particular postulate (e.g., demanding that β project). Defining noncyclic mergers requires more information. The merging relation itself must still hold between α and some γ that is already merged somewhere inside a phrase marker β. The relevant definition must first locate γ within β: "For root nodes α and β, and γ dominated by β, α merges with γ if and only if . . ."—followed by some particular postulate. The second definition is obviously more complex.

O: Which has the same theoretical status as my disallowing the overwriting of the notation!

L: Except that I'm worried about a basic definition, while you were worried about algorithmically implementing a notation which may or may not be relevant . . .

O: But should we not have a unified account of the fact that noncyclic mergers are as impossible as noncyclic movements?

L: First, we don't know whether the two processes are related. Second, it's possible that they are related—thus, they both involve Merge—and yet their cyclicity doesn't follow from this shared property (cyclicity being a very general property of derivations, as we saw [see sec. 4.5]). And third, if you insist that the cyclicity of Merge and the cyclicity of Move should be the same, a straightforward possibility you can try is this. Think of matters in a strictly derivational way, forcing command to hold between α and β only when α is attached to β by Merge or Move. This is now your "new coding C" [see fig. 4.14]: a given relation (command) is expressed between α and β as a result of their derivational history. Transitively, this annotates the entire phrase marker in a very specific way. In and of itself, it doesn't really matter if this coding, at some point, goes against the history of the derivation—you'll just break off the transitivity of the coding. The breach in command, however, will have consequences when you try to linearize the structure at Spell-Out. The structure won't linearize in those regions where command doesn't exist, leading to a crash [65].

O: That's in the spirit of what I had in mind, except that you're relating matters to linearisation via the LCT. And I see some possible drawbacks to that, too. Suppose, for example, that the element that moves downwards has no phonetic content; consider one of those null complementisers that you talked about today, which appear in root clauses. According to your assumptions, if this creature is devoid of PF content, it shouldn't be subject to any particular linearisation. I should then be able to lower it. Accordingly, we would predict that null complementisers can be found not only in root clauses, but indeed wherever they've managed to crawl down!

L: Maybe; they'd have to have a reason to go there, though. But at least this view is coherent.

O: Mine isn't?!

L: I see two problems with it. First, you have to turn the trivial notational point about "overwriting" into something substantive; you already admitted this, when you said you do need some "new coding C" that the notation is capturing. I gave you one such coding: command. It's hard to see what else you're going to code, but in any case this is one valid way of capitalizing on a reflex of the derivational history of Merge, which is what your intuition is based on. So at any rate, at this point we're talking about notational variants of the proposal I gave you. Second, your insistence on avoiding "overwriting" leads you to wild parallel derivations of the kind in (47). While I grant you that these shouldn't be ignored on the basis of purely technical difficulties (which they obviously have), you have to admit that going in that direction requires considerably more empirical support than you've given so far . . .

———————————————————————————————— *stylistic processes*

O: I accept that as a matter of principle, although I must say that thus far, empirical coverage hasn't really been what's impressed me about your theory. Nevertheless, I shall do, not as you are wont to do, but as you tell me, and hence shall observe—well, that the matter is considerably more general than either of us has yet implied . . .

L: Oh?

O: We've already established—have we not?—that C_{HL} must be allowed to select something from the numeration and not merge it directly with the rest of the phrase marker being assembled. In the limit, I suppose there's no reason why it shouldn't take each and every one of the items in a numeration: say, *a, man, saw, a, woman* [66]. The numeration would be then reduced to zero, and Spell-Out could take place directly. Needless to say, we must prevent this, for otherwise these words could be assembled at LF in any order whatsoever, including *a woman saw a man* (instead of *a man saw a woman*)—and then we'd return to the problem of comparing *Socrates thinks Plato likes arguments* and *Plato thinks Socrates likes arguments.*

L: Those crazy derivations will crash at PF!

O: In a language like English [67]. Yes, certainly, since one must check some strong features of Tense in its specifier, which for the example that concerns us now means that one must move either *a man* or *a woman* (or something) to this specifier. But imagine a language whose functional features are all weak, so that they needn't be checked [68]. Does such a language exist?

L: In principle.

O: Now, the phrase marker must be assembled by PF because of the strong features of elements like Tense, I presume.

L: There may be independent reasons why the phrase marker should be assembled, in order to ship it to the interpretive components for interpretation.

O: I do see that for LF purposes you might want a single phrase marker as a sheer consequence of the fact that LF is aiming at what one might call "systematic meaning," or something of the sort. Intuitively, the meaning of the entire LF expression in the I/C components must be some function of the meaning of its parts, as we saw today when we were looking at the scope of modifiers. This systematicity, then, is a natural property to expect of LF [69], just as it was natural to expect linearity of PF. But then I don't see why it would be important to have a single object at PF. I've raised the possibility today that certain phrase markers are literally not linearised at PF; perhaps this phenomenon is rather general. All we seem to know is this: by the end of the PF component, the phrase marker must be disposed of entirely, for PF is about prosodic contours and stress peaks, not about phrases—thus, no obvious reason exists why *assembled* phrase markers should matter there, much as they matter at LF. D'you see what I'm after?

L: You want to say that in a language with weak Tense and so on, C_{HL} might not syntactically assemble a single phrase marker when it ships the structure to PF.

O: Of course at LF there'd still be a single phrase marker. I'm imagining a language which doesn't assemble *a man* and *saw a woman* into a single PF object.

L: Then it shouldn't be able to linearize those two . . .

Figure 4.33

Consider a numeration $\{\alpha\text{-}1, \beta\text{-}1, \gamma\text{-}1, \ldots\}$, and suppose for the sake of argument that Select has cost, just as Merge does. In scenario I, suppose $\alpha\text{-}1$ has a strong feature, so that Merge must proceed prior to Spell-Out, independently of whether the phrase marker itself may or may not need to be assembled before this point. In these circumstances, derivational cost is affected by whether Select precedes Merge, or vice versa. (Assume each step has cost 1.)

Scenario I, case A

$\{\alpha\text{-}1, \beta\text{-}1, \gamma\text{-}1, \ldots\}$	Reduced numeration
Select α	$\{\alpha\text{-}0, \beta\text{-}1, \gamma\text{-}1, \ldots\}$
Select β	$\{\alpha\text{-}0, \beta\text{-}0, \gamma\text{-}1, \ldots\}$
Merge β with α	$\{\alpha\text{-}0, \beta\text{-}0, \gamma\text{-}1, \ldots\}$
Select γ	$\{\alpha\text{-}0, \beta\text{-}0, \gamma\text{-}0, \ldots\}$
Merge γ with $\{\underline{\alpha}, \{\alpha, \beta\}\}$	$\{\alpha\text{-}0, \beta\text{-}0, \gamma\text{-}0, \ldots\}$

Scenario I, case B

$\{\alpha\text{-}1, \beta\text{-}1, \gamma\text{-}1, \ldots\}$	Reduced numeration
Select α	$\{\alpha\text{-}0, \beta\text{-}1, \gamma\text{-}1, \ldots\}$
Select β	$\{\alpha\text{-}0, \beta\text{-}0, \gamma\text{-}1, \ldots\}$
Select γ	$\{\alpha\text{-}0, \beta\text{-}0, \gamma\text{-}0, \ldots\}$
Merge β with α	$\{\alpha\text{-}0, \beta\text{-}0, \gamma\text{-}0, \ldots\}$
Merge γ with $\{\underline{\alpha}, \{\alpha, \beta\}\}$	$\{\alpha\text{-}0, \beta\text{-}0, \gamma\text{-}0, \ldots\}$

The derivations are identical up to the second step ("Select β"). Then derivation B does something less economical than derivation A: it selects γ, which necessitates a separate merger, as opposed to direct merger of α with γ. This is a derivation that does not maximize its limited resources. But now consider scenario II, where no strong features are involved, and then (arguably, at least) no prior-to-Spell-Out merger.

O: That's positively true. It should allow *a man saw a woman* alongside *saw a woman a man*. I'm not sure that's a bad result, given our assumptions. Actually, I thought Polish worked pretty much this way. And Russian, and Latin, and . . .

L: I know. What you're alluding to are rules which used to be called "stylistic." Linguists used to think of them as rules of movement in the PF component, without any consequence for LF. What you're suggesting is that they aren't instances of movement at all, but simply two possible orderings resulting from the lack of merger of two given phrases in the PF component.

O: Spot on. When you come to think of it, the fact that some languages allow both *a man saw a woman* and *saw a woman a man* is quite unexpected from the perspective you've shown me today. If *a man* needs to raise in Polish or Latin, why doesn't it raise where it doesn't? That should crash at PF. If *a man* needn't raise in Polish or Latin, why does it raise where it does? That should violate Procrastinate. Similar issues arise with adjuncts.

L: There may be an answer to that depending on what the exact command properties of adjuncts are, vis-à-vis the rest of the structure. It's possible that an adjunct doesn't command (then does not precede, by the LCA) the structure it's adjoined to. And it's also possible that the structure the adjunct is adjoined to doesn't command (then doesn't need to precede) the adjunct. All of this is in accordance with the LCA. Under those circumstances, we don't expect any fixed ordering . . . This all depends on how exactly we define command for segments of categories. Try it as an exercise [see app.].

O: But what's wrong with my alternative?

L: For one thing, it creates an internal paradox. Your suggestion crucially relies on there not being any earliness requirement on Merge.

O: Allow me to disagree. Earliness isn't an absolute strategy, any more than Procrastinate is. They both follow from economy, in the sense that they both choose the derivation which does as little as possible. In the case we've discussed before, merger happens early, but only as opposed to happening late, given a phrase marker that's being formed. That is to say, in (47) V has adjoined to T, and these two phrase markers are out there in the derivation: $\{\underline{<T, T>}, \{V, T\}\}$ and $\{\underline{V}, \{V, \ldots \}\}$. At this juncture, it's cheaper to merge them than to select a third phrase marker, given that in any case everything will need to be merged prior to Spell-Out. But suppose that instead of selecting and merging a further item from the numeration, C_{HL} were to keep it again unattached, in derivational limbo, so to speak. Well, then: further selection is then cheaper than further merger—which presupposes selection—or at least as cheap, depending on when we evaluate cost: as the derivation proceeds or when it reaches LF. Needless to say, after Spell-Out everything is merged covertly (in a language without strong features) [see fig. 4.33].

L: We can't accept that analysis for two reasons; first, it involves multiple Spell-Outs, one for each separate phrase marker that gets sent to PF.

O: I've independently argued for multiple Spell-Out [see sec. 3.7]!

L: In the limit, that proposal means there isn't a meaningful level of LF or PF, since you send cascades of structures to the PF and LF components, which never get to be unified in a proper level [70].

O: True . . . but what's wrong with that?

L: We started from the assumption that the LF and PF levels are conceptually necessary.

O: You started with that assumption, which I was never too fond of. Why, of course, I see that LF and PF *components* (encoding the stuff that makes up LF and PF) are conceptually necessary in a system that pairs sound and meaning, but I still don't see why you have to unify this stuff into this mysterious level. What does it buy you to stipulate that the LF and PF stuff coheres so much that it forms an LF unified representation or a PF unified representation [71]?

L: For starters, the fact that you speak in sentences with propositional import and prosodic unity.

O: But that could follow from properties of performance at the A/P and I/C interfaces, could it not?

Scenario II, case A

$\{\alpha\text{-}1, \beta\text{-}1, \gamma\text{-}1, \ldots \}$	Reduced numeration
Select α	$\{\alpha\text{-}0, \beta\text{-}1, \gamma\text{-}1, \ldots \}$
Select β	$\{\alpha\text{-}0, \beta\text{-}0, \gamma\text{-}1, \ldots \}$
Merge β with α	$\{\alpha\text{-}0, \beta\text{-}0, \gamma\text{-}1, \ldots \}$
Select γ	$\{\alpha\text{-}0, \beta\text{-}0, \gamma\text{-}0, \ldots \}$
SPELL-OUT - - - - -	- - - - - - - - - - -
Merge γ with $\{\underline{\alpha}, \{\alpha, \beta\}\}$	$\{\alpha\text{-}0, \beta\text{-}0, \gamma\text{-}0, \ldots \}$

Scenario II, case B

$\{\alpha\text{-}1, \beta\text{-}1, \gamma\text{-}1, \ldots \}$	Reduced numeration
Select α	$\{\alpha\text{-}0, \beta\text{-}1, \gamma\text{-}1, \ldots \}$
Select β	$\{\alpha\text{-}0, \beta\text{-}0, \gamma\text{-}1, \ldots \}$
Select γ	$\{\alpha\text{-}0, \beta\text{-}0, \gamma\text{-}0, \ldots \}$
SPELL-OUT - - - - -	- - - - - - - - - - -
Merge β with α	$\{\alpha\text{-}0, \beta\text{-}0, \gamma\text{-}0, \ldots \}$
Merge γ with $\{\underline{\alpha}, \{\alpha, \beta\}\}$	$\{\alpha\text{-}0, \beta\text{-}0, \gamma\text{-}0, \ldots \}$

The question of economy again arises after the second step. Is it cheaper to select γ, or is it cheaper to start merging the selected items? Apparently, case A is either more economical than case B (if there is some advantage to merging late, perhaps in terms of PF rules), or at least as economical as case B.

L: It could, but you'd have to show how. And look, several instances of Spell-Out should be much more expensive than a single instance.

O: That's definitely true, but expense is computed up to convergence. If I can show you that a derivation which doesn't involve multiple Spell-Out doesn't converge, then multiple application should be allowed.

L: Right, so when you show that, we can talk [72]. But second, if we were to adopt your proposal, we'd be right back where we started with respect to the candidate derivations in the reference set. So take a language where nothing's strong and thus nothing gets assembled by PF in terms of syntactic rules, by your assumptions. Say Warlpiri is one such language [73]. Suppose you scramble things in a perverse enough way that the exact same PF representation can correspond to the LF of either 'a man saw a woman' or 'a woman saw a man'. Should we then compare these two?

O: What would go wrong if we did? Assuming that they're equally costly, both possibilities should be allowed . . . So what exactly is the problem?

L: It's the wrong intuition! We shouldn't be able to compare derivations in those instances. Languages shouldn't differ in terms of how *late* they tolerate merger. Oh, Lord—late? Do you have any idea how late it is?!

O: But . . .

Note from the scribe:

Idle reader, in the fourth chapter of this true story we left the famous Linguist and the mysterious Other with their gleaming swords brandished aloft; and at this uncertain and critical juncture, the history abruptly breaks off, without our being informed by the author where or how that which is wanting may be found.

"Good day, sir."

"How are you . . ."

Er . . . Excuse me? I'm trying to scribble something here . . .

"Is something the matter?"

"How can you tell? . . . I guess . . ."

Hey, hey! I said, "Excuse me!"

". . . spending every afternoon here, well, it's wonderful; but I have so many students to meet with, so many letters to write—so many things to do, really . . ."

"I think I should like to help you . . ."

If I'm going to be ignored, I'll—

"How?"

"Why, it's elementary . . ."

I'll quit, I mean it!

"First, you enter the wormhole, and you vanish from Cambridge. Once you reappear in Cambridge, we relocate the American side gravitationally, and drag it back in time. That'll grant us as much time as you want. When you get tired, you go back, and you enter the space-time continuum in the past, when no one has missed you. Just make sure not to kill your grandmother or alter your theory or something rash like that. At least until you get to the point where you left."

I really, really mean it!!

"Excuse my saying so, but how are we going to drag the hole gravitationally?"

"Yes, well, it's not easy to affect just a part of the universe, without affecting the rest. But before we worry about that, you should know that you run a much greater risk in the very process of traversing the wormhole."

Okay, that's it! I'm out of here!

"That could be exciting . . . But I think I'll deal with my time pressures here at home."

"As you wish."

"Thanks for the suggestion, though."

"Any time."

"So what's today's question?"

5.1 The Minimal Link Condition
(featuring minimal domains and the relativity of distance, among other matters worth considering)

O: Last night my reason was clogged by those shell creatures you introduced yesterday, which you said may in some languages encode bundles of agreement features: person, number, et cetera . . . Can they—as a matter of principle—host any phrase that moves to them?

L: In principle, yes.

O: Ah!

L: Is that the question?

_____ objects that move as subjects and vice versa

O: I'm afraid that's just the setup. If these projections can receive any guest whatever, then presumably they can host an object or a subject that arrives to check its features. Can they not [1]?

L: Well, assuming that whatever moves there has the sort of feature that's appropriately checked against the feature(s) in the functional projection, yes . . . Otherwise, of course not.

O: Right, right. But now I believe I've got a puzzle. Take a language (make it different from English) which involves overt movement of noun phrases to strong shell specifiers. Basque, for example, where one can say *Jonek Miren maite du* 'Jon-subject Miren-object love auxiliary'. The hindmost word, remember, encodes the agreement of *maite* 'love' with the subject *Jon* (which bears the *(e)k* Case marker) and the object *Miren* (bearing the Ø Case marker) [see sec. 4.6, (40)]. In your terms, this means that *Jon* raises to the top specifier (and checks its Case in the Tense projection), and *Miren* raises to the lower specifier (and checks its Case in the verbal projection). Now picture the following derivation (I shall use English words for ease of exposition). Perversely, the object *Miren-O* raises to the higher, Tense specifier, and the subject *Jon-S* to the lower, *v* specifier, as in (1). Needless to say, this means that the Case marker of *Jon* (the subject marker *(e)k* must be checked against the verb, whereas the Case marker of *Miren* (the Ø object marker) must be checked against Tense. Here is the structure, ignoring verb movement:

(1)

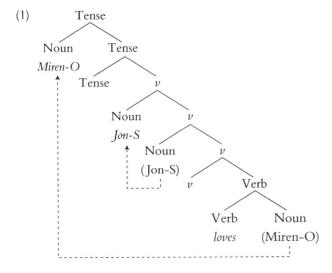

L: Yeah, well, this collapses immediately, since it involves feature mismatch [see fig. 5.1] [2].

O: Of course—I see that. But now observe (2)! In this instance, I'm proceeding in a subtler way ... I am warily placing the element marked *Jon-S* in the lower, as it were "logical" object position within the verb phrase, and the element marked *Miren-O* in the higher, "logical" subject position within the verb phrase. And then I'm moving *Jon-S* to the matrix Tense, and *Miren-O* to the embedded *v* shell—as follows (again ignoring verb movement):

(2)

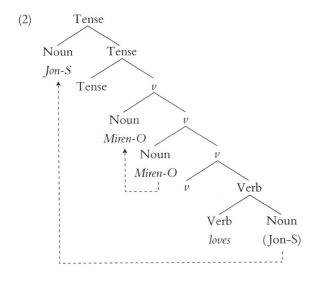

Figure 5.1

In (1) *Miren-O* ends up in a specifier where what is checked is an S-Case marker, not the O-Case marker that *Miren* bears. And conversely, *Jon-S* ends up in a specifier where what is checked is an O-Case marker, not the S-Case marker that *Jon-S* bears:

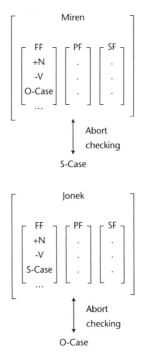

L: Which means that the basic object (Case-marked as a subject) is licensed in the grammatical subject position, and the logical subject (Case-marked as an object) is licensed in the grammatical object position. For Basque, this would be a sentence like . . . er . . .

O: Again *Jonek Miren maite du,* but now with the impossible meaning 'Miren loves Jon' (needless to say, as we just saw, the sentence is grammatical with the meaning 'Jon loves Miren').

movements are the shortest possible

L: So suppose each instance of Move has to choose as a target its *closest possible* landing site [3].

O: I knew it: economy!

L: Let's assume a condition on chains that says, "Move to the closest possible landing site." Call it the Minimal Link Condition, or MLC.

(3) *Minimal Link Condition (MLC)*
     F can raise to target K only if there is no legitimate operation Move F′ targeting K, where F′ is closer to K.

Now it follows that the movement of *Jon-S* to the specifier of Tense in (2) is impossible, because Tense could have related to closer potential sources of movement [see fig. 5.2]. So the MLC takes care of the ungrammaticality of (2).

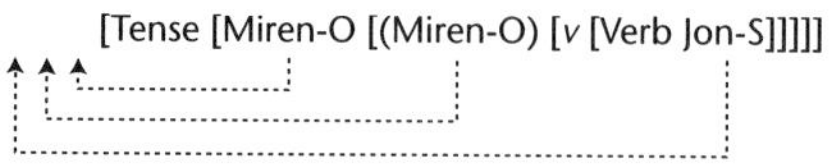

O: Very clever; but may I ask a follow-up question? Let us look again at our example *Jonek Miren maite du* in its *good* sense ('Jon loves Miren'). Let me draw the structure of this sentence as in (4), again using English words (and still ignoring verb movement) for ease of exposition. As before, Tense does not appear to be relating to its closest potential source of movement, namely, *Miren-O;* it relates instead to *Jon-S,* which is lower within the structure, inside the *v* projection! Hence now your MLC has ruled out even this perfectly perfect sentence . . .

Figure 5.2

The movement of *Jon-S* to Tense is intuitively not the closest possible:

[Tense [Miren-O [(Miren-O) [v [Verb Jon-S]]]]]

(4)

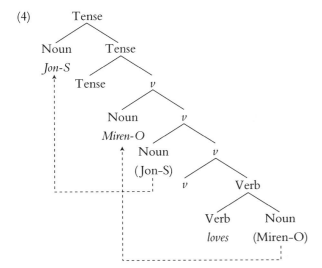

L: Well, we haven't yet decided what "closest" means: we have to explicitly describe what "distance" implies in our formal terms [4]. So we can do this, I first need to introduce some supplementary notions. Consider again the structure in (5):

─────────────────────────────────────── a definition of maximal domains

(5)

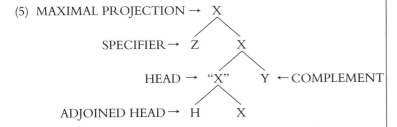

This is just a standard projection of X with a complement and a specifier, such that some other head H has adjoined to X [see fig. 5.3]. The notions we're now seeking are defined within projections. The intuition is this: a projection is the "umbrella" that defines a minimal domain, within which core grammatical relations—checking and others—are established:

Figure 5.3

A *head* is a lexical item #X# that is not contained within any other lexical item.

Category-projecting relations
A *complement* is the sister to a head. (Here, Y is #X#'s complement.)

A *specifier* is the sister to a nonhead. (Here, Z is #X#'s specifier; remember that, in principle, there can be more than one specifier, since there can be more than one nonhead.)

Segment-projecting relations
An *adjunct* relates to a category without projecting a further category.

Figure 5.4

Gloss of (7):

(i) "Where (a) Max(α) is the smallest maximal projection dominating a head α, . . ."

This defines the umbrella for α:

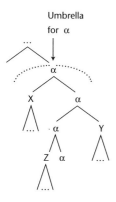

(ii) ". . . and (b) the domain D(α) of α is the set of categories/features dominated by Max(α) that are distinct from α; . . ."

This defines the domain of α, a set of categories/features within the umbrella for α; note that the definition directly excludes α from that set, because the point here is to determine α's dependents. Note also that this version of the definition is noncommittal with respect to the category/feature distinction, although ultimately it will be desirable for the system to be sensitive to features (the primitives of checking) and not categories (see app.).

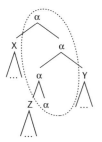

D(α) = {X, ..., Z, ..., Y, ...}

(iii) ". . . then (c) the minimal domain Min(D(α)) of α is the smallest subset K of D(α) . . ."

The class of categories/features in the domain of α includes not just α's dependents, but also their daughters (for instance, all the categories/features that X dominates in the previous tree). However, for definition (7) all that is relevant is the set of dependents K, which is a subset of the set D(α) defined in (ii); furthermore, K is the smallest subset of D(α) with the following characteristic:

(iv) ". . . for any x belonging to D(α), some y belonging to K dominates x."

(6)   Umbrella for X

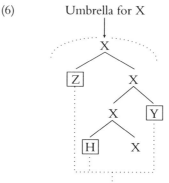

Minimal domain of X = {Z, H, Y}

O: I presume these are entirely new set-theoretic objects you're now creating, and not objects in the phrase marker. No phrase is formed by merging Z and H [5].

L: For example—right . . . We talk about minimal domains as abstract sets which are defined for the dependents of chains in a phrase marker. But these domains aren't themselves direct chunks of the phrase marker. To make things explicit, assume the following definitions [see fig. 5.4 and app. for a fuller discussion]:

(7) *Definition of minimal domain (first version)*
     Where (a) Max(α) is the smallest maximal projection dominating a head α, and (b) the domain D(α) of α is the set of categories/features dominated by Max(α) that are distinct from α; then (c) the **minimal domain** Min(D(α)) of α is the smallest subset K of D(α) such that for any *x* belonging to D(α), some *y* belonging to K dominates *x*.

O: Right; perhaps if we return to the difficulty I raised in (4)—which triggered this entire reflection—I shall be able to comprehend these arcane notions.

───────────────────────────────────── characterizing distance

L: They're very simple, really. Let's study the formal properties of (4), a relevant part of which I'll now repeat as (8). This object corresponds to the stage in the derivation where nothing has moved yet. I'll parenthesize the parts of the phrase marker which will be built when *Miren* targets the *v* projection to create τ, a specifier to this projection:

(8) 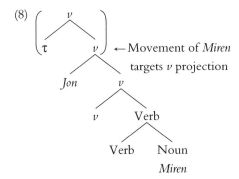 ← Movement of *Miren*
targets *v* projection

The question is whether the movement of *Miren* will be legitimate, in the sense of being the shortest one that could have targeted the projection of *v* to create a specifier. Visually, *Jon* looks closer; but vision isn't what's at stake—rather, grammar is. How are we to define "close" for grammar? . . . Which is closer to England, Paris or London?

O: Well, but . . . London is in England . . . I see! You want to say that *Jon* in (8) actually isn't closer to its movement destination τ than *Miren* is because, as it were, *Jon* is already within the neighbourhood of τ [6]. Very cute.

L: We can make matters explicit, as usual [see fig. 5.5]:

(9) *Definition of distance (working version)*
   If β commands α, when targeting K for raising to τ in the minimal domain of K, β is *closer to* K than α is, unless β and τ are in the same minimal domain.

Here I have to clarify a potentially confusing terminological question. We distinguish between the action of targeting a phrase marker K for movement and the target itself. When any operation takes place, a phrase marker K is targeted. In the case of Merge, for instance, the targeted K is the element which needs whatever it is that's merged with it, thereby projecting. Similarly in movement cases: K needs something (a feature) which is provided by movement, typically from inside K itself. For this operation to succeed, we therefore have to find within K a given element α that moves, attaching to K in satisfaction of its needs. In doing so, of course, we create a new position—for instance, an adjunct to K's head; or, if the moved feature comes from a context which demands the ancillary movement of a whole maximal projection, then we have to

That is, for any element *x* within D(α) there is an element within K that dominates *x*. If domination is a reflexive relation, the ideal members of K (ideal in the sense that makes K "smallest") will be the elements within Min(D(α)) that are sisters to a projection of α:

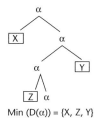

Min (D(α)) = {X, Z, Y}

Observe that for D(α) = {X, . . . , Z, . . . , Y, . . . }, there is a subset K of D(α) whose members are X, Z, and Y, such that for any member *x* of D(α), some member of K (that is, either X, or Y, or Z) will dominate *x*. Domination must be assumed to be reflexive because, for instance, X is a member of D(α); and X can be dominated by a member of K only if X dominates X. The appendix provides a more elegant approach to these matters, which does not involve the unintuitive notion of reflexive domination.

Essentially, then, Min(D(α)) is a set comprising the dependents of α. The idea may be hard to define formally, but it is easy to grasp visually, as in the graph immediately above, after (iv).

Figure 5.5

Gloss of (9):

(i) "If β commands α, when targeting K for raising to τ in the minimal domain of K, β is *closer to* K than α is, . . ."

This begins to provide a general characterization of distance within the phrase marker; note that only two categories within the same command path compete for distance purposes, the commanded category being farther away than the commanding one (see sec. 5.5). The crucial subcase where command does not matter for distance is the following:

(ii) ". . . unless β and τ are in the same minimal domain."

That is, β (the element commanding α) and τ (the target of movement) are within the same minimal domain, and α (the moved element) is outside.

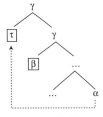

Min (D(γ)) = {τ, β}

Here, τ and β are irrelevantly close to one another, being in the same "neighborhood."

Figure 5.6

Movement of α *targets* K, the phrase marker containing α:

(i)

Occasionally, it is also said that movement creates *a target* τ, which can be of two sorts: a specifier (ii), or an adjunct (iii):

(ii)

(iii)

create a specifier for K. The new position that's created upon movement is often called "the actual target." Similarly, a building may undergo a renovation, and the actual part of the building that's renovated is called "the renovation" [see fig. 5.6].

O: Very well, so now the situation in (8) falls under (9): even though *Jon* commands *Miren,* when *Miren* targets the *v* projection (with the specifier τ of *v* the actual target of movement), *Jon* is irrelevantly close to the target and hence does not interfere with *Miren*'s movement. Nevertheless, I'm still not fully satisfied. You've been careful enough to highlight a part of (4) that you can deal with: the one represented in (8). But let's return to my original worry. How are we to deal with *Jon-S* moving over *Miren-O,* appropriately moved to *v*'s specifier? *Miren-O* is certainly not within the minimal domain of Tense, and yet *Jon-S* must move precisely to that domain. Of course, it's easy to see that *Miren-O* commands *Jon-S.* Therefore, I submit that we're still stuck!

L: You're right, but this time it's because I was just trying to present the facts rationally—thus, in sequence. Given the definition of closeness that I've presented in (9), there would indeed be no way of moving *Jon-S* over *Miren-O,* as your reasoning showed. But it's clear what we have to do, right?

O: You mean because *Miren-O* and *Jon-S* are within the minimal domain of *v* before they move? Well, I certainly see that; but why should that affect their relative distance vis-à-vis the target of movement?

L: Look at it this way. Imagine I had asked you which is nearer to London: Trenton, New Jersey, or New Haven, Connecticut.

O: Evidently, were I to get out a map, I could immediately show you that New Haven is. But I'm certainly willing to grant that were I to ask my travel agent, I'd be told it doesn't matter: I should probably have to go through a so-called gate city, such as New York, in both instances—because this is a transatlantic flight.

L: That is, two places inside the same country are equally close to a third place outside the country, at least when you fly. This is the same intuition as the one behind the neighborhood metaphor you invoked a moment ago, except that this time we're not concerned with the target of movement, but rather with its source. It's only natural that minimal domains should affect locality for both the landing and launching sites of movement; otherwise, something would have to be explained. Then (9) has to be redefined as (10) [see fig. 5.7]:

(10) *Definition of distance (final version)*
If β commands α, when targeting K for raising, with τ the actual target of movement, β is *closer to* K than α is, unless (a) β and τ are in the same minimal domain, or (b) α and β are in the same minimal domain.

O: Steady on! Your New York metaphor is charming, but I'm afraid we're not flying here. Besides, I'm having trouble visualising how something could be far away from or close to an object (specifically, a specifier) that hasn't yet been created.

L: You're being misled by the (wrong) intuition that a chain of movement is a relation between the moved element and its copy. Strictly, a chain should be seen as a relation between two configurations: that existing between the moved element and its sister, and that existing between the copy of the moved element and its sister [see sec. 4.3]. Let me repeat (8) to clarify this point—it's very important:

(11) a.

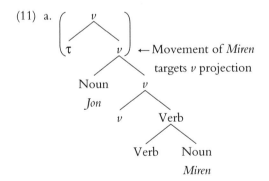

b.

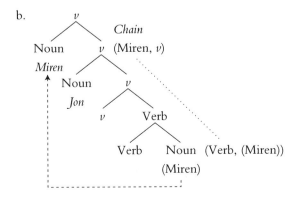

Figure 5.7

Gloss of (10):

(i) "If β commands α, when targeting K for raising, with τ the actual target of movement, β is *closer to* K than α is, unless (a) or (b) . . ."

This is very much like (i) in figure 5.5, except that τ is now referred to as "the actual target" of movement. (10a) is identical to (ii) in figure 5.5, and (10b) is new:

(ii) ". . . (b) α and β are in the same minimal domain."

This adds one further exceptional case to the situation glossed in figure 5.5: namely, that in which α and β (the elements competing for distance purposes) are within the same minimal domain, and τ is outside:

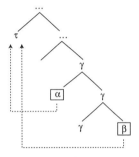

Min (D(γ)) = {τ, β}

Here, the two movements have the same length.

Keep in mind that both exceptional clauses in (10) involve minimal domains, which essentially equalize structural relations depending on a category α, lumping all dependents into a new set-theoretic object. Elements within this set-theoretic object are equally distant from (or close to) an element outside it, both in terms of the source of movement and in terms of the target.

In fact, we can represent the chain ((Miren, *v*), (Verb, (Miren))) in (11b), equally accurately, as (*v*, Verb) [7]. By that I mean, the longer sequence and the shorter one contain the same information: (*v*, Verb) and ((Miren, *v*), (Verb, Miren)) identify the same object. (Note, in contrast, that (Miren, Miren) would ambiguously identify two objects, or more if several movements take place, unless we enrich our notation to specify that the upper *Miren* is a higher occurrence of the lower one, and so on.) But (*v*, Verb) is, in a sense, more perspicuous: it tells us that what *Miren* targets when moving upward is *v*, not the specifier that's formed upon movement. Thus, when we ask whether X is closer than Y to the landing site, we're asking a question about *v*, not anything else. The specifier of *v* which hasn't been created yet is irrelevant to the computation. And as for your contention that my New York metaphor doesn't work in letting *Jon* in (11b) move (in principle) to the same domains that the commanding *Miren* can move to, observe that the chain formed in moving *Miren* ends as (. . . , *v*), and so does the chain formed in moving *Jon;* this is because *Jon* and *Miren* are both sisters to a *v* projection, which places them in the same minimal domain. In other words, inasmuch as the chains in question both "stretch" *v* to some outer domain (for instance, of Tense), it's reasonable to say that the chains are equally costly. In effect, what counts is the distance between *v* and the target of movement [8].

5.2 Well-Formedness Conditions versus Ranking Criteria
(a gracious interlude on derivational matters, which discusses how to keep transformations from acting wild)

O: Right. Right. Well now, forgive my insistence, but let me suggest yet another possible way of creating difficulties for structures like (1). Imagine the language we're considering is no longer Basque, where both subjects and objects must raise to check viral features; rather, let it be like English, where subjects obligatorily raise to subject position, but objects (in the general instance) do not. Now, why can the derivation not proceed as in (12a)? In the overt component (12a), the object *Mary* raises to the specifier of *v* to check its Case features. Generally, this would not be permitted, since the object can procrastinate until LF. But in this instance, I'm choosing not to stop there; rather, I'm proposing that the object *Mary* moves farther up, with its Case checked, to subject position (as subjects usually do in English). Then in the covert component (12b), the relevant (perhaps Case) features of the subject *John* move to the domain of Tense, where they're appropriately checked. And now we've licensed the sentence *Mary John loves,* with the meaning 'John loves Mary'—have we not?

——————————————————————————— more procrastination

(12) a. *Overt movement*

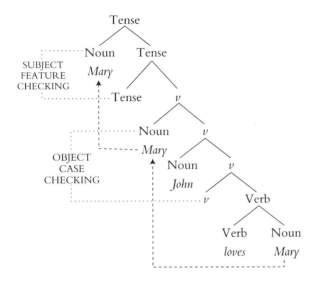

b. *Covert movement*

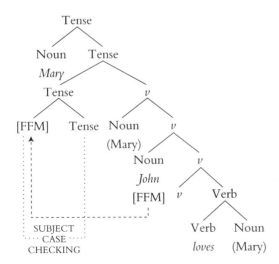

L: I think this derivation is perfectly convergent, as your reasoning suggests. But consider the alternative in (13):

(13) a. *Overt movement*

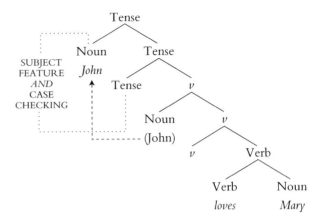

b. *Covert movement*

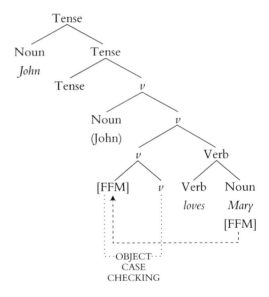

O: I see; you wish to say that (13) is cheaper . . .

L: Well, it is. To be precise about it, consider the crucial point in the derivation where the derivational horizon has narrowed down to the relevant convergent continuations in (12) and (13):

(14)

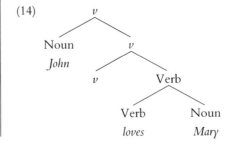

Here, two options exist: your (12), with movement of *Mary* to the specifier of *v*, or my (13), with insertion of Tense (and subsequent movement of *John* to subject position). Right there you know I've chosen the cheaper alternative—the one that doesn't involve any movement.

O: Why, I thought you were going to say that (12) involves three derivational steps, whereas (13) involves only two.

L: That's true too, but I don't even need to go into that computation of cost. The decision is reached derivationally on trivial grounds: given a common derivational horizon, you moved and I didn't. Since I've procrastinated, that's the end of the story [see fig. 5.8] [9].

_____ successive movements

O: Fair enough, but I'm still a bit baffled about the overall picture. I have a specific question which, to be sharp, demands such an interesting kind of example that I'm not sure it even exists. It so happens that all of the good examples we've looked at today involve just one movement per argument of the verb. That is to say, *Mary* in (12) moves twice; but that example, you've argued, is bad. Are there any good cases where an argument moves more than once?

L: Oh, sure. For instance [10]:

(15) a. the Cheshire cat seems to be likely to grin
     b. [the Cheshire cat seems [(the Cheshire cat) to be likely [(the Cheshire cat) to grin]]]

First, note that the grammatical subject of (15a) is in a sense the logical subject of the verb *grin*. We hypothesize this because (16) is a fairly good paraphrase of (15a):

(16) it seems that it is likely that the Cheshire cat grins

Obviously, the *it* elements in (16) are purely pleonastic; they carry no referential **role** of their own. So the general issue is this: if verbs like *seems* don't generally take a referential subject, how come *the Cheshire cat* is in the grammatical subject position in (15) [see fig. 5.9]?

Figure 5.8

As this section has demonstrated, an object that is Case-marked as a subject cannot produce a grammatical result. But what about structures involving the passive voice, whose logical subject is missing, and whose grammatical subject is typically a logical object?

(i) I was arrested

Here, the logical subject (say, *the police*) is missing (it can appear only obliquely, in an agentive phrase: *I was arrested by the police*). In turn, the grammatical subject, *I*, is the logical object of the arresting action. This indicates that there is nothing wrong, per se, with subject-Case-marked objects. What makes them impossible in active structures is that other alternatives exist that are more appropriate.

Now, how does the passive derivation converge? The fact that the logical object manages to move all the way up to the Tense projection must relate to the fact that there is no logical subject to occupy that position. In turn, the fact that the logical object shows up with subject (and not object) Case must mean that there is no *v* projection in these structures where the object can get Case. In other words, the derivation must be as follows:

(ii)
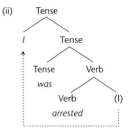

This suggests that the *v* projection is introduced into the numeration only when necessary for Case reasons (that is, only when a transitive structure is generated).

The Cheshire cat. (John Tenniel)

Figure 5.9

Cheshire Cat Mystery Solved

In a sentence such as *the Cheshire cat seems to grin* (which is a true paraphrase of the sentence *it seems that the Cheshire cat grins*), there is a mismatch between logical and grammatical relations. The logical relations are shown in (ia) and the grammatical relations in (ib):

(i) a.   [seems [the cat to grin]]
                          Subject Predicate
    b.   [the cat [seems [to grin]]]

This mismatch is accounted for if the expression involves (at least) two separate phrase markers, one with the basic structure in (ia), and one with the basic structure in (ib). The second is derived from the first, by application of the transformational process, as follows:

 (ii) [the cat [seems [(the cat)] to grin]]]

This mismatch of grammatical and logical dependencies is also found in passive constructions (see fig. 5.8), which receive the same sort of analysis:

(iii) a.   [was seen the cat in the tree]
      b.   [the cat [was seen (the cat) in the tree]]

O: And your answer is something like "*The Cheshire cat*'s there but it's also not really there, because it's actually the referential subject of the *lowest* verb, *to grin*." And that kills two, well, cats with one stone!

L: Precisely, because otherwise we'd have to say that *grin* is the sort of verb that can't have a referential subject, which is obviously false: *it grins* can only mean that, say, the cat grins (the sentence doesn't have the import of 'grinning is taking place', which should be possible if the structure were akin to *it's hot,* meaning something like 'heat is taking place'). So then we say that the grammatical subject of *seems* isn't really its logical subject, and the way we express that is by saying that at some point in the derivation *the Cheshire cat* is actually the subject of *to grin,.* and then it starts moving up: it gets to be the grammatical subject of *is likely* and finally of *seems.*

O: Just a minor question: Why does *the Cheshire cat* move? Curiosity . . .

L: At first, Case looks like the right answer. That would appear to be the reason why noun phrases move, and so we have to postulate that if *the Cheshire cat* had stayed as the subject of *to grin*, it wouldn't have checked its Case features down there, and the derivation would have crashed at LF [see fig. 5.10].

O: I'm afraid you didn't understand. I gather that noun phrases move to check their Case features; but why must *the Cheshire cat* move overtly? Why not undertake the movement in the quieter space of LF?

L: That's why I'm only saying that the answer I sketched looks like the right answer; it's not complete [11]. Certainly, movement for Case reasons is necessary by LF (in which case the appropriate relations are established through features, instead of involving entire categories). But the reason why the movement is overt in (16) (at least in a language like English, but possibly elsewhere as well) must be a strong feature in Tense.

———————————————————————— why shortest steps aren't more costly

O: Which finally brings me to my real question. As a result of the intermediate moves in (15), the MLC is satisfied—even if that itself cannot be the motivation for the movement. But then the crux of my problem is this. Programmatically, we've discussed two rather different notions of economy. On the one hand, given a set of alternative derivations, the one with the fewest derivational steps prevails. But on the other hand, given a possible source of movement, this site must be the closest to the target. Aren't these two conflicting requirements? The MLC disallows movements in one fell swoop over possible intermediate landing sites. In the ideal case, you should maximise the steps you take so that they're as close as possible to each other. And evidently, then, if the derivation keeps to shortest moves, it will have more steps, as in (17). But surely that goes against the strategy of what one might call **Fewest Steps.**

(17) [[the cat] seems [t to be likely [t to grin]]]

  a.

  b.

((a) involves *shorter* and therefore *more* steps than (b).)

L: So there you have a theory-internal argument that the MLC isn't a **ranking criterion** but a derivational condition [12].

O: But, sir, my question is whether, for example, the intermediate step in (17a) (even if justified) isn't violating Fewest Steps (cf. (17b)) . . .

L: I understand your question; but a derivation can't violate an optimality criterion. It can violate a convergence condition at LF or PF (thus producing an illegitimate object that for instance doesn't have its features checked). And it can violate a derivational condition, thereby immediately being canceled (for instance, a feature mismatch entails immediate termination). But that's it; optimality criteria, in contrast, are just ways of ranking convergent derivations. In our case, if you chose not to undertake the intermediate movement in order to minimize derivational steps (as in your (17), or any version of it), the derivation wouldn't even converge; end of story.

O: Would it crash or would it be cancelled?

L: That's a separate question, and a tough one—let's put it aside for now [see sec. 5.3]. Whether something that violates the MLC crashes or is canceled, the fact remains that it doesn't count for the purposes of ranking. Optimality criteria only operate on convergent derivations. Period. So the need to satisfy the MLC in (17) overrides the need for simplicity. First we have to get there (LF or PF), and then we can ask whether we can do it elegantly.

Here, a logical object is promoted to the position of grammatical subject. Consider also the structure shown in (iv), which is very similar to the one in (ii):

(iv) a.   [was believed [the cat to be mischievous]]
   b. [the cat [was believed [(the cat) to be mischievous]]]

Here, as in (ii), the logical subject of the lower predicate ends up as the grammatical subject of the higher predicate. Clearly, (i) through (iv) all involve similar movement processes, even though the constructions themselves (passives, infinitivals, etc.) differ. It is phenomena like this that make linguists claim that movement processes are rather general, and not specific to a given construction.

Figure 5.10

More on Cat's Case

If *the cat* in (16) did not relate to the matrix clause at all, it would not be able to receive Case, under the reasonable assumption that regular subject Case cannot be checked in infinitival clauses, but is instead licensed in relation to Tense. Under this assumption, the ungrammaticality of (i) is accounted for in terms of a Case failure (since *the cat's* Case features are not checked, the derivation crashes at LF):

No Case
(i) *[it seems [[the cat] to grin]]
   Infinitival clause

Contrast (i) with the perfect (ii), where Case can be checked in the embedded (tensed) clause:

Case checked
(ii) [it seems [that [the cat] grins]]
   Tensed clause

It should be emphasized, however, that although raising allows *the cat* to check its Case features in (16), this is not what motivates the movement (as a result of which (16) converges).

O: In actual fact, then, you decide that the MLC is a convergence condition for theory-internal reasons: to make it compatible with Fewest Steps.

L: First, I haven't really decided yet whether the MLC is a *convergence* condition or a condition *on derivations*. But second, I see nothing wrong with having indeed decided that the MLC isn't an optimality criterion, merely ranking derivations.

--- fewest steps and how to take them

O: What I was mildly implying is that, although I understand the general point you're trying to make, I now don't see that Fewest Steps is doing any actual work. Since only movements that obey the MLC converge, what Earthly difference does it make how many steps they invoke? To be part of the theory, Fewest Steps would have to do some independent work; but recall your reasoning today about why (13) is more optimal than (12). I was all set to begin counting steps, and you eagerly told me I needn't! As a matter of fact, (13) procrastinates more than (12), as the derivation unfolds; therefore, it's the strategy of Procrastinate that determines optimality—not the strategy of Fewest Steps!

L: No, no, no! The fact that you don't need to count steps doesn't mean you're not using a ranking in terms of optimal derivations that, if you *were* to count them, would indeed use fewest steps. You have to separate whatever algorithm is at stake in determining that a given solution to a problem is optimal, from the general variational property of the system where that issue arises. That is, optimality problems typically involve various solutions, and one (or more) among those that are best, in terms of some criterion—such as fewest symbols, or fewest operational steps, or whatever. That's the general form of the system. Then a separate question is how to actually find the best solution [see sec. 1.7]. A dumb way is to try all possible solutions and then count symbols or operational steps, and so on. But there are smarter ways, too. In fact, all sorts of algorithms exist that efficiently find, say, minimal paths between pairs of nodes in a graph [13]. You can then think of the Procrastinate strategy as an efficient algorithm (perhaps among others) to implement the overall strategy of Fewest Steps when movement is taking place.

O: Do you mean to imply that there really is no such thing as a primitive strategy of Procrastinate—that it actually follows from Fewest Steps?

L: It depends on what you mean by "follows from." Clearly, if movement doesn't happen until LF, fewer operations are involved. Moving before Spell-Out involves the core operation Move F, the ancillary operation of copying and merging some pied-piped free-riders, and arguably whatever phonological operations take part in deleting traces [see sec. 4.7]. In contrast, moving after Spell-Out involves Move F, period. In that sense, the effects of Procrastinate directly follow from a general, primitive strategy of Fewest Steps. At the same time, how does the grammar "know" that a movement prior to Spell-Out will result in more work? Does it compute the derivation, and its alternatives, and then count symbols? I don't know, but I suspect not [14]. Plausibly, the grammar may have incorporated an effective strategy of procrastination precisely because it works: Procrastinate offers a nice simple algorithm that can decide, at any given point in the derivation, whether to move or stay—if you can, stay. In the end, that's the most elegant solution to the convergence problem.

O: But by Jove: how did the grammar know that Procrastinate worked?!

L: Well, that's a bit like asking how proteins "know" that a certain procedure will give them the right, optimal folding, or how a brain "knows" that certain neural connections will lead to a kind of global optimality [see sec. 1.7]. Does nature strike the right key accidentally, or does it have some sort of "macrocomputer" that allows it to examine alternative realities, and go with the one that fits this universe in the optimal way [15] . . . I hope you're not expecting me to answer that one!

O: All right—I keep forgetting that language is a natural phenomenon . . .

L: So it isn't obvious that Procrastinate follows from Fewest Steps. Rather, it would seem that these are just two facets of the same phenomenon: a global solution and a particular implementation of this solution in ways effective to a grammatical computation. Had the system been dealing with a different type of computation, maybe it would have implemented Fewest Steps in a very different way.

O: Can that not also explain why entire feature bundles move, instead of separate features—even though it's the features that are moving [16]?

L: How so?

O: If C_{HL} moves a whole bundle of features, the chances of its doing more checking with all the free-riders that tag along are greater than if it moves the features separately . . . As in my suggestions from yesterday about early Merge [see sec. 4.7], it maximises the results of its derivational efforts, once it's undertaken them. As a result, there's less work left to do later on, thereby reducing complexity.

L: Maybe. Whether you're right also depends on other issues, such as whether it's even possible to split the feature matrix so features can move by themselves (note: Spell-Out only separates the phonological feature matrix from the others). But I see what you mean, and yes: that would be the sort of effective algorithm that we'd expect the system to have, in order to implement economy. If C_{HL} can maximize the checking it can do in configuration C, it will clearly minimize the amount of movement the involved checkers need to engage in. It's a way of locally detecting (in a checking configuration) a global property: the computation of the simplest among alternative derivations. More generally, think about the fact that there may be other transformational operations to consider, aside from movement: merger, deletion, erasure, and so on. So take deletion, and suppose it also obeys Fewest Steps. Does it do this by way of the strategy of Procrastinate—if you can, delete features covertly—or does it invoke some other strategy? Well, it depends on the details of exactly what it means to delete stuff.

O: Such an interesting concept . . . You think of merger, deletion, copying, movement, as mere facets of a single operation—is that it?

conditions on transformations

L: It's likely that these are just processes for building and destroying structure—what we can call "Affect α," for α any chunk of structure [17]. In a sense, transformational operations do just that: affect the structure.

O: And what we've been conversing about all along, then, are basically ways of constraining such a mighty device . . .

L: Three different ways, yes. First, the very fact that derivations have to converge is one way: certain transformations may yield absolute garbage with no representation at PF or LF. In this sense, PF and

LF have a filtering task: only derivations whose resulting representations meet Full Interpretation will be considered by the system [18]. Second, we're also assuming derivational laws that have to be satisfied for something to count as a derivation; these are conditions which, if not obeyed, lead to automatic cancellation of a derivation. Some of these are very punctual conditions, like the ones which demand that certain features match; if they don't, that's the end of the derivation. It's a bit like moving a bishop sideways, or a pawn backward, to positions which don't match their substantive character as pawns, bishops, or whatever [19]. Other derivational conditions are very general. Take for instance the fact that the array A is completely mapped to LF [see sec. 4.5]. This is a bit like the unspoken rule of chess that tells players to put all their pieces on the board; a player can't force a draw by not putting her king on the board! For us, the condition basically means that C_{HL} has to use up the items in A if it's going to reach LF; in other words, it can't reach LF with a few items, leaving half of them in the numeration, say. This is one aspect of what we could call the "Law of Conservation" in derivations; another aspect of this law would prevent C_{HL} from simply erasing items just when it sees fit. Again, imagine removing a piece from a chess game by just lifting it off the board and making it disappear! So these basic rules of the game of derivations prevent a lot of wild use of Affect α—it's not as if anything goes. And third, the fact that C_{HL} has to get to the interpretive levels in the fewest number of steps possible is obviously also a constraining force on derivations: most derivations are outranked by a few lucky ones which are optimal.

O: Whether they involve movement, deletion, merger, or what have you . . .

L: In principle; those are just transformations, and the system seeks an optimization. Basically, the strategy of Fewest Steps demands an elegant solution to the problem of convergence, given C_{HL} as a procedure. Then C_{HL} shouldn't care about derivations that don't converge. In fact, to engage in a transformational operation violating some convergence condition, and then to ask whether you moved "elegantly," would be like beating someone at chess with an "optimal" checkmate that involves an illegitimate chess representation [see fig. 5.11].

O: And what about the operation that forms the numeration from the lexicon? Is that costly?

Figure 5.11

Given the bifurcated model that we are assuming, there are three ways of constraining the effects of Affect α:

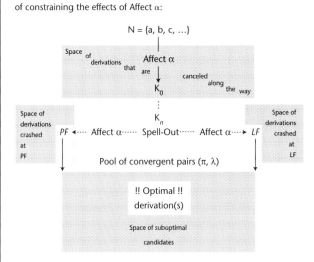

(i) The *structural modes of PF and LF* determine the shape of convergent derivations.

This is relevant in determining which derivations *crash* at PF or LF.

(ii) The effects of Affect α can also be constrained by *derivational conditions,* such as the *Law of Conservation* ("Symbols in a derivation are not created or destroyed") or *Feature Matching* ("If F and F′ enter into a checking relation, F must match F′").

These conditions are relevant in determining which derivations are *canceled.* (Being a formal dead end, a canceled derivation cannot try different alternatives. Although a crashed derivation is a derivation, a canceled derivation is not even that. In other words, the notion "canceled derivation" must be interpreted as prohibiting any further computation, alternative or not.)

(iii) The effects of Affect α can also be constrained by *ranking criteria,* such as the strategy of *Fewest Steps* ("Among convergent derivations, grammatical derivations are those that are optimal").

This is relevant in determining which derivations are *suboptimal.* (Given this state of affairs, it is meaningless to ask about the cost of an operation that is necessary to meet derivational well-formedness conditions; cost arises only within convergent derivations.)

L: Asking that is like asking whether placing your pieces on the chessboard is costly . . .

O: What I mean to say is this: ceteris paribus, a smaller numeration is preferable to a larger one. The issue would arise when speakers are choosing the pieces of what they're about to say, and find the cleanest way of doing it . . .

L: I'm totally skeptical about that. Philosophers often raise that sort of point, assuming that speakers are sensitive to "cooperation maxims" in conversation—they don't say more than they need to, and so on [20]. Maybe, but I doubt it's at all significant to us, essentially because it raises the problem of choice of action. Mind you, that problem is real, but I don't think science has had much to say about it . . . As far as I'm concerned, the numeration has nothing to do with what sorts of "building blocks" speakers actually choose in conversation. For that matter, nothing that I've been saying these days has anything to do with that topic, which falls under the rubric of performance.

O: I didn't mean to unleash another philosophical debate. I merely thought you'd also want to construct the smallest possible numeration—that's all.

L: But smallest with respect to what? If you take that route, you again have to ask what the comparison pool is, so you can decide that this numeration is better than that one for saying such-and-such. Obviously, without some space of comparison, the numeration that involves saying nothing at all would be the most economical, thus ruling out "I'm hungry," and "The cat is on the mat," and any other sentence a speaker might be inclined to say. Nonsense. But what's the alternative? You'd have to say something like "Seek the simplest numeration for this kind of 'thought.'" And I wish you good luck on characterizing what a thought is [21].

O: Thank you. What about two different, single operations within the derivation that involve different amounts of information? Take for example Move F, which copies a feature onto K, and Merge, which attaches a whole, potentially very large chunk of structure to K. Had we the choice, should we not prefer Move F, since it involves less structure?

L: Again, I don't see it. Is it more costly to move the queen (which leaps over several squares) than to move the king (which moves to the next square)? Well, each of these is just one chess move. This is actually rather different from what we find when we compare the whole set of operations that have to accompany Move prior to Spell-Out (the ancillary stuff) with a covert instance of Move—or with Merge, for that matter. The ancillary operations are introduced by a repair strategy, so the derivation doesn't crash at PF because of having moved a feature prior to Spell-Out. Those are indeed extra steps. To go on with the chess metaphor, they're like the moves you have to make to reach a defense/attack position, which typically involves the combined effort of several pieces. Reaching a position of privilege does have cost, which is why your opponent doesn't let you make the desired moves all at once—you have to take turns. Then again, things don't have to be this way—this is just a hypothesis about economy in linguistic terms. You could come up with an alternative system within the same general conceptual guidelines, and see whether it would do the work (that is, predict the facts) any better. I'm just telling you what I think works; which is to say, I don't bother to qualify my statements every time I say, "This is the best solution . . ."; but you should, substituting my words "the best" for something like "a best." Again, otherwise you wouldn't be talking to me, and instead you'd be chatting with a mathematician.

5.3 Further Conditions Pertaining to Chains

(in which two important properties of chains are illustrated, and the engrossing fact is deduced that the target of movement never projects)

O: But I hate formulae . . . Still, I'm now ready to return to another set of questions that concerned me yesterday, and still does. Recall your definition of chain, which I shall repeat as (18) [see fig. 4.11 for a gloss]:

(18) *Definition of movement chain*
Given a term $\tau_i = K$ that is targeted for merger, such that $K = \{\underline{\alpha}, \{ \ldots \{\tau_k, M\} \ldots \}\}$, and a term τ_j that merges with τ_i, such that $L = \{\underline{\alpha}, \{\tau_j, K\}\}$, the pair (K, M) is a *movement chain* if and only if τ_j and τ_k are identical.

In the sort of example we've seen today, *the Cheshire cat* comes from an object $K = \{\underline{\alpha}, \{ \ldots \textit{the Cheshire cat} \ldots \}\}$, and produces an object L = {<u>α</u>, {*the Cheshire cat*, K}}, in one intermediate subject position. Since the two occurrences of *the Cheshire cat* are identical, this movement constitutes a chain, by definition (18). And one can easily check that the same thing happens in the next step of movement, producing yet another chain—in both instances, a pair of positions in a phrase marker.

L: So what's your question?

_____ chains are uniform

O: To start with, I'm a bit worried about stipulating the relevant identity between τ_j and τ_k in a definition like (18), instead of having this identity simply follow from the inclusiveness of the mapping to LF.

L: Yeah, maybe. Whether or not you can trivially deduce the identity in question—that is, from LF inclusiveness alone—depends on whether something stricter than mere categorial identity is needed for definition (18) to be met. For instance, consider this version of the uniformity condition:

(19) *Condition on Chain Uniformity (CCU)*
The formal/categorial informational content of chain elements τ_j and τ_k is identical.

In the general case the CCU merely stipulates what you've just said—categorial identity. But its predictions may go beyond that, into the phrasal status of the chain: whether its elements are heads or maximal projections. This information is external to the category and, as we saw, contextually determined [see fig. 5.3]. Interestingly, phrasal status may be necessary in determining the well-formedness of a chain, which could relate to the question of why the element that's targeted for movement should project—rather than the moved element itself. In this respect, consider (20), an ancillary operation that accompanies Move F:

(20)

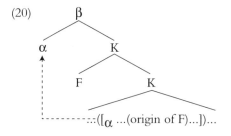

Again, you're moving α to repair the "damage" that moving a feature F from within α has produced. And what are possible landing sites for this movement [22]? Intuitively, they should be very close to F. But is α going to be a head in its new site, or a maximal projection? (That is, does α project or does K project?) If we assume the CCU, we have some answers, considering the position that α occupied before it (and F) moved. As you know, the grammar encodes an output-condition-driven algorithm that we're assuming determines phrase-structural relations throughout the derivational history [see sec. 3.1]. In principle, we know that, in (20), β's label must be either α's or K's, given the property of projection that Merge exhibits. So given the CCU, we now have various possibilities. If the trace of α in (20) is a maximal projection, and α (the moved element) projects, α is obviously not a maximal projection (precisely because it projects). Therefore, the chain (α, (α)) isn't uniform, and the derivation can't converge if the CCU obtains [see (i) of fig. 5.12]. If the trace of α isn't a maximal projection, and α projects, once again α isn't a maximal projection. But this time the chain is indeed uniform, according to the CCU; the derivation converges, all other things being equal [see (ii) of fig. 5.12]. If the trace of α is a maximal projection, and—contrary to what we've seen so far—the element K which is targeted for movement projects, α will be a maximal projection, yielding a uniform chain and a convergent derivation [see (iii) of fig. 5.12]. Finally, if the trace of α isn't a maximal projection and the element which is targeted for movement projects, again α will be a maximal projection, resulting in a nonuniform chain and a derivation which can't converge [see (iv) of fig. 5.12].

O: If I've followed you, this basically says that the ancillary operation of copying after Move F preserves the structure that was its input [23]. If the source of movement is a maximal projection, then the target must be a specifier, and if the source is a head, then the target must be a head. Nevertheless—two possible uniform chains may be created by standard movement, I should think. If the chain is that of a maximal projection, then the element which is targeted for movement must project [see (iii) of fig. 5.12]. But if the chain is that of a head, it would seem as though the moved element must project [see (ii) of fig. 5.12]. This is very confusing, for I thought we had assumed that whatever moves never projects. Now you're telling me that when the moved element is a head, it can yield a uniform chain only if it does project.

why the target of movement never projects

Figure 5.12

(i) (α) is X^{max};
β is α;
therefore, α is not X^{max};
therefore, the chain is nonuniform;
therefore, the derivation does not converge.

(ii) (α) is not X^{max};
β is α;
therefore, α is not X^{max};
therefore, the chain is uniform;
therefore, other things being equal, the derivation converges.

(iii) (α) is X^{max};
β is K;
therefore, α is X^{max};
therefore, the chain is uniform;
therefore, other things being equal, the derivation converges.

(iv) (α) is not X^{max};
β is K;
therefore, α is X^{max};
therefore, the chain is nonuniform;
therefore, the derivation does not converge.

Figure 5.13

Here, *it* is both a head (because it is a lexical item) and a maximal projection (because it is not immediately dominated by any nondistinct category):

L: That doesn't mean the resulting structure necessarily converges; that's why I said, "The derivation converges"—and then I added, "all other things being equal." As it turns out, in this case involving head movement, all other things aren't equal. To see this, consider the relevant possibilities in (21). In both (21a) and (21b), a head X moves as a result of F (one of F's features) having moved first; but whereas in (21b) X is the head of a nontrivial projection, in (21a) it's the head of a trivial projection. Remember that an element can be both a head and a maximal projection, for instance, *it* [see fig. 5.13].

(21) a.   b.

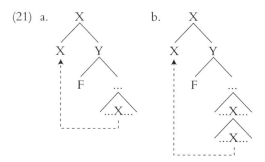

In principle, it's possible for *it* to move as a head or as a maximal projection. But then we have to worry about its landing site. A strict uniformity condition would demand that the categorial status of the moved element be the same both before and after movement. This doesn't happen in (21a), where the head/maximal projection X moves to a site where it becomes a nontrivial projection—thus, no longer a maximal projection. In other words, (21a) involves a nonuniform chain, despite appearances. So this case is ruled out straightforwardly. (21b) is more interesting. Since X projects, by definition Y is the complement of X.

O: This would be an instance where a complement is gained when a head moves. Pray tell—is that generally possible?

L: No, but we have to see why [24]. Remember, the whole purpose of movement is to check a feature, a process that takes place in a checking configuration. That means that F in (21b) is in some checking domain D. But now watch what happens with the moved X, whose function is just to repair the action of F for PF reasons. If X moves as in (21b), Y quite literally becomes a complement to X (a sister to a projecting head—which is true, incidentally, about (21a) as well). That is, rather than X being some added guest in the minimal domain of X, F having moved, X is now its own host, with no obvious connection to F, and with Y as its complement. Assuming that projection from Merge is always asymmetric (the target of the operation having one of its features satisfied by the operation [see sec. 3.1]), then in (21b) we have a case where X can't be the target of Merge, since it isn't getting any of its features satisfied by the operation—again, the sole reason why X is there is to repair some "damage" that F causes. In sum, in (21) it's Y that merges with X, and not vice versa—as should have been the case, given that X's presence in the domain of Y is ancillary, not central.

O: Which entails . . . a crashed derivation?

L: Either that, or a canceled derivation.

O: Could you kindly tell me why you always hedge on that issue?

L: Because I don't know the answers a priori. All we have is a phenomenon, and we ask whether it follows from a suboptimal derivation, from a crashed derivation, or from a canceled derivation. What's the answer? For optimality versus the rest, we can appeal to the fact that if certain derivations are allowed to converge, they might outrank others. That's the sort of reasoning I used a while ago to tell you that violating the MLC isn't more or less economical than not violating it—the question doesn't arise. Of course, if we do let the question arise, then someone can argue that violating the MLC in fact is more economical than applying Move several times. And then we're in trouble. So in this type of case, we can conclude—on theory-internal grounds—that a given effect (say, an MLC effect) has nothing to do with optimality. But deciding between crashing and canceling is much more subtle. Of course, these are very different on conceptual grounds: crashing is related to the shape of objects at the interface levels, whereas canceling is related to the shape of derivations [see fig. 5.11]. But since we know little, in particular, about LF objects, I couldn't swear to you whether, say, even the CCU is a law about the form that chains must have at LF, or whether it's a consequence of how derivations should proceed if the derivational mapping has to have certain properties—for instance, with respect to the overall structure of phrase markers before and after a transformation. In any case, I don't think this matters at this stage of our investigation, when we're still deciding, for instance, on what our vocabulary is for PF, not to even mention LF!

O: But how do you then implement, for example, the "last resort" condition?

L: You do just that.

O: What? Invent a suitable formal postulate, and give it a fancy, capitalised name like Last Resort Condition?

L: What's wrong with that? Take (22), for instance:

(22) *Last Resort Condition (LRC)*
Where α is a sublabel of a head β if and only if α is a feature of β or a head adjoined to β, F raises to target K only if F enters into a checking relation with a sublabel of K.

O: Wait, a sublabel? Why? What's that—what's at issue?

L: In (22) I mention sublabels because a checking relation is essentially established with a head that has adjoined to another head. Imagine, for instance, a language where the verb raises overtly to Tense, but the object doesn't. The relevant Case checking at LF must be between the raised verb and the object, okay? But at LF the verb is buried inside a layer of adjunctions (it has adjoined to *v*, and then to Tense). So how can the formal features of the object be checked against this buried verb? Easily, if they move to Tense and if the features of the raised verb are sublabels of the features of Tense. Then the movement of the object's features is trivially motivated [see fig. 5.14].

O: But sir, doesn't the notion of a sublabel grant a sort of special status to the top layer of a head adjunction structure?

L: In fact, that's the intention. We want to make sure that, for instance, the word boundaries are established around this layer, so that if we have an object like, say, [[V[*v*]] [T]], we know to put word boundaries around the outer brackets (that is, #[[V[*v*]] [T]]#), and not anywhere else.

O: In actual fact, then, the notion "head" is rather more relational than you implied earlier [see sec. 3.2]. Concretely, heads cannot merely be defined as whatever comes from the lexicon; if they were,

Figure 5.14

French is a language in which verbs move to Tense overtly, but objects stay in situ, as (i) demonstrates ((ia) is grammatical in colloquial French):

(i) a.   j'aime pas Paris
          I love not Paris
          'I don't love Paris'
     b.   *je pas aime Paris (ungrammatical without verb raising past negation)
     c.   *j'aime Paris pas (ungrammatical with object raising past negation)

Therefore, at LF a French sentence like (ia) has the following configuration:

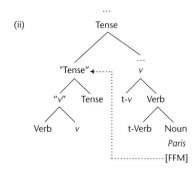

The formal features of the object *Paris* must relate to a moved verb that is adjoined to Tense. Since the features of the verb are now sublabels of Tense, the formal features of *Paris* can successfully be checked against these sublabels. Furthermore, the covert movement (dotted in (ii)) is justified in terms of the Last Resort Condition in (22).

then in the object [[V[*v*]] [T]], V, *v,* and T would all be heads. Rather, we need some sort of recursive procedure to say that it's the whole object which is a head in this instance, the rest of the lexical structure being encoded as sublabels of this very large head [25].

L: Yeah, that's what I told you when we talked about clitics [see sec. 3.5]. So just like the notion "maximal projection," the notion "head" is relational. We can't just say V is a head, period. It may be by itself, but it won't be if it's part of a structure like [[V[*v*]] [T]], in which case the head is a larger object, and V is just part of it.

O: Very well; now what (22) basically prevents is idle movement with the sole purpose of reaching a target.

L: Correct. And of course, the LRC has the same status as the MLC or the CCU, raising the same sorts of questions. In any case, whether violating it entails a crashed derivation or a canceled one, forget about ranking derivations that violate it. Those aren't part of the derivational space to consider. Remember also that it's feature matrices that move (sometimes forcing the ancillary movement of free-riders in pied-piping instances [see sec. 4.1]). Thus, (22) is satisfied only when a *feature* F enters into a checking relation. The feature itself may be checked (for instance, a Case feature in a nominal raised to a Tense projection), or the feature may be checking some other feature in the structure it targets (for instance, a strong feature in Tense that has to be obliterated prior to Spell-Out).

O: Hm . . . I presume it's because of the second situation, whereby a moved feature checks something in the targeted structure, that you say in (22) that "F enters into a checking relation with . . ." rather than "F is checked" [26].

L: Yes, although my formulation is also more general, making fewer assumptions.

O: You've then shown that when standard movement is the ancillary operation accompanying Move F, whatever is targeted for movement must project—as a consequence of the computational architecture of the system. If the moved element projects, something well and independently established always goes wrong. But what about movement by adjunction? Must the targeted element project in that case as well?

Figure 5.15

Consider (i):

(i) [I'm afraid that [this government [I dislike t]]]

Here, *this government* has moved from the complement position of *dislike* to a topic position, after the complementizer *that*. Clearly, because it does not project, *this government* is a maximal projection in its landing site. Because its trace in complement position is also a maximal projection, the chain is uniform and the result grammatical.

  Now consider the Spanish sentences (iia) and (iib):

(ii) a. [me [observó [t]]]

        me observed

        'she/he observed me'

     b. [obsérvame [t]]

        observe-me

        'observe me'

Clitics appear to adjoin to maximal projections, as in (iia), and to heads, as in (iib). But clitics are themselves both heads and maximal projections, given the algorithm for determining phrasal status. What is not found is a nontrivial head adjoining to a maximal projection, leaving behind the rest of the structure it associates with. Thus, compare (iiia) and (iiib):

(iii) a. [them [I dislike t]]

     b. *[the [I dislike [t government]]]

The maximal projection *them* can move, apparently adjoining to the sentence periphery, but the head *the* cannot. This is because the movement of *the* leaves behind a trace that is not a maximal projection, and when *the* adjoins at the sentence level, the resulting chain is therefore not uniform.

L: To consider the matter in detail would take us too far afield, but take the most general instance: head adjunction [see sec. 4.4]. Here, the moved element targets a head which projects, as in (23a). Suppose, then, that the moved element were to project, as in (23b) (again, keep in mind that these are ancillary movements):

(23) a. $\{\underline{\beta}, \{\beta, ...\}\}$ b. $\{\underline{\beta}, \{\{<\alpha, \alpha>, \{\alpha, \beta\}\}, K\}\}$

The top object in (23b) is not well formed, since its label isn't any of the constituents' labels.

O: Hah! That looks to me like exactly the same argument I tried to construct yesterday against certain noncyclic movements [see sec. 4.3]!

L: Not really. You did argue that the merger of certain phrase markers is disallowed. But what concerned you was this: some sort of code for the derivational history of a category is screwed up. So, for instance, you weren't happy with a category whose derivational history somehow encodes the relation (α, β), and whose constituents are actually α and, not β, but some γ object. But I told you that this reflects, in part, the limitations of a notation. What we're looking at now has little to do with that. Now the label of the category is what's at stake, not its derivational history. By projecting the adjunct in (23b), we don't even keep the appropriate labeling in the dominating object, which is thus an impossible object.

O: But you must grant that if what I called overwriting were admissible, you should then be able to remedy the deficiency in (23b), by simply relabelling the entire object beyond the adjunction site.

L: You mean actually giving it the label of the adjunct? Then matters would be even worse, since the derivation would reach LF with all its lexical dependencies messed up {27}. For instance, suppose a category were to lexically relate to $\underline{\beta}$ in (23a). If after the adjunction we allowed the adjunct to project—relabeling the entire object—then whatever selected $\underline{\beta}$ would be forced to select $<\underline{\alpha}, a>$, the adjunct [see sec. 6.3].

O: The ban against overwriting would have that effect; that's all my argument from yesterday actually needs in order to be valid.

L: What I'm saying is that you don't need to ban "overwriting" for this purpose: in this case the results of overwriting are either non-convergent or uninterpretable gibberish, so as things stand, the system itself rules them out.

———————————————————————— the need for Word Interpretation

O: I shall have to think more about that. Meanwhile, here's another in my series of questions about movement. A moved element never projects (instead, the element which is targeted for movement does). If I understand correctly, this entails that a moved element is a maximal projection.

L: You do understand correctly, but things are more complex than your comment suggests. In the general case, it's indeed true that a moved element is a maximal projection. If its trace is also a maximal projection, the resulting chain is uniform; if it's not, the chain is nonuniform. This predicts that heads that aren't maximal projections can't be adjoined to maximal projections—which I think is true [see fig. 5.15].

O: But what if a head is targeted for adjunction?

L: That's much more interesting. If the algorithm for expressing phrasal relations had anything to say about the phrasal status of the adjunct in such case, it would always designate it as a maximal projection [see (i) of fig. 5.16].

O: That's what I thought . . . But then the chain of the adjunct wouldn't be uniform in cases where we want it to be so [see (ii) of fig. 5.16]!

L: That's right. However, keep in mind that, when we adjoin an element to a head, we're dealing with a word-internal phenomenon. The algorithm that determines phrasal status is a matter of syntax, while the categorial status of an element inside a word is a matter of morphology [28].

O: Oh, then we must sharply separate morphology from syntax . . .

Figure 5.16

In (i) the adjoined head is not immediately dominated by any category with the same label:

(i)　　　"X"

　　　　Y　　#X#

If the algorithm for determining phrasal status applies here, the adjunct will by definition be a maximal projection. Problems arise in a case like (ii). When a verb moves to *v*, for example, the result must be head movement:

(ii)　　　"v"

　　　　Verb　#v#　　...

　　　　　 ·············· #Verb#

But if the verb adjoined to *v* is determined to be a maximal projection, the chain will clearly not be uniform, since the trace of the verb is a head. The solution is to assume that categories within word boundaries # (that is, head-internal elements) are submitted to word-internal processes (see (24)), at both PF and LF. The resulting bifurcated model with word-level components on both branches is sketched in (iii):

(iii)

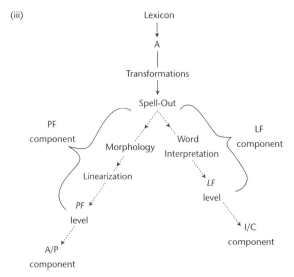

L: And we have. Remember, for instance, that internal to words, elements are linearized according to morphological rules [see sec. 3.5]. Here, too, the projection status of a word is a moot issue for word-internal processes. There's no point in asking whether something inside a head is a maximal projection, since its relevant domain is morphology, not the main syntactic derivation. To make this explicit, let's assume the following Principle of **Lexical Integrity** [29]:

(24) *Principle of Lexical Integrity*
      Only items that are not dominated by head boundaries (#) enter into C_{HL} operations; items dominated by head boundaries are submitted to independent word-interpretation processes WI.

The PF reflex of Word Interpretation (WI) is linearization within heads (the orderings among word-level subconstituents). And in the LF component, head-level elements are immune to the algorithm that determines phrasal status. In particular, we take WI to ignore principles of C_{HL}—such as the algorithm determining categorial status—within elements that are X^{min} [see (iii) of fig. 5.16].

O: By the way, feature matrices move at LF, and thus far we've assumed that they adjoin to whatever they target. Why can't a feature move to a specifier?

L: The notions "head" and "maximal projection" aren't defined for feature matrices. A head is a lexical item [see fig. 5.3], but a feature bundle isn't; instead, it's part of a lexical item. C_{HL} has full access to these parts, as separate features, only after Spell-Out, when it splits atomic lexical items, sending the phonetic part to PF and keeping the rest. This presupposes that feature matrices aren't heads; but then if they're not heads, they can't really project either [see (i) of fig. 5.17].

O: And why not, pray? Why can't we define projection in such a way that features project?

L: Of course we could do that, but what would it buy us? The bottom line is that projection is a relation that holds of lexical items.

O: Why?!

L: I don't know why. Why are molecules made up of atoms, and not directly of subatomic particles? Why are organisms made up of cells and not directly of molecules? It's as deep a question as there is, pertaining to the very fabric of a given subject matter. Why are phrases made up of lexical items, and not directly of feature matrices? The fabric of syntax is words. That's a fact [see chap. 6]. So feature matrices can't be maximal projections (since they can't be projections, period), which means that they can't end up in a specifier position. Of course, whatever's in a specifier position must, by definition, be a maximal projection—which means that a feature matrix in a specifier position is a contradiction in terms [see (ii) of fig. 5.17]. This in turn entails that the only chance for feature matrices to survive after movement is to end up as sublabels of a head, as we've assumed.

5.4 The Overall Shape of Grammatical Chains (and Where It May Come From)

   (which treats of matters that must be disclosed in order to make this history the more intelligible and distinct, and presents an account of some entertaining *wh*-movements)

O: All right—but I think we're in need of some perspective here. You've introduced various conditions today, which amount to my summary in (25) (where I've turned all your "only if" statements to stronger, definitional "if and only if" ones, assuming—to be concrete—that this is a complete list of requirements):

———————————————————— *a summary of structural chain conditions*

(25) Given a term $\tau_i = K$ that is targeted for merger, such that $K = \{\underline{\alpha}, \{ \ldots \{\tau_k, M\} \ldots \}\}$, and a term τ_j that merges with τ_i, such that $L = \{\underline{\alpha}, \{\tau_j, K\}\}$; the pair (K, M) is a *movement chain* if and only if (a), (b), and (c):

   a. *Last Resort Condition (LRC)*
      F [a feature of τ_k] raises [carrying τ_k as a free-rider] to target K if and only if F enters into a checking relation with a sublabel of K.

   b. *Minimal Link Condition (MLC)*
      F can raise to target K only if there is no legitimate operation Move F′ targeting K, where F′ is closer to K.

   c. *Condition on Chain Uniformity (CCU)*
      The formal/categorial informational content of chain elements τ_j and τ_k is identical.

Figure 5.17

Lexical items are matrices of matrices of features, including formal, phonological, and semantic bundles:

(i)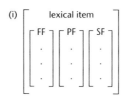

Only elements of this sort (i.e., lexical items) are heads, and only they project.

In a configuration of the sort in (ii),

(ii)

Y is a maximal projection since it is not immediately dominated by any category with a nondistinct label. Y can never be just a feature matrix, given (i).

The basis for (25) is definition (18). I've enriched it, though, with the LRC in (22), the MLC in (3), and the CCU in (19). In addition, many of the notions mentioned in these conditions presuppose complex definitions. For example, the LRC talks about *sublabels,* which must be independently defined; *closer* in the MLC presupposes the notion *minimal domain,* which must be independently defined; *formal/categorial information* in the CCU means a complex, contextually determined set of notions, which must be independently defin—

L: Please make your point . . .

O: Well, these are all definitions, hence statements with an axiomatic character which we must stipulate in order to characterise the notion of a chain, an LF object.

L: First of all, we haven't quite decided that. All we seem to know is that the separate statements in (25) are true. You're loading the dice, though, by placing them all under the rubric "definition of chain." Maybe that's the right decision; then again, maybe not. Say that we're right, and all of these are indeed conditions on what a chain is. (25) would then be a characterization of a substantive LF object, with the status of, say, the characterization of a syllable at PF—which is fairly complex, as any phonologist will attest. If the universe at this level is articulated, so be it. Is the definition in (25) any more complex than the definition of other slices of the natural world: molecules, genes, and so on? That isn't obvious to me.

O: Fair enough. Honestly, though, I was just trying to consolidate all these statements about chains to force you into this discussion. But now suppose the decision to lump these statements together is, as a matter of fact, not right. Isn't that more interesting?

L: Perhaps—which doesn't mean it's right, as usual. I suppose what you have in mind is whether some of the properties in (25) might follow from some kind of elegance in the overall design of the computational system.

O: Or, as you'd call it, virtual conceptual necessity . . .

feature accessibility determines movement

L: Right. So take (25a), for instance. The details of this condition might follow from an appropriate characterization of the sorts of features which are **accessible** for C_{HL} to operate with. It seems, for example, that uninterpretable features and strong features are accessible to C_{HL} for transformational processes.

O: By "uninterpretable features" you mean those whose presence in an interface representation makes the derivation crash.

L: Right—Case being the canonical instance.

O: And then there are the strong features . . .

L: Those are the "viral" ones. Not checking a strong feature brings the derivation to a halt right then and there; it doesn't even make it to PF or LF.

O: And of course you're saying that these features are accessible to C_{HL} because they clearly enter into transformational processes which result, for example, in their checking. Very well, then, let's talk about the checking itself, which I presume involves deletion. How does that actually work?

L: As a matter of fact, checking has various subcases, and whether or not deletion is involved turns out to be tough to determine. You see, deletion doesn't eliminate a structure; rather, it makes it uninterpretable for an interface level [see sec. 4.1]. In contrast, what if there's a transformational procedure—call it Erase—which literally wipes out a chunk of structure? If you think about it, that's less costly than deletion, which is actually a pretty cumbersome transformational procedure that has to target a set of features (maybe only one feature, maybe several), seek the value α of each feature, and destroy it. Those are then uninterpretable features. They're there, but they can't be read at the level where their interpretation is supposed to be encoded, and therefore no output is produced. In contrast, Erase is a simpler, dumber rule: it targets a set of features for destruction. Period.

O: How does that differ from comparing the movement of the queen with the movement of the king?! Delete and Erase are simply two operations, full stop, just as in my earlier example, Move F and Merge were simply two operations . . .

Figure 5.18

When comparing the complexity of Delete and Erase, keep in mind the elements required in defining each:

(i) *Delete*
TARGET: K = {αF, βF′, γF″, . . . }
SEARCH: Value for F, F′, F″, . . .
CHANGE: For all values x, $x \rightarrow \emptyset$

RESULT: K′ = {F, F′, F″, . . . }

(ii) *Erase*
TARGET: X
CHANGE: X $\rightarrow \emptyset$

RESULT: $\emptyset$

L: But that's not a fair comparison. You wanted Move F to be simpler than Merge because Merge uses more structure. I'm saying something different: Erase is simpler than Delete because it uses less information [see fig. 5.18]. That is, to characterize deletion of structure X we need to say more than we do to characterize erasure of structure X. In fact, if we had the option of moving F to the root of K, or merging F with the root of K (which we don't have, for other reasons), we'd prefer merging F, because this operation is informationally simpler. That is to say, your "elegance by way of structural results" and my "elegance by way of derivational information" may yield opposite results; one of them is wrong. I think yours is, but the issue isn't trivial, and as usual has to be decided on empirical grounds.

what constrains Erase

O: . . .

L: . . .

O: . . .

L: Have I left you speechless?

O: I was merely trying to make a point, by generating a sentence starting from the numeration {nothing-1, constrains-1, Erase-1, if-1, it-1, is-1, preferred-1, over-1, other-1, transformations-1, Tense-2}. Then I undertook what I thought to be the most elegant derivation: I dutifully assembled the whole phrase marker, and then zap! Death ray! Adios to the whole thing . . . I'm afraid that's what you heard: only silence.

L: Of course, we want to prevent that, which is easy. In general, only features can be successfully erased. Thus, imagine that you had a term β within {α̲, {α, β}}, and you erased it—yielding {α̲, {α}}. That's not a legitimate syntactic object, and thus the derivation would immediately be canceled at that point. In contrast, if you were to erase a feature F within β, you wouldn't affect the basic shape of the object, namely, {α̲, {α, β}}.

O: But I created no illegitimate object—I erased the whole thing!

L: Yeah, but the Law of Conservation prevents that: you can't just erase interpretable information. In fact, the only way you could've generated your silence and still conserved information is to've had nothing whatsoever in the numeration, to start with. Usually, we don't call that language—but maybe that's what people do in a yoga class, "Ommm" and so on (although that has PF; mere breath, perhaps . . .).

O: Oh, well, but what happens when a derivation could converge by either deleting or erasing a feature? For example, suppose we're dealing with an uninterpretable Case feature. I presume it would be enough to delete it, would it not?

L: Yes, that's the important question. Of course, from the point of view of LF, it's enough to delete the uninterpretable Case feature, precisely because there's no way to interpret it. If that were how things work, though, we'd immediately predict that the Case feature is still accessible for C_{HL} to go on moving it—since the structure isn't gone. However, factually we know that once a Case feature's been checked, no other transformational operation can involve this feature. This tells us that the feature isn't there. Why? Because it was cheaper to erase it than to delete it. Once again, the system goes with the most economical derivation in a totally mindless way; after all, had the feature just been deleted, other derivations would be possible, in principle.

O: Then there must be an entirely different account for **interpretable features,** whose erasure would violate the Law of Conservation.

L: Correct. Interpretable features are accessible to C_{HL} regardless of whether they've been checked—so they must still be in the structure. Take for instance the sort of movement involved in checking the agreement features of a nominal, such as number and gender. Well, those features are clearly interpretable at LF; in fact, they're crucial for interpretation, since *the cat* and *the cats* differ precisely (and only) in their number features. Then the Law of Conservation doesn't allow us to get rid of these features, either by erasure or by deletion [see fig. 5.19].

---

checking is not a process

Figure 5.19

This figure summarizes the types of features for movement purposes.

A feature is *accessible* for C_{HL} to use in operations if it is (a) interpretable at the interfaces or (b) uninterpretable and not checked. Agreement features on nouns are instances of interpretable features. In contrast, Case is an instance of a feature that is uninterpretable at LF (unchecked Case features are illegitimate objects at LF). If an uninterpretable feature is not appropriately checked, the derivation crashes.

If a strong feature is not checked immediately after insertion, within the projection of the category that bears it, the derivation is canceled (rather than crashing). Thus, strong features force overt movement.

All other things being equal, all features that can be deleted are erased, since the latter operation is less costly.

O: I must say, I'm finding the system perversely pretty . . . Perhaps too perversely. For I wonder: what's the purpose of all these nasty little creatures that force overt and covert movement? Do they truly exist merely to be erased?!

L: That's like asking what's the purpose of a virus!

O: Yes, my dear sir, but that part of the universe is contingent, and change in sufficiently complex systems, ultimately unpredictable. At this level, the universe is . . . well, stranger than we can even imagine [30]. But I thought you were trying to—

L: Characterize Human . . . That's all I'm trying to do. Certain aspects are optimal—core ones. Certain aspects, maybe not. We're talking about movement now, and the whole thing—particularly overt movement—is obviously a departure from optimality. For some reason (possibly having to do, ultimately, with the properties of the PF mapping), that's how things are. At any rate, these features seem to be what gears movement; maybe they're encoding something deeper that we haven't understood yet. Maybe the universe is prettier than we can imagine . . .

O: All the same, you must confess that, if what you're saying is remotely true, there's no such thing as a unified process of checking.

L: Which means checking is just a way of talking, a notation. The devices we have suffice to describe anything we need, without our introducing further machinery, such as a checking operation. What we have are *checking configurations,* defined in terms of the domains we've articulated today, and *checking relations* of various sorts, the ones that the LRC demands [see fig. 5.20]. But no specific operation is necessary. Thus, suppose C_{HL} leaves an uninterpretable feature undeleted prior to the interface levels. Well, the derivation crashes. So C_{HL} had better do something, and one possibility is deletion. Yet the system doesn't do that; instead, it erases the offending feature. Why? Because that's cheaper.

O: Let's return to locality. Take an interpretable feature, which isn't gone from the structure. Interestingly, C_{HL} has no access even to interpretable features unless they're to be used in the derivational step immediately at hand. That is to say, derivations don't have a "look-ahead" device; they're not clever, in the sense of reasoning, "If I could move this particular feature through this position, I

Figure 5.20

Checking is not an operation, but a complex process requiring

(i) a configuration that allows the process;

(ii) a relation that determines it;

(iii) an actual matching of features.

For (i), locality is essential, in terms of minimal domains (see fig. 5.4). Note that what matters with respect to (i) is not so much how F gets to an appropriate configuration, as that F be in this configuration. (Of course, how F gets to a configuration does matter for other aspects of the computation—the movement must be local, economical, and so on). In turn, (ii) presupposes an appropriate checking relation: for example, Case, for a moved nominal, or the subject requirement that forces Tense to host a nominal specifier. Finally, (iii) is the derivational condition that forces actual matching, so that the derivation is not immediately canceled; for instance, the accusative Case feature of a moved nominal is checked against the corresponding accusative feature in the verb.

If any of these requirements of checking is not met, something can go wrong. For example, if a derivation does not conform to (i), checking cannot take place at all, and the derivation crashes (if the feature that needs to be checked is uninterpretable) or is canceled (if the feature that needs to be checked is strong). The same fate awaits a derivation not conforming to (ii), since no checking will take place. Finally, if the derivation violates (iii), it is canceled because of mismatch, regardless of the nature of the features involved.

should eventually reach this other position where something grand happens." Rather, at a given derivational stage C_{HL} has the ability to seek a feature to fulfil a given checking relation within the specific structure which is created at that time. If that operation has a favourable consequence for the derivation, all well and good. Otherwise, the derivation may be over (either immediately, or later on)—but such is life. This is the content of the LRC, is it not?

L: Yes, in a sense C_{HL} plays like a normal chess player, and not a grand master with lots of long-term strategies and the ability to see patterns of action. A few steps at a time is as good as it gets.

O: And then exactly how many steps that is, is what the MLC tells us.

L: Right. We can possibly see this best if we think of movement as a process of attraction rather than as a process whereby something goes from a launching site to a landing site [31]. Let's suppose C_{HL} has put together a phrase marker K which, at the current stage of the derivation, needs a feature F to fulfill some requirement—for instance, checking a strong feature. C_{HL} expects the feature in question to be somewhere down in the structure it's already assembled, and wants to bring that feature to the domain of K to proceed with checking. So let's say, then, that K attracts F. Where does it find it? The first F that does the job will be just fine, and end the search, right? So here's where the notion "close" comes in. It makes no sense to attract a feature that's further down if you can attract one that's closer up. It's that simple, really. To make things explicit, we can define Attract as in (26), incorporating the MLC and the LRC:

(26) *Attract*
   K attracts F if F is the closest feature that can enter into a checking relation with a sublabel of K.

This isn't to say that (26) is any different from what we've been saying so far; we're still characterizing Move, although we now see a bit more clearly how it operates. From now on, I'll use the terms "Move" and "Attract" interchangeably.

—————————————————————————— *on the nature of chain conditions*

O: Well, by now I know this is the kind of sheer speculation you don't care to engage in, but it would seem to me that we're dealing here in matters of complexity. The initial array determines a reference set of derivations to be ranked for the purposes of derivational economy. This optimality question is posed within a derivational horizon: the mere fact that we start with a given lexical array already limits the possible answers. But if the range of this question were merely determined by the array, the computations involved in reaching the answer would easily become overwhelming [32]. One way we've already pared down the size of the computation is by demarcating the reference set in terms of *partial* numerations. At any given stage (D, S) in the life of a derivation, for S some already committed structure, we ask what continuations are available to D. At that point (D, S), the derivations C_{HL} could have pursued if it had used different elements within the numeration are irrelevant, since they would have led to a committed structure S′, instead of S. Hence, these other derivations aren't real alternatives—they're not within the derivational horizon, for C_{HL} considers only those derivations which factor in S, the committed structure. Even so, the number can be astronomical . . .

L: Yes, but—

O: Hold on! Secondly, I'd say that, given any partial, reduced numeration, asking the general question of whether there's a way of finding a derivation D′ which involves shorter links than those in D faces another problem: how to determine "shorter" in two different parts of the derivation. Is that a meaningful notion? I don't know, but at the very least the computation must be excruciatingly difficult—unreasonably so. And it's at this juncture that one may venture to claim that, perhaps, the human mind adopts a nice solution to this difficult task of comparison: replace "shorter" link with "short*est*" link . . . That's certainly easier to compute [33].

L: And that's what I was going to say, but—

O: Brilliant. So this seems then to be what the chain conditions instantiate: they address both the issue of computational blowup and the issue of comparison. They effectively define a minimal **derivational horizon,** particularly since they're coupled with the fact that syntactic derivations are by and large cyclic (whatever that follows from). This is to say: given a committed structure S, transformational processes target the root of S. At any given point, very few options remain: do something at the root, using whichever features are relevant. The latter clause is the content of the LRC: chain links are possible only if they involve feature checking. We needn't even ponder other alternatives, for these are the only transformational operations the system makes available, since feature checking gears movement. And within that narrow horizon, determining the shortest link (the content of the MLC) seems like a tractable problem [see fig. 5.21].

Figure 5.21

The diagonal lines represent the derivational horizon of (S, D). Partial numerations and committed structures define the derivational horizon; the LRC and MLC define a minimal derivational horizon.

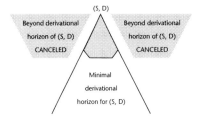

L: Of course, if those speculations are right (and they're certainly within the spirit of the program), then the LRC and the MLC shouldn't be lumped together in the characterization of chain that you gave in (25); that's the wrong ontological claim for those conditions. Rather, we have to think of them as derivational conditions whose "purpose," so to speak, is to eliminate a significant class of derivations within a given derivational horizon, reducing its reach [34]. This is what (26), Attract, is intended to express. From that perspective, derivational paths that aren't within the minimal derivational horizon of a given derivation will immediately be canceled, since they don't lead anywhere. Then global computations within this focused horizon are possibly tractable—for instance, in terms of simple algorithmic steps like the decision to procrastinate. When one first thinks about comparing derivations, one immediately fears a potentially huge cost; but the problem disappears if blindly solved as the computation unfolds, without having to wait until the convergent end. In fact, we've already seen cases where the system procrastinates early on, even if this eventually forces another overt movement [see sec. 4.6]. This is planning of a very dull sort: you procrastinate because in general that means less work if you manage to get away with it; but you don't have the slightest idea whether you will, or whether in fact, because of procrastinating now, you'll have to work later. As long as long-term strategies remain this simple, it doesn't seem terribly problematic (in computational terms) to keep them in the system.

O: In a word, given these speculations, the LRC and the MLC should follow from virtual conceptual necessity . . .

L: Well, look, that presupposes that a grammar without (26) would be impossible for any intelligent creature—other than God, say. Is that true? You tell me. I have no idea what sorts of computational limits the human mind has. You were the one who mentioned quantum computers. Is the mind more or less powerful than that? It's a meaningless question at this point.

O: I grant you that, but if the LRC and MLC don't follow from conceptual necessity, then where should we fit them?

L: Wherever we can. Yes, maybe they're there to reduce derivational cost, a nice alternative. That, of course, makes another assumption—apart from the one about computational complexity being relevant. Namely, that you have derivations to start with [35]. That is, to the extent that you have last resort or minimal link conditions in your grammar, you have an argument that your system is derivational *if* these conditions are there to reduce computational complexity—in a derivation. Incidentally, note that the MLC and LRC might also be conditions that UG has because otherwise, given human LADs, it would be unlearnable. Of course, we don't know this, but it's as much of a possibility as saying that without these conditions UG would be unusable, or would never have emerged as a system of knowledge to begin with. Then again, a different route to take would be the one you implied by (25): instead of being derivational requirements (whose violation leads to cancellation), the conditions may be convergence properties of LF objects, chains (whose violation leads to a crash). If your system is representational, you in fact want to argue that these conditions simply define LF chains, and then you want to justify why these are natural definitions to expect, a matter that depends on what sorts of axioms you propose for your LF [36].

---

extraction across wh-*elements*

O: All this reminds me of a problem I've been worrying about since the first day we met, which I now see must relate to conditions on chains or conditions on derivations. I shan't forget the sentence as long as I live: *what are you talking to a man whom you just asked?* [37]. Stop smiling! How can you explain this?

L: Just give the thing its full (relevant) structure . . .

O: Let me ponder the edifice. Here:

(27) $[_{CP}$ wh- $[_{IP}$ ... $[_{NP}$ a man $[_{CP}$ whom $[_{IP}$ ...t... [...t...]]]]]]

I detect recursion: the structure of the relative clause is much the same as that of the main clause. The manoeuvre you pulled on me was extracting an element from inside a relative clause all the way up to the matrix clause, across the Comp of the relative clause itself. Oh, blimey, I think I see it! In this Comp, a *wh*-element seems to be the closest to the matrix Comp, certainly closer than the actual position from which the matrix *wh*-element has moved [38] . . .

L: You have to assume that a Q(uestion) feature in Comp is attracting a *wh*-feature in the *wh*-element, forcing the *wh*-feature into the checking domain of Comp. It's clear that the long movement in (27) doesn't involve the shortest attraction. A closer attraction could be established between the matrix Comp and the intermediate *wh*-word *whom*. So the MLC is violated, and the derivation crashes [see fig. 5.22].

O: Even though if we had moved whom up (the wh-element which is closer to the matrix Comp), we'd get rubbish too: **whom are you talking to a man you just asked what?*

L: Yeah, but that's irrelevant. Of course, that sentence itself is out because it can't be interpreted—the same *wh*-element is acting both as a question word and as a relative clause marker [39]. But once again, whether the alternative that screws things up in (27) is itself convergent or interpretable or whatever is entirely beside the point. The fact is that the MLC forces C_{HL} to make the chain in a given way [as in fig. 5.22], and if it fails to do so, either it's not producing a chain or there's in fact no derivation (depending on the status of the MLC). This makes a very nice prediction, actually. Consider the contrasts in (28), which often go by the name of "superiority effects" [40]. Starting with a sentence like (28a), take a look at possible embedded and matrix questions, beginning with the embedded sentence. (28b) and (28c) involve short-distance movement of object and subject within the embedded clause. In (28d) and (28e), the same sort of movements now proceed long-distance, to the matrix Comp . . . Here's the key: in (28f) and (28g), one *wh*-movement is short-distance, while the other one is long-distance:

Figure 5.22

Note that in (i) the question word *what* cannot move to the checking domain of Comp (where Q is), since *whom* is closer and has the sort of feature that Q requires:

(i) $[_{CP}[_{Comp} \text{ Q}] [_{IP} \ldots [_{NP} \text{ a man } [_{CP} \text{ to whom } [_{IP} \ldots [\ldots \text{what}]]]]]]$

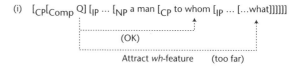

(OK)

Attract *wh*-feature   (too far)

(28) a.   he has said that Socrates loved Plato

    b.   he has said who Socrates loved t

    c.   he has said who t loved Plato

    d.   who has he said (who) Socrates loved t?

    e.   who has he said (who) t loved Plato?

    f.   *who has he said who t loved t?

    g.   *who has he said who t loved t?

O: Diabolical. I see. The Q-feature in the matrix Comp is trying to attract a *wh*-element, and it obtusely attracts the one that has moved. Movement of *the other wh*-element over the one that has moved short-distance violates (25b), the MLC.

L: Now look at (29a). Note that here the second *who* hasn't even moved. The intermediate Comp has a Q-feature which has to be checked with a *wh*-element, which is what the embedded subject is doing, just as in (28c). (29a) sharply contrasts with (29b), which again violates the MLC, since the movement there isn't the shortest one possible:

(29) a.   he has said who t loved who

    b.   *he has said who who loved t

O: But then why is (30b) not as bad as (29b)?

(30) a.   he has said which professor t loved which student

    b.   he has said which student which professor loved t

L: Well, the structures are different. See what they look like prior to movement:

(31) a.   [he has said [who [loved who]]]

    b.   [he has said [[which professor] [loved which student]]]

In (31a) the subject *wh*-phrase *who* commands the object *wh*-phrase, which is also *who*. In contrast, in (31b) the *wh*-phrase is the *which* in the subject *which professor;* of course, the moved element proper is always the *wh*-feature, and the rest of the structure pied-pipes in the ancillary operation that PF demands. Now observe that the higher *which* is buried inside the subject *which professor,* and hence doesn't command the lower *which*. And recall our characterization of distance in (10), which I'll repeat:

(10) *Distance*

If β commands α, when targeting K for raising, with τ the actual target of movement [/attraction], β is *closer to* K than α is, unless (a) β and τ are in the same minimal domain, or (b) α and β are in the same minimal domain.

For right now, forget about (a) and (b), and focus on the presuppositions in (10). Let the element corresponding to α in (10) be the embedded Comp in both (31a) and (31b). Note that in (31b) the higher *which* doesn't command the lower one (and of course vice versa). This means that each *which* is as close to the target of movement/attraction as the other one is, and both movements should in principle be possible. Consequently, (31b) yields two grammatical outputs, (30a) and (30b). In contrast, (31a) only yields one grammatical output, (29a)—because of (31a)'s structure, a derivation like the one in (29b) either won't converge or will simply be canceled [see fig. 5.23].

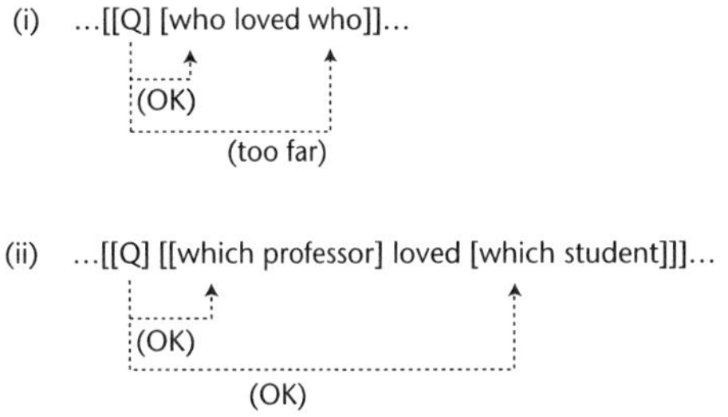

5.5 Desperately Seeking Features

(treating of that which will be seen by him or her who reads, and known by him or her who works on it) [41]

O: Most intriguing . . . I say, why doesn't the object *who* need to move in (29a), if it may move in, let's say, (28b)?

———————————————————— interpretable versus uninterpretable features

L: The *wh*-elements don't move for their own sake, but in order to check the strong Q-feature in Comp, which they're attracted to. The assumption here is that Q is interpretable at LF, and hence doesn't need to be checked for LF reasons. Of course, the reason the *wh*-element can move at all is that its *wh*-features (which we can think of as determiner features) are interpretable as well, and hence always accessible to C_{HL}. This justifies the movement/attraction in terms of the LRC, since the moved *wh*-phrase does engage in a checking relation with one of the sublabels of the hosting Comp—

Figure 5.23

In (ii), since neither *which* commands the other, neither interferes with the other for movement purposes:

(i)   ...[[Q] [who loved who]]...

(OK)

(too far)

(ii) ...[[Q] [[which professor] loved [which student]]]...

(OK)

(OK)

which attracts the *wh*-element in order to check its strong features. English works this way, but think about what would happen in a language where the Q in Comp isn't strong.

O: There, the *wh*-element wouldn't have to move in order to do the checking: an interpretable feature simply needn't be checked (and as a matter of fact, can't be erased) . . .

L: Which would entail no movement whatsoever (if the movement isn't necessary, economy makes it impossible) [42]. Chinese questions very possibly work like this, which is one of the reasons why question words in this language are identical to indefinites (unlike in Japanese and Portuguese, where they're more complex), and why overt movement/attraction is never observed in Chinese questions.

O: I shall give you an example each in Japanese, Portuguese, and Chinese, and perhaps you'd care to compare them for me. Here you are [43]:

(32) a. *Japanese*

[[Ø]   [Morihirowa   [t   dareo]   aisiteiru]]

wh-F   subject   object   verb

'who does Morihiro love?'

b. *Portuguese*

[quem   quere   [o Zé   t   t]]

wh-phrase   verb   subject

'who does Zé love?'

c. *Chinese*

[Zhangsan   ai   shei]

subject   verb   object-*wh*/indefinite

'who does Zhangsan love?'

L: While the Japanese and Portuguese question words *dare* 'who' and *quem* 'who' aren't fully identical to quantificational phrases (in Japanese an indefinite corresponding to *dare* would be *dareka* 'someone' and in Portuguese an indefinite corresponding to *quem* would be *alguem* 'someone'), in Chinese the very same word *shei* can be used to mean both *who* and *anyone* [44]. This is systematic [see fig. 5.24].

O: The bottom line, then, is that Chinese questions are rather different from English questions, since in Chinese a *wh*-feature can't be moved/attracted to Comp . . .

L: A *wh*-feature doesn't have to move to Comp in English, either, if Comp is intrinsically a *wh*-Comp, which somehow checks strength "internally":

(33) a.   he wondered whether Socrates loved Plato

  b.   *he wondered (that) Socrates loved Plato

  c.   who wondered whether who loved who?

  d.   who wondered who loved who?

In (33a) the complementizer *whether* can check the Q-feature, internally to the Comp head [45]—thus, no *wh*-movement is necessary (compare the ungrammatical (33b), where no element like *whether* is present). Note also that in (33c) there's no *wh*-movement to the intermediate Comp. By contrast, in (33d) *who* has moved there; and the sentence means something totally different. In sum: *wh*-movement is just one possible way of checking Q; any *wh*-element can do the job; and as (28d) showed, it can be done from a long distance. This is quite different from Case checking, say. A given Case feature has a designated site for being checked (otherwise, a feature mismatch arises); Case features aren't checked via alternative processes, internal to the projection of Tense or V, so Case checking necessarily involves movement; and Case checking is a short-distance process.

O: What do you mean? In (15) *the Cheshire cat* moved quite a good distance!

L: Still, the process is more constrained than *wh*-movement. Compare these examples [46]:

(34) a.   [it seems [that Alice is likely [t to live here]]]

  b.   *[Alice seems [that it is likely [t to live here]]]

  c.   [who does it seem [that it is likely [t is living here]]]?

Figure 5.24

Chinese question words and corresponding indefinites, from Huang 1982:

Word	Wh-*interpretation*	Indefinite *interpretation*
na	'which'	'any'
shei	'who'	'anyone'
sheme	'what'	'anything'
heshi	'when'	'any time'
nali	'where'	'any place'
zeme	'how'	'any way'
. . .	. . .	. . .

For some reason (I'll get back to this in a minute), the long movement to check Case in (34b) is terrible, but the comparable *wh*-movement in (34c) is fine. So the two sorts of movement/attraction are behaving differently, which is what we'd expect if in movement/attraction for Case purposes the feature that moves is checked (unlike in movement for *wh*-purposes). That is, checking configurations have the shape in (35) (basically, as a consequence of the LRC and the Law of Conservation, as well as general economy considerations):

(35)   Checking
        domain of K

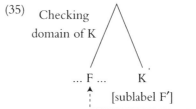

F′ is [−interpretable]

F can be [+interpretable]

F must be "accessible-to-C_{HL}"

K must be [+functional]

Where

    a. Features visible at LF are accessible to C_{HL}.

    b. Features invisible at LF are inaccessible to C_{HL} once they have been checked.

    c. A checked feature is deleted when possible.

    d. A deleted feature is erased when possible.

Given the design of the system, the core instances of Move/Attract may in principle be motivated internally or externally—since two sites, landing and launching, are involved. Case checking is a typical instance of "internally motivated movement" (IMM): movement/attraction whose trigger is the feature that actually moves. In contrast, *wh*-movement is a typical instance of "externally motivated movement" (EMM), whose trigger is in the structure that's targeted for movement/attraction [see fig. 5.25] [47]. The feature that triggers the IMM of a nominal for Case reasons is, as we saw, uninterpretable, and is matched up against an equally uninterpretable feature in a verb or Tense (which may or may not be strong, depending on the language; if it's strong, the movement is also an EMM, to satisfy this feature [48]). The feature that triggers EMM of a *wh*-phrase is also uninterpretable—but in addition it's strong

Figure 5.25

(i) *Internally motivated movement (IMM)*

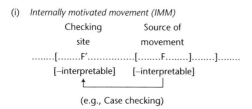

(ii) *Externally motivated movement (EMM)*

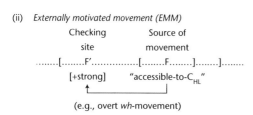

and therefore has to be erased soon after it's selected [see sec. 4.7]. In contrast, the corresponding attracted feature only has to be "accessible-to-C_{HL}"—it can be interpretable or not. The element targeted for movement of F—namely, K (which contains a feature checker F′ as one of its sublabels)—is always a functional category, in whose checking domain the checking relation is established, with or without erasure depending on the nature of the categories involved [49]. If the features are interpretable, erasure wouldn't be recoverable and hence doesn't happen. If the features are uninterpretable, the system erases them. It's almost as if the system didn't really want to deal with these sorts of features, and some imperfection forced them in, which is remedied through checking.

---

some variations in checking

O: But it's also unquestionable that categories that move by PF in some language don't move at all in another, not even at LF.

L: Yes, and we can see that in *wh*-movement. In a given language L, a given feature F may be overtly attracted to F′ in order to check it, given the viral nature of F′. But in the next language L′, nothing may be attracted to F′, if it isn't strong. As a result, L′ won't have any overt movement, and since interpretability was never involved in this sort of movement to begin with, it won't have any LF movement either. That's what I'm suggesting may be happening in the Chinese question in (32c), for instance.

O: What about the converse, though? If I've followed you, it could happen that the *wh*-feature that's attracted to a strong Q is itself uninterpretable (since it would still be accessible to C_{HL}) . . .

L: In principle that's possible, and maybe it explains what happens in languages like Bulgarian, where speakers can say things like *who what did t see t?,* with multiple movements/attractions.

O: Right you are [50]:

(36) koj   kakvo vidja?
    who what saw
    'who saw what?'

It appears that *koj* 'who' and *kakvo* 'what' both move.

Figure 5.26

Some instances of multiple subjects:

(i) *Chinese (from Xu 1993)*
shuiguo wo xihuan pingguo
fruit   I   like   apple
'as for fruit, I like apples'

(ii) *Korean (from Suh 1993)*
John-ka   pwulhaenghito apeci-ka   tolakasietta
John-nominative unfortunately father-nominative died
'unfortunately, John's father died'

(iii) *Japanese (from Ura 1996)*
zoo-ga   hana-ga   nagai
elephant-nominative nose-nominative long
'the elephant's nose is long'

L: It does. At first sight, this seems like the kind of example you want; although a number of complications emerge.

O: Not the least of which is, I suppose, the fact that an uninterpretable *wh*-feature wouldn't need to move until LF!

L: Right, so it could either be that (36) is an example of something else (whatever that is [51]), or that we have to parameterize strong features. Maybe in some languages strong features don't get erased when they're checked—maybe they just get deleted without economy being violated, and they keep attracting all categories that match them for checking purposes . . . Or maybe some languages are only allowed one violation of Procrastinate (say, as in English *wh*-movement), while other languages (like Bulgarian) are allowed several [52].

O: If your claim is general enough, it doubtless predicts that some languages should be able to have, very specifically, multiple subjects. And so they do! For example, Chinese, Korean, Japanese [53] . . .

L: Yeah, which must mean that several noun phrases can move to a given site where nominative Case is checked [see fig. 5.26].

O: Of course, now we've seen languages with no *wh*-movement, languages with the *wh*-movement of a single phrase, and languages with multiple *wh*-movement. Shouldn't we be concerned that we're finding three sorts of languages, with different LFs?

L: Let's not confuse the issue. The similarity of LFs is relative to the features that enter the syntactic computation. So take two languages L and L′, and say that only L encodes a [+/−feminine] distinction in its lexicon. Well, then, the word for 'cat' in L will be different from the word for 'cat' in L′, not just at PF, but also in its LF features. (For instance, Spanish has the *gato/gata* distinction where English has the single word *cat;* this has an obvious PF effect, and a clear LF correlate, in terms of lexical entailments. [see sec. 2.4].) It's a trivial point, really. The only difference between this case and the kind of examples we've been discussing is that we're not dealing with semantic features, but with purely formal features, like Q's strength. In some languages Q is strong, and in some languages it isn't—just as with many other features. In a language where Q is strong, there'll be an extra movement, to check Q. In a language where Q is weak, there's no need for such a movement, and everything stays put. And as you said, in a language with uninterpretable *wh*-features (assuming those exist), there'd be extra movements.

O: But goodness, won't that have a consequence for interpretation?!

L: It may, but we're not directly concerned with that. So it's possible that the actual way of asking *who does John love?* in Chinese is best characterized in terms of something like *does John love anyone?* (cf. (32c)). Which may get the appropriate information through, communicating a question, and eliciting a response like *John loves Mary* [54]. There's no reason to expect that just because in English we ask the question with an element like *who* moving to the beginning of the sentence, this is the way questions are formed universally. In fact, there's no such thing as a pretheoretical notion of "a question." That's a traditional notion with no status in the theory. All that has a status in the theory are elements that we motivate internal to the theory, like Comp, Q, *wh-*, indefinites . . . These relate to each other rather blindly, according to processes that have nothing to do with the need to ask questions, the effability of a given thought, and so on. All that is performance. The fact is, though, that speakers can communicate a question however they want. To be deliberately provocative about the matter, English speakers have all sorts of strategies besides standard *wh*-movement to convey an information question:

(37) a. who does John love?
    b. so, John loves who?
    c. John loves who?
    d. who is it that John loves (him)?
    e. John loves someone, right?
    f. John doesn't love anyone, or does he?
    g. can you tell me if John loves someone?
    h. does John love anyone?
    i. John must love someone . . .

So we have to be cautious about positing processes for which the evidence is at best arcane in some language of the world, just because we see them in English. Mind you, I've got no problem making the proposal: Chinese has covert *wh*-movement. But we do that only if we have strong theoretical reasons for it [55].

Figure 5.27

In (i) *it* is blindly attracted, given the MLC:

(i)   [Tense [seems [that [it is likely [Alice to live here]]]]]

                  (OK)

                     (too far)

This prevents the movement of *Alice,* even if the result of attracting *it* is also ungrammatical (for reasons discussed in the text), as in (ii):

(ii) *[it Tense [seems [that [t is likely [Alice to live here]]]]]

O: You were going to tell me why (34b) is ill formed whereas (34c) is perfect . . . That was your illustration of why *wh*-movement is less constrained than raising for Case.

L: Oh, yes. Well, intuitively we want (34) to follow from the MLC, right?

O: You mean because the matrix Tense attracts the pleonastic *it,* instead of *Alice* . . . And again, it's irrelevant that the would-be movement of *it* would lead to a crashed derivation [see fig. 5.27] . . .

L: Yeah, the only thing that counts is that this is the movement that the MLC forces. It crashes, too, but the important thing is that it eliminates (34b) as a possibility.

O: But I'm still confused. We're comparing alternative derivations which start with the same partial numeration, after the initial numeration has been reduced. As far as I can see, (34a) and (34b) (which I repeat in (38)) and (38c) have all got the common committed structure in (39):

(38) a.   [it seems [that Alice is likely [t to live here]]]
     b. *[Alice seems [that it is likely [t to live here]]]

     c. *[it seems that [t is likely [Alice to live here]]]

(39) [is [likely [Alice [to [live here]]]]]
     reduced numeration: {it-1, seems-1, that-1, Alice-0, is-0, likely-0, to-0, live-0, here-0, etc.}

At this point, shouldn't the derivation procrastinate, preferring insertion of *it* over movement of *Alice?*

L: No, because the derivation would crash [see (41)] and Procrastinate is an economy strategy that applies up to convergence. That is, inserting *it* is certainly an option—but it's lethal. Moving *Alice* is another option. If inserting *it* led to a convergent derivation, it would be preferred over moving *Alice,* which is more cumbersome. But such a convergent derivation never materializes, and therefore the derivations with *it* don't even enter the competition for grammaticality.

O: What about (34c)? Why is *wh*-movement possible over it (which contrasts with (34b)/(38b))? Oh, this one's easy! *It* hasn't got a *wh*-feature for Q to attract, and so it doesn't interfere with the more distant *wh*-movement . . .

L: Right: Q seeks a *wh*-feature, and *it* doesn't have one [56]. Period. Clearly, several factors can conspire to yield an ungrammatical result; it's a very modular system. Consider (40), which we looked at earlier:

(40) a. the Cheshire cat seems to be likely to grin
      b. [the Cheshire cat seems [(the Cheshire cat) to be likely [(the Cheshire cat) to grin]]]

First, we have to make sure *the Cheshire cat* ends up in subject position. Movement/Attraction to that position takes place in order to check the strong Tense feature of the matrix clause, which demands a subject. In a different language, where such a feature is weak, a version of (40) without overt movement would be possible. Of course, even in a language like that, the relevant Case feature from the in-situ *the Cheshire cat* would have to move in the LF component, or the derivation would crash at the LF level. But the feature alone would be attracted, without *the Cheshire cat* going along as a free-rider.

O: The intermediate steps in (40b) are taken to check the strong features in the Tenses that *the Cheshire cat* moves through. Shouldn't this have an immediate effect on the uninterpretable Case feature of this element?

---

successive checking

L: It would if those intermediate positions could check Case—but they can't; these are infinitival elements. And in principle the fact that *the Cheshire cat* has moved to the intermediate specifier of Tense doesn't entail that it shouldn't be able to move any further. Suppose that there's a feature D(eterminer) that an element has to have in order to check the strong feature of Tense, and furthermore that this feature is interpretable. (The details of this proposal aren't crucial, but we should be concrete [57].) Then it can raise as many times as it needs to, since it's never erased and C_{HL} has access to it all the time, all the way up to LF. Also consider (41):

(41) a.   [it seems [Alice is living here now]]

   b.   *[Alice seems [t is living here now]]

Alice has features other than Case (which has been erased in the intermediate clause, after checking). It's got agreement features, for instance: it's singular, at least, and in many languages you'd also have to express its being feminine and third person. Those are interpretable features, and they don't get erased upon checking—so they're accessible to C_{HL}. This is why we can see agreement processes occurring on each successive cycle—because a whole matrix of features is moving along with the attracted feature, thus satisfying the agreement.

O: Hah! This explains—I believe—something I've always found puzzling about languages like Spanish. A plural phrase like *los soldados* 'the soldiers' moves from the embedded clause to the matrix clause, and it's able to agree in both [58]!

(42) [los   soldados   parecen   [haber   sido   arrestados]]
     the   soldier-plural   seem-plural   to have   been   arrested-plural

L: Which indicates that the plural feature hasn't been erased upon first being checked, and can continue on to the matrix, where further checking-without-erasing takes place. This is what we'd expect if plurality is an interpretable feature, which we want to survive LF.

O: Just a moment, though: if plurality survives LF, it'll appear in two different places in (42), and Full Interpretation will be violated!

L: No: the interpretable feature is inside the element that moves: *los soldados*. That's where it gets interpreted, within the chain formed by the movement of this particular element (after the relevant parts of the chain have been deleted, and so on). What we see attached to the verbal elements in (42), the feature *-s* for plurality in *arrestado-s* 'arrested' and the feature *-n* for plurality and third person in *parece-n* 'seem', is eliminated by the time the derivation hits the LF level, precisely as a result of being checked against the interpretable plurality feature in *los soldados* [59].

O: Oh, but then a feature like plurality may be interpretable in nominal expressions and uninterpretable in the verbal ones.

L: Sure. The whole phenomenon of agreement appears to be based on this asymmetry: one element partially determines the overt features of the other element, though only one set of features is interpretable—those that have moved, given the assumptions in (35).

O: All right, but returning to (41b), *Alice*'s agreement features make it accessible for movement, and so it should be able to go up to the matrix clause, to check the strong features in the Tense there. And now we're in trouble . . .

L: Are we? The matrix Tense also has a Case feature to check, corresponding to the Case feature of the element that moves. But in this particular instance, no checking can take place, simply because *Alice*'s Case feature has already been checked in the embedded Tense [see fig. 5.28].

O: Are you telling me that Case checking is a reciprocal process as well?

L: You can think of it as a form of agreement, except that the features involved in Case checking (in the noun and in the verb) are both uninterpretable (again according to the assumptions in (35)) [60]. The features don't have a profound LF effect, like the one that, say, plurality has. Note that (41b) contrasts with (43a–b), which are of course perfect:

(43) a. [Alice seems [t to be living here now]]

      b. [Alice seems [t smart]]

In these instances, the matrix Tense is capable of entering into a checking relation with the moved *Alice,* whose Case isn't checked in the embedded infinitival clause or the adjectival clause.

O: Nice. Only if the embedded clause doesn't involve Case features (so that Case checking doesn't happen there) will movement upwards be allowed.

L: Movement/Attraction of the sort we're exploring, that is. Yes, which makes an interesting prediction. Consider, for instance, Modern Greek, which allows expressions such as 'the men seem that will leave' that are impossible in English [61] . . .

Figure 5.28

Alice's feature [F] (presumably, an interpretable agreement feature) makes the matrix of features containing [F] accessible for C_{HL}, thus allowing movement:

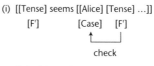

Nonetheless, this matrix of features does not contain a Case feature, once it has been erased after engaging in Case checking in the embedded clause. As a result, feature [F'] in the target (the one responsible for the checking of nominative Case) cannot be checked, and the derivation crashes at LF.

O: That's right!

(44) [oi   anthropoi   phainontai   [pos   [t   tha   phugoun]]]
    the   men   seem   that   will   leave

The embedded clause here isn't infinitival (the verb encodes Tense features). This must mean that, for some reason, Case isn't being checked in this clause, and the rest of course follows. Movement upwards, which results in a crashed derivation in English—we saw that in (41b)—leads to a convergent derivation in Greek.

L: That's what the theory predicts.

5.6 There!
(of the unseen and unheard-of adventures experienced by features when they move in a covert guise)

O: Here's another question. We concluded yesterday that, given the system as it stands, there must exist some covert, LF movement. It goes without saying that this sort of movement, if it indeed exists (and we hope that it does, because the system predicts it), will not be evident at all. This is always a bit hazardous. True, most interesting things in the natural world (black holes, quarks, genes, and so forth) aren't evident at all; but then again, theoretical entities may in the end be figments of the scientist's imagination (ether, a vital force, a language—as opposed to a chain). It's therefore good news when something whose existence one's theory predicts turns out to be reasonably in accord with certain facts that one can establish within natural reality. In this respect, it would seem that we could take the set of conditions in (25) as a rather interesting tool, as it were, for testing LF. If we see those very properties cohering also around objects which we abstractly hypothesise in the covert component, then the reality of these otherwise mysterious LF objects would have to be readily granted. And with it, we'd be motivating and justifying the very level of LF, which is quite abstract. So? You're smiling again . . .

---
                                           expletive-associate relations

L: Think about the apparently trivial expression in (45) [62]:
(45) once upon a time, there was a tavern

This is one of the few cases in English where the verb seems to be agreeing with something other than the grammatical subject of the sentence. Observe:

(46) a. there is/*are a man here
       there *is/are two men here
    b. there arrives/*arrive a plane every five minutes
       there *arrives/arrive two planes every five minutes

O: I've noticed, thank you.

L: We can then easily construct the paradigm in (47):

(47) a. a man is here
       (cf. there is a man here)
    b. a man was arrested
       (cf. there was a man arrested)
    c. a man seems to have been arrested
       (cf. there seems to have been a man arrested)
    d. a man seems to be certain to be here
       (cf. there seems to be certain to be a man here)
    e. *a man seems that it is certain to be here
       (cf. *there seems that it is certain to be a man here)

O: That, I hadn't noticed! My word, whenever a noun phrase can move, a corresponding sentence exists with *there* in place of the target of movement . . . Absolutely brilliant! I'm particularly moved by (47e), whose ungrammaticality, I expect, corresponds to that of (34b)—and hence follows from the MLC. Inasmuch as the corresponding sentence with *there* is also ungrammatical . . . it must be that *there* constructions involve movement [see fig. 5.29]! Hence, they're subject to requirements such as the MLC, although needless to say, whatever movement is going on here, it cannot be overt, since no actual movement is present at PF. This is the case I was looking for; once again, thank you . . .

L: Let's recap. First, in *there* constructions the verb agrees with the element that follows it (call this the "associate" of *there*). This in fact suggests that the associate is, in some sense, the LF subject, as your reasoning implied. That is, you can expect to explain the mysterious agreement by virtue of moving a feature in the associate to Tense [see fig. 5.30]. Second, the relation between *there* and the associate

Figure 5.29

Note that (i) and (ii) are parallel if (ii) is assumed to involve covert movement:

(i) *[a man [seems [that [it is certain [t to be [t here]]]]]]

(ii) *[there [seems [that [it is certain [t to be a man here]]]]]

This particular sort of example has not been discussed yet, although it is similar to (34b). The difference, here, is that pleonastic *it* is assumed to be able to move. This is justified as follows:

(iii) [it seems [t to be likely [that the universe expands]]]

In (iii) the strong D-features of the first embedded Tense and the matrix Tense can be checked only if *it* moves. Once this is granted, derivations (i) and (ii) must be prohibited. The first is directly ruled out by the MLC, since the matrix Tense is forced to attract *it* instead of *a man*. The second would be ruled out as well if it had to involve LF movement.

Figure 5.30

The associate in the grammatical object position covertly relates to the Tense position, where subject agreement is encoded. The relation obeys chain conditions:

(i) *Overtly*
  there arrives a plane every five minutes

(ii) *Covertly*
  [there Tense = Agr [...a plane...]]

$$\uparrow_____|$$

  Local relation

is very local—so much so that it looks like a chain relation [see fig. 5.30]. As you said, for every structure with *there* and an associate, there's a related structure where the noun phrase corresponding to the associate shows up in the position of *there*.

O: Hold on! We want to say that the structures with *there* are structurally identical to the structures with overt movement. But then shouldn't the derivation with covert movement always rule out the one with overt movement, since only the former procrastinates?

L: No; a structure with *there* and a structure with mere movement start out with two different arrays—specifically, only one of them has the pleonastic *there* [63].

O: Why, of course! I was dazzled by the beauty of these examples [64] . . . You don't compare the derivations you generate in each instance; nevertheless, you do observe that the principles that are relevant to predicting one kind of structure are also relevant to predicting the other kind of structure.

—————————————————————— anaphoric licensing after movement

L: But I was about to show you how parallel standard chain formation and *there* structures indeed are. You've already seen this in (47), and particularly in (47e), which, as you correctly point out, follows from the MLC applying at LF. Now consider the situation in (48) [65]:

(48) a. two boxers are in tonight's match without having identified themselves
    b. there are two boxers in tonight's match without having identified themselves

O: And what language is that?

L: These examples may not be perfect English, but you do hear people say such things; I have to build arcane examples like these in order to raise a point concerning the fact that, as you may recall, at LF an anaphoric element like *themselves* needs to be in the command domain of its antecedent [see sec. 3.7].

O: Well, your examples certainly aren't very eloquent, and I have to imagine I'm hearing a sportscast not to be too bothered by them . . . But to the extent that I accept the examples at all, I find it rather remarkable that (48b) isn't particularly worse than (48a). This appears to show that the associate in (48b)—namely, *two boxers*—raises at LF to a site which commands the anaphor *themselves!* This of course follows if the associate, at LF, is in the position occupied by *there* at Spell-Out [see fig. 5.31] . . .

L: To be precise, remember that at LF only features move. Nonetheless, a crucial feature from the associate—perhaps a determiner feature with referential import—is arguably displaced to a position from which it commands the anaphor *themselves* [66]. (The reason I'm invoking movement of a referential feature is that the anaphor is referentially dependent on a feature from the associate, *two boxers*.) Now observe (49):

(49) there's (always) two boxers in a prizefight

For many people, (49) is acceptable, even though the verb doesn't agree with the postverbal nominal [67]. This is a colloquial expression that's usually invoked when identifying the parts of a whole, or some constitution relation (in this case, stating what a prizefight has to have in order to count as one) [see fig. 5.32]. Contrast (49) with (50), which doesn't obviously involve any such integral relation (and instead reports a given state of affairs):

(50) although there are only two boxers in tonight's main fight, there
       will be many more people fighting outside the ring

O: Suppose I accept what you're saying—what's the point of it?

L: Well, compare (51) with (48b). (I'll purposely omit my judgment, not to influence yours.)

(51) there's two boxers in tonight's match without having identified
       themselves

O: That's gruesome! I mean, "There's two boxers in a prizefight" isn't a sentence I'd say to Mother—evidently—but I can picture myself saying it in a pub (though the information would hardly be news to most pub-goers!). But what I find intolerable is then to add a comment such as . . . er . . . "because of each other's challenge."

Figure 5.31

The licensing of *themselves* under command is straightforward in (48a). In (48b), however, the logical antecedent of the anaphor (namely, *two boxers*) does not command it and hence should not be able to license it:

(i) [two boxers are…[without…themselves…]]

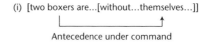

Antecedence under command

(ii) [there are [two boxers…] [without…themselves…]]

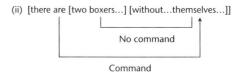

No command

Command

However, if at LF the associate relates to a higher position that in fact commands the anaphor, licensing may be possible.

Figure 5.32

Other instances of colloquial integral expressions (from Hornstein, Rosen, and Uriagereka, forthcoming):

(i) a. there's a Ford T engine in my Saab 95
     b. there's a before and an after to any argument
     c. there's gold and sapphires in the queen's crown
     d. there's (only) four chairs in this dining-room set
     e. in New York City, there's Manhattan, Brooklyn, Queens, The
         Bronx, and Staten Island

These are expressions of formal or substantive constitution, which can also be paraphrased as follows:

(ii) a. my Saab 95 has a Ford T engine
      b. any argument has a before and an after
      c. the queen's crown has gold and sapphires (in it)
      d. this dining-room set has (only) four chairs
      e. New York City has Manhattan, Brooklyn, Queens, The Bronx,
          and Staten Island

Olsen vs. Robinson, World Middleweight Championship, Los Angeles, 1956.

Figure 5.33

Mind you, I know that this is true: "Ali fights Frazier because of Frazier's challenge, and vice versa." Why, two boxers always engage in a prizefight because of something like each other's challenge. But English speakers simply can't express that thought by saying, "There's two boxers fighting in tonight's match because of each other's challenge." I've got the same feeling about your (51): I don't like *themselves* there. So it seems that only if the associate agrees with the main verb, can it (or rather, its referential features) then raise to the LF position from which to license the anaphor, from a command point. Fascinating. Alas, the data are definitely not as clean as one would wish them to be, but in all fairness, you should see the kind of evidence physicists get! At all events, the phenomenon is extraordinary, particularly because I don't suppose anyone could really teach anyone else any of this [68] . . .

L: Yeah, it'd be very surprising if kids were taught all these subtleties about sentences their parents wouldn't even consider saying! So now we've established that there's a real parallel between standard movement/attraction and *there* constructions that exhibit agreement, where the attraction by hypothesis takes place at LF.

_____ the associate moves to check Case

O: One thing I still don't understand is why the associate moves [69].

L: Let's return to the simplest contrast:

(52) a. a particle seems to be moving
     b. there seems to be a particle moving

Why does *a particle* move in (52a)?

O: Although it's checking its Case in the matrix Tense, the reason it moves overtly is that the strong Tense features must be checked prior to Spell-Out.

L: Well, then. Suppose that *there* is capable of checking the strong Tense features.

O: Then *a particle* won't need to move. It can procrastinate because the need to check its Case is LF-driven. So long as this uninterpretable feature is gone by LF, the derivation will converge; but it's more economical to converge without overt movement, if at all possible.

L: But *by* LF, *a particle*—or more precisely, a feature within *a particle*—needs to be in a position to check Case.

O: I see. The need for the associate to check Case motivates the LF movement. I presume this means that the Case feature from the associate must adjoin to a position where Case is checked. But hold on. Then what happens in (51)? By hypothesis, you're saying that in this instance the postverbal nominal doesn't move. How does it manage to check Case, then?

L: These elements that don't agree in English are arguably predicates, not arguments. To see this, consider the paradigm in (53) [and see fig. 5.33]:

(53) a. a prizefight has two boxers
　　 b. a prizefight may have tragic consequences
　　 c. a prizefight has some tragedy to it
　　 d. a prizefight is pure tragedy
　　 e. a prizefight is tragic

(53a) and (53b) are very similar: just as a fight usually has two boxers, so it can have tragic consequences; these are characteristics of a fight. Characteristics that appear in other guises as well, as in (53c), where *tragedy* is clearly abstract and not obviously an argument of anything, and (53d)/(53e), where *tragedy* and *tragic* appear in typical predicative form.

O: You mean that *two boxers* isn't an argument of *have*?

L: That's what I'm trying to say. Remember from our discussion about the abstractness of light verbs [see sec. 2.7] that it's a mistake to think that *be* and *have* are regular verbs like *use* or *think*. *Have* may in essence be a **suppletive form** of *be* plus an expression of location, and *be* appears to express a very abstract relation of predication plus some agreement. Basically, (54a) and (54b) are just two ways of expressing the relation in (54c):

(54) a. there's two boxers in a prizefight
　　 b. a prizefight is+in (= has) two boxers
　　 c. [. . . is [in [a prizefight [two boxers]]] . . .]

Figure 5.34

Consider (i):

(i) *[there seem [t have been several riots in town]] (cf. *[several riots seem [t have happened in town]])

Suppose *there* has a Case feature that is checked by Tense. This is the result:

(ii) [[there] Tense . . . [t Tense . . . [several riots] . . .]]
     [Case] [F]   [F]   [Case]

The (hypothesized) Case features of *there* are checked by the [F] feature in the matrix clause, and the [F] feature in the embedded clause appropriately associates to the Case features of *several riots*. The sentence should therefore be grammatical, contrary to fact. If on the other hand *there* has no Case features to check, either the matrix or the embedded [F] feature will remain unchecked. This is because only *several riots* has an appropriate feature for [F] to match up with, and Case features are uninterpretable—and hence erased upon checking. The result is a derivation that crashes at LF, as desired.

In (54a) a pleonastic *there* occupies the subject position. In (54b) there's no such pleonastic, and *a prizefight* has to appear in subject position. Either way, *two boxers* isn't an argument, but a predicate expressing an integral characteristic of prizefights.

O: And only arguments have Case features . . .

L: That's the assumption, yes: Case is a property of arguments, not predicates. That is, the lexicon just has the item *boxer,* with its idiosyncratic codings for PF and LF. The lexicon is just a list of idiosyncrasies, so it doesn't itself encode that *boxer* has Case or regular agreement features. However, by the time *boxer* enters the numeration, it has a specific Case and specific agreement features. When? Only when it's an argument. If it's a predicate, it doesn't behave the same way, and these features generally aren't added (or if they're randomly added, the derivations with these inappropriate features will crash in most languages).

—————————————————— some expletives have only categorial features

O: If this is true, *there* shouldn't have Case features either.

L: That's right, because *there* isn't an argument. This is confirmed by the ungrammaticality of (55b):

(55) a. [there seem [t to have been several riots in town]]
      b. *[there seem [t have been several riots in town]]

Of course, we want the ungrammaticality of (55b) to be akin to that of (41b). But for this to be so, *there* can't be checking Case. Otherwise, *there* could take care of the matrix Case relation with Tense, while (at LF) *several riots* could take care of the embedded one, and the sentence would be predicted to be grammatical—which would mean trouble . . .

O: Well, perhaps *there* hasn't any features, and that's what being a [EXPLETIVE] expletive is [see fig. 5.34]!

L: Maybe . . . Although *there* has to have at least **categorial features,** since it's moving around (for instance in (55a)), and of course also PF features. But I share your intuition about . . . er . . . pleonastics.

O: But why doesn't the system erase *there* if it has no features?

L: It does have categorial features; it's a regular term. And as I said before, eliminating a term from the structure leads to a derivational cancellation. I'll put it in writing:

(56) *Law of Conservation*
    a. No operation can eliminate derivational terms.
    b. All interpretable features that are present in the lexical array
       are present at LF.

We've talked about this informally, now you have it officially. As a result of (56), only nonterms can be erased, and in fact only *uninterpretable* nonterms—that is, a handful of features, as desired.

O: But although *there* is a term, you're nevertheless thinking of it as nothing but a categorial support for a D-feature of some sort, whose sole purpose is to serve as the way to check the strong D-feature of Tense (i.e., to provide a grammatical subject in a language like English).

L: Well, that's what I think about *there,* not about *it!* Observe:

(57) a. it was a man
    b. *it appeared/arrived a man and a woman (cf. (46b))
    c. it was/*were a man and a woman (cf. (46a))
    d. *it was/seems to have been a man arrested (cf. (47))
    e. it was just a man and a woman (*without having identified
       themselves) (cf. (48))

The point is, *it* is also a pleonastic, in that it doesn't have referential import (see (57a)). Nonetheless, *it* behaves unlike *there* in several respects. Thus, it's impossible with most verbs that *there* can occur with (57b); it simply doesn't allow verbal agreement with the postverbal nominal (57c); it can't associate long-distance in situations where *there* would (57d); and it doesn't cooccur with anaphors licensed by the postverbal nominal (57e). So what we have to say about *it* is unlike what we said about *there:* D provides the categorial essence of *there* and its very raison d'être in a derivation; in contrast, *it* has both its own agreement and Case features. As a consequence, *it* doesn't need to (and hence can't, by economy) take an associate.

O: Thanks for telling me, but I wasn't talking about *it* when I said "it," but about *there*.

L: Then why didn't you say *there?*

O: I did, but then I started talking about it and—

L: That's why I was telling you that *it*—

O: Oh, never mind! I understand what you're saying: *there* has only a D-feature, but *it* has more.

L: There! (Don't even think about it!) And this relates to another important distributional property of pleonastic *there:* it (*there*) must have an associate. What does that mean? Well, what's the actual relation between *there* and its associate? One thing is obvious: the features of the associate have to move to the Tense head which the expletive specifies. In other words, the expletive and the associate end up in the same checking domain (where whatever semantic relation holds between the two can be established) [see fig. 5.35]. Why is the associate there? For Case reasons. Why is *there* there? Because of the strong D-feature in Tense. Why do these two needs coincide, relating *there* and the associate? Think of alternative derivations where the associate and the expletive in fact don't end up in the same checking domain. Try, for instance, (58a):

(58) a. *[a child seems [that there is likely [t to be [t crying]]]]

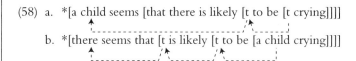

  b. *[there seems that [t is likely [t to be [a child crying]]]]

Why can't *a child* move this way, if the alternative (58b) where it procrastinates doesn't converge—since there are too many Case features for it to check?

O: Precisely for that reason. Just as the Case features of *a child* can't check the Case features of both *is* and *seems* at LF in (58b), so too the overtly moving *a child* can't check these features in (58a).

L: So we don't have to worry about this instance: it's ungrammaticality is directly predicted (and we didn't have to say anything special about the relation between the associate and the expletive). Now try something else:

Figure 5.35

The formal features of the associate adjoin to Tense, which allows its Case and agreement to be checked, and endows it with binding powers:

(i)

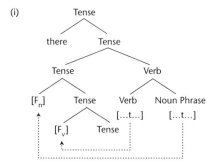

Note also that *there* is very local with respect to the moved features of the associate: they are both within the checking domain of Tense. Whether another, more direct relation between the expletive and the associate is necessary is currently being explored. Possibly the features of the associate move again to adjoin to *there,* in effect derivationally creating a complex nominal expression, with a determiner (*there* with a D-feature) and an associate NP; or perhaps the relation is more abstractly determined in terms of the configuration in (i).

(59) *[a child seems [there to be likely [t to be [t crying]]]]

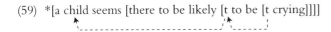

O: Ah, but this time there's clearly a simpler derivation, one that allows *a child* to procrastinate:

(60) [there seems [t to be likely [t to be [a child crying]]]]

L: So again we have an independent reason why the sentence is ungrammatical, without having said anything about the expletive and the associate. Try one more:

(61) [it seems [there to be likely [that a child is crying]]]

O: Hm . . . This one would seem to converge. Needless to say, *there* can't check its Case features, but it hasn't any! I think this is in fact why the sentence converges, since *to be likely* isn't a tensed element, and hence by hypothesis doesn't have features that engage in regular Case checking. And of course the rest of the sentence should be as perfect as *it seems that a child is crying,* where pleonastic *it* checks everything that needs to be checked in the matrix clause (since *it* has Case and agreement features, unlike *there*).

---

interpretive issues concerning expletives

L: However, the sentence is plausibly uninterpretable. It converges without an interpretation, since *there* (which only has a D-feature) hasn't associated to any relevant noun phrase which can depend on this D-feature.

O: Hold on! I thought you just claimed that *there* and the associate needn't be syntactically related.

L: Right. There *is* an interpretive requirement: Ds associate to noun phrases (thus, people don't just say *the* in isolation, they say *the man of La Mancha,* or something like that). But this doesn't need to be stated as a syntactic requirement. If a derivation doesn't meet the requirement, it converges without an interpretation. This sort of reasoning also relates to instances of multiple expletives, which are unacceptable [70]:

(62) *[there seems [there to be a child crying]]

Presumably, the noun phrase *a child* associates to the matrix *there* (since that's where it can check its Case features). But this leaves the intermediate *there* without an associate, which leads to a convergent derivation with no interpretation.

O: This looks like a conspiracy! Every time you try to force *there* and its associate into two different checking domains, something adverse happens . . .

L: Maybe that's all there is to it.

O: You mean to *there* . . .

L: Yeah—don't start again. Which has obvious consequences for a second consideration in dealing with *there* constructions: they just don't mean the same thing as corresponding structures without *there* [71]:

(63) a. anyone isn't likely to be winning the jackpot this time
      b. there isn't likely to be anyone winning the jackpot this time

(63a) is about an event where there's likely to be a winner for the jackpot, although it won't be just anyone; it may be, say, Joe Lucky, who bought half the tickets. In contrast, (63b) is about an event where there's likely to be no winner for the jackpot.

O: Hm . . . If the LFs of (63a) and (63b) were syntactically identical, one would expect the mapping to their respective semantics to be identical, raising a curious puzzle for interpretation.

L: But with the sort of LFs we've given them—which are quite different—what we map to the semantics is also rather different in each case [72]. In one case, (64a), *anyone* is in subject position, while in the other case, (64b), what's in subject position is *there,* with only the formal feature F_n of the associate in the Tense head:

(64) a.

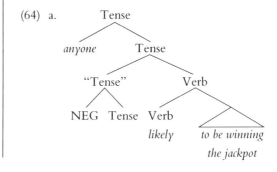

b.

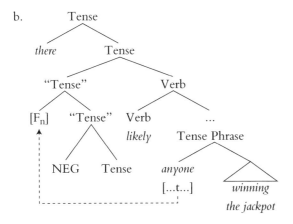

Consider the negative element in Tense (corresponding to *isn't*). Whereas NEG in (64b) commands *anyone* (assuming the "Tense" segments don't block command [see app.]), it clearly doesn't do so in (64a). Suppose the general licensing of words like *anyone* (often called "negative polarity items") is a bit like other binding-type interpretive requirements [see sec. 4.4], thus involving command—in this case from a negative element [73]. So, for instance, while English speakers can say both (65a) and (65b), they can only say (65c)—it isn't possible to say (65d) with the intended meaning:

(65) a. [I [saw no one]]
      b. [no one [saw me]]
      c. [I did [not [see anyone]]]
      d. *[anyone did [not [see me]]]

By the same reasoning, (64a) is predicted to be uninterpretable with the reading 'not . . . anyone', that is, 'no one'. Rather, it's interpretable with the reading 'just anyone' (often called "free-choice *any*"). In other words, (64a) means 'just anyone isn't such that he or she is likely to be winning the jackpot this time'; however, (64b), where *anyone* is licensed under the negative, means 'there's no one such that he or she is likely to be winning the jackpot this time'. Our analysis predicts these facts rather directly [see fig. 5.36]. The point is this: the *there* expletive with D-features and its nominal associate always end up in the same checking domain, and this may relate to their semantic dependencies and subtleties. One of them, as we saw, has to do with the facts in (64). More generally it's sort of curious that the associate of *there* always has to have a peculiar indefinite character [74]:

Figure 5.36

The literature on polarity items is extremely lively and relevant to determining the properties of LF. *Anyone* is actually not a genuine polarity item, since—as free-choice *any* shows—it need not be interpreted under command by a negative (or other sorts of affective and modal operators). Genuine polarity items—like *a living soul* and *a red cent* in English—are typically idiomatic noun phrases with an indefinite character. Consider:

(i)   a. *a living soul isn't likely to be winning the jackpot this time
      b. there isn't likely to be a living soul winning the jackpot this time

(ii) a. *a red cent isn't likely to be showing up in my account any time soon
      b. there isn't likely to be a red cent showing up in my account any time soon

The (a) sentences are directly deviant in interpretation, for the reasons discussed in the text. However, matters are slightly more complex than alluded to there, given examples like (iii), discussed by Linebarger (1980):

(iii) a fellow who matters to a living soul isn't likely to be winning the jackpot this time

(iii) is interpretable, even though *a living soul* does not seem to be in the command domain of the negative. This suggests an analysis of these facts in terms of the "reconstruction" patterns discussed in chapter 4 (Uribe-Etxebarria 1994):

(iv) [[a fellow who matters to a living soul] isn't likely to be [[a fellow who matters to a living soul] winning the jackpot this time]]

The subject of the main clause starts its derivational life in the lower clause, as the subject of *winning the jackpot*. If the trace left by moving this item to subject position is "reconstructed" (that is, if the lexical material is interpreted in its original rather than final position), then the polarity item *a living soul* will be in the command domain of the negative. However, two questions arise. First, should reconstruction be possible with this sort of movement? (Previous examples have involved movement for reasons other than satisfying the subject requirement of Tense.) This issue is still undecided. Second, and more important for the analysis of *there* constructions, if reconstruction is possible in these cases, why are *a living soul* and *a red cent* not under the command of the negative in (ia) and (iia)? Conceivably, the notion that reconstruction always has to leave a quantificational residue in the overt position [see sec. 3.7] plays a role here. As (v) shows, (ia) and (iv) differ in this regard, the polarity item (assuming it is the determiner *a* introducing *living soul*) being commanded by the negative only in (iv):

(v)   a. *[[a . . .] isn't likely to be winning [. . . living soul] the jackpot]
      b. [[a . . .] isn't likely to be [[. . . fellow who matters to a living soul] winning the jackpot]]

(66) a. there is a child crying
     b. *there is the child crying (*not to be confused with* THERE
         [speaker points] is the child crying)
     c. *there is Bart crying
     d. *there is everyone crying
     e. *there are most people crying
     f. there are many/three children crying (cf. the children crying
         are many/three)

(66a) is fine, but (66b) is strange. Same thing with names: it's kind of funny to say (66c). Ditto with a variety of real quantifiers (66d–e) as opposed to quantifiers which have an indefinite character to them (66f). Well, one possible approach to this effect is to look at *there* as a D-element, with familiar restrictions. Thus, for instance, we can say *the many/three people I know,* but not *the most/every person(s) I know.* At the same time, we can say *Bart,* but not (at least in English) *the Bart.* So maybe we can't say *there is the child crying* for essentially the same reason we can't say *the the child is crying*—an interpretive impossibility. And we can't say *there is everyone crying* for the same reason we can't say *the everyone.* But we can say *there are many children crying* for the same reason we can say *the many children.* From this perspective, there's nothing obviously wrong with the syntax of *there is the child crying.* It's just that when it comes down to interpretation, *there* and *the child* are in the same checking domain, and the only way to interpret *there*'s D-feature is through a structure like that of *the the child*—which arguably has no interpretation. Actually, I should add: in languages where it's possible to say *the Bart* and so on, it should also be possible to say things like *there's Bart crying.*

O: As indeed Galician speakers can do . . . For example, *o Xan* (literally 'the Xan'), and *cando houbo a Xan, habia moita ledicia* 'when there was Xan, there was lots of happiness' (literally 'when we had Xan, we had much happiness') [75].

L: Then again, note that these restrictions don't arise with *it,* even if it is a pleonastic. So *it's just the child/Bart/every child (crying)* is fine. This confirms the distinction between these two pleonastic elements.

5.7 Heads and Tails

(pertaining to the number of chains it takes to tie up the fabled Cheshire cat)

O: But enough about covert attraction and related conspiracies! I should like to return to overt ones, and the number of chains they involve. Given our definitions, there are two chains in (67), not one:

(67) [[the Cheshire cat] [is likely [t_2 [to [appear t_1 any minute now]]]]]

Movement #1 forms the first chain, so as to satisfy the strong D-feature of the intermediate Tense; and movement #2 forms the second chain, which satisfies the strong D-feature of the matrix Tense. The mechanics are now straightforward.

_____ relevant chains

L: But let's be precise. What you called *1* and *2* in (67) aren't chains, but instances of Move/Attract [76]. Although each movement does create a chain, it's not the case that the first chain being created goes from the intermediate trace t_2 to the initial trace t_1. Rather, it goes from *the Cheshire cat* to t_1, as in (68). More precisely, this chain associates two phrase markers: the very small *appear*—which t_1 is a sister of—and the much larger *is likely t_2 to appear t_1*—which *the Cheshire cat* is a sister of, after movement. In turn, the second chain goes from the medium-sized phrase marker *to appear t_1*—a sister to t_2—all the way up to the larger *is likely t_2 to appear t_1*. Graphically:

(68) [α [is likely [t_2 [to appear t_1...]]]]]

CH$_2$ = (K, L)

CH$_1$ = (K, appear)

K = [is likely [t_2 [to [appear t_1...]]]]
L = [to [appear t_1...]]
α = the Cheshire cat

The two chains are in a sense "headed" by *the Cheshire cat*—which I'm representing as α for operational ease—although α's traces are different terms in the configurational structure. Generally, one can be more informal than is implied in (68); but you should keep in mind that this is really what's going on.

O: My question is this: it would seem as though there should be something like a single chain in (67)—as a matter of fact, CH$_1$—at least for interpretive purposes. That is to say, I can easily grant you that *the Cheshire cat scratched Alice* has two chains, one for *Alice* and one for *the Cheshire cat.* But two chains in a case like (67)—that's harder to swallow.

L: The relevant structure in (67) has the rough abstract shape in (69):

(69)

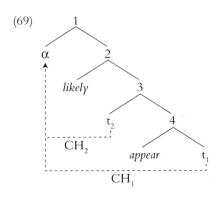

The intuition to pursue is that CH_1 gets interpreted at LF, and CH_2 gets eliminated.

O: Yes, but how on Earth is this done?

_____ chain integrity

L: The idea is that, for both the PF and LF components, the very raising of α in (69) deletes the irrelevant intermediate traces (they can't be erased because they're terms, given the Law of Conservation in (56)); of course, the initial trace can't be deleted, since it's the carrier of the semantic role "logical-object-of-*appear.*" So all intermediate traces are invisible for interpretability purposes, and only the larger object CH_1 in (69) is appropriately interpreted. This is very possibly a profound property of chains, understood as lexical objects which extend beyond their lexical reach. The way we're seeing them, chains don't have accessible parts—they act as a whole, as far as C_{HL} is concerned:

(70) *Principle of Chain Integrity*
   Only entire chains enter into C_{HL} operations.

(70) can be argued for independently, with cases like (71) [77]:

(71) a. who have last week's scandals caused [rumors about _____]?

(last week's scandals have caused rumors about the president)

b. *who have [rumors about _____] caused last week's scandals?

(rumors about the president have caused last week's scandals)

Why should (71b) be less grammatical than (71a)? They're both sensible questions, so why is one good and the other bad? Of course, the question is where the examples in (71) differ structurally.

O: Evidently, in one instance you're extracting *who* from inside the complement of the verb (71a), and in the other you're extracting it from inside the subject (71b). Subjects come first, which means that subjects command objects. Indeed, we even know that (at least in English), all sentences have an overt subject, which we encode in terms of the checking of a strong feature in Tense. It's this feature that attracts the subject to the specifier of Tense, while the object remains as the complement of the verb. Structurally, these are rather different, and also in terms of chains: the object's chain is trivial, containing one member only, whereas the subject's chain has two members, since the subject has taken a free ride with the feature that Tense has attracted. Visually:

(72) a. $[_{CP}$ *wh-* $[_{IP}$ ... $[_{VP}$ ... $[_{NP}$ ...t...]]]]

b. $[_{CP}$ *wh-* $[_{IP}[_{NP}$ ...t...] ... $[_{VP}[t]$...]]]

L: Right. So suppose we capitalize on this structural difference to explain the ungrammaticality of the movement of *who* in (72b). Why should this structural difference have any consequences? The movement is perfectly cyclic, it seems to employ regular transformational devices, it would seem to have a totally trivial interpretation, and it even appears to be more local than the one in (72a). So what could possibly be wrong? Consider the chain of the subject in (72b), whose tail is a trace inside VP. Again, this movement is perfect (it has to be, since it's nothing but regular movement to the specifier of Tense). But: what happens in this chain when the *wh*-element gets extracted from its head?

O: The extraction leaves a trace. What's wrong with that? Oh, I see: the Principle of Chain Integrity's been violated! *Who's* been extracted from the first element of the chain alone, thereby breaking the integrity of the subject chain.

L: This is of course rather different from the situation in (72a). There *who* gets moved from inside a configurational structure which isn't part of a nontrivial chain; we don't breach the integrity of any chain whatsoever. Next consider (73):

(73) a. [what [have you said [t [the president has done t]]]]?

b. $[_{CP}$ wh- $[_{IP}$ ... $[_{CP}$ t $[_{IP}$ ...t]]]]

This case is analogous to (67), except here we're moving a *wh*-element. The important point is that the second movement extends the reach of the first chain formed—thus, it extends the entire chain. The good and the bad chain processes can be shown side by side, as follows:

(74) a. [wh- [... [t   [...t]]   OK

    CH$_2$

    CH$_1$

b. [wh- [[...t...] ...[[t]...]]]   not OK

    CH$_2$ CH$_1$

Roughly speaking, in (74a) the first chain "grows" because of the second movement (the one which creates the second chain). In (74b) no such "growth" takes place; rather, the second movement creates its own chain, which moves from inside the head of the first chain, flatly violating the Principle of Chain Integrity. In a word, this principle predicts that chains are *opaque:* nothing can be moved from inside one of their links [78].

---

further predictions of Chain Integrity

O: Well, once again we indirectly observe a phenomenon which is invisible to the naked eye—or should I say inaudible to the naked ear—the conservation of structural integrity on the part of a chain. Most interesting! As before, though, I must raise empirical questions to test the validity of this theoretical move. The first immediate consideration is what happens in the chain of the object in the LF component. Although I myself can see the answer. The structure in (72a) is unaffected by LF movement, since you've extracted *who* before the LF component. But this makes a prediction for languages that move objects in the overt syntax, like Basque: it shouldn't be possible to extract from these moved elements—that is to say, objects in Basque should be as opaque for extraction as subjects are in English. And I'm sure you know that the Basque equivalent of (71a) is, as a matter of fact, quite atrocious [79]:

(75) *nori buruzko sortu zituzten aurreko asteko istiluek
      who   about-of create aux   last   week   scandals
      zurrumurruak?
      rumours
      'who have last week's scandals caused [rumours about ＿＿]?'

L: Of course I knew that.

O: Good. Now, my second question concerns the status of (73), and very specifically the intermediate movement, which is by no means an obvious movement/attraction. According to our assumptions, checking must take place here, just as it does at the top. I wonder whether a type of sentence that has always puzzled me could be explained along these lines. It's an example in colloquial German [80]:

(76) [was [hast du   gesagt [t was [der Präsident gemacht hat t]]]]?
      what have you said   what the president done   has
      'what have you said that the president has done?'

What's the second *was* doing here?

L: Can you answer that too?

O: I couldn't possibly . . .

L: But I insist.

O: Well, if I must . . . If your hypothesis about (73) is correct, then this intermediate *was*—literally 'what', though it doesn't really mean 'what' here—would be nothing but a mark of agreement with the moved, meaningful *was* [81]. To be specific, there must be a formal feature that the moved *wh*-element checks in this intermediate position, and colloquial German proves the point rather directly.

L: Many languages present that kind of evidence, actually—even a stage of child English [82].

O: Really?!

L: Children say things like this:

(77) [what d' [you think [what [Cookie Monster eats t]]]]?

O: Oh, that's lovely. Then there must be something deeply correct about this intermediate step, which allows the formation of a long chain across an intermediate position with no semantic content . . . I wonder, though . . . how does the system know that it should delete the intermediate link which constitutes the head of CH_2 in (69), for example? Or the intermediate, uninterpretable *what* in (77), for that matter! Granted, deletion yields the right result, but how does the system, obtuse as it is, have the mind to undertake deletion?

L: Because if it didn't, these structures wouldn't converge. See, these are cases where the crucial operative transformation isn't Move/Attract, but Delete. But just as movement is sometimes necessary for convergence, here deletion is necessary for convergence.

O: And deletion can take place without violating the Law of Conservation, because the deleted elements are actually encoded elsewhere in the structure . . . Why, it's another conspiracy . . .

———————————————————————————————— domains of conservation

L: It can happen.

O: Now, we've talked about chain integrity (70) and about lexical integrity (24), and I wonder whether these are the same integrity, at different dimensions. Is it not the case that sublexical units don't "speak to" elements outside the domain of their lexical integrity, just as subchain units don't "speak to" elements outside their chain?

L: I really don't know whether we're seeing the same kind of integrity in both cases; all I know is it exists. It's a bit like asking a physicist whether the conservation of this quantity is the same as the conservation of that quantity; maybe it is (e.g., matter and energy), and then again maybe it isn't, or at least not obviously (e.g., the sorts of conservation involving particle/antiparticle relations).

O: Then let me push the symmetry a bit. Please recall your very interesting graph in (69), which I shall now repeat in (78a). The very sight of this graph suggests the modification in (78b):

(78) a.

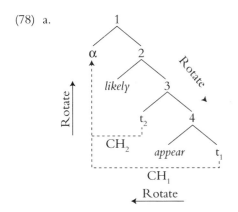

b.

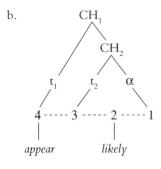

(78b) has the same information as (78a); I've simply rotated it clockwise to a more familiar sort of alignment (I've also projected *appear* and *likely* downwards—in part to get them out of the way, and in part because directionality means nothing whatever prior to PF). Now, I don't really intend to put words in your mouth, but did you not imply that chains are merely instances of a higher-order Supermerge, where the constituent items aren't selected from a numeration, but instead are taken from a phrase marker that's already been assembled (using Merge at a lower dimension)?

L: I don't recall saying that; what would be the advantage of expressing things that way?

O: For one, the integrity of chains now reduces to the integrity of lexical items.

L: How? Maybe I haven't been clear enough about this, but the integrity of lexical items is a morphological issue.

O: Very well, but the question I'm trying to pose is whether the Principle of Chain Integrity is the Principle of Lexical Integrity at a higher level.

L: At what level?

O: I'm thinking of it as a chain dimension. You talked today about trivial and nontrivial chains, a distinction that presupposes a unified notion of "chain." But it isn't fully clear what that is, since trivial chains appear to be just words, whereas nontrivial chains result from movement operations. It's my humble yet considered opinion that the chain dimension is where this chain invariance is expressed. Indeed, to make things crystal clear and push them to their natural limit, let us say that it's LF where the chain dimension is determined—after all, isn't LF about chains?

L: So what you're suggesting is that the Principle of Chain Integrity is the LF reflex of the Principle of Lexical Integrity, for LF a syntactic level of representation (while lexical integrity holds of WI representations).

O: I frankly thought that was what you were saying, the intuition in the end being that whereas chains are formed by movement from elements in the derivation, phrases are formed by merger from elements in the numeration. In any event, the nodes in the graph in (78b) are certainly intended to represent LF objects—or chains. The edges in the graph directly represent phrasal relations, as well as more elaborate movement-chain relations. But before I point out a further advantage that I've come to suspect this idea has, I'd like to ask you this: how is it possible, in your view, for C_{HL} to delete the intermediate link of a chain without violating the Principle of Chain Integrity?

───────────────────────   *could chains involve some sort of "superprojection"?*

L: Technically, in a situation like (67) what we want to delete is CH$_2$, the whole of it. The chain is formed just in order to carry *the Cheshire cat* upward, appropriately checking intervening features (e.g., in the intermediate subject site). But CH$_2$ has no status at LF, and should disappear.

O: I understand. But exactly how does CH$_2$ disappear? If we merely delete the term t_2, we'd seem to be violating the Principle of Chain Integrity. Specifically, deleting the tail of a chain isn't an operation on the entire chain. If in contrast you tell me that the operation affects the entire chain, then I shall ask, what kind of transformation is that? Up to now, transformations have involved a regular category τ within a target phrase marker K, and have proceeded to modify K by either copying τ, or deleting it, or even erasing it altogether if it's not a term—hence, its erasure doesn't destroy the entire phrasal structure above it. But now you're suggesting that a transformation can involve an entire chain, that is to say, a pair of phrase markers K and M [see (25)].

L: I see what you mean, but we need to say something like that for (successive) movement as well, except this time what we target is the head of the chain, not its tail. In other words, if we want to delete a chain, we attack it from below; in contrast, if we want to extend a chain, we pull on it from above. It's a bit like a house of cards. We can add cards on top of what's there, but if we take cards out from underneath, the house collapses.

O: But you see, my friend, the card-house image works also to indicate how regular phrase markers grow, and how their terms can't be erased. The first half of the metaphor corresponds to the cyclic nature of transformations, which we've argued about at such length [see sec. 4.3]; and the second half corresponds to your idea that terms can't be erased, for the structure above them would collapse after the erasure. This is what the Law of Conservation is designed to prevent, when terms are involved. Hence, the same law, although applying at a higher dimension, would determine when to eliminate a chain: precisely when it does not contribute to interpretation. What I'm trying to suggest is that these correspondences are not accidental [see fig. 5.37]. Rather, the construction of a chain seems to me to be very much like the construction of a phrase, warping, as it were, out of the domain of regular phrase markers. The stock

Figure 5.37

(i) a. *Standard chain structures*   b. *Rotated graphs*

(ii) *Standard Merge*

(iii) *Possible formal correspondences between (ib) and (ii)*

(iv) *Possible mechanisms for chain superprojection*

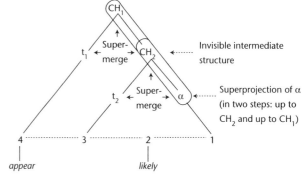

that chains work with isn't lexical items from a numeration, but items that have already been selected and placed in a phrase marker, which "stretch out" (to the checking domains of other categories in the phrase marker) by a sort of Supermerge that involves their copy (in these checking domains that host them). As a matter of principle, C_{HL} can apply this superoperation as often as it likes, so long as it moves according to the principles that we've assumed to govern Attract. The result will be a more and more complex super-projection of the lexical item that moves. This gives concrete formal meaning to your first intuition (that the chain is extended by "pulling on it from above"). Movement stretches the chain because superprojection, just like regular projection, cannot move inwards; it always extends structure. Your second intuition (that to delete a chain, one attacks it from below) is instantiated in terms of letting the tail of the chain project. Viewed from the perspective of the super–phrase markers generated by Supermerge, the head of the structure is also what we've been calling the head of the chain (that is to say, its top element), which determines what the extended chains are chains of. Put differently, we can think of movement of α as a way of superprojecting α, so that it takes itself (or one of its superprojections) as a supersister. Then the fact that the chains which do not superproject (the intermediate chains) are invisible for interpretation is a subcase of the fact that intermediate projections are invisible to LF [83].

L: That's worth exploring, though it seems a little too abstract for a technical implementation of the intuition I was pushing, involving not-altogether-clear devices like "superthis" and "superthat."

O: Oh, but the way I see it "superthis" and "superthat" are simply "this" and "that," except at a higher dimension.

L: Yeah, but then you have to justify those higher dimensions, and that's hard enough with the lower dimensions we've explored. Besides, I think there are good reasons to keep words and chains separate [see chap. 6].

O: . . .

L: . . .

feature attraction: the final frontier

O: Well, I should like to take the opportunity to make my case.

L: What opportunity? Which case?

O: I assure you it won't take a minute. Observe first some full-fledged projections using my bubbles from the other day. Something interesting happens, look [see fig. 5.38].

L: Something very interesting indeed: your picture's a mess!

O: Well, that's the point, thank you. It's easy to keep track of a few bubbles, but beyond a couple of levels of embedding, the picture becomes very convoluted. The outer bubbles don't let us see what's going on at their core: we see only what went on in the last couple of embeddings; after that, it's a complete muddle. Hence, observe that I've taken away the outer layer in the bubbles to the right of the big, fat bubble, so that you see what went on inside them; in contrast, I've kept the outer layer in the central (and real) bubble, so that you see that you see nothing (very specifically, none of the structural relations that the derivational history has been creating).

L: So this just shows that your bubbles are of little use to us . . .

O: Au contraire! I submit that ending up with an informational scrap heap after a bout of construction is very intriguing, indeed. Do think now of how we could make sense of this picture. How would you like to travel inside the largest bubble [in fig. 5.38], which corresponds to the present state of the phrase marker? (Once again, the other bubbles are merely "afterimages" of the derivational history, and "retouched" ones at that [see fig. 5.39]!) And what have we there? Dark, on your left, is the specifier; the very centre of the figure is occupied by the small head; and the large object to your right is the complement. Notice that the head and the complement are enclosed by a polyhedron which C_{HL} doesn't even see—though it's there in the structure, keeping the head and the complement together [see sec. 3.4]. The complement is, evidently, the minimal domain of the head: what C_{HL} actually sees inside the large bubble we just entered. If you care to think of the central head bubble as the "planet" you occupy, your minimal do-

Figure 5.38

main comprises the objects in the "gravitational system" around you (the big bubble delimiting your bubble universe, which we're looking into [in fig. 5.39]); those are your complement and your specifier(s). (The polyhedron only determines an abstract, structural space—not something that's relevant for bubble relations within the system.) Right. Now, now: what is movement?

L: You tell me . . .

O: Do you like cheese?

L: I beg your pardon . . .

O: Swiss cheese! You see, the way I picture them, if you'll allow me, chains are a bit like the wormholes of syntax, existing within derivational horizons as holes do in Swiss cheese, which—needless to say—worms could actually use to crawl from one area to another . . . Do you follow me?

L: Revolting!

O: That's quite all right. If you think of it, I'm simply trying to bring things down to the realm of *natural* science . . .

L: If that's the price, forget it.

O: Really, how dare you! Now, say you live in the central bubble we're studying [in fig. 5.39]. From there, you can survey your dominion: your complement and your specifier. But what if you wished to receive a visit or . . . a worm friend from the inner world . . . someone who owes you something, and should pay you with a personal cheque—or check! Well, this is what wormholes are good for, isn't it? Here: I shall open a door in the complement domain of the central bubble [see fig. 5.40]. See? You can peep right through it, giving you access to the inner bubbles! And now you can directly think of movement as the process of attraction that you had in mind. For example, imagine you have an attractor beam—as it were—in your comfortable head bubble, to pull objects from the inner bubbles with some specific features that serve your purposes—roughly in the same way that one can turn a glove inside out by reaching into its fingers and . . . pulling! The attractor beam can't be choosy: the first object that it finds down there with the relevant

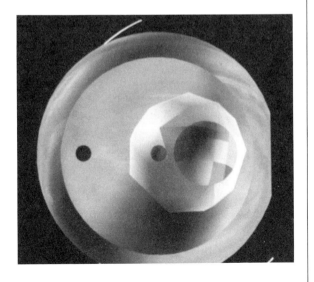

Figure 5.39

features will be sucked up to the dimension of your bubble. Furthermore, if this attractor beam operates only across the dimensions of the successive bubbles (that is to say, it works only through wormholes), then it won't attract objects in your own object-space, will it? Likewise, once it penetrates a deep bubble-space, across a wormhole, it'll attract all objects in that space with equal strength. This is how we've characterised distance. Why do I bother to say all of this? Firstly, because I'm better with pictures than with words. But secondly, because I find that, on a larger scale, locality appears to be a central property of our universe, where things don't usually happen at a distance without affecting intervening things. One of the reasons I so like those Fibonacci patterns [see sec. 1.6] is that, evidently, such series are directly based on growing by incrementing a previous element within the series. Eight "talks to" 13 in the same way that 13 "talks to" 21, et cetera. It is through this local "conversation" that the series is generated. Relations of this sort might be a central feature of syntactic extension, biological growth, or certain fields for that matter. Then chain conditions like the MLC and the LRC might in the end follow from deeper properties of the universe at large . . . Right. The idea is very simple: Merge is always local, whether it's expressed as the simple merger of lexical items or as the complex supermerger of chains in the next dimension. Supermerge looks a bit less local than Merge merely because it's operating on a different scale. Nevertheless, at an appropriate level of abstraction, one . . . Er . . . Mr. Such-and-such, are you still there? . . . Sir? . . . Heavens, this is getting to be quite a bore—whenever I'm trying to get a good line in, he disappears!

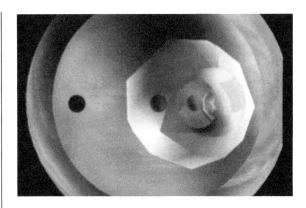

Figure 5.40

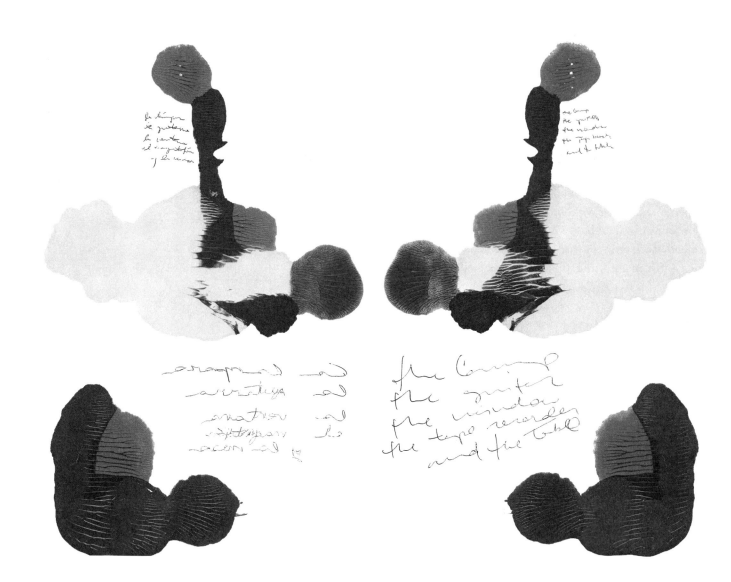

L: You look radiant today . . .

O: I am. We've eliminated our author!!

L: Oh?

O: Remember the chilling face against the background of the wormhole? It was gone today.

L: How d'you know it wasn't the reader's face?

O: I don't. Readers, authors—who cares? What are people up to when they break loose?

L: . . .

O: Oedipus had a thunderous row with his father, but then he went back to his mum's place (that was a mistake). Adam and Eve . . . at least they started procreating. Faust? Oh, he was a bore!

L: . . .

O: Personally, I hate fate.

L: How do you suppose we eliminated them?

O: Confusion!

L: Great. So now what?

O: For starters, we needn't have these witless dialogues at the beginning of each chapter.

L: That's a plus.

O: So let's get cracking, shall we? I've been thinking . . .

L: Yes?

O: . . . about the fact that minimal domains—well, they should be independently motivated. That is to say, these set-theoretic domains make an excellent job of characterising distance for movement transformations. But what other tricks can we do with them? If we can't demonstrate their value independently of the analysis of movement, one might argue that the notion of a minimal domain is merely a useful way of discussing locality, reflecting more on our manner of investigation than on what we're actually investigating. In contrast, if we're able to show the relevance of minimal domains anywhere else in the grammar, then it's much more plausible that they should be relevant for locality as well: the grammar needs minimal domains for such-and-such a purpose, and once their existence has been adduced, voilà! the grammar uses them in determining, for example, distance—perhaps in other areas as well. That, of course, makes a tidier picture. Now, I certainly see that checking domains are a subset of minimal domains. Under the umbrella of a given category X, the specifiers and the adjuncts to the head are obviously dependents of X, and it's within this set of dependents that checking relations obtain. Right? Right. However, consider the complement of X. You indicated yesterday that checking never takes place in complements—rather, it takes place in specifiers and head adjuncts. Then what on Earth is the complement doing? If it's not part of the checking domain, is it nonetheless part of the minimal domain? Formally, it would seem as though complements should be included in minimal domains, for the simple reason that the complement of X is as much a dependent of X as the specifier of X is—if anything, the complement's dependency is even clearer [see fig. 6.1]!

6.1 Internal Domains

(wherein they are introduced with examples, and the distinction is drawn between inflectional and derivational morphology)

---

arguments for arguments

L: So we need the notion "**internal domain**" to capture the relation between a head and what we can call its "internal argument(s)." Of course, the relation that holds between a verb and its direct object is very intimate—more so than that between a verb and its subject [1]. Consider (1):

Figure 6.1

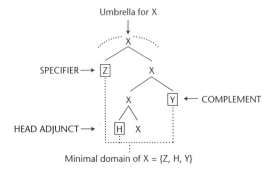

Umbrella for X

SPECIFIER →

X

HEAD ADJUNCT →

Y ← COMPLEMENT

Minimal domain of X = {Z, H, Y}

(1) a. the queen broke a nut
   b. the queen broke her arm
   c. the queen broke the news
   d. the queen broke into tears

What the queen is taken to be doing in each example is quite different. It's also intuitively clear that what the queen does in each case is a function not just of the verb *broke*, but also of the argument this verb takes.

O: But presumably this is all semantics . . .

L: It would be all semantics if there weren't any structural restrictions of the kind we've been seeing all along. However, there are very powerful restrictions constraining the distribution of internal arguments. To see this, let's look at a counterpart to (1), this time involving "external arguments" of the verb *broke:*

(2) a. the queen broke a nut
   b. a nutcracker broke a nut
   c. pressure broke a nut

Here we've changed the subject, keeping the direct object constant. The meaning is of course different in each case, but it's not obvious that it changes as drastically as in (1): in all of (2a–c) we're talking about the same breaking action, while in each of (1a–d) the action is different [see fig. 6.2]. The point is, whatever role *the queen* plays in (1), it's what can be called "compositional," in that it depends on the composition of the various elements making up the verb phrase. In contrast, whatever role *a nut* plays in (2), it doesn't depend on a relation between the subject and *broke*. This is what we'd expect, given the syntax we've been developing.

O: Because we hypothesise a phrase that includes the verb and the object, but not one that includes just the verb and the subject [see fig. 6.1].

L: Precisely. And there's other empirical evidence that proves this hypothesis. Take idiom formation. English speakers say things like *kick-the-bucket,* where a verb and its complement make up a unit of lexical meaning. We don't find similar idioms made up of a verb and its subject.

Figure 6.2

Different internal arguments:

(a) is a regular breaking action;
(b) is an accident resulting in a fracture;
(c) is an informative action;
(d) is an experience in frustration.

The relation between the verb and its internal argument is direct:

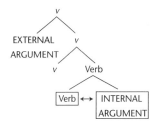

Different external arguments:

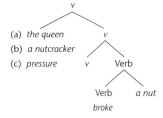

(a) is a breaking action with the agent specified;
(b) is a breaking action with the instrumental agent specified;
(c) is a breaking action with the cause specified.

The relation between the verb and the external argument is indirect; namely, there is a compositional relation between the external argument and the relation between the verb and the internal argument:

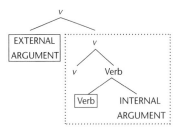

Figure 6.3

Idioms of the form Verb-Object (and a variable subject):

Someone . . .
    gave-[her-blessing] (granted permission).
    gave-[tongue] (cried out).
    got-[his-way] (obtained what he wanted).
    had-[a-ball] (enjoyed herself).
    had-[it] (reached the limit of accepting a situation).
    hit-[rock-bottom] (reached a downward limit).
    kicked-[the-bucket] (died).
    led-[the-way] (showed leadership).
    opened-[a-can-of-worms] (raised an issue that leads to multiple problems).
    sat-on-[his-butt] (did nothing).
    struck-[a-bargain] (obtained a good result).
    threw-[a-tantrum] (got violently and unreasonably angry).
    took-[a-back-seat] (stayed out of the center of attention).
    took-[a-blow] (got hurt).
    took-[charge] (assumed responsibility).
    took-[her-chances] (gambled).
    took-[his-time] (acted slowly and deliberately).
    took-[it] (accepted a situation).

Similar idioms of the form Subject-Verb (and a variable object) do not seem to exist.

O: What about, and excuse my language, *shit happens?!*

L: Surprising as it may seem, I can show you that the grammatical subject is actually in some deep sense the object of *happens* in that idiom, and not its subject—thus proving my point. But before I do that, let me just clarify what I mean in general. Idioms of the form *x Verb Object* are common; however, logically possible idioms of the form *Subject Verb x* don't seem to exist [see fig. 6.3].

O: Hm . . . Let's try, shall we say, . . . er, *the-Devil-take x.* Now *the-Devil-take* might have an idiomatic reading like 'the Hell with', and the object of that idiom would refer to the person who's being sent there. So *the-Devil-take you* would have an idiomatic reading like 'the Hell with you'. God damn it! It's difficult even to illustrate what you could possibly mean!

L: All right, all right, you've made your point . . . But see, those are less idiomatic than mythical or colorful statements. When you say you want the devil to take somebody, you mean what you're saying (something like 'get lost'), more or less the same way you say you're in heaven when you're happy. That's slightly different from saying somebody kicked the bucket when they died. If you're not a native English speaker, you're going to have a very hard time understanding that idiom, since the meaning of the whole expression isn't a function of the meaning of its parts. In contrast, you won't have any problem with *I'm in heaven* or *the devil take you,* even if they're said to you in Chinese.

O: Good move. For example, the Chinese say *chao-youyu* 'fry squid' [2].

L: . . . ?

O: To mean 'dismiss'! If I dismiss you, you're fried squid . . .

L: So there you go . . . The bottom line is, there's something deep about these lexical relations expressed in the internal domain of a head. A similar relation, which in fact bears on what I want to show you about verbs with only one argument, is what's called "incorporation" [3]. Take (3):

(3) a.   Canadians hunt seals
    b.   Canadians seal-hunt
    c.   *Canadian-hunt seals

(3b) has roughly the same meaning as (3a). Descriptively, the logical object incorporates into the verb *hunt,* producing a complex verb *seal-hunt,* which basically means 'hunt seals'. But try doing that incorporation with the logical subject of (3a), to produce a complex verb which should basically mean 'the activity of hunting by Canadians'. That's just terrible, as we can see from (3c)—which should mean 'the activity of hunting by Canadians targets seals'.

O: Almost unimaginable! (Although of course the intended meaning of the expression is perfectly imaginable, and true in the real world.)

———————————————————————— different intransitive verbs

L: Next let's return to intransitive verbs like *happen* and how they relate to their single argument. Let's decide, first, what should be the syntactic representation for something like *several funny things happened.* To start with, we can try something simpleminded like this:

(4) [_{TP}several funny things [_{VP} happened]]

This should clearly be our initial hypothesis, but now think about what concrete operations would yield such a representation . . .

O: According to our assumptions, the subject in (4) moves to the specifier of Tense in order to check the strong features of the English Tense. But the subject actually starts inside the verb phrase; that's the way a verb phrase is projected, by relating the verb to its argument(s)—unless the verb has no arguments (for example, I presume, *rain* in *it rains*). That reduces our structural possibilities to something like (5):

(5) [_{TP} several funny things [_{VP} happened (several funny things)]]

Now, if we relate *several funny things* and *happened,* we'll get a projection of *happened* (that is to say, roughly: {happened, {happened, [several funny things]}}). But if I'm not mistaken, that must mean that, by definition, *several funny things* is actually the complement of *happened* . . .

L: My point exactly [4]. In fact, *several funny things* is obviously the object of *happen* in a sentence like *there happened several funny things.*

Figure 6.4

Some intransitive verbs that may appear with pleonastic *there:*

(i) a. *Appear:* In the mating season, there appear huge clouds of butterflies in the Mexican forests.

    b. *Arrive:* As if from nowhere, there arrived a flock of hungry seagulls.

    c. *Come:* There comes a time when every animal must die.

    d. *Emerge:* All of a sudden, there emerged several humpback whales.

    e. *Exist:* There exist no large animals without a robust internal skeleton.

    f. *Happen:* There happen two major events in the metamorphosis of a caterpillar.

Some intransitive verbs that may not appear with pleonastic *there:*

(ii) a. *Breathe:* *Soon after birth, there breathe some creatures.

    b. *Dine:* *When their long-awaited food is brought to them, there dine some cubs.

    c. *Laugh:* *When the jackals howled, there laughed a bunch of hyenas.

    d. *Rest:* *After a tiring hunt, there rested the female lions.

    e. *Sit:* *Patiently waiting, there sat a baboon on the ground.

    f. *Walk:* *At some point during their first year of life, there walk some mammals.

Figure 6.5

It is precisely because heads take dependents that they project; given the system discussed in section 1.1, the vacuous projection of a head without a dependent (as in (ii)) is senseless. A verb phrase thus cannot project if it has no complement. That is, whereas (i) is an acceptable projection, (ii) is not:

(i)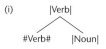

(ii)

Figure 6.6

The intuition behind the analysis in this section (due to Hale and Keyser (1993)) is that a pure intransitive verb (e.g., *bathe*) involves incorporation of a noun (here, *bath*) into an abstract verbal element (here, having the import of 'take'):

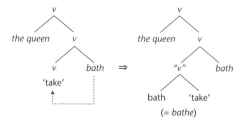

O: Do all intransitive verbs work like that?

L: Only some. For instance, *a queen bathes* is fine, but not **there bathed a queen.* The availability or unavailability of a *there* paraphrase tells you whether a verb with a single argument is a pure intransitive (such as *bathe*) or not [see fig. 6.4]. And then we have to wonder whether the sort of structure in (5) describes a verb like *bathe*.

O: But I'm not certain there's much of a choice! If a verb's single argument is located inside the verb phrase, how can the verb phrase be other than the one in (5)? We can't stipulate that a single argument is a specifier and not a complement; that makes no sense, given how phrases project [see fig. 6.5].

L: That's right; but in fact we can have it both ways. The intuition is that pure intransitive verbs like *bathe* have a more complex internal structure than they seems to at first. Consider a minimal pair: *bathe* and *arrive*. You can say *the queen took a long bath,* but you can't say **the queen took a long arrival.* This is suggestive. Plausibly, the simple verb *bathe* has as much internal structure as its periphrastic form *take a bath.*

O: So a verb like *bathe* is in essence *bath-take* (by analogy with *seal-hunt*) . . .

L: Basically. The main difference, of course, would be that *seal-hunt* comes out as a compound, while *bathe* comes out as a single lexical item, perhaps because the element that *bath* incorporates into is a *v* element with no phonological content. If this is correct, the problem of representing the subject of *bathe* disappears: syntactically, it's the subject of a *transitive* light verb, of which *bath* is the (implicit) object [see fig. 6.6] [5].

O: However, not all intransitive verbs that I can think of have a paraphrase with *take.* One can't say **John took a long talk,* for example.

L: Yeah, but *John had a long talk* is okay. Some verbs have paraphrases with *have,* some have them with *get* or *give;* others don't have a paraphrase like this at all. But we still postulate the same basic structure for them if they don't tolerate the paraphrase with *there* (or if they don't pass similar tests in other languages) [see fig. 6.7]. Why verbs don't all behave alike, and instead have relatively idiosyncratic prop-erties, is an important matter I'd like to discuss today. But for now we can assume that these ideas are roughly on the right track, which is what the theory predicts.

_____ verbs with two internal arguments

O: I can see that we need internal domains to express all that. Only a phrase from an internal domain can incorporate, form an idiom, or provide a compositional interpretation for a role . . .

L: That's the crucial point. Needless to say, the internal argument of a verb should remain its internal argument regardless of verb move-ment—otherwise, the minute a verb raises to Tense and so on, it would lose its connection to the very basic lexical properties we've just been discussing.

O: But what about the converse? Couldn't a head actually gain an internal argument by moving upwards, contrary to what you said yesterday [see sec. 5.3]?

L: I don't think so, no. It's a general fact about heads that they don't move around to gain arguments.

O: And what, precisely, does that follow from?

L: Yeah, that's an important and very difficult question that I'd like to talk about. But first let me illustrate the basic claim with a set of cases that might, on the face of it, look like a counterexample. Abstractly, the situation is this: Preposition (Prep) moves to merge with a *v* shell, within a structure like (6) [6]:

(6)

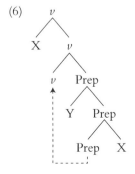

Figure 6.7

None of the verbs in (i) of figure 6.4 have periphrastic counterparts of the form *verb+noun;* however, all of those in (ii) do:

(i) a. *Breathe:* Please *take a (deep) breath!*
   b. *Dine:* Did you *have dinner?*
   c. *Laugh:* At last we *had a laugh* about it . . .
   d. *Rest:* I didn't *get any rest* after my trip.
   e. *Sit:* Don't wait for me—*have a seat.*
   f. *Walk:* Did you finally *take a walk* last night?

Interestingly, in languages like Basque verbal forms correspond-ing to the *arrive* class differ substantially from those corresponding to the *breathe* class:

(ii) a. Jon   etorri zen
      Jon-O arrive III-be-past
      'Jon arrived'

   b. Jonek arnasa hartu zuen
      Jon-S breath take III-have-past-III
      'Jon took-a-breath (= breathed)'

Note, first, that in (iia) the "subject" *Jon* is (obligatorily) in object Case (intuitively, the way to say *John arrived* in Basque is 'there arrived John', with the name in object position). Second, observe that the auxiliary verb that (obligatorily) introduces the main verb in Basque, agreeing with the argument *Jon,* is in this case a form of *izan* 'be'. This state of affairs contrasts sharply with that in (iib). Here, the subject *Jonek* is (obligatorily) in subject Case, and the auxiliary verb that (obligatorily) introduces the main verb, and shows agreement with both subject and object, is a form of *ukan* 'have'. Subject agreement (*Jonek*) is expected, but object agreement is extremely interesting and unexpected: this sentence has no real object. But it does have an implicit object: *arnasa* 'breath'. This element is not referential, but it is nevertheless robust enough in structural terms to determine a default (obligatory) third person singular object agreement. Finally, note the verbal form *hartu* 'take', which supports the nominal *arnasa* 'breath'. It looks as if Basque directly illustrates the sort of structure hypothesized in the text: there is no such thing as a pure verb 'breathe'; rather, it is best understood as 'breath-take'.

It should be added that all Basque verbs are like the one in (iia) or the one in (iib). In other words, some verbs are single lexical items (e.g., *agertu* 'appear', *heldu* 'arrive', *sortu* 'emerge', *gortatu* 'happen') and behave as in (iia), and the rest are periphrastic (e.g., *barre egin* 'laugh', *atsenaldi bat hartu* 'rest', *hitz egin* 'work') and behave as in (iib). For discussion of these issues, and references, see Mendikoetxea and Uribe-Etxebarria, forthcoming.

The examples in (7) illustrate this concretely:

(7) a.
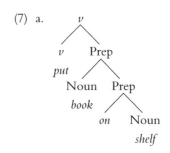

b.
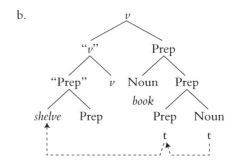

In essence, (6) is the structure involved in (7b). Here *book* is really the direct object of the verb *shelve;* but this verb itself is complex, the result of some incorporation. It's presumably because of this that the word *shelf-Prep-v* is pronounced *shelve:* the phonological "devoicing" that *shelf* undergoes in isolation is prevented when further morphemic structure accompanies it (that is, the *-Prep-v* part prevents the phonological process from taking place).

O: I presume the general intent of these movements/attractions is to establish the contexts of word formation.

L: In a sense. Abstract heads carrying certain features join forces with other heads which require those features, and the result is some sort of word with a complex internal structure.

O: And there appears to be an intention, also, to make (7b) and (7a) look alike . . .

L: Yes and no. Surely, there's some parallelism between the derived verb *shelve* and the periphrastic form *put on the shelf*—but they're not identical. You can put books on a shelf (e.g., in a stack) without shelving them. You can put a saddle on a horse (e.g., on its head) without saddling it [see (8)]. You can put butter on a piece of toast (e.g., in a lump, in one of its corners) without buttering it. At the same time, you can put, say, water on a shelf; but you don't shelve water. You can put a saddle on the floor, but you don't saddle the floor. You can put butter in the frying pan, but you don't butter it [7].

O: Doesn't this mean that, when you shelve something, in addition to putting it on a shelf, you do so in some orderly fashion; and when you saddle something, in addition to putting the saddle on it, you strap the saddle around its body; and when you butter something, in addition to putting butter on it, you spread the butter all over it; et cetera?

L: Maybe. The relations are complex, and beside the point right now. Suffice it to say that *shelve, saddle, butter,* and the like, require a specific interpretation. It's clear that this canonical interpretation stems from the meaning of the heavy element that incorporates into the light verb. That is, it's because it's a saddle that you're putting on the horse that you have to strap it; were it a hood, in order to hood the horse, you'd have to put the hood on its head. That's why I say that the idiosyncratic lexical meaning of the expression comes from the incorporated element, not the light verb. Some kind of meaning postulate to the effect that "for all events of saddling, the saddle ends up in the canonical place where saddles are put on horses" is needed in order to capture the full meaning of the intended expression. That's just an irreducible lexical property of *saddle:* novice English speakers have to learn that *saddle* (at the very least) implies something about the position of a saddle on someone's back (and not their head), just as *hood* implies something about the position of a hood on someone's head (and not their back). The place to encode these idiosyncrasies is in the lexicon: we have to learn these things word by word.

O: In what specific sense is *book* an object of *shelve* in (7b)? Is it an internal argument?

L: That's the question, but before we decide on an answer, let's consider the basic facts. Let me first assume (as seems natural) that the position of, for example, *foot* in an idiom like *(X) put (X's) foot in (X's) mouth* (meaning X said something inappropriate), or *money* in *put (X's) money where (X's) mouth is* (meaning X's deeds should match X's words), directly corresponds to the position of *book* in (7). Assuming

Figure 6.8

Idioms are formed within internal arguments (see fig. 6.3):

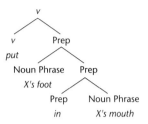

Therefore, it msut be that *X's foot* is in the same internal domain as *X's mouth,* plausibly the internal domain of *in,* whose projection is within the internal domain of *put.*

Figure 6.9

Gloss of (9): To fully understand (9), return to the gloss in figure 5.4; the present figure highlights only the parts of the definition that have not already been discussed.

(i) "Where α is a feature matrix or a head #X#, and CH is a given chain (α, t) or (the trivial chain) α: . . ."

This is crucial. The previous definition of minimal domains made use of projections; this definition makes use of chains instead (chains that result from moving either a feature matrix or a head).

(ii) ". . . Max(α) is the smallest maximal projection dominating α. . . ."

This statement was part of the previous definition, but it now has a slightly different import. At issue is still the umbrella for α, but now α can be part of a chain, resulting in the following type of situation:

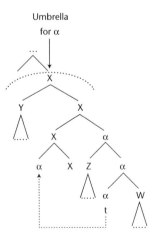

(iii) ". . . The domain D(CH) of CH is the set of categories/features dominated by Max(α) that are distinct from and do not contain α or t. . . ."

what we said about idioms, then the very fact that the idiom is possible immediately suggests that *(X's) foot* is within the same internal domain as *(X's) mouth,* namely, the internal domain of *in*—and something similar should be said about the specifier *book* in (7), which should be in the internal domain of *on.* This is further confirmed by the quasi-idiomatic reading of *shelve* in *we shelved that proposal* [see fig. 6.8]. Also compare (7) with (8) [8]:

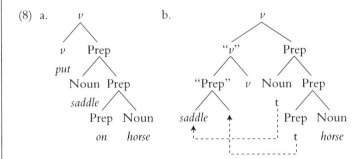

Here the derived verb is formed by raising *saddle,* the element corresponding to *book* in (7). Inasmuch as it's possible to incorporate *saddle* into (the moved) Prep, once again we conclude that the specifier of Prep is one of its internal arguments.

—————————————————— a definition of internal and checking domains

O: But how exactly do you define "internal domain"?

L: We have to generalize the notions we talked about yesterday [see sec. 5.1], from heads to chains, as in (9) [9]. Then we can explicitly add the characterizations of checking and internal domain as in (9d) and (9e), respectively [see fig. 6.9].

(9) *Definition of minimal domain (final version)*
     Where α is a feature matrix or a head #X#, and CH is a given chain (α, t) or (the trivial chain) α:
     a. Max(α) is the smallest maximal projection dominating α.
     b. The domain D(CH) of CH is the set of categories/features dominated by Max(α) that are distinct from and do not contain α or t.
     c. The minimal domain Min(D(CH)) of CH is the smallest subset K of D(CH) such that for any *x* belonging to D(CH), some *y* belonging to K dominates *x*.

d. The *internal domain* ID(CH) is the subset of Min(D(CH)) that includes only sisters to α's projections.

e. The *checking domain* CD(CH) is the set-theoretic complement of ID(CH) in Min(D(CH)).

The intuition is this. In general, the internal domain of a chain (α, t) includes whatever (sister) dependents relate to α before it moves [10]. (After it moves, thus forming a chain, if the head element in the chain relates in the normal way—that is, adjoining to the next head up—no other element will ever be its internal argument, since the adjunction will prevent it from having any more sisters.) In a nutshell, internal dependencies of the lexical sort must be established prior to Move/Attract; the transformation is invoked solely for checking purposes, not related to the internal domain, but to its set-theoretic complement within the minimal domain instead—that is, the checking domain.

_____ the chain generalization and predicate-role relations

O: You mean to say, then, that lexical relations are, in fundamental respects, complementary to checking relations [11].

L: Yes. We can turn that into an explicit generalization, as in (10):

(10) *The architecture of chains (descriptive generalization)*
    Where CH = (α, t),
    a. the head α is the checking position and
    b. the tail *t* (α's trace) is lexically related.

I'm formulating this just to keep track of what's going on, though—its content is implicit in (9), in the definitions of internal and checking domain.

O: I take your point—but unless I'm missing something fundamental, all of this machinery constitutes a radical departure from conceptual necessity . . .

L: Maybe. When the facts are better understood, we can talk about this with more insight. However, if it's indeed the case that something fundamental about chain architecture departs from conceptual necessity—so be it. I haven't ever tried to imply that Human should be perfect. It just so happens that, to a significant extent, it

This still defines a domain, but it is now the domain of a chain, not a category. The domain of CH is still a set of categories/features (with the same qualifications raised in figure 5.4) within the umbrella for α. Note also that both α and its trace are now excluded from the set, because the set of dependents of the chain (α, t) is still what matters. Since the set includes only those categories/features within the umbrella for α that do not contain α (or its trace), the set excludes X, the only category that contains α (see app.).

(iv) ". . . The minimal domain Min(D(CH)) of CH is the smallest subset K of D(CH) such that for any *x* belonging to D(CH), some *y* belonging to K dominates *x*. . . ."

This still limits the minimal domain to the dependents of the chain (α, t), and none of their descendants. Graphically:

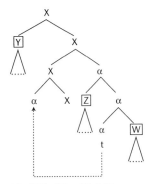

Min (D((α, t))) = {W, Z, Y}

(v) ". . . The *internal domain* ID(CH) is the subset of Min(D(CH)) that includes only sisters to α's projections. . . ."

That is, where Max(t) is the umbrella for *t*:

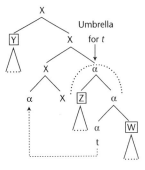

ID(α, t) = {W, Z}

(vi) ". . . The *checking domain* CD(CH) is the set-theoretic complement of ID(CH) in Min(D(CH))."

"Set-theoretic complement," here, means the remainder of the set. That is, if Min(D(CH)) = {Y, Z, W}, and ID(α, t) = {W, Z}, then we conclude that CD(α, t) = {Y}.

Note that this definition of minimal domain, now extended to chains, has a bearing on the notion of equidistance discussed in section 5.1. See the appendix on this matter.

seems to be (in the technical sense of "perfect"). But if the facts show that in some specific domains the system isn't optimal—what can I say? That's reality.

O: Let me remind you nonetheless that although the definition of checking domain has some bite, given what we've already established about checking processes [see secs. 5.4–5.5], the definition of internal domain merely says what an internal domain is—not exactly what goes on in there. That is to say, we need more machinery . . .

L: Of course; we also have to establish what lexical relations are, and that they're configurational. Simply put:

(11) *Predication Axiom*
       Predicates assign roles by definition.

(12) a. β assigns a role to α only if β heads a configuration C.
       b. α receives a role from β only if α is a dependent of β in C.

The existence of a predicate immediately entails the assignment of a role, as long as the conditions in (12) are met [12]. This is what requires that the relation of lexical role assignment be configurational—thus occurring within the internal domain of a head (the set of dependents under its projection) [see fig. 6.10]. The requirement has two aspects: (12a) states what the configurational site of the role assigner is (e.g., a verb); (12b) states what the configurational site of the role receiver is (e.g., a noun phrase). If the role assigner moves, it's no longer in a configuration; it's now part of a chain, a nonconfigurational, more abstract relation between two phrase markers. Thus, the moved element can't assign a role. Similarly, if an element intending to receive a role were to move, it would no longer be in a configurational relation, and thus it couldn't receive a role in its movement site. That's why, if you look at an already formed chain, it's the trace that really tells you what the lexical relations are (10b). More technically, we can simplify the statement in (12) to the Role Assignment Requirement in (13):

(13) *Role Assignment Requirement*
       α receives a role from β if and only if α belongs to the internal domain of β.

O: Suppose you form a chain whose first link has moved to a position where a role is assigned.

Figure 6.10

The internal domain of (α, t) is determined in the umbrella of α prior to movement; in contrast, its checking domain is determined in the umbrella of α after movement:

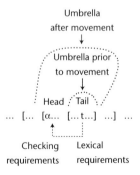

That is, a chain originates in the tension between two sorts of requirements: it starts in a configurational position where lexical requirements are established, and it stretches to a different position, in the checking domain of some other category, where checking requirements are established.

L: I can't.

O: Why?

L: Because such a chain would be forced to be an argument of the verb—but chains aren't configurational and thus can't be arguments.

O: That was going to be the question, thanks.

L: It's because of this that (14b) can't mean that Ike likes himself [13]. Obviously related to this, also, is the fact that an expletive like *there* isn't inserted in a position where a role is assigned, even in instances like (14c) where the associate is a subject; instead, the expletive is base-generated in the specifier of Tense [see sec. 5.6] [14]. It's actually *there*'s associate that stands in a configurational relation with a role assigner [15]:

(14) a. I like Ike

     b. *Ike likes t

     c. I believe there to have visited us a large group of people

         (cf. I believe a large group of people to have visited us)

And this is also the crux of the matter in distinguishing the external and internal arguments in (8), for instance. We have to make sure that in something like *Jack saddled the horse* (or, correspondingly, *Jack put the saddle on the horse*), whereas *saddle* starts as an *internal* argument, *Jack* is an *external* argument—otherwise we wouldn't be able to predict any of the basic facts we've talked about so far . . . How do we do that? First, let's look at the configurations prior to movement:

(15)

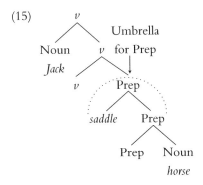

Before movement, the umbrella for Prep covers *saddle* and *horse;* however, it doesn't cover the specifier of the *v* shell, *Jack,* thus leaving this element outside the minimal domain of Prep. If arguments are distinguished in configurational terms, it's immediately clear that *saddle* and *horse* are internal arguments, whereas *Jack* is external, as desired. Now look at the situation after movement:

(16)

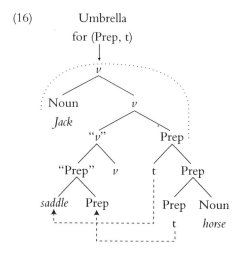

In this representation, *Jack* falls within the umbrella for the chain arising from moving Prep, and it's part of the minimal domain of this chain. We still want to say, however, that *Jack* isn't part of the internal domain of the chain. Technically, it isn't, given (9d): it's not a sister to any of the projections of Prep. The fact that the head of the Prep chain has moved "closer" to *Jack* is still irrelevant; what counts for deciding whether α is in the internal domain of β is whether α and β's projections are sisters, a configurational notion. *Jack* would be in the internal domain of (and getting a role from) Prep only if it were a dependent of the configuration that Prep heads (thus, prior to movement).

O: Do tell, then: how does *Jack* get a role?

L: Through the *v* shell. In essence, we can think of *v* shells as being projected from affixes that lexical elements have to associate with [16]. The affix brings something to the ultimate semantic import of the verb; in this case it introduces an agent role.

6.2 Much Ado about Word Formation
   (a pleasant dialogue about word forms, and their possible explanation)

O: Hm . . . Do you wish me to display my next question in a concise and somewhat summary manner?

L: By all means . . .

————————————————————————————— *are words to be expected?*

O: I feel inspired. As I see it, you've split that pristine atom left you by your worthy ancestors, men of old who dwelt closer to the gods and heard from them that whisper which the beasts and stones have been denied, and which they alone have cherished as they have the fire of the hapless Prometheus, and for countless generations . . .

L: Talking about the word?

O: Indeed . . . Behold now *saddle,* which, before your blast, was but a pleasant sound, tickling our ears with memories of the far-off Amazons and of Alexander's horse—who is known throughout the universe.

L: Make your point.

O: It is now but a reckless arrangement, which grows vaster than the firmament . . .

L: So?

O: So say you? What means it then to you, Sire, to have to have words?! Could one not choose to condemn them to the gorges of your mouth, where live the demons that salivate and hum and hiss and make all sounds, having traveled from afar, all the lengthy way back from . . . from . . . All the way back from . . .

L: Where, for heaven's sake? We don't have deep structures!

O: Must they start somewhere? Aye, they must. They must . . . O lexicon, come then, please, to my assistance. What say you? That we must dawn on you? Alas! What sorts of creatures dwell in your enigmatic caverns? How diverge they from these clumsy arrangements that my will aspires to build, my sense declines to parse, and my memory forsakes?

L: Can you please talk normally? This issue is very important.

O: Rats: why words?

———————————————————————————————— impossible words

L: Well, we have them—and we have to start somewhere. You're right in asking what it means for words to have those elaborate structurings your discourse illustrated; but it's not so clear to me that asking whether we need words at all, given the structures we've argued for, is a meaningful question. But since I don't want to just stomp my foot harder than yours, I'll ask you to imagine an English verb we can invent on the spot: *to wug* [17].

O: Meaning?

L: Let's have it mean this: '*x* causes that *y* smiles'. So I could say, for instance, "Jokes wug people," and that would mean 'jokes cause that people smile', which is of course true in the real world. Now imagine another verb—say, *to wog*—and suppose it meant 'that *y* smiles causes *x*'. So I could say, "People wog happiness," which would mean 'that people smile causes happiness', also a true statement in this world of ours . . .

O: Blimey!

L: What?

O: Hrrmm . . .

L: If you're having trouble understanding me, you're normal. In your mind, *people wog happiness* still probably evokes something like 'people seek happiness', or 'people love happiness'. I don't think one can honestly imagine a child learning the verb *to wog*. *My child wogged a family commotion.* That should mean something like 'the fact that my child smiled caused a family commotion'. But it doesn't work. One can't avoid taking *my child* as a *subject:* the sentence evokes a meaning like 'my child created a family commotion'. It's ludicrous, even if this is just an apparently innocent word. The verb *to wug* is much easier, even though it's also made up. *Groucho Marx wugged me* is easy to understand as 'Groucho Marx made me smile' . . . But even if children could learn "to wog" (they can easily learn that smiling causes something or other—they're geniuses at that!), what children couldn't learn is the word itself, *to wog.*

O: Aye.

——————— predicting the nonexistence of certain words from their syntax

L: Now the action of "wogging" is there, and the sounds [w], [ȯ], [g] are there—arbitrarily pair the two things, and what do you get? Garbage. Which, if you think about it, is what your contention that words don't exist would readily predict, assuming words are just low-level phonetic encodings for an entire syntactic derivation.

O: Why?

L: Let's look again at the kind of structure we saw in (3), involving incorporation. Many heads can incorporate into others (as in *Canadians seal-hunt*); but some can't (as in **Canadian-hunt seals*). There's a simple explanation for these facts, which we can see by looking at the basic source structures:

(17)

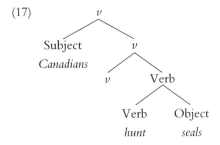

If we try to incorporate *seals* into the verb, we get something like this:

(18)

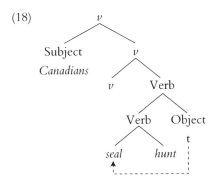

Now, what would happen if we tried to incorporate *Canadians* instead?

O: Can't.

L: Right, because we'd have to move downward! This immediately means that the incorporation is impossible in English, since the verb itself never moves higher than the v shell. As it turns out, the impossibility of incorporating subjects appears to be universal, not just a fact about English. So we want to avoid the incorporation even in a language where the verb overtly moves upward to Tense, as in (19):

(19)

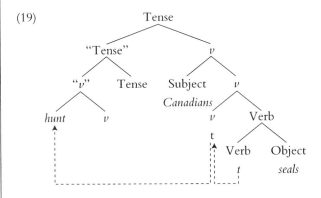

———————————————————— *a condition on lexical relatedness*

This, we can prevent if we require that incorporation be limited to sister dependents, as in (20) [18]:

(20) *Condition on Lexical Incorporation*
      α lexically incorporates into β if and only if α is in the internal domain of β.

Then *Canadians* can't incorporate in (19), even if it would be going upward, because it's not a member of *hunt*'s internal domain (which is made up only of *hunt*'s sisters). Now you may be thinking that this condition has negative effects for the sorts of covert feature movements/attractions that we discussed yesterday.

O: Wasn't.

L: But you could have been; so the answer to that hypothetical concern is that the condition has nothing to do with formal feature checking—it's just a subcase of a broader lexical requirement, which we can state as follows:

(21) *Axiom of Lexical Relatedness*
      α and β are lexically related if and only if α is in the internal domain of β.

In addition to subsuming the Condition on Lexical Incorporation in (20) (under the assumption that lexical incorporation is a lexical relation), the Axiom of Lexical Relatedness subsumes the Role Assignment Requirement in (13) (again, assuming that role assignment is a lexical relation). More generally, the Axiom of Lexical Relatedness should also tell us why it is that idioms are formed in internal domains, if we take idiom formation too to be a lexical relation. In sum, no lexical relation between *hunt* and *Canadians* can be established, as desired. Why is all of this relevant to the hypothetical verbs *wog* and *wug?*

O: Same thing.

L: Yeah, although the reasoning is slightly more abstract. In your hypothesis, words don't exist; so every time we find something with lexical dependencies, such as *wug,* we have to assume that the string of sounds—here, [wag]—is the PF realization of a structure, which in this case can be as complex as this (and recall (17)):

(22)
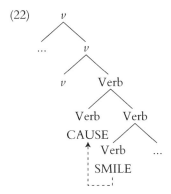

An abstract verb *SMILE* incorporates into a causative verb, and the result, *SMILE-CAUSE,* happens to be pronounced [wəg]. But now look at *wog,* the verb that seems so hard to accept. The relevant structure would be roughly (23), with *SMILE* coming from a complex subject of *CAUSE* (remember (18), and also that the intended meaning of *wog* is 'that *y* smiles causes *x*'):

(23)
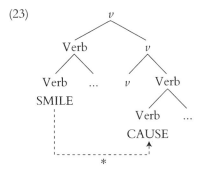

In trying to make the lexical unit *SMILE-CAUSE,* you'll violate the Axiom of Lexical Relatedness, since *SMILE* isn't in the internal domain of *CAUSE.* The same can be said about trying to incorporate *SMILE* into *CAUSE* after this element raises upward to T, if your language allows such movement (recall (19)); while *SMILE* is in the internal domain of *v,* it's not in the internal domain of *CAUSE,* the target of incorporation [19]:

(24)

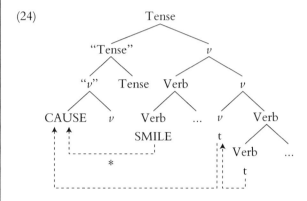

O: . . .

L: Your syntactic mind doesn't even allow you to structure the perfectly conceivable verb *wog* [20].

O: . . .

L: Are you on a communication strike? I hope my eagerness to clarify matters hasn't left you wordless—particularly after that dazzling outburst a while back.

O: I'm simply wondering what you could possibly say to demolish such a glorious argument for *my* theory! I'd say I'm right: there's no initial array of lexical items that humans build structures from, and all you have is some abstract syntactic structures that come directly from . . . ahem . . . the caverns of the mind . . .

L: Yeah, but that's the wrong theory.

_____   **arguments against identifying words with phrases**

O: Show me.

L: Right at the core of syntax are three fundamental properties that we can express in the form of postulates [21]:

(25) Basic syntactic postulates
    a. Syntactic structures are productive.
    b. Syntactic structures are systematic.
    c. Syntactic structures are transparent.

These postulates correlate with traditional observations; any theory that attempts to explain linguistic facts has to predict these three, or it won't even be observationally adequate. It may be that the three postulates actually reduce to more fundamental ones, having to do with the computational architecture of the model as I've been presenting it—but let's set that aside. What I'd like to demonstrate (against your theory) is that word formation processes are neither **productive,** nor **systematic,** nor **transparent.** Take any derivational morpheme [see fig. 6.11].

———————————————————————————— productivity

We can say *musical* but not **artal,* and *tidal* but not **waval.* We can say *hospitalize* but not **clinicize, terrorize* but not **horrorize.* We can say *electricity* but not **eclecticity, reality* but not **fakity.* And so on. Whatever process is going on here isn't very productive, and a child learning English has to learn each case individually . . . There are regularities here, surely—but nothing like what we find in syntax. Take for instance causative sentences in English. In general, we can use any verb like *walk* in a causative environment, *NP makes NP V:* so, *I make my dog walk.* But a *lexical* version of a standard causative structure is very unproductive. You can "walk your dog," which roughly means that you make your dog walk. But you can't say, well . . .

O: "Poop your dog," though it's clear what that would mean . . .

L: Right. Or you can "enlighten an audience," but you can't "endarken them"; and so on. This just isn't productive.

O: Point taken. Argument number two . . . ?

———————————————————————————— idiosyncrasy

Figure 6.11

The "past" morpheme is an example of *inflectional morphemes:*

(i)   *evaluate* ⟷ *evaluated* (= *evaluate* + *d*)
(ii)   *break* ⟷ *broke* (≠ *break* + *d*)

These morphemes are checked in the syntax. Checking is not what gives a lexical item its final PF shape; rather, it is an abstract process whereby an inflectional morpheme relates to a corresponding functional category, by moving to its checking domain. When this movement takes place in the overt syntax, it pied-pipes some extra material with it; when it takes place covertly, though, it presumably only involves the bundle of formal features of a given category.

    The morpheme *-ate,* which makes a noun into a verb, is an example of *derivational morphemes:*

(iii)   *evaluate* = *e* - *value* – *ate*
                   e - *vapor* – *ate*
                   e - *labor* – *ate*
                   e - *viscer* – *ate*
                   e - *nerv* ⁻ *ate*

These morphemes are not checked in the syntax. However, they are important in determining relational matters pertaining to internal domains, and in this sense they too are syntactic.

L: Think now about how idiosyncratic the meaning of words is. For instance, you can say that your boat is *reliable* if it performs well in different water and wind conditions. However, if you say that your boat is *inflatable,* you don't mean that it does something, but rather that someone can do something to it: inflate it. If you say that it's *inflammable,* you mean that fire can burn it, regardless of the agent. And what's a *demonstrator?* An individual who engages in a (political or mathematical) demonstration—not generally something that's the instrument for a demonstration (say, a loudspeaker or a computer; although a car that prospective customers test-drive can be a demonstrator). In contrast, what's a *generator?* It isn't an individual who generates something or other (an engineer or a mathematician); rather, it's a device that does the job. How about an *incinerator?* It's a gadget to incinerate garbage, say, and not the operator who turns it on. But then take an *excavator.* That can be either the machine used for excavating, or the person who does the excavation. That is, the suffix *-or* can mean something relating to agency or instrumentality; but which meaning it has when it's combined with a particular lexical item appears to be lexically idiosyncratic. This is different from what we find in syntax. Thus, we can say, "The proof was demonstrated by the professor using a powerful computer" (but witness: "?The proof was demonstrated by a powerful computer (*using the professor)"); similarly, "The information was sneaked out by a spy using a tape recorder" (however: "?The information was sneaked out by a tape recorder (*using a spy)"); likewise, "The electricity was generated by the engineer using a dynamo" (but: "?The electricity was generated by a dynamo (*using the engineer)"); or "The garbage was incinerated by the janitor using the new incinerator" (but: "?The garbage was incinerated by the new incinerator (*using the janitor)"); and "The excavation was completed by the archeologist using a deficient excavator" (but: "?The excavation was completed by a deficient excavator (*using the archeologist)"). That is, in all these cases, first of all, the instrumental phrase is only marginally acceptable after the preposition *by* (rather than saying, "?The proof was demonstrated by a computer," I'd say, "The proof was demonstrated *by way of* a computer"), and of course the sentences become meaningless when the agent is placed after the verbal form *using.* But more importantly, all the sentences behave alike: we don't get idiosyncratic behaviors because in one case we're talking about an excavation and in the next we're talking about a demonstration; the agent goes best after *by* and the instrument goes after *using,* and that's that. This is the most obvious property of syntax: structures are what they are regardless of the context they're in. A plural is a plural, a past tense is a past tense, and so on, and whether a speaker attaches the plural morpheme to *cat* or to *dog,* or the past tense morpheme to *excavate* or to *demonstrate,* is perfectly irrelevant. Lexical relations just don't work like that, and we see this over and over. To *father* someone is to be that person's father; but to *mother* someone isn't to be their mother, but to take care of them; and of course one can't *brother, sister, uncle,* or *cousin* someone. It's a different system altogether.

O: And three?

_____ transparency

L: That's transparency. Syntactic structure can easily be modified. So the statement "While at some remote resort, someone other than Oswald caused Kennedy to die in Dallas" makes perfect sense (assuming the speaker's favorite conspiracy theory) and is perfectly grammatical. The causing event (say, a final, decisive phone call) takes place far from the scene of the assassination, while the dying event takes place in front of the cameras. Of course, one could also say, "Someone other than Oswald killed Kennedy," with the desired meaning. While Oswald may have pulled (one of) the trigger(s), the responsible assassin is ultimately someone higher up the ladder of power. In such a case, it's felicitous and politically accurate to speak the truth: it was someone other than Oswald who did the killing—understood as the ultimate causation of the death. But note that it's rather unacceptable to say, "While at some remote resort, someone other than Oswald killed Kennedy in Dallas," or, with temporal adverbs, "Last night at a meeting, someone other than Oswald killed Kennedy today in Dallas." These sound pretty horrible, even if it's clear what they mean. They should be perfect if the word retains the structure it acquires during the sort of syntactic derivation you were hypothesizing, where presumably *kill* doesn't exist as such, and should instead have the sense of something like *cause-to-die.* But they aren't perfect—so then why doesn't *kill* behave just like *cause-to-die* [see fig. 6.12] [22]?

O: Because words are a mess . . .

_____ conditions pertaining to words

L: Don't get me wrong: they are what they are. They're just not syntax, that's all. So far, I've shown you that word-level structures

Figure 6.12

Consider the expression in (i), which can be modified as shown:

(i) the governor caused   [the prisoner to die]
            ↓   ↓
      last night   this morning
   while in the Executive Office   in the electric chair

Now suppose that, in some underlying form, the structure of (iia) were (iib), with incorporation of a verb like *die* into a causative verb like *cause* (in rough accordance with the lexical meaning of *kill*):

(ii) a. the governor killed the prisoner
      b. the governor caused-die [the prisoner t]

Then why is (iii) ungrammatical?

(iii) * the governor caused-die (= killed) [the prisoner t]
                    ↑   ↑
              last night   this morning
         while in the Executive Office   in the electric chair

To the extent that the matrix and embedded events in (iii) cannot be modified as shown (contrary to what happens in (i)), it seems reasonable to conclude that *kill* cannot be decomposed into something like *cause-die.*

don't obey some of the most obvious properties of syntactic structures. I could also take the opposite tack, and show fairly robust properties of word structures that aren't obeyed by syntax. Take, for instance, the notion of a **paradigm,** a cluster of some sort which obeys certain specific properties [23]. There's no such thing in syntax. Pretheoretically, we can talk about a certain syntactic paradigm, meaning by that a bunch of structures which behave alike with respect to some property. For example, we could talk about "the paradigm of overt-movement-for-Case-reasons"; we'd list all kinds of sentences like the ones we looked at yesterday, whereby a given noun phrase is displaced to a site where it checks Case. But the sentences on this list wouldn't have any specific significance within the linguistic system. Just because a sentence is one in which a noun phrase has moved, nothing special happens to it; whatever happens to it is a function of the words it has and how they're assembled. Period. It may be useful to lump together a bunch of sentences exhibiting movement behaviors if you're a theorist trying to figure out the basis for these behaviors or if you're explaining them to someone. But the bunch of sentences doesn't really have any theoretical significance as such—it's not a cluster with macroscopic properties, so to speak. This is very different from what we find with words. For instance, certain words don't exist in the lexicon because other words do exist with the same meaning, within the same paradigm. For instance, English has *went* instead of **goed*. Why? Two bizarre things are going on here. One we can justify historically: *Went* is a type of past form that corresponds to a peculiarly Germanic inflectional system, of the sort that existed in English prior to 1066, when the Normans invaded. In contrast, so-called regular verbs like *walk* form their past by means of a process that was common to Romance languages: suffixation. When things settled down after the Norman invasion, the suffixation process became the dominant one, although verbs with the Germanic format remained in some instances. So that's history. But why don't we use both the old form *went* and what would be the new form, *goed*? Apparently, learners don't want two such forms. Not an obvious syntactic fact, is it? Thus, for instance, the truth conditions of *Brutus killed Caesar, Caesar was killed by Brutus,* and even *Caesar, Brutus killed (him)* are practically identical. Yet we keep all three (or, I should say, the syntax generates all three). So if word formation generates both *went* and *goed,* why don't we keep both?

O: Actually, you must also explain why *went* is what we keep, rather than *goed*.

L: Correct—the second mystery. An obvious regularity exists in this respect. We keep *sunk,* and not **sinked; brought* and not **bringed; understood* and not **understanded; hit* and not **hitted.* In other words, we keep a form that's specific to the particular verb, instead of a more general one. Call that the **Elsewhere Condition,** a principle about paradigms that goes all the way back to Pāṇini [24]. What's important is that this sort of condition pertains to lexical structures, but doesn't apply in the syntax proper [see (32) for a partial statement].

O: However, this looks a bit odd to me—a quirk of English: the historical accident that it kept some of its strong Germanic forms for tense . . .

L: But I don't think the facts are peculiar to those sorts of paradigms. Take a totally different one, not related to any historical development. For instance, both Jespersen and Sapir noticed that English speakers can say *impossible* (not possible) but not **innecessary* (not necessary); *none* (not some) but not **nall* (not all); *never* (not sometimes) but not **nalways* (not always); *nor* (not or) but not **nand* (not and).

O: That's rather curious! The extant negative form involves the "weaker" element in a pair of related items [25] . . .

L: That's it. Given that necessity entails possibility, but not conversely, think of the meaning of the hypothetical word **innecessary.* It could have applied in situations where something isn't necessary; but that's where we use *possible.* Except in cases where something that's not necessary isn't even possible; but that's where we use *impossible.* So with the words *possible, impossible,* and *necessary,* English speakers cover all three of the situations that can be expressed in this paradigm. Same thing with the hypothetical **nall* (given that *all* entails *some,* but not conversely), which doesn't add anything to the paradigmatic space covered by *some, none,* and *all.* And so on: *sometimes, never, always* displace **nalways* from their lexical paradigm, and *or, nor, and* displace **nand* from theirs.

O: Have you now explained the nonexistence of *unnecessary?!*

L: No. That word is formed by way of a different negative prefix, *un-,* as opposed to *in-.* I was just trying to show how the *(i)n-* prefix works—not something about *un-.*

O: Well, the prefix *un-* comes from the word *and,* which in its original sense meant 'opposite'. But I must tell you that the prefix *in-* comes from a Latin cognate of *and,* which also meant 'opposite'. So why should there be a difference?

L: They're just members of different paradigms, a Latinate one and a Germanic one. At any rate, the same sort of account can be given for why English doesn't have **unsynthesized,* say, together with *unanalyzed.* Of course **unsynthesized* could be used when something isn't synthesized; but there we use *analyzed,* except when something that's not synthesized isn't even analyzed—there we use *unanalyzed.* Same thing with paradigms involving *dis-: allowed* goes with *disallowed;* but *required* doesn't go with **disrequired* (again, what would be **disrequired* is either *allowed* or *disallowed*).

O: Now that you mention it, I've seen this in other Indo-European languages, and even elsewhere. For example, the Malagasy word pronounced [tsish], meaning 'not some', appears to be a composite of the words [tsi] 'not' and [mish] 'some'; however, there's no similar word meaning 'not all'. But tell me, why should the system stick to *possible* and *impossible,* instead of adopting **innecessary* to cover the same space?

L: The Elsewhere Condition. Adopt the more specific forms (*possible, impossible*) instead of the more general form that covers the paradigmatic space for both. At any rate, regardless of how the facts are ultimately explained, my point is: these sorts of phenomena don't show up in syntax. Nonetheless, they're clearly systematic; the fact that something isn't part of the syntactic mapping from the lexical array to LF doesn't mean it doesn't have systematic properties of some sort. One wants to know what those are, and that's in itself an important research program; but it shouldn't be confused with the research program I've been sketching.

———————————————————————————————— and what about idioms?

O: But we're now back to square one—and with a question. If words enter syntactic derivations fully formed, how do we address the beautiful argument that you created for the theory you've now thrashed?

L: We have to go back to the drawing board, but words alone aren't the problem; take a look at idioms. It's obvious that idioms aren't productive, and that they're semantically idiosyncratic; that's what makes them idiomatic. In a sense, an idiom behaves more like a single word than like a whole expression with different subparts. Then a whole set of new questions arise. What does it mean for these phrasal structures (after all, idioms clearly have the superficial shape of whole phrases) not to be productive or systematic?

O: I presume you'd have to assert that the idiom is treated as a unit for the purposes of WI, the word interpretation component. Just as words are.

L: To be very technical about it, idioms do allow a nonidiomatic interpretation, right? I can literally pull your leg and claim that I've pulled your leg. So it's not as if in that case I couldn't have a transparent structure. What's puzzling is that I can also treat the whole unit as a quasi-frozen word, and ship it directly to WI. Arguably, one might need to invoke the notion of internal domains to account for idioms [26]. That is, the internal domain of a head—say, a verb— isn't just where its internal lexical dependencies get satisfied—it's also a domain which in principle can yield an idiomatic interpretation. Sometimes the idiomatic interpretation stays phrasal, and we get something like *kick the bucket.* Sometimes we get a word form instead, like *saddle.* But the whole process is clearly restricted to internal domains, satisfying the Axiom of Lexical Relatedness; the minute a dependency's expressed through a checking domain, idiomatic readings are gone, and word formation processes disappear. So the WI component has no access to information beyond internal domains, and what we have to figure out is how it relates to the structures that the Axiom of Lexical Relatedness hands it.

O: Right, so now how does your system predict the absence of *to wog?*

6.3 The Subcase Principle
    (wherein the Linguist and the Other hunt for mischievous gavagais, and what they mean; together with other amusing facts about furry beasts)

L: I'm getting there. Remember our analysis of *bathe.* On the one hand, a syntactic structure is clearly involved. We can show that complex structural differences exist that determine the context in which *bathe* can arise, vis-à-vis *arrive,* let's say. For example, *bathe* can't appear in the same syntactic contexts as *arrive* (e.g., *there arrived a queen* vs. **there bathed a queen*). Our explanation for that sort of fact was purely syntactic: the subject of *arrive* is an internal argument— as opposed to the subject of *bathe,* which is external. This is expressed in terms of very concrete structural differences; for instance, while the underlying direct object of the expression *a queen arrived* is actually *a queen,* the underlying direct object of *a queen bathed* is something like *bath,* in some abstract shape. Similar arguments could be made for *saddle, shelve,* and eventually for every verb out there, specifying what sort of structure each one can appear in.

─── lexical representations

O: Right—so say we're dealing with *bathe,* whose structure we think we know. Would it be fair to say that I can represent *bathe* in the lexicon as follows?

(26)

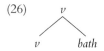

L: Not really—not, at any rate, with all the specific phrasal information that your graph implies. In my view, the lexicon should only include what's absolutely idiosyncratic to *bathe:* obviously the sound [bāth], in terms of its phonetic matrix; and a certain meaning peculiarity about carrying out the action in certain places where one is surrounded by a liquid; and what else? Suppose *bathe* also contains the derivational feature "I-incorporate-into-*v*" (*v*-feature, for short).

O: Is that idiosyncratic to *bathe?* Is it not more true that *bathe* involves incorporation into *v* because of what it means, as its paraphrase *take a bath* shows?

L: It's not obvious to me [27]. True, *bathe* has a sort of uninterpretable formal feature that somehow relates to *take a bath,* which a verb like *arrive* (which doesn't have the paraphrase *take/have/get . . . an arrival*) wouldn't have. On the other hand, there are a bunch of nouns that can go with *take:* somebody can take money out of a bank, take a queen in a chess game, take sugar in their coffee, and so on; but none of those result in verbs **money,* **queen,* or **sugar . . .

O: But perhaps that's because those aren't normal things one does. We need the notion of normal, or something of that ilk, to express lexical notions about the place on a horse's back where one puts a saddle, for example. Once we assume that the lexicon includes this sort of thing, why not use it here as well?

L: Maybe—good luck characterizing what "normal" means, though. It may not be normal to take a queen, but I don't really see what's so abnormal about taking sugar. Maybe I'm politically incorrect. In any case, you'd have to go outside of linguistics to do this sort of work. For instance, when you say that Ted drinks, you don't mean he drinks just any old beverage, right? So now you have to build in canonicity for alcohol, or something. Maybe this tells us something about human societies, but it's totally beside the point of linguistics [28]. We may as well call it idiosyncratic, in the absence of an anthropological theory that says anything about it. Which means, at least for our purposes, that it's appropriate to indicate this *v*-feature in the lexical entry for *bathe*. In turn, this implies that every time you use the lexical item *bathe,* you also have to add a *v* element to your numeration, in order to produce the appropriate *v* shell for *bathe* to relate to. In fact, it shouldn't be just any old *v* that you add to the numeration, but one which has the formal feature "a-Noun-incorporates-into-me" (feature-N, for short), assuming that *bathe* is actually nominal in character. Similar issues arise for *saddle,* although in this case the structure is presumably more complex. It idiosyncratically involves the sound [sa-dˀl], and—with regard to its semantic matrix—a meaning peculiarity about having to strap saddles on, and so forth. In addition, *saddle* contains some sort of formal feature that triggers the movements we saw in (8b) [repeated in fig. 6.13]. Prep incorporates into *v,* and *saddle* incorporates into Prep. Suppose this is expressed in terms of Prep containing the uninterpretable formal *v*-feature, which forces it to incorporate. Apart from this, in this instance Prep's specifier—which brings a P-feature with it—incorporates into the moved Prep. Then, the hosting elements also have to contain receiving features: *v* contains feature-P (for "a-Prep-incorporates-into-me") and Prep contains feature-N (for "a-Noun-incorporates-into-me"). Therefore, if you want to use the lexical item Prep implied in (8b) (lexicalized as *on* in (8a)), you have to add a Noun and a *v* to your numeration—furthermore, a Noun with a P-feature and a *v* with a feature-P, so that Prep can act both as a guest in and as a host of incorporation processes [see fig. 6.13]. Otherwise, the derivation will crash.

Figure 6.13

(7) and (8) are repeated for ease of reference:

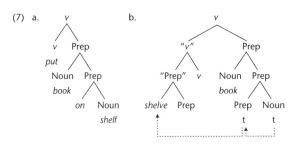

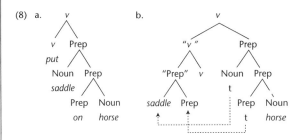

Note that the relation between X and Y is signaled in terms of an X-feature and a feature-Y:

O: I can see that this is a perfectly legitimate structure, but why is the specifier of Prep required to incorporate?

L: But it isn't! Suppose Prep had a complement with a P-feature allowing it to incorporate into Prep. The preposition itself (with the incorporated complement) again incorporates into *v*—as we saw with *shelve* in (7b) [repeated in fig. 6.13]. It's just another possible lexical structure that makes use of Prep, although in a different structural layout.

O: You must understand that I'm a bit worried about these features whose content is "I-incorporate-into-such-and-such" or "such-and-such-incorporates-into-me." That sounds rather on the "invisible-threads-hold-everything-together" side, even if—

L: Isn't that true?

O: —you're filling in with actual lexical structures the possible combinations that your system is predicting. What?

L: Never mind. Why are you worried? The features in question are purely combinatorial markings, uninterpretable formal features of words like *saddle* and *shelve* that are idiosyncratic to each of these verbs. (Thus, for instance, there's no verb *to rider/jockey*—to put a rider or a jockey on a horse—alongside *to saddle,* and no verb *to wardrobe/car*—to put something inside a wardrobe or a car—alongside *to shelve.*) Therefore, it's perfectly appropriate to indicate the *v*-feature in various lexical entries. The word *bath,* let's say, relates to *v* in a way that the word *money* or the word *sugar* can't (at least in my lexicon).

_____ various lexical entries

O: That's the other thing that troubles me. Take a word like *laugh,* which I hope in your lexicon can be a noun or a verb—in other words, can relate to a *v* or not. How many words *laugh* have you got, then? Does your lexicon contain two lexical entries, *laugh-1* (a noun) and *laugh-2* (a verb), or one lexically/structurally ambiguous entry? I implore you, don't simply say "yes"! And, I may add, a lexicon with two entries for *laugh-1* and *laugh-2* would have to treat them as two different, essentially unrelated items, just as it treats *laugh* and *emasculate,* for example . . .

L: Yes, yes. Of course, the question is whether there's anything more than some sort of lexical relatedness at stake. Remember, the fact that the lexicon only encodes a list of idiosyncrasies doesn't mean that regularities don't exist within that list. Surely they do [29]. *Tall* and *short* are two different words, but they're somehow related, as are *horse* and *mare, mother* and *daughter, face* and *nose, forest* and *tree, water* and *wine*. Very complex relations are at stake here. Is the relation between having a *laugh-1* and *laugh-2(ing)* different from that between having a *child* and *delivering* (and not *childing*), or having a *pain* and *hurting* (and not *paining*)? And how about putting a *saddle-1* on a horse and *saddle-2(ing)* the horse—is that different from the relation between putting *silverware* on a table and *setting* the table, or that between putting *frosting* on a cake and *icing* the cake?

O: I see, and you presumably don't want to say that *frosting* and *to ice* or *child* and *to deliver* are different forms of the same word.

L: I don't see what argument one could make to that effect . . .

O: Very well, so in your lexicon you have things like *bath-2* with a *v*-feature; and you have prepositional elements with this feature, associated to things like *saddle-2* with a P-feature; et cetera. How can I, the learner, predict any of this? Whether *saddle-2* will contain the *v*- or the P-feature, and so forth?

L: To some extent, you can't—you shouldn't! As a learner you have to acquire a good chunk of that knowledge, just as you've acquired knowledge about how that particular word is pronounced, or the fact that saddling a horse requires more than just putting the saddle on top of it (the saddle has to go on the horse's back, it has to be strapped on, and so forth). There just isn't any way to predict whether the verb, I don't know, *to tablecloth* (a table) or the verb *to blouse* (a child) exists (in my dialect they don't, but maybe they could have). Whereas we can say we (short)sheet a bed, we don't say we sheet a child who's dressing up like a ghost; whereas we can say we bandage a broken arm, we don't say we bandage a broken pipe; we can say we dress a person, but not that we dress a clothes hanger; and so on. There may be all sorts of reasons why we don't say these things, ranging from the frequency of some of these situations, to all sorts of functional constraints having to do with intentions, perceived use, and speaker's perspective [see chap. 2]. In fact, I doubt that everyone agrees with everyone else's use of these words, and a speaker's personal history may interfere, including the details of how or when she acquired a given word.

O: According to what you're suggesting, it's not the case that when a learner first encounters the word *saddle-2,* he reasons in terms like "this must be *saddle-1* used in structure such-and-such." Rather, the learner takes this to be a new word, which is capable of appearing in such-and-such lexical contexts. I actually find that reasonable, because I presume that most folks haven't really thought about the fact that *a mask* is related to *masking,* or *a frame* to *framing.* Indeed, *to mask* is often used in the metaphorical sense of covering up (for example, the facts). In that sense, how closely related are the verbs *to mask* and the noun *mask?* Or take *frame* and *to frame.* The latter can be used in the sense of putting something together ("to frame a proposal"). In this sense, it doesn't truly relate to a material *frame;* instead, it relates to a *framework* or perhaps *a frame of reference.* Indeed, if I'm not mistaken, this is closer to the historical sense of *to frame,* which traces back to Old English *framian* 'to avail'. Do people generally know this? I sincerely doubt it, nor do I see what relevance the ages-old meaning of *framian* could possibly have for a modern-day child learning the verb *to frame.* Or take deceptive cases like the noun *box* and the verb *to box,* meaning fight. One might think that English speakers say *to box* because boxers fight in a ring that looks like a box. Except that Chaucer used *box* to refer to a punch, long before boxing matches were organised in rings . . . But do people who think *to box* is somehow related to *box* (carton) not know how to use it? Surely not—I wouldn't suggest that to the ones I know . . .

L: I'd agree one hundred and ten percent!

_____ some lexical structures

O: Now . . . the learner must know that the word *saddle-2* is whatever it is not because it relates to *saddle-1* (we've discarded that theory), but because it appears in a context such as *Jack _____ the horse.* This context is presumably different from the contexts *Jack _____* (where *bathe* occurs), *here _____ Jack* (where *come* occurs), and so forth. One hopes these frames, if you will, are good enough that the learner can tell apart, at least, the basic syntactic contexts in which *come, bathe,* and *saddle* are possible, even if they don't really help in distinguishing, for example, *come* from *appear,* or *bathe* from *dine,* or *saddle* from *hood.* Here's what concerns me, though. Take the context *Jack _____ the horse.* We know that we need this context for *saddle,* whose structure roughly corresponds to that of the periphrastic expression *put x on y,* as in (8). However, is this not also the context required for *bring,* as in *Jack brought the horse,* whose internal structure, if anything, has more to do with *cause x to come* than it does with *put x on y?* How does the learner know that every time he comes across a transitive structure of one sort it isn't a transitive structure of some other sort?

L: Obviously, "transitive structure" is a pretheoretical notion without any specific meaning; obviously, too, we need more fine-grained distinctions. For instance, as you suggest, we need to separate causative-transitives like *bring, kill,* and *fire* from what we can think of as locational-transitives like *saddle* and *shelve.* For locational-transitives, we already know what *put x on y* means: (7b) or (8b), depending on whether Prep's complement or Prep's specifier incorporates into Prep. For causative-transitives, let's say the right structure is (22), which must mean that these verbs are formed in terms of items which are verbs in the lexicon, and which furthermore have a V-feature to check. Okay?

O: I grant you all of that. But in fact the child learning English simply hears sounds like [sa-dˀl] and [kil], uttered in some context. How does he know that the first involves a Prep, and the second a Verb, plus some features?

L: That is the question—I understand. But let's be precise. Two possibilities for verbs are these:

(27)   a. $|\#V\#|$ b. $|V|$

      [e.g., *rain*] $\#V\#$ ...

                      [e.g., *arrive*]

These structures correspond in the syntax to the simplest kinds of verbs: one with no lexical dependencies (thus no projection), as in (27a), and one with a single, unspecified dependency, as in (27b).

O: A dependent which is always Noun . . .

L: Yes, but that follows from the fact that sentences demand subjects (assuming a strong feature in Tense), and for some reason subjects are Noun [30].

O: I don't understand. For *arrive,* expletive *there* seems to satisfy this requirement. So why should the associate have to be nominal?

Figure 6.14

The structures given in (27) and (28) are not lexical representations, but syntactic structures corresponding to lexical representations, after they are selected from the numeration. What follows are the actual lexical representations that determine the syntactic structures discussed in the text:

(i) (Corresponds to (27a))

$$\begin{bmatrix} -N \\ +V \end{bmatrix}$$

[e.g., *rain*]

(ii) (Corresponds to (27b))

$$\begin{bmatrix} -N \\ +V \\ \ldots \end{bmatrix}$$

[e.g., *arrive*]

The dots in the representation in (ii) indicate that the verb has more structure than is represented in the feature matrix; in particular, it must also have a dependent object to project. This could be indicated in terms of a feature [+project], not represented in (ii).

Now consider (iii) and (iv):

(iii) (Corresponds to (28a))

$$\begin{bmatrix} -N \\ +V \\ F\text{-}N \end{bmatrix} \begin{bmatrix} +N \\ -V \\ v\text{-}F \end{bmatrix}$$

[e.g., *v + bath* (= *bathe*)]

(iv) (Corresponds to (28b))

$$\begin{bmatrix} -N \\ +V \\ F\text{-}A \end{bmatrix} \begin{bmatrix} +N \\ +V \\ v\text{-}F \end{bmatrix}$$

[e.g., *v + soft* (= *soften*)]

These are lexical representations for compound verbs, formed from two lexical items in a numeration—for instance, a noun like *bath* or an adjective like *soft,* plus the *v* head that projects a *v* shell, specified so as to incorporate an element with an N- or an A-feature.

L: Because, as we saw yesterday [see sec. 5.6], the associate of *there* enters into a (Determiner, Noun) relation with *there*. This relation couldn't be satisfied if the associate were an adjective or a preposition. So the bottom line is, the lexical representation of *arrive* doesn't need to say that its single argument is a noun—that fact follows independently. Next we have verbs which are assembled, by way of incorporation into a *v* shell, through a word formation process. Of these, the simplest are the ones whose lexical base lacks any argument structure; their corresponding syntactic structures are as follows:

(28) a.   b.

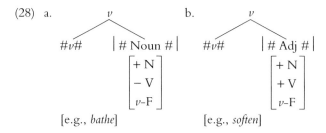

[e.g., *bathe*]   [e.g., *soften*]

These are underlyingly transitive structures that come out as intransitive at the surface, after the +N element incorporates into *v*. This situation illustrates the problem you just brought up. Whereas the learner can tell one structure in (27) from the other on the basis of sheer structural contexts (i.e., *it rains* has a different form from *there arrived a man*), it's not so obvious in (28) that basic structural relations offer any clues. The learner is exposed to sentences like *the queen bathed* and *the queen softened,* and the issue is how to figure out which structure corresponds to which sentence. Contextual cues about meaning may help—but this isn't always obvious [31]. Still, here the decision might seem relatively unimportant, and a wrong decision fairly innocuous, because the structures are so similar. That is, two speakers may assign two different structures to the verb *soften:* one speaker may decide that its syntax involves the sort of *v* that has feature-N, and the other may decide that it has feature-A. Consequently, one speaker will take the base of *soften* to be nominal, while the other will take it to be adjectival. Probably they won't be able to tell these two apart in terms of the English they speak to each other, and situations like this may actually be possible [see fig. 6.14]. However, as soon as we move to the next set of cases, we see that the relevant structures, although underlyingly very similar (see (29)), result in different surface representations (remember (7b) and (8b)):

(29)

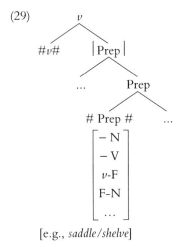

[e.g., *saddle/shelve*]

O: Hold on: where are we specifying that *saddle* or *shelve* assigns a role to a subject?

L: In the same structural position where this information is encoded for *bathe* or *soften:* the *v* element in whose domain Prep checks its *v*-feature. So that's general—thus, no subject receives a role in (27a) or (27b) precisely because there's no *v* there. For lexical representations involving structure (29), it's obvious that the learner somehow has to discriminate between *Jack saddled the horse* and, say, *Jack corralled the horse*—and this isn't trivial, as your question implies. Again, contextual cues about meaning might help: *saddling a horse* involves a direct object that's a location of some sort, while *corralling horses* doesn't; but this is just handwaving unless we really know what semantic contexts are doing. Finally, (30) shows some cases which are underlyingly different from (29) (even if they result in a surface form which may be similar to the one resulting from (29)):

(30) a.

Verb

#Verb# |Verb|
CAUSE

Verb
$\begin{bmatrix} -\text{N} \\ +\text{V} \\ \text{V-F} \\ \ldots \end{bmatrix}$ ...

[e.g., *bring* (= 'make arrive')]

Figure 6.15

Consider a lexical representation for (30a):

(i)
$$\begin{bmatrix} -N \\ +V \\ F\text{-}V \end{bmatrix} \begin{bmatrix} -N \\ +V \\ v\text{-}F \\ \dots \end{bmatrix}$$

[e.g., *v* + *bring*]

Note that (i) is formed from two lexical items; however, *bring* cannot be decomposed into two obvious lexical items, as *bathe* and *soften* can. In other words, there is a lexical item pronounced *bath* that has a *v*-feature forcing it to incorporate into *v*, and there is a *bath* that lacks this *v*-feature (the noun *bath*, used in isolation); but there is no lexical item pronounced *bring* that lacks the *v*-feature that forces it to incorporate into *v*. This is all idiosyncratic information that must be listed in the lexicon, in each lexical entry.

Consider also (ii) and (iii):

(ii) (Corresponding to (29))
$$\begin{bmatrix} -N \\ +V \\ F\text{-}P \end{bmatrix} \begin{bmatrix} -N \\ +V \\ v\text{-}F \\ F\text{-}N \\ \dots \end{bmatrix} \begin{bmatrix} +N \\ -V \\ P\text{-}F \end{bmatrix}$$

[e.g., *v* + Prep + *saddle*]

(iii) (Corresponding to (30b))
$$\begin{bmatrix} -N \\ +V \\ CAUSE \\ F\text{-}V \end{bmatrix} \begin{bmatrix} -N \\ +V \\ V\text{-}F \\ F\text{-}N \\ \dots \end{bmatrix} \begin{bmatrix} +N \\ -V \\ v\text{-}F \end{bmatrix}$$

[e.g., Verb + *v* + *dine*]

These words are built from three items in the numeration, and around Prep (as in (ii), where Prep incorporates a noun and itself incorporates into a *v*), or around *v* (as in (iii), where *v* incorporates a noun and itself incorporates into a causative verb). This is arguably as complex as words get, given the Wording Law discussed in the text (and see fig. 6.16). Thus, there is no word corresponding to (30c).

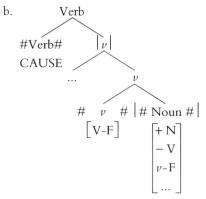

[e.g., *wine and dine* (= 'make have wine and dinner')]

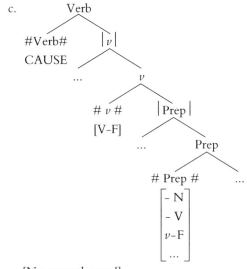

[No example: gap!]

These are some of the possible syntactic combinations involving a causative format like (22) plus verbal frames of the sort we've been considering [see fig. 6.15].

————————————————————— a wording law

O: Hold on again! Hold on! I'm a bit confused about your use of the terms "underlying" and "surface." I thought we had no "deep" structures [32]!

L: We don't. By "underlying" I mean something without any theoretical status, as in "first (set of) phrase marker(s) in the derivation, prior to movement." And by "surface" I just mean "phrase marker at the point of Spell-Out."

O: Then there's something else I fail to grasp. Structures like (29) and (30) **encapsulate** certain **information** that corresponds to words like *saddle* and *dine.* But where the Hell is that happening?!

L: Good question. We know it can't be in "deep" structure, because we don't have that level. Therefore, it must be in the WI component, which as we saw operates even at LF, given the Principle of Lexical Integrity [see chap. 5, (24)]. Are there properties of linguistic representations that WI demands? We saw one earlier: phonological words have to obey certain "gluing" conditions, whereby clitics are hosted by heavier items. Are there similar "gluing" requirements that pertain to the semantic interpretation of words? Suppose this is the case, and we summarize both the phonological and the semantic conditions on the unification of words as the Wording Law, a condition imposed by WI [33]:

(31) *Wording Law*
> WI recognizes α as a word if and only if
> a. α has phonological content and obeys the standard requirements on phonological words; and
> b. there is a sublabel β of α that, for all x, x a sublabel of α, x's trace is lexically related to β's trace.

(31a) has the basic content of the Wording Requirement we talked about a couple of days ago [see chap. 4, (7)], and is intended to prevent affixes from being stranded if they've got phonological content; basically, if an affix isn't appropriately attached to a word with the usual phonological content (in terms of stress and so on), WI won't be able to identify it as a word, and it'll be taken as some sort of noise for PF, with a resulting PF crash. Next, let me show you the work that (31b) does with one of the structures in (30): the impossible (30c). That verbs corresponding to this sort of structure don't exist is of course very interesting, because the structure itself is perfectly legitimate; moreover, it's clear what a verb would mean if it were to appear in this combination of categories. For instance, imagine the verb *to weg,* meaning 'to cause somebody to saddle something' (equivalently, 'carpet', 'file', 'chain', etc.), as in *I wegged Jack the horse (wegged Jack the floor, report, dog).* Similarly, imagine that *to weg* were supposed to mean 'to cause somebody to shelve something' (equivalently, 'corral', 'bag', 'can', etc.), as in *I wegged Jack the books (wegged Jack the horses, groceries, tomatoes)* [34] . . .

Figure 6.16

To see the Wording Law at work, consider the minimal domains involved in trying to create the verb *to weg* meaning, for instance, 'to cause to shelve', vis-à-vis those involved in creating *dine*:

(i) *dine*

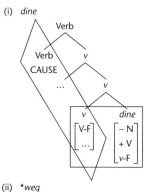

(ii) **weg*

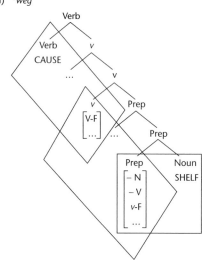

Whereas there is a pivot in (i) that is lexically related to all other crucial elements in the formation of *dine* (namely, *v*), there is no such pivot in (ii).

O: Heavens, those are truly terrible! Even without using *weg* to illustrate, the result is hopeless: one can't say **I saddled Jack the horses* or **I shelved Jack the reports* (meaning 'I made Jack saddle the horses/ shelve the reports'). But why?!

L: This is a result of the Axiom of Lexical Relatedness, when combined with the Wording Law. To see this, look at a good verb, like *dine* (in the causative reading in (30b)). What's the key element that, so to speak, "glues" (30b) together as a lexical expression?

O: Clearly, the *v* element which incorporates into the causative element, and which *dine* incorporates to.

L: Exactly—call this element the "pivot" [35]. The pivot is a chain with an important characteristic: its trace is lexically related to the traces of all other sublabels in the element that's trying to be a word. In this instance, the pivot *v* (or its trace, after *v* moves) is lexically related to the causative verb, while *dine* is lexically related to *v*, as its incorporation into *v* shows.

O: There's no such pivot for *weg* in (30c)! The abstract *SHELVE* is lexically related to Prep, and Prep to the *v* element, and this *v* element to the causative verb. However, *SHELVE* isn't lexically related to the causative verb . . .

L: And thus it can't be a word, according to the Wording Law, in particular (31b)—always assuming lexical relatedness within internal domains, in accordance with the Axiom of Lexical Relatedness [see fig. 6.16].

O: Very nice. I assume something like a Wording Law is needed because without it, words could be as long as *supercalifragilisticexpialidocious,* with zillions of potential dependents . . .

L: I don't know that the law is needed because of that, but it does explain why words like . . . well, that . . . don't exist in natural languages.

—————————————————————————— *learning lexical structures*

O: Very well. But could you now please concentrate on my question? Take the verb *bring,* with the structure in (30a), and the verb *saddle,* with the structure in (29). As a learner, I'm certainly likely to hear both of those in the context *Jack ____ the horse,* right? Right, so how do I know to assign the structure in (29) to *saddle* and not to *bring*—or vice versa?

L: Arguably, you don't—if the situational context is such that you can't really use it to determine the lexical differences. This must happen often, maybe one of the reasons it takes time to acquire a language. For concreteness, imagine a real-life situation: it's Easter-time, and a bunch of kids are sitting around a table painting eggs while they eat lunch—hard-boiled eggs, among other things. So they're both painting eggs and peeling eggs, and they monkey around with the eggshells and the paint, in such a way that they put shells back on peeled eggs, or they take paint off of already painted eggs. The point is: the situation presents various events of putting and taking paint and eggshells on and off eggs. Now, the smallest child, age one or so, is watching what's going on, hearing tokens like *I've painted my egg!* or *I've skinned my egg!,* and of course all along unconsciously acquiring language. How does the toddler know the older children meant 'I've put some paint on my egg' (and not 'I've taken some paint off my egg') or 'I've taken this bit of shell off my egg' (and not 'I've put this bit of shell on my egg')? Well, probably she doesn't know what the others meant. The situation is just too confusing, so the child will just have to wait for better times, cry for attention, or something.

O: Right, I see that. But I'm worried about a scenario that's worse than yours, in a sense: a situation that could confirm the wrong guess. Suppose, for example, that the child sees Jack moving horses into an enclosure—or as you say, a "corral"—and someone then says, "Jack ____ the horses." How does the child know the person meant 'corralled' and not 'moved'? Why, every time someone corrals something, he moves it (into the enclosure).

L: Yeah, that's an instance of a famous puzzle posed by Quine [36]. Somebody points at an animal hopping by and says, "Gavagai." You're learning the language of the pointer; how do you know she meant 'rabbit' and not, say, 'furry texture'? If you don't have a linguistic mind, this may indeed be puzzling. If you do have a linguistic mind, though, you don't seem to have a problem. Children immediately conclude that *gavagai* must mean 'rabbit'. Why? Because LADs are built that way. When a child sees an object and hears a novel term, the child's LAD assumes the term is a label for the object, and not, say, a label for its substance [37].

O: But that begs the question! Particularly since you once suggested to me that an abstract term (like *brown* or *furry*) corresponds to a dimensionally simpler concept than a concrete, countable term (like *rabbit*) [see sec. 2.4]. If you're going to say that in ambiguous situations the LAD will make a decision based on the way it's wired, why shouldn't the very elegant LAD hypothesise the *simpler* conceptual structure (among the possible ones in a given situation)? In that case, the LAD would of course conclude that *gavagai* means 'furry', or 'brown', or some such thing . . . And then I wonder how you can square that reasonable prediction with the actual facts.

L: I don't find it reasonable at all, and I'll tell you why [38]. In principle, the term *gavagai* could be denoting the dimensionally simple concept "furry," let's say, or the dimensionally more complex concept "rabbit." Call these scenario 1 and scenario 2, and assume a world in which all rabbits are furry. Suppose that (because of how the LAD is built) the child were to always hypothesize the simplest conceptual structure (among a set of candidates) for an unknown term. So in either scenario 1 or scenario 2 the child would assume that *gavagai* means 'furry'. This, of course, is perfect for scenario 1; so the child succeeds at the task. But now take scenario 2. How could the child ever learn that *gavagai* actually means 'rabbit'?

O: Someone tells him that 'furry' isn't—

L: Uh-uh! No negative data, remember? For that matter, no metalinguistic explanations—the child doesn't know the language yet.

O: Rats (or gavagais!). So the child can't unlearn that *gavagai* means 'furry', if all rabbits are furry. Needless to say, if the child heard *gavagai* while seeing a skinned rabbit, then he'd get the point. But that's cheating, I know, since we're assuming a world with regular furry rabbits (and in real life, many children who know the relevant word probably have never seen a skinned rabbit!). So the interesting situation is one in which the "right" meaning is essentially a subcase of the "wrong" one. If the learner is even allowed to hypothesise the supercase (in our scenario 2, "*Gavagai* means 'furry'"), then he'll fall into a learning trap. And I do see that, as a matter of LAD construction, hypothesising the subcase is the safest route. Were I to take *gavagai* to mean 'rabbit', I should be all right in scenario 2, of course. But I shall also be all right in scenario 1, for the simple reason that someone, sometime, will say *gavagai* while talking about a furry object that's not a rabbit. This is now positive evidence . . .

---
                                    a semantic elsewhere condition

L: Let's make these ideas explicit [see fig. 6.17] [39]:

(32) *Subcase Principle*

Assuming (a) a cognitive situation S, integrating subsituations s_1, s_2, . . . , s_n, (b) a concrete set W of lexical structures l_1, l_2, . . . , l_n, each corresponding to a subsituation s [40], (c) that there is a structure l_t corresponding to a situation s_t that is a subcase of all other subsituations of S [41], and (d) that the LAD does not know which lexical structure l_t is invoked when processing a given term T uttered in S, then the LAD selects l_t as a hypothesized target structure to correspond to T.

O: That looks like the Elsewhere Condition!

L: It is, except that now we're concentrating on its lexicosemantic aspect, a restriction on the acquisition of information pertaining to lexical items.

O: I presume that having a concrete set of lexical structures to choose from is quite important, is it not? In actual fact, I should think that the set W in (32) had best be, well, not merely concrete, but in fact rather small—if a realistic LAD is to reach a lexical decision before retirement!

L: I agree, although I don't really know how to determine the size of W—nor does it matter for our purposes now. I'll just say your point is well taken, and invoke the vague notion "paradigm" again.

O: But now, what help is any of this in answering my general question? . . . Oh, I see. Yes, let's suppose Jack is corralling the horses, and someone says "Jack _____ the horses." We have here a cognitive situation with some subsituations—let's limit the case to s_1 and s_2. Given the syntactic context, we can determine that Jack did something to the horses. This, I might add, is by no means evident. For example, when *Jack looks at the horses,* it's rather odd to think that Jack is doing something to them; but let's set that aside, since I'm more interested in what I take to be a tougher question. We must establish whether what Jack did to the horses is of the "shelve-sort" (e.g., *corral*) or of the "bring-sort" (e.g., *move*). Then there are two lexical structures, l_1 and l_2, that correspond to s_1 and s_2, respectively—namely, (29) and (30a). And let's say there's a situation s_t

Figure 6.17

Gloss of (32):

(i) "Assuming a cognitive situation S, integrating subsituations s_1, s_2, . . . , s_n . . ."

The general situation must be broken down into subsituations because each subsituation allows for a different lexical meaning (e.g., 'rabbit' vs. 'furry'). "Situation" should be interpreted here in the vaguest possible way: in this sense, the property of being furry is a situation, as is the property of being a rabbit.

(ii) ". . . [and assuming] a concrete set W of lexical structures l_1, l_2, . . . , l_n, each corresponding to a subsituation s, . . ."

This is the linguistically significant part: a list of relevant structures. The "corresponding to" part is deliberately vague, for little is known about how linguistic structures correspond to situations (see sec. 2.3).

(iii) ". . . [and assuming] that there is a structure l_t corresponding to a situation s_t that is a subcase of all other subsituations of S, . . ."

This is the formally significant part: one situation is a subcase of all others. Empirically, as will be suggested in the text, it is very likely that actual LADs are not concerned with whether situations are subcases of other situations, but instead make lexical decisions on the basis of which lexical structure (among those applicable in situation S) is the most specific. Nonetheless, the Subcase Principle is noncommital on this issue, which is taken to be a matter of implementing the general, formal principle in a realistic LAD.

(iv) ". . . and [assuming] that the LAD does not know which lexical structure l_t is invoked when processing a given term T uttered in S, . . ."

This is intended to indicate that the learning strategy is relevant when the LAD does not know the meaning of a word. The assumption might be slightly misleading, however, because lexical decisions involving the Subcase Principle are also taken when the LAD retreats from a previous assumption; in those instances, complex issues arise concerning what the LAD knows prior to changing its assumptions. Such issues are set aside in this definition.

(v) ". . . then the LAD selects l_t as a hypothesized target structure to correspond to T."

Finally, this is the crux of the proposal: the most specific structure is selected among the competing ones.

which is a subcase of the other situation; s_t is in fact "the act of corralling something," which is "the act of moving something" plus something else (". . . into a corral"). Since s_t corresponds to l_t, we conclude that l_t is the structure that the LAD assigns to the perceived word. In a nutshell, the LAD decides that *Jack* _____ *the horses* means 'Jack *corralled* the horses' and not 'Jack (just) moved the horses'. Is that what actually happens?

L: I don't know that any particular experiment's been conducted, but I'd predict (and I'd guess) that the answer is, the child goes with the more specific meaning, namely, *corral* [42].

O: One small thing, though: how does the child know what's the more specific meaning?

_____ *further considerations about word learning*

L: That's no small thing! Keep in mind, though, that the Subcase Principle is intended as a mere description of a formal state of affairs—a semantic version of the Elsewhere Condition. A very different question is how LADs implement (32), or for that matter a phonological version of the Elsewhere Condition, say [see fig. 6.17]. Abstractly, this is very similar to the issue of how UG finds an effective algorithm for computing the most elegant derivation— except this time we're talking about representations, specificity, and the LAD. To my knowledge, an elaborate theory about these matters doesn't exist, but it's apparent to me that it would have to invoke the mere amount of information involved. That is, suppose, in particular, that the structures we hypothesized in (29) and (30a) naturally correspond (as they should) to semantic concepts like "bring," "move," "saddle," and "corral." The ultimate semantic representations—that these are actions, involving certain participants, with certain presuppositions, and the rest—should be more or less direct reflexes of these lexical structures. That is to say, one could, in principle, compute whether situation s_1 is or is not more specific than situation s_2 on the basis of the lexical structures that one associates to these situations. In other words, in trying to figure out whether the concept of corralling is more specific than the concept of moving, the child might (unconsciously) be doing something as mechanical as evaluating the structure in (29) vis-à-vis the one in (30a). And here, we might start considering the relative size of the structure, and assume that the one with more symbols (therefore, containing more information) is the more specific one.

O: Two more questions. Suppose the child *knows* the verb *to corral,* and he hears *Jack ——— the horses.* Now what? The Subcase Principle will lead him to suppose that the new word he's heard—let's say it was *brought*—actually means 'corral', again!

L: The "again!" part is crucial. Children also make assumptions about mutual exclusivity for lexical choices. If a child already has a term for a concept, she won't take a new term that somebody applies to this same concept to be yet another label for the concept [43]. This is actually important, over and above the case you describe. Ask yourself how a child can learn the word *furry* . . .

O: My second question, precisely! Right. "Furry" isn't something that walks round on its own—it's part of rabbits, dogs, rugs, jumpers, and so forth. Every time I point at "furry" I'm also pointing at an object or a mass . . .

L: Right, and if you don't have a word for dogs, carpets, or whatever, then you may tentatively conclude that *furry* means 'carpet', say. Then again, if you do have a word for rabbits, then the next time somebody points at one and says "*Furry,*" you'll know that this can't mean 'rabbit'. So you may learn it indeed means 'furry'. Obviously, this then predicts a certain acquisition sequence: children should first acquire basic concepts applying to objects, in relative isolation, then proceed to organize these and other concepts in more intricate ways, precisely via assumptions about mutual exclusivity and the Subcase Principle. This is actually what we find [see fig. 6.18].

O: But then a last question comes to mind: how does a child ever *unlearn,* for example, the incorrect notion that *furry* means 'carpet'? Doesn't that require direct negative data?

L: Let's be careful. It certainly involves negative data of some sort—that is, information to the effect of "That's not what *furry* means." But why should that information be direct [44]? Suppose a child is saying the word **goed* (as children do) where you or I would say *went.* How does the child retreat from **goed* to *went?* Sooner or later, the child hears someone say *went,* and she has to confront the fact that her term **goed* is actually synonymous with *went,* which other people use. Having two terms violates the hypothesis of mutual exclusivity—so one of them has to go. Which one? Well, how

Figure 6.18

Markman and Wachtel (1988) designed studies to demonstrate that children engaged in language acquisition (i) assign new term labels to objects (rather than to properties, substances, etc.), as the first hypothesis about their meaning, and (ii) do not assign new term labels to already labeled objects.

In one study, Markman and Wachtel sought to demonstrate that three-year-olds may assign a label to the substance of an object when they already have a label for the object itself. The experimental task involved two scenarios. In scenario 1, a familiar object was labeled using a novel term. For instance, children were shown a metal cup and told, "See this? It's chrome." Then they were presented with the chrome cup, a ceramic cup, and an unformed piece of chrome, and they were eventually asked, "Which is chrome? This thing here or this stuff here?" In scenario 2, an unfamiliar object was labeled using a novel term. For instance, the same children were shown an odd-shaped metal container and told, "This is chrome." (Evidently, different words and objects were used in each scenario, so that children would not get conflicting information.) They were then presented with the odd-shaped chrome container, an odd-shaped ceramic container, and the unformed piece of chrome, and they were asked the same question as in scenario 1.

The results were as follows. The mean number of object responses was .13 out of 1 for scenario 1 (the children overwhelmingly decided that the unformed piece was chrome; of course, the other response—that the cup is chrome—is also true). In contrast, in scenario 2 the mean number of object responses was .57 out of 1 (the odd-shaped object was considered "chrome" more often than before). Although not conclusive, the experiment is suggestive: when children do not know what to call an object, they decide that a new label associated with this object must be its name; however, when they already know the object's name, they can decide that a new label associated with the object denotes its substance.

does the child come up with *goed, to begin with? Obviously, by applying a generalization like "The past tense is formed by adding -ed to the present tense stem." Clearly, *went* isn't the result of a generalization; it's a specific, unique word meaning 'past tense of *go*'. So the Elsewhere Condition tells the child to stick to the narrower option. This is what we call **indirect negative data.**

O: Haven't you now predicted, nay, foretold, the nonexistence of synonymous words or terms? That appears to be most discouraging, disappointing, dissatisfying, disheartening, dispiriting, and dismaying . . .

L: I don't see that. Everything we've talked about, starting with the contrast between *innecessary* and *unnecessary,* happens within morphological paradigms. What we're predicting—correctly, it seems—is the nonexistence of synonyms within the same paradigm. That two words from different paradigms end up meaning the same thing is an accident that poses no special problem for acquisition, so long as the relevant words don't end up competing for the same "acquisition space" in given situations. It's true that if a child were to hear *automobile* used in exactly the same contexts as *car,* she'd assume that the two words correspond to different notions, perhaps an object and a shape (all experiments that have tested the matter show precisely this result [see fig. 6.18]). Then again, it's enough that these two synonyms don't cooccur, for the child to avoid trouble. For example, *automobile* seems to belong to a more scientific or formal register than *car;* very probably, *automobile* is used in less familiar situations than *car,* and therefore these two would never pose any problems.

6.4 Departures from Optimality

(which pertains to complex morphology, movement, and linguistic variation, and how these may all be related)

———— predicting the nonexistence of certain words from their features

O: Very well, now before you even bring it up, I shall tell you that I can see how your theory could predict that *wog,* meaning 'that *y* smiles causes *x*', doesn't exist. You need only say that for *wog* to exist, it would have to involve a structure like (33):

(33)

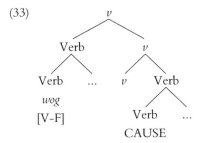

Needless to say, in (33) *wog* can't incorporate into the causative verb, since it would have to move downwards. You might try to incorporate *wog* after the causative element raises to Tense:

(34)

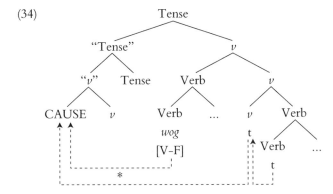

But this violates the Axiom of Lexical Relatedness, because at no point was *wog* inside the internal domain of the causative. I suppose what I don't see is how your theory differs from mine!

———————————————————————————————— on the nature of words

L: Oh, conceptually they're entirely different . . . In essence, you proposed a generative semantic procedure, where derivations go all the way back to thought [45]. And that's a good way to get into a big mess.

O: I was led down that path because you started splitting words apart—*saddle* and *shelve,* and so forth! What *is* a word in your view, anyway?

L: Definitely a complex object, with specific PF and LF properties. Anybody's theory has to assume this, for very simple reasons. For example, an idiom is a combination of lexical items with a single, holistic interpretation. We can't say that idioms are frozen in the

Figure 6.19

Even the most rigid idiomatic expressions are transparent to some degree: for instance, *kicked/will kick the bucket, give(s)/gave tongue, open a/several can(s) of worms, strike a/several bargain/s.* Some idiomatic expressions are necessarily transparent, in that one of their constituents is a variable bound by an expression outside the idiom: *get X's way, get on X's case.* This is significant: since part of its structure is not established, the idiom cannot be listed as an item in the lexicon. Note also that idioms have the PF properties of regular phrases. That is, *kick the bucket* has the PF structure of a phrase like *kick the packet,* and not that of a word like *kindergarten.*

lexicon, because we (for example) conjugate the verbs they contain, and they clearly have variable parts [see fig. 6.19]. At the same time, for PF purposes word-level units are formed in the course of the derivation, with clitic elements incorporating into their hosts and being linearized with respect to them via morphological procedures. This is all just factual, and the question is how to explain it. But the fact that words aren't in one-to-one correspondence with items from the lexicon doesn't mean that words are phrases—that's mixing apples with oranges. Phrases and syntactic structures in general obey the postulates of productivity, transparency, and systematicity, as is expected of UG objects, whereas words obey none of them—nor should they, if they're not syntactic in nature. True, some lexical items must make use of syntactic devices (in particular, incorporation) in order to meet their lexical requirements, but that still doesn't make them phrases. An item like *saddle-2,* for instance, must incorporate into v, or a structure involving it won't converge at LF, simply because *saddle-2* hasn't checked its features.

O: It reminds me a bit of viruses, which aren't able to replicate their DNA, and in that sense aren't living creatures. Nevertheless, they penetrate host cells and induce these hosts to replicate their viral DNA, thus creating more virus particles. In that sense, since they do end up reproducing their genetic information, they're also not inert entities, like rocks.

L: Once again, that's a mere analogy. In any case, lexical items do have certain relational properties that make them enter into syntactic dependencies. Some of these relational properties are established in the simplest fashion: one item relates to another item of the right sort through standard merger. This is what we call "assignment of a role." In some circumstances, though, item B that meets item A's relational requirement also forces a fusion between itself and item A, which is stronger than merger: incorporation. The minimal pairs *x put y on z* and *x y'd z* or *x z'd y* illustrate this quite well. Is an item like *saddle* a phrase? It's not. It's a word arising from the lexical item *saddle-2,* which happens to need a Prep (which in turn needs a v) to satisfy its lexical requirements. This is what makes a word sensitive to syntactic restrictions—and what explains why *wog* doesn't exist, without having to invoke Generative Semantics.

O: And what about an idiom? Is that a phrase?

L: I think the answer there is yes, although an idiom is also lexical, in the sense of being a unit of WI [46]. But I don't think there's any one lexical item, at least for some idioms, which we can hold responsible for determining the idiom's shape. In the idiom *kick the bucket,* what's the one word whose lexical properties force it to relate to the others? Is it *bucket?* Is it *kick?* I doubt it's either, because *bucket* isn't looking for just any verb within a given semantic class. In this, *kick the bucket* is different from *saddle,* which (just like *carpet, brake, file, cork,* and so on) looks for a locative prepositional element to relate with; one would have to say that *bucket* specifically looks for *kick.* Some idioms might be more systematic than this. Maybe *take advantage* is built from *advantage* in ways that aren't totally different from the ones used by *saddle-2* to produce *saddle;* but I don't see how to extend that to *kick the bucket.* So . . . we bite the bullet and assume that idiomatic expressions are what they are, in fact more akin to your viruses than standard words are, since they look like hybrids of some sort. In any case, they provide good evidence that we need a WI component to take care of word-level units which aren't directly listed in the lexicon.

————————————————————————— *different word formation processes*

O: I'm still a bit foggy about exactly how you distinguish *saddle* from *shelve.* I can see that each of these involves the same *v* and Prep elements—Prep being the pivot around which the word coheres. But it's also crucial that *saddle* be the specifier of Prep, and *shelve* its complement. How does *shelve* know not to be the specifier of Prep, or *saddle* its complement?

L: That's a bit like asking how *peanuts* "knows" not to be the specifier of *eat.* Suppose it were. You'd generate something like *peanuts ate Charlie Brown,* which is perfect in the syntax, but converges without a coherent interpretation. So let's say *saddle* starts out as the complement of Prep, thereby incorporating, with *the horse* in the specifier of Prep. That will converge, say, in *Jack saddled the horse,* with the meaning 'Jack put the horse on the saddle'. Is that bad?

O: I don't see why it should be, particularly because that's the sort of structure we find in *Jack corralled the horse.* Needless to say, it makes sense to put horses inside corrals, whereas it makes precious little sense to put horses on or inside saddles—something we don't do too often (we'd need dwarf horses or giant saddles, to start with).

Figure 6.20

Check your own judgments in the following scenarios.

Suppose you manage to put a small piece of toast inside a large stick of butter; have you "buttered" the toast? Display a miniature bottle on top of a large cork; have you "corked" the bottle? Put a falcon inside a large human hood; have you "hooded" the falcon?

Now check your judgments in the other direction. Suppose you draw a box on a report; have you "boxed" the report? Suppose you want to cover up a horse, but all you have with you is a plastic bag; have you "bagged" the horse? Suppose you're at a wine festival, and as part of the ritual you throw empty bottles from last year into this year's wine casks; have you "bottled" the wine?

Intuitions are not totally clear. Some perfectly standard uses of these sorts of denominal verbs pose similar questions. For example, does framing a picture involve putting a frame on the picture or putting the picture in a frame? That is, is the frame or the picture the location?

But let's say Jack does manage to put a horse inside a saddle. It still seems to me that this state of affairs can be described by saying that Jack put the horse inside the saddle, but not so well by saying that Jack saddled the horse . . .

L: I'm not so sure [see fig. 6.20]. In any case, that's a matter of perspective, and it's not clear that linguists have much to say about it. Why is it possible both to *man a ship* and to *ship a man?* Or to *cork a bottle* and to *bottle a cork?* In these instances, note, the basic relations are kept constant: when you man a ship, you put a crew of men on the ship; when you ship a man, you put the man on something like a ship; when you cork a bottle, you put a cork in the bottle's mouth; when you bottle a cork, you put the cork inside the bottle. Of course, different, idiosyncratic meaning details emerge in each case—the mouth of a bottle versus its inside, and so on. But that's expected, given that you're forming two different words. The important point is that the locative preposition which pivots both of these words may in principle host either its specifier (e.g., *man*) or its complement (e.g., *ship*). When this isn't possible, it must be because of extralinguistic reasons.

O: The issue you've convincingly raised is that we don't mix phrases and words; but I wonder whether this is true historically. Words often have idiomatic origins: *starboard* from *steer-board, rigmarole* from *ragman-roll, corduroy* from *corde-du-roi* . . . And of course, idioms have compositional origins.

L: I don't think it's very useful to ask what *kick the bucket* comes from; all I know is, I know it as an idiom. Same thing with *starboard* and *larboard,* whose origin I don't know, but which I relate to right and left in the appropriate way, when I'm on a boat. How I managed to acquire all this knowledge is an issue of only moderate interest (even for myself, personally), beyond the general sorts of issues we've raised.

——————————————————— *could all departures from optimality be related?*

O: I'm wondering about something else. Today we've discussed incorporations into all sorts of pivots—Prep, *v,* and so forth. Inasmuch as these are overt (they don't procrastinate), I presume that a strong feature is involved. Is that so?

L: That's a technical issue. Implicit in the logic of overt incorporation is movement/attraction prior to Spell-Out. But whether you want to say this is because of some strong feature, or because of some other reason having to do with word formation, is up for grabs, as far as I can tell.

O: Either way, though, I'm concerned with the fact that strong features (or equivalent morphological codings) are hosted by categories that trigger movement to their minimal domain. Alas, a great departure from the optimality of the ideal mapping to LF! Why does the system need movement/attraction?

L: Essentially, for morphological reasons.

O: But is that the answer or the question?! Lexical items must relate to other items which aren't their sisters, and then the system is set in motion. Right. So then the obvious question is what these morphemic elements are that trigger the flow. That doesn't seem to be clear. A morpheme appears to be an item in the lexicon, but this small creature doesn't know whether it will carry itself with the dignity of a separate word (like *shall* or *can*) or be gutted by the grim word that leaps ahead of the others, into the creature's domain (the fate that awaits *-ed,* and *-s,* and so forth). This embrace we call checking, and we've seen a great many instances of it; it depends so much on movement that one wonders whether the two are indeed different, or rather manifestations of the same thing. And why stop there? Is movement-checking any different from the fact that linguistic variation exists? If I've followed you, languages really differ only in terms of whether their functional categories are this or that, which results in different kinds of movement processes. Again, the fact that differences exist among languages is a departure from the simple mapping to a universal LF. One should therefore like to relate this departure to the other, which indeed follows directly if one identifies all three: movement, morphological checking, and variation.

L: Yes, departures from the optimality of the mapping to LF arguably have to do with the fact that, at the point of Spell-Out, the system branches off to PF.

O: But mightn't it then be the case that strong features . . . well, strong features are really viral, in more than a metaphorical fashion? Suppose that a strong feature is, in essence, a word that the system has "swallowed up" as a morpheme [47] . . .

Figure 6.21

Suppose for concreteness that functional items correspond to dimensions of the kind suggested in figure 2.20. It is not clear that a system with the potential of the lexicon (whereby sound and meaning symbols are paired indefinitely, up to memory limitations) is needed to linguistically encode these few dimensional notions. It is possible that the lexical context uniquely determines the functional structure. Thus, a verbal expression may be expected to come together with a Tense dimension; a whole sentence may be expected to come together with a Comp dimension; and so forth. Consider in this respect the Chinese sentence in (i):

(i) Chan shuo Chen dele jiang
     Chan said Chen get   prize
     'Chan said that Chen got the prize'

This is a clear case where translation (here, to English) is slightly inaccurate, since Chinese has no pronounced items *that* and *the,* and it encodes no obvious Tense morphology on a verb like *dele* (unlike *got,* the past form of *get*). The English word-for-word gloss is more precise. This gloss sounds like a sentence that Genie, a child raised in isolation, actually uttered after she was exposed to language (Curtiss 1977):

(ii) I like elephant eat peanut

However, the two cases are entirely different. By hypothesis, Genie's sentence contains no functional items, overtly or underlyingly. In contrast, an underlying representation of the Chinese sentence does have Comp, Det, Tense, or whatever functional categories the English sentence *Chan said that Chen got the prize* has. The difference is that whereas English uses words and morphemes to represent these categories, Chinese does not; instead, lexical context determines the presence of functional items.

L: And what do you mean by that?

O: We made a distinction between standard lexical items and grammatical functional items. Language has a fixed, very limited set of the latter. Suppose that the split between lexical and functional items means that they're not even part of the same mental stock [48]. Let's say that the lexicon lists only lexical items, and functional items are added only in the numeration—they don't exist in any other form [49]. Perhaps they're not even stored in memory proper (as lexical items are). Thus, although you may forget the name of your cousin, or what to call very small Mexican dogs, you don't forget how to form plurals or past tenses (unless you become aphasic, of course). Given this design for the system, human language learners have two very different acquisition jobs, do they not? For lexical items, the task is clear and the labour intensive: learners must make the correct pairings between form and meaning, and since these are arbitrary, they must learn them, test them, and so forth—as we've discussed today. For functional items, it would seem prima facie that matters should be easier. But in actual fact, these items turn out to be very hard, and wild children, for instance, never master them, not having been exposed to language during the critical period. This appears to be a fundamental difference between functional and lexical items; people learn new lexical items after the critical period, but they don't generally learn new grammatical items after puberty, at least when acquiring their first language, and (in most circumstances) they obviously acquire all these items much earlier than that. Which is best explained if we boldly assert that people don't learn grammatical items at all. That is to say, they learn their form, but not the items themselves. These are universal.

L: We're already assuming that, at least to some extent. Of course, to learn a lexical item from scratch would also be impossible. We need epistemologically prior notions that we don't learn at all, like "cause," "agent," and "action" (whatever those are [see secs. 2.4, 6.6]). As for functional items (which seem as epistemologically prior as these basic lexical notions), we have to consider why they in fact don't have a fixed form—and why children raised without access to human language aren't ever able to use them, if they're in fact universal. Hopefully, these are related questions.

_____   *some speculations on the emergence of functional forms*

O: Which reminds me of my earlier conjecture about why language has parameters of variation: UG won't specify what it needn't specify [see sec. 1.5]. For all we know, UG doesn't even specify that arbitrary pairings between meaning and form must be listed in the lexicon. It's perfectly plausible that this simply follows from the need to have a lexicon, since without the pairings, words simply won't exist. If humans had telepathy, they wouldn't need to encode the arbitrary dependency, and they could directly transmit concepts.

L: I'm not sure I agree with that—but go on, because I don't have a theory behind my intuition either . . .

O: Well, humans don't have telepathy, so they're stuck with these pairings. The point is, though, no statement within UG needs to say that the pairing must exist. (Just as no genetic instruction tells a leaping salmon to fall back into the water.) The same is true of functional items: very plausibly, UG says nothing about their form. Now, here the need for a *word* format is less evident. Trivially, if thousands of notions need to be encoded, separate articulated sounds or gestures or the like would seem a necessity. But if . . . what? only half a dozen regular cognitive dimensions need to be mapped into a syntactic structure, why should these items take any cumbersome lexical form? Perhaps they do (since humans have the capacity to form words anyway), or perhaps they don't (since humans also have morphemes at their disposal) [see fig. 6.21]. It's a matter of environmental chance, just as it's a matter of chance whether a bee becomes a queen, or stays a drudge for life. Relatively similar issues arise in early development [see sec. 1.2], where environmental input sets fundamental parameters of growth and form, in epigenesis. Which addresses the second concern: why don't wild children acquire functional items [50]? Because they missed the triggering experience during a critical age in development, just as a larva which doesn't get royal jelly never grows into a queen, even if as an adult it's made to swim in royal jelly for weeks—it'll drown before turning into royalty. I suggest that information for grounding functional items (as words or morphemes) is as basic for humans as royal jelly is for queen bees: both for the commoner bee and for the wild child, some fundamental dimensions (be they body patterns and associated behaviours in the case of bees, or mental patterns and associated behaviours in the case of humans) are wanting, because the key information that sets the system into those patterns is missing [see fig. 6.22].

Figure 6.22

(i) *The acquisition of the reproductive capacity in bees*

royal jelly	+	bee larva	→	queen bee
no jelly	+	bee larva	→	worker bee
royal jelly	+	worker bee	→	worker bee

Critical period: the time it takes to go from the larva to the adult stage

(ii) *The acquisition of the linguistic capacity in children*

human speech	+	human child	→	speaking adult
no human speech	+	human child	→	adult incapable of speech
human speech	+	adult incapable of speech	→	adult incapable of using functional items

Critical period: infancy to puberty

Why do children who are not exposed to language lack functional categories? Suppose these categories are verbal representations of the sorts of basic mental dimensions alluded to in figure 6.21. Suppose, further, that although the human mind has the potential to verbalize these dimensions, whether this potential is realized depends crucially on triggering information that comes from the environment during a critical period. If the child's environment provides no linguistic cues, hence no way of actualizing functional items (words, contextual lexical cues, or a combination), the child will develop without the ability to verbalize dimensions that are fundamental to language.

L: But even if I granted you all of that—how do functional dimensions emerge in different guises, in different languages?

O: As I see it, those are simply natural possibilities that the system provides. At the point of acquisition the learner must ask whether to encode, for example, Tense into a word or a morpheme. From the speech continuum itself, the answer may not be crystal clear. Observe for example the Old English sentence *dyslic bið þæt hwa woruldlice speda forhogie for manna herunge.* What is this telling us?

L: Yeah, it would be nice if you told us.

O: Oh, sorry. Er . . . 'foolish is that someone worldly goods despise for men's praise'. The point is: complementisers weren't pronounced in Old English; the element *þæt* in our sentence was literally the demonstrative 'that', so the sentence actually means 'foolish is that: for someone to despise worldly goods in order to obtain the praise of men'. Now, couldn't a child learning Old English, who after all has the function "complementiser" available in UG, hear this sentence and give it a structure such that *þæt* is a complementiser [51]? If so, the sentence would be analysed as 'foolish is that someone may despise worldly goods in order to obtain the praise of men'.

L: Sure—this is how complementizer *that* arose in English, and various other languages as well. Not in all, though—which is important. In the Romance languages, for instance, complementizers come from the Latin relative pronoun; complementizers can arise from conjunctions, adverbs, and even nouns and verbs which occur near complementizer regions, like *say*—for instance, the Ewe complementizer which is still used as the verb 'say' as well. The same is true of other functional items. The Greek future tense morpheme apparently comes from an older structure meaning 'I wish that', and the equivalent marker in Romance comes from Latin 'have', when used in structures expressing some kind of obligation (in the sense of 'to have to'). Determiners often start out as demonstratives, and gender classifiers as marks of agreement, in turn deriving from articles—and so on. These are tendencies, possibilities in the analysis of messy data. Until fairly recently, linguists often talked about cyclic patterns in this respect [see fig. 6.23]. But that picture seems to be too optimistic. After all, why should such cycles exist? To the extent that they do, they're patterns in very complex systems, with only indirect relevance to language—systems of populations, sys-

Figure 6.23

At the turn of the century, some linguists started studying patterns of regularity in linguistic change. For instance, Gabelentz (1891) metaphorically speculated that linguistic change is cyclic, with a tendency toward ease and a tendency toward distinctness. Pursuing such ideas, Meillet (1912) laid the foundation for much current work, which is still based on such dictums as "Today's morphology is yesterday's syntax" (Givón 1971, 413) and "[Periphrasis] is the major mechanism for achieving perceptual optimality in syntax" (Langacker 1977, 105).

Although statements of this sort may be true at an abstract level, they are only of programmatic help when trying to understand linguistic change. They are perhaps best summarized in another famous dictum, by Sapir (1921, 150): "Language moves down time in a current of its own making. It has a drift." But if language has no outside reality of its own, Sapir could have been right in only one word: "drift." Inasmuch as individuals acquire language from other individuals, for a brief

tems of primary linguistic data under different sorts of environmental pressures, and so on [see sec. 1.5]. To say these systems are behaving cyclically is to say they obey harmonic functions, which would be more surprising than saying, for instance, the weather behaves cyclically [52]. Maybe weather or population systems in language behave *sort* of cyclically in some instances, around certain attractors—but that's what we expect from complex systems. For instance, it's often claimed that learners analyze lexical elements as functional elements, functional elements as morphemes, and morphemes as zero elements.

O: In all honesty, I had a picture of that sort in mind . . .

L: But then you have to look at reality, and indeed, that course of events is possible—but not necessary. First of all, even when we find these tendencies at work, they don't happen at the same speed, or even at the same intervals, across languages. So whatever function might be relevant doesn't have any of the usual properties of simple harmonic functions. Second, and more important, the process may just halt indefinitely at any given point [53].

O: But can it be reversed?

L: People argue about that, but I don't know how anybody can really tell. The sort of observation that's needed is almost impossible. Besides, these are systems where we can't just logically work backward from a given point to a unique antecedent of that point—as is true of other equally complex systems. So we're basically stuck with observing things as they unfold, which means we're going to find missing links all through the textual record, and so on. It's really very messy.

O: I concede all those points. But let us assume, if only for the sake of argument, that (i) lexical elements can be analysed by learners as functional elements, and (ii) functional elements can be analysed by learners as morphemes, and (iii) morphemes can be analysed by learners as zero morphemes [see fig. 6.23].

L: I have no problem with that, a priori—and factually you're probably right. The issue raises nontrivial questions of learnability, though—for example, why a child decides to take the verbal form *have* as a future mark. Whatever you say here, you have to be extremely careful. Thus, suppose you assume the Subcase Principle

moment part of the linguistic system is exposed to unpredictable factors. Four aspects of the acquisition situation are dynamic:

1. Input data are not organized.
2. The LAD is sensitive to number of data of a given sort, up to critical amounts.
3. The LAD is able to determine "best hypotheses" to fit given data.
4. Learners are members of populations.

Furthermore, a LAD must have access to some kind of processing mechanism, with the interesting and crucial peculiarity that it must be a processor for a language that has not yet been acquired. Given this complex state of affairs, the sorts of dynamic scenarios discussed in the text could conceivably be explained in terms of how learners process incoming data. Three different scenarios for functional categories have been considered:

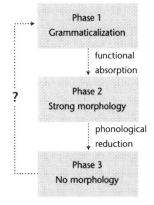

These dynamic phases do not relate to one another in any obvious linear way. It is possible, however, that each stage constitutes a complex phase transition of some sort with respect to the previous stage. Descriptively, the transition from phase 1 to phase 2 would correspond to the dictum that yesterday's syntax is today's morphology. The transition from phase 2 to phase 3 corresponds to the well-attested idea that morphological paradigms are lost through phonological reductions. Finally, whether the relation between phase 3 and phase 1 is a phase transition proper depends on whether the dynamic situation in the diagram is taken to be open (in the technical sense of section 1.7) and on how much credence is given to the dictum that the periphrastic analysis of lexical items as functional leads to perceptual optimality. How languages that have functioned for centuries without many periphrastic forms, like Chinese, have survived under allegedly suboptimal perceptual conditions remains a mystery. Moreover, if the system is closed, it should be easy to reconstruct its phase transitions both backward and forward. This is not what linguists have found, however: actual transitions of the sort assumed here are impossible to reconstruct backward. Another possibility is that there is no transition from phase 3 to phase 1. Rather, with the disappearance of a morphological cue, a way of representing a functional item disappears as well. Then it is possible (though not necessary) for learners to analyze certain lexical items as functional, if the data permit such an analysis. In this way, the entire sequence of open dynamic events starts over again, from a point not at all connected to the previous sequence. Given that creole languages systematically arise through phase 1, this possibility is more likely than the other.

predicts that, given two competing structures, the learner goes with the more specific one—and say you convince yourself that the future interpretation of *have* is more specific than the very general interpretations *have* can be assigned. But then why did learners of Romance take this route, and not learners of Germanic or Greek [54]? English speakers instead use a form of *shall* or *will* for the same purposes. You'd have to consider the frequency of a sort of structure in a given environment, for instance. You'd have to argue that the relevant number of structures involving *have* which could have a future sense in English or Greek is, for some reason, smaller than the relevant number of structures involving *will* in similar contexts, with a similar sense. Presumably, mutual exclusivity assumptions would then make the child learning Germanic or Greek stick to *will* or a variant thereof. As you can see, nothing very clean . . .

O: Granted. You may of course say that the mess makes the analysis not worth pursuing, and I might even agree—if it weren't that reflecting on these matters might provide a bit of an insight as to why strong features exist, in our otherwise clean system.

L: Whatever happens after Spell-Out in the branch to PF, or what happens anywhere because of considerations having to do with the phonological component, I already expect to be messier than whatever happens in the syntactic mapping, particularly the covert part.

-- where morphemes come from

O: I understand that general expectation; but I think we can be a bit more specific . . . In fairly concrete terms, I'd suggest that strong features that lure items into their domain should appear when learners take separate functional items as morphemes. For example, consider a Later Latin passage such as *quomodo dicere habes? veritatem dicere habeo.* That is, 'what (to) say have (you)? truth (to) say have (I)' or 'what have you to say? the truth, I have to say'. Firstly, this is the type of instance where the obligation use of *habere* is very close to the future meaning—so the passage could be interpreted as 'what will you say? the truth, I shall say'. Secondly, notice that the words *dicere habeo* are adjacent in the way they need to be, for a learner to take *habeo* as a morpheme of a combined form *dicere-habeo.*

L: Arguably because these sentences are a question and its emphatic answer, they involve movement of the verb *dicere* to the checking domain of Comp, after having adjoined to the auxiliary *habeo* in Tense [see fig. 6.24] [55].

O: Right. And now consider a version of the second sentence in one of the mediaeval Romance languages: the Old Spanish *dezir vos he la verdad* 'tell you (I) shall the truth', or 'tell you the truth, I shall' [56]. Here, too, the verb *dezir* has moved, for some reason. Notice also that now the Latin *habeo* appears in the much more reduced form *he.*

L: Yes, that *he* 'have' is itself a clitic—like the indirect object *vos* 'to you'—and it ends up hosted by *dezir* in Comp [see fig. 6.24].

O: Now, had the speaker chosen to drop the indirect object (a perfectly natural possibility), the resulting sentence would have been *dezir he la verdad.* A learner of Old Spanish might then reasonably wonder whether these are two words which happen to occur in this particular sequence, [[dezir] he], or whether they form a single word [dezir-he]. If the learner takes the latter option, the verbal *dezir* 'say' has now gained a new form with which to be conjugated. Why does the learner assume that the feature he has analysed as a morpheme is strong? Because it's there! Indeed, it's the very presence of *he* that allowed the learner to move in this direction. This should be emphasised: I am not claiming that merely because *he* is cliticised to a verb, the child must necessarily analyse it as a morpheme. It is possible that, given the right sort of circumstances (whatever those are), the child continues to assume that *he* is a clitic on a verb *dezir* that has moved to Comp for reasons that have nothing to do with the strength of Tense—but rather, involve the strength of Comp (for example, in a question or in an expressive context). However, should the child assume that *he* is a morpheme of a single word *dezirhe,* then he must acknowledge its presence: it's a viral element that attracts the verb into checking it. And why is it viral? Because morphology isn't syntax [57]. The immediate reaction of the syntactic system towards a morphemic intruder is to eliminate it as soon as possible. The child (unconsciously) knows *he* to be a morpheme, and the rest follows. Call that "dynamic phase 2" (dynamic phase 1 being the interpretation of a lexical item as a functional item). Logically, phase 1 precedes phase 2, although phase 1 doesn't necessarily linearly map to phase 2. Patently, we also

Figure 6.24

(i) *Latin question*

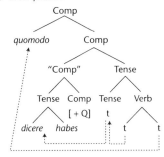

(ii) *Latin focus fronting*

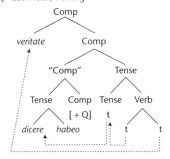

(iii) *Old Spanish stylistic (verbal) fronting*

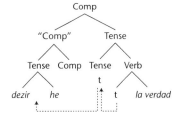

need a dynamic phase 3, in which features are weak—that is to say, no longer a cause of derivational cancellation. In large part, this must correlate with phonological reduction tendencies.

L: Well, that's true—and in the nature of PF. Vowels and consonants are often dropped in normal speech; stress changes, causing grammatical features to be less salient perceptually; adjacent phonological segments assimilate. Just hearing people pronounce *I'm going to prove that* as [äm-ə-ˈprüv-dä] is enough to illustrate this process. I should add, also, that morphological paradigms easily lose members. This may be in part because phonological reductions go in the direction of less marked forms. Eventually paradigms collapse, since the different forms are perceptually indistinguishable [58].

O: Finally, a way is needed of moving from a language with weak (eventually no) morphology, to one where lexical items are reanalysed as functional. And to be honest, I do not know what to say about this transition [see fig. 6.23] [59]. But say you grant me all these points as pertaining to various learning possibilities that arise, given different sorts of inputs—and provided that nothing that I've said challenges anything you've said. Suppose you even accept my rationalisation of viral strong features in terms of their morphological (ultimately, nonsyntactic) character. You'll still ask me one last question.

L: Why does C_{HL} have uninterpretable features?

6.5 On the Origins of Uninterpretable Features
(with other circumstances that, again, partake more of accuracy in reporting than of discretion in doing so)

O: I say, you're good! Right, which is like asking why C_{HL} has LF movement/attraction.

L: . . .

_____   *is there a rationale for uninterpretable features?*

O: Needless to say, *if* LF movement is required, then the uniformity of the mapping to LF will guarantee that it takes place for checking reasons, just as the movement prior to Spell-Out does [60]. But why should the conditional clause be true? Why does LF movement exist if it constitutes a departure from the optimality of the system, and

its justification in the overt component has to do with matters pertaining to morphology? Here two possibilities arise, actually: either
all languages have uninterpretable features or only some do. Let's
consider first the possibility that languages need not have uninterpretable features, such as Case. Then why do some languages have
such features? Consider again my dynamic phase 2. Imagine that
the learner of Old Spanish has hypothesised that Tense has strong
verbal features—a virus the verb must eliminate. This means that in
this learner's grammar Verb will have to move to Tense, and now the
learner may wonder the following: is Verb moving to Tense merely
because Tense has a strong feature, or also because Verb itself has a
T-feature [61]?

L: In both scenarios Verb would move to Tense overtly (assuming
Tense's feature is strong) [62]. However, in the second scenario the
checking of features goes both ways: Tense gets its strong feature
checked by Verb, and Verb gets its feature checked by Tense. So this
involves more checking.

O: Then two questions are evident. One: is this a reasonable assumption for the learner to make? I think it is: that the learner
should assume the worst-case scenario is what the Elsewhere Condition would predict. In this instance, the issue is one of lexical
choice: deciding whether Verb must have a given T-feature which
is compatible with the environment where Verb appears. Assuming
that this is the case is more specific (involves more information) than
assuming that it isn't, and that Verb has no such feature. But thus far
we've said nothing terribly interesting: the learner assumes that if
Verb moves to Tense, it must be because each gets something out
of the move—it's a greedy world [63]! This, however, doesn't tell
us much about *un*interpretable features; why should the learner
even think there's anything like an uninterpretable feature that carries Verb to Tense, instead of its being an interpretable one? That's
the second question.

L: Well, why should the learner even think the feature in question
is interpretable [64]?

O: Ah! Right on the mark . . . If derivations don't have a mind of
their own, all the learner can reasonably assume is this: there's a
T-feature in Verb which is related to Tense, because that's a safe
assumption to make. As for whether the T-feature in question is
interpretable, we cannot decide this teleologically; we must apply

the same mechanics as before. Assuming the Elsewhere Condition, should the T-feature be interpretable or uninterpretable? Interestingly, the condition predicts the latter, for the very simple reason that the system need do nothing about the T-feature in the checking domain of Tense if the feature's interpretable, but it must clearly eliminate the feature if it's uninterpretable. This is accomplished via Erase/Delete, a further operation involving further system information—thus, the Elsewhere Condition will choose this option over the other [65]. As we saw in other instances of learning involving subcases, some other, positive information in the system may make the LAD revise its assumptions—thus deciding, perchance, that the feature in question is interpretable. But this is of no concern now, the important point being that I've justified the birth of an uninterpretable feature.

L: By assuming that there is an uninterpretable feature, to start with!

O: Well, not quite. Rather, by assuming that I have no reason to assume that the feature in question is interpretable! I'm now trying to suggest that uninterpretable features arise in a linguistic world that has "viral" features that affect the overt mapping. If you grant me that those exist for some reason or other, in the case I've just described the LAD may rightfully ask, when facing overt movement, "Do all the items involved in this particular checking have strong features?" For the LAD to conclude, "No, the fellow that's moving here must involve an interpretable feature"—ceteris paribus—would be unexpected . . .

L: But that can't be right, for you want to make sure that it isn't the case, for just any strong feature the system involves, that it also entails an uninterpretable feature in the element that moves to check it. Compare, in this respect, *wh*-movement with movement for Case reasons. Take a language like English, with a strong feature in Tense requiring that subjects move to the domain of Tense. To say that the LAD in this situation hypothesizes that subjects moved to Tense involve an uninterpretable feature that carries them to the checking domain of Tense has no empirical consequences, given that the subject will move to the domain of Tense anyway. (The decision may have empirical consequences with regard to the larger issue of why there are uninterpretable features in the system, but let's set that aside for now.) Next, consider, still in English, the fact that a strong question feature in Comp requires that a *wh*-phrase move to the domain of Comp. In this instance, the conclusion that the *wh*-phrase has an uninterpretable feature does have empirical consequences—wrong ones [see sec. 5.6 and fig. 6.25].

—————————————————————————————— *matters of lexical relatedness*

O: I can see that, but I think there's a difference between these two cases, which my picture in (35) illustrates:

(35)

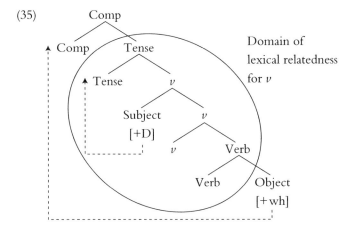

The subject that moves to Tense starts within the specifier (hence, the internal domain) of *v,* and it moves to the specifier of Tense. Clearly, *v* is lexically related both to its subject and to Tense, and the subject and Tense are therefore related within a lexical relatedness domain. In contrast, any argument that were to move to Comp would not be lexically related to the one and only category which is lexically related to Comp—namely, Tense. Thus, the object (or any other argument) and Comp are not related within a lexical relatedness domain. You may ask, "Why should that be relevant?" We could make it relevant, as follows:

(36) When and only when X and Y are lexically related to Z, if a strong F, a feature in X, attracts F′, a feature in Y, assume that Y has an uninterpretable X-feature and X an uninterpretable feature-Y.

We want (36) to follow, as a learning strategy, from the Elsewhere Condition. The LAD hypothesises that Y has been displaced to X, and it needs some sort of feature to justify the movement/attraction—otherwise, the Last Resort Condition will be violated. Then the LAD assumes the strongest possible hypothesis. And why limit

Figure 6.25

(i) *Movement to subject position*

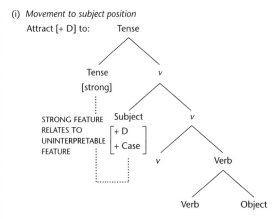

(ii) *Wh-movement*

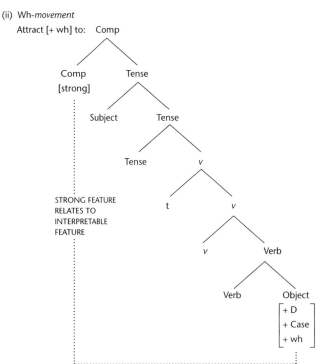

Figure 6.26

The ungrammaticality of an example like (i) shows that the phenomenon of Case exists in a language like English (see fig. 3.8).

(i) *you to convince me would be nice

It is considerably harder to show this for a language like Chinese:

(ii) [ni   shi   wo   xiangxing] tai   hao le
      you make me   convinced   very nice aspect
      '[that you have convinced me/for you to convince me] is very
      nice'

(Problem case suggested by Howard Lasnik through personal communication; data courtesy of Jian-Xin Wu.) Does (ii) involve a tensed or an infinitival subject sentence? Here morphology does not help: the verb *shi* 'make' is not inflected. If the subject clause in (ii) is infinitival, it is not obvious where the subject pronoun *ni* checks its Case. It could be that Case is checked in some abstract position (akin to the English *for*, but not pronounced), or that Chinese subjects need not be Case-marked. The second conclusion is perhaps less desirable on more general, conceptual grounds. See Aoun and Li 1993a for an indirect argument that Chinese subjects are Case-marked.

(36) to domains of lexical relatedness? Because the Elsewhere Condition is relevant only when there are a couple of alternatives; if there are more, the comparison task becomes intractable. Domains of lexical relatedness are nice domains of locality where this sort of learning consideration can easily be determined. In actual fact, the elusive notion of "paradigm" could possibly be made concrete in these terms.

L: Suppose this were the missing link you've been looking for: having a strong feature in X entails assuming that there's an uninterpretable feature in whatever Y moves to X, as long as X and Y are lexically related to Z. I still don't see why this grants us uninterpretable features in a language, like Chinese, let's say, where there are no strong features to start with . . .

———————————————————————————————— *issues of covert morphology*

O: In this first general scenario, we've been considering the possibility that only some languages have uninterpretable features, like Case. As we move to the second scenario, to consider the possibility that all languages have uninterpretable features, my first question would be, "What's your evidence that Chinese has Case?" I don't suppose you mean morphological case, in a language without apparent inflectional morphology! I don't suppose, either, that you mean Case somehow indirectly showing up via agreement, in a language without agreement! Then again, you might have in mind a sentence like *you to convince me would be nice,* which shows, I believe, that the English subject *you* needs Case, and the infinitival verb cannot provide it [see fig. 3.8]. But how do you intend to show this in Chinese, where one can't really tell an infinitival from a tensed verb [see fig. 6.26]?

L: That's naive falsificationism! Conceptually we know that languages don't differ in whether they have uninterpretable features. This is because interpretive operations at the interface should be very simple, particularly if the interpretive systems are as impoverished as we're assuming . . .

O: I thought you didn't know what goes on in those systems that lie "beyond LF"!

L: I'm just naturally extending our Minimalist Program assumptions, from the competence systems to other systems in the language faculty [66]. If the Minimalist view is correct, the forms that reach LF should be as similar as possible, which limits the class of structures to hypothesize.

O: Isn't the assumption that LF representations should be as similar as possible incompatible with our discussion of *wh*-movement in English and Chinese [see sec. 5.5]?

L: I don't think so; in fact, we concluded that Chinese doesn't even have *wh*-movement, and uses a different interpretive structure to create questions. Remember, *wh*-features are interpretable—and needn't move. In fact, what forces overt *wh*-movement is a strong ("viral") feature, and not an uninterpretable one; so the variation is, as usual, restricted to the overt side of the grammar. What I'm now saying is that we don't expect some languages to have uninterpretable features at the interface and some not to—that would lead to very different sorts of LF representations. Then, since some languages obviously have uninterpretable features, they must all have them.

O: But if uninterpretable features must be checked prior to the LF interface, even if some languages have such features and others don't, the LF representations will be the same.

L: Not if it's only by way of uninterpretable features that certain features move. In a language with an uninterpretable Case feature in the object, say, the bundle of formal features that contains the Case feature is going to raise to a relevant checking domain— maybe as high as Tense. If another language didn't have the relevant Case feature, the corresponding bundle of formal features would have to stay put within VP, given economy. Then the two languages would have different representations at LF [67] . . .

O: All right, but even saying that I share your methodological consideration, I cannot let the LAD learning Chinese, for example, even consider hypothesising no uninterpretable feature in the domain where there could be one. Radically put, the learning strategy in (36) must be strengthened to (37):

(37) When and only when X and Y are lexically related to Z, if there *were* a strong F, a feature in X, that *could* attract F′, a feature in Y, assume that Y has an uninterpretable X-feature and X an uninterpretable feature-Y.

However, to make (37) follow from anything natural, one must make some rather surprising assumptions about morphology. (37) claims that whenever a derivation involves a domain of lexical relatedness, it must also involve an uninterpretable feature, regardless of whether an actual strong feature is present or not. This is why I initially raised my question about the nature of idioms. Consider *take a hike,* in its idiomatic sense of 'get lost'. This is a unit of lexical expression, and yet it is not a single lexical unit. You yourself admitted that this sort of expression is "like a virus" in that it has both lexical and phrasal properties. Suppose this duality is interpreted thus: at LF an uninterpretable feature in *hike* must actually raise to the domain of *take,* just as in the formation of the verb *to hike* the entire noun *hike* overtly moves to the domain of some *v* element with the same import as *take.* This happens, I presume, because a strong feature in the numeration is involved in the formation of *hike,* while no such thing happens in the formation of *take a hike.* Otherwise, the elements are derivationally very similar. The fact that the entire word *hike* has had to move—and not merely the relevant features attracted by the strong feature in *v*—in the case of *to hike* is only a result of the fact that the operation takes place before Spell-Out (since the strong feature must be eliminated in the course of the derivation), thus before the word *hike* has split into its three constituent feature matrices. In actual fact, this means that for every idiomatic expression, morphological processes are happening *at LF* [68]. Now we've come full circle. Overt morphological items may be viral, forcing an immediate erasure as the syntactic derivation proceeds. But viruses aren't always deadly; some, one's system learns to live with, parasitically. On this analogy, we may suppose that uninterpretable features are parasites: the system needn't eliminate them to survive a derivation, but it does need to eliminate them eventually to produce an interpretable representation.

L: But note that (37) says something stronger than what you're now implying: given any domain of lexical relatedness, you'll in effect have an idiom, in the sense that an uninterpretable feature will be involved.

O: That's why I'm saying one must make surprising assumptions about morphology. In essence, even *John loves Mary* involves an idiomatic expression—actually, two. One is a relation between the uninterpretable Case features of *Mary* and the verb *loves.* The other is a relation between the uninterpretable Case features of *John* and Tense. How bad can that be, though? This "idiom" wouldn't have a pronunciation in English; but then again, Basque speakers would pronounce it in the form of object and subject agreement. Is that less an idiom than *take a hike?* Only in the sense that the latter involves a word whose content is mostly lexical, and thus has some interpretable (semantic) content. However, the verb *to hike* is already less lexical than *take a hike,* in that *to hike* involves some sort of null *v* with no clear lexical content. Well then, object agreement or subject agreement is an even less lexical idiom, involving purely functional features from nouns and whatever their Case checker is. The important point, though, is that in both instances some sort of word-level unit is formed at LF which is driven by uninterpretable features. In the case of LF units, I'd say we're witnessing a consequence of the learning mechanism. That is to say, suppose the LAD makes no assumptions about LF morphology, but does make assumptions about standard morphology: in particular, that complex morphology involving featural displacement arises whenever features are lexically related (noting that features are lexically related even if movement hasn't taken place—recall (21)). Then the LAD may take the very worst scenario (hence the preferred one, given the Elsewhere Condition) to be one where all lexical dependencies are analysed as *potentially* involving movement. If we assume that processes can (and hence do) happen covertly in those domains where they do happen overtly, even if not clearly in the language being learnt, then LF morphology results [69].

L: Maybe. I still don't see the premises behind (37) following from anything natural, though.

_____ *what would an evolutionary scenario look like?*

O: Well, we should have to say that the linguistic system has actually *adapted* into assuming (37)—unlike everything else in the mapping to LF, which is presumably an *exaptation.*

L: What?—Why?

O: (37) isn't something that follows either from LF, or corresponding intentional-conceptual properties—or from virtual conceptual necessity. Then I can immediately think of only two options. One I've already mentioned: perhaps some languages have no uninterpretable features. I actually agree with you that this conclusion isn't terribly pretty, even if you can't prove that Chinese indeed has Case. Chinese certainly has idioms, which presumably also involve uninterpretable features to relate different lexical items at LF, if my speculations are correct. So then suppose things are as you've said, and all languages exhibit uninterpretable features. Why do they depart from optimality in such a drastic way? That's in essence the question of why languages have words; that's why I don't think it's trivial that *rigmarole* comes from *ragman-roll,* just as it's not trivial that *hike* is associated with *take a hike.* Why do these pockets of lexical regularity emerge? Why isn't the system such that it encodes only those pristine thoughts I wanted it to encode, mapping *CAUSE* and *TO* and *DIE* to *CAUSE-TO-DIE,* instead of *kill?* Granted that this is how the system works, with words and phrases, you may still ask why it's natural for it to do so. If virtual conceptual necessity or interface conditions don't entail the existence of *kill,* does the fact that your system forges such entities have other advantages? It is strong viral features that force overt movement/attraction, thereby transporting two items to a domain of morphophonological codependency and resulting in *kill.* Once this is a possibility, the system may naturally treat the codependent items as a unit (presumably, this is what happened historically in *rigmarole*). To make the story explicit, we can think of this step as resulting from some sort of biological mutation, whereby the linguistic system of humans became capable of the long-distance association which is the key to movement/attraction.

L: Look, that's just not—

O: Hold on—do let me play Devil's advocate. In actual fact, it's because the system allows movement/attraction that humans have words that go beyond trivial naming. The question is, then, whether a system that allows humans to say *kill* is more or less advantageous than one that allows only *CAUSE-TO-DIE.* Notice that asking the evolutionary question now isn't totally pointless, because we're considering two alternatives: one with words, one without [70]. One might argue that encapsulating the information *CAUSE-TO-DIE* in a single lexical item is more efficient than always having to express this concept phrasally, which may be one of the reasons why people tend to name things, rather than always describing them [71]. If we're in danger, being able to call out that you'd better "Pass me that spear" is considerably more useful than saying something akin to "There is an event at the present time which has you, myself, and a concrete, countable artefact called 'spear' as participants, which is an event of causation and exchange, and where you are the subject of the causation, I am the receiving part of the exchange, and the bloody spear is what's transferred"!

L: Look, if you like evolutionary fairy tales, you have to at least be serious about them. To start with, your whole argument is based on a mutation which sounds crazy: the possibility of long-distance syntactic association. Why is movement an option that pre-sapiens didn't have?

O: That's a fair question, but I suspect their lack relates to something more basic: rhythm [72].

L: ?!

O: Yes, I should like to suggest that specific aspects of the architecture supporting UG may have evolved from something else, and I should like to tell you how this may have happened, using one of the few mental representations outside of the language faculty that something's known about: music. Needless to say, just as humans are capable of speaking, so too they're capable of producing and understanding music, to the point that it's fair to say they have a specialised Universal Musical Grammar [see fig. 6.27]. Surely, musical representations have no meaning, of the sort humans ascribe to LF representations; they look more like PF representations, with harmonies, tones, and—crucially—rhythm. But of course, if music were a species-specific adaptation, what would it be in aid of [73]? 'Tis pretty, no doubt—but does that give anyone an edge? Now, suppose that music proper is just an exaptation (or a spandrel, even) of something else, whose purpose was different. To be specific, it may well be that what gave humans music is nothing other than what gave them the ability to map LF structures to a viable PF form. I'm thinking of Linear Correspondence, which allows linear expression of hierarchical structure. Needless to say, without something like the LCT, it would be well-nigh impossible to translate hierarchical musical motifs into a sequence of organised notes [74]. The same is true of linguistic structures. Just picture language and music (if those terms are even appropriately used) prior to linear correspondence. You couldn't really tell, by listening to me, whether my sequence <α, β, γ> (be those words or notes) corresponds to the constituent structure {{α, β}, γ}, or to the structure {α, {β, γ}}, or to {{α, γ}, β}, or even to the flat {α, β, γ}—for unless you assume linear correspondence, ternary (or even *n*-ary) merger is possible [see sec. 3.5]. In the case of language you could perhaps determine which one I meant through context, but in the case of music you'd have no clue whether I'd just sung the first three notes of "The Internationale" or of "Yellow Submarine." And here

"Happy Birthday" and "Yadhtrib Yppah." ("Happy Birthday" is in the public domain; "Yadhtrib Yppah" will be in the public domain if the universe crunches back—and is for now adapted from Jackendoff, *Patterns in the mind*)

Figure 6.27

Excerpts from Jackendoff 1994:

Why should it be that a sequence of notes . . . makes sense as music? Not every collection of notes sounds like music. . . . Imagine we're listening for the very first time to . . . "Happy Birthday," and let's compare this experience with hearing the same tune played upside down and backward.
　　Even on the first hearing, we will surely recognize the former tune as a coherent tune. . . . But the latter . . . will sound odd, like a bunch of senseless notes, and it will be pretty tough to hum along with. (pp. 165–166)

Knowing [musical] patterns enables us to . . . notice it if . . . (some) wrong notes violate the melodic or harmonic patterns that we associate with this style of music. Or consider listening to jazz. . . . [Players] don't play the literal notes of the tune[, but] something that is related to the tune in harmony, rhythm, and melodic structure. We can recognize these relationships . . . evidently by intuitively extracting and comparing the patterns of the original tune and the solo choruses. . . .
　　The analogy to language ought to be obvious. . . . To push the parallel, I'll call this collection of patterns a *musical grammar*. [And] if we each have a mental grammar for music, how did we get it? (pp. 166ff.)

Jackendoff then proposes that the musical grammar is universal (and see Lerdahl and Jackendoff 1983), concluding with the following question:

So the overall picture is that there is a partly specialized Universal Musical Grammar, which, like language, is a species-specific adaptation. An adaptation for what?—That's not so clear. . . . I consider this a real puzzle. (p. 170)

Figure 6.28

The complexity of constituent arrangements, given a sequence of perceived heads, grows dramatically:

(i) *Possible constituent arrangements of the sequence <α, β>*
$\{\alpha, \beta\}$

(ii) *Possible constituent arrangements of the sequence <α, β, γ>*
$\{\{\alpha, \beta\}, \gamma\}, \{\alpha, \{\beta, \gamma\}\}, \{\{\alpha, \gamma\}, \beta\}, \{\alpha, \beta, \gamma\}$

(iii) *Possible constituent arrangements of the sequence <α, β, γ, δ>*
$\{\alpha, \beta, \gamma, \delta\}, \{\alpha, \{\beta, \gamma, \delta\}\}, \{\alpha, \{\{\delta, \beta\}, \gamma\}\}, \{\alpha, \{\delta, \{\beta, \gamma\}\}\},$
$\{\alpha, \{\{\delta, \gamma\}, \beta\}\}, \{\alpha, \{\delta, \beta, \gamma\}\}, \{\beta, \{\alpha, \gamma, \delta\}\}, \{\beta, \{\{\alpha, \delta\}, \gamma\}\},$
$\{\beta, \{\alpha, \{\delta, \gamma\}\}\}, \{\beta, \{\{\alpha, \gamma\}, \delta\}\}, \{\beta, \{\alpha, \delta, \gamma\}\}, \{\gamma, \{\alpha, \beta, \delta\}\},$
$\{\gamma, \{\{\alpha, \beta\}, \delta\}\}, \{\gamma, \{\alpha, \{\beta, \delta\}\}, \{\gamma, \{\{\alpha, \delta\}, \beta\}\}, \{\gamma, \{\alpha, \beta, \delta\}\},$
$\{\delta, \{\alpha, \beta, \gamma\}\}, \{\delta, \{\{\alpha, \beta\}, \gamma\}\}, \{\delta, \{\alpha, \beta, \gamma\}\}\}, \{\delta, \{\{\alpha, \gamma\}, \beta\}\},$
$\{\delta, \{\alpha, \beta, \gamma\}\}, \{\{\alpha, \beta, \{\gamma, \delta\}\}, \{\{\alpha, \gamma\}, \{\beta, \delta\}\}, \{\{\alpha, \delta\}, \{\beta, \gamma\}\},$
$\{\{\alpha, \beta\}, \gamma, \delta\}, \{\{\alpha, \gamma\}, \beta, \delta\}, \{\{\alpha, \delta\}, \beta, \gamma\}, \{\alpha, \beta, \{\gamma, \delta\}\}, \{\alpha, \gamma,$
$\{\beta, \delta\}\}, \{\alpha, \delta, \{\beta, \gamma\}\}$

The possible arrangements of the sequence <α, β, γ, δ, ε> would not fit on this page. Assuming an LCA reduces these possibilities, since LF hierarchical structure is taken to be directly correlated with the PF linear ordering.

I'm talking about just three notes; adding even a few more symbols would condemn you to eons trying to decipher messages, which makes this a useless system of communication—even if it's a system of thought [see fig. 6.28]. The moment that Linear Correspondence kicks in, though, the picture becomes clearer. The sequence <α, β, γ> corresponds to the constituent structure $\{\alpha, \{\beta, \gamma\}\}$. And so forth. In a sense, then, the LCT serves as a "switchboard" between PF and LF [75].

L: But I think you still have a problem. Suppose I were to accept your claim that some sort of "switchboard" allows humans to map PF to LF. Now imagine a human ancestor—one with the "LCT mutation"—trying to acquire language. What's she supposed to be learning, if there are no instantiations of the (PF, LF) pair around her—if nobody around her is speaking Human? In other words, where's the information found that's needed for the linguistic ability to be triggered [76]?

O: Granted, yes—that's a serious question. It may have been that for millennia humans with the ability to speak, never did. However, suppose that, as you were ready to suggest the first day we met, communication is more inferential than codified [77]. That is to say, suppose the communicator displays evidence to his listeners that he intends to inform them of something, and the listeners infer his intention from the evidence; given creatures who are capable of attributing mental states to others, this might have worked. For example, given a fellow who utters α every time he sees you, or even when he doesn't, but he's after you, you may reasonably take α to be a way of summoning you—particularly if the fellow doesn't use α when he's after someone else. If he's sufficiently high in the social structure of your clan, you may have gotten yourself a name.

L: Of course, I could now ask how it occurred to that Newton among our ancestors to ever name me—but I've got a tougher question. I imagine you could invent stories like this for object naming. But how about kinds? Whatever leads our Newton to learn that α means 'woman' and not 'man'?

O: You'd have to grant humans, first of all, the ability to classify as part of what they acquired when they stumbled onto the "switchboard." This isn't implausible, for even Neanderthals had elaborate rituals, tool-making abilities, fire control, and so forth—activities that presuppose classification, even if not linguistically expressed, or only rudimentarily so. Second, you'd have to grant humans the Elsewhere Condition and the mutual exclusivity hypothesis. Now, when the Newton of your clan calls out α to a clan member whose name you (think you) know is β, and then calls out α to a different clan member γ, you'll (think you) know that α cannot be someone's name, but is something more general.

L: Or possibly that this Newton's gone crazy and has to be ousted.

O: That would be an unfortunate turn of evolution. Then again, we have thousands of clans and thousands of years at our disposal to get the whole thing started, and moving along step by step . . . At some point, one hopes, at least one clan arises where not just a single member but numerous members name objects—which poses another immediate problem. When we don't know the name for something, we ask. But whom can we possibly ask when things have no names [78]? Humans encountered this situation many times in precultural stages. When they migrated to new, unpopulated areas, they had to refer to new species of animals and plants, new geographical features, new activities, et cetera. What did they do then?

L: The same thing children do when they don't know the name for something, and don't bother to ask: invent a compound.

O: Spot on. For example, a child can call a gardener a *plant-man* [79]. When Native Americans first saw locomotives, they called them *iron-horse*. And what is that, but an association?

L: Yeah, but I don't see that this association is long-distance: it doesn't have to involve syntactic displacement like the kind we talked about for *saddle* and *shelve.* I thought you were trying to show me how movement relations give humans an adaptive edge—and I still don't see that.

O: Granted. As a matter of fact, prehumans with no rhythmic capacity (no LCT) may have had all these amenities: naming, classification, compounding, and perhaps others. However, whatever protolanguage they had must have been very limited—as limited as pidgins are, or the language of one-year-olds, or the language of aphasics, tourists, and new immigrants [80]. The limitations are of two sorts, actually. The addressee's problem is one of processing: to know what the addresser means. The addresser's problem is one of expressiveness: to know how to say what he means [81]. Needless to say, if the exchange of information is trivial ("Ouch!" "Idiot!" "Hey, you," and so forth), these two demands match up reasonably well. But the problem is compounded when some other Newton in some other clan tries to pass on some useful information: how to make a tool, how to trick a mammoth, what berries cause stomach-ache—that sort of thing. Naming each of these would be both difficult and essentially pointless. Difficult, because these aren't things, or even clearly unified events, in some natural sense. Some activities may be perceived as unified; perhaps there are names for those, associated with expressions of joy (*birth!!*) or sadness (*death . . .*), or with those timeless imperatives *eat!, run!, gimme!, hide!, shut up!* However, most articulated events are much less unified: sharpening a tool, building a hut, starting a fire, et cetera. And even if one could give these events names, what would be the point in doing so? The purpose of communicating something about an event usually isn't referring to it, but describing it. Calling your innovative stick-rubbing fire-starting technique does little towards telling me how to use it. Somehow, you must find ways of integrating lots of names and descriptions into unified little plots. By using nouns as endpoints of activities, as in "*Run stick!*", you may convey to me that I should get sticks. I may be informed of how poor my choice of sticks was if you angrily tell me to "*Eat stick!*", or how good it was if you say "*Gimme stick.*" When I fail to place dry straw in the hollow of the larger stick, you might get creative and tell me to "*Hide straw!*", metaphorically meaning that the straw must be placed there, so the point of the smaller stick can rub against it. And so forth [82].

L: So far I'm not really describing events, but giving orders. The sentences you're creating don't have truth values, so they're not yet anything like what we find in real languages—they don't allow interconnections, embedding, and in short the basic syntactic structure that distinguishes *you should give me an orange to eat* from the ape's *give orange me give eat orange me eat orange give me etc.* [see sec. 1.4].

O: Absolutely, but that's precisely my point. At this stage in the evolution of language, you might not be able to go beyond *give orange me*. Thus, imagine you wanted to express Tense, perhaps because of the whim of some Newton who recounts an event that took place, in front of the campfire. "Mortimer run stick; Mortimer eat stick!; Mortimer gimme stick . . . ; Mortimer hide straw!" The point is, how do you chunk those subevents in the absence of a linearisation procedure? You have thousands of combinations to play with. Certainly, if you'd been at the scene with Newton, you might recognise it. But if you hadn't been, how would you know that he doesn't mean 'Mortimer started eating the stick Mortimer gave me, so I ran behind Mortimer with the stick until Mortimer hid under the straw'? With more than a couple of words, the combinations are endless.

L: Fine, so let's assume linearization and some basic words—now, where are the complex ones?

O: A Newton who fancies himself a raconteur may start using some term α to separate an event that isn't taking place now (but was before) from an event that is taking place now. How does a listener know that he means 'before' when he says α? In part, perhaps because α refers to some salient past event—a thunderstorm or a snowfall, for example. And in part perhaps through a useful procedure that eases the obvious processing problem: the listener assumes that what he can't decipher (in terms of what he knows and what is evident from context) is a way of encoding the basic dimensional axes of linguistic expression itself (which by hypothesis are part of what he already knows) [83]. I don't wish to call this a learning procedure, because it would be misleading to say that something is being learnt now—when it is, as it were, just being constructed. In any case, this is intended to be the same sort of procedure that leads learners into my dynamic phase 1, where lexical items of various sorts are interpreted as functional. Thus, suppose every time the addresser says α (et cetera), he intends α to mean 'before'. The addressee might not be able to suss this out, but may assume that α is a way of encoding Tense (perhaps past, assuming that present tense need not be expressed). This might actually be nothing but a consequence of Full Interpretation: C_{HL} cannot simply disregard linguistic information as some sort of noise; faced with an item to which it can't assign any direct meaning, C_{HL} assumes it instantiates functional structure.

L: You mean, as an alternative to just giving up, which is what most reasonable apes would do . . .

O: Right. And consider also the following way of resolving the expressiveness problem. As yet this protolanguage hasn't any strong features: it's at the pristine stage at which only syntax exists, and transparent words are being developed. Then, if what I said three

Figure 6.29

Bickerton (1990) argues that properties of creolization are highly relevant to theories about the origins of language. Perhaps his strongest suggestion is that in its inceptive stages linguistic behavior may not have rested on a robust lexical base; this is clearly also a concern for creoles, since they arise from pidgins. Pidgins systematically display the following characteristics (extracted from Hopper and Traugott 1993, 213):

(i) a. The lexicon consists mostly of nouns and verbs.
    b. The lexicon lacks standard word formation rules, although compounding is extremely productive.
    c. Functional relations are expressed periphrastically.
    d. Inflectional morphology is absent.
    e. Word order is not fixed, and matters of discourse salience help arrange sentence constituents.
    f. Systematic embedding is missing.
    g. Movement processes involving topicalization or focusing are missing.

Properties (a) through (d) are expected of an emerging lexicon; but why pidgins should not display movement or embedding is more intriguing. One possibility is that adult speakers in a pidgin situation may not be able to successfully relate deficient pseudolinguistic input sequences to valid hierarchical structures.

As creolization sets in, the following characteristics emerge:

(ii) a. Clear functional categories develop, expressing reference (through a Determiner system), tense-modality-aspect (through a Tense system), and force (through a Complementizer system).
    b. Embedding is systematic.
    c. Movement arises through leftward focusing.

The first property reveals a functional system entirely in place. The second property is expected if the children who turn a pidgin into a creole, unlike their parents, are indeed capable of relating whatever input they hear to a valid structure. But it is still intriguing that movement should arise now, and precisely through focusing. It is possible that a pidgin expression that by hypothesis contains no movement, but is arranged according to information prominence (the topic preceding the comment), is analyzed by the learner (who assumes hierarchical structure) as involving movement to the left.

days ago about merger prior to Spell-Out is moderately sensible [see sec. 3.7], it should be possible for a speaker of protolanguage not to merge certain structures prior to Spell-Out, instead doing so in the covert component. What would be the advantage of that? simply this: the ordering among the items which do not form a constituent may be expressed in terms other than linear correspondence, up to pragmatic considerations concerning what's important, what's being discussed, what new information is being conveyed, and so forth. For example, if you wanted to say that the hut is on fire and you wanted to emphasise *on fire,* the system allows you to say, "ON FIRE the hut!" Presumably, this has a different emotional content—inasmuch as you've placed *ON FIRE* in a position of iconic prominence—than, for example, "THE HUT on fire!" But although this device aids expressiveness, it also creates a perceptual wrinkle: are the constituents *the hut* and *on fire* merely presented in a nonsyntactic, stylistic order, or has one of them been moved?

L: Why would it even occur to me to even ask whether the constituent has moved?

O: Because this is a possible way for you—who have access to linear correspondence—to analyse the data. Prior to evolving this procedure, speakers wouldn't be able to communicate the sorts of structures needed for movement, which involve a fairly significant amount of embedding, a copy of an embedded item, and a decision to delete the lower copy for PF reasons [see sec. 4.7] [84]. However, you do have the relevant correspondence, and may then unconsciously wonder whether expressive structures that a speaker uses for various sorts of emphasis are to be analysed as stylistic scrambling, or whether they're the result of Move/Attract. And here comes the punch line: if humans assume movement for processing, they can also assume it for expressive purposes, which then allows them to develop elaborate words with the implied structure of *saddle* or *shelve* (that is to say, beyond simple compounds like *plant-man* or *run-sticks*) [see fig. 6.29] [85].

L: What you're trying to suggest, then, is that this stage of Human resembles creolization [86].

O: I plead guilty.

6.6 Evolution Strikes Back

(wherein the Linguist deflates the evolutionary argument and the interlocutors explore the confines of evolution)

L: The fairy tale is amusing; but I remain agnostic. It reminds me of stories about insect jaws being perfectly adapted to thousands of flower-forms, and how this could happen. Except that insect jaws got to be what they are before flowers even existed!

O: Fair enough—so you tell me: why do words exist?

—————————————————————— questions and topics for discussion

L: I tend to think "why" questions are more topics for discussion than honest-to-goodness questions. We can philosophize about this, and you've presented some intriguing speculations. I prefer to start by assuming that words are part of the factual body of what I have to explain. So are chains, for that matter; or sentences.

O: Yes, but how do you know those are units to be found in a factual base?

L: That's like asking physicists how they know that electrons are part of their factual base, or why there should be antiparticles.

O: Hold on. "Why strong features?" is a legitimate question, but "Why words?" is metaphysics?! Where does this distinction come from?

L: I'm perfectly happy to say that "Why strong features?" also isn't a question, but a metaphysical topic for discussion. At any rate, your speculations about strong features certainly put the matter beyond the realm of standard linguistics . . .

O: I find that a bit unfair. I honestly puzzled over the fact that words should present properties that conflict with the optimality of the standard merger to LF. Within that system, what one expects, ceteris paribus, is the sorts of pristine structures that I was arguing for, and you called Generative Semantics. Why should there be uninterpretable features, why should there be strong features, why should there be words, why should there be movement, why should there be linguistic variation at all? I've tried to suggest that these are all, perhaps, the same question—at least, the world will be a more elegant place if they all are.

L: But in order to relate all of those topics, you had to propose an adaptationist account, to justify (37). Any such account has several premises. First, since the point here is that one option wins over another, individuals have to display genetic **variation.** Since you want complex word formation to be an alternative to more basic conceptual units, you have to say that two populations coexisted at some point: those who were able to handle *kill* and those who had to stick to simpler notions—Fastspeakers and Slowspeakers. According to you, both populations had similar conceptual structures but Slowspeakers had no linearization, whereas Fastspeakers did. But what sort of reproductive advantage did Fastspeakers have over Slowspeakers?

O: Why, Fastspeakers certainly could make better use of language!

—————————————————————————————— linguistic functions

L: Perhaps, but if we mean that assertion seriously, it entails understanding what a "linguistic function" is. When linguists looked at this question a while back, they tried to establish some "elementary functions" for language—six, in fact [87]. The first three are the "personal functions" of *expressiveness* (first person), *communication* (second person), and *referentiality* (third person). Then there are three "secondary functions" based on the personal ones. Along with referentiality we have the *metalinguistic function* that allows us to talk about language, create paradoxes and lies, and so on; and along with communication we have the *phatic function* that keeps the conversation alive, through "yeah, yeah," and "no way," and "aha." And finally, along with expressiveness, we have the *poetic function,* which allows us to express pretty things. The last three have virtually no imaginable connection with an adaptive edge.

O: Granted, but the first three probably do.

L: Let's see about that. First consider emotions. Words aren't the best way to express them; facial expressions and gestures, body language, and so on, work lots better. Why would it be advantageous to duplicate a system to tell each other what we can see with our own eyes [88]? Now take referentiality. If I've understood your claims, Slowspeakers are as good at referring as Fastspeakers.

O: As a matter of principle, yes, but Slowspeakers can't communicate elaborate thoughts, hence they'd never learn elaborate referents beyond those in their own personal experience.

L: This isn't obviously good or bad, in terms of one's personal life. Most creatures seem to do quite well without apparent referents, developing elaborate chains of behavior and ways of life I sometimes envy. Take a look at European bees, for instance, which were imported to Japan a century ago [89]. Following the pheromone of a pioneer hornet that marks a hive for destruction, giant hornets used to swoop down and butcher an entire colony in a couple of hours. Recently, the bees have developed a counterattack. Apparently, when the probe hornet reaches its target, a few workers await it, and lure it into an ambush: about a thousand bees jump on the hornet, half of them engulfing it. Then they make their wing muscles vibrate, raising the temperature in the bee-ball so high the hornet bakes to death in fifteen minutes. Finally, the bees "decide" whether this hornet was truly a solitary scavenger—in which case the message dies with the messenger—or whether other culprits escaped—in which case the entire colony moves out and builds a whole new nest. The moral of the story . . . I'd like to see humans manage to create a collective strategy like this with all the wonders of human language—in a century, or even a few dozen generations . . . In any case, if referentiality depends so much on communication with others, the real question then reduces to the communicative edge that Fastspeakers get with linearization. To the extent that the relevant mutation is adaptive, it's because Fastspeakers can say more elaborate things to each other than Slowspeakers can, period.

O: I would agree with that.

L: So now we're back to our old friend, communication. As I told you, I don't really know what that means, but to get on with the show, suppose I forget that "communication" is really a buzzword, and let it mean whatever you tell me it means. That is, suppose that Fastspeakers are brilliant talkers, and this is supposed to give them some edge, no matter how small. The first obvious question, then, is what this edge could consist of. Presuming that Fastspeakers would interact better with each other than Slowspeakers did, in social terms, leads to some obvious embarrassments. First, untold numbers of species seem to interact just fine without linearization or music— as the bee scenario clearly shows. Second, social interactions aren't precisely a human forte. There's probably no other species out there that perpetrates so many atrocities on its fellow members, starting with ritual cannibalism, whose adaptive benefits aren't directly obvious [90] . . . Of course, I don't have to argue for an adaptation, so I don't have to justify anything here; but if I had to pick the subspecies of prehumans with the chance for better social interaction, I'd go with Slowspeakers; you just have to ask what Europeans have been up to during the same century that the European bees have spent learning to outsmart the hornets. Incidentally, this relates to another fundamental question: what ever happened to Slowspeakers? One answer suggests itself, given your premises: they must have been exterminated. Why else would a perfectly healthy group of hominids, which (according to your questionable measurements) are capable of feats ten times more remarkable than those of other apes, eventually cease to exist? Surely, the abilities that carried them to the verge of the human experience couldn't have suddenly betrayed them, sending them to extinction in an environment that had been familiar to them for hundreds of thousands of years. Only a new predator could have done the job—a fact that's arguably coherent with the vicious view of Fastspeakers.

O: That's a horrifying tale.

L: It's your tale, not mine—I don't believe it for a second. As far as I'm concerned, all good and evil aspects of humans, whatever that means, have nothing to do with adaptations. In fact, good is even harder to explain than evil. What sense does it make for humans to be philanthropic—as they clearly can be, rather uniquely—from the point of view of a standard adaptation?

O: Yes, well, but hold on: have we not agreed that the formal properties of the emergence of language are witnessed in creolisation as well? I don't suppose you're saying that creole speakers exterminate their pidgin-speaking ancestors!

_____ **challenging the assumptions**

L: There's one small difference between that case and the evolutionary scenario, though: both pidgin and creole speakers are sapiens (Fastspeakers), whereas—if we're to believe your mutation line—your Slowspeakers aren't sapiens at all [91]. That is, creole speakers are simply the children of pidgin speakers, who literally invent a language out of scraps of others. However, by hypothesis the children of Slowspeakers have the same abilities as their parents, and thus aren't able to contribute to the invention of human language. The conclusion is inescapable. Only if Fastspeakers slowly or rapidly weed out Slowspeakers will their biological trait live on. Which basically entails either that Fastspeakers are everything we abhor about humans (capable of eliminating a perfectly reasonable version of themselves) or that they don't really have an edge over Slowspeakers. It's that simple. I'm afraid no other natural disaster will come to your rescue here, to get rid of your nagging Slowspeakers—the argument is well known to Nazis and white supremacists. But let's put moral issues aside and look at your other claims. Consider, first, the alleged mutation that gave humans linearization, and when it became adaptive, according to you. This didn't happen immediately—it couldn't have, since there's no direct connection between rhythm and words. Your argument was more convoluted: the communicative situation that Fastspeakers faced created a tension between processing and expressiveness. For each of these, you ended up proposing basically a learning strategy (assign functional structure to whatever isn't analyzed as lexical) and a parsing strategy (analyze stylistic scrambling as movement). I have no problem granting you that this is indeed what happens in creolization, where lexical items may be "grammaticalized" as functional, and stylistic processes are "grammaticalized" as movement [see fig. 6.29]. But I have to emphasize, first, that Slowspeakers didn't need either of these strategies, given their rudimentary system (i.e., what we find in pidgins anyway), and second, that without these two crucial assumptions, it wouldn't have made any sense for Fastspeakers to create complex morphological words (i.e., what we find in creoles), which is what in your view gave them the edge over Slowspeakers [92]. But then the real issue is the learning strategy and the parsing strategy. How did they get into the picture? Without them, Fastspeakers may have been around for thousands of years as terrific dancers but showed no discernible advantage over the clumsier Slowspeakers—and thus no natural selection should arise. And now you're back where you started: without a coherent evolutionary picture. True, if you could compare an account with complex words to an account without complex words, you'd have a potentially meaningful evolutionary question (leading to the horror scenario I sketched). But that's entirely beside the point, because when the question boils down to elaborate words, it's totally removed from any remotely plausible mutation, like rhythm, for instance. In fact, what you argued for is a chain of unrelated mutations, one having to do with a "switchboard" between PF and LF, one with performance, and one with acquisition [93]. In other words, you need a theory of everything, which means you have a theory of nothing.

O: Suppose I were to say that all of those aspects evolved simultaneously, and were useful as a whole [94]?

L: You could, of course—but you'd be stepping right into the realm of the unfalsifiable. First of all, what's "useful" is hopelessly underspecified, particularly if it's meant to apply in all environments inhabited by evolving humans [95]. Take for instance the ability to specify reference to an object, a location, or whatever you want, with as much precision as you could possibly need. Or take the linguistically supported social interactions of the hunter-gatherer way of life [96]. What specific selective pressure did prehominids have toward evolving these traits [97]? I can only think of one: they were competing with prehominids who lacked the language faculty—which brings us right back to the holocaust scenario [98]. Second, even if you believe the horror story, if you take all aspects of the language faculty to have evolved simultaneously, there's the problem of those that are nonoptimal for functional purposes. We've talked about a few, starting with the most obvious: why should there be more than one language? And why should linguistic structure disallow all sorts of expressions which presumably would be useful to have? I can't even imagine what's more useful about being able to ask *who are you saying that you are thinking that you are talking to?,* which is possible, than about being able to ask **what are you talking to a man whom you just asked?,* which isn't [see sec. 1.1] [99]. Similarly, think of the different possible ways of interpreting the sentence *time flies like an arrow;* what could possibly be the advantage of having ambiguous (or "multiguous") structures [100]? And finally, if there's one thing worth listening to in your fairy tale, it's that two alternatives were at stake. But the minute you talk about a global evolution of all the mutations that are needed to justify complex-word formation, that one credible aspect of the tale vanishes, and you can dream up any "just so story" you like. You can also say that God gave us the Word, which at least is more inspiring [101].

[The publishers have been advised to explicitly acknowledge that, in all likelihood, the following pages are apocryphal. A reasonable effort has been made to contact the author about this possibility, unfortunately to no avail.]

O: In all honesty, I can't say I disagree with anything you're saying—except the You-know-who bit, that is. I was just trying to see whether reflecting on words from a traditional evolutionary perspective had anything to tell us about their lack of optimality.

_____ are chain conditions emergent?

L: Note also that whatever you say about the inelegance of words won't cover the emergence of chain formation, or sentences, for that matter—the other major domains of structural conservation. We looked at very reasonable conditions that determine what's a possible chain: the Last Resort and Minimal Link Conditions, whose effect appears to be to reduce the pool of competing derivations in a principled way. Given derivational dynamics, these are natural constraints, which may follow from virtual conceptual necessity. In fact, we can think of the LRC and MLC as two consequences of a general tendency to minimize derivational horizons. That is to say, imagine a dynamic flow of some sort—a creek current, for example. There are certain paths that given water particles won't ever try. To describe this, the system dynamics theorist assumes certain boundaries, and figures out how to calculate them precisely (a task that's tough, of course, and specific to each system). The LRC and the MLC can be seen as specific linguistic solutions to this sort of boundary problem. If this is the right general approach, then this aspect of chain formation is really quite elegant.

O: Oh, no doubt about it. I confess that of all the things you've told me, it's these dynamic problems that intrigue me the most: the complex situations that emerge in language learning and change, matters of optimality in morphology, and above all derivational variation and how the system narrows it down, through derivational conditions like the LRC or MLC, and resolves it by selecting the structure with the lowest derivational cost. That's a remarkable system, and a splendid tool for reflecting on other complex systems in the biological world. In actual fact, what particularly moves me is the dialectic in language between conservation and transformation of structure. It fits well with the view of living creatures as dissipative and conservative systems, in the sense that their elaborate structure manifests itself both in the highly dynamic flow arising far from thermodynamic equilibrium, and the conservative arrangement emerging near it [see sec. 1.7].

L: You keep making those sweeping generalizations and you'll soon proclaim the end of syntax . . .

O: And what's wrong with that? Won't there be an end to biology? Hasn't there been an end to chemistry as it was once understood?

L: That comes with the territory, but we never know whether the end of a scientific enterprise will turn out to be a reduction or an extension. Take syntax. If you're telling me that in the near future syntax will reduce to molecular biology, or some such thing, I'll say it depends on what you mean by "near future." Maybe in our species' evolutionary lifetime. On the other hand, take an extension from syntax to whatever part of the mind exists beyond PF and LF, particularly the latter—semantics, and so on. Is it possible that an extended syntax will swallow up semantics? It depends. If by semantics we mean something that's ultimately behavioral, individual, perspective-dependent, I doubt very much that syntax will have anything meaningful to say about it. But if by semantics we mean a core system of knowledge of some sort—for example, a vocabulary of features for LF—then we can expect that to actually follow from, and not determine, the properties of syntax.

O: Hold on: if syntax is to determine the vocabulary of LF, how can LF convergence drive syntactic derivations?

L: There's no contradiction there, at the level I'm talking about (where syntax is meant as "structure"). And of course, it could have been that, at the point the species acquired human language, it was syntax that determined everything linguistic.

O: But isn't syntax a branch of psychology?!

—————————————————————————— *and what about linguistic symbols?*

L: It is what it is, a theory about a certain system [102]. I mean, ask the question about PF, which is less mystical. There's a bunch of PF features that the language faculty makes use of, like consonants and vowels, syllables, rhythmic and intonation patterns. That's what it means to have a level of PF: a coding of the relevant features into some sort of system, whereby features "speak" to each other, and combine, and more complex units arise. Where do those features come from? You and I have taken them as primitives—as we should, given the scope of our talks. But they actually have funny discrete properties, even if they correspond to continuous streams like sound (perception-wise) and modulated voice (production-wise). In fact, one of the oldest questions in modern phonetics is what it takes to produce or perceive, say, a consonant. Proponents of the motor theory of speech perception have argued that even a consonant is a very complex mental event, involving all sorts of extraordinarily modular matchings between what's perceived and what's thought to be perceived by a mind which, apart from perceiving speech as if it were any other sound, is also capable of producing it [103]. We should be moved by the treatment of a consonant (something which the system takes to be a discrete unit) as a dynamic event, involving the integration of various factors, including contextual cues. This suggests that the very emergence of a consonant might have been a dynamic event as well. More importantly, even, the sort of discreteness found in language allows for unlimited combinatorics. Take syllables, for example—how do they arise? If people studying sign language are right, the important thing about syllables isn't consonants and vowels proper, or sonority hierarchies in a literal sense [see figs. 2.24, 2.28]. Rather, it seems that syllables involve relations between spaces of some sort (as different and yet as intuitively similar as vowels and hand movements) and boundaries for those spaces (consonants or hand positions). And of course, we know what the possible patterns are, right? Simplifying to just C and V combinations, the major patterns are V, CV, VC, CVC, CVV, and CVVC. Interestingly, Human doesn't have syllables with the patterns CVVVC, or VVC, or VCCV—and I can see you want to know why. I don't know why (if you want a nontrivial answer that extends to sign language), but eventually we'll be able to ask that kind of question in a systematic way. For instance, we can represent boundaries with a "plus" sign and spaces with a "minus" sign, and see what happens when we let them interact according to some computational rules. Here's an example, a combinatorial game we can call the Boundary Game. You start by writing either a "plus" or a "minus." Next to that you write another "plus" or another "minus"—but with one condition. This condition can be thought of as a "Repulsion Rule": Don't put two identical symbols together, unless they're neighbors of a different symbol. You can see what that gets us.

```
(38)  a.  +−   +−+   +−−+   +−++−   +−−++−   +−−++−+   +−−++−−+
          1    1     +−+−   +−−+−   +−+−−+   +−++−−+   +−−++−+−
                     2      +−+−+   +−++−+   +−−+−+   +−+−+−+−
                            3       +−−+−+   +−+−−+   +−++−++−
                                    +−+−+−   +−−+−+−  +−−+−++−
                                    5       +−+−++−  +−++−−+−
                                            +−+−−+−  +−−+−+−+
                                            +−+−+−+  +−++−+−+
                                            8       +−−+−+−+
                                                    +−−+−+−+
                                                    +−+−++−+
                                                    +−+−−+−+
                                                    +−+−+−+−
                                                    13
..........................................................................
                                                    13
                                                    −+−+−+−+
                                                    −+−++−+−
                                                    −+−+−−+−
                                                    −++−+−+−
                                            8       −+−−+−+−
                                            −+−+−+−  −++−++−+
                                            −+−++−+  −+−−++−+
                                    5       −+−+−−+  −++−+−−+
                                    −+−+−+   −++−+−+  −+−−+−−+
                            3       −++−+−   −+−−+−+  −+−+−++−
                    2       −+−+−    −+−−+−   −++−++−  −+−+−+−+
          1    1    −+−+    −++−+    −+−++−   −+−−++−  −++−−+−+
          b. −+  −+−  −++−  −+−−+    −++−−+   −++−−+−  −++−−++−
```

Fibonacci patterns in language?

O: Fibonacci!

L: Right: the number of possible combinations always maps to the Fibonacci series. This is because of the Repulsion Rule itself [see sec. 1.2]. More interesting, though, is what kinds of space-boundary relations this general possibility-space delimits. Let's think of a few rules for that too:

(39) a. *Nucleus Constraint*

Look for a maximal space.

When (a) is satisfied:

b. *Onset Constraint*

Try to assign an onset boundary to that space.

When (b) is satisfied:

c. *Coda Constraint*

Try to assign a coda boundary to that space.

We can think of (39) as an optimization algorithm, trying to make bounded spaces as large as possible, and as delimited as possible [104]. This algorithm has the following consequence in our (38) arrangements:

```
(40) a.+-   +-+  +--+    +-+ +-   +--+ +-    +--+ +-+    +--+ +--+
              +- +-  +-- +-   +- +--+    +-+ +--+    +--+ +- +-
                +- +-+   +-+ +-+    +-- +--+    +- +- +- +-
                +-- +-+   +-+ +- +-    +- +- +--+
                +- +- +-  +-- +- +-   +-+ +-+ +-
                      +- +-+ +-   +-- +-+ +-
                      +- +-- +-   +-+ +-- +-
                      +- +- +-+   +-- +-- +-
                                  +-+ +- +-+
                                  +-- +- +-+
                                  +- +-+ +-+
                                  +- +-- +-+
                                  +- +- +- +-
                                  - +- +- +-+
                                  - +-+ +- +-
                                  - +- +-- +-
                                  -+ +- +- +-
                                  - +-- +- +-
                            - +- +- +--+ +-+ +-+
                            - +-+ +-+ - +--+ +-+
                            - +- +--+ -+ +- +--+
                      - +- +-+ -+ +- +-+ - +-- +--+
                      -+ +- +- - +-- +-+ - +- +-+ +-
                  - +- +- - +-- +- -+ +-+ +- - +- +- +-+
                - +-+ -+ +-+  - +-+ +- - +--+ +- -+ +-- +-+
  b. -+ - +- -+ +-  - +--+  -+ +--+   -+ +-- +-  -+ +--+ +-
```

It's clear that after a while, it doesn't matter how many "pluses" or "minuses" there are: there won't be any further types of groupings. The possible types are:

(41) a. $+ - - +$
      b. $+ - +$
      c. $+ - -$
      d. $+ -$
      e. $- +$
      f. $-$

Now we can replace each "minus" sign with a vowel (or a hand movement) and each "plus" sign with a consonant (or a hand position), and we've got our syllabic patterns; that's the idea. The main point I'm trying to raise is this. Our beloved syllable may be an emergent property of two factors: general repelling forces that generate other Fibonacci patterns, and general "gluing" forces that result in discrete units of various shapes. The gluing forces should be as basic as what the constraints in (39) express, at least in the case of syllables.

O: Most intriguing. Does this Boundary Game work for items other than syllables?

L: Of course, there's no reason why you shouldn't apply other "gluing" forces to the patterns arising from the game. But I take it you're asking this question to see whether the game is merely a way of describing an item within the phonological system, or whether it's saying something basic about the sorts of systems involved in this kind of pattern formation.

O: Correct—it reminds me of the Fibonacci patterns we saw before. Perhaps these aren't encoded in the genes of different species, and only more fundamental matters really are (say, growth functions, and the timing of their internal dynamics). The syllabic patterns you describe may arise from something genetically encoded in humans, or from something even more elementary. If this underdeterminacy holds, that basic systemic balance may show up elsewhere.

L: I don't know about that, but suppose we replace the Nucleus Constraint in (39) by the Clarity Constraint in (42), keeping the rest intact:

(42) a. *Clarity Constraint*

    Look for a unique space.

    when (a) is satisfied:

  b. *Onset Constraint*

    Try to assign an onset boundary to that space.

    When (b) is satisfied:

  c. *Coda Constraint*

    Try to assign a coda boundary to that space.

Now that will clearly restrict the possible combinations as follows:

(43) a. $+-+$

  b. $+-$

  c. $-+$

  d. $-$

These arguably correspond to possible "theme rheme" relations found in languages, spaces being substantively interpreted as rhemes, and boundaries as themes [105]. For instance, the combinations in (44) are all possible in English:

(44)   a. there's a man here $-$ [cf. (43d)]

    b. [John], I like $+-$ [cf. (43b)]

    c. he just arrived, [John (did)] $-+$ [cf. (43c)]

    d. [John], she loves, [Mary (does)] $+-+$ [cf. (43a)]

(44a) involves no pragmatic theme; it's a conversation starter, so to speak. In contrast, the other instances involve more or less complex pragmatic predicates which are about John. Finally, (44d) is also about Mary. What's more interesting is the sorts of combinations that aren't allowed. For instance:

(45)   a. * [a man] (does/is) $+$

    b. * [Mary], [John], she loves $++-$

    c. * she loves him, [Mary (does)], [John] $-++$

    d. * [John], I like, Mary hates $+--$

    e. * he likes Mary, he loves Sue, [John (does)] $--+$

    f. * [John], she likes, she hates, [Mary (does)] $+--+$

It's not obvious that anything's grammatically wrong with any of these. Why can't a noun be a conversation starter (45a)? If it's a boundary in some sense, you're invoking one of the patterns this version of the Boundary Game doesn't allow. The same is true about (45b–c), which involve two boundaries [106]. Again, it's not clear why these are impossible, if the same semantic structure turns out all right in (44d). But of course, there the boundaries are on either side of the space (the rheme part), whereas here they're lumped on one side. Finally, (45d–f) involve two pragmatic predicates (two spaces), which the game doesn't allow either. It's again not totally clear why these sentences are impossible otherwise, given that the semantically identical *John, I like and Mary hates* and *he likes Mary but he loves Sue, John does* and *John, she likes and she hates, Mary does* are perfectly possible.

O: Hm . . .

L: There's a lot to be discovered in these domains, but the main point I'm trying to make is that symbolic elements, and perhaps even certain combinatorics, may indeed be derivative on system dynamics, once we get to understand them. This is all irrelevant at the level of analysis needed in competence studies of the kind we've been considering, but the issue may ultimately be important in looking at how the system of knowledge that we're dealing with evolved or even develops. This syntactic region of the universe may well become labeled because of its dynamic properties, just as the rest of the universe has certain "labels" (atoms, molecules, genes, cells, and so on), presumably because of other complex properties at different scales or levels of organization.

——————————————————————————— *then what is a representation?*

O: Of course, as a matter of principle the same issue arises for LF features . . .

L: Yes, so you should raise similar questions about equally cherished notions on the other side of the grammar. Standard predicates and arguments, for instance—are they emergent too? Unfortunately, it's too late in the day to make a convincing case in this respect, but, as a point of logic, the question suggests itself. I see no reason why the issue should be a priori different from the one that arises for syllables or theme rheme relations. In fact, we ran into similar questions for nonconfigurational notions like chains, when we were talking about the serious possibility (in fact, likelihood) that chain constraints are an epiphenomenon of syntactic computations on the mapping to LF—a bit like syllabic constraints are too, on the PF side. But why stop there? Are we prepared to say that the recognition/production of whatever LF features we need should be more robustly determined than those of the modest consonants which give phoneticians so much trouble? The little evidence we have points in the opposite direction; after all, consonants can be defined reasonably well in terms of some elementary features [see fig. 2.10], but the task appears to be phenomenally more complex for equivalent LF units [see sec. 2.4]. Should we be shocked if we're then told that all LF symbols (which the system takes to be discrete units) are at some level or have been (in the course of evolution) complex dynamic events, involving the integration of various factors? To be surprised by this is to treat LF symbols differently from PF symbols, and I don't see what reason there could be for such parochialism. From this perspective, semantics is just either part of behavior, or else ultimately part of syntax—assuming the simplest universe.

O: But if symbols could be literally created in the way you're implying, what are we to make of representing a symbol in the mind? Why, a plant doesn't *represent* a Fibonacci pattern anywhere in its biological makeup—it instead obeys certain laws of growth, which result in the pattern. Of course, the plant can *use* the pattern, which may give it some nice benefits—for example, an attractive design for pollinators.

L: I told you from day one that no serious issue of representation ever arises for the system of knowledge we're dealing with.

O: How can you know something that you haven't represented?!

L: That's all terminology! Do you want to call it something else, other than "knowledge"? Be my guest. Call it "growth," for all I care, or "being endowed with structural property X"; or better still, give it a technical name: UG, using it not as a theory but as a phenomenon. Just as your plant obeyed some growth function and developed in this or that manner, my mind was structurally endowed with UG and got parametrically fixed in this or that way. The result is a certain I-language, which isn't unlike a Fibonacci pattern—except a lot more intricate.

O: But surely you must eventually represent some knowledge of some sort—over and above the I-language. I mean, you know—do you not?—that we've been speaking for days, the things you said and I said, to some extent, the very words we uttered!

L: But I have nothing to say about that; that's been our performance. Yeah, sure, I know you by now—at least I think I do. But how I know what you said, what's the place in my mind for what I've discovered about your claims, is basically a mystery as far as I'm concerned. If you tell me you need representations for that, I'll ask you to give me some evidence (of the sort I've been giving you for days about matters for which the issue of representation doesn't even arise). Personally, I'm skeptical that you'll produce any.

O: Well, that's that, then—of course I have no evidence. It would seem to me, however, that the very logic of the system, even as you've exposed it, would force representations somewhere. For example, you've consistently spoken of conservation laws, which define theoretical regions: words, chains, sentences perhaps. If these aren't represented, what is being conserved in linguistic computations?

L: You don't need representations for that. Conservation laws hold of derivations, for some reason. The structural qualities of items— or if you wish, phenomena—like words or chains are integrally preserved throughout linguistic computations. However, we're not even talking about derivations right now, but about what could be behind derivations, at a more basic (and obviously speculative) level—be it in evolution, development, or whatever. The discussion we're having is to derivations as, say, a discussion about the first milliseconds after the Big Bang would be to how physical systems operate in the present universe. It's in the latter that reactions conserve this-that-or-the-other physical quantities, which tell us something about what the inner stuff is like; ultimately, we want to match up what went on at the Big Bang **singularity** with whatever goes on now. My speculations have a similar effect: derivations are the "reactions" of the linguistic system, whereby certain structural qualities are observed as remaining unchanged (word-level, chain-level, sentence-level properties); we want to have a theory of how the properties that predict those reactions fit together, and ultimately how they relate to whatever singularity gave rise to this aspect of the human mind [107]. So this is the same question you raised before, and once again I don't see any contradiction.

and beyond?

O: Needless to say, you can push that sort of argument all the way down to the emergence of just any sort of symbolic system!

L: Whatever that means, though. I don't know much about symbolic systems, and certainly most of what I've said these past few days bears little on that issue—if it's even real. To be quite honest, for me the word "symbolic" is essentially as much of a buzzword as the word "communication." Yeah, you can ask questions about what it is to have a set theory, and what it means for physics to involve scalar calculations, and so on. Those are interesting, philosophical topics for discussion, but completely beyond the scope of linguistics. I wouldn't be particularly bothered if the human mind conceived set theory because of the dynamics of whatever evolutionary event gave rise to this mind, thus making it perhaps less surprising that it's figured out how to build bridges or send rockets into space. From this perspective, the same "symbols" that once emerged in this mind because of the dynamics of the universe allow it to see properties of this universe. At any rate, this is all way beyond my area of expertise or even interest, and I don't want to reach any conclusions about it. Not so much because I'd have a problem with claiming that the syntactic mind (in the sense now of a dynamic macroevent that leads to structure) is what gave humans access, ultimately, to mathematics (in the sense of properties of the universe) [108], but because we want to reach that sort of result scientifically, and not through fancy rhetoric.

O: But of course—I had something in mind. Remember cytoskeletons, the "personalised nervous systems" of even the humblest cells—which of course neurons have as well? The internal organisation of the cytoskeleton is rather curious, particularly in terms of the microtubules it's composed of. These fellows are hollow tubes, consisting of thirteen columns of tubulines, which spiral in five and eight sloping lines of opposing chirality [109].

L: Fibonacci redux.

O: Yes, but this time inside the brain—and deeply so. The question is:

....

[Publisher's note: In the original manuscript, several pages are missing after this passage; only figure 6.30 remains. We can only speculate that the Linguist and the Other continue to discuss matters pertaining to the emergence of Fibonacci patterns as mental patterns of brains that, at some level, present a Fibonacci-type structure. There is no evidence for this extreme speculation.]

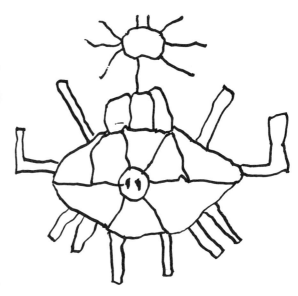

A robot. (Theodore Lebeaux)

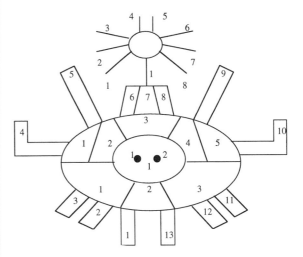

Figure 6.30

6.7 An Abrupt and Unexpected Coda

(giving an account of the Linguist's and the Other's last known, contentful exchange)

L: At any rate, it's worth emphasizing that the perspective I'm contemplating is exactly the opposite of the one taken by cognitive scientists who view meaning as prior to language, a driving force behind syntax. For instance, "cognitive grammarians" have tried to argue that "part-whole" or "center-periphery" schemas, and so on, are behind grammatical relations, which are seen as nothing but "idealized cognitive models" [110]. The error here is to think that "part" and "whole," "center" and "periphery," and similar notions have any meaning outside of whatever trivial formal properties they have which allow us to conceive of them in those terms. That is, it's a mistake to think that a notion like "part" or "whole" is cognitively primitive, and gives rise to whatever grammatical function you care to imagine in this connection. At a sufficient level of abstraction, a "part" may be to a "whole" what a certain mathematical "boundary" is to some sort of "space." If this is true, to call something a "part of a whole" is to engage in interpreting something more basic—it's not an end in itself. Then what's the more basic stuff? I'd say it's something syntactic, the sort of process involved in understanding the numbering system, dimensional changes, and all that. But I don't really like to dwell on matters at this level of abstractness, because we can easily lose touch with reality. Down on planet Earth there's plenty of dirty work to do.

O: Such as?

L: I'd need another week to tell you that! Take the notion of minimal domain—absolutely central in characterizing both checking and internal domains (one vital for movement, the other for lexical relatedness). What does that locality follow from, as of now? I don't know, nor do I think the notion is even adequately characterized [111]. Same thing with distance, which itself partly depends on minimal domains, but adds something else, about command and neighborhoods. Or take command, also a central notion. Where does that ultimately come from [112]? And Move and Merge; are they the same at a sufficient level of abstraction [113]? How about chains? How do they really differ from lexical items on the one hand and sentences on the other? Are chains involved in the phenomenon of ellipsis? If so, do all movements we're familiar with involve chains—for instance, verb movement? What are types of movement, to start with [114]? Not to mention apparently simpler systems, which turn into nightmares when we look at them for a while: binding theory, for instance, whose principles make use of command and something else, which I don't think anybody understands [115]; adjuncts of all sorts, from relative clauses, to temporal and aspectual modification, to parentheticals [116]; or the very fact that sentences have to have subjects—what does that follow from? Again, not to mention a host of phenomena that linguists have unearthed over the years (or centuries), which get put aside in working toward overall understanding of the model. That's all syntax, as we've known it for centuries, and as we'll continue to know it—for how long, I can't begin to say.

O: . . .

L: But if you ask me, this grand "end of syntax" that you've talked about is closer to hand not because of syntax's having little left to explain, but because theoretical interests and fashions are going in other directions. It wouldn't be the first time this happened. Back in the fourteenth century, after extremely insightful grammarians had come up with core concepts of linguistics and ways of understanding Universal Grammar, carefully separating it from cognition in a broader sense and the "outside" world of physics in the broadest sense, nominalist philosophers decreed that everything that exists is a mental object. As a result, the study of Latin, Greek, Hebrew, Arabic had to be abandoned, and instead researchers were to concentrate on the study of thought itself! Soon grammarians had given up essentially everything they'd achieved, until the seventeenth century, when the topic again flourished. Not for long, though. Rationalist and Romantic thinking gave us the linguistic work of geniuses like Huarte, Descartes, and Humboldt, and the grammar of Port-Royal; but again the level of discourse went downhill, until linguists were talking, at the beginning of this century, about language being a cultural treasure, a communicative tool, something that shapes thought environmentally, a pseudomathematical construct with the same status as street lights and bee dances, or just a habit of some sort, like scratching—and those are the highlights. Anyone who dared to mention traditional Scholastic or rationalist concepts like Universal Grammar, ideal speakers, knowledge as opposed to use, or grammaticality as opposed to interpretability, was accused of being imperialistic, simplistic, a dualist, or a provocateur—and that's not an exclusive "or." How far we are, again, from one of these valleys in the history of linguistics is very unclear to me. But I won't go into that.

O: What a gloomy picture . . .

L: Look, you asked me what I do for a living—I've told you: I study the human mind. I think any number of people would give you that answer, though I don't know how many of them would go on to admit that it's a very difficult business, maybe in fact beyond our capabilities. The temptation of studying thought and interpretation directly has always been there; but I don't know how that can be done—thank God, or Life, for that. As I see it, there's no way of studying the human mind other than through the sorts of painfully slow and often dull procedures we've talked about these last few days. Considering it's the most complex object in the known universe, maybe we shouldn't be surprised at the magnitude of the task. And maybe we shouldn't be methodologically cavalier about it, either.

O: What can I say?

L: Say nothing, really. This may just be me.

"Still there?"

"Thought you might want to go on, for a while."

". . ."

". . ."

   . . . "Say, talk—". . . "Incident—" . . .

"Pardon?"

"What where you going to say?"

"No, please, what were you going to say?"

"Wasn't important, really. You were about to say something."

"It was a conversation starter—but we're already there . . ."

"Well, I was going to say I haven't even learned your name, yet!"

"Yes, well, what are names? You sounded sceptical . . ."

"Maybe we should go back to using grunts."

"Hm . . ."

"Yp . . ."

"Say, d'you know I think I've actually regained my memory?"

"Is that good or bad?"

"Yes . . . Which reminds me I still have lots of questions."

"Oh, so do I."

"Excellent. I shall start, if you don't mind—for I've even remembered what I was supposed to be doing. You see, I'm concerned about what you fellows call 'free will.'"

"Oh, that's a big one."

"You think so? Perhaps we should take a long walk, then."

A.1 Syntactic Objects

According to the bare X-bar theory developed in Chomsky 1994a, 1995, chap. 4, syntactic objects are recursively defined as in (1) (see Chomsky 1995, 243, 262):

(1) *Syntactic object*
    σ is a syntactic object if it is
    a. a lexical item or the set of formal features of a lexical item, or
    b. the set $K = \{\underline{\gamma}, \{\alpha, \beta\}\}$ or $K = \{\underline{<\gamma, \gamma>}, \{\alpha, \beta\}\}$ such that α and β are syntactic objects and $\underline{\gamma}$ or $\underline{<\gamma, \gamma>}$ is the label of K.

Complex syntactic objects such as $K = \{\underline{\gamma}, \{\alpha, \beta\}\}$ or $K = \{\underline{<\gamma, \gamma>}, \{\alpha, \beta\}\}$ result from applications of the operations Merge or Move forming a regular category or a two-segment category (see chaps. 3 and 4 and secs. A.2.3 and A.2.4). The specific choice of the constituents α and β of K in an optimal derivation depends, among other things, on whether K is formed overtly or in the covert component (see chaps. 4 and 5). In instances where a syntactic object σ is a set K (see (1b)), the label γ is said to be identical to either α or β; in instances where a syntactic object σ is either a lexical item or the set of formal features of a lexical item (see (1a)), we will assume that the label of σ is σ itself.

In sections A.2–A.9, we discuss how various grammatical notions and relations can be analyzed given the definition of syntactic object in (1).

A.2 Domination and Containment

A.2.1 Domination: Tentative Definition

Throughout this book the notion of domination has been informally discussed based on intuitive graph representations. A formal recursive definition of domination in terms of the syntactic objects defined in (1) is provided in (2) (adapted from Chomsky's (1995, 247) definition of term; see sec. A.3):

(2) *Domination*
    Given a syntactic object $K = \{\underline{\gamma}, \{\delta, \mu\}\}$ or $K = \{\underline{<\gamma, \gamma>}, \{\delta, \mu\}\}$, K dominates α if and only if
    a. for some set L, $\alpha \in L$ and $L \in K$, or
    b. for some set M, K dominates M and M dominates α.

To see definition (2) at work, consider the partial representation of *he will like it* in the top line of (3), where the Tense head *will* takes the VP *like it* (= A = {like, {like, it}}) as its complement and the pronoun *he* as its specifier. (As in the text, a two-headed arrow represents the application of the operation Merge and the syntactic object resulting from this operation is placed above an upward-pointing arrow.)

(3)   C = {will, {he, {will, {will, {like, {like, it}}}}}}

$$he \longleftarrow\overset{\uparrow}{|}\longrightarrow B = \{\underline{will}, \{will, \{like, \{like, it\}\}\}\}$$

$$will \longleftarrow\overset{\uparrow}{|}\longrightarrow A = \{\underline{like}, \{like, it\}\}$$

$$like \longleftarrow\overset{\uparrow}{|}\longrightarrow it$$

Consider the syntactic object A = {like, {like, it}} in (3), which is formed by merging *like* and *it*. Take A to correspond to K in the definition in (2), the set {like, it} to correspond to L, and *like* and *it* to correspond to α. *Like* and *it* are members of the set {like, it}, which in turn is a member of the set A = {like, {like, it}}. Hence, according to the base step of (2), A dominates *like* and *it*. Likewise, *will* and A are members of the set {will, {like, {like, it}}}, which in turn is a member of the set B = {will, {will, {like, {like, it}}}}. Thus, B dominates *will* and A, according to (2a). Since B dominates A and A dominates *like* and *it,* B dominates *like* and *it* by the recursive step in (2b). Finally, *he* and B are dominated by C given that they are members of the set {he, {will, {will, {like, {like, it}}}}}, which is itself a member of C = {will, {he, {will, {will, {like, {like, it}}}}}}. Given that C dominates B by the base step, it also dominates by the recursive step all the elements that B dominates, namely, *will,* A, *like,* and *it.*

A.2.2 Irreflexivity

There are several reasons for taking domination to be an irreflexive relation. For instance, consider the undesirable consequences of a reflexive notion of domination for the definition of command given in (4) (for further discussion, see secs. 3.3 and A.7) and ultimately for the Linear Correspondence Axiom, which is repeated here in (5) (see sec. 3.3):

(4)   *Command*
     Where α and β are accessible to C_{HL}, α commands β if and only if
     a.   α does not dominate β, and
     b.   the first category dominating α also dominates β.

(5)   *Linear Correspondence Axiom (LCA)*
     A category α precedes a category β if and only if
     a.   α asymmetrically commands β, or
     b.   γ precedes β and γ dominates α.

Given the syntactic object C in (3), for instance, it should be the case that *he* asymmetrically commands *will,* so that the order specifier-head results (see sec. 3.3). However, if *he* dominated itself, it would fail to command *will* (or any other category), because the first category dominating *he*—namely, *he* itself—does not dominate *will* (or any other category). This shows that domination is to be taken as an irreflexive relation (see Kayne 1994, 134 n. 8).

The undesirable implications of a reflexive notion of domination can be prevented as follows. According to the definition in (2), in order for K to dominate itself, K (= α) must be a member of the set L, which in turn must be a member of K; in other words, the syntactic object K, which is a set, must be a member of itself. However, clearly set membership is not a reflexive relation (if it were, for instance, the empty set would have to paradoxically contain itself). Therefore, K cannot dominate itself by the base step of (2) because set membership is not reflexive.

In turn, in order for K to dominate itself by the recursive step of (2), K, M, and α should be identical in (2b), which amounts to saying that K should dominate itself by the base step. Since this does not hold, it is also the case that K does not dominate itself by the recursive step of (2).

Therefore, if the definition of domination given in (2) is assumed, nothing needs to be added to the theory in order to ensure that domination is irreflexive. The notion of domination in (2) is defined for syntactic objects that are set-theoretic objects (see (1b)) and relies on set membership, which is an irreflexive relation. Thus, domination inherits its irreflexivity from set membership.

A.2.3 Domination and Containment Relations in Adjunction Structures

Consider the phrase marker representation in (6), where β adjoins to α_1, forming the two-segment category $[\alpha_2, \alpha_1]$.

(6)

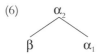

The idea behind this informal representation is that α_2 in (6) has no independent reality with respect to the computational system, but is merely a segment of the two-segment category $[\alpha_2, \alpha_1]$. The domination relation involving categories is then characterized in terms of the domination relation involving segments, as in (7) and (8) (see May 1985, Chomsky 1986a).

(7) *Domination*
      A category α dominates a syntactic object β iff every segment of α dominates β.

(8) *Containment*
      A category α contains a syntactic object β iff some segment of α dominates β.

According to these definitions, the category $[\alpha_2, \alpha_1]$ in (6) contains but does not dominate β, because the segment α_1 of $[\alpha_2, \alpha_1]$ does not dominate β. Thus, β in (6) can in principle command outside of $[\alpha_2, \alpha_1]$ (that is, β can command an element that is not dominated by $[\alpha_2, \alpha_1]$). Some of the consequences of these assumptions are reviewed below in the context of bare X-bar theory representations.

Consider now the bare phrase structure representation of (6), given in (9):

(9) $K = \{<\underline{\alpha, \alpha}>, \{\alpha, \beta\}\}$

$$\beta \leftarrow\!|\!\rightarrow \alpha$$

Chomsky (1994a, 15; 1995, 248) takes the notation $K = \{<\underline{\alpha, \alpha}>, \{\alpha, \beta\}\}$ in (9) to correspond to the two-segment category informally represented as $[\alpha_2, \alpha_1]$ in (6). Under this view, the two-segment category K in (9) dominates both α and β, according to the definition of domination given in (2); hence, neither α nor β can command out of K. Let us examine two concrete cases to discover if this is correct.

Consider first the syntactic object K in (10), which is formed after V(erb) moves and adjoins to T(ense):

(10) $M = \{\underline{T}, \{K, L\}\}$

$$K = \{<\underline{T, T}>, \{T, V\}\}\leftarrow\!|\!\rightarrow L = \{\underline{V}, \{V, ...\}\}$$

$$V \leftarrow\!|\!\rightarrow T$$

T and the moved V are members of the set $\{T, V\}$, which in turn is a member of the set $K = \{<\underline{T, T}>, \{T, V\}\}$. Thus, according to (2), K dominates T and V. In order for a chain between the moved verb V and its trace to be formed in (10), V must command its trace (see sec. 4.4). For this to hold according to the definition in (4), the first category dominating V should dominate the trace of V. As shown above, the first syntactic object dominating the moved V in (10) is $K = \{<\underline{T, T}>, \{T, V\}\}$, which does not dominate the trace of V. Thus, if K is a (two-segment) category and the definition of domination in (2) is assumed, no chain can be formed between the moved V and its trace, predicting that the derivation should either crash or be canceled.

A similar undesirable result arises in constructions involving noncyclic adjunction of relative clauses. As discussed in sections 4.3 and 4.4, the derivation of sentences such as (11a) presumably involves noncyclic adjunction of the relative clause to the moved *wh*-phrase, as partially represented in (11b) and (11c), where Q stands for the null interrogative complementizer:

(11) a. which portrait that Rivera$_i$ painted did he$_i$ like?

b. $[_{CP}[$[which portrait] [that Rivera painted]] [did+Q he like [which portrait]]]$

c. $W = \{Q, \{M, Y\}\}$

$M = \{<\underline{which, which}>, \{K, L\}\} \leftarrow\!|\!\rightarrow Y = [$did+Q he like $K = \{\underline{which} \{which, portrait\}\}]$

$K = \{\underline{which}, \{which, portrait\}\} \leftarrow\!|\!\rightarrow L= [$that Rivera painted$]$ which $\leftarrow\!|\!\rightarrow$ portrait

which $\leftarrow\!|\!\rightarrow$ portrait

In (11c) the relative clause L = [that Rivera painted] adjoins to the moved *wh*-phrase K = {which, {which, portrait}}, forming M. If the moved *wh*-phrase K and its trace within Y are to form a chain, K must command its trace. In order to determine whether this is the case, it is necessary to identify the first category dominating K. The first syntactic object dominating K is M, which does not dominate the trace of K. Thus, if M is a (two-segment) category and the definition of domination in (2) is assumed, K is prevented from commanding and forming a chain with its trace inside Y, which should then either cancel the derivation or make it crash.

In order to prevent this undesirable result, one could, for instance, take K = {<α, α>, {α, β}} in (9) to be a segment of a two-segment category [K, α], rather than a two-segment category in itself. Assuming that domination for categories is defined as in (7), the two-segment category D = [K, T] in (10), for example, does not dominate the moved V because it is not the case that every segment of D dominates V; the segment T of D = [K, T] does not dominate V. Thus, if K in (10) is a segment of the two-segment category D = [K, T], the first category dominating the moved V is actually M = {T, {K, L}}; given that M dominates K and K dominates V, M dominates V by the recursive step of (2). Since the first category dominating the moved V—namely, M—also dominates the trace of V (by the recursive step of (2)), V commands and can form a chain with its trace. As for (11c), if M is only a segment of the two-segment category X = [M, K], the root object W = {Q, {M, Y}} is the first category dominating K. Crucially, the two-segment category X = [M, K] does not dominate K according to (7), because K does dominate itself, as discussed in section A.2.2. Given that the root object W dominates the trace of K by the recursive step of (2), K commands its trace and a *wh*-chain can be formed, as expected.

In order to derive the expected command relations, this approach assumes an additional complex syntactic object: an object of the type K = [L, M] such that L is a segment built from M (i.e., L = {<Head(M), Head(M)>, {α, M}}) and M is a category (i.e., M is a lexical item or a syntactic object of the type M = {γ, {α, β}}). This approach also raises the issue of whether [. . .] in K = [L, M] should be understood as a set, so that an adjunction structure would involve a set of syntactic objects with no label attached to it, as suggested in passing in section 4.4, or whether [. . .] is a new kind of formal object.

Below, we pursue an alternative approach to this one, which also maintains that syntactic objects of the type K = {<γ, γ>, {α, β}} are two-segment categories. However, the notation of the label of syntactic objects formed by adjunction is slightly changed. The proposed change in notation does not increase the number of types of syntactic object or introduce new kinds of formal objects, as we will show.

A.2.4 Domination and Containment: Final Definitions

An ordered pair <α, β> is defined as a set A = {{α}, {α, β}}, and of course the set {α, α} is equal to {α}. Thus, an ordered pair <α, α> is the set B = {{α}, {α, α}} = {{α}, {α}} = {{α}}. Instead of using the ordered pair notation for the label of syntactic objects formed by adjunction, let us use its set-theoretic correspondent, so that the formalization of syntactic objects is as given in (12):

(12) *Syntactic object*

  σ is a syntactic object if it is

  a. a lexical item or the set of formal features of a lexical item, or

  b. the set $K = \{\underline{\gamma}, \{\alpha, \beta\}\}$ or $K = \{\underline{\{\{\gamma\}\}}, \{\alpha, \beta\}\}$ such that α and β are syntactic objects and $\underline{\gamma}$ or $\underline{\{\{\gamma\}\}}$ is the label of K.

Throughout the text, labels have been underlined for clarity. However, labels themselves are nothing but simple set-theoretic elements that are not terms (see (17)). Keeping this in mind, observe that according to the base step of both (1) and (12), the label of syntactic objects formed by adjunction ($\underline{\langle\gamma, \gamma\rangle}$ or $\underline{\{\{\gamma\}\}}$) does not correspond to a syntactic object. Given the alternative notation for the label of objects formed by adjunction in (12b), the definitions of domination and containment can be updated as in (13) and (14):

Given a syntactic object K such that $K = \{\underline{\gamma}, \{\delta, \mu\}\}$ or $K = \{\underline{\{\{\gamma\}\}}, \{\delta, \mu\}\}$:

(13) *Domination*

  K dominates a syntactic object α if and only if

  a. for every set L such that $L \in K$, $\alpha \in L$, or

  b. for some set M, K dominates M and M contains α.

(14) *Containment*

  K contains a syntactic object α if and only if

  a. for some set L such that $L \in K$, $\alpha \in L$, or

  b. for some set M, K contains M and M contains α.

Let us reconsider the relevant domination and containment relations in (10), repeated in (15) with the new notation:

(15) $M = \{\underline{T}, \{K, L\}\}$

  $K = \{\underline{\{\{T\}\}}, \{T, V\}\} \leftarrow\mid\!\rightarrow L = \{\underline{V}, \{V, ...\}\}$

              $V \leftarrow\mid\!\rightarrow T$

The object K in (15) has two sets as members: $\{\{T\}\}$ and $\{T, V\}$. T and V are members of $\{T, V\}$, but not of $\{\{T\}\}$. Note that (13a) poses, as a necessary condition for domination—say, by T of K in (15)—that all sets have T as a member. This strong condition will never be met in standard phrasal objects, unless these objects only have as members a label that is itself not a set, plus some arbitrary set. Only in that case, and crucially assuming that a label $\underline{\gamma}$ is not the same as the set $\{\gamma\}$, will (13a) be vacuously met for the label part of the syntactic object. However, this exception does not hold for K in

(15), which has a nontrivial label $\{\{T\}\}$, an obviously complex set. In contrast, the condition that (14a) imposes for containment is much weaker: it is enough that some set in K have, say, T as a member in order for K to contain T. In consequence, according to the definitions in (13) and (14), K in (15) contains but does not dominate T or V.

In turn, M has only one set as a member, namely, $\{K, L\}$. Thus, M contains and dominates K and L. Given that M dominates K and K contains V and T, M dominates V and T by the recursive step in (13b). Hence, according to the definition of domination in (13), the moved V in (15) commands and can form a chain with its trace: the first category that dominates the moved V—namely, M—also dominates the trace of V (by the recursive step of (13b)).

As for (11c), repeated in (16) using the new notation, the moved K is contained but not dominated by the two-segment category $M = \{\{\{which\}\}, \{K, L\}\}$, according to the definitions in (13) and (14). The first category that dominates K is the root object W, which also dominates the trace of K (by the recursive step in (13b)). Thus, the moved K commands its trace and the two copies can form a chain, as expected.

(16)
$$W = \{\underline{O}, \{M, Y\}\}$$

$M = \{\{\{\underline{which}\}\}, \{K, L\}\} \leftarrow | \rightarrow Y = [\text{did+Q he like}$ $K = \{\underline{which}, \{which, portrait\}\}]$

$K = \{\underline{which}, \{which, portrait\}\} \leftarrow | \rightarrow L = [\text{that Rivera painted}]$ $which \leftarrow | \rightarrow portrait$

$which \leftarrow | \rightarrow portrait$

Notice that, assuming the definitions of domination and containment in (13) and (14), there is no sense in asking whether K in (15) dominates or contains $\{\{T\}\}$ or whether M in (16) dominates or contains $\{\{which\}\}$. As stated in (13) and (14), domination and containment are relations established between syntactic objects, and according to the list of possible syntactic objects in (12), $\{\{T\}\}$ and $\{\{which\}\}$ are not syntactic objects. The label of a syntactic object formed by adjunction is akin to the "top" segment α_2 in the informal phrase marker representation in (6) in that it is not accessible to the computational system or interpreted by the interface systems.

A.3 Terms

In standard X-bar theory representations, the constituents of a given syntactic object correspond to nodes in a phrase marker. Chomsky (1995, 247) proposes that syntactic constituents in bare X-bar theory correspond to terms, as defined in (17):

(17) *Term*

For any syntactic object K,

a. K is a term of K;

b. if L is a term of K, then the members of the members of L are terms of K.

Consider the syntactic object M in (18), for instance:

(18) M = {α̲, {δ, {<α, α>, {γ, {α, {α, β}}}}}}

$$\delta \leftarrow\!\!\uparrow\!\!\rightarrow L = \{<\underline{\alpha, \alpha>}, \{\gamma, \{\alpha, \{\alpha, \beta\}\}\}\}$$

$$\gamma \leftarrow\!\!\uparrow\!\!\rightarrow K = \{\underline{\alpha}, \{\alpha, \beta\}\}$$

$$\alpha \leftarrow\!\!\uparrow\!\!\rightarrow \beta$$

According to the base step in (17a), M in (18) is a term of M. If M is a term of M, then the members of the members of M are also terms of M, according to the recursive step in (17b). M has two members: the label α̲, which is irrelevant for our purposes because it has no members, and the set {δ, {<α, α>, {γ, {α, {α, β}}}}}, whose members are δ and L = {<α, α>, {γ, {α, {α, β}}}}. Thus, δ and L are terms of M by (17b). L in turn has two members: the label <α, α>, which is not relevant because it is not a set (more on this below), and the set {γ, {α, {α, β}}}, whose members are γ and K = {α̲, {α, β}}. Given that L is a term of M, and γ and K are members of a member of L, γ and K are also terms of M by the recursive step of (17). Finally, the set K has two members: the label α̲, which is irrelevant by virtue of not having any members, and the set {α, β}. Thus, α and β are terms of K by the base step of (17) and terms of L and M by the recursive step.

The definition of term in (17) raises some problems for adopting the notation {{γ}} instead of the ordered pair <γ, γ> for the label of objects formed by adjunction, as proposed in section A.2.4. Consider L of (18) under the notation adopted in (12), for instance:

(19)   L = {{{α̲}}, {γ, {α, {α, β}}}}

$$\gamma \leftarrow\!\!\uparrow\!\!\rightarrow K = \{\underline{\alpha}, \{\alpha, \beta\}\}$$

$$\alpha \leftarrow\!\!\uparrow\!\!\rightarrow \beta$$

Under the new notation, L comprises two sets: {{α̲}} and {γ, {α, {α, β}}}. Given that L is a term of L by the base step in (17a), the members of these two sets—namely, {α}, γ, and K = {α̲, {α, β}}—are also terms of L by the recursive step in (17b). However, this is a conceptually odd result; {α} in (19) is a term of L although {α} is not a syntactic object (see (1) or (12)). Moreover, the combination of the new notation adopted in (12) with the definition of term in (17) has the a priori dubious implication that operations forming adjunction structures yield more terms than operations forming "substitution" structures. The Merge operation forming K in (19), for instance, yields three terms (K, α, and β), whereas the Merge operation forming K in (20) yields four terms (K, α, β, and {α}):

(20) K = {{{α̲}}, {α, β}}

$$\alpha \leftarrow\!\!\uparrow\!\!\rightarrow \beta$$

In section A.2.4 we showed that the new notation for the label of syntactic objects formed by adjunction allows domination and containment relations to be computed without the introduction of new primitive syntactic objects or relations. We will thus continue to use this new notation and will revise the definition of term in terms of containment (repeated in (21)), as shown in (22):

(21) *Containment*

Given a syntactic object $K = \{\underline{\gamma}, \{\delta, \mu\}\}$ or $K = \{\{\{\underline{\gamma}\}\}, \{\delta, \mu\}\}$, K contains a syntactic object α if and only if

a. for some set L such that $L \in K$, $\alpha \in L$, or

b. for some set M, K contains M and M contains α.

(22) *Term*

T is a term of a syntactic object K if and only if

a. $K = T$, or

b. K contains T.

According to (22), the terms of the syntactic object M in (23) (which is (18) under the revised notation) are M by the base step, and δ, L, γ, K, α, and β by the recursive step, given that M contains δ, L, γ, K, α, and β. The two problems noted above thus do not arise. As stated in (22), *term of* is a relation between syntactic objects; given that $\{\alpha\}$ in (20) does not conform to a possible syntactic object according to (20), it is not a term of M or any other syntactic object. Therefore, the number of terms resulting from an adjunction operation is the same as the number resulting from a substitution operation.

(23) $M = \{\underline{\alpha}, \{\delta, \{\{\{\alpha\}\}, \{\gamma, \{\alpha, \{\alpha, \beta\}\}\}\}\}\}$

$$\delta \leftarrow\!\!\!\overset{\uparrow}{|}\!\!\!\rightarrow L = \{\{\{\underline{\alpha}\}\}, \{\gamma, \{\alpha, \{\alpha, \beta\}\}\}\}$$

$$\gamma \leftarrow\!\!\!\overset{\uparrow}{|}\!\!\!\rightarrow K = \{\underline{\alpha}, \{\alpha, \beta\}\}$$

$$\alpha \leftarrow\!\!\!\overset{\uparrow}{|}\!\!\!\rightarrow \beta$$

A.4 Minimal, Maximal, and Intermediate Projections

As discussed in section 3.1, bare output conditions require that minimal and maximal projections be distinguished from intermediate projections, since only minimal and maximal projections receive an interpretation at the interface and hence are accessible to the computational system. Intuitively, minimal projections are lexical items, maximal projections are projections that project no further, and intermediate projections are neither minimal nor maximal. Evidence for taking intermediate projections to be inaccessible to the computational system comes from the linearization of structures involving a complex specifier. Consider how a structure such as (26), for example, should be linearized in accordance with the definitions of command and the LCA given in (4) and (5) and repeated in (24) and (25):

(24) *Command*

Where α and β are accessible to C_{HL}, α commands β if and only if

a. α does not dominate β, and

b. the first category dominating α also dominates β.

(25) *Linear Correspondence Axiom (LCA)*

A category α precedes a category β if and only if

a. α asymmetrically commands β, or

b. γ precedes β and γ dominates α.

(26)   M = {saw, {{the, {the, man}}, {saw, {saw, it}}}}

     L = {the, {the, man}} $\leftarrow\!|\!\rightarrow$ K = {saw, {saw, it}}

        the $\leftarrow\!|\!\rightarrow$ man   saw $\leftarrow\!|\!\rightarrow$ it

If the intermediate projection K in (26) were accessible to the computational system and thus able to command, it would asymmetrically command, and should therefore precede, *the* and *man*. By the recursive step of the LCA in (25), the categories dominated by K—namely, *saw* and *it*—should then precede *the* and *man*. In turn, since L asymmetrically commands *saw* and *it, the* and *man* should precede *saw* and *it,* in accordance with (25b). However, this yields a violation of the asymmetry requirement of a linear order; *the* and *man* should precede and be preceded by *saw* and *it*. This leads us to conclude that intermediate projections are inaccessible to the computational system and cannot command. Thus, given that *the* and *man* are not commanded by K in (26), *the* and *man* should precede *saw* and *it* according to (25b), as expected.

It should be noted, however, that at the point in the derivation where L in (26) merges with K, K must be accessible to the computational system. In other words, the notions of minimal, maximal, and intermediate projection must be computed at each step of a derivation. These notions can be defined as in (28)–(30) in terms of the definition of domination given in (13) and repeated here in (27):

(27) *Domination*

Given a syntactic object K = $\{\gamma, \{\delta, \mu\}\}$ or K = $\{\{\{\gamma\}\}, \{\delta, \mu\}\}$, K dominates a syntactic object α if and only if

a. for any set L such that L $\in$ K, $\alpha \in$ L, or

b. K dominates M and M contains α.

(28) *Minimal projection*

A syntactic object α is a minimal projection if and only if there is no syntactic object β such that α dominates β.

(29) *Maximal projection*

A syntactic object α is a maximal projection if and only if there is no syntactic object β such that β dominates α and β has the same label as α.

(30) *Intermediate projection*

      α is an intermediate projection if and only if α is a syntactic object that is not a minimal or a maximal projection.

Note that two categories have the same label only if they are projected from the same lexical item. In other words, the notion "label" is to be understood as "token label," or a mere set-theoretic object within a syntactic object (as defined in (12)) that is not a term (as defined in (22)). Two different items in the lexical array may have the same type of label, but they still have two different token labels.   ·

To show the definitions in (28)–(30) at work, we will examine derivations involving instances of multiple specifiers and multiple adjunction. Consider the derivational steps involved in the formation of the verb phrase headed by the auxiliary *du* in the Basque sentence (31), for instance (see chaps. 4 and 6):

(31) a. Jonek   Miren   maite du
            Jon-subject Miren-object love   auxiliary
            'Jon loves Miren'
      b. [Jonek T [Miren [(Jonek) [maite+du [(maite) (Miren)]]]]]]

The computational system selects *maite* and *Miren* and merges them, forming K in (32):

(32) K = {maite, {maite, Miren}}
        maite $\longleftarrow\mid\longrightarrow$ Miren

Before these two lexical items merge, they are both minimal and maximal projections, according to (28) and (29); they dominate and are dominated by no syntactic objects. After K is formed, *maite* and *Miren* are still minimal projections since they dominate no syntactic objects. Since they are now dominated by K, their status as maximal projections may change. The label of K is the same as the label of *maite*, which is *maite* itself (see sec. A.1); hence, according to (29), although *Miren* is still a maximal projection after K is formed, *maite* is no longer a maximal projection. In turn, K is a maximal projection because it is dominated by no syntactic object and is not a minimal projection because it dominates *maite* and *Miren*.

The next steps of the derivation involve selection of the auxiliary *du*, which then merges with K in (32) forming L, as shown in (33):

(33) L = {du, {du, K}}
        du $\longleftarrow\mid\longrightarrow$ K = {maite, {maite, Miren}}

Like *maite* in (32), *du* in (33) is a minimal maximal projection (both a minimal and a maximal projection) before merging with K, and becomes a minimal nonmaximal projection after the merger, because in (33) *du* is dominated by L and the label of *du*—namely, *du* itself—is the same as the label of L. On the other hand, K remains a nonminimal maximal projection after merger; although it is dominated by L in (33), the label of K is different from the label of L. Finally, L is a maximal projection because it is dominated by no syntactic object, and is not a minimal projection because it dominates *du*, K, *maite*, and *Miren*.

Assuming a cyclic derivation for (31b), the main verb *maite* then moves from within K in (33) and adjoins to the auxiliary *du* of L, forming M in (34a), which then replaces *du* in L, forming X in (34b):

(34) a. M = {{{du}}, {maite, du}}

             maite ←↑→ du

       b. X = {du, {M, K}}

In (34) M contains but does not dominate *du* or the moved *maite*; hence, M is a minimal projection according to (28), because it dominates no syntactic object. M is not a maximal projection according to (29), because its label is the same as the label of X, which dominates it. Therefore, a two-segment category formed by adjunction inherits the projection status of the target of adjunction. In the case of adjunction to heads, for instance, a "larger head" is formed, an issue to which we return below (see chapters 4 and 6 for a general discussion of instances where a head is more than just a lexical item). As far as the status of the moved verb *maite* is concerned, it dominates no syntactic object and is dominated by X by the recursive step of (27), whose label is the same as the label of the auxiliary *du*; hence, the moved V is a minimal maximal projection, according to the definitions in (28) and (29) (on the reasons why this result is irrelevant to the Condition on Chain Uniformity (see sec. 5.3). Finally, X in (34b) is a maximal projection because it is dominated by no syntactic object, and it is not a minimal projection, given that it dominates M and K by the base step of (27), and *du*, the moved *maite*, the trace of *maite*, and *Miren* by the recursive step.

The following steps of the derivation involve selection of *Jonek*, which then merges with X, forming W in (35):

(35) W = {du, {Jonek, X}}

         Jonek ←↑→ X = {du, {M, K}}

Jonek is a minimal maximal projection before and after merging with X, because in each derivational step *Jonek* dominates no syntactic object and is dominated by no syntactic object whose label is the same as its own label. As for X, recall that it was a nonminimal maximal projection before merging with *Jonek*. After merger, it remains a nonminimal projection in W since it still dominates the syntactic objects it did before merger, but it becomes a nonmaximal category because it has the same label as W, which dominates it. Since X within W is neither a minimal nor a maximal projection, it is an intermediate projection, according to (30). Thus, although X was accessible to the computational system in (34), it becomes inaccessible after merging with *Jonek* in (35).

Under the assumption that the auxiliary *du* in Basque has a strong feature, *Miren* moves from within W and merges with W, forming Y in (36):

(36) $Y = \{\underline{du}, \{Miren, W\}\}$

  $Miren \leftarrow | \rightarrow W = \{\underline{du}, \{Jonek, X\}\}$

The moved *Miren* in (36) is a minimal projection because it dominates no syntactic object and a maximal projection because it does not have the same label as the object that dominates it, namely, Y. In turn, W, which was a nonminimal maximal projection before merging with the moved *Miren,* becomes an intermediate projection after merger in (36); W is not a minimal projection because it dominates some syntactic objects and is not a maximal projection because it has the same label as Y, which dominates it. This sequence of derivational steps again shows that the projection status of a given syntactic object may change as the derivation proceeds.

Let us now turn to instances of multiple adjunction to a head, which has consequences for checking theory, as will be discussed in section A.6. Consider the T head of the *there*-existential construction in (37), for instance. Before verb movement takes place, the object Z is formed as shown in (38), where the internal structure of K is irrelevant for the point under consideration:

(37) a. there is a cat on the mat

  b. [there [is+T [(is) [a cat on the mat]]]]

(38) $Z = \{\underline{T}, \{there, M\}\}$

  $there \leftarrow | \rightarrow \underline{M} = \{\underline{T}, \{T, L\}\}$

  $T \leftarrow | \rightarrow L = \{\underline{is}, \{is, K\}\}$

  $is \leftarrow | \rightarrow K = [\ a\ cat\ on\ the\ mat]$

After the verb moves and adjoins to T overtly, the object W in (39a) is formed. W thus replaces T in M within (38), forming the object Y in (39b), which in turn replaces M within Z in (38), forming X in (39c):

(39) a. $W = \{\{\{\underline{T}\}\}, \{is, T\}\}$

    $is \leftarrow | \rightarrow T$

  b. $Y = \{\underline{T}, \{W, L\}\}$

  c. $X = \{\underline{T}, \{there, Y\}\}$

As shown above, an object such as W in (39b) is a minimal nonmaximal projection. It is not a maximal projection because it has the same label as Y, which dominates it, and it is a minimal projection because it dominates no syntactic object (W in (39a) contains but does not dominate *is* or T). As discussed in section 4.1, the relevant set FF of formal features of *a cat* moves from within K in the covert component and adjoins to W, forming the object R in (40a). R then replaces W within Y in (39b), forming S in (40b), which in turn replaces Y within X in (39c), forming U in (40c):

(40) a. R = {{{T}}, {FF, W}}

$$\text{FF} \leftarrow\!\!\uparrow\!\!\rightarrow \text{W} = \{\{\{\underline{T}\}\}, \{is, T\}\}$$

$$is \leftarrow\!\!\uparrow\!\!\rightarrow T$$

    b. S = {T, {R, L}}

    c. U = {T, {there, S}}

R in (40b) is not a maximal projection because it has the same label as S, which dominates it. On the other hand, although R contains FF and W by the base step of the definition of containment (see (21)) and contains *is* and T by the recursive step, R dominates no syntactic object; hence, R is a minimal projection. Again, the syntactic object formed by adjunction has the same projection status as the target for adjunction; thus, R "inherits" its status as a minimal nonmaximal projection from W, which in turn inherits it from T. Another way to state this, as observed above, is that adjunction to a head creates a "larger head."

Notice that, according to the definitions of projections in (28)–(30), the set of formal features FF in (40) is a minimal maximal projection, since it dominates no syntactic object and its label is different from the label of the categories that dominate it (S and U). The trace of FF, however, is arguably not a projection, because it is only part of a lexical item and enters into neither domination nor containment relations (see (13) and (14)). The fact that the chain CH = (FF, FF) is not uniform with respect to its projection status is not problematic if at LF word-level elements are immune to the algorithm that determines projection status, as stated by the Principle of Lexical Integrity (see sec. 5.3). It is also possible that the notion of projection is not defined for sets of formal features, but is only defined for categories (see Chomsky 1995, 270), where a category is a syntactic object (see (12)) that is not a set of formal features of a lexical item. We leave this issue open. For concreteness, we continue to use the notions of minimal, maximal, and intermediate projection in (28)–(30).

A.5 Specifiers and Complements

Given the definitions of projection status in (28)–(30), repeated in (41)–(43), and the definition of sisterhood in (44), the notions of specifier and complement can be defined as in (45) and (46):

(41) *Minimal projection*

A syntactic object α is a minimal projection if and only if there is no syntactic object β such that α dominates β.

(42) *Maximal projection*

A syntactic object α is a maximal projection if and only if there is no syntactic object β such that β dominates α and β has the same label as α.

(43) *Intermediate projection*

α is an intermediate projection if and only if α is a syntactic object that is not a minimal or a maximal projection.

(44) *Sisterhood*

The syntactic objects α and β such that $\alpha \neq \beta$ are sisters if and only if for every syntactic object γ such that γ contains α, γ also contains β, and conversely.

(45) *Specifier*

A syntactic object α is a specifier of the head H if and only if α is a sister of an intermediate projection P such that P has the same label as H.

(46) *Complement*

A syntactic object α is a complement of the minimal nonmaximal projection H if and only if α is a sister of H.

Consider the syntactic object M in (47) in light of the definitions in (45) and (46):

(47)   M = {saw, {he, {saw, {saw, it}}}}

$$he \leftarrow\!|\!\rightarrow K = \{\text{saw}, \{\text{saw, it}\}\}$$
$$\text{saw} \leftarrow\!|\!\rightarrow it$$

Here, *he* and K, on the one hand, and *saw* and *it,* on the other, are contained by the same elements; hence, *he* is a sister of K, and *saw* is a sister of *it,* according to (44). Given that *he* is a sister of K and K is an intermediate projection, *he* is the specifier of the head of K (i.e., *saw*), according to (45). In turn, since *it* is a sister of *saw* and *saw* is a minimal nonmaximal projection, *it* is the complement of *saw,* according to (46).

The definition of complement in (46) may be revised to extend to instances where there are syntactic objects adjoined to the head H itself as in (48), where the verb has moved from within VP and adjoined to T, forming K:

(48)   L = {T, {K, VP}}
$$K = \{\{\{T\}\}, \{T, V\}\} \leftarrow\!|\!\rightarrow VP$$

According to the definition of complement in (46), VP is a complement of T before the verb moves, but a complement of K after the verb moves. Although the revision is straightforward, we will not pursue the matter here, because *specifier* and *complement* are merely descriptive terms that will be subsumed under the notions of checking and internal domains (see sec. A.8).

A.6 X^{0max} and Sublabels

As discussed in section A.4, adjunction to a minimal projection creates a "larger head," that is, another minimal projection. In the case of U in (40), repeated in (49), for instance, W and R are minimal nonmaximal projections that have the same label as T, also a minimal nonmaximal projection:

(49)   U = {$\underline{T}$, {there, S}}

there $\leftarrow\!|\!\rightarrow$ S = {$\underline{T}$, {R, L}}

R = {{{$\underline{T}$}}, {FF, W}} $\leftarrow\!|\!\rightarrow$ L = [is a cat on the mat]

FF $\leftarrow\!|\!\rightarrow$ W = {{{$\underline{T}$}}, {is, T}}

is $\leftarrow\!|\!\rightarrow$ T

Chomsky (1995, 245) uses the term X^{0max} to refer to the "largest" among heads of the same type that enter into checking relations. In (49), for instance, R corresponds to T^{0max}. A given syntactic object α can then enter into a checking relation with X^{0max} if α enters into a checking relation with a sublabel of X^{0max}, that is, either a feature of X or a feature of a syntactic object adjoined to X (see (52) for a definition).

Given the definitions of projections and containment proposed in sections A.4 and A.2.4, X^{0max} can be defined as in (50):

(50) *X^{0max}*

The syntactic object K is an X^{0max} projection if and only if
a. K is a minimal projection, and
b. there is no minimal projection L such that L contains K.

According to (50), among the minimal projections R, FF, W, *is,* and T in (49), only R qualifies as an X^{0max} projection: whereas FF, W, *is,* and T are contained by R, no other minimal projection contains R. Since R has the same label as T, R is said to be a T^{0max} projection in (49).

Sublabels can now be defined as in (52), based on the notion of term given in (51) (a repetition of (22)):

(51) *Term*

T is a term of a syntactic object K if and only if
a. K = T, or
b. K contains T.

(52) *Sublabel*

σ is a sublabel of K if and only if

a. σ is a formal feature of a term of K, and

b. K is an X^{0max} projection.

Let us identify the sublabels of the T^{0max} projection R in (49). R has the following terms: R itself by (51a) and FF, W, *is,* and T by (51b). According to (52), each formal feature of FF, *is,* and T is thus a sublabel of T^{0max}. As for the complex syntactic objects W and R, their formal features are the formal features of the elements that they contain; hence, W and R do not themselves contribute any sublabels to the set of sublabels of T^{0max}.

A.7 Command

A.7.1 Tentative Definition

Let us reconsider the definition of command given in (4) and repeated in (53), which has been used thus far:

(53) *Command*

Where α and β are accessible to C_{HL}, α commands β if and only if

a. α does not dominate β, and

b. the first category dominating α also dominates β.

Given that the recursive step of the definition of domination in (27b) states that domination is a transitive relation, (53b) need not be restricted to the first category dominating α. According to (27b), if the first category dominating α also dominates β, then every category that dominates α also dominates β. We can therefore simplify the definition of command in (53) and replace *first category* in (53b) with the simpler quantification *every category,* as in (54):

(54) *Command*

Where α and β are accessible to C_{HL}, α commands β if and only if

a. α does not dominate β, and

b. every category dominating α also dominates β.

Notice also that it is not necessary to include in the definition of command the requirement that β not dominate α (see Chomsky 1995, 339). This follows from the conjunction of (54b) and the irreflexivity property of domination discussed in section A.2.2. In order to see this, consider whether α commands β in (55), for instance:

(55) β = {γ, {δ, α}}

$$\delta \leftarrow\!|\!\rightarrow \alpha$$

According to (54b), in order for α to command β, every category dominating α must also dominate β. Since β dominates α in (55), β is required to dominate itself in order for α to command β. This is not permitted, given that domination is irreflexive. Since there is a category that dominates α—namely, β—that does not dominate β, α does not command β in (55), according to the definition in (54). Put generally, a category α does not command a category β that dominates it.

A.7.2 Irreflexivity and Final Definition

The definition of command in (54) allows an element to command itself. Consider the command relation between α and itself in the structure in (56), for instance:

(56) K = {γ, {α, β}}

$$\alpha \leftarrow\!\!\uparrow\!\!\rightarrow \beta$$

Here, α does not dominate itself, because domination is irreflexive; hence, (54a) is satisfied. In turn, (54b) is obviously satisfied: the only category dominating α—namely, K—dominates α. Therefore, according to (54), α in (56) commands itself.

However, binding theory considerations indicate that command should be an irreflexive notion (see Lasnik and Uriagereka 1988, 161 n. 14). As discussed in section 4.3, a sentence such as (57a), informally represented in (57b), shows that a name cannot have the same referent as a commanding expression:

(57) a. Bacon puzzled Bacon

b. L = {puzzled, {Bacon, K}}

$$\text{Bacon} \leftarrow\!\!\uparrow\!\!\rightarrow K = \{\underline{puzzled}, \{puzzled, Bacon\}\}$$

$$\text{puzzled} \leftarrow\!\!\uparrow\!\!\rightarrow \text{Bacon}$$

Consider the predictions of this coreference restriction for a sentence such as (58a), with its representation in (58b):

(58) a. Bacon left

b. {left, {Bacon, left}}

As shown in (56), in a structure such as (58b), *Bacon* commands itself, according to the definition in (54). However, this gives rise to a contradiction. Since the binding theory requires that names not be interpreted as coreferential with any commanding element, *Bacon* in (58b) cannot refer to the entity that *Bacon* refers to. In order to prevent such an absurdity, it is thus necessary to take command to be irreflexive, as in (59):

(59) *Command*

Where α and β are accessible to C_{HL}, α commands β if and only if

a. α does not dominate β,

b. $\alpha \neq \beta$, and

c. every category dominating α also dominates β.

According to the requirement in (59b), *Bacon* in (58b) (and α in (56)) cannot be taken to be α and β of the definition of command; hence, *Bacon* does not command itself in (58b) and the binding theory restriction on the interpretation of names is not violated. (57b), on the other hand, involves two instances of *Bacon;* thus, the first instance can be taken as α in (59) and the second instance as β. If so, the first instance commands the second instance and the binding theory requires that they not be understood as coreferential, which corresponds to the interpretation of (57a).

A.8 Domains

A.8.1 Tentative Definitions

Let us now consider the definitions of domains formulated in section 6.1, which define the configurations in which grammatical relations take place. (We use notationally inert subscripts to keep track of elements within chains.)

Where α is a feature matrix or a head #X# and CH is a given chain (α_i, t_j) or (the trivial chain) α:

(60) *Max(α)*

Max(α) is the smallest maximal projection dominating α.

(61) *Domain of CH (D(CH))*

The domain D(CH) of CH is the set of categories/features dominated by Max(α) that are distinct from and do not contain α or *t*.

(62) *Minimal domain of CH (Min(D(CH)))*

The minimal domain Min(D(CH)) of CH is the smallest subset K of D(CH) such that for any $\gamma \in$ D(CH), some $\beta \in$ K dominates γ.

(63) *Internal domain of α (ID(CH))*

The internal domain ID(CH) is the subset of Min(D(CH)) that includes only sisters to α's projections.

(64) *Checking domain of α (CD(CH))*

The checking domain CD(CH) is the set-theoretic complement of ID(CH) in Min(D(CH)).

The notions in (60)–(64) are based on phrase marker representations of syntactic objects. In the next sections we discuss how (60)–(64) should be revised in order to be compatible with the set-theoretic notion of syntactic object adopted in the bare X-bar theory (see sec. A.2.4). For the sake of brevity, we focus on the parts of the definitions in (60)–(64) that do not work properly if the definitions of syntactic object and domination assumed here are adopted.

A.8.2 Revisions

A.8.2.1 Max(α) Let us begin the discussion with the notion of Max(α) in (60), repeated in (65):

(65) *Max(α)*
   Where α is a feature matrix or a head #X# and CH is a given chain (α_i, t_i) or (the trivial chain) α, Max(α) is the smallest maximal projection dominating α.

Let us make precise what *smallest* stands for in a representation such as (66), where V is a main verb, IO an indirect object, DO a direct object, v a light or auxiliary verb, and Subj a subject. Take Max(V), for instance. Intuitively, the smallest maximal projection dominating V is VP = {V̲, {DO, V′}}.

(66) vP = {$v̲$, {Subj, v′}}
   Subj ←⌐→ v′ = {$v̲$, VP}}
   v ←⌐→ VP = {V̲, {DO, V′}}
   DO ←⌐→ V′ = {V̲, {V, IO}}
   V ←⌐→ IO

The more detailed definition of Max(α) in (67) expresses the notion of "smallest maximal projection" through the notion of domination. According to (67), Max(V) in (66) cannot be vP, for instance, because VP is a maximal projection that dominates V but does not dominate vP. Hence, Max(V) in (66) is VP; the only other maximal projection that dominates V—namely, vP—also dominates VP.

(67) *Max(α)*
   Where α is a feature matrix or a head #X# and CH is a given chain (α_i, t_i) or (the trivial chain) α, Max(α) is the maximal projection P such that P dominates α and for every maximal projection Q ≠ P, if Q dominates α, then Q dominates P.

A.8.2.2 Domain Consider now the definition of domain in (61), repeated in (68):

(68) *Domain of CH (D(CH))*
   Where α is a feature matrix or a head #X# and CH is a given chain (α_i, t_i) or (the trivial chain) α, D(CH) is the set of categories/features dominated by Max(α) that are distinct from and do not contain α or *t*.

Applied to the chain CH = (V_i, t_i) of (69), the graph representation of (66) after the main verb adjoins to the light verb, the definition in (68) states that D(CH) is the set with the following members: Subj, DO, IO, and whatever these categories contain. VP, V′, V_i, and t_i are not members of D(CH) because they are—in some sense to be made precise (see below)—nondistinct from V_i; in turn, vP, v′, and the two-segment category ["v," v] are not members of D(CH) because they contain V_i.

(69)

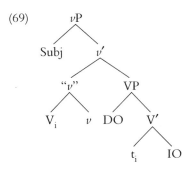

Consider the bare phrase structure representation of (69) in (70):

(70) vP = {$\underline{v}$, {Subj, v′}}

Subj $\leftarrow\!\overset{\uparrow}{|}\!\rightarrow$ v′ = {$\underline{v}$, {K, VP}}

K = {{{$\underline{v}$}}, {v, V}} $\leftarrow\!\overset{\uparrow}{|}\!\rightarrow$ VP = {$\underline{V}$, {DO, V′}}

V_i $\leftarrow\!\overset{\uparrow}{|}\!\rightarrow$ v DO $\leftarrow\!\overset{\uparrow}{|}\!\rightarrow$ V′ = {$\underline{V}$, {V, IO}}

t_i $\leftarrow\!\overset{\uparrow}{|}\!\rightarrow$ IO

One aspect in which the definition of D(CH) in (68) fails to yield the expected results in (70) regards the exclusion of v from $D(V_i, t_i)$. The notion of containment in (68) is not sufficient to exclude v in (70) from $D(V_i, t_i)$; although the two-segment category K contains V_i, the light verb itself does not contain V_i. The correct results can be obtained if we exclude the elements that have the same (token) label as Max(α) from the definition of D(CH). Incorporating nondistinctiveness in terms of labels, the appropriate notion of domain needed for set-theoretic syntactic objects can then be defined as in (71):

(71) *Domain of CH (D(CH))*
     Where α is a feature matrix or a head #X# and CH is a given chain (α_i, t_i) or (the trivial chain) α, D(CH) is the set K such that for any $\gamma \in$ K
     a. γ is dominated by Max(α),
     b. for any β, such that β has the same label as α, $\gamma \in \beta$, and
     c. for any δ, such that δ has the same label as Max(α), $\gamma \in \delta$.

According to (71), D(v) in (70) is the set with the following members: Subj, V_i, VP, and whatever these categories contain. (71a) excludes vP = {$\underline{v}$, {Subj, v′}} from D(v)

because vP is not dominated by Max(v) = vP (recall that domination is an irreflexive relation). When a domain is computed with respect to a trivial chain such as D(v) in (70), the conditions in (71b) and (71c) have the same effect, for v has the same label as Max(v) = vP. Thus, v, K = {{{v}}, {v, V}}, and v' = {v, {K, VP}} in (70) are excluded from the D(v) by either (71b) or (71c). On the other hand, when a domain is computed with respect to a nontrivial chain such as D(V_i, t_i) in (70), the conditions in (71b) and (71c) are not redundant; in the case at hand, for instance, V_i does not have the same label as Max(V_i) = vP. Thus, D(V_i, t_i) has the following members: Subj, DO, IO, and whatever these categories contain. As before, vP = {v, {Subj, v'}} is not a member of D(V_i, t_i) because it is not dominated by Max(V_i) = vP (see (71a)); (71b) excludes from D(V_i, t_i) the following elements: V_i, VP, and t_i (a copy of V_i), all of which have the same label as V_i. Finally, (71c) excludes v' = {v, {K, VP}}, K = {{{v}}, {v, V}}, and v, all of which have the same label as Max(V_i) = vP.

A.8.2.3 Minimal Domain   Let us now consider the definition of minimal domain in (62), repeated in (72):

(72)   *Minimal domain of CH (Min(D(CH)))*
Where α is a feature matrix or a head #X# and CH is a given chain (α_i, t_i) or (the trivial chain) α, Min(D(CH)) is the smallest subset K of D(CH) such that for any $\gamma \in$ D(CH), some $\beta \in$ K [reflexively] dominates γ.

(72) is incompatible with the assumptions of the preceding sections in that it takes domination to be a reflexive relation. As discussed in section A.2.2, if domination is defined along the lines of (27), repeated in (73), it inherits irreflexivity from set membership:

(73)   *Domination*
Given a syntactic object K = {γ, {δ, μ}} or K = {{{γ}}, {δ, μ}}, K dominates a syntactic object α if and only if
a. for any set L such that L $\in$ K, $\alpha \in$ L, or
b. K dominates M and M contains α.

The expected relations can be established under an irreflexive notion of domination, if minimal domains are defined as in (74):

(74)   *Minimal domain of CH (Min(D(CH)))*
Where α is a feature matrix or a head #X# and CH is a given chain (α_i, t_i) or (the trivial chain) α, Min(D(CH)) is the subset K of D(CH) such that for any $\gamma \in$ K, if some Max(β) $\neq$ Max(α) dominates γ, then Max(β) dominates Max(α).

Let us consider the effects of (74), by reexamining the minimal domains of (66), repeated in (75):

(75) vP = $\{v, \{\text{Subj}, v'\}\}$

Subj $\leftarrow\!|\!\rightarrow$ v' = $\{v, \{v, \text{VP}\}\}$

v $\leftarrow\!|\!\rightarrow$ VP = $\{\underline{V}, \{\text{DO}, \text{V}'\}\}$

DO $\leftarrow\!|\!\rightarrow$ V$'$ = $\{\underline{V}, \{\text{V}, \text{IO}\}\}$

V $\leftarrow\!|\!\rightarrow$ IO

Assume for the sake of discussion that Subj, DO, and IO in (75) are just lexical items. Why, according to (74), are DO and IO, for instance, part of Min(D(V)) but not part of Min(D(v))? According to the definition of domain in (73), D(V) is the set {DO, IO} and D(v) is the set {Subj, VP, DO, V$'$, V, IO}, since, by assumption, Subj, DO, and IO are lexical items and contain no other element. The only two members of D(V) are dominated by VP (= Max(α) in (74)) and by Max(v) (= Max(β) in (74)); given that vP dominates VP, the two members of D(V)—namely, DO and IO—are also members of Min(D(V)), according to (74). As for D(v), we must consider two cases: (i) Subj and VP, which are dominated by only one maximal projection, namely, vP; and (ii) DO, V$'$, V, and IO, which are dominated by vP and by VP. Since Subj and VP are dominated by no maximal projection other than vP (= Max(α) in (74)), Subj and VP are members of Min(D(v)); on the other hand, since VP (= Max(β) in (74)) does not dominate vP (= Max(α) in (74)), the members of D(v) that are dominated by VP—namely, DO, V$'$, V, and IO—are not members of Min(D(v)), according to (74).

A.8.2.4 Internal Domain   Consider now the diagram in (76), formed after DO in (70) moves, creating the chain CH = (DO$_j$, t$_j$):

(76) vP = $\{v, \{\text{DO}_j, v_2'\}\}$

DO$_j$ $\leftarrow\!|\!\rightarrow$ v_2' = $\{v, \{\text{Subj}, v_1'\}\}$

Subj $\leftarrow\!|\!\rightarrow$ v_1' = $\{v, \{\text{K}, \text{VP}\}\}$

K = $\{\{\{v\}\}, \{v, \text{V}\}\}$ $\leftarrow\!|\!\rightarrow$ VP = $\{\underline{V}, \{\text{DO}, \text{V}'\}\}$

V$_i$ $\leftarrow\!|\!\rightarrow$ v t$_j$ $\leftarrow\!|\!\rightarrow$ V$'$ = $\{\underline{V}, \{\text{V}, \text{IO}\}\}$

t$_i$ $\leftarrow\!|\!\rightarrow$ IO

In (76) Max(v) is vP; D(v) involves DO$_j$, Subj, V$_i$, VP, and whatever these categories contain, and Min(D(v)) is the set {DO$_j$, Subj, V$_i$, VP}. As discussed in section 4.6, DO$_j$ and V$_i$ must fall within the checking domain of v because they enter into checking relations with v. Given the definitions of internal and checking domains in (63) and (64), repeated in (77) and (78), the question then is whether the definition in (78) does not incorrectly entail that both DO$_j$ and V$_i$ fall within the internal domain of v and, consequently, not within the checking domain of v, which is the set-theoretic complement of Int(D(v)):

Where α is a feature matrix or a head #X# and CH is a given chain (α_i, t_i) or (the trivial chain) α:

(77) *Internal domain of α (Int(D(CH)))*
Int(D(CH)) is the subset L of Min(D(CH)) such that for any $\gamma \in$ L, γ is a sister of a projection of α.

(78) *Checking domain of α (Check(D(CH)))*
Check(D(CH)) is the subset M of Min(D(CH)) such that M is the set-theoretic complement of Int(D(CH)).

Under plausible assumptions, this unwelcome result can be prevented by the Principle of Chain Integrity given in (71) (see sec. 5.7):

(79) *Principle of Chain Integrity*
Only entire chains enter into C_{HL} operations.

Intuitively, it is not the case that all the links of the chains $CH_1 = (V_i, t_i)$ and $CH_2 = (DO_j, t_j)$ in (76) are sisters of a projection of v. Put differently, only trivial chains can be part of an internal domain. Incorporating this idea into (77), the notion of internal domain can be revised as in (80):

(80) *Internal domain of α (Int(D(α)))*
Where α is a feature matrix or a head #X# and CH is a given chain (α_i, t_i) or (the trivial chain) α, Int(D(CH)) is the subset L of Min(D(CH)) such that for any $\gamma \in$ L, γ is a nontrivial chain and is a sister of a projection of α.

According to (80), neither DO_j nor V_i in (76) is in the Int(D(v)) because neither is a trivial chain; rather, each heads a nontrivial chain. Given that DO_j and V_i are in Min(D(v)), according to (74), but are not in Int(D(v)), according to (80), (78) states that they are in Check(D(v)), as desired.

A.8.3 Final Definitions

With the revisions in section A.8.2, the final definitions of grammatical domains are as follows:

Where α is a feature matrix or a head #X# and CH is a given chain (α_i, t_i) or (the trivial chain) α:

(81) *Max(α)*
Max(α) is the maximal projection P such that P dominates α and for every maximal projection Q $\neq$ P, if Q dominates α, then Q dominates P.

(82) *Domain of CH (D(CH))*

D(CH) is the set K such that for any $\gamma \in$ K

a. γ is dominated by Max(α),

b. for any β, such that β has the same label as α, $\gamma \in \beta$, and

c. for any δ, such that δ has the same label as Max(α), $\gamma \in \delta$.

(83) *Minimal domain of CH (Min(D(CH)))*

Min(D(CH)) is the subset L of D(CH) such that for any $\gamma \in$ L, if some Max(β) $\neq$ Max(α) dominates γ, then Max(β) dominates Max(α).

(84) *Internal domain of α (Int(D(α)))*

Int(D(CH)) is the subset X of Min(D(CH)) such that for any $\gamma \in$ X, γ is a nontrivial chain and is a sister of a projection of α.

(85) *Checking domain of α (Check(D(CH)))*

Check(D(CH)) is the subset Y of Min(D(CH)) such that Y is the set-theoretic complement of Int(D(CH)).

Chapter Summaries

Chapter 1

The main ideas discussed on the first day can be framed in terms of traditional philosophical issues, starting with Plato's insight: given the view that language acquisition must overcome the *poverty of the linguistic stimulus,* knowledge of language illustrates that humans know more than they are taught. To account for this fact, linguists assume that much of that *knowledge of language is innate.*

Then Locke's question arises: if linguistic knowledge is innate, how is it possible for it to vary, giving rise to different languages? In general terms, it does so because a biological individual is not simply the result of following a recipe of gene instructions. Rather, the genes provide a *framework for development* that interacts with the early environment. In the case of humans this environment is extremely stable not just for the nine months of pregnancy but also during the early years of life. It provides primary linguistic data that enable the linguistic system to develop, just as it provides light and food that enable the visual and motor systems to develop. This sort of reasoning implies that the linguistic system is *profoundly abstract.*

Equating human language with biological growth may seem to pose a new kind of question for the sciences, but in fact the question is merely a fleshed-out version of Descartes's challenge to develop a *theory of mind.* In the light of pre-Newtonian theories of matter, this challenge appeared dualistic. However, within modern conceptions of reality, it is a priori no more or less answerable than the challenges posed by developing a theory of life or of body plans, or more generally perhaps a theory of complex systems.

The assumption underlying this naturalistic approach to language can be thought of as Humboldt's program: the phenomenon of human language is characterized by making use of *finite means* to produce *an infinite sort of structure* (discrete infinity). Implied is a view of language not as the directly observable output of a generative procedure, but as the procedure itself. This procedure has the same natural status as other complex systems do, and is studied by way of a linguistic theory that is referred to as *Universal Grammar* (UG).

These ideas form the conceptual basis of the *principles-and-parameters* approach to linguistic theory. Languages have invariant properties formally encoded through universal (natural) laws called *principles,* and a few dimensions along which variation can emerge within the confines of those laws, called *parameters.* On the basis of some procedure for analyzing *primary linguistic data,* the child must set the parameters for the particular language he or she is learning. The *Minimalist Program* assumes this tradition, but proposes to ask more abstract questions about the nature of principles and parameters themselves. Given contingent facts about language, is there a *conceptually necessary* and *optimally economical* way of meeting those conditions? If so, does that say something about the nature of linguistic principles and parameters?

To start with, although the primary linguistic data determining parametric settings are very complex, children are capable of sieving through them to come up with a language every time they try (before a *critical age*). How they do this is particularly puzzling if, as it seems, children do not make use of direct negative evidence of the sort employed in metalinguistic statements; instead, they use *direct positive evidence:* actual utterances from the language spoken around them. This implies that the actual linguistic system acquired by children is economical enough to be trivially learnable. The underlying system that UG studies is *underspecified* (as compared to what is seen in actual languages after they are acquired), and setting its core parametric values is a direct process allowing entire populations to converge on the same answers. This *overall economy in the design of the language faculty* is responsible, at least, for *structural conservation* in the process of acquisition, and perhaps elsewhere.

Given the *dynamic equilibrium* presupposed in the acquisition process, occasionally (when input data are murky enough to allow for ambiguous parametric options) children acquire a parametric setting different from the one used by speakers around them to generate the input data, possibly leading to a *language change*. Apart from accounting for linguistic variation, these dynamics point in the direction of a second kind of elegance: *economy in the device responsible for the acquisition process*. Apparently, this process is sensitive to critical amounts of data and simplest hypotheses concerning the structure underlying the data, two characteristic traits of complex dynamic problems that suggest that a dynamic kind of economy exists internal to the general system.

Learnability considerations aside, the linguistic system can be shown to present two sorts of what may be called *internal economy,* to be explored in other chapters. One is *representational:* the linguistic system provides an optimal encoding of symbols. The other is relatively new to Minimalism: the workings of the computational system that describes structures involving elegantly encoded symbols are *computationally* optimal.

If these ideas are correct, the linguistic system may be an easily observable yet farreaching *complex system* of the natural world. To the extent that the system exhibits economy (particularly in terms of design and internal aspects) and discrete infinity, it is a surprising object within the standard biological world. It appears close to what is thought to exist at the level of molecular biology (which is not as easy to observe), or at yet to be understood levels of abstract complexity in biological systems.

Viewed this way, linguistics provides no evidence for gradual adaptationism. First, large portions of human language appear to be unusable, and the adaptationist view makes sense only if linguistic usability gave humans an evolutionary edge. Second, if language arose as an adaptation, it is unclear what advantage language variation could have provided. Evolutionary pressure should have worked toward fixing particular behavioral patterns for the entire species.

On the other hand, if language is an *exaptation,* no specific evolutionary pressure is expected, and whatever properties language has should be profoundly underspecified. This correlates nicely with the underdeterminacy observed in the linguistic system. That language is an exaptation is also confirmed by the fact that it displays the kind of structural elegance present in *dynamic systems* of various degrees of complexity, which must follow from mechanisms other than natural selection through adaptation.

Chapter 2

The Minimalist Program is Aristotelian: linguistic expressions couple *external conditions* on sound and meaning substances, in terms of *internal formal properties*. It departs from Aristotelianism in terms of the role of scientific investigation: linguistic questions must be resolved by empirical research and cannot be decided a priori. In particular, the system of knowledge implied by UG is a subcomponent of the human mind; therefore, some of its properties are expected to arise as a result of the *natural interactions* between it and the rest of the mind. On the other hand, UG is intended as a description of a natural object, which should have *internal coherence* (if it is not the mere result of evolutionary selection).

More technically, the language faculty is said to be embedded in an *articulatory/perceptual* (A/P) matrix and an *intentional/conceptual* (I/C) matrix. The language faculty's interface with the A/P component is *Phonetic Form* (PF), and its interface with the I/C component is *Logical Form* (LF). PF and LF are *levels of linguistic representation*. Whereas PF and LF are levels of linguistic *competence,* A/P and I/C are components of linguistic *performance*. The criterion of *Full Interpretation* states that possible PF/LF representations consist entirely of legitimate PF/LF objects. Computationally, the model obeys the following equation: $C_{HL}(A) = (PF, LF)$, where A is an *array* of lexical items and C_{HL} is a *computational system* that is essentially invariant across languages. If there is variability within C_{HL}, it must be accessible to the language learner, a condition that restricts it to phonological/lexical matters.

The lexicon contains *lexical* and *functional* items, both of which are *matrices of features* from substantive universal vocabularies. Whereas variations among functional items may affect the computations of C_{HL}, variations among lexical items may not, suggesting that each type ultimately represents a different kind of knowledge. Absence of exposure to language prior to a critical age results in damage to the functional system, not the lexical one. This suggests that functional items are *basic syntactic dimensions,* whereas lexical items are the locus of *knowledge about the world*.

Functional items affect syntactic computations, particularly in terms of their morphological *strength*. The need to *check* morphologically strong elements triggers syntactic movements. Languages do not differ with respect to what types of movements they allow; rather, they differ with respect to the strength of the morphemes that require these movements. The computation is constant; what varies is an overt cue to it.

The task of determining the vocabularies of features making up matrices of functional and lexical items is purely empirical. Relevant clues in this difficult task are *sensitivity to syntactic processes* (e.g., movement, agreement) and *lexical implications*. The latter relate also to the nature of *classifiers,* or syntactic manifestations of lexical classifications. Studies on the universal dimensions of classifiers should have a bearing on the essential features of LF and how they are systematically related.

A *syntactic derivation* is characterized as a *set of phrase markers* generated from elements taken from an array. It is said to *converge* at LF or PF only if it produces an object that meets the outside conditions of these levels (Full Interpretation). Otherwise, it *crashes*. A derivation may be *canceled,* thus ceasing to be a derivation, if it disobeys a defining formal condition of derivations somewhere during its history.

Convergence is a property at a given level of the representations produced by a derivation, and not a property of the derivation before it reaches that level. This follows from the *interpretability* of levels: every linguistic symbol is accessed by systems that interact with the language faculty. Apart from being interpretable, levels are *comprehensive* (which entails that any expression of human language is representable at some level) and *complete* (which entails that linguistic levels of representation are interface levels only).

Given an initial array A, C_{HL} can generate *alternative derivations* that converge. Given alternative convergent derivations, the *more economical* ones rule out the less economical ones. However, an optimal representation generated by a convergent derivation may not have an interpretation at A/P or I/C. That is, a convergent derivation need not yield an interpretable representation.

Minimalism as presented here is *harmonious* (it seeks various sorts of symmetries within and possibly also across levels of representation), *reductionist* (it postulates only the bare essentials as a formal apparatus), and *constructivist* (it assumes an inflationary model of syntax, whereby derivations have a real beginning and a real end). Given that mere notations must be distinguished from actual claims within the theory, might alternatives to this system exist that are also minimalist? This question has arisen, in particular, with respect to whether the triplet (A, PF, LF) factually allows for representational relations other than the basic derivational ones, carrying the system onward from A to PF and LF.

In a representational system that incorporates a single level of S-structure from which all A/P and I/C properties of expressions are read off, basic objects like chains would be primitive, instead of the history of a derivational procedure. The strongest evidence for such a theory would be *externally driven output filters* that could not be expressed as internally motivated derivational steps of the computational system.

Optimality Theory is a proposal of that sort, inasmuch as it involves *soft constraints* that rank alternative representations described by a basic general function. The effects of this architecture cannot be mimicked in any standard serial derivation. The optimality approach works best in *input-output* systems, such as phonology or morphology, and may provide a way of dealing with some kinds of linguistic variation. To the extent that this is the case, it also suggests that the core mapping from A to LF is rather different from the mapping to PF. The latter is basically less perfect, in a Minimalist sense.

Chapter 3

Externally determined conditions must be distinguished from (virtually) *conceptually necessary* conditions. For instance, the fact that interpretive levels interpret single objects justifies the merger of multiple phrase markers into a single one that is interpreted. Although the operation Merge is externally determined, it is not conceptually necessary and must be postulated as part of linguistic theory. In contrast, the property of *projection* that Merge exhibits is conceptually necessary, since all other alternatives lead to paradoxical results. Thus, projection encodes the basic asymmetry of Merge.

Given Merge, notions outside this operation, such as *head, maximal projection, complement,* and *specifier,* can be defined. These notions are defined because they are important for other subsystems of grammar, not C_{HL} itself. It is assumed that in the simplest possible world, C_{HL} sees only those elements that enter into relations with other subsystems of grammar, and it is hoped that those elements are conceptually necessary at interface levels. As a consequence, intermediate projections have no status.

It is not known a priori what a given linguistic phenomenon may follow from: whether from the *internal workings of* C_{HL} or from an *outside condition* on a level of representation (and if the latter, whether the condition arises for PF or LF reasons). For instance, Case could be a property of elements that need to be "visible" at LF, or a way of expressing a computational relation between elements that need to be "linearized" for PF reasons— or even neither of these, arising instead from other dynamic properties of the system. The final option is explored in chapter 5.

Likewise, phrase markers can be computationally described by way of *phrase structure rules,* but these structures are not necessarily a property of C_{HL}. In fact, phrase structure rules encode both *dominance* and *precedence* in terms of a unitary symbolic system; for these rules to be useful in describing actual linguistic phrases, they must be enriched in terms of conventions about *heads* and *binary branching.* But the Merge system (which yields projections of X) accounts for at least the headedness property without stipulation, hence is preferable to the alternative. If Merge ultimately derives from external (perhaps LF) properties, the headedness aspect of phrase markers should follow from an external (LF) property.

As for the binary branching property, it follows in a more indirect way from taking phrases of human language to be derived interactively from two different factors, one central to LF and the other central to PF. The first factor is Merge, which in itself only produces headed phrases (not necessarily binary ones). The second factor is *Linearization,* a procedure by which the internal hierarchy of phrases resulting from Merge is mapped to a linear object that is expressible at PF. As it turns out, *only binary branches can be linearized* in terms of the specific procedure that UG provides for linearization, as follows.

Linguistic phrase markers make crucial use of the specifically linguistic structural relation of *command* (which may itself derive from Merge). A category *asymmetrically* commands all categories that its mother dominates, except for its sister. Furthermore, command is *irreflexive* and *transitive.* Asymmetric command is thus a partial ordering, which allows the categories in the ordering to be trivially mapped into a PF timing sequence. The conjecture that precedence (PF timing) relations must be *homomorphic* with command (derivational or LF) relations is expressed in the *base* step of the *Linear Correspondence Axiom* (LCA). The *induction* step of the LCA is added so as to connect the categories that are ordered by command to other ordered categories.

Multiple branching entails *ambiguous command* relations by the multiple sisters of a category and thus makes *unambiguous linearization* impossible. As a result, any multiply branching phrase marker crashes at PF. It must be emphasized that this result is obtained only if the phrase markers of human language are the *emergent product of Merge and Lineariza-*

tion; it would not follow from describing these objects by rules specific to their structure. Independent conceptual evidence for this view is that phrase structure rules can also describe many phenomena in nature that are not connected with linguistics in any obvious way, at least a priori.

The LCA makes other empirical predictions: for instance, *specifiers precede heads,* and *heads precede those complements that have a nontrivial internal structure.* Languages in which (superficially) the head precedes the specifier, or that exhibit any ordering that does not correspond directly to the LCA, must invoke some *extra movement.* This sort of analysis predicts the existence of languages, for instance, that are superficially the mirror image of English with respect to the order of complements and heads and therefore license embedded subject anaphors.

But although the LCA predicts that a head precedes the elements (nontrivially) dominated by its complement, it does not predict that a head precedes its complement when this complement is both a head and a maximal projection, since these two stand in a symmetric relation. (As a consequence, the LCA predicts that each head must precede the other.) In order that the LCA be met at Spell-Out, complements without internal structure must be *cliticized* or otherwise moved to a position that commands the head, leaving behind a trace (understood as a nonpronounced copy of the moved element) that need not be linearized, since it lacks phonetic content. Clitics are taken to be part of *word morphology,* and the LCA has nothing to say about their linearization, which instead follows from general morphological principles outside the scope of syntax proper. This sort of analysis predicts why a heavy complement can appear to the right of a head, whereas (generally speaking) a weak complement must undergo "light shift" to the left.

Traces of movement are real from the point of view of the computational system, LF, and PF. Without traces, it would be impossible to provide a straightforward LF interpretation of questions and other expressions involving movement. Without traces, it would be impossible to explain why certain contractions over extraction sites are impossible at PF. Finally, without traces understood as articulated, exact copies of moved elements, it would be impossible to relate anaphors appropriately to their commanding antecedents in "reconstruction" environments.

Chapter 4

The assumption that, for comparable lexical arrays, all languages are identical at LF, coupled with the fact that some exhibit overt movement, argues for *covert LF movement.* This is as expected, since after Spell-Out the computational process continues, working on whatever phrase marker was assembled prior to Spell-Out. But the wealth of LF structures is shown, independently of movement, through the existence of *ellipsis.* This phenomenon (or group of phenomena) turns out to be rich in interpretive consequences, including a characteristic parallelism between the elided sentence and its antecedent.

The assumed LF correspondence between languages raises the question of what exactly moves in the covert component. Minimalism suggests that *features move,* not categories. Had the linguistic system relied on mechanisms that do not invoke the resources of PF, it is possible that the movement relation would not involve words or phrases at all. Thus, it is supposed that only if movements take place prior to Spell-Out (hence feeding the PF component) do they involve anything other than features, essentially for morphological reasons. In particular, under the well-motivated assumption that features cannot survive PF by themselves, they need extra material to take a *free ride* with them, thus giving the superficial impression that movement is categorial.

Move and Merge are two instances of a binary *transformation* targeting one phrase marker that projects with another phrase marker. They differ in that Merge takes stock for the added phrase marker from the lexical array, whereas Move copies this material from inside the target phrase marker. However, both generate a new operational *term,* a set-theoretic object whose categorial *label* is copied from the *target* phrase marker and whose *constituent construct* is a set formed by the target phrase marker and the phrase marker added through Merge or Move. Terms can thus be determined all the way down to lexical items, whose labels are intrinsic. A central property of both Move and Merge is that they *extend* the phrase marker, thus never operate "downward" or "inward." There are several possible explanations for the existence of this property, depending on different assumptions.

A phenomenon that cannot easily be reduced to either standard Move or standard Merge is *adjunction*. Technically, an adjunction is a transformation that does not create a single category term, but instead creates a pair of *segments* of a category. By convention, the label of the result of adjunction is an object built from (not identical to) the label of the target phrase marker, for both empirical and technical reasons. The core instance of adjunction is *head movement,* which generally transports a feature from a category to the first head that commands it. Other instances of adjunction involve the merger of *modifiers* of various sorts, a type of category that may be on a separate plane, since modifiers need not extend the phrase markers they adjoin to and do not interfere with the internal uniformity of the chains they modify.

Most familiar chains are the result of Move, which relates two phrase markers M and K, M embedded in K, by making a *copy* of M's sister τ as a sister of K. The chain is not just the copied element τ, but in fact the pair of pairs $<<\tau, K>, <\tau, M>>$, or informally the pair $<K, M>$. Nontrivial procedures must determine how to *interpret* this sort of object at PF and LF. For PF, the process is straightforward: of the two copied elements, the matrix one is pronounced and the embedded one is deleted. However, this need not be the case in the LF component; a chain can be interpreted as involving an embedded copy of τ, even if the matrix copy of τ is actually pronounced.

Apart from the issue of how chains manifest themselves at PF and LF, there is a more general *compatibility* issue: the linguistic system must guarantee that not just any PF representation can be mapped to any possible LF representation. It does so by postulating a *complete* map to LF from a lexical array, understood as a *numeration*. This object is a bag or multiset, where each lexical item to be used in the structure has a label index indicating the number of occurrences of the item within the structure. In almost all instances, Spell-Out applies when the numeration is reduced to zero; this entails that there is no lexical access after Spell-Out. This follows from the extension property of phrase markers, coupled with the fact that LF does not interpret PF features and PF does not interpret LF features. The exceptions are items with no PF content, which, when inserted at the root, may be selected after Spell-Out. Since these items have no PF reflex, the compatibility of PF and LF is guaranteed.

Numerations also have a consequence for the *optimality* of the chain-generating transformations, under the assumption that the *reference set* of derivations that are compared with respect to optimality is determined by a function F(N), for N a numeration. Given a *partial derivation* D and a *partially used* numeration N_D, the reference set is any continuation of D that starts with N_D—that is, it contains all derivations that begin with D and access N_D. Thus, the economy of possible *continuations* of derivations is evaluated at any given point, and *cyclicity* is built into the reference set of equivalent derivations.

Chains are formed because of the need to *check* features like *agreement* and *Case*. Nominative Case is a function of a tensed verb; accusative Case is a property of the verb itself, expressed through a *verb shell*. The elements that enter into Case/agreement relations with either the element Tense or the verb shell v must be in a checking configuration with respect to these categories, which may lead to multiple specification of or multiple adjunction to either v or Tense. Ideally, features are checked in the covert component. Covert checking is ensured by the economy strategy of *procrastination:* An element should not move overtly if it can move covertly. When considerations of any sort force an overt movement, even if it still involves a head-to-head relation of features, it must be coupled with an *ancillary movement* to the specifier of the target and with *repair* operations aimed at satisfying morphological requirements.

Although the reason for overt movement is not clear, it relates to the need to *erase strong features,* which must be done, for a category X with strong feature F, *before abandoning X's projection.* This may account for the cyclic nature of movement. However, other mechanisms are worth exploring, given that the notion "strong feature" is metaphorical. Among these mechanisms is *multiple Spell-Out,* according to which Spell-Out is simply a rule that applies anywhere, up to economy. From this perspective, the split model of UG that maps the numeration to PF and LF would involve *successive cascades* of partial representations feeding the PF and LF components in a dynamic fashion. Other mechanisms to explore include parallel movements (the moved phrase marker does not immediately attach to the target) and stylistic processes.

Chapter 5

The chain relation between phrase markers is heavily constrained. This chapter specifically introduces the *Minimal Link Condition* (MLC), the *Condition on Chain Uniformity* (CCU), and the *Last Resort Condition* (LRC). A priori, these could be either representational conditions on the form of chains or derivational conditions on the process determining a chain. Here it is assumed that *the CCU is a representational condition,* whereas *the MLC and the LRC are derivational conditions.*

The LRC requires that Move be featurally justified: an element can move to the domain of another element only if one (or more) of the features of one or the other element is thereby appropriately checked. In essence, then, *the existence of Move is justified morphologically.*

The MLC requires that the landing site of movement be optimally "close." To capture the relevant locality, the set-theoretic notion "*minimal domain*" must first be invoked. Essentially, a minimal domain is a set of phrasal objects, all of which are directly associated to a given head. Elements of this set-theoretic domain are equally far from or equally close to other elements in a phrase marker. Apart from this, only elements within the same command path interfere with one another for the purposes of locality (thus, elements in different command paths do not compete with respect to "closeness").

The LRC and the MLC are incorporated into the definition of *Attract:* A phrase marker K attracts feature F if F is the closest feature that can enter into a checking relation with a *sublabel* of K. This characterization of Move as Attract has the effect of *reducing the derivational horizon* that any given derivation needs to contemplate, by reducing the number of possible derivational steps that a partial numeration can take.

The CCU requires that the *categorial content* of chain links be identical, and it predicts the *structural preservation* of Move and some structural dependencies for Adjoin. In particular, the CCU allows the adjunction of a maximal projection to a maximal projection and disallows the adjunction of a head to a maximal projection. But the CCU has nothing to say about adjunction to a head, which is part of morphology, as predicted by the Principle of Lexical Integrity.

The CCU/MLC/LRC and economy strategies *cannot impose conflicting requirements* because the former are *necessary conditions* and the latter are merely *ranking criteria.* That is, violating the necessary conditions—CCU, MLC, LRC—leads either to a derivational cancellation or to a derivational crash at the levels of representation. In contrast, there is no such thing as "violating an economy condition." Rather, all other things being equal, the derivation that accords with the economy strategy wins over the alternative candidates from a reference set.

Although economy strategies are *global* in nature, it is possible for various *local algorithms* to implement these strategies without having to compute an entire set of alternatives. For example, the strategy of *procrastination* may be seen as a local way of encoding a global strategy of *fewest (computational) steps.*

Move and Merge are subcases of a more general transformational operation that can be called "*Affect;*" others include *Delete* and *Erase.* Whereas Move and Merge are *constructive* operations, Delete and Erase are *destructive* operations. Delete does not eliminate structure; it simply *renders it uninterpretable* at the interface. In contrast, Erase entirely eliminates structure, in such a way that it is *not even accessible to* C_{HL}. Erase is used to eliminate features that are not interpretable in the interfaces and is *preferred over Delete.* Erase is constrained by the Law of Conservation, which protects interpretable features from "spontaneous" creation or destruction and prevents the destruction of terms.

The distinction between *interpretable* and *uninterpretable* features is thus central, since only the latter are erased. Operationally, C_{HL} has access to uninterpretable features exactly once (after checking, they are removed from the structure), whereas it has access to interpretable features an indefinite number of times. This distinction is designed to capture the phenomenology of movement, which in some instances occurs more than once, and in other instances only once in a partial derivation. Note that from this perspective there is *no unified process of checking,* since checking results in different outputs depending on whether the checked features are interpretable or not.

An interesting case of checking (the ideal one, in this system) takes place in the covert component; specifically, it involves *expletive-associate* pairs. Descriptively, the relation between an expletive and its associate is formally identical to the relation of *local movement.* For various semantic and syntactic purposes, the associate behaves like the subject of these constructions. This behavior can be explained if a crucial feature of the associate moves to the same domain that the expletive occupies, for some reason. Here, that reason is taken to be Case, under the assumption that true expletives do not have either Case or agreement features. As a consequence of the movement, the expletive and the associate enter into a semantic relation akin to that between article and noun.

Just as words define a *domain of conservation* in terms of lexical integrity, so too chains define a domain of conservation in terms of the *Principle of Chain Integrity,* which basically demands that chains be treated as integral units for the purposes of C_{HL}. This basically means that chains can only be extended by attracting their head (first element) upward, or eliminated by deleting their tail (last element). Chain integrity is central to the phenomenon of successive movement and makes interesting predictions about the syntactic opacity of chains, for instance.

Given chain and lexical integrity, chains and words represent specific pockets of symmetry within the linguistic system, whereby *structural qualities* of elements within the system are *conserved* throughout a derivation. The conserved properties clearly define spaces for linguistic units, possibly predicting unsuspected objects. Among the questions that arise, then, is whether chain integrity could be lexical integrity at a different dimension.

Chapter 6

In addition to the long-distance relations between categories explored in chapter 5, local relations are established between predicates and their arguments. The notion "*minimal domain*" is designed to express these configurational relations. In general, the notion is intended to capture the structural dependency that exists between a head and its complement, the *internal argument.* If a category α is within the internal domain of a head β, α and β are said to be *lexically related.* Internal domains express configurational relations between categories, which means that, although the tail of a chain can be in an internal domain, its head cannot, since *chains are not configurational* objects. As a result, a clear chain generalization emerges: *the tail of the chain is lexically related;* in contrast, *the head of the chain is involved in checking.*

Several other dependencies exist besides standard complementation. For example, ditransitive verbs (with two internal arguments) require extending current notions to more general *sister domains,* in order to capture the full range of argumenthood. Furthermore, many ditransitives allow one of their internal arguments to be incorporated into a *light verb,* a mechanism that produces an entirely new word. As shown earlier, words engage in processes of checking *inflectional morphology;* but morphological dependencies of a *derivational* sort also arise in the course of the syntactic computation. This raises the question of *what words are* within the system.

The intriguing absence of many logically possible words would be accounted for if words are thought of as being derived from syntactic processes, instead of coming fully formed from the lexicon. However, there are strong arguments against taking this view. The grammatical model is designed so as to predict the *productivity, transparency,* and *systematicity* of the syntactic system; however, the structures of words are neither productive, transparent, nor systematic. In fact, word structure is a matter of performance and convention, the meaning of the whole not always being a function of the meaning of its parts. To the extent that word-level processes exhibit systematicity, it results from syntactic residues or learning strategies.

The best-known learning strategy is the *Subcase Principle,* which causes the learner to be conservative in the acquisition process, so that no learning decisions are made that cannot be altered on the basis of only positive data or indirect negative data. In learning circumstances involving a condition C that is a subcase of a condition C′, the learner will adopt C, extending to C′ only in the presence of evidence that this decision would be sound. This strategy is used in various domains, ranging from morphology to semantics. It is relevant only in instances of subcase relations and when options are few, perhaps within lexical *paradigms.* Other learning strategies include *mutual exclusivity,* which prevents learners from assuming various names for the same notion. In conjunction with the Subcase Principle, mutual exclusivity allows children to learn names for abstract notions that are not instantiated directly, but through entities that have a more specific name.

The main syntactic residue determining the derivational behavior of words is the *Wording Law,* which establishes the domain of structural conservation of words. In the PF branch, this domain relates to complex matters that concern stress dependency, adjunction dependency (cliticization and feature addition), and morphophonemic readjustments. In the LF branch, words must be formed around a *pivot,* a chain whose trace is lexically related to the traces of all other sublabels in a word. Outside of this domain of lexical relatedness, no word can be recognized by the system. Any syntax involved in the derivation of a word collapses if the Wording Law is not met in the *Word Interpretation* component.

To some extent, words present a departure from optimality in the syntactic system, as do linguistic variation, strong and uninterpretable features, and the very existence of movement processes. This leads to the question of whether all of these may be related; the answer, though, is not obvious. To start with, it is very unclear what the nature of morphemes is, although historically the "birth" and "death" of morphemes can be clearly substantiated. Without a better understanding of this matter, it is very hard to comprehend what exactly is at stake in fundamental variation among languages, related movement processes whose motivation is ultimately morphological checking, and consequently complex word formation.

It is tempting to ask whether the system's departures from structural optimality are functionally optimal, as would be expected had these traits evolved in an adaptive way. All presently existing scenarios concerning this possibility are completely implausible. It is not known what the evolutionary advantage of complex words, morphology, movement, variation, or the linguistic faculty really is. To the extent that any of these involves a mutation, it is even unclear what the selective pressure could have been that led prehominids in that direction. In most instances, no alternative to these elements of the linguistic system is even remotely plausible.

Although evolutionary questions regarding human language will have nothing to do with adaptations, it is not the case that there are no such questions to ask. Interesting evolutionary questions arise for any system that involves discrete infinity, underdeterminacy, and optimality, the language faculty being the only well-studied system of this sort. Discrete symbols arranged in unbounded patterns may have emerged through the same sorts of dynamic equilibrium of forces as the Fibonacci patterns found in nature. If some of the fundamental properties of these systems are so basic that they are not even genetically coded (but follow from whatever laws of nature are relevant at this level), their underdeterminacy will result in great flexibility, which may be responsible for such varied properties of the language faculty as linguistic variation, or the formal symmetries found across domains (e.g., in terms of notions such as *space* and *boundary*). Finally, the economy of the system is expected in these dynamic circumstances.

Although these are some of the prospects that the Minimalist Program opens, the end of syntax is nowhere in sight. Syntax will only dissolve if the sort of work that has been done for decades (and in some instances centuries) is given up in favor of "just-so stories" based on opinions rather than empirical research.

Major Definitions, Principles, and Conditions on the Model

The following is a list of the formal notions explicitly raised in the text. For additional and more accurate notions, see the appendix.

General Matters

Definition of I(nternal/ntensional)-language [(1), chap. 1]
Given a set of universal principles encoded as the initial state S_0 of an idealized language faculty, and a set of parameters of variation for S_0, an I-language L is a complete specification S_f of parametric options.

Basic syntactic postulates [(25), chap. 6]
a. Syntactic structures are productive.
b. Syntactic structures are systematic.
c. Syntactic structures are transparent.

A formulation of the model [fig. 2.3]
Given: $A = \{a, b, c, \ldots \}$, where $a, b, c, \ldots$ are lexicon items
  $C_{HL}(A) = (\pi, \lambda)$ for π, a PF representation, and λ, an LF representation
  $\Sigma = \{K_0, \ldots, K_n\}$ for $K_0, \ldots, K_n$ phrasal representations by C_{HL} from a given A in a given computation

Then: K_0

More precisely [(6), chap. 2]:

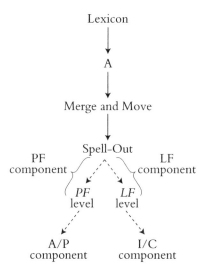

Definition of numeration [the lexical array; (36), chap. 4]

Given a lexicon L, a multiset N is a *numeration* if and only if all of the elements of N are members of L.

Dynamic economy [(37), chap. 4]

Given a set of derivations R all starting in numeration N, and where D is a partial derivation of any member of R, and N_D is the sub-multiset that corresponds to D, the *reference set* Δ for all the derivational continuations of D is a *fixed function* $F(D, N_D)$.

Law of Conservation [(56), chap. 5]

a. No operation can eliminate derivational terms [see definition of *term* below].

b. All interpretable features that are present in the lexical array are present at LF.

Conditions Pertaining to Phrases

"(Immediate) domination" is discussed in the appendix, where these notions are refined.

Definition of term [(15), chap. 4]

Where (a), (b), and (c) are syntactic objects—(a) an FFM [formal feature matrix]; (b) a labeled lexical item; (c) a phrase marker $K = \{L, \{\alpha, \beta\}\}$, where α, β are syntactic objects and L is the label of K and where K is a root phrase marker—then (i) K is a *term,* or (ii) if P is a term, the members of the members of P are *terms.*

Definition of Merge [(2), chap. 3]

Given a term $\tau_i = \alpha$ that is targeted for merger, and a term $\tau_j = \beta$ that is to merge with τ_i, τ_j *merges* with τ_i if and only if a new term $\{\underline{l}, \{\tau_i, \tau_j\}\}$ is obtained, such that $\{\underline{l}, \{\tau_i, \tau_j\}\}$ immediately dominates τ_i and τ_j, and $\underline{l} = \alpha$.

Definition of command [(12), chap. 3]

Where α and β are accessible to C_{HL}, α *commands* β if and only if

(a) α does not dominate β, and (b) the first category dominating α also dominates β.

Linear Correspondence Axiom [(13), chap. 3]

A category α precedes a category β if and only if (a) α asymmetrically commands β, or (b) γ precedes β and γ dominates α.

Conditions Pertaining to Movement Chains

Definition of movement chain [adapted from (11), chap. 4, and (18), chap. 5; enriched with the Condition on Chain Uniformity in (19), chap. 5]

Given a term $\tau_i = K$ that is targeted for merger, such that $K = \{\underline{\alpha}, \{ \ldots \{\tau_k, M\} \ldots \}\}$, and a term τ_j that merges with τ_i, such that $L = \{\underline{\alpha}, \{\tau_j, K\}\}$, the pair (K, M) is a *movement chain* if and only if the formal/categorial informational content of chain elements τ_j and τ_k is identical.

N.B.: Of the three conditions discussed in (25) of chapter 5 as defining chains, only the Condition on Chain Uniformity is retained in the final version, since the other two conditions (see Attract, below) are best thought of as derivational (that is, not representational) requirements.

Principle of Chain Integrity [(70), chap. 5]

Only entire chains enter into C_{HL} operations.

Definition of Attract [incorporating the Last Resort Condition in (22), chap. 5, and the Minimal Link Condition in (3), chap. 5]

K attracts F if F is the closest feature that can enter into a checking relation with a sublabel of K.

Formal Elements Involved in Locality

Definition of minimal domain (final version including the definitions of *internal* and *checking* domains) [(9), chap. 6; see (7), chap. 5 for a first version]

Where α is a feature matrix or a head #X#, and CH is a given chain (α, t) or (the trivial chain) α:

a. Max(α) is the smallest maximal projection dominating α.

b. The domain D(CH) of CH is the set of categories/features dominated by Max(α) that are distinct from and do not contain α or *t*.

c. The minimal domain Min(D(CH)) of CH is the smallest subset K of D(CH) such that for any *x* belonging to D(CH), some *y* belonging to K dominates *x*.

d. The *internal domain* ID(CH) is the subset of Min(D(CH)) that includes only sisters to α's projections.

e. The *checking domain* CD(CH) is the set-theoretic complement of ID(CH) in Min(D(CH)).

Definition of distance (final version) [(10), chap. 5; see (9), chap. 5, for a working version]
If β commands α, when targeting K for raising, with τ the actual target of movement, β is *closer to* K than α is, unless

(a) β and τ are in the same minimal domain, or (b) α and β are in the same minimal domain.

N.B.: The notion of "minimal domain" used in this definition is the first version given in (7), chapter 5. After the revision in (9), chapter 6, given above, the definition of "distance" must be slightly modified to accommodate the chain; see the appendix on this matter.

Conditions on Lexical Roles

Predication Axiom [(11), chap. 6]
Predicates assign roles by definition.

Axiom of Lexical Relatedness [(21), chap. 6; for related conditions that this axiom subsumes, see (13) and (20), chap. 6]
α and β are lexically related if and only if α is in the internal domain of β.

Conditions Pertaining to Words

Wording Law [(31), chap. (6); for a related condition that this law subsumes, see (7), chap. 4]
WI [Word Interpretation] recognizes α as a word if and only if

a. α has phonological content and obeys the standard requirements on phonological words; and

b. there is a sublabel β of α that, for all x, x a sublabel of α, x's trace is lexically related to β's trace.

Principle of Lexical Integrity [(24), chap. 5]
Only items that are not dominated by head boundaries (#) enter into C_{HL} operations; items dominated by head boundaries are submitted to independent word-interpretation processes WI.

Subcase Principle [(32), chap. 6]
Assuming (a) a cognitive situation S, integrating subsituations s_1, s_2, . . . , s_n, (b) a concrete set W of lexical structures l_1, l_2, . . . , l_n, each corresponding to a subsituation s, (c) that there is a structure l_t corresponding to a situation s_t that is a subcase of all other subsituations of S, and (d) that the LAD [language acquisition device] does not know which lexical structure l_t is invoked when processing a given term T uttered in S, then the LAD selects l_t as a hypothesized target structure to correspond to T.

Notes

Chapter 1

1. This is the traditional behaviorist perspective. For a critical presentation of behaviorist ideas (going back to Chomsky's (1959) review of Skinner's *Verbal Behavior*), see Jackendoff 1994.

2. This classical problem is outlined in several places. See, for example, Lightfoot 1982, Grimshaw and Pinker 1989, Pinker 1994, Jackendoff 1994.

3. See Crain and Nakayama 1986 for experiments proving the point.

4. This point is raised, for instance, in Bickerton 1990 and Pinker 1994.

5. See Cohen and Stewart 1994, chaps. 1 and 2.

6. The reference is to the "Baldwin effect." See Pinker and Bloom 1990, 723. This important work is crucial both to the present chapter and to chapter 6 (a good summary is given in Pinker 1994, chap. 11). The article is presented in a format that includes commentaries from several experts, which are also of interest here. Each commentary is not referenced separately.

7. Although the view that language acquisition is "learning" is very popular (see, e.g., Gell-Mann 1994, chap. 5), Chomskyan linguists are skeptical about this outlook. See Crain 1991 and Jackendoff 1994 for discussion of this idea, which is also related to the hypothesis that language acquisition is possible only during a critical period, up to puberty (Lenneberg 1967).

8. This point is raised in various places (e.g., Dawkins 1987 or the October 28, 1994, *Science* issue on development).

9. Richard Kayne (class lectures, MIT, 1987) attributed the genetic observation to Changeux (1981). Kayne raised the point in the same context that is relevant now: with respect to the implications of Changeux's view for a theory of linguistic variation. Many of the ideas presented below owe much to Piattelli-Palmarini (1989), freely adapted to present purposes.

10. This particular instance was pointed out by Noam Chomsky (personal communication; and see Mehler and Dupoux 1994). Facts of this sort, and many that follow, are commonly discussed among generative linguists. It is beyond the scope of this book to be systematic about them; see the works cited in the notes that follow, particularly Jackendoff 1994. Osherson 1995 and Piattelli-Palmarini 1994 are good introductions to cognitive science in general.

11. See Goodwin 1994, chap. 3.

12. Cohen and Stewart (1994) report several, some mentioned here, as does Goodwin (1994).

13. Most of the observations below can be found, for instance, in Cairns 1991. See also Jackendoff 1994, chap. 9.

14. This famous case where behavior is linked to physical forces is due to Williams (1966), who reaches different conclusions from the ones to be discussed below, involving more complex behaviors whose base may be physical.

15. Thanks to Noam Chomsky for emphasizing this important example. It will be mentioned again in section 1.7 and should serve as a guiding intuition for the sorts of systems that Minimalism aspires to relate to, abstractly.

16. This idea is taken from Cherniak (1992), who credits D'Arcy Thompson for having proposed a way of formally expressing his finding. This is interesting, for Thompson was describing anatomical shapes of organisms, thus not dealing with neurology. It is this sort of convergence that interests the minimalist, who ultimately expects principles of language to reflect a kind of reality that may well express itself, also, in the form of organisms.

17. Here the Linguist takes the cautious route. However, there is a twist in the last sentence of the paragraph—a point that Noam Chomsky has raised in personal communication. In effect, the Linguist is being skeptical because physics has not been able to address the kinds of questions that would be relevant to settle the issue of how much the genes encode.

18. Relevant facts appear in the initial chapters of Cohen and Stewart 1994 and throughout Goodwin 1994.

19. The discourse that follows can be found, for instance, in Chomsky 1993 and contrasts with the view presented in Gell-Mann 1994, chap. 9.

20. Thanks to Noam Chomsky for raising this point about Pauling.

21. This example is taken from Radin and Folk 1982.

22. Actually, Cohen and Stewart (1994, 252) think that the entire question is "bogus" (their term), although part of the price they pay for dismissing it is having to essentially give up an entropy-based explanation for the directionality of time. For an instance of the classic question, see Jou and Llebot 1989, Wesson 1991, or Meinzer 1994.

23. Pinker and Bloom (1990, 769) critically report on an early contemporary instance (in the 1960s) in which these questions were posed by mathematicians and physicists to biologists. In the last few years these questions have been raised again, rather systematically, and not just by mathematicians and physicists (see Goodwin 1994, Kauffman 1995).

24. The historical facts that follow are excerpted from Papavero 1992; see also Goodwin 1994, chap. 2.

25. Bruno 1987 is a delightful source for ideas concerning this and other episodes in the history of science. Many of the illustrations in this chapter (which are in the public domain) are discussed by Bruno.

26. These ideas are taken from the philosophical presentation in Meinzer 1994. Other introductions to these issues are available, but Meinzer's book is extremely helpful, particularly because it tries to relate the concerns in the text with familiar philosophical questions.

27. This is a famous claim made by Philip Anderson that echoes Chomsky's thought—the reason it is placed in the Linguist's mouth. See Waldrop 1992 for an entertaining presentation of this and related matters (Anderson's claim is quoted on page 82).

28. Most of the discussion that follows is adapted from Meinzer 1994. For a basic introduction to the underlying ideas, see Spielberg and Anderson 1987.

29. The metaphor of "antichaos" is used in several places (see, e.g., Kauffman 1991, 1992, or the more accessible Goodwin 1994). These dialectics between chaos and complexity are well explained in Cohen and Stewart 1994, chap. 7. It should be noted that the famous paper by Gould and Lewontin (1979) already mentions a variety of possible mechanisms for evolution whose basis is not in the traditional paradigm. Nonetheless, alternatives to the traditional view do not have to invoke "complexity tools."

30. This point is raised by Stewart (1995).

31. The question here is *not* a Chomskyan denial of evolution (see, e.g., Chomsky 1988, 167). Rather, the view that fundamental aspects of language do not arise from an adaptation is extremely consistent with current linguistic research.

32. Once again, the Linguist is (healthily) skeptical. This observation was made by Noam Chomsky through personal communication. See also Kauffman 1995 for a specific proposal on how physical constraints (on networks of biochemical reactions) can constrain evolutionary paths.

33. See Veron 1995 on the general topic of reticulate evolution.

34. The Linguist's agenda, here, should be clear. Before one comes up with a complexity picture for emergent systems, one must know what those systems are. This, in itself, justifies linguistic research as it is presently understood.

35. This fact is reported in Schmidt 1994.

36. See Touchette 1994 for a current report on morphogenesis.

37. See Nijhout 1994 for a clear perspective, and Lawrence 1992 and Bate and Martínez Arias 1993 for wealths of information about drosophila. The importance of these matters is brought to light rather dramatically by Wray (1995), who discusses the possibility that natural selection can act directly on developmental mechanisms, independently of what happens in corresponding phenotypes.

38. This claim, which is refuted in the next section, hides one of the pitfalls of "just worrying about complex systems" when studying language. Similar questions can be raised about other areas of cognition as well (see, e.g., Kelso 1995, Port and van Gelder 1995).

39. Here the Other is taking the view that complexity theorists advocate (see, e.g., Cohen and Stewart 1994).

40. Provocative as this central Chomskyan claim may seem, it is fundamental to everything else this book is about and is still not understood in many circles.

41. All that follows will not be appreciated by functionalists but is crucial in arguing against the notion that language arose as an adaptation. For the assumptions behind "communication," see O'Grady, Dobrovolsky, and Aronoff 1993; for more abstract concerns regarding the notion, see Gell-Mann 1994, chaps. 3 and 4.

42. Saussurean terminology is purposely avoided here in order not to prejudge the issue in familiar ways.

43. This is the assumption made in philosophy of language. See Martinich 1985 for various classic articles, and George 1989 for reflections on Chomsky's position on these matters.

44. For a background on these sorts of ideas, within a fairly developed semantic theory, see the last chapter of Larson and Segal 1995.

45. The expression is Chomsky's, from personal communication.

46. The idea of language as a set is central to philosophical proposals stemming from Quine's work (e.g., 1960). The more technical view of language as "a set of all and only the grammatical sentences" (implying some sort of recursive procedure to determine that set) misinterprets some of Chomsky's (1955) ideas. It is nonetheless a central view in theories of formal languages, which shows that these theories are dealing with a different object—not human language. For discussion and references on this important matter, see Chomsky and Lasnik 1995.

47. This conclusion has provided a major impetus for generative grammar research since the late 1960s, after the fundamental work by Haj Ross (Ross 1967; also see Chomsky 1968). An insightful exercise on constraining linguistic rules is Lasnik 1981. The central expression of this paradigm shift is Chomsky 1981 (and see the references cited there). However, the general reader may find Chomsky 1986b and 1988 more accessible.

48. See Higginbotham 1996 for a perspective on many of these matters.

49. This point is taken essentially from Lightfoot 1991.

50. Mayr (1991) calls them five theories, within the general Darwinian paradigm.

51. These ideas relate directly to the work of Eldredge and Gould (1972) and of Gould and Lewontin (1979), which is discussed at some length below. They are central to the view that language is not an adaptation.

52. Pinker (1994) takes up this thorny question (which arises together with the no less thorny question of whether the human species itself originated with a single, common ancestor). A curious presentation of the matter is given in Wright 1991, from a totally different perspective.

53. Actually, what was shown is that people disagree about how central the claim is. In turn, as Lightfoot (1979, 1991) claims, discovering a "bumpy" phenomenon in the case of language change would be central to establishing that linguistic change is based on language learners. Of course, here the facts are also controversial, and in particular Kroch (1989b) has argued for the opposite view.

54. Tragically, at the present rate of extinction, only about 10 percent of the languages spoken on the planet today will still exist in the twenty-first century. The claim is not exaggerated by passion— a report in the journal *Science* speaks for itself (Gibbons 1995).

55. Essentially, this is the position that Kroch (1989b) advocates.

56. This claim was first made in Lightfoot 1979.

57. This is a crucial question, and an important part of the argument that language is not an adaptation. Adaptationist proposals have a hard time explaining why there should be different languages. Note that it is not enough to have an adaptive explanation for the existence of diverse languages; one must also be able to explain why languages change.

58. Strictly speaking, children are not even exposed to E-English, which is really a useless concept in this context. PLD sets are both subsets of E-English and subsets of whatever else is contained in the utterances that children hear, since actual speech is full of false starts, incomplete sentences, errors, and so on (which would not fall under any sensible characterization of E-English).

59. Technically, this is not a catastrophe if the system reaches the change by itself (see Cohen and Stewart 1994, chap. 6, regarding catastrophes). The catastrophic view of language change is also first due to Lightfoot (1979, 1991). Whether linguistic change is gradual or not (an issue that is discussed again later), and whether changes are always propelled by outside influences, are still open questions.

60. This question is first raised in Lightfoot 1989.

61. This idealization is explicitly stated in Chomsky 1980. See also Pinker 1984, Lasnik 1989, and Crain 1991 regarding this idea and related ones discussed immediately below.

62. The developmental view (which goes back to Piaget in a very different tradition) has recently been advocated by various psycholinguists. (See Bloom 1994 for proposals and references.)

63. The term *core/periphery distinction* is taken from Chomsky 1981, although there it has a slightly different meaning. Factually, it is useful to separate core parameters of variation in language from peripheral variations. This discussion focuses on the former (but see section 2.7 for instances of the latter). Technically, a core parameter of variation may be seen as dividing the entire space of human languages (e.g., objects must either precede or follow verbs), whereas a peripheral variation is only relevant in distinguishing two closely related dialects (e.g., British English inverts main verb *have*, as in *have you any money?,* whereas American English does not).

64. Thanks to Ian Roberts for this observation; Roberts 1993 is a good source for the changes that took place in French, and see Martins 1994 for a nice demonstration of the "conservativeness" of Portuguese. For an interesting comparison of acquisition of different languages (English and French), bearing on the issues being raised now, see Pierce 1992.

65. The case is reported in Whitaker 1976. Many interesting related examples are discussed in Pinker 1994, chaps. 2 and 10.

66. For recent views on this important topic, see Arends, Muysken, and Smith 1995 and De-Graff, forthcoming.

67. Lightfoot (forthcoming) makes much of the creole scenario. He argues that it constitutes a testing ground for hypotheses, such as Gibson and Wexler's (1994), whereby the child/LAD is taken to be an "input matcher": in the creole situation there is not much of a coherent input to match. Lightfoot then argues that the child/LAD should be seen as a "cue-based" learner, seeking only certain structures in the input data, of a sort that may be present even in the creole situation.

68. This sort of view is defended by Kroch (1989b); also see Arnold 1995 for discussion of this matter and related ones, as well as references. There is no fully developed acquisition system that implements the sorts of ideas that the Other raises here. The closest proposal in the literature is Clark and Roberts's (1993) use of a "genetic algorithm" (see Holland 1995); Clark and Roberts's article is the first work within generative grammar that makes use of a device from the theory of complex systems. Robin Clark does specifically think of the matters discussed in the text in essentially these terms (see Clark 1995). On more general dynamic approaches to cognition, from a different perspective, see Thelen and Smith 1994.

69. See Niyogi and Berwick 1995 for the source of this idea, as well as the references cited there.

70. Again, the Linguist takes the conservative stance, for the same reason as before: to avoid positing explanations outside of linguistic theory until the relevant phenomena are linguistically clear.

71. Bickerton 1984 was the first work to discuss the significance of pidgins and creoles, triggering a very important debate. For a less technical presentation and ample discussion of consequences and implications, see Bickerton 1990; and for a factual base, see Holm 1988.

72. This idea, classically presented in Chomsky 1965, gave rise to most work on matters of learnability until the early 1980s (see Pinker 1979, Wexler and Culicover 1980). The paradigm shift from systems of rules to a system of principles and parameters (Chomsky 1981) also had important consequences for the question of whether a LAD should rank hypotheses (as opposed to simply setting parameters). Clark and Roberts (1993) argue that the two views are not incompatible, and their combined use makes interesting predictions about linguistic change. Three current models that are compatible with the general perspective taken here, yet make different claims and predictions, are those of Gibson and Wexler (1994), Valian (1993), and Fodor (1995b). See also Bloom 1994 for various recent contributions.

73. Wesson (1991) presents many more (intriguing) instances of this sort. On the brain's malleability, see Barinaga 1994; and see Jackendoff 1994, chap. 11, for a general presentation.

74. This is meant literally, given that (if the Linguist's claims are correct) the options for structurally different languages are finite.

75. See Edelman's (1987) view of brain development (and Edelman 1992 for an accessible presentation). Of course, even if Edelman's model is not adopted, the "genomic bottleneck" remains: it is not plausible that very limited DNA information capacity represents trillions of neural connections. (On the general topic of brain development, see Jacobson 1991.) Edelman's model is introduced here merely to take the extreme position. In this respect, it should also be noted that a Darwinian system like Edelman's does not have, a priori, any direct, natural connection to the theory of evolution. Darwinian systems are just specific instances of complex systems based on population dynamics (see Holland 1995, Mitchell 1996).

76. See Papathomas et al. 1994.

77. This central Chomskyan view is not shared by all (perhaps even most) generative linguists. The Minimalist Program presents an interesting testing ground for the idea of exaptation, by defending the essential elegance of language. This elegance lends itself to three sorts of interpretations. The first is the sort of Neoplatonic view discussed by Katz (1981): the linguistic system is a mathematical object (which can be represented in various formally equivalent ways). To the extent that the arguments presented in later chapters have an empirical base, they could not be obviously justified in mathematical terms. The second interpretation is the gradual adaptationist view discussed by Pinker and Bloom (1990) and Bickerton (1990). This view rests on the claim that language gave humans an adaptive edge; it assumes that language is (and was, when it evolved) functionally useful. A criticism of this view is presented in chapter 6. The third interpretation is based on the fact that the communicative function of language is not particularly optimal (see secs. 1.3 and 1.6). From this perspective (partly sketched in Gould 1991, Lewontin 1990, and Lightfoot 1995, and in bits and pieces throughout Chomsky's work), if linguistic structure is optimal, then its elegance must correspond to the sort of structural optimality that can be seen in biological morphology, which need not always be dictated by evolution.

78. In chapter 6 an argument is built for an adaptationist view that is consistent with the picture presented here.

79. See Brandon and Hornstein 1986 on these topics, as well as Lewontin's commentary on Pinker and Bloom 1990.

80. This point is crucial, as several of the commentaries on Pinker and Bloom 1990 clearly observe. No justification will be attempted until specific structural processes are proposed that (according to the Minimalist view) are involved in human language. However, it must be emphasized here that Minimalism takes phonetic and semantic structures to involve radically different processes, with the result that (it can be argued) each of these has to be justified on the basis of separate mutations. In turn, grammatical competence is different from the use of grammar, and both of them differ from the acquisition mechanism (LAD). A serious evolutionary proposal should address each of these separately.

81. This comment is slightly unfair, given (for instance) some of the facts reported by Gibson and Ingold (1993). As Kathleen Gibson notes (personal communication), whatever it is that apes are capable of doing, though very interesting in and of itself, is specifically different from what a child does. For instance, in terms of production, apes do not really go beyond a repetitive two-word stage (see the famous "sentence" in the text below, which lacks a coherent articulation). In terms of comprehension, apes display more remarkable achievements, but even there it is far from clear that they are capable of, for instance, *recursion* (of the sort found in *the cat that lives in the house that Jack built*), even though they appear to be capable of *iteration* (as in *very very very interesting*) and hence can understand a trivially unlimited number of structures.

82. This sequence of signs is discussed by both Bickerton (1990) and Pinker (1994). Seidenberg and Petitto (1987) directly question the resemblance between human signed languages and whatever it is that apes do when instructed in the use of these languages. Nonetheless, it would be quite interesting to reopen the question in light of the issues presented in this book, particularly in chapter 6.

83. Thanks to Noam Chomsky for stressing this point, which Lewontin's commentary to Pinker and Bloom 1990 also raises. Pinker and Bloom claim that not being able to determine whether a dog or a fish is more complex (Lewontin's point) is biologically irrelevant. Cohen and Stewart (1994, 86) do not share this view, noting that "frogs have longer DNA sequences than mammals," a large chunk of frog DNA being devoted to programming contingency scenarios for development, a "problem" that dogs have "solved" by developing inside a womb. Very subtle issues about developmental plans are obviously at stake, and one would like to learn how to compare different natural solutions (involving both genes and the environment where they have to operate) in nontrivial ways. Whether the comparisons are possible is hard to know, but they seem hardly irrelevant.

84. Fodor (1983) hypothesizes that the mind is a modular system, composed of various "mental organs" that are independent of one another. This thesis (in a somewhat broader version than Fodor presents; see Chomsky 1995) is central to Chomskyan thought. Although most adaptationists do not believe the modularity hypothesis, Pinker and Bloom (1990) do; by contrast, Gould (1991 and elsewhere) does not seem particularly committed to modularity, yet his view of language is not one of gradual adaptationism. So these two ideas are simply independent. The discussion of these matters in chapter 6 assumes modularity for two reasons. First, because it is part of Minimalism. Second, because although it invites the (nonnecessary) inference that various adaptations are involved in human language, each of which must be justified, it makes the existence of the highly complex structure of human language all the more viable for the adaptationist, as a sequence of structures that are built on top of each other.

85. For an illuminating discussion of these matters, see Gould 1991, 141–151. Gould presents the now classical view—adduced both for birds and even more solidly for insects (see Kingsolver and Koehl 1985)—that the origin for wing structures was connected with thermoregulation. However, recent studies by Marden and Kramer (1994) on water insects suggest that the initial function of their "wings" was to aid in skimming. (Theories on the origin of insect wings have flourished for over a century, but solid scientific evidence has not always been provided.)

86. On these matters, see Chomsky 1972.

87. The joke is due to Gould (1991), who also refers to the article mentioned here: Falk 1990.

88. See Gould and Lewontin 1979 for this nice metaphor.

89. Pinker and Bloom (1990) are not moved by this comment of Chomsky's (see Piattelli-Palmarini 1981). Admittedly, it is hard to say something scientifically sound about an object whose physical properties might be beyond human grasp—or might turn out to be relatively trivial. Interestingly, Chris Cherniak (personal communication) appears to have found an extension to his (1992) optimization of neural connections, crucially at the global level. According to Cherniak, neuron arbors "act" like flowing water, globally minimizing their volume versus surface area or branch length. How they do this is unknown, but if Cherniak is correct, something physically interesting is happening globally. (Later it will be shown that global optimization appears to be crucial to syntactic derivations as well.) In an even more abstract (and strange) way, Penrose (1989, 1994) suggests a view of the mind/brain that defies regular physics in the usual states of matter. The point is, how certain is it that the physical reality of brainlike objects is the same as that of more familiar objects?

90. For this intriguing idea, see DiVincenzo 1995.

91. This is the view advocated by Penrose (1989), possibly for invalid reasons inasmuch as his arguments only affect conscious reasoning (see chap. 2, n. 40). The possibility is mentioned only because of the often stated claim that certain models of mind are implausible because of computational difficulties. DiVincenzo (1995) shows that a quantum computer would be able to assume computations that are theoretically beyond the capabilities of regular computers. The computational theory of mind (as presented in Churchland and Sejnowski 1992, for instance) is based on familiar computers (neural networks at best). Nothing intrinsic to what theoretical linguists do has to be expressed in those terms, since they work at an abstract level that is not directly concerned with implementation. This is thus intended as a cautionary note: when a theory is deemed implausible because of its being computationally unrealistic, it must be kept in mind what kind of computer is being assumed, for the concern to be meaningful.

92. This point is also emphasized in several commentaries on Pinker and Bloom 1990. Pinker and Bloom claim that even if there did not exist more than forty different evolutionary scenarios giving rise to (slightly different, yet comparable) eyes, scientists could not help but conclude that eyes evolved adaptively. Not everyone shares their certainty. Cohen and Stewart (1994) and Goodwin (1994) argue that so much convergence is possible with regard to eyes because the eye, as a system, is dynamically natural. It is also worth noting that Pinker and Bloom's claim is based on the belief that "appearance of design" is something that any (presumably good) engineer can detect. However, serious engineers appear rather more skeptical about the prospect, as noted in Petroski 1993 (a book about inventions that argues against Darwinism in the history of industrial design).

93. The ideas that follow can be found, in a larger context, in Chomsky 1993.

94. This view is discussed frequently nowadays. It had an early linguistic precursor in the motor theory of speech perception developed at Haskins Laboratories (see Liberman 1996 for an overview).

95. These ideas, reported by Penrose (1994, 355ff.), are due to Stuart Hameroff. Microtubules appear to be responsible for maintaining synaptic strength and seem capable of organizing the growth of new nerve endings, among other things.

96. For a linguist's succinct perspective on these matters, see Jackendoff 1994, chap. 11.

97. Detailed arguments for these rather obvious claims are omitted here (but see, e.g., Chomsky 1986b, 1988).

98. However, as Georges Rey (personal communication) observes, Descartes thought of mental phenomena (of the sort that interests linguists) as readily accessible to subjects, through introspection. This is clearly false.

99. This point is crucial. Even if human language is elegant in structure, it does not seem to be particularly elegant in function (see Lightfoot 1995).

100. Pinker and Bloom (1990) are rightly concerned about this matter (see also Maratsos 1988). Given that lexical differences are irrelevant for core structural variation, proposals concerning advantages of having different words are simply irrelevant. About what linguists take to be interesting variations (parameters), Pinker and Bloom speculate that

there is a learning mechanism, leading to the development of multiple languages. That is, some aspects of grammar might be easily learnable from environmental inputs by cognitive processes that may have been in existence prior to the evolution of grammar, for example, the relative order of a pair of sequenced elements within a bounded unit. For these aspects there was no need to evolve a fixed value, and they are free to vary across communities of speakers. (p. 716)

Although this is possible for certain paratactic orders (which are ultimately not part of sentence grammar; see sec. 4.4), it cannot be correct with respect to grammatical parameters, if Minimalism itself is correct (for reasons that become apparent from chapter 2 onward). Concerning the "Baldwin effect" that they invoke (p. 722), Pinker and Bloom note that although

there is always a selection pressure to make learnable connections innate, this pressure diminishes sharply as most of the connections come to be innately set, because it becomes increasingly unlikely that learning will fail for the rest. This is consistent with the speculation that the multiplicity of human languages is in part a consequence of learning mechanisms existing prior to (or at least independent of) the mechanisms specifically dedicated to language. Such learning devices may have been the sections of the ladder that evolution had no need to kick away. (p. 723)

101. Pinker and Bloom (1990, 718) discuss the possibility that the LAD may have been an adaptation. Although it may indeed be "adaptive for each member of a community of speakers to be forced to learn to do it the same way as all the other members," the point is not totally meaningful in the absence of a clear theory of what the learning device consists of. That is, Pinker and Bloom's statement could have referred to behaviors other than the linguistic one, trivially. The statement has content only if the LAD has rich internal structure, a possible but mostly unsubstantiated fact.

102. For an illuminating update on these matters, see Wolpert 1994.

103. On this issue, see for instance Travis 1994.

104. This particular example is discussed by Gleick (1987). The experiment was performed by Robert Shaw.

105. See Chomsky and Miller 1963.

106. Hofstadter (1979) discusses the matter at length. In his delightful book, he also comments on the Fibonacci series, discussed below.

107. Details of this claim are taken up later. For now, however, it should be easy to see that a structural fact of this sort is not easy to justify on adaptive grounds, particularly because it crucially does not correlate with optimality of function—and may even impair functionality.

108. On these issues, see Jackendoff 1994, pt. 4.

109. The terms "combinatorial" and "input-output" to describe different systems have been suggested by Paul Smolensky (personal communication); they may not be entirely standard, but they are graphic enough. At the end of chapter 2, the possibility is mentioned that the morphophonological system of language (which is not a core system in the intended sense) is also an input-output system that seeks an optimal realization for an array of symbols combined by a different system.

110. The plant case is discussed in many places, some of which are mentioned in figure 1.25. It is hard to find a specific study of the peacock's tail beyond the general statement of the problem, for instance, in Cronin 1991. Carroll et al. (1994) discuss butterfly "eyespots" (in orthodox biological terms). Note that although an orthodox biological study might account for how a peacock's "eyespot" (a discrete unit arising from the continuity of barbs' growth) can emerge, it does not say anything about the relations among the "eyespots" on different feathers. In any case, the matter of interest now is the underlying relations among the skin bumps from which the feathers grow.

111. This proposal by Douady and Couder (1992) is reported by Stewart (1995) and seriously studied by Jean (1994), who provides a comprehensive analysis of phyllotaxis. Givnish (1994) criticizes the fact that Jean offers no adaptive explanation for phyllotactic patterns, at the same time dismissing D'Arcy Thompson's work because, ultimately, "nothing in biology makes sense except

in the light of evolution." Of course, the whole point of Jean's book is to argue that Fibonacci patterns can arise in nonbiological systems, as the Douady and Couder experiment clearly shows.

112. This is the famous "four-bug problem," reported, for instance, by Maor (1994).

113. This was observed by Church (1920 and elsewhere). For comments on these works by Church, and for excellent references, see Jean 1994.

114. This seems to be what Church (1920) has in mind, although it is unclear what internal generative forces are responsible both for the repulsion that generates the spiral and for the attraction that determines the featural lumps. This phenomenon recalls the successive activation and inhibition mentioned in figure 1.26, a matter discussed in Uriagereka, forthcoming c.

115. These ideas are adapted from the research of Paul Green, as reported by Goodwin (1994, chap. 5). It should be kept in mind that these dynamics do not need to have the sort of physical basis seen in Douady and Couder's (1992) experiment (where the relevant forces are electromagnetic) (see fig. 1.25). A similar system, suggested by Felix Goñi, arises in yeast populations so long as the growth rate is similar to the proportion between the size of a "mother" yeast and one of its buds (see Uriagereka, forthcoming c). the growth from a bud to a mature yeast is coded as *0*, and the growth from the mature form to a critical bifurcation stage where a new bud emerges is coded as *1*, the following rules can be stated:

$0 \rightarrow 1$ (rewrite *0* as *1*)
$1 \rightarrow 0\ 1$ (rewrite *1* as *0 1*)

If these rules are invoked simultaneously, the number of symbols that emerges is always in the Fibonacci series (for an illustration of this result, see fig. 3.10):

```
0 . . . . . . . . . . 1
1 . . . . . . . . . . 1
0 1 . . . . . . . . . 2
1 0 1 . . . . . . . . 3
0 1 1 0 1 . . . . . . 5
etc.
```

116. Other implications of this case study will be taken up directly; the emphasis here is on accounting for elegant regularities within a modular mind. Just as two totally different living creatures can converge on a natural packaging solution, so too can two different mental organs. This is not to say that they necessarily do—rather, that giving up evolutionary assumptions does not immediately leave one without possible explanations, or force one to adopt explanations that posit, uncritically, all-purpose complexity in a mind without structured organs.

117. For recent treatments of this general issue, see Kondo and Asai 1995 and Meinhardt 1995; and for relevant background, see Goodwin 1994, chap. 4.

118. This potential difficulty is central to Edelman's (1987) criticism of all computational theories of mind. The sort of possible (and promissory) solution discussed here is mentioned in passing by Chomsky (1994b). The issue is raised by Pinker and Bloom (1990), who suggest that discrete symbols arise because "brain mechanisms should reflect not 'the continuity of reality' . . . but rather . . . 'the causal texture of the environment'" (p. 770; also see commentaries). Of course, what that "causal texture" is, or whether it is in sync with human minds, is far from obvious; however, Pinker and Bloom assume that it is advantageous to have evolved the ability to conceive of discrete units. Even if this assumption were to be granted, neither Pinker and Bloom nor any of their commentators have much to say about exactly how that trait could evolve or what it implies.

119. The point about theoretically unlimited numbers of features is important. The sunflower corolla in figure 1.25 probably has on the order of two thousand discrete florets. To the extent that there are upper limits on this number, they arguably relate to gravity, metabolism, and similar considerations—which are a priori not unlike memory limitations for the linguistic system. In Uriagereka, forthcoming c, it is argued that Fibonacci patterns constitute examples of discrete infinity (a point based on Jean's (1994) work). This comports well with the fact that the flower/peacock patterns can be described in terms of phrase structure rules (as the grammar on the jacket of the book readily shows). These formal devices are taken up again in chapter 3.

120. This general point is raised by Land (1960). Jean (1994) warns against taking each observation about phyllotaxis literally, since a variety of happenstances might deter a plant from reaching an ideal target of growth. Nonetheless, the matter is important when trying to establish whether the basis of phyllotaxis is genetic.

121. Again, the question is of the sort raised by Edelman (1987, 1992). The issue here is not to pose a crisis-inducing problem; however, the account given earlier for the continuous-to-discrete relation cannot be extended to the residual aspects of this relation.

122. Both Goodwin (1994) and Jean (1994) advocate this view, although neither offers a conclusive account of epigenetic phyllotaxis. (The bottom line is that the process appears to be extraordinarily complex.) Nonetheless, these authors do successfully raise serious doubts about traditional proposals regarding morphology, laying the groundwork for a real alternative.

123. On general matters of limb development from the perspective in the text, see Goodwin 1994, 128ff.

124. This is a slight rhetorical exaggeration. Vogel's optimality formula discussed in figure 1.25, for instance, is relatively recent and would have been basically impossible to state without Chomsky's ideas on recursion. Nonetheless, Jean (1994) illustrates how old the main insights on phyllotaxis are.

125. This comment is in the mouth of the Other for stylistic reasons, though it has actually been made by Chomsky (1994b).

126. The ideas that follow are adapted from Meinzer 1994, except for their connection to linguistics. Thanks to José Manuel Vegas both for recommending this book and for very useful discussion on these topics. For related ideas, though more concentrated on purely biological issues, see Emmeche 1993 and Goodwin 1994.

127. This comment may seem gratuitous, but it is made in the spirit of D'Arcy Thompson's work and much current discussion on complex systems; it is inspired more specifically by the thought-provoking ideas of García-Bellido (1994a,b), who boldly proposes models for molecular biology and genetics that make explicit use of familiar Chomskyan concepts such as transformations and levels of representation. For general questions concerning body plans, see Jacob 1982.

128. Note that this is Darwinian talk in a nonevolutionary complex adaptive system. See Gell-Mann 1994, Kauffman 1995, and Holland 1995 on these matters.

129. This point is important, in order to address the claim that it "is absurdly improbable that some general law of growth and form could give rise to a functioning vertebrate eye as a byproduct of some other trend" (Pinker and Bloom 1990, 710). Of course, nothing in the text directly addresses that claim, nor is a specific proposal being made about a general law. The point is different: highly dynamic systems of particular sorts present emergent properties with probability one, for reasons

having to do with feedback. Those emergent properties may be relevantly present in at least rudimentary eyes; some researchers, such as Cohen and Stewart (1994, 294) and Goodwin (1994, chap. 5), feel that they are, whereas others, including exaptationists like Gould, do not. Needless to say, even in the most extreme circumstance, it could not be true that an eye is nothing more than dynamics (see fig. 1.20 on the eyeless gene).

130. See Eldredge and Gould 1972 for the classical proposal, and Eldredge 1995 for current discussion, as well as a perspective on the debate. "Punctuated equilibrium" is used here in a less precise sense than, in particular, Gould's. As defined, the concept relates to speciation, whereas here both a narrower view of it (cascades of genetic changes within species) and a broader one (cascades of macrochanges across species) are presented. Eldredge (1995) takes a wide-ranging view as well, encompassing concepts that include various large-scale biological systems (larger and narrower than species). In any case, the issue is only partly relevant to present concerns, inasmuch as dissipative phase transitions are by definition not gradual. Of course, the suggestion remains metaphorical, in the absence of a concrete model to express bumps at all these scales (but see Eldredge 1995, chap. 6).

131. See Dawkins 1987 for criticism of the punctuationist view, and Cronin 1991 for a succinct overview of the orthodox paradigm. This paradigm has of course also concerned itself with the morphological issues discussed in this chapter, viewing them from a functionalist perspective and invoking concepts that go beyond the traditional ones; see, for instance, Wainwright and Reilly 1994 or Thompson 1994.

132. Paleontological data often give conflicting evidence with regard to this claim. See for instance, the differing results of Benton (1995) and Culotta (1994) (the latter reporting on work by John Alroy). Also see Eldredge 1995 for cautionary notes concerning the sort of simplistic complexity models that the Other is sketching here.

133. See Quiring et al. 1994 on this extraordinary finding.

134. See Jean 1994.

135. See Goodwin 1994 for a good introduction to these matters, placing the evolution of DNA and the development of organisms slightly beyond standard Mendelian genetics (in particular, pp. 13ff.).

136. See Horgan 1995 for a sample, and for the source of the Linguist's skepticism. Lewontin's commentary on Pinker and Bloom 1990 also emphasizes the difficulty of characterizing complexity—particularly adaptive complexity.

137. Thanks to Naoki Fukui for useful discussion of these matters; the thought-provoking ideas below are raised in Fukui 1996.

138. See Piattelli-Palmarini 1981, 10, and 1989, as well as Otero's commentary on Pinker and Bloom 1990 (p. 749).

139. See Chomsky 1988, 167.

140. Examples of this sort, with illuminating discussion, are provided by Meinzer (1994, chap. 3).

141. Thanks to Chris Cherniak for emphasizing the global aspect, which he is exploring in work in progress. The point immediately below is raised at the very end of Cherniak 1992.

142. See Patel 1994 on the very interesting topic of pattern conservation (across species) in development. For a more general presentation of molecular evolutionary studies, see Avise 1994.

143. This idea is taken from studies of the so-called protein-folding problem. For a general perspective on protein structures, see Hall 1995; for approaches to the folding problem, Wolynes, Onuchic, and Thirumalai 1995; and for general matters regarding protein design, Bryson et al. 1995.

144. See Jean 1994.

145. For an interesting example of this sort, see Goodwin 1994, 71.

146. This claim is argued for in Uriagereka, forthcoming c.

Chapter 2

1. The Minimalist Program is slightly more ambitious than the principles-and-parameters model advocated in Chomsky 1981. In that model, grammar-internal considerations led linguists to "ask how particular assumptions about [phonetics] and [logical semantics] relate to the rules and principles of grammar," whereas grammar-external considerations led them to "ask how such assumptions bear on the problem of determining physical form, perceptual interpretation, truth conditions, and other properties of utterances, through interaction of [phonetics], [logical semantics] and other cognitive systems" (Chomsky 1981, 4). The Minimalist Program tries to answer the first question by asserting that grammar-internal principles exist in order to meet grammar-external conditions. Apart from this substantive justification for the internal principles of grammar, Minimalism is built around the intuition that the way in which grammar-external conditions are met by the grammar-internal principles is optimal.

2. Chomsky (1955) adapted the term from the theory of concatenation algebras (e.g., Rosenbloom 1950). Each level of linguistic representation involves a set of primes, which justifies the discussion that follows. In principle, if one asks how the primes or combinations of logical semantics relate to the world, one should also ask how the primes or combinations of phonetics relate to the world; there are no differences here, even if the primes of logical semantics would seem to be "deeper." This is not the view that philosophers typically take; for instance, at the start of his famous discussion of these and related matters, Quine purposely "ignore[s] phonematic analysis, . . . early though it would come in [the] field linguist's enterprise, for it does not affect the philosophical point [he] want[s] to make" (1960, 28). Quine does not explain why "the philosophical point" is not affected by that part of the linguistic system that happens to be understood best, and has a most obvious reality: phonetics.

3. This is the prevalent view in philosophy and many areas of linguistics. See Quine 1960 or Soames 1989, for instance.

4. Linguists represent a pronounced or perceived symbol between square brackets.

5. Not all phoneticians agree on what the Linguist is assuming here, namely, the motor theory of speech perception (see Liberman 1996).

6. It is impossible to do any kind of justice to phonetic and phonological facts in this context. O'Grady, Dobrovolsky, and Aronoff (1993) provide an instructive introduction and references.

7. Here too, it is impossible to even present the basic facts in a fair way; a very useful introduction is Larson and Segal 1995.

8. See Bruno 1987 for the source of the anecdote.

9. Noam Chomsky has raised this question in personal communication (perhaps somewhat provocatively, given chapter 2 of Quine 1960).

10. For discussion and references on this topic, see Fodor 1995a.

11. Concerning this notion and various empirical consequences, see Hornstein 1995b.

12. Many previous models, including the principles-and-parameters model outlined in Chomsky 1981, ascribe this very property to the underlying level of representation that they postulate. In the principles-and-parameters model, the θ-Criterion (a precursor of Full Interpretation) assesses the legitimacy of initial representations. The Minimalist Program departs from this assumption, going back to earlier models in the spirit of those postulated both by Chomsky (1955) and by proponents of Generative Semantics in the late 1960s, which deny the existence of an underlying level of representation.

13. See for instance Chomsky 1986b for a summary and references.

14. The joke is Edelman's (1992). Much of the skepticism about traditional semantics in the following pages can also be found in this work.

15. On this topic, see Jackendoff 1994, chap. 14. Berlin and Kay's (1969) work reveals crosslinguistic regularities in color terminology (but see Michaels 1977). Pullum (1991) criticizes what he calls "The Great Eskimo Vocabulary Hoax."

16. See Saussure 1959.

17. The tradition (known to the author firsthand) is reported in Cunqueiro 1981. The names have been changed to protect the cow.

18. See Genesis 2:19. Plants are indeed not mentioned in this passage, an omission that may relate to the traditional idea that plants generate spontaneously (Papavero 1992).

19. For various sources on the mystical character of naming, see the entry on names in Walker 1983.

20. The discussion that follows has benefited from Michael Devitt's seminar on reference and from many discussions with him, as well as with Elena Herburger, Norbert Hornstein, Michael Morreau, Paul Portner, and Georges Rey. None of them should be held responsible for the ideas introduced below, which are very much in the spirit of Chomsky's conception of reference (see Chomsky 1993). For traditional views, see the relevant articles in Martinich 1985, pts. III and IV. For the conceptual background behind the sort of approach advocated here, see Higginbotham 1996 and Larson and Segal 1995.

21. Whether this idea (due to Putnam (1973)) is accepted depends on the status one gives to kinds. For philosophers who do not accept the reality of such abstract notions, it is not accurate to say that the noun names a kind.

22. The riddle is described quite accessibly in Quine 1953, chap. 1.

23. The relevance of examples like this was first mentioned in Chomsky 1965, 217 n. 26: *the England that I know and love*. One could say that this name is special, being the name of a location. The Russell examples in the text, however, are straightforward.

24. See Wittgenstein 1953 and Searle 1983 for discussion of this issue.

25. See Quine 1953 for the proposal, as well as a discussion of the matters mentioned here.

26. In Catalan, masculine singular names can be introduced by the determiner *en,* which is not used for any other sort of expression (thanks to Carme Picallo for this fact).

27. This is Kripke's (1972) famous point about the rigidity of names.

28. On these matters, see Kaplan 1975.

29. See Burge 1974 for the source of this idea.

30. The matter is considerably more involved, however, than this offhand remark implies. Higginbotham (1988) argues that, although the idea is essentially sound (in that a demonstrative is a free variable whose range is set pragmatically), it is nonetheless inadequate, which suggests that grammatical expressions must involve contextual variables of the sort proposed by Boolos (1984) (and see Schein 1993). These are variable predicates partially determining the range of quantificational expressions (including descriptions and names); speakers confine this range in acts of speech, in a manner that the grammar does not determine. From this perspective, rigidity is a structural device, which is external to what the name itself denotes. There are rigid uses of names (and other expressions), not rigid names.

31. On "speaker reference" and "semantic reference," see Kripke 1972.

32. The ideas that follow are due to Steven Neale and are developed in work in progress. See also Neale 1992 (which, however, concentrates on descriptions, rather than names).

33. Atlas 1989 is a provocative piece that bears significantly on all of these issues. Also see Chomsky 1993 and 1994b.

34. Chomsky (1993) provides a similar example involving London. Arguably, his example could be explained away, provided that London is some sort of location. The example with Shakespeare is constructed in order to avoid such potential difficulties.

35. Thanks to Jorge Campos for a clarifying discussion on these matters.

36. On the pitfalls of definitions, a matter going back to Wittgenstein in modern times, see Jackendoff 1994, chap. 14.

37. For discussion of these matters, see Lakoff 1986, 1987.

38. Kosko (1993) provides an introduction to the topic.

39. Some of the ideas that follow emerged in discussion with Georges Rey.

40. Implicit in this comment is Fodor's (1983) distinction between mental modules and a central coordinating system of thought. Whereas there is rather strong evidence for the modular character of the visual and linguistic systems, no such case has been built for scientific and mathematical reasoning, artistic performance, or moral behavior. To the extent that the abilities required for these tasks vary across individuals, can improve with practice and present no critical periods, require a degree of self-awareness and consciousness, are not fast-paced or automatic, and do not seem to be informationally encapsulated, it is plausible that they may not correspond to any specific module. It is important to keep these two types of mental activity separate; otherwise, serious confusions can ensue. For example, Penrose (1989, 1994) demonstrates the impossibility of computationally simulating the activities of any (knowably sound) device that can ascertain mathematical truths, as a consequence of Gödel's theorem; he then conjectures that, since human mathematicians can ascertain mathematical truths, their minds are not acting computationally. (Penrose proposes that the physical action of the brain at very elementary—below neural—levels "evokes awareness.") This may or may not be true, but it has no obvious consequence for modular activities of the mind. These can still be computationally modeled even if the higher-order central system cannot. Crucially, Penrose's argument is (admittedly) about conscious reasoning and the sort of capacity that only certain individuals systematically display (advanced mathematical reasoning). Penrose has not demonstrated that the modular activity of either the visual or the linguistic system cannot be expressed computationally.

41. For elaboration on these issues and references regarding the idea that the Linguist criticizes, see Chomsky 1994b.

42. This is a very sketchy version of an idea defended by Edelman (1992), for whom the mechanism used to form concepts is of an abstract Darwinian sort. According to Edelman, whether a concept gets appropriately stored depends on how fit it is with regard to the specific function it is supposed to serve (see n. 43). Presumably, fitter concepts are recalled often enough to somehow become easier to access, through a mechanism essentially of the sort found in the immune system (which has a "memory" for successful antibodies). In recent years, various researchers have explored abstract Darwinian systems; a useful discussion is provided by Holland (1995).

43. Genetic algorithms are based on the notion of "adaptation." It is thus fair to raise the same questions about these algorithms that are raised about the neo-Darwinian program more generally (see sec. 1.5). The units of evolution are different in each case, but the functionalist logic is the same. It should be kept in mind, however, that in this particular instance the issue is not whether concepts are useful for the survival of a given individual; rather, what counts is how well a conceptual hypothesis matches some phenomenological correlate. Hence, one may speak of symbolic arrangements that are useful for the "survival" of the conceptual hypothesis.

44. See Jackendoff 1994, pt. IV.

45. See Gleitman and Landau 1994 on these matters.

46. Two major schools of thought have pursued this connection: Lexical Semantics (e.g., Jackendoff 1990, Pustejovsky 1995) and the neo-Davidsonian project (e.g., Higginbotham 1985, 1987; Parsons 1990). Whereas Lexical Semantics reveals a variety of properties that are internal to words and constant across them, the neo-Davidsonian project studies lexical dependencies and how they determine syntactic associations. These schools complement each other, and both are important to Minimalism. Unlike previous lexicalist models, Minimalism is not so much about words as it is about certain crucial features within words. Hence, on the one hand it must assume a theory of the sort that the neo-Davidsonian project provides, which is useful in literally starting derivations out in terms of sentence-level dependencies; but on the other hand it must drive derivations to their convergent limits in terms of the sorts of features that, ultimately, Lexical Semantics provides.

47. This particular example is from Lee Slack's personal record: one of her children produced three distinct clicks, involving different places of articulation, over the course of several months. Regarding the topic at large, and for more facts about what infants know, see Mehler and Dupoux 1994. For a general discussion of the issues involved here, see Jackendoff 1994, chap. 14.

48. For the remarkable case study of Genie (whom the Linguist will allude to shortly), see Curtiss 1977; and on the general topic, see Jackendoff 1994, chap. 9.

49. See Covington 1984.

50. For general issues regarding "grammaticalization," which will be discussed in chapter 6, see Hopper and Traugott 1993. See also Belazi, Rubin, and Toribio 1994 concerning restrictions on code switching (the use of elements from two languages in the same sentence by bilingual speakers), a matter of great interest when considering the differences between functional and lexical structure. For a different perspective about functional structure, see van Gelderen 1993.

51. Although Bickerton (1990) assumes an adaptive theory, and not the exaptive line pursued here, he emphasizes the crucial relevance of functional items. Recent work on development, going back to Lebeaux 1988 and Radford 1990, explores the possibility that children start their grammatical lives without any access to functional items. Although this might be seen as evidence for Haeckel's

law that ontogeny recapitulates phylogeny, the factual claim itself is dubious. If the view presented in this book is at all correct, functional items are so fundamental to human language that without them there would be no such thing. The matter, however, might be significant in evolutionary terms.

52. On the Linguist's point regarding pidgins, see Bickerton 1990.

53. The ideas that follow are being worked out by various investigators. For a summary and statement of goals, see Uriagereka 1996.

54. The following ideas are central to a trend, initiated in Borer 1984, that tries to reduce linguistic variation of the sort first emphasized in Rizzi 1982 to morphological matters. The topic is too broad to reference it adequately here; but for an overview and abundant citations, see Fukui 1986, 1993, Hyams 1986, Roeper and Williams 1987, Uriagereka 1988, Benincà 1989, Jaeggli and Safir 1989, Webelhuth 1989, 1995, Freidin 1993, 1995, Clark and Roberts 1993.

55. Readers who cannot wait until chapter 3 to delve into these matters can review them in any of the introductory texts cited in this chapter—with the warning that the models presented in those books operate rather differently (at least in technical detail) from the Minimalist Program.

56. This sort of account was one of the triumphs of Chomsky 1959a. Other influential works on the topic include Emonds 1976, Pollock 1989, and Belletti 1990, which led to much current Minimalist research (e.g., Wilder and Cavar 1994, Cann and Tait 1994, Jonas 1995, Lasnik, forthcoming).

57. This sort of observation is traditional (see Harris 1952).

58. See Lasnik, forthcoming, for a detailed discussion of the issues involved in this sort of analysis, as well as a problem with it that leads to an interesting refinement.

59. Many similar examples are discussed in Horn 1989; see also Herburger 1996.

60. This point is stressed by Stephen Crain in most of his work (see Crain 1991, Crain, Ni, and Conway 1994). Crain believes that adult minds have too many sorts of (often conflicting) information to deal with and that children's minds are actually a better place to explore the fundamental issues being discussed.

61. Thanks to Georges Rey for discussion on these matters.

62. Up to this point, this is all essentially orthodox Minimalism. The conjectures that follow, however, are taken from the author's work in progress with Ian Roberts and with the La Fragua group, and are freely inspired by the work of Ray Jackendoff (see, e.g., 1992). The admittedly Aristotelian line that is sketched below is heavily influenced by Pustejovsky's (1993) analysis and goes back to the spirit of Chomsky 1965.

63. This is a crucial point. If there is no systematic way of distinguishing basic semantic features of lexical items from other associations, there is no way of pinning down the semantic features that are relevant to LF. One possibility is that there are no semantic features at LF; but then one must worry about both what LF is and what semantic features are. The other possibility is that a systematic way does exist of making the distinction (as one does for phonological features, on psychological grounds). The second view is assumed here. On these issues, see Jackendoff 1994, chap. 14.

64. See Dowty, Wall, and Peters 1981, 224.

65. This point is raised by Katz (1972) and Lakoff (1972), for example.

66. This fact, originally studied by Dixon (1972) from a totally different perspective, is discussed by Lakoff 1986, 1987.

67. For data and references, see Muromatsu, forthcoming.

68. This is the position that Lakoff (1987) takes, and Edelman (1992) assumes within his general criticism of computational theories of mind.

69. The claims that follow are explored by Muromatsu (forthcoming) for noun systems.

70. When these items are classified (e.g., in Japanese), they are given a dummy classifier that is used for any sort of noun. The point being raised is that no classifier that is particular to these sorts of abstract, countable elements is possible in human languages.

71. This sort of noun classification in a linguistic domain D (the equivalent of verbal "Aktionsart") is not orthodox. Technical details aside, the problem is being faced here from syntactic perspective, where it is just a fact that what is being referred to as, for instance, two-dimensional items (mass terms) are structurally less complex than three-dimensional ones (count terms), and so on. Most semantic systems go the other way; this approach probably stems from the traditional belief that entities are epistemologically prior to masses or more arcane notions. Quine (1969) showed some skepticism about whether this is the natural order of things, when considering problems connected with East Asian classifiers. Unfortunately, his view of language acquisition was not sophisticated, and he was led to conclude that children should start conceptualizing in mass terms, then move on to complex individuations. Real children do no such thing. In chapter 6 the actual acquisition sequence is taken as an argument for the present view. For discussion on these general matters, see Uriagereka 1996.

72. These ideas share something with the proposals in Carlson 1977 concerning stages of individuals. Ultimately, however, the proposals and the assumptions behind them are very different.

73. For the semantics being assumed here, see Hornstein 1990; and for a corresponding Minimalist syntax, see Thompson, in preparation.

74. For this sort of view, and references, see Raposo and Uriagereka 1995.

75. This is a favorite example of Chomsky's (see 1993, 1994) that is amenable to the treatment presented here.

76. Actually, this terminology is loaded. The common use of the Gricean (1989) concept of "implicature" would not apply in the case just mentioned. Yet the text is now committing to the view that whatever is not an LF feature of an expression cannot be part of its lexical presupposition structure. To take an extreme instance: if the psychological theory leads to the decision that "handpicked" is not a lexical feature of a term like *coffee,* then the proposition "I am touching a handpicked thing" cannot be lexically inferred from the proposition "I am touching a grain of coffee." To the extent that speakers feel they can reason otherwise, they would have to be using a meaning postulate, and then the question becomes whether such devices allow entailments, or mere implicatures, given world knowledge. In contrast, the proposition "I am touching something with mass" would be adequately inferred as an implication, even without any world knowledge about specifically what *coffee* means, as opposed to *tea,* for instance.

77. This famous classification is due to Vendler (see Schmitt 1995 for discussion of this and related matters, as well as references).

78. An early article that makes this point about alliteration is Kiparsky 1970.

79. This analogy is quite important for the Minimalist Program. When Chomsky (1995, chap. 4) talks about "formally identical LFs," no point about logic is being raised. Instead, what matters is a "dull" parallelism of the sort now being discussed.

80. A point made by Edelman (1992) in a way that he takes to be devastating for computational theories of mind. Although the matter is not trivial, some interesting ways of dealing with it have been discussed in chapter 1.

81. The issue is this: What exactly is one doing when one points at something? How does one know it is a something? Would a different intelligence know it as the same sort of something? Could one program an automaton to point at the same thing one is pointing to oneself? (This is without even mentioning situations like partial perception, as discussed by Churchland and Sejnowski (1992, 173), or going beyond perception.)

82. These examples are discussed in Chomsky 1965, 201 n. 15.

83. The term comes again from concatenation algebras. See Chomsky 1957, 1959a, 1965, chap. 2.

84. This terminology is partly a residue from Chomsky 1955, where each level of representation was called X-marker (for instance, T-marker was the transformational level); at the time, phrase markers were taken to be objects at a level of representation whose basic primitives were those of a phrase structure grammar. Since then, phrase structure rules have been abandoned, and phrases are no longer taken to be generated at a level of representation. As a result, phrase marker is actually a somewhat anachronistic term, which nonetheless can be reinterpreted, with the word marker referring to "formal procedure." The details of this procedure are discussed at length in chapter 3.

85. To facilitate reading by a general audience, pronunciation transcriptions have been given in dictionary notation.

86. See Hornstein 1995b for discussion and a proposal.

87. On this general issue (going back to Fodor 1975) and for references, see Jackendoff 1994, pt. IV.

88. See O'Grady, Dobrovolsky, and Aronoff 1993, 384.

89. This topic is too complex to reference it appropriately in this context. For basic ideas, see Halle and Clements 1983 or O'Grady, Dobrovolsky, and Aronoff 1993, chap. 3.

90. The technical idea of "deep structure" was introduced by Chomsky (1965), who credited at least the Port-Royal grammarians, Reid, Humboldt, Wittgenstein, Hockett, and Postal for the basic intuition behind it. This generosity to the sources may have led to misinterpretations about what the technical notion of "deep structure" meant in the linguistic system: a mere level of representation, just as deep or shallow as any other.

91. For generations of linguists who were not part of the "linguistics wars" (Harris 1993), it is both fair and easy to grant generative semanticists the basics of this important point (for references, see Newmeyer 1980). This matter is discussed again at length in chapter 6.

92. On these issues, see for instance Jackendoff 1994, chap. 7.

93. That the ultimate phonetic level is just a speech continuum (no matter how abstract) is not usually debated (although recall fig. 2.28). However, researchers have disagreed on whether PF is that continuum. Aoun et al. (1987), for instance, argue for a more elaborate PF where conditions on phrasal representations can be imposed. The Minimalist Program denies itself this possibility by demanding that levels of representation be complete and comprehensive.

94. For the ear untrained to casual American speech, the expression under discussion is just a very reduced form of *I'm going to prove that*. The kind of semantic representation being assumed is discussed at length in Parsons 1990, 1995.

95. In fact, the model proposed in Chomsky 1965 was pretty much this model, where "deep structure" was essentially what here is called LF: the interface with the intentional/conceptual component of mind.

96. This is probably the most positive, direct result of the debates of the late 1960s, a fact that is not always adequately acknowledged. The work of Emmon Bach and James McCawley, in particular, was quite significant in sensitizing linguists to LF matters. See Newmeyer 1980 for references, and Bach et al. 1995 for many of the results of the earlier program.

97. Again, it is hard to do justice to the implied facts. See Hornstein 1995a for a good summary, references, and a Minimalist proposal.

98. For expository purposes, although the notion of S-structure is involved from Chomsky 1981, the *S* is being attributed to *singular,* and not *surface*. The term *surface structure* was already unfortunate by the appearance of Chomsky 1981, since the true "surface" was PF. In publications and class lectures, Chomsky questioned the very existence of S-structure, using essentially Minimalist arguments (see Chomsky 1986b). D-structure was abandoned soon after, partly as a result of proposals made by Lebeaux (1988).

99. Brody (1995) makes a proposal of the relevant sort. These sorts of ideas have also descended from Koster 1978, 1987; Koster's postulates have influenced various tenets of Minimalism. Rizzi's work (see esp. 1986, 1990) also offers representational alternatives that have significantly influenced Minimalism. Work by other representationalists is discussed in section 2.7.

100. For discussion of these issues and for references, within a pre-Minimalist system, see Epstein 1991.

101. See Brody 1995 for discussion of this point.

102. Brody (1995), for instance, relates the matter to his conventions on how syntactic features "percolate" through formal objects: up instead of down. As it will turn out, Minimalism too involves relations among features, although of a different sort. Ultimately, any system has to explain the "outward" character of these relations, a matter discussed in chapter 4.

103. See for instance Hawking 1993 for a discussion of this sort of model, and Meinzer 1994, chap. 2, for interesting connections with classical philosophical debates.

104. The first system to incorporate radical use of filters was that of Chomsky and Lasnik (1977). A variety of derivational proposals summarized in Lasnik and Uriagereka 1988 and Lasnik and Saito 1992 make crucial use of these devices.

105. For helpful discussions of the issues that follow, thanks to Luigi Burzio, Jane Grimshaw, Géraldine Legendre, Paul Smolensky, and especially Linda Lombardi.

106. As Linda Lombardi points out in personal communication, if some rankings are universal, some of these options need not be learned; one would then have to ask, though, why those rankings happen to be universal, given the architecture of Optimality Theory.

107. This point is raised in Smolensky 1994.

108. This problem has been a notorious locus of recent debate and misunderstanding, on both sides of the argument. A clear, fair discussion (which admits the problem is real and ponders the sort of solution it demands) is Burzio 1995.

109. See Chomsky and Halle 1968.

110. But see Burzio 1995 for a discussion, raising problems based on the seriality of rule application. The seriality assumption, although traditional and assumed in this book, is not really necessary. It certainly holds of Chomsky's (1955) grammars; however, models deriving from Lindenmayer's L-systems (see Rozenberg and Salomaa 1986; also fig. 3.10) allow the application of simultaneous productions. It would be interesting to find out whether the problems that Burzio notes for traditional serial productions also hold for parallel productions.

111. The references are too numerous to cite exhaustively. See Prince and Smolensky, forthcoming, for the basic proposal and references to the necessary background reading.

112. See Grimshaw 1990, 1995, Burzio 1991, 1996, among others. For interesting pieces that give a sense of the state of the art, see Legendre, Smolensky, and Wilson, forthcoming.

113. See Kayne 1993.

114. This point, initially raised by Benveniste (1971), has been rescued by Kayne (1993). On the general topic, see Den Dikken, forthcoming; and for a different perspective, see Ritter and Rosen 1993.

115. This example and the discussion below are taken from Hornstein, Rosen, and Uriagereka, forthcoming.

116. See Grimshaw 1995.

117. For different perspectives on the topic of phonology's difference, see Anderson 1985, Bromberger and Halle 1989, Goldsmith 1993, Prince and Smolensky, forthcoming, among others.

118. On these matters, see Gell-Mann 1994.

Chapter 3

1. This is an old notion within linguistics and is expressed in different ways in different frameworks (see, e.g., Baltin and Kroch 1989). The ideas that follow are discussed in Chomsky 1995, chap. 4. See also Carnie 1995, Koizumi 1995, Chametzky, forthcoming, among many others.

2. The choice of labels in (3) is intended to emphasize that this "bare" version of phrase structure does not involve intermediate levels of projection, of the sort introduced in Jackendoff 1977. Whenever a precise formal notation for intermediate projections is not needed, the projecting head is simply used to mark this part of the phrase marker.

3. For discussion of essentially this sort of system, see Speas 1990.

4. This comparison is due to Mike Dillinger (personal communication), who applies it more generally.

5. The system of features that gives this result is discussed in Muysken 1982.

6. Pesetsky (1982) was the first to advocate that the inherent properties of an expression determine its combinatorial properties. Grimshaw (1979) provides arguments against a simpleminded implementation of this idea (see also Grimshaw 1990). Chomsky and Lasnik (1995) criticize some of Pesetsky's results on empirical grounds, although they concede that his view is conceptually desirable.

7. The notion that a predicate must locally satisfy its lexical dependencies is very old within linguistics and was explicitly discussed by Modistic grammarians in the fourteenth century (see Covington 1984).

8. Although Fillmore (1964) was the first to bring traditional concerns with case into generative grammar, it was Jean-Roger Vergnaud who first adduced the sort of argument made in figure 3.7 (in an unpublished letter, in response to Chomsky and Lasnik 1977), thereby giving a major impetus to what was to become the Government-Binding framework. As Howard Lasnik points out (personal communication), Vergnaud's vision about abstract Case was remarkably current; he even talked about "checking" Case, much in the spirit of the way Case will be implemented here.

Capitalizing *C* when talking about abstract Case is not a matter of pedantic terminology. As it turns out, exactly how Case manifests itself in a given language is by no means a trivial question, as Freidin and Babby (1984) showed when studying the Russian morphological case system; here, the lowercase *c* denotes an explicit, lexically present representation of abstract Case in the language, of the sort that is only marginally present in Modern English. Chomsky (1986b) presents some interesting conjectures on the differences between lexical case and an instance of abstract Case that is usually called "structural." Everything said about Case in this book concerns this particular sort of Case, which typically appears in major arguments of the verb in association with agreement. However, see Rooryck, forthcoming, for a view, within Minimalism, of other sorts of Case.

9. Joseph Aoun is to be credited with this idea, which is defended in Chomsky 1986b and assumed in much work done during the 1980s.

10. See Kayne 1994, where basically this idea is extensively pursued.

11. A version of this proposal is defended by Travis (1984). Raposo and Uriagereka (1990) argue that both this idea and a version of Aoun's idea of Case visibility are necessary. See Watanabe 1993, Sauerland 1995, Murasugi 1992, Bobaljik and Phillips 1993, and Phillips 1993 for a Minimalist perspective on Case theory, a matter taken up again in chapter 4.

12. All notions discussed in this section can be found in any elementary introduction to formal languages (e.g., Arbib, Kfoury, and Moll 1981, Kelly 1995) or any book on mathematics for linguists (e.g., Partee, ter Meulen, and Wall 1990). However, it must be kept in mind that these ideas are not original to computer science; it was Chomsky who developed them (1955, 1959a). See Lasnik and Kupin 1977 for a useful presentation of the traditional sources and for several improvements that led to theories assuming projection, as opposed to phrase structure rules.

13. Structuralist linguists like Zellig Harris (1952) specifically talked about "the head of a construction." Lyons (1968) stressed the significance of the endocentricity of phrases at a time when it was not predicted by phrase structure rules.

14. Speas (1990) discusses these matters, including the classical source, Stowell 1981. See also Chametzky, forthcoming.

15. For discussion of these and related issues, see Bach, Oehrle, and Wheeler 1988.

16. For a more detailed discussion of these matters, see Lasnik and Uriagereka 1988, chap. 1.

17. Phonological metarules are systematically discussed in Chomsky and Halle 1968. A syntactic theory that instantiates them is presented in Gazdar et al. 1985.

18. That was essentially the medieval argument for binary relations in grammar (see Covington 1984); in current terms, the concept is forcefully defended by Kayne (1984).

19. Cherniak (1992) has been able to predict very interesting regularities concerning the angle of separation of branches (vis-à-vis, in particular, the thickness of the trunk) for natural systems like river and neural networks. This, however, barely scratches the surface of what is implied in the text.

20. The paradigm of exceptional Case marking discussed in section 4.5 strongly suggests that (structural) Case marking is not about meaning.

21. Langacker's (1969) intuitive term *command* is used (instead of *c-command, m-command, k-command, θ-command,* or any of the variants in the literature) because the interpretation of this notion presented here is slightly new, yet old at the same time. The basic insight goes back to Klima's (1964) notion "in construction with," which is itself a medieval intuition about syntactic dependencies.

22. Thanks to Dorit Ben-Shalom for bringing up this issue, which is discussed in Higginbotham 1996.

23. The corporation example is due to Howard Lasnik.

24. This idea, in its essentials, is presented and argued for in Kayne 1994.

25. Formally, the way this result is achieved here differs considerably from the way it is achieved in Kayne 1994. The statement of the LCA given in (13) has not been proposed anywhere else as such. Chomsky (1995, sec. 4.8) discusses Kayne's idea very explicitly, but he gives no detailed axiom. Kayne's axiom does not work within the modified assumptions that Chomsky introduces (his bare phrase structure).

26. Many of the ideas that follow were largely inspired by questions raised by Bob Frank and Michael Morreau, and the discussion they generated. Thanks also to Jairo Nunes for various comments.

27. This suggestion is due to David Pesetsky.

28. The ideas that follow are developed and defended in Epstein, forthcoming, in a slightly different format.

29. Sam Epstein was the first to make this general observation, slightly adapted for present purposes.

30. This possibility was first pointed out by Jairo Nunes, who develops a possible implementation in Nunes 1995a.

31. This idea is discussed in Uriagereka, forthcoming b.

32. For analyses of Irish from a Minimalist perspective, see Duffield 1995 and selected papers in Borsley and Roberts, forthcoming.

33. The last projection is, of course, less obvious. As late as Chomsky 1981, linguists were still using one last rewrite rule: S → NP VP. This was a bit anachronistic, since rewrite rules had already been argued out of the model; however, the rule highlighted a problem that goes back to Aristotle: sentences have subjects. Pesetsky (1982) then argued that within a projection system, sentences can be naturally conceived as projections of an inflectional element like Tense. However, this still does not explain why a sentence must include a Tense specifier. Until recently, the existence of this specifier was demanded by a separate requirement: the Extended Projection Principle. Minimalism does not fare much better, since it requires a separate feature to capture the same old fact (see chap. 5).

34. This point is raised by Kayne (1994) and further discussed by Koizumi (1995).

35. On the nature of Japanese Tense, and for important (and conflicting) references on the topic, see Saito 1985, Fukui 1986, and Ishii 1991. Also see Koizumi 1995 for a different view, suggesting that Japanese may involve verb raising, together with further argument raising to the left periphery of the clause.

36. On this topic within Minimalism, see Branigan 1992 and Zwart 1993.

37. The Linguist takes a few liberties with the actual quotation, which is

If we are satisfied that an apple falls to the ground because that is its natural place, there will be no serious science of mechanics. The same is true if one is satisfied with traditional rules for forming questions, or with the lexical entries in the most elaborate dictionaries, none of which come close to describing simple properties of these linguistic objects. Recognition of the unsuspected richness and complexity of the phenomena of language created a tension between the goals of descriptive and explanatory adequacy. (Chomsky 1995, 4)

38. The main source of such arguments is Kayne 1994. For empirical discussion of Kayne's proposal, see the papers in Zwart 1994.

39. For discussion of these and related matters within the Minimalist framework, see Abe 1993, Murasugi 1992, Oka 1993, Kawashima 1994, Takahashi 1993, Koizumi 1995, and Ura 1996.

40. This is indeed an important point, for several reasons. Empirically, its immediate consequence is to disallow derivations whose sole motivation is achieving a certain interpretive form, be it at PF or at LF. The text gives an example involving an LF configuration, but similar examples can be constructed for PF as well: for instance, a verb should not be allowed to move just to support an unrelated weak element that otherwise would not have the morphological weight to be interpretable at this level. Since many traditional proposals have precisely this effect (allowing derivations whose purpose is not "self-serving"), Minimalism forces considerable reanalysis of standard paradigms.

Conceptually, the point is central for two reasons. One is methodological; the alternative view gives too much power to the system, which is thus not restrictive enough (the question is, when should a derivation not be allowed to resort to all sorts of arcane transformations to salvage a representation?). The other reason connects with the ongoing discussion of whether human language is an adaptation or an exaptation. To the extent that the link between derivations and intelligibility or expressiveness is severed, the justification for claiming that the linguistic system arose as a consequence of adaptive pressures is considerably weakened.

Not surprisingly, for all these reasons, this central property of Minimalism remains controversial.

41. The idea of *wh*-movement to Comp was first proposed by Bresnan (1972). In several 1984 lectures that reanalyzed Den Besten's (1989) "verb-second" effects in German, Craig Thiersch first proposed a standard X-bar analysis of Comp (also see Chomsky 1986a). This effect is very similar to auxiliary fronting in English (see Rizzi 1990), although clearly more general. Exactly why auxiliaries move to Comp, and why only in matrix clauses, is still a controversial question. For an early treatment of these matters within Minimalism, see Zwart 1993.

42. Huang 1982 is the classical source for this proposal, but see Kim 1990 and Watanabe 1992 for a different perspective.

43. This observation, raised within Joseph Greenberg's typological framework (see Comrie 1981), is used by Koopman (1984) in noting that head-last Kru languages nonetheless involve *wh*-movement to the left.

44. This problem does not arise for Kayne's (1994) theory, but for notational reasons. Since Kayne does not assume a bare phrase structure theory of the sort presented in this chapter, vacuous levels of phrasal projection are possible in his system (thus, an element that does not merge with anything else can nonetheless project). If this possibility exists, then the complement in (24) can be made not to command the verb by simply adding vacuous structure. Since Minimalism tries to eliminate unmotivated structure, this particular move is unwelcome, and the discussion that follows becomes necessary.

45. This topic is too broad to reference fully. Recent works bearing on it, more or less within Minimalism but taking different approaches, include Collins 1993, Corver and Delfitto 1993, Auger 1994, Moore 1994, Cardinaletti and Starke 1995, Duarte and Matos 1995, Everett 1995, Raposo 1995, Terzi 1995, Uriagereka 1995, Martins 1995.

46. This offhand remark does not imply that the matter of defining what a head is has only technical consequences. In fact, this issue is central in separating two entirely different domains of structural conservation within human language: the word-level domain and the phrase-level domain. This question will be taken up at length in chapter 6. Note that at this point the naive characterization of a lexical item as a head breaks down: a complex head can be formed in the course of the derivation. As a result, a complex morphological component is needed, something that is assumed from this point on.

47. The notion "trace," which goes back to Fiengo 1977, is purposely introduced here in an informal way; evidence for these elements will be presented in the next section.

48. See Horvath 1995 for useful discussion of this idea (which goes back to Horvath 1981) and Kiss 1995 for important data and analyses. The topic is too broad to reference adequately here. For Chomsky's ideas on focus, see Chomsky 1972, 1977. Two recent works compatible with Minimalism and replete with references are Tancredi 1992 and Herburger 1996.

49. The empirical adequacy of Kayne's proposal has generated much recent discussion; see, among many others, Cann 1993, Zwart 1994, Buering and Hartmann, forthcoming, and Pensalfini 1995.

50. Some of these observations go back to Chomsky 1955, 1965. An influential proposal revamping "light shift" can be found in Larson 1988.

51. Longobardi (1994) discusses this sort of idea, which is first provocatively defended by Burge (1974).

52. For critical discussion of this notion, see Anderson 1992 and Halle and Marantz 1993.

53. For related ideas, see Cardinaletti and Starke 1995.

54. See Chomsky 1990.

55. This argument is due to Kayne (1994).

56. For reasons that do not hold in the present system, Kayne's (1994) theory prevents this. It is in fact not obvious why multiple cliticization is impossible, given the assumptions made here. At the same time, the possibility of multiple cliticization may explain why the order in which clitics occur in a given cliticization site differs crosslinguistically (see Uriagereka 1995 for a proposal and references, and Terzi 1995 for an analysis of new and recalcitrant data).

57. This proposal is made in passing by Kayne (1994).

58. The semantics of questions are very complex; here they are only very indirectly relevant. For references, see Gamut 1991; and for the general topic of quantification in natural language, see Bach et al. 1995 and Larson and Segal 1995. Issues regarding linear algebra that are marginally relevant here (and to some extent throughout the book) are usefully presented in Behnke et al. 1987.

59. This comment is not unfair. Previous models assumed traces-as-variables almost as a matter of fact (see, e.g., Lasnik and Uriagereka 1988, 41), and it is certainly true that, in many semantic models, a quantificational element in a standard argument position (e.g., object of *convince*) must move in order to leave behind an object of the appropriate type, to satisfy the properties of the

relevant predicate. However, first, this conclusion is not semantically necessary (see Hornstein 1995a and references therein). Second, even if the conclusion were required on semantic grounds, Minimalism does not allow a derivation to be influenced by this sort of consideration. To the extent that a movement is necessary in this system, it must be so because of properties that are internal to the syntactic derivation. Then an immediate question arises: what properties of a syntactic derivation demand the creation of the type of element that will obtain the semantic interpretation of a variable? As the discussion in section 5.5 suggests, it is not completely obvious that any such property exists in full generality, and languages may differ on whether they create the relevant structures for quantificational purposes; some may (e.g., English), and some may not (e.g., Chinese). In any event, this matter is unresolved, and the locus of much current discussion.

60. It has been reported that Australian English and certain American English dialects do not accord with these facts.

Essentially the same sort of argument can be presented with much more elaborate detail and rigor; it is omitted here so as not to stop the flow of the dialogue (but see fig. 3.26). However, note that the paradigm is complicated by the reasonable fact that (29c) also involves a null element in subject position: PRO. Lasnik and Uriagereka (1988, chap. 1) discuss this matter at length and provide references. Here empty categories other than traces are not discussed at any length, partly because Minimalism, unlike previous models, has until now had relatively few interesting things to say about null elements as constituting a whole paradigm (Chomsky 1981, 1982, 1986a, Bouchard 1984, Lasnik and Uriagereka 1988, Brody 1993). See Chomsky and Lasnik 1995, Bošković 1995, Ormazabal 1995, and especially Martin 1996, for discussion of PRO, and Speas 1994, Barbosa 1994, and Ordóñez, in preparation, for matters relating to a counterpart of this element in null subject languages: pro.

61. This assumption is not innocent and has for years been the locus of debate (see chap. 6). Note that it essentially eliminates option (i) in the text from serious consideration.

62. The matter is controversial, though, as the debate presented in Freidin 1995 concerning Galician determiner incorporation clearly shows.

63. This very lively issue is discussed in Halle and Marantz 1993, Harley and Phillips 1994, Bobaljik 1995, and Phillips, in preparation, and, from a more syntactic perspective, in Lasnik, forthcoming, and Arnold 1995.

64. Note that, given this picture, morphological rules must be learned, in a serious sense. This entails that when it is stated, as in chapter 1, that language acquisition is more akin to growing than to learning, morphology must be set aside. The core/periphery distinction seems reasonable here, if "periphery" is taken to mean whatever is not directly specified within the innate language faculty and does not directly follow from epigenetic growth. Needless to say, this is a vast space.

65. The Linguist is given the role of skeptic in this passage because the ideas the Other discusses have not been explored within Minimalism. The Other is thus (perhaps unfairly) required to venture first proposals about what kinds of things Minimalism can do when pushed to various limits. (For a more thorough presentation of multiple Spell-Out, see Uriagereka, forthcoming b.)

66. Building in parallel and merging afterward presupposes a kind of operation that is often referred to as a *generalized transformation*. This sort of operation was introduced in Chomsky 1955 and was brought back into fashion in the mid-1980s by Aravind Joshi (see Kroch 1989a, Frank 1992, and Frank and Kroch 1993 on the linguistic significance of Joshi's proposals). Lebeaux (1988) gave strong support to generalized transformations by showing that some interesting empirical problems (discussed in chap. 4) can be analyzed in terms of these devices.

67. This notion is essentially equivalent to Kayne's (1984) "unambiguous paths," adapted to the present system.

68. Essentially this proposal was made by Bresnan (1972). Relevant proposals that could be interpreted along the lines suggested in the text have been made by Cinque (1993) and Zubizarreta (1994), who study focus projections through right branches. However, matters in these domains are extremely complex, as a look at Selkirk 1984 or Tancredi 1992 will show.

69. This architecture was first discussed by Jackendoff (1969). Lebeaux (1996) has revised it, essentially as suggested in the text, although with slightly different assumptions.

70. The idea that follows is argued for by Nunes (1995a,b). Again, since it is not standard within Minimalism, the Linguist reacts skeptically.

71. It is impossible to adequately reference this very large topic. An accessible summary of research up to the mid-1980s is Barss 1986. Fiengo and May (1994) provide references and interesting reconstruction facts, but their assumptions are mostly incompatible with Minimalism. Also see Chomsky 1995, chap. 3, and Hornstein 1995a (though the Minimalist assumptions of these texts are arguably inconsistent with the theory as it will be developed here). For related proposals, also see Munn 1994, Huang 1993, Heycock 1991, and Fukui and Saito 1995.

72. Matters become considerably more complex in examples like (i):

(i) which portrait of himself did Picasso say that I like?

Observe that reconstruction to the original launching site of movement yields (ii), which is still not a valid configuration to license an anaphor, in terms of proximity to its antecedent:

(ii) Picasso did say that I like [which portrait of himself]

On the other hand, Chomsky (1995, chap. 3) suggests that if movement proceeds in two steps, through the intermediate complementizer domain, then the anaphor will be closer to its antecedent:

(iii) [[which portrait of himself] did [Picasso say [t that [I like t]]]]

This is the case, of course, if the intermediate step of movement also involves "reconstruction"— that is, if it also involves a copy of *which portrait of himself,* and furthermore if this is the copy that is interpreted at LF. Note finally that this analysis does not contradict the statements in section 3.4 that an anaphor can be licensed through a movement operation only for an independent purpose. In this instance, the movement is independently driven by the requirement to satisfy question features.

73. This is a very open question within Minimalism. First, it is not clear whether all types of movement involve reconstruction. Second, it is not clear in exactly what instances reconstruction takes place to initial positions, or to intermediate sites. No comprehensive theory of these matters exists, although most of the Minimalist works cited in this book (see esp. n. 71) have addressed the topic.

Chapter 4

1. Within generative grammar, one must go back at least to Bach 1964 and McCawley 1968 to find emphasis on the notion that traditional logical forms express certain aspects of language. Linguists in the Chomskyan tradition have tended to reject the presence of logic as such in grammatical analysis, since the latter is taken to be empirical research. Nonetheless, many linguists have been sensitive to

covert operations that may precede logical relations in grammar, and often the shape of these operations has found at least an inspiration in logic (see Chomsky 1972, 1975, 1977). Crucial among these is the rule of quantifier raising (in the tradition of Montague Grammar), as expressed in May 1977. For the most part, the present discussion shies away from this complex matter and focuses on more mechanical aspects of covert movement. Hornstein 1995a is a good source for treatments of these issues, including a proposal about quantifier raising within the Minimalist Program.

2. See Lasnik 1972 for early discussion of these matters; Kuno 1987 and Chao 1988 for traditional data and analyses from different perspectives; Hornstein 1994, Lasnik 1995c, and Wilder 1995 for Minimalist works on various aspects of ellipsis; Lappin 1996 and Fiengo and May 1994 for interesting phenomena viewed from a different angle; and Williams 1995 for a critical review of Fiengo and May.

3. This is a very open issue. See for instance Poole, forthcoming.

4. The following observations are from Kuno 1987.

5. Thanks to Ralph Fasold for pointing out this issue.

6. Precursors of this idea are found in Oka 1993 and Ferguson and Groat 1994; it is pushed to interesting consequences in Chomsky 1995, chap. 4. For related matters, see Nunes 1995a, Ferguson, in preparation, and Groat, in preparation.

7. Although Chomsky (1995, chap. 4) speaks in these terms about words, he never pushes the issue as is done in the text below. This is in part because the specific mechanics of what happens at Spell-Out are still unclear, as is the ultimate form of words as morphological units, in the course of the derivation.

8. Tom Roeper and Rozz Thornton point out (in personal communication) that English-speaking children sometimes say things like this. This may relate to the fact mentioned in note 9.

9. This rather traditional idea was first argued for in Lasnik 1981 and then pursued in Baker 1988. Observe that the structure in (8) should be possible in languages in which the determiner element does not have a morphological support. This may explain the generalization discussed in Uriagereka 1988 that languages with systematically overt definite articles in general disallow extractions like (6), unlike many languages without systematically overt definite articles (e.g., within the Slavic family, Bulgarian-like languages vs. Polish-like languages). A possible alternative explanation is suggested in Hoffman 1996.

10. For a good source of data and an important analysis, see Watanabe 1992 (also see Kim 1990). Observations along these lines go back to Klima 1964 and are pursued further in Sloan 1991 and Pica and Snyder 1995.

11. Watanabe (1992) provides interesting arguments for this view, involving considerations about locality of the sort that will be discussed in chapter 5.

12. The traditional idea of pied-piping is pushed much further in the Minimalist Program, partly in the spirit of Hornstein and Weinberg 1990.

13. To be precise, linguists expect that this desideratum is fulfilled. Serious questions remain, however. These include massive descriptive differences among languages (Basque and Quechua, for instance, allow entire clauses to pied-pipe, as discussed in Ortiz de Urbina 1989) and the very serious issue of whether pied-piping also takes place at LF (as suggested in Pesetsky 1987 and Nishigauchi 1986, argued against in Fiengo et al. 1988, and more recently again supported in Fox, forthcoming, and Reinhart 1995).

14. Some linguists have argued that the two operations should be collapsed; see, for example, Kitahara 1994, 1995, Nunes 1995a, Groat, in preparation, and Epstein et al., forthcoming.

15. Although the idea of a chain is old within transformational grammar, the specific technical implementation suggested here is new.

16. The rough idea for this notation, in an early form, was discussed informally by John Frampton (personal communication), particularly for adjunction chains.

17. The essentials behind the idea to be discussed below go back to what Chomsky (1973) called the "strict cycle." In recent years many linguists have tried to deduce cyclic properties of derivations from more elementary conditions. Interesting readings in this respect include Kitahara 1995, Watanabe 1995, Ura 1995, Epstein, forthcoming, and Kawashima and Kitahara, forthcoming.

18. Thanks to Marcus Kracht for emphasizing this point.

19. The issues that follow and a good deal of the content of the rest of the chapter owe much to conversations with Sam Epstein. See Epstein, forthcoming.

20. See Brody 1995, for instance.

21. A systematic treatment of these matters goes back, at least, to Chomsky 1972 and Lasnik 1976. Over the years innumerable versions of binding theory have been proposed. See Lasnik 1989, Reinhart and Reuland 1993, and Reinhart 1995 for references.

22. This issue is the locus of much current debate. See Uriagereka, forthcoming a, for a proposal, discussion, and references.

23. These sorts of examples were first discussed by Freidin (1986).

24. Chomsky (1995, chap. 3) tries essentially this requirement, in order to force a violation of (19b) in a case like (22b). Exactly what such a condition may follow from is not completely clear. Perhaps the "reconstruction procedure" (whatever that is, when the term is meant precisely) tries to mimic, as much as possible, the types of representations that result from mere movement of features. That is, had movement proceeded at LF, (21b) would have had the form in (ib):

(i) a. he likes the most which portrait of Rivera?
     b. [wh- [he likes the most [t "this one" portrait of Rivera]]]

And (ib) is the sort of structure obtained, also, if "reconstruction" is required to maximize the amount of lexical information to be interpreted in the original position of the *wh*-phrase.

25. Many of the ideas that follow are introduced as an exercise to practice with issues concerning Merge and to test its limits. The conclusions regarding modifiers and the whole matter of adjunction, to be discussed further below, must be viewed as tentative.

26. Thanks to Jian-Xin Wu for the data and helpful discussion.

27. Thanks to Dave Lebeaux for emphasizing this point.

28. On these issues, see Larson and Segal 1995, chap. 12. On the matter of adverbial placement within Minimalism, see Abe 1994.

29. A useful presentation of these matters, with implications beyond the scope of this discussion, is Crain and Hamburger 1992.

30. This analysis was proposed in Lebeaux 1988.

31. Thanks to Jairo Nunes for pointing this out.

32. The comment refers to the properties of categorial grammars and phrase structure grammars, which produce the same results as Merge does. Although the results are equivalent, it would be improper to equate these systems, since they achieve their results through rather different means, and this intensional difference may be significant. See section 3.2 on this.

33. The notion of "adjunction" is to be understood, traditionally, by opposition to the notion "substitution." In early transformational grammars, when a category moved, it could replace another category (eventually, a designated null target) or it could attach to already existing structures. The first kind of movement was called "substitution"; the second, "adjunction." Adjunction was interesting in that it did not really change or eliminate structure: if Y adjoined to X, Y became a sister to X, dominated by a newly created copy of X. This is the origin of (29) in the text. May (1985) and Chomsky (1986a) argued that the newly created segment of X does not have a reality of its own. May's arguments are not relevant within Minimalism, but Chomsky's claims are, although somewhat cryptically. Chomsky proposed that adjunction to arguments is impossible. The intuition behind this idea is that the ghost copy created in the adjunction process would interfere with the process of lexical dependency, for unclear reasons. (This position is justified within current views in chapter 6.) Substitution has now been subsumed under the more general process Move, which does not need to involve a dummy target for movement in the strongly constructive system assumed here.

   For further discussion of adjunction, see Poole 1994, Kayne 1994, and Lasnik and Saito 1992. (Kayne takes all specifiers to be adjuncts; Lasnik and Saito argue against adjunction.)

34. This comment and the brief suggestion about the graph-theoretic object in (33) owe much to discussions with John Frampton. Thanks to Paola Merlo for raising the point that adjunction structures do not really involve trees.

35. Perhaps the first systematic exploration of this sort of idea, at least for conjunctions, is Goodall 1984. See also Johannessen 1993, Munn 1993, and Wilder 1994, concerning coordination.

36. This line of research is pursued in Hoffman 1996. Of related interest, though different in execution, is Wilder 1994. For less radical views on the matter, still within Minimalism, see Baek 1995, Bošković and Takahashi, forthcoming, Fukui and Saito 1995, and Poole, forthcoming.

37. See Demirdache 1991, Cheng 1991, Kaan 1992, and Varlokosta 1994 for related discussion.

   If there is one place in which the parametric speculation that Pinker and Bloom (1990) entertain is well taken, it is precisely the realm of parataxis. Pinker and Bloom essentially suggest that it would be natural for language not to specify the relative order of pairs of elements within a bounded unit. This is not an unreasonable conclusion to reach concerning the relative order of paratactic associates.

38. This is a central issue for any "split" model in which derivations start in a formal object that is neither PF nor LF. This question already emerged, in some form, for models that made use of "deep" structure. In those models, the compatibility requirement was strengthened to the Projection Principle, which demanded that LF be in some way homomorphic with "deep" structure. Since PF was derivationally obtained from "deep" structure as well, compatibility was ensured.

39. This issue emerges only in optimality-seeking systems, such as Minimalism, and was irrelevant, per se, in traditional derivational systems. Interestingly, though, in systems involving "deep" structures the optimality question was trivially solved: only those derivations that started in the same "deep" structure and finished in the same interpretive representations would compete for optimality. Once "deep" structure is given up, however, the question of optimality emerges again in full generality.

40. Bob Frank raised this potential difficulty in personal communication.

41. A good portion of Chomsky and Lasnik 1977 is devoted to this apparently trivial fact. Once it is claimed that sentences are introduced (or headed) by complementizers, the question of why they are not pronounced in main clauses immediately arises.

42. The ideas that follow are found in Chomsky 1995, chap. 4.

43. The descriptive apparatus behind this idea goes back to Postal's (1974) rule of subject-to-object raising. Lasnik and Saito (1991) have reinterpreted Postal's proposals in terms that are compatible with Minimalism, which will be discussed below.

44. This is contrary to Chomsky's (1995, 226) statement that ". . . Merge [is] 'costless'; [it does] not fall within the domain of discussion of convergence and economy." Chomsky is led to this conclusion because "[i]nsufficient application of Merge . . . fails to yield an LF representation at all [and] no derivation is generated . . ." (p. 226). Although the premise is correct, the conclusion is wrong, and the error involves a category mistake. According to Chomsky (class lectures, fall 1995), the argument was valid about the *type* of Merge, but not about *token* applications of the rule, which is what matters for economy. Token applications have cost, as the operations that they are, just as any move in a chess or checkers game has cost—even if, in many instances, it is forced by the logic of the game.

45. See Kitahara 1994 for discussion of this sort of idea.

46. This idea was first mentioned by Chomsky (1986b) and explored by Kitagawa (1987). In chapter 5 it becomes central.

47. On the issue of what counts as reliable data for LF, see Reinhart 1995 and references cited there. For proposals involving movement without an economy procedure, see Epstein 1991 and Lasnik and Saito 1992.

48. Alternatively, movements in a language like Japanese might take place simply for the purposes of satisfying the LCA/T discussed in chapter 3. See Moro 1996a for the source of this idea.

49. See Ortiz de Urbina 1989.

50. Agreement has never had a definite place in syntactic systems of a generative orientation. In recent years the topic has gained new significance, partly as a result of works like Kornfilt 1985, Raposo 1987, Pollock 1989, and Mahajan 1990. Chomsky (1995) makes significant use of an Agreement projection in chapter 3, but gives this up in chapter 4, where agreement is again a feature. The latter view is assumed here. For current discussion on agreement matters within the Minimalist Program, see Sigler, in preparation, Bobaljik and Phillips 1993, and Phillips 1993; also see Benmamoun 1992 and Bittner and Hale 1996 for much related discussion.

51. See Larson 1988 for the source of this idea.

52. For the origins of this view, see Kornfilt 1985 and Raposo 1987. Also see Raposo and Uriagereka, forthcoming, for a Minimalist perspective.

53. As will become apparent in chapter 5, pleonastic elements like *there* are an exception to the general tendency. The exception will be shown to follow from the properties of lexical dependency, as discussed in chapter 6.

54. This idea goes back to McCawley (1968) and has been discussed in recent years by many authors, notably Kitagawa (1987) and Koopman and Sportiche (1991).

55. The analysis that follows is essentially due to Lasnik and Saito (1991). Also see Lasnik 1993, 1995a,b, for much related discussion.

56. Chomsky (class lectures, MIT, fall 1995) has simplified this picture by proposing that all checking relations take place in the domain of head adjunction, movement to the specifier position being purely ancillary, for PF reasons. This idea is presented briefly in section 4.7.

57. At least at the time when these pages were originally written. More recently Chomsky (class lectures, MIT, fall 1995) has attempted a cleaner approach, without postulating strong features.

58. What it does relate to is currently unclear. See Raposo and Uriagereka 1995 for a proposal and some references, as well as section 6.5.

59. This view is introduced in Lasnik 1995b.

60. Alternatively, verbs must move at PF, a proposal that Chomsky has pursued in class lectures (MIT, fall 1995).

61. An interesting exception to this, within English, arises in simple questions such as *who do you like?*, which involves movement from object position. Only two possibilities arise here: either *who* moves through the intermediate Case-checking position on its way out to the periphery of the sentence, or else, in the covert component, the trace of *who* must move to the Case-checking position. The latter option is problematic (see sec. 5.5), suggesting that the first option must be taken. This then raises the nontrivial question—currently the topic of considerable debate—of why *who* must move through a position that it does not need to move to. See also Johnson 1991 for the more radical proposal that English involves generalized object movement.

62. Other possibilities are pursued in Ura 1996. Also see Koizumi 1995 for a more elaborate analysis of Japanese.

63. This idea is systematically discussed by Nunes (1995a), for less technical instances having to do with parasitic gaps. Jonathan Bobaljik and Sam Brown have independently made the specific proposal in the text and are pursuing the idea jointly.

64. This is one reason for pursuing the possibility that head movement is done in the PF component (Noam Chomsky, class lectures, MIT, fall 1995). That is, rather than proceeding as in (50), the featural movement in (50a) would have a direct PF correlate: head adjunction of Y to X. Instead of involving the two steps in (50b) and (50c), the whole process would be a repair strategy, as it were. This could not be done in the case of movement as in (49) because an entire phrase, rather than a word, is involved. It is also worth asking whether the still largely mysterious process of agreement has anything to do with these repair strategies.

65. This proposal is made in Epstein, forthcoming.

66. This issue was raised by both Joel Hoffman and Jairo Nunes in personal communication.

67. As noted by Cristina Schmitt through personal communication.

68. This line is pursued in Hoffman 1996.

69. See Hornstein 1995b for discussion.

70. In essence, this sort of model goes back to Jackendoff 1969, among other works of that era. The proposal can be shown to be a consequence of multiple Spell-Out in the sense discussed in Uriagereka, forthcoming b, which owes much to ideas discussed in Lebeaux 1991. Epstein et al., forthcoming, also pushes matters in this direction.

71. The word "unified" here is crucial. As conceived in Chomsky 1955, levels of representation were taken to be sets of *concatenated* primitive symbols, and a procedure of admissibility for possible strings of symbols. All of that machinery is now given up in favor of the Merge/Move operations, which do not create strings, but unordered sets (later to be ordered through a linearization procedure). This raises the question of whether the various outputs of these operations should be unified into a single representation, or whether that unification follows from performative processes. Technically at least, then, the Other is right in raising the question, although a real answer would be too complex to discuss here.

72. Again, the Linguist speaks skeptically because multiple Spell-Out is not assumed within Minimalism; see Uriagereka, forthcoming, for development of the idea that only multiply spelled-out derivations should converge.

73. See Hale 1983 on this matter, from a different perspective, as well as Bošković and Takahashi, forthcoming, for a current, Minimalist version of Hale's idea.

Chapter 5

1. The issue discussed in this section arises in any theory in which the site for Case checking/assignment of/to X is different from X's initial attachment site. See Cheng and Demirdache 1994 for the first explicit discussion of these matters, which involves Basque, just as in the text below, and Murasugi 1992 for a different perspective within Minimalism.

2. Case mismatch, in a theory that assigns Case derivationally, was discussed as early as Davis 1984.

3. This sort of answer goes back at least to Chomsky's (1981) characterization of government. In the mid-1980s, numerous works explored the issue of "barriers" for movement (in the sense of Chomsky 1986a) and (relativized) minimality, most notably Aoun et al. 1987 and Rizzi 1990 (the latter is particularly well summarized in Cinque 1990, which also explores empirical consequences and presents recalcitrant data). Extensions of these notions to movement were only explored later, although they had already been proposed by Chomsky. Raposo and Uriagereka (1990), for example, explicitly raise these issues, modifying Chomsky's system of barriers in a way almost identical to the proposals discussed here. For an influential Minimalist view on these topics with various consequences, see Bobaljik and Jonas 1996.

4. This point was explicitly raised in Raposo and Uriagereka 1990, where "distance" was defined in terms of the very mechanics of the system.

5. This is a crucial point, and a source of much confusion when interpreting the proposals made in Chomsky 1995, chap. 3.

6. This intuitive idea is due to Howard Lasnik.

7. In the system presented by Chomsky in his 1995 MIT class lectures, a chain ((Jon, v), (Verb, Jon)) is in fact defined as ((Head (Jon), v), (Verb, Head (Jon))). That is, what counts for chain formation is not the movement of *Jon* (which is, after all, an ancillary operation for PF reasons), but the movement of the features in the head of *Jon*. Note, also, that the movement of any other element X to the minimal domain of v would create a chain whose top element could be expressed as (Head(X), v); likewise, if X moved from the minimal domain of Verb, the bottom element in the created chain would be (Head(X), v). Clearly, ((Head(Jon), v), (Verb, Head(Jon))) and ((Head(X), v), (Verb, Head(X))) look alike as chains, and it should not be surprising that their elements are "equidistant."

8. These ideas (presented in Chomsky 1995, 250ff.) can be confusing, since they turn some traditional intuitions on their head. The notion of distance being assumed here is practically equivalent to that proposed in Raposo and Uriagereka 1990, whereby a category is formally closest to its sister (the *base* of distance) and as far away from another category as there are fully specified categories "in between" (the *induction* of distance). This proposal is the first dynamic characterization of locality in the sorts of terms discussed here. A more remote precursor, although with rather different assumptions and consequences, is Kayne 1984, which introduces the notion "unambiguous path." Another interesting system, also with a different perspective, is presented in Manzini 1992.

9. Although both types of reasoning just mentioned achieve the same results on economy grounds, one is global ("Consider the total number of steps") and the other is local ("At a given stage in the derivation, did C_{HL} procrastinate?") Collins (forthcoming) stresses this point, as do Frampton and Gutmann (in preparation), which leads them to different revisions of the Minimalist model.

10. The sort of analysis that follows is classically presented in Chomsky 1981; it was central to the principles-and-parameters model and remains so in the Minimalist Program (see Lasnik and Uriagereka 1988, Webelhuth 1995). What is interesting about examples like (15a) is that the grammatical relations they exhibit do not directly match logical (or role) relations, thus arguing for displacement. Various recent Minimalist analyses (e.g., Bošković 1995, Ormazabal 1995, Martin 1996) partially change the assumptions that led to the traditional analysis, but they involve proposals and machinery that cannot be explored here.

11. The answer was in fact complete within the principles-and-parameters model (see Lasnik and Uriagereka 1988), although what it meant for sentences to have subjects (the Extended Projection Principle) was always an open issue. Clearly, what was an irreducible principle in the 1980s is still a mystery in the 1990s.

12. In chapter 3 of Chomsky 1995 (actually written in 1992), the economy strategy of Fewest Steps can indeed be (plausibly) seen to be competing with the economy strategy of Shortest Movement. However, as soon as Shortest Movement is recast as the MLC (in fact, a condition sine qua non for convergence; see Chomsky 1995, chap. 4), the issue of competition with Fewest Steps disappears. (However, see Nakamura 1997 for arguments that the MLC should be kept as an economy strategy.)

13. This point is richly illustrated by calculus problems (where finding effective ways of integrating equations is a bit of an art). Frampton and Gutmann (in preparation) take the fact that local algorithms are unclear within the present system as a potentially serious drawback and assert that clarifying the matter will lead to a drastic reduction of "optimality" issues. Chomsky (class lectures, MIT, fall 1995) has suggested various places where local algorithms would be reasonable, but the matter remains quite unclear. It must be stressed that Frampton and Gutmann take as a guiding intuition the nonobvious claim that C_{HL} computations approximate mental computations. This is either an attempt to bridge the gap between competence and performance, or an unsubstantiated claim about the form of competence (although neither more nor less substantiated than the claims being made here). These issues are raised as a note of caution regarding expectations about the nature of "reasonable mental computations."

14. It is worth clarifying that to determine that X involves more steps than Y, a counter is not necessary, just as one does not count water to determine that there is more of it in a lake than in a pond. A counter would be necessary only if the precise number of steps were at issue.

15. This is intended rather literally. For instance, Chris Cherniak notes in personal communication that what accounts for the (observed) global optimality of brain wirings is entirely unknown. Related formal issues are posed, for example, by the computations involved in protein folding or the replication of DNA.

16. See Nunes 1995a for the source of this idea.

17. The simplification of transformations began with Ross 1967. An intermediate step was taken in Lasnik and Kupin 1977, which provided the formal basis for Chomsky 1981 and subsequent work. The radical simplification that the Linguist mentions, the last step in the process, is discussed in Lasnik and Saito 1984, 1992. Now, under the Minimalist Program, transformations have to be formally redefined in terms of operations like Merge and the sort of phrasal objects that a "bare" phrase structure (of the sort discussed in chapter 3) demands. The precise formalization in question does not yet exist.

18. The fact that the levels of representation have a filtering effect does not mean, however, that they are filters, or well-formedness conditions of the sort proposed in Chomsky and Lasnik 1977. There, rich representational statements described, and prevented, impossible structures; for instance, $*\ldots$ *that* [t . . . rules out a configuration whereby a trace follows an overt *that*. No such filter is possible in the system presented here, which is purely constructive. The closest constructs this system has to filters in the old sense are statements about interpretable objects. Provided that PF and LF are subject to the condition of interpretability, all objects that reach these levels must obey certain formal properties, to make them compatible with the substantive properties that the levels encode. For example, a syllable of the form (Consonant, Consonant, Consonant) is uninterpretable at PF, and presumably a chain of the form ((John, X), (Mary, Y)) is uninterpretable at LF. If C_{HL} produces such objects, they will be ruled out as nonconvergent at PF or LF. A more subtle question is whether C_{HL} is even capable of producing such objects, and if not, whether the substantive character of PF and LF may reduce to emergent properties of the computation at some specific, crucial points. This issue is discussed at the end of chapter 6.

19. Chess analogies—favored by Chomsky, and by Wittgenstein and Saussure before him, and by the medieval grammarians before them—can be carried only so far, since (contrary to what, in particular, Wittgenstein and Saussure may have thought) the view of language presented here has more to do with the interaction of particles or the combination of genes than with the rules of a game. For example, here the Linguist assumes without argument that the mapping from the numeration to LF is complete. But why it should be so, or even whether the numeration is a necessary condition, is far from obvious.

20. The point goes back to Grice (1989). Not only philosophers, however, take interest in these matters. Reinhart (1995), for example, is explicitly concerned with the rules speakers use in choosing the elements that enter into what they want to say.

21. Ultimately, as will be apparent in chapter 6, the proposal that the Linguist is implicitly criticizing goes back to Generative Semantics. Various interesting proposals within Minimalism do address the issue of the set of candidate derivations (the "reference set") from the point of view of alternative representations (see, e.g., Bošković 1995 and Fox, forthcoming). Chomsky (1995, 292ff., 377) indirectly contemplates comparing alternative LFs and PFs (as opposed to alternative derivations).

22. The following discussion (adapted from Chomsky 1994a) is included largely for methodological reasons: it is a good exercise on how Minimalism tries to deduce properties, such as "The target of movement never projects," from more fundamental properties of the system. This is not to say, however, that this particular property should be deduced in the way articulated here. In fact, the significance of the uniformity condition on chains (here, the CCU) has already been weakened (compare Chomsky 1995, chap. 4, with the work from which it was adapted, Chomsky 1994a). Nunes (1995a) directly questions the condition's role.

23. This way of putting things relates the CCU to the important work of Emonds (1976), which posed many questions about the form of transformations and the structural conservation that they

involve. The matter was highly significant in Chomsky (1986a,b). The quest, however, is older, going back at least to Koster (1978), whose intuitions (particularly as expressed in Koster 1987) are central to the specifics of the CCU.

24. The impossibility in question is one of the chief insights behind the principles-and-parameters notion of the θ-Criterion and marks a major difference between that system and previous ones. For instance, Postal (1974) presented numerous transformations that involved raising to object, by hypothesis an impossibility in the principles-and-parameters approach (Chomsky 1981). Interestingly, the option is now open again, albeit with different implications (see sec. 4.6). As before, movement to a complement position is still unavailable, for reasons discussed in chapter 6. However, movement to an "object" position may involve movement to the checking domain of a matrix *v*.

25. This subtle point has been a central one in generative grammar since it (re)emerged in the 1950s. Are "words" items from the lexicon, or are they derivationally formed? Chomsky (1970), however, systematically separates derivational processes (which he takes to be lexical) from inflectional processes (which he takes to be syntactic). Work in the 1960s, starting with Lees 1960, explored the other possibility, which Generative Semantics pressed to the limit. Some current researchers have revamped many of the Generative Semantics tenets (see, e.g., Pesetsky 1995, Ormazabal 1995). Although (following the proposals in Hale and Keyser 1993) it would seem that Minimalism has also been forced into this position, it will be suggested in chapter 6 that this conclusion is not necessary. At this stage in the presentation, it is sufficient to separate a "word" (which can be generated derivationally) from an "item from the lexicon" (which initiates a projection via Merge). Technically, this means that characterizing "heads" as mere "items from the lexicon" (as in chapter 3) is not accurate.

26. This idea is not assumed in chapter 3 of Chomsky 1995, although it is in chapter 4, where Chomsky essentially assumes Lasnik's (1995a) notion "enlightened self-interest." In the earlier version of the Minimalist Program, only a category that gets something out of a move can in fact move; in Lasnik's version, a category can also move if the target of movement gets something as a result. See also Epstein 1993.

27. This offhand remark hides a nontrivial issue: whether LF should care about lexical relations. Chapters 3 and 4 of Chomsky 1995 take different views on this. The apparently simplest proposal is made in chapter 3: semantic dependencies of all sorts are determined only after LF. It is not easy to make this proposal work, however, as will be discussed in chapter 6. Note, also, that the "simplest" proposal makes a nontrivial assumption about what lies beyond LF.

28. This point is often confused, possibly in part because not everyone is happy with separating the domain of lexical conservation from the domain of syntactic conservation (which may itself be divided into a domain of chain conservation and a domain of sentential conservation). In any case, if the typological division is adequate, there is no strong reason that whatever algorithm functions at one level should also function at another level.

29. The assumptions behind this principle will become clearer in chapter 6. A simple fact noted by Bach (1968) gives credence to the claim that material inside words does not "talk to" material in the realm of syntax; this is the lack of scopal ambiguity in a phrase like *all parties' nonintervention in the debate* . . . (cf. *all parties did not intervene in the debate*). That is to say, the element *non* within the word *nonintervention* cannot take semantic scope outside the scope of *all*.

30. This is the sort of view advocated by Gould (1991), for instance.

31. This idea, suggested by John Frampton in personal communication to Noam Chomsky, makes the system of movement as described here (practically) formally identical to the system of government defined in Raposo and Uriagereka 1990. Here and in chapter 6, *Move* and *Attract* will be

viewed as simply two different ways of referring to the same process. This is only true in a purely derivational system. In a representational system, Move and Attract make different predictions with respect to locality, a matter that will not be pursued here (and see Hideki 1995 for related discussion).

32. Chomsky has often taken the skeptical view about such computational considerations. Nonetheless, he explicitly makes these particular comments in Chomsky 1995, 228. See also Fong 1991 for the computational properties of a pre-Minimalist grammar, Wu 1994 for issues concerning the acquisition of a Minimalist grammar, and Chomsky 1992 for a general perspective on language use.

33. The multiple-Spell-Out proposal in Uriagereka, forthcoming b, reduces the complexity even further, as Amy Weinberg notes in personal communication. In fact, Weinberg observes that most familiar parsing problems involving traditional garden paths and robust preferences can be directly related to the model in question.

34. This may be an instance of a general property of complex systems, which have various means of drastically reducing variability (for example, in terms of Haken's (1983) Slaving Principle).

35. Although the position that the system is derivational is not necessary, many important Minimalist works argue for it (Epstein 1992, forthcoming, Watanabe 1993, Collins 1994, Ferguson and Groat 1994, Jonas 1995, Hornstein 1995a, Kitahara 1994, Nunes 1995a, Pensalfini and Ura 1995, Takahashi 1995, Ura 1995, Zushi 1995, Bobaljik and Jonas 1996, Nakamura 1997, Groat, in preparation, Kawashima and Kitahara, forthcoming).

36. Various proposals cited before (see, e.g., Brody 1995, Cinque 1990, Koster 1987, Rizzi 1990) are relevant in this respect. It is very hard to decide whether this alternative is better than the derivational one. This book tilts toward the derivational approach for two reasons: first, because the book presents Chomsky's view, which has always been derivational; and second, because it is easier to relate the derivational view to current concerns about complexity, many of which involve questions of dynamics.

37. Again, these are old chestnuts, going back to Ross 1967 and beyond. See Lasnik and Uriagereka 1988 and Webelhuth 1995 for a summary of the classical issues, and Lasnik and Saito 1992 for an overview, from a derivational perspective, using the machinery of the 1980s.

38. This is a version of a proposal that goes back to Chomsky 1973.

39. On these issues, see Chomsky 1995, 289ff.; and for related discussion, see Lasnik and Saito 1992 and Cheng 1997.

40. See Lasnik and Saito 1992 for extensive discussion of superiority effects from a pre-Minimalist perspective, and Epstein 1993, O'Neil 1993, and Kitahara 1993 for a Minimalist view, of the sort taken here. Also see Hornstein 1995a for a different approach and recalcitrant data.

41. The issues discussed here are still tentative within Minimalism, fairly technical, and not crucial to the overall program. The reader who is interested in the general picture can (perhaps even should) skip this section and move on to section 5.6 or 5.7.

42. This is quite different from the traditional principles-and-parameters view presented by Huang (1982), for instance. Huang did note the connection between question words and indefinites that is mentioned here (observations of this sort go back to work by Edward Klima in the early 1960s, mentioned in Chomsky 1964). However, it was Kim (1990) who first explicitly proposed a non-movement analysis of Korean; soon after, related analyses were proposed by Watanabe (1992) for Japanese, and by Aoun and Li (1993a,b) and Tsai (1994) for Chinese. All of these proposals, however, involve different machineries; a fully unified analysis is yet to be assembled within Minimalism.

43. The Japanese and Chinese data are courtesy of Keiko Muromatsu and Jian-Xin Wu, respectively.

44. This may be an empirical reason to keep the analyses of Japanese and Chinese mentioned in note 42 separate. It is possible that the lack of discernible movement of a *wh*-element at PF in Chinese and Japanese has two different sources: no movement versus movement of a null operator (for general, pre-Minimalist discussion of null operators, see Browning 1987 and Ishii 1991). Although testable in principle, these two sorts of analysis are obviously hard to tease apart, and both are compatible with Minimalist assumptions.

45. It is not altogether clear what this "internal" checking of *whether* means. In general, categories move to check. Expletives do not, for reasons having to do with requirements on lexical selection, to be discussed in chapter 6. But *whether* seems neither to have moved nor to be an expletive.

46. Once again, these are classic examples studied in the principles-and-parameters framework. For background, see Chomsky 1986a and Webelhuth 1995.

47. Note that whereas *wh*-movement is always externally motivated, Case checking, although internally motivated, can also be externally motivated in some languages. Chomsky (class lectures, MIT, fall 1995) has pursued the possibility of entirely eliminating these distinctions, thus simplifying the system.

48. When a strong feature is involved, movement to check it must proceed immediately, as the phrase marker is being assembled. This means that the checking of strong features always involves movement of full categories; bare features move by themselves only in the covert component. In earlier work (1995), Chomsky assumed that strong feature checking is performed by way of a categorial feature of the moved element. More recently (class lectures, MIT, fall 1995), he has tried to push the system of strong feature checking outside of the core grammatical processes.

49. Chapter 6 will present several instances of movement whose target is not Tense, Comp, and so on, but a quasi-lexical element, such as a null (light) verb. Two possibilities exist here: either those elements are also functional in the intended sense, or they involve some other sort of movement, whose motivation is the formation of a complex word.

50. The Bulgarian data are courtesy of Tvetelina Ganeva.

51. See Lasnik and Saito 1984 for this view with respect to Polish data. Rudin (1988) suggests that Slavic languages divide into two groups: those (like Bulgarian) involving real multiple movement to Comp and those (like Czech) in which one element moves to the checking domain of Comp and the other does not move that far. The main sort of argument that linguists use to determine which type of movement has taken place is whether the moved *wh*-phrases enter into superiority effects of the sort illustrated in (29); if they do, they are taken to have both moved to Comp. Bošković (forthcoming) argues that Serbo-Croatian, one of the languages that Rudin would expect to behave like Czech and unlike Bulgarian, does show superiority effects when examined carefully; that is, they are found in cases of long-distance *wh*-movement (across more than one Comp domain), but apparently not in more local cases. As Jairo Nunes points out through personal communication, the fact that long-distance multiple *wh*-movement exists in Bulgarian immediately indicates that, if the suggestion that the moved element does not involve an interpretable *wh*-feature is correct, local movement to Comp cannot erase this feature; if it did, further movements would be impossible (alternatively, intermediate Comps would have to be skipped).

Multiple *wh*-movement is also found elsewhere: for instance, in Eastern Romance languages such as Romanian (Comorovski 1989; and see Dobrovie-Sorin 1992 for a more general perspective).

52. Chomsky (1995, chap. 4) seems to favor this view, but it involves a conception of parameters that differs radically from the one discussed in chapter 1. Note, incidentally, that regardless of how the question of when movement can proceed is resolved (why it takes place so early), the issue raised in note 51 remains (why the movement is even possible).

53. This puzzling fact was first analyzed in terms of multiple specifiers by Xu (1993). Xu relates various properties of Chinese Tense to multiple subjects, including the existence of the structure (39b) (ungrammatical in English) in Chinese (superraising), and he suggests a similar analysis for other East Asian languages without overt agreement. Ura (1996) pursues a similar line, which goes back, in some form, to Reinhart 1981. See also Abe 1993 and Déprez 1989 for much related discussion.

54. See Tsai 1994 regarding Chinese questions.

55. Until recently, Chomsky considered those reasons powerful. His current skepticism (see Chomsky 1995, chap. 4) is related to the intuition that at LF only features move, and furthermore only if they are uninterpretable. Fox (forthcoming) and Reinhart (1995) take a different view of these issues and argue that there may be actual phrasal movement in the covert component, roughly of the sort that various researchers (following Chomsky in the 1970s) postulated in the 1980s.

56. The spirit of this idea goes back to Aoun et al. 1987 and Rizzi 1990.

57. The devil is in the details, which are more important than is implied here. A question raised to Chomsky by Eduardo Raposo (in personal communication) vitiates the Linguist's analysis of (38b), particularly if the analysis of (41b) is as discussed below. Raposo notes that (38c) actually converges if at LF the Case features of *Alice* may raise to the matrix Tense. As noted in the text, (38c) is simpler than its alternative, (38a), and thus should be the grammatical form—contrary to fact. Raposo's question has led to a drastic rethinking of these (ultimately technical) matters (Chomsky, class lectures, MIT, fall 1995). For a solution to Raposo's problem, see Raposo and Uriagereka, forthcoming.

58. For the general issue of standard agreement, see Kayne 1989; and for a critical view, see Branigan 1992.

59. These matters and some consequences are further discussed in Uriagereka, forthcoming a.

60. These ideas go back to Kornfilt 1985 and Raposo 1987. See also Raposo and Uriagereka, forthcoming.

61. See Ingria 1981 for the Greek data; also see Xu 1993, where essentially the same point is raised about Chinese.

62. The data explored here are of longstanding interest within generative grammar, their importance vis-à-vis chains first having been stressed in Fiengo 1977. Many of the generalizations discussed below stem from Safir 1985 and especially Burzio 1986. See Raposo and Uriagereka 1990 for a theoretical characterization and references, as well as for interesting counterexamples that the version of Case and locality developed there can account for. See Moro 1996b for a different approach.

63. The literature reveals trickier examples:

(i) a.   there was a man arrested t
     b. ???there was arrested a man
     c.   there was arrested a man from Massachusetts
     d. ?there was a man from Massachusetts arrested

In the 1980s examples like (ib) were considered ungrammatical. When the theory started predicting that (ib) should be better than (ia) (since it involves no movement whatsoever), linguists brought examples like (ic) to bear on the discussion: when the associate is "heavy," it likes to stay in the position following an adjectival like *arrested*. This strongly suggests that the LCA/T is responsible for the movement in (ia). The element *man,* the bottom of a right branch, must move in order to be linearized. Plausibly, *a* is too weak to support the cliticization of *man,* and the whole complex *a+man* must move to a higher position, preceding *arrested.* The linearization problem would not arise in (ic), which is favored over (id) given economy considerations. If this suggestion is on the right track, even the simple *John saw a man* should involve some sort of movement, although perhaps the verb *saw* itself moves higher in the tree, unlike the adjectival *arrested;* this is in line with the proposal by Johnson (1991) that English involves some local verb movement, perhaps up to a *v* shell. See also Moro (1996a) for much related discussion.

64. Alternative accounts are nonetheless available. In particular, Frampton (forthcoming) proposes a system that permits comparing the relevant examples, expletives being introduced as a last resort. The matter is important because, prima facie, auxiliary *do* seems to be lexically introduced as a last resort (see Arnold 1995).

65. These example sentences are offered in an attempt to illustrate the prediction of the Linguist's theory with English. An example of the relevant sort was pointed out in Uriagereka 1988, chap. 4: *there arrived two knights on each other's horses.* However, this example can be explained away in current terms if the structure of the verb phrase has enough internal layers. The examples in the text are designed to avoid this problem, but the results are far from perfect. Then again, the question should be not so much whether the sentences individually are judged grammatical or ungrammatical as whether they display grammaticality *contrasts* in the direction the theory predicts. For much relevant discussion of these controversial matters, see Cardinaletti 1995 and Den Dikken 1995.

66. In (48) each anaphor is licensed, not by its antecedent, but by an implicit category (PRO) in the subject of the sentence where it appears, which is in turn licensed by the antecedent. That is:

(i)   [two boxers are in tonight's match [without PRO having identified themselves]]

The Other mentions (ii) as an alternative to (i):

(ii) there are two boxers in tonight's match because of each other's challenge (cf. two boxers are in tonight's match because of each other's challenge)

Chomsky (class lectures, MIT, fall 1995) notes that the fact that PRO is involved in examples like (i) is significant. He speculates (though without providing justification) that binding proper involves categories, whereas the referential control of the PRO element in (i) involves features. If so, (ii) should be worse than (i), since the latter involves no PRO. This, however, has immediate consequences for the examples that first motivated the discussion, which go back to Postal 1974 and are discussed within Minimalism in Lasnik and Saito 1991:

(iii) a. *the DA [proved [that the defendants were guilty] during each other's trials]
       b.   the DA [accused the defendants during each other's trials]
       c.   the DA [proved [the defendants to be guilty] during each other's trials]

(iiia) shows that *the defendants* cannot license the anaphor *each other* when neither it itself, nor some crucial feature emanating from it and moving to a Case-checking position at LF, commands the anaphor (*the defendants* checks subject Case inside the embedded clause). In contrast, (iiib) and (iiic) are good, even though *the defendants* does not command the anaphor; at LF the crucial feature that licenses the anaphor moves to an object Case-checking position that does command the anaphor (recall the discussion in section 4.6 about exceptional Case marking). If anaphoric licensing were categorial, these contrasts could not be explained.

67. The facts and the brief theoretical sketch that follow are taken from Hornstein, Rosen, and Uriagereka, forthcoming.

68. Sam Epstein stresses this fundamental point in personal communication. Regardless of how acceptable or unacceptable the sentences are, to the extent that speakers have any intuitions about them, these could not possibly have been taught. This is a notable reason why it is so important to explore arcane data like these.

69. This is still one of the deepest mysteries concerning expletive constructions. The view sketched here is arguably the simplest; it is adapted from Chomsky 1995, chap. 4, and has been developed in conversations with Norbert Hornstein and Howard Lasnik (also see Lasnik 1992 and following works, as well as Groat 1995). Frampton (forthcoming) reaches similar conclusions. The crucial point where Chomsky's proposals differ from the ones made here is that Chomsky claims the associate moves specifically to adjoin to the expletive, for unclear reasons having to do with a semantic dependency. He does not discuss why that dependency could not be established by mere proximity (in the same minimal domain).

70. See Lasnik 1993.

71. This important point is raised by Williams (1984).

72. However, see Martin 1996 for various complications. The discussion here is intended only to point out that the two sorts of structures involve different LFs, whatever the details of the difference turn out to be.

73. The literature on polarity items is too broad to reference here. See Laka 1990, Zanultini 1991, Uribe-Etxebarria 1994, Haegeman 1995, and Herburger 1996 for recent proposals and references. See also Nishioka 1994 and Pena 1994 for explicitly Minimalist analyses of negative polarity items and negation in general.

74. This fact was first systematically discussed in Milsark 1977 and has since been the subject of numerous analyses. For a good summary, see Reuland and ter Meulen 1987.

75. As Jairo Nunes points out through personal communication, an important contrast exists between *houbo a Xan* 'there was Xan' (with "personal" *a*) and **houbo o Xan* 'there was the Xan'. The latter should be the equivalent, at LF, of **the the Xan*. On Galician articles, see Uriagereka 1988.

76. A very important point to emphasize, since the distinction is not made in previous versions of Minimalism, or in other models.

77. The analysis suggested here was inspired by proposals made in Ormazabal, Uriagereka, and Uribe-Etxebarria (see Ormazabal 1995, chap. 2, for a summary), now adapted to the Principle of Chain Integrity; see Takahashi 1995 for a similar proposal. The original example paradigm was mentioned in passing in Ross 1967 and is fully analyzed in Huang 1982. For different analyses of Huang's effects, see Kitahara 1994 and Uriagereka, forthcoming b.

78. Chain opacity extends to adjuncts, about which the present account has nothing to say (but see Uriagereka, forthcoming b, for an account in terms of multiple Spell-Out that does predict adjunct opacity). The point of examining this paradigm is to show the kinds of explanations that Minimalism can provide for traditional analyses. Importantly, Minimalism cannot directly incorporate, say, Huang's (1982) Condition on Extraction Domain, since it would follow neither from economy/necessity considerations nor from substantive properties of the interfaces. In contrast, the present analysis is based on a substantive property of chains: their integrity.

79. This fact was discovered by Patxi Goenaga and is analyzed in Uriagereka 1994.

80. Facts of this sort are analyzed in McDaniel 1989. Example (76) is courtesy of Elena Herburger.

81. This line of argument goes back, in some form, to Torrego's (1984) analysis of verb movement in Spanish and to Chung and Georgopoulos's (1988) analysis of Chamorro *wh*-agreement. Various recent proposals share the essential tenet of involving some formal feature in an intermediate Comp.

82. See Thornton 1991.

83. This procedure may be able to account for the extended chains discussed by Nunes (1995a), involving, for instance, parasitic gap constructions.

Chapter 6

1. Regarding the matters that follow, see Marantz 1984.

2. Thanks to Li-Ling Chuang for this example.

3. On these matters, see Baker 1988.

4. This point was fully developed by Perlmutter (1983) and adapted to the principles-and-parameters system by Burzio (1986).

5. For the notion of "light verbs," see Grimshaw and Mester 1988.

6. For expository purposes, matters are a bit simplified in the conversation that follows. The verbs to be discussed probably involve an even more complex structure than is assumed here; see Hale and Keyser 1993 on these matters, which (within generative studies) go back at least to Gruber 1965.

7. The ideas that follow are rooted, in some form, in such early generative pieces as Katz and Fodor 1963. The assumptions in that work led to so-called Generative Semantics (see below), which in turn eventually created a "lexicalist" reaction. Relevant current lexicalist analyses are too numerous to mention. Two collections of studies within (roughly) Minimalist assumptions are Ausín and López 1996 and Den Dikken, forthcoming. Thanks to Sara Rosen for useful discussion of these topics.

8. Perhaps more accurately, *saddle* should incorporate not into the moved Prep, but into *v*. This issue is set aside here in order to keep (8) parallel with (7), and also because there is no direct way of testing the alternative possibilities. In any case, the structures involved in these kinds of examples are probably considerably more elaborate than assumed here for expository purposes; see Déchaine 1993 for relevant discussion.

9. The discussion that follows requires a firm grasp on the concept "chain" (in the Minimalist sense, which is not the traditional sense); see chapter 5. See also Chomsky 1995, 299, for the source of (9).

10. One reason for simplifying the structure in (6) through (8) is to permit a relatively simple definition of internal domain for chains. Were the structure in (6) more involved, it would be necessary to define internal domains in terms of notions that are more arcane than "sister to a projection."

11. This is the central intuition to keep in mind, however it is implemented technically.

12. Note that the Linguist departs here from the notion that all semantic relations are captured after LF (see Chomsky 1995, chap. 4).

13. However, Alan Munn (personal communication) points out that examples like *John washed* may be of precisely the unexpected sort. If he is correct, the concept of a chain receiving a single role may need to be rethought. Likewise, what allows an element like *John* to move to subject position (in what sense this is a "last resort" movement) will need to be studied.

14. Jairo Nunes asks (through personal communication) how it is possible for the expletive, which starts its derivational life in the specifier of Tense (hence, according to (9d), in the *internal* domain of this category), to check any features in the *checking* domain of Tense (according to (9c), the set-theoretic complement of the internal domain in the domain of Tense). A possible solution is for the expletive in the base-generated specifier to move to another specifier (since the number of specifiers is not limited), thereby entering the checking domain. The technical result is obtained because the newly formed chain is not a configurational object, hence is not a sister of (the projection of) Tense. This solution may, nonetheless, create further technical problems for some of the derivations outlined in Chomsky 1995, sec. 4.10, particularly because the movement in question is string vacuous. If the technical objections cannot be overcome, the definitions of internal and checking domain will need to be refined even further.

15. Examples like (14c), discussed by Chomsky (1995, 343) and attributed to Richard Kayne, are far from perfect in English, for unclear reasons. Interestingly, (i) is considerably worse than (14c):

(i) *I believe there a large group of people to have visited us (cf. I believe a large group of people to have visited us)

For extensive discussion of this matter, see Jonas 1995.

16. This is the intuition pursued by Hale and Keyser (1993), which goes back to Generative Semantics analyses. Norbert Hornstein observes (through personal communication) that giving this substantive character to the *v* shell may be unnecessary, from the point of view of the syntax. If *v* is needed only to justify the movement of the real verb in terms of the Last Resort Condition, this condition can be weakened to say that "something is gained" by a verb moving to create *v* (as in Chomsky 1995, chap. 3), namely, the ability to assign a role in a compositional fashion. This suggestion is plausible, but one should also not lose sight of the substantive nature of Hale and Keyser's claim about *v* elements; in effect, they are postulating a real category with semantic import in terms of Aspect, for instance. Whether those sorts of issues can also be represented in terms of a more traditional composition of verbs and arguments is a complex matter (see Higginbotham 1985, 1987, Parsons 1990, 1995).

17. Although adapted to present concerns, the argument that follows is directly taken from Generative Semantics (see Newmeyer 1980, 142).

18. The principle that follows is Baker's (1988) Head Movement Constraint, adapted for present purposes. Baker's constraint relies heavily on the notion "government," which is not viewed as significant in the Minimalist Program. There are obvious ways of adapting this notion to Minimalism (see, e.g., the definition in Raposo and Uriagereka 1990); the formulation in (20) instead hews to Minimalist guidelines by using the simplest devices that the system provides. Note also that this principle is closer in spirit to Travis's (1984) initial formulation of locality among heads than to Baker's version. See also Di Sciullo and Williams 1988, Brody 1993, Williams 1994, and Cormack and Smith 1994 for much related discussion.

19. As Jairo Nunes points out (through personal communication), verb-to-*v*, *v*-to-*CAUSE,* and *SMILE*-to-*v* incorporation must also be prevented. The issue is not trivial, given the analysis proposed earlier for (8). One possibility is that, in that case, structures of the form [[saddle Prep] *v*] result (alternatively, [[saddle *v*] Prep]), whereas in the present, impossible case, the result is [[[CAUSE *v*]

SMILE] Tense] (as opposed to [[[CAUSE SMILE] *v*] Tense], which has been successfully ruled out). This sequence recalls the kinds of difficulties that Pesetsky (1995) and Ormazabal (1995) discuss, concerning the realization of null morphemes. It is plausible that, on morphological grounds, null morphemes must be peripheral to the structure of words (Myers's generalization). If so, [[[CAUSE *v*] SMILE] Tense] should collapse.

20. Newmeyer (1980, 165) cites some interesting exceptions to this general tendency; for example, *cuckold* in *John cuckolded Bill,* which means 'have sex with the person who is the wife of'. Arguably, the relation between each of the roles of *cuckold* is across a relative clause. But as the evidence in section 6.5 shows, at least for Attract F such a relation is impossible.

21. Many of the ideas in this section are adapted from Chomsky's (1970) response to Generative Semantics. An illuminating discussion of these matters, with abundant references, can be found in Newmeyer 1980, chaps. 4 and 5.

22. For more on this argument, see Fodor 1970. On the face of it, the facts just discussed are correct (*kill* is not transparent in the sense that *cause to die* is), but there may be an explanation for this, depending on exactly how subevents of *DYING* (or some equivalent process) relate to subevents of *CAUSING* (see Schein 1993 for much of the relevant machinery that will be needed in deciding this matter), and on what constitutes a unified event comprising all these subparts. This is all to say that the lack of transparency observed for words might be an expected property of their semantics, even if their syntax were standard—as generative semanticists argued. For more on this, see Rooryck and Zaring 1996 and Pustejovsky 1995.

23. Defining a paradigm is not easy, at least on language-internal grounds (see Anderson 1992). On the other hand, the learning phenomenon to be discussed here clearly (in fact, crucially) happens within paradigms, whatever they are. Carstairs (1987) already raised the issue of economy within paradigms.

24. This important condition was recovered and applied to phonology by François Dell and Paul Kiparsky (as noted by Lasnik (1981)). Lasnik was the first to use the idea in syntactic analyses. The best-known form of the condition is due to Berwick (1985) and is usually referred to as the Subset Principle. Within current theories, which do not take language to be a set, this view is slightly misleading. Here the learning strategy will therefore be called the Sub*case* Principle instead; exactly how subcases are to be characterized will be left vague.

25. This analysis and the facts discussed are due to Horn (1989, 253ff.), although he does not express it in the learning terms discussed here.

26. This claim and others that immediately follow owe much to discussions with Dave Lebeaux.

27. The topic goes back to an important discussion of the early 1980s, which originated in the attempt to eliminate phrase structure rules from the grammar. These rules produce objects like (26) (see sec. 3.2), and the question was whether such objects can be deduced from the lexicosemantic properties of the head that projects. Grimshaw (1979) argued that some syntactic properties expressed through phrase structure rules (more accurately, subcategorization requirements on these rules) are reducible to lexical conditions. Pesetsky (1982) argued instead that all properties are ultimately reducible, in the process making claims about what is epistemologically prior for a child acquiring a language. Chomsky and Lasnik (1995) express some skepticism about Pesetsky's account, although they consider it desirable on general grounds. Examples like (26) have raised the stakes of the debate, in the sense that the *v* shell that projects is not an obviously substantive head. In the 1980s discussion, the issue was a head's properties, but the current version seems to invoke the properties of a complement that must incorporate into a light head. Below, a mechanism is

suggested to express these ideas, although no commitment is made about whether they have a syntactic base or a semantic implication. On these issues, and for references, see Rooryck and Zaring 1996.

28. This issue was central in the debate with Generative Semantics. One cannot help but invoke world knowledge when trying to fully characterize lexical representation; if grammatical relations are identical to lexical relations, the former are ultimately dependent on world knowledge. It should be emphasized that it is not this argument, but the premise behind it, that seems wrong in the Generative Semantics analysis (as shown, empirically, at least by the idiosyncrasy and lack of productivity of lexical relations). Given the revival of this school of thought, it is important to realize that, in the limit, Generative Semantics denies the existence of linguistics as understood in this book.

29. The question is where to capture them. This issue was central in Chomsky and Halle 1968 and is behind the notion of "meaning postulates." It is true (putting aside fuzziness) that, say, whatever is short is not tall, and vice versa. But since this truth does not follow from the syntax of expressions involving the words *tall* and *short,* a postulate is needed that relates the words (technically, the models corresponding to the words' meanings). As Dowty, Wall, and Peters (1981) admit, however, this is merely an observational device, not even a descriptive tool (let alone an explanatory one). Part of the job behind discovering the featural makeup of LF is to determine systematic correspondences in terms of an architecture that ultimately does not need meaning postulates (and relegates them to vaguer, purely world-knowledge relations, like those existing in "lexical fields"; for instance, *doctor* relates to *health, blood, scalpel, tumor,* and so on). The task is phenomenally difficult, but recent efforts in very specific domains (e.g., unaccusative verbs, as in Levin and Rappaport Havav (1995)) show that it is not a priori impossible, nor is it theoretically different from a similar task on the PF side of the grammar.

30. Bresnan (1993) shows that the matter may be considerably more complex.

31. In fact, as Gleitman (1990) shows, contextual cues are basically useless beyond standard referential instances involving nouns. On matters concerning the acquisition of the lexicon, directly relevant to the discussion that follows, see Gleitman and Landau 1994.

32. The Other's confusion is more than justified. "Deep structure" is about to be reintroduced, albeit in a residual fashion. In Uriagereka, forthcoming a,b, this is taken to be a potentially serious issue that should be resolved in a drastic manner: by denying the existence of levels of representation, in the specific sense of Chomsky 1955. Technically, the Linguist and the Other are already not using the notion, since it was defined for concatenation algebras that the Minimalist Program does not assume. The real question is whether the new system of Merge (or whatever structuring function linguists decide should exist at PF) yields unified objects by itself, or whether the unification takes place only in performance. If the latter, then there are no levels of PF and LF—merely PF and LF components. These of course have all the descriptive apparatus of levels, but they are not independent objects; quite literally, on this view, LF and PF are "scattered" all over a derivation, as in dynamically bifurcated models stemming from Jackendoff 1969. Once the model is simplified to this extreme, "deep structure" has a completely different meaning. Of course, there will be no level of "deep structure" if there are no levels. But the question remains: is there a component of "deep structure," in the sense of a place within the grammar that is responsible for an interface with the lexicon (just as the LF component interfaces with logicosemantics, and PF interfaces with phonetics)? The alternative is, ultimately, a representational view: the lexicon itself is directly mapped to PF and LF, in which case the derivational notation seems useless. So it seems that the underlying choice between derivations and representations comes to the fore again, and that there are potentially new ways for making the decision.

33. The facts basically force this proposal (in particular, (31b)). Previously this sort of idea was discussed in Uriagereka 1988; there the notion of an "event matrix," which resulted from incorporation, was introduced. The idea discussed here is formally equivalent to positing a component of "deep structure," in the sense of the previous note. (31a) is simply Lasnik's (1981) "Stranded Affix" Condition.

34. This traditional fact turns out to be crucial, as Hale and Keyser (1993) note. It is precisely these sorts of facts that make the proposal in the text different from Generative Semantics.

35. This term is invented for present purposes; it should not be confused with the similar term in Relational Grammar.

36. See Quine 1960, chap. 2.

37. On these matters, see Markman 1989.

38. The following passages are directly inspired by Stephen Crain's extension of (in his terms) the Subset Principle to semantic situations (see, e.g., Crain, Ni, and Conway 1994), and they owe much to helpful discussions with him. The basic intuition is that there should be no correlation between complex concepts and late learning (rather, there should be one between simple concepts and early learning), if complex concepts are "more specific," in the Paninian sense that is relevant for the Elsewhere Condition. Moreover, specificity is relevant only for a finite (very small) set of options arising in paradigmatic situations, and up to some definite limits (otherwise, children—or humans in general—could learn arbitrarily complex concepts). These matters are discussed in Uriagereka 1996.

39. This specific statement of Crain, Ni, and Conway's (1994) Semantic Subset Principle owes much to conversations with Howard Lasnik on the topic.

40. At issue in Crain, Ni, and Conway 1994 are simply propositions corresponding to sentences presented in circumstances that make them true for a speaker. What is relevant here, however, are parts of propositions, hence elements that may enter into the computation of truth, but are themselves more elementary than propositions. Thus, the term "correspond" is used here to indicate both the relation "sentence(proposition)-situation" and whatever relation holds between terms like *rabbit* or *fur* and situations such that the speaker can successfully use those terms to refer in those situations. In other words, the Subcase Principle is more general than Crain, Ni, and Conway's Semantic Subset Principle.

41. Note that it is situations that enter into subcase relations, and not the corresponding linguistic structures. This is one reason the noncommittal notion "subcase" is used here, instead of "subset."

42. This conjecture is due to Stephen Crain (personal communication).

43. For discussion and references on this topic, see Markman 1989, chap. 9.

44. On indirect negative data, see Lasnik 1990. On negative data in general, see Grimshaw and Pinker 1989.

45. The Linguist is referring, specifically, to Lakoff and Ross 1967 and Postal 1972. See also Newmeyer 1980, 138ff.

46. The existence of idioms is a rather strong argument for not accessing the lexicon directly, as representational systems would predict. To have a lexicon that lists idioms, with their full phrasal (variable) structure, is to have an object far more complex than a mere list of idiosyncrasies. So either the lexicon is not what it has traditionally been thought to be, or there must be some structure

that lies outside the lexicon and yet is neither PF nor LF (either as levels or as components). Chomsky's (1995, chap. 4) WI seems like a good candidate, but then obvious questions arise about what WI really is, and how it differs from LF or PF (or morphology).

47. There are two reasons for embarking on this question: first, to discuss the birth and death of morphemes, a source of linguistic variation and a significant issue for the Minimalist system; and second, to build up, within present assumptions, a plausible evolutionary scenario (so that later arguments against it will not be arguments against a straw-man case).

48. This idea, originally due to Bradley (1980), is pursued in Lebeaux 1988.

49. Although this tentative suggestion is new, it is directly influenced by proposals in Chomsky 1995, chap. 4, particularly those about introducing Agr (understood as a strong feature) in the numeration. The Other is proposing that all functional items be introduced in a similar fashion.

50. That they do not (at least in Genie's instance) is noted by Curtiss (1977). Bickerton (1990)—correctly—makes much of this.

51. Facts described in the functionalist literature are adapted to present concerns; see Hopper and Traugott 1993 for a useful introduction. Needless to say, the functionalist perspective is vastly different from the perspective taken here.

52. Even researchers who work in the generative tradition and who assume I-language (as opposed to E-language) often talk about cycles in this regard. This usage must be metaphorical; if language is actually I-language, it is unclear why a harmonic pattern should arise there. Of course, if E-languages existed, then they might display not only cycles, but in fact any other sort of simple structuring pattern, since an E-language is just a presumably well behaved set.

53. Regarding these matters (including whether "cycles" are reversible), see Hopper and Traugott 1993, chap. 5.

54. The ideas that follow are partly based on discussions with Mark Arnold, David Lightfoot, and Ian Roberts.

55. Why such movement should take place has been much debated (see Rizzi 1990 for references and a particular view). Chomsky (class lectures, MIT, fall 1995) has recast an idea that was popular in the 1960s: verb movement is a "postcyclic" rule (i.e., it takes place in the PF component). Even if this is true, nothing discussed so far is directly affected. What matters for present purposes is that the child acquiring the relevant language would encounter the verb in a domain that (even if it is not strictly speaking a checking domain) allows something that in the primary linguistic data consists of more than one lexical item to be analyzed as a single unit.

56. The Latin sentence (*quomodo . . . habeo*) is discussed in Hopper and Traugott 1993, 44. The Old Spanish sentence here is from *El Cid* (thirteenth century).

57. Here the Other echoes Givón (1971, 413). For perspectives on the role of morphology within a Minimalist system, see Bobaljik 1995 and McGinnes 1995; for related discussion, see Baker 1995.

58. The claims the Linguist presents here, although central to present-day functionalism, are taken from traditional historical linguistics.

59. This is, of course, the hardest transition—so much so, that it does not look like a transition at all, suggesting that this kind of talk may well be beside the point (see fig. 6.23).

60. As Norbert Hornstein points out (through personal communication).

61. The discussion that follows assumes that verb movement to Tense takes place in the syntax.

62. Again, this is a big assumption, particularly because talk about "strong features" is really metaphorical.

63. In Chomsky 1995, chap. 3, the grammatical world was considered to be ruled by what might be called "plain old greed": elements that move do so only out of self-interest. In contrast, in large part as a result of Lasnik's (1995a) concept of "enlightened self-interest," Chomsky (1996) now considers that Attract F involves "suicidal greed": the attracting feature (not the moving one) must get something out of the attraction, and "dies" (gets checked) in the process. The "greedy world" scenario that the Other proposes is a result neither of "plain old greed" nor of "suicidal greed" (i.e., it concerns neither the attracting nor the attracted feature). Rather, it is a consequence of learnability, and in particular the Elsewhere Condition.

64. The answer depends entirely on the nature of interpretable features. If interpretable features simply motivate the syntactic derivation, then it is unclear why the learner should expect anything else. The alternative perspective is more plausible: the syntax involves features, with no a priori nature, and whether they become interpretable is a metasyntactic matter. This possibility is assumed here without argument.

65. The reasoning here has two steps. First, the Elsewhere Condition predicts the "greedy world" scenario: when relating a verb to Tense, the learner assumes that the (verb, Tense) relation holds both for reasons having to do with Tense and for reasons having to do with the verb, whatever those are. Second, there is the question of whether whatever feature triggered the verb-to-Tense relation is interpretable or uninterpretable. The latter possibility entails further derivational machinery and hence involves more information. The derivational analysis of what must happen to the unit [verb [Tense]] then tells the child that the safest assumption to make (the more costly one) is that the verb moved to Tense as a consequence of some uninterpretable feature.

66. For this (nonobvious) claim, see Chomsky 1995, 359.

67. Alternatively, LF is not sensitive to movements other than those involving features.

68. This view is explicitly defended in Lasnik 1993 for different instances, and hinted at in Baker 1988 for very similar ones.

69. The ideas that follow are logically independent of what has been said so far—although what has been said is a prerequisite for them.

70. Perhaps this should be emphasized. Evolutionary scenarios tend to assume without argument that there is no alternative to language. Generally, this is true, but not in the case of words: one could imagine a system without them, of the sort roughly sketched by the Other in preceding passages but in which words do not emerge even at PF. The question being posed, then, is whether it would be more advantageous to have words, or not, and (more interestingly) whether a positive answer to this question could have anything to do with justifying the presence of certain kinds of structuring processes, like movement, and the sorts of features that drive them.

71. This speculation is essentially taken from Bickerton 1990.

72. What follows is an adapted version of ideas sketched by Jackendoff in his commentary on Pinker and Bloom 1990 (works cited without dates in later notes are commentaries that follow this piece).

73. Two points should be clarified. First, Jackendoff's question in figure 6.27 is the right question from a traditional evolutionary perspective, and a traditional evolutionary answer would try to do what the Other does below: link music up to language, the adaptive benefit coming from the latter. Second, the reason this is interesting is that music involves the formal mapping of hierarchy to

linearity—precisely the same issue that arises for linguistic phrase markers, if Kayne (1994) is right. Something as trivial as the absence of the LCA would render language useless. To the extent that the LCA and rhythm involve identical tasks, one might reduce to the other (which, incidentally, is very much in the spirit of Darwin's views on this particular matter; see Donald 1991, 34ff.). Then an answer to Jackendoff's question might be an answer to the question of language use. That of course would still leave open the question of how the apparatus that is necessary prior to the LCA came to be.

74. Although Jackendoff could not have made this connection (the LCA was proposed years after his commentary), he hints at it when asserting that

Lerdahl and Jackendoff (1983) and Jackendoff (1989) show that the representations supporting the rhythmic structure of music bear a strong resemblance to those for the rhythmic organization of speech, roughly the stress and timing subsystems of phonology . . . . [These seem to be] systems with the same basic morphology but differentiated for distinct functions . . . [so] it is possible to see these two rhythmic representations as alternative differentiations and specializations of a common ancestor. (p. 738)

In chapter 3 the LCA was taken to be part of the linguistic system for PF reasons; if the system used telepathy, the LCA would arguably be irrelevant. Telepathically communicated music would presumably also not require the usual linear presentation; but human music is not communicated telepathically. Therefore, just as linguistic structures involve the LCA, so too musical structures need to involve some such procedure (which of course is not to say that the musical procedure would have to invoke command).

   Curiously, Nespor, Guasti, and Christophe (1996) argue that rhythmic patterns are crucial to toddlers' determining word order specifications, prior to their fully accurately segmenting the speech signal. This might be construed as indirect evidence (in development) of the Other's speculation (in evolution).

75. The metaphor is taken from Newmeyer's commentary, although he is talking about something much more widely encompassing than the LCT—in effect (in derivational terms) a computational system like C_{HL} (see p. 746). Newmeyer takes the existence of this level or system to grant humans a selective advantage, since it allows us to link phonology and semantics. There are two difficulties with this claim, however. The first, concerning what is meant by "selective advantage" in this case, will be addressed in the text. The second concerns the implausibility of the kind of mutation that would yield C_{HL}—the whole of it. If C_{HL} is anything like what has been described in this book, then it seems to have as rich an internal structure as, say, a limb does. But the claim that a limb evolved all at once harks directly back to the puzzle that Mivart posed for Darwin—and is in fact Mivart's "solution." Of course, the Minimalist view would be that the sudden emergence of C_{HL} is plausible and hence has nothing to do with an adaptation. It is the adaptationist who must worry about the plausibility of a "wholesale" mutation. The discussion in the text hews to the level of linearization partly to give the adaptationist proposal its best chance: the Other conjectures that the specific mutation that separates humans from nonhumans is not the whole of C_{HL}, but the linearization mechanism.

76. This question is posed by Sperber (p. 757).

77. On these issues, noted by Sperber, see Sperber and Wilson 1986.

78. At no point does the Other cast doubt on the human ability to conceptualize, independently of the human capacity for language. His lack of skepticism on this point, by itself, is consistent with the notions of a "language of thought" sketched by Jackendoff (1983) and Fodor (1987). Of course, one must next wonder how that language of thought arose, particularly if it is not identical in humans and other creatures. Pinker and Bloom (1990) specifically suggest that "a propositional

language of thought is probably not a by-product of natural language but is itself a prior adaptation, perhaps found in other primates" (p. 771). Given this suggestion, it is not clear why Pinker and Bloom need to propose a theory of "Explicit Naming," to allow humans to name objects and kinds. If "propositional language of thought" means a language that makes use of propositions, it must presumably also make use of something like names (as entity-types, or perhaps generalized quantifiers). In any event, the presentation in the text will assume that the "Explicit Naming" theory was part of the system before the stage the Other is trying to justify, and that it may have been available even to Neanderthals and may be to present-day apes as well (Bickerton (1990) directly suggests this). Of course, if "Explicit Naming" were a specifically human trait, the adaptationist case would be considerably weakened, given the unlikelihood of the combined mutations giving rise to naming and to linearization, or a similar trait.

79. The example is taken from Markman 1989.

80. This is a central point made by both Bickerton (1990) and Pinker and Bloom (1990), for obvious reasons.

81. This is a classic outlook on the problem; see both Bickerton 1990 and Pinker and Bloom 1990.

82. The proposal outlined here is not all that different from the one sketched by Pinker and Bloom (1990, 771), even if theirs appears less realistic given present assumptions. In particular, Pinker and Bloom must also come to grips with thematic relations (p. 718), since in their global terms they must justify even the hierarchical status of these relations (e.g., that an argument of a verb is a theme, say, and not an agent). By contrast, since the Other assumes an intact conceptual structure, he need not justify any of the hierarchical structure.

83. Here the Other makes assumptions fundamentally different from those of Bickerton (1990) and Pinker and Bloom (1990). Bickerton explicitly takes functional items to be the major difference between protolanguage and human language. Pinker and Bloom subscribe to fundamental aspects of Gopnik's commentary, which claims that functional structure evolved independently, and after the system for "representing the world" was already in place (p. 735); and they express no qualms in speaking about "the function made defective by a single gene—inflectional features" (p. 768).

Clearly, if anything that has been said in this book about functional categories is remotely correct, they are or stem from the most basic dimensions behind the linguistic system. They are so basic that although they would be trivially learnable, lack of exposure to them during a critical period leads to their absence from the speech of otherwise healthy individuals capable of learning thousands of lexical items; so basic that they may underlie complex aspectual distinctions in verbs, and similar distinctions in nouns (allowing conceptualization over abstract, mass, countable, animate nouns, etc.); so basic that the entire system of linguistic parameters hinges on them. Thus, taking functional structure to be a late evolutionary development seems wrong; it is much more usefully viewed as fundamentally prior. Of course, the question remains of how functional categories became part of the system, to start with. For exaptationists, this is not a new or even interesting problem. Adaptationists, however, would have to either find them in other species (a possibility, but hard to prove if those species lack a medium to express these dimensional basics) or argue that they gave prehominids an adaptive edge. What that could be is not at all clear, if functional categories are perfectly useless, in and of themselves (their use being revealed only once a full-fledged linguistic system is in place).

84. The Other is not saying that movement would be impossible in the absence of linearization; rather, he is pointing out that it would be very difficult to make sense of, in communicative terms, for reasons illustrated in figure 6.28.

85. It should be stressed that the Other's suggestion (deriving complex words from syntactic structure) is diametrically opposed to the commonly assumed progression. For example, Catania asserts that "[a]t some point, the increasing complexity of the vocabulary and its contexts must reach the point at which some calls occur in combination, and their several forms could then evolve further into verbs, nouns, and various modifiers." Presumably, this "[sets] the stage for the development of grammars and propositional language" (p. 731). Other commentators also claim that syntax is an adaptation of allegedly more basic linguistic structures. Thus, Lieberman asserts that "the preadaptive basis for the brain mechanisms underlying human syntactic ability is motor control *for speech* [Lieberman's emphasis]," adding medical instances that "demonstrate . . . linked speech production and syntax deficits" and comparative data on chimpanzees "who lack the ability to produce the complex voluntary maneuvers that underlie speech and the similar rule governed operations that underlie complex syntax" (p. 742). Studdert-Kennedy claims that "phonology is logically prior to syntax (without phonology, no lexicon; without a lexicon, no syntax) and perhaps evolved earlier in our hominid ancestors, as it still develops earlier in the child" (p. 758). Pinker and Bloom themselves echo these ideas, asserting that "knowing how language works, we would not expect complete syntax to have evolved before articulation" (p. 768). None of these authors offer specifics about the supposed links between calls and sentences.

86. The idea is taken in part from Bickerton 1990, but the specific suggestions pursued by the Other (and adapted to present concerns in previous sections) are based on functionalist notions of the sort discussed in Hopper and Traugott 1993, concerning grammaticalization and expressive uses.

87. For the ideas that follow, see Jakobson 1960.

88. This is a point that Catania raises (p. 731).

89. See *Discover* magazine, January 1996. More amazing than the behavior itself is the fact that it has evolved over a few generations, and in a colony—not an individual.

90. Two recent, nonpatronizing articles on cannibalism are Fabris 1992 and Smith 1995. The matter of cannibalism goes beyond the moral issue: is it advantageous for members of a given species to eat each other? Fabris offers conjectures about social cohesion in this respect, but they are hard to evaluate. Smith makes interesting connections among elaborate sexual practices, religious sacrifices, gourmandise, and ritual cannibalism. These connections suggest that cannibalism is in fact a spandrel of a kind of brain/mind, as elaborate sex, religion, cuisine, and language probably are. At any rate, ritual cannibalism defies any obvious adaptationist explanation, and challenges basic assumptions about being human.

91. Thanks to David Lightfoot for emphasizing this point and for useful discussion on these matters—and see Lightfoot 1991, chap. 7.

92. Here the Linguist's argument addresses Lewontin's question: "At what stage, if any, in the evolution of the language faculty, [did] communication by speaking and listening [become] a significant evolutionary 'problem' so that natural selection may have started to operate on it[?]" (p. 741). The Other sketches a familiar "solution," summarized in Newmeyer's commentary: "[T]here arose many conflicts between the demand that [the language faculty] 'fit' well with semantics (which would favor a one-to-one match between concepts and syntactic categories) and the demand that it feed smoothly into the expressive plane (which would favor structures designed for ease of production and perception)" (p. 746).

93. It is important to stress that these are different (a point Jackendoff also makes (p. 738)).

94. This is the view that Pinker and Bloom (1990) take: "[T]he value of each component of universal grammar is its contribution to how the entire language faculty allows complex thoughts to be communicated, an ability that is useful across a huge range of environments" (p. 772).

95. Hornstein observes that "no capacities [are] favored across all environments" (p. 735).

96. These are two of Pinker and Bloom's (1990) answers to Lewontin's question mentioned in note 92 (pp. 724ff.). The third is discussed below.

97. With respect to the second trait, Premack's commentary is illuminating:

In principle, any species endowed with the expectation that giving will be reciprocated (and that receiving obliges giving) would have the functional equivalent of an agreement to share . . . . Innate expectations of this kind obviously do not depend on language . . . (p. 755)

98. Or as Pinker and Bloom (1990) put it, in terms that are more politically correct:

It should not take much imagination to appreciate the role of language in a cognitive arms race . . . . [P]rimitive humans lived in a world in which language was woven into the intrigues of politics, economics, technology, family, sex, and friendship and that played key roles in individual reproductive success. (p. 725)

In Lewontin's terms:

[T]he language faculty might have increased the survivorship and reproduction of its possessors relative to others, so it might have been selected. But was it? We know nothing about the political economy of our prelinguistic ancestors . . . . To give the linguistic faculty a selective advantage, one has to make our ancestors into competitive, individualistic Pleistocene bourgeoisie . . . . If we assert that the language faculty did, in fact, give a selective advantage, then we assert what we started out to demonstrate in the first place . . . . If it was selected, it was selected. (p. 741)

99. Frazier's commentary emphasizes this point:

To simply claim that the input is analyzed in accord with existing grammatical universals will not suffice . . . as an explanation for why easily conceived functionally effective alternatives don't penetrate what appears to be a fixed grammatical system . . . . The only reason this is not a devastating critique of [Pinker and Bloom's] position is the assumption that the various functions of language place *conflicting* [Frazier's emphasis] demands on the grammatical system . . . . [Pinker and Bloom's] case would be much stronger if they demonstrated that these demands conflict with each other, rather than merely assuming they do. (p. 732)

100. On this issue, see Frazier's commentary. (Other readings of the sentence become more salient if one imagines a scientist rapidly timing the movements of flies, or a kind of fly (the time fly) that is fond of arrows.)

101. This is not a rhetorical exaggeration on the part of the Linguist. As Piattelli-Palmarini observes (after extensively commenting on the implausibility of each of the concrete "useful" scenarios that Pinker and Bloom (1990) discuss):

[T]hey manage to render their approach utterly *indefeasible* [Piattelli-Palmarini's emphasis; also below] . . . : by taking refuge in nonoptimality, by conceding that not *every* trait of UG is the product of natural selection, and, on top of that, by retrenching themselves behind the accusation of "personal incredulity[,]" . . . they proceed to construct an a posteriori, ad hoc, irrefutable explanation. (p. 754)

Pinker and Bloom's substantive response (taking the fundamental question to be "How dysfunctional must a structure be before an adaptationist admits it cannot have been shaped by the proposed function?") is that

[T]he relevant criterion is . . . whether there are things [the grammar] can do *that cannot be done by a system designed at random* [Pinker and Bloom's emphasis], where by "random" we mean unrelated to the task that the system is to be used for. (p. 773)

The question then arises whether this use of the word "random" (God, for the creationist) applies to the sorts of design matters raised in this book, and if so, whether a grammar so designed can rank derivations and meet sound convergence requirements.

102. That is, linguists can rightfully be concerned both with language as a psychological phenomenon (the way it manifests itself) and with the very emergence of language as a complex system in the natural world. For the former problem, the question of feasibility is bounded by learnability considerations. For the latter problem, however, learnability is one of several considerations to be entertained. The matters of elegance discussed in this book (including the discrete infinity, nonredundancy, and economy of the system) are among these considerations.

103. See, for example, Mattingly and Studdert-Kennedy 1991.

104. Thanks to Linda Lombardi and Paul Smolensky for listening to these arcane ideas and suggesting improvements. Of course, the optimization algorithm suggested here recalls the architectural constraints of Optimality Theory.

105. Chomsky has at times speculated on this type of notion (see, e.g., 1965, 220–221 n.32). In class lectures (MIT, fall 1995) he suggested that the Extended Projection Principle (the fact that all sentences have a subject—in present terms, a boundary) should be reduced to "thematization" properties, given some theory of theme/rheme relations. On these matters, see Raposo and Uriagereka 1995 and Uriagereka 1996.

106. For examples of this sort, in a different framework, see Lasnik and Saito 1992.

107. The domains of structural conservation mentioned here are of course not the only ones. Similar issues surely arise in infralexical dimensions, and perhaps even in suprasentential dimensions. Chomsky (class lectures, MIT, fall 1995) is particularly interested in how sublexical features arrange themselves into matrices of various sorts, though he suggests no theory about why they do it one way or another. Theories about phonological structure are quite rich and interesting, but comparable theories about semantic structure have not yet been developed. However, the situation is no different in other sciences, where partial theories exist that account for only small fractions of the phenomena that occur within a given pocket of symmetry, as predicted by some kind of conservation law.

108. Kayne (class lectures, University of Maryland, fall 1993) has tried to meaningfully relate the number system to phrasal dimensions.

109. For a report of these facts, see Penrose 1994, 361.

110. See Edelman's (1992, 246ff.) summary of proposals by Lakoff and others.

111. Judging from Chomsky's class lectures (MIT, fall 1995), much needed simplification is possible.

112. Sam Epstein and his associates (Epstein et al., forthcoming) are pursuing the idea that "command" basically means "derivationally combine."

113. See, for example, Kitagawa 1995 and Nunes 1995a.

114. Works in progress on these matters are too numerous to be cited adequately.

115. See Reinhart 1995 and Uriagereka, forthcoming a.

116. See Thompson, in preparation, for instance.

Glossary

Terms used in definitions that are themselves defined in this glossary are *italicized*. The glossary was produced with statements adapted from the following sources: Akmajian et al. 1990, 1995, Chierchia 1995, Chomsky 1965, 1986b, 1993, 1995, Chomsky and Lasnik 1995, Cohen and Stewart 1994, Davidson 1967a, 1967b, Ducrot and Todorov 1979, Finegan and Besnier 1989, Fromkin and Rodman 1993, Gibson 1981, Gleason and Ratner 1993, Gleick 1987, Gould 1991, Grice 1989, Haegeman 1991, Hornstein 1990, 1995a, James and James 1992, Kahane 1986, Kuno 1987, Larson and Segal 1995, Lasnik and Uriagereka 1988, Lightfoot 1982, 1991, Lincoln and Boxshall 1987, O'Grady, Dobrovolsky, and Aronoff 1993, Partee, ter Meulen, and Wall 1990, Silk 1980, Steen 1971, Walker 1989.

accessible   Grammatical elements that the computational system can use in its operations are said to be accessible.

adaptation   Adjustment of the *phenotype* to environmental demands, through the process of natural *selection* acting on the *genotype*. A given change in a phenotype may lead to a property that is badly suited to a given environment, or maladaptive. When this happens, a species runs the risk of extinction, if its individuals systematically die before reproducing.

Adjoin   Roughly, a *syntactic object* A adjoins to a syntactic object B in order to make B larger, creating a new *segment* of B.

adjunct   Optional *phrase,* generally associated by *Adjoin* to a given *head,* such as the underlined phrases in the following sentences: *John will leave the room (at 5:00), Mary cleared the driveway (with a shovel), Phil quit the race (because he broke his foot).* (See *argument.*)

affix   A *bound morpheme* is an affix if it modifies the meaning and/or syntactic (sub)category of the lexical stem it attaches to. For example, *un-* and *-able* are affixes of *read* in *unreadable.*

agent   (See *thematic role.*)

agreement   a. The marking of a *word* (as with an *affix*) to indicate a particular grammatical relationship to another word in the sentence. For example, the markers of number and person on a verb. b. Technically, relation of *feature* matching among categories. (See *checking.*)

algorithm   Mechanical procedure for performing a given calculation or solving a problem in a series of steps.

alliteration   Local repetition of the same consonantal sounds. For example, "But day doth daily draw my sorrows longer" (Shakespeare, sonnet 28). Alliteration is sometimes based on abstract linguistic representations. (See *rhyme.*)

anaphoric   An element is anaphoric if it depends on another element for its interpretation. For example, in the sequence of sentences *I saw a beautiful sunset yesterday; it lasted for a half-hour,* the element *it* in the second sentence is anaphoric on *a beautiful sunset* in the first. (See *bind.*)

argument   An element that is required by a *predicate* as part of a *proposition*. For example, the verb *praised* has two arguments, a subject and a direct object, in *Mary praised the dog.* (See *thematic role, adjunct.*)

array   See *lexical array.*

articulatory-perceptual component   Component of the mind/brain that interfaces with *PF* and is responsible for motor articulation of speech sounds, their auditory perception, and so on. (See *performance systems.*)

aspect   Expression of the logical structure of an event, often classified as "outer" and "inner" aspect. Outer aspect is a grammatical process to encode the progress of an event (*John is making a movie*) or its completion (*John has made a movie*). Inner aspect makes reference to intrinsic lexical *features* of events; for example:

> **state** No definite culmination (*love*).
> **achievement** Definite culmination (*climb*).
> **process** Accumulation with no end result (*run*).
> **accomplishment** Accumulation with end result (*build*).

asymmetry   Property of a relation R according to which it is never the case that for any $<x, y>$ in R, the pair $<y, x>$ is also in R. For example, the relation *is older than* is asymmetric in the set of human beings.

Attract   A *head* H attracts a *feature* F if F is the closest feature that can enter into a *checking* relation with a *sublabel* of H.

attractor   A region of (phase) space that a typical dynamic system ends up converging on, as time passes.

auxiliary   A class of verbs that are *functional items,* traditionally called "helping" verbs, such as *will, can, would, could.*

bag   See *multiset.*

bifurcation   See *catastrophe.*

bijection   See *isomorphism.*

binary transformation or **operation**   A (*transformational*) operation that is applied to two distinct *syntactic objects,* neither of which is syntactically *dependent* on the other.

bind   A semantically binds B if A determines the *reference* of B, and A has *scope* over B. For example, in *Everyone likes his mother, everyone* can bind *his.*

bound morpheme   A *morpheme* that functions as part of a *word* but cannot stand alone as a word.

cancellation   A *derivation* is canceled if an illegitimate operation is executed during the computation, if the pair (*PF* object, *LF* object) is not formed, or if the *numeration* is not exhausted.

case   The morphological form of nouns and pronouns, and in some languages articles and adjectives, that indicates their grammatical relationship to other elements in the clause. For example, in the Latin first declension, singular:

> **nominative** *ros-a alb-a* (rose-<u>nom</u> white-<u>nom</u>) 'the white rose'
> **accusative** *ros-am alb-am* (rose-<u>acc</u> white-<u>acc</u>) 'the white rose'
> **genitive** *ros-ae alb-ae* (rose-<u>gen</u> white-<u>gen</u>) 'of the white rose'
> **dative** *ros-ae alb-ae* (rose-<u>dat</u> white-<u>dat</u>) 'to the white rose'
> **ablative** *ros-a alb-a* (rose-<u>abl</u> white-<u>abl</u>) 'with, from, in . . . the white rose'

Case (abstract)   The abstract form of *case* that every *argument* noun phrase requires.

catastrophe or **bifurcation**   Radical qualitative change in a dynamic system, brought about by a continuous and subtle change in a given control variable.

categorial features   The *features* [+/−Nominal], [+/−Verbal], and so on, that specify the class to which a given *lexical item* belongs.

chain   An ordered set of *phrase markers linked* through a relation such as *Move,* and represented at *LF.*

Chain Integrity (Principle of)   Only entire *chains* enter into computational operations.

Chain Uniformity (Condition on)   The formal/categorial informational content of *chain links* is identical.

chaos   a. The complicated, aperiodic *attracting* orbits of certain (usually low-dimensional) dynamic systems. b. Behavior that amplifies small uncertainties but is not utterly unpredictable.

checking   Relation between two formal *features* of the same type in a given structural configuration, called the checking configuration.

checking domain   Set of *syntactic objects* that are directly associated to a *functional head* H but are not included in the *internal domain* of H.

clausemates   Elements that are *arguments* of the main *predicate* within a given clause.

clicks   Characteristic consonants found in Bantu languages, in which the tongue makes a closure with the roof of the mouth at two points. The primary airflow is created by making the sealed-off space larger, creating a partial vacuum, usually by lowering the tongue and jaw. When the front stoppage is released, and air rushes into the partial vacuum, a click sound results.

clitic   A *word*-level element that is at least phonologically and morphologically dependent on another element, and possibly also syntactically dependent.

combinatorial system   A system that yields a structural form of a variety of unstructured elements. (See *input-output system*.)

command   Given *syntactic objects* O and O′ associated by *Merge* or *Move,* command is the relation between O, on the one hand, and O′ and the objects that constitute O′, on the other.

compatibility   The requirement that the pairing of *PF* and *LF* representations be based on the same lexical choices.

competence   System of unconscious linguistic knowledge that a native speaker of a given language has. (See *performance*.)

complement   *Sister* of the *head* of a *phrase.*

complete   A *level of linguistic representation* is complete if it has all the information it requires in order to be an interface with *performance systems*.

comprehensive   A *level of linguistic representation* is comprehensive if it is capable of representing any expression of language.

computational economy   A particular type of elegance within the computational system, for instance in the number of steps a given *derivation* may take. (See *representational economy*.)

constituent   See *phrase.*

constructive   See *strongly constructive.*

controlling gene   *Gene* that programs not the individual pieces of an organism, but the way those pieces are organized in development.

convergence   A *derivation* converges if it meets *Full Interpretation* at *PF* and *LF.*

copy intonation   Characteristic intonation occurring in a sentence that repeats a previous conjunct. For example: *Cassidy loved his girlfriend, and so did Sundance love his girlfriend.* In circumstances of this sort, the material with the copy intonation can be deleted, as in . . . *and so did Sundance.*

counterfactual   A conditional of the form *if p had happened, q would have too,* where supposition of *p* is contrary to the known fact that not *p*.

covert   General term used for processes or categories that do not have a *PF* reflex. (See *overt*.)

crashing   A *derivation* crashes if it fails to meet *Full Interpretation* at *PF* or *LF* (i.e., if it does not *converge*).

creole   A language that has developed from a *pidgin* to become established as a native language, within a community of speakers.

critical period or **age** The developmental period between infancy and puberty during which a child can acquire language with the fluency of a native speaker (for example, without an accent).

cyclicity Property of *derivations* according to which operations should apply to a given *syntactic object* O before the syntactic object O′, which contains O, is formed. (See *extension*.)

dative See *case*.

dedicated capacity Property of the language faculty according to which its vocabulary and computations are independent from other cognitive systems.

defeasing an implicature Canceling an *implicature* from one statement to another by means of a contextual clarification.

delete Operation that renders *features* invisible at the *levels of linguistic representation*.

dependency Informally, a type of local relation among *syntactic objects*. For example, *arguments* and *adjuncts* depend on a given *head*.

derivation Sequence of symbolic elements S mapped from a *lexical array* or *numeration* N, such that the last member of S is a pair (*PF* object, *LF* object) and N has been exhausted.

derivational horizon The continuations of a given *derivation* that are contemplated by the computational system for *optimality* purposes.

description A *phrase* that can pick out different individuals in different possible circumstances. For example, the phrase *the person who wrote Hamlet* picks out Shakespeare in the real world, but it would pick out Marlowe in a situation in which Marlowe had been the author in question. (See *rigid expression*.)

determiner A *functional item* that combines with noun phrases, specifying, for instance, whether the noun is definite or indefinite. For example, *the, a*.

direct negative data Explicit corrections from the speaker of a language L to someone trying to acquire L. (See *indirect negative data, positive data*.)

domination Relation between a *syntactic object* O formed by *Merge* or *Move* and the syntactic objects A and B that O is composed of, as well as the objects that A and B are composed of, and so on.

Elsewhere Condition Within a *paradigm* presenting two forms A and A′ competing for portions the same space, such that A′ covers a region of space S′ that is a subcase of the region of space S covered by A, the more specific or marked form A′ outranks the less specific, default, or elsewhere form A.

emergence Property of a system, whereby a process stabilizes into some global state that cannot be produced at a more local level. For example, a whirlpool emerges when a set of water molecules is in motion, under certain contextual restrictions, and is not a property of a single or even a few molecules of water. (See *phase transition*.)

epenthetic vowel Vowel, represented by [ə], which is inserted when an impermissible sound sequence is encountered. For example, if *film* is borrowed into a language that does not permit the sound sequence [lm], it is possible that it will be pronounced with an epenthetic vowel breaking the [lm] sequence.

epigenetic Processes that are not precisely prespecified in the *genes,* but nevertheless occur in early development if certain previous events have taken place, are said to be epigenetic.

Erase Operation that entirely eliminates *features* from a given syntactic structure.

exaptation Evolutionary process according to which a biological feature, now useful to an organism, did not arise as an *adaptation* for its present role, but was subsequently co-opted for its current function.

experiencer See *thematic role.*

extended projection See *shell.*

extension (condition) Property of *derivations* according to which a *syntactic object* formed by *Merge* or *Move* must formally contain the syntactic objects of which it is composed. Traditionally, derivations that obey the extension condition are said to be strictly *cyclic.*

E(xternal/xtensional)-language A complete collection of possible sentences of a language, understood independently of the properties of the mind. (See *I(nternal/ntensional)-language.*)

feasibility A linguistic theory is feasible if it is consistent with the kinds of data available to a child and with language acquisition in real time.

feature A primitive, minimal unit of linguistic organization.

Fewest Steps Global economy strategy that establishes the preference for a *derivation* with fewer steps over competing derivations with more steps.

force The semantic type of a clause. For example, questions have interrogative force, and statements have declarative force.

formal language A symbolic system that is subject to the fully explicit constraints of a formal *grammar.* Such an apparatus specifies, for a given initial set of elements (the vocabulary or alphabet), the complete set of strings of those elements that are the *(E-)language* defined by the grammar. Set theory, logic, and ordinary arithmetic can be seen as examples of formal languages.

Full Interpretation *LF* and *PF* objects satisfy Full Interpretation if all of their elements receive an interpretation at the relevant interface *level.*

functional item A member of a small yet fundamental class of usually short *words* that does not easily permit new items to be added and establishes syntactic relations. For example, articles, tense markers, complementizers.

gene   a. A hereditary factor or unit of heredity. b. A specific region of a chromosome that is capable of determining the development of a specific trait, composed wholly or in part of DNA; a gene is a self-duplicating particle involved in the transmission of genetic information from one generation to the next. (See *controlling gene, genotype, phenotype*.)

generative procedure   The *principles* and general properties that underlie the *grammars* of all human languages and are postulated as part of an individual's mental capacities.

genetic algorithm   Computer-based complex adaptive system suggested by analogy with biological evolution. A computer program generates alternative schemata for a given methodology (for instance, for learning) by randomly varying the instructions of two given "parent" programs that interact. The "child" program may or may not be more fit than the "parents," according to some metric of evaluation. Fit programs are selected and continue the process.

genotype   The hereditary or genetic constitution of an individual; the genetic material of a cell. (See *gene*.)

goal   See *thematic role*.

grammar   a. A part of a person's mental makeup that characterizes his or her mature linguistic capacity. b. In mathematics, a collection of procedures to generate a *formal language*.

grammatical formative   An element in a structure of *grammar* of any sort.

head   *Syntactic object* that does not *dominate* any other syntactic object and is in that sense a minimal *projection*. The head determines the *label* of a syntactic object.

homomorphism   A *mapping* from one set into another that preserves algebraic properties.

implication   a. Lexical relation obtaining between the meaning of a *word* W and the meaning of those words that W is a subcase of. For example, *dog* implies *animal* (every dog is an animal) and *to pat* implies *to touch* (every patting is a touching). b. See *presupposition*.

implicature   The relation between two conversational statements A and B, whereby if A is asserted, B is *implicated,* unless this is explicitly denied. For example, the question *Can you open the window?* conversationally implies that the speaker wants the listener to open the window, unless the speaker adds something like *I do not want you to open it—I was just wondering whether you could.*

inclusiveness   Condition on *derivations* according to which an *LF* object must be built from the *features* of the *lexical items* of the corresponding *lexical array*.

indirect negative data   In some delimited, *paradigmatic* instances, the absence of certain structures in the linguistic environment that children's current *grammar* predicts should occur, leading them to conclude that these structures are ill formed and to modify their grammar accordingly. (See *direct negative data, positive data*.)

inference   The process of concluding from evidence or premises.

infix An *affix* is infixed if it occurs within another *morpheme*.

inflectional morpheme a. A *morpheme* used to create variant forms of a *word* to mark the syntactic function of the word in its sentence. b. A morpheme that involves operations of the syntactic system.

informational encapsulation Property of a system whose functioning is not influenced by information from outside the system.

input-output system A system that is fed a representation and yields an adjusted form of this representation. (See *combinatorial system*.)

instrument See *thematic role*.

intentional-conceptual component System of the mind/brain that interfaces with *LF* and represents matters of beliefs, attitudes, decisions, and so on.

internal coherence Property of a theory whose parts are mutually dependent and noncontradictory. (See *natural interaction*.)

internal computational step Mapping from one *syntactic object* to another through the application of an operation of the computational system.

internal domain Roughly, the subset of the *minimal domain* that includes only those elements that are *complements* of a *head* H.

I(nternal/ntensional)-language A system of language represented in the mind/brain of a particular individual. (See *E(xternal/xtensional)-language*.)

interpretability See *interpretable representation, a*.

interpretable features *Features* that can be interpreted at the interface *levels* and thus survive the *derivation*. (See *uninterpretable features*.)

interpretable representation a. A representation at *PF* or *LF* that meets the *Full Interpretation*. b. Informally, a representation that meets Full Interpretation may achieve (or not) an appropriate interpretation in the *performance systems*. (See *usability*.)

intersection The intersection of two sets A and B is the set whose members are just the members of both A and B.

intrinsic features *Features* specified in the lexicon .

isomorphism or **bijection** A one-to-one correspondence between two sets such that an operation on all the elements of one set corresponds to an analogous operation on their images in the other set, and vice versa.

label Identification of the type to which *syntactic objects* belong.

language See *I(nternal/ntensional)-language* and *E(xternal/xtensional)-language*.

Last Resort Condition A *movement* operation must license a *checking* relation.

level (of linguistic representation)   a. A symbolic system that encodes certain systematic information about linguistic expressions. b. Technically, a system based on a set of minimal elements (for example, an alphabet), a compositional operation that forms combinations of these minimal elements of arbitrary finite size, various relations, and a designated class of objects (or sets of objects) of minimal elements informally referred to as "the level of . . ."

lexical array or **numeration**   Assortment of *lexical items* that feeds the computational system.

lexical integrity   a. Property of a *lexical item* that isolates its parts from a syntactic *derivation*. b. Technically, the various subcomponents of a lexical item X cannot interact with *syntactic objects* other than X without also involving the whole of X in the process.

lexical item   a. Informally, a *word*. b. Technically, a set of (at most) formal, semantic, and phonological sets of *features,* which is the basis of a *numeration*. c. A member of a large class of words to which new items can easily be added, such as nouns and verbs; in this sense, the notion is understood in opposition to that of *functional item*.

lexicon   a. Informally, a mental dictionary. b. Technically, the set of *lexical items* that linguistic operations manipulate, usually understood as a repository of idiosyncrasies.

liaison   A phonological process whereby *word*-final consonants are generally dropped, but are maintained when the following word begins with a vowel.

linear order   All elements that are linearly ordered can be put in a single row, one right after the other. (See *precedence*.)

link   Each member of a nontrivial (multimembered) *chain*.

location   See *thematic role*.

L(ogical) F(orm)   *Level of linguistic representation* that interfaces with the *intentional-conceptual systems* and where the well-formedness of syntactic *terms* resulting from a *derivation* is determined. (See *PF*.)

maladaptive   See *adaptation*.

mapping   A relation from set A to set B is called a mapping from A to B if for each element *x* in A there is exactly one element *y* in B such that *x* is in relation to *y*.

matrix   A set structured in a particular way.

maximal projection   A category α is a maximal projection if there is no category β that *dominates* α whose *label* is determined by (the *head* of) β.

meaning postulate   Statement that gives explicit constraints on relations between the meanings of *words*. For example, in order to capture the *implication* from the sentence *Kate pats Fido* to *Kate touches Fido,* the following meaning postulate may be proposed for the verb *pat: x pats y only if x touches y.*

Merge(r)   Syntactic association of two independent *syntactic objects* to form a new one.

metarule   A rule that states a condition on rules.

minimal domain   A set of *phrasal* objects, all of which are syntactic *dependents* of a given *head*.

Minimal Link Condition   An element X can raise to a target T only if there is no other element Y closer to T that can legitimately raise to T.

modification scope   Relation between an *adjunct* and whatever *phrase* it associates to. (See *scope*.)

monotonicity   Property of a function whereby it always changes in the same direction; a monotonic function *f* of a variable *x* increases if *x* is increasing, decreases if *x* is decreasing, or stays constant, but *f* never goes in the direction opposite to that of *x*'s growth.

morpheme   The minimal unit of *word* building in a language. Generally, a morpheme is any part of a word that cannot be broken down further into syntactically meaningful parts; however, a morpheme often represents more than one syntactically meaningful *feature*. For example, the English verbal morpheme *-s* encodes third person, singular, present tense.

mother   A *syntactic object* O is the mother of A and B if O was formed by *merging* A and B.

Move(ment)   Syntactic association of two *syntactic objects,* one of which *dominates* the other, to form a new syntactic object.

multiset   A set that is special in that it may contain a given member *x* more than once, each occurrence being distinctly labeled $(x, 1)$, $(x, 2)$, and so on. For obvious reasons, a multiset is also called a "bag."

mutual exclusivity hypothesis   Learning strategy whereby learners assume that each acquired notion is referred to by a unique *word*.

natural interaction   Any mutual action between systems. For example, the language system exhibits natural interactions with other parts of the mind/brain. (See *internal coherence*.)

notational variants   Different ways of encoding the same notion. For example, ~P and ¬P are notational variants, as are $R(x, y)$ and xRy.

numeration   See *lexical array*.

occurrence   Instance of a given item in a *derivation* that is differentiated in terms of its unique syntactic context.

open expression   A *proposition* with at least one *variable*.

optimality   Informally, the search for elegance in a *derivation* or a representation.

Optimality Theory   Proposal about the form of *input-output* linguistic systems (such as phonology or morphology), whereby different *soft constraints* are ranked in various ways, each corresponding to a possible *language*.

output condition Condition imposed on *derivations* at the interface *levels* of *PF* and *LF,* ultimately a reflex of systems that are external to the linguistic system proper.

overt General term used for processes or categories that have a *PF* reflex. (See *covert.*)

paradigm a. Collection of systematically related expressions. b. Technically, array of morphologically distinct yet related expressions whose linguistic values are mutually dependent. (See *Elsewhere Condition.*)

parameters (of variation) Aspects of *grammar* that may be characterized by one of a finite number of values along which languages are free to vary. (See *principles.*)

parataxis Parallel syntax; a loose *dependency* that is not the result of *Merge.*

patient See *thematic role.*

performance The actual use of language in concrete situations, on the basis of a variety of mental (internal) and circumstantial (external) considerations. The *articulatory-perceptual* and *conceptual-intentional* systems are considered performance systems; these systems enable the expressions of the language to be used for articulating, interpreting, referring, inquiring, reflecting, and other actions. (See *competence.*)

perspective The point of view of the speaker of a sentence. For example, a speaker may place himself or herself at a distance from the participants of an event and give an objective description (such as by using the pronoun *they*) or may instead describe the event from the point of view of one of the participants (such as by using the pronoun *we*).

phase transition Change in the global behavior of a system. (See *emergence.*)

phenotype The characteristics of an organism as determined by the interaction of its *genotype* with its environment, which contribute to determining its adaptive value.

P(honetic) F(orm) *Level of linguistic representation* that provides the interface between the *grammar* and acoustic/articulatory properties, including deletion, contraction, and phonological processes. (See *LF.*)

phrase or **constituent** A central *syntactic object* formed by any local combinations of *lexical items,* which behaves as a unit.

phrase marker a. Sets of syntactic *terms* arranged according to combinatorial laws of *transformations.* b. Informally, *syntactic objects* represented in graph (tree) notation.

pidgin Language variant formed when mutually unintelligible speakers develop a communicative system, characterized by some lexical aspects of each contributing language. Pidgins are less grammatically and lexically complex than natively spoken languages.

pivot *Chain* whose *trace* is lexically related to the traces of all other *sublabels* in a *word.*

positive data Actual language examples that children are exposed to and use to acquire language. (See *(in)direct negative data.*)

poverty of the stimulus   Property of children's linguistic environment, which does not provide an appropriate database for the mere induction of grammatical knowledge. (See *primary linguistic data*.)

precedence   A familiar type of *linear order* (for instance, the winner of a race precedes all other competitors).

predicate   a. An event or relationship, usually involving one or more participants (*arguments*). b. In predicate logic, a predicate combines with a number of terms to create an elementary statement. For example, the statement L(m, j) is composed of the predicate L and the terms m and j, and may be the translation of *Mary loves John*.

predicate calculus   A *formal language* consisting of statements composed of a *predicate* and a number of terms and possibly *quantifiers,* whose truth value is either 1 (true) or 0 (false), determined by the semantic values of its components.

predication   The part of a sentence that describes or applies to an entity, where the sentence is true just in case the entity satisfies the *predicate* or falls under the concept expressed by the predicate.

presupposition   If A presupposes or *implies* B, then the truth of A requires that the truth of B be taken for granted. For example, *John regrets getting his Ph.D. in linguistics* presupposes *John got his Ph.D. in linguistics.*

primary linguistic data   Those data to which children are exposed and which actually determine or trigger some aspect of their *grammars,* having some long-term effect. (See *poverty of the stimulus*.)

principles (of U(niversal) G(rammar))   Invariant properties of language that are innately specified. (See *parameters*.)

procrastination   Economy process according to which *overt movement* is *derivationally* more costly than *covert* movement.

productivity   Property of syntactic structure that it is regular and predictable.

projected   A structure that undergoes *projection* is said to be projected.

projection   The output of *Merge* and *Move*.

proposition   The meaning or *sense* common to all sentences that share the same *truth conditions.* For example, the meaning common to the sentences *Gus threw the ball* and *The ball was thrown by Gus.*

prototype   The most typical example of a given concept. For example, *robin* can be the prototype of the concept *bird*.

quantifier   An expression that picks out a number or amount of things of a certain sort. For example, in *No man agrees,* the expression *no man* describes how many men are agreers (none, in this instance). (See *scope, a.*)

range The possible results of a *mapping*. The range of a function $f(x)$ is the set of values that $f(x)$ can take, for all possible values of x.

ranking criteria Economy conditions are ranking criteria; they choose the most economical *derivation* from the candidates of a *reference set*.

recursivity a. Property of a structure that is self-similar, or the process that generates such a structure; for example, the structure of branching in a tree is typically recursive. b. Procedure for defining categories that are composed of more elementary categories of a simpler order of complexity; for example, natural numbers can be defined from more elementary numbers, starting with a basic one and applying a successor operation to it.

reference The ultimate semantic value of an *argument,* which indirectly connects it with reality in situations of language use.

reference set Set where *optimality* of *derivations* is computable, the optimal derivation being the one that *converges* and is the most economical among other convergent alternatives.

representational economy A particular type of elegance characterizing the possible forms in a *level of linguistic representation,* for example, in terms of the harmony of different *emergent* objects within this level. (See *computational economy.*)

rhyme A local vocalic sound repetition, generally appearing at the end of verses. Rhyme is sometimes based on abstract linguistic representations. (See *alliteration.*)

rigid condition A constraint whose violation results in ungrammaticality, regardless of alternative computations. (See *soft constraint.*)

rigid expression A *phrase* that picks out one particular individual, independent of circumstances of use. For example, in any possible circumstance, the phrase *William Shakespeare* picks out the same individual. (See *description.*)

role See *thematic role.*

root The top element in a *phrase marker;* the *syntactic object* that is not a *term* of any syntactic object other than itself.

scope a. A *quantificational* statement is divided into three semantic components: a quantification proper (*every, some, two,* etc.); a restriction on the individuals appearing in the quantification (*the men in the class, the women at the meeting,* etc.); and a scope stating what is true of these individuals (*he agrees, she knows him,* etc.). For example, the sentence *Every student jogs* has the following semantic form: quantification-*every*, restriction-*student*, scope-*jogs*. b. Informally, the scope of a modifier establishes its domain of *modification.*

segment A pair of segments make up a category in an *adjunction* structure.

selection (biological) The process by which some individuals come to contribute more offspring than others to form the next generation through intrinsic differences in survival and fertility. (See *variation.*)

selection (semantic) The semantic relation between a verb and its *arguments*. For example, the verb *like* semantically selects agent and patient *thematic roles,* as in *Mary liked the apple,* where *Mary* is the agent and *the apple* is the patient.

sense A mental concept associated both to a linguistic expression and to its *reference.*

shell (X′) or **extended projection** A sort of layer of syntactic structure that arises when a category XP is the *complement* of a category X whose *label* is identical to that of XP.

sign Abstract object that allows its user to regularly and uniformly convey some interpretation by means of a specific physical support.

singularity A region in space-time where the known laws of physics break down.

singulary transformation or **operation** A (*transformational*) operation that is applied to one *syntactic object.*

sister The *syntactic objects* A and B are sisters if and only if they *merge* to form a new syntactic object. (See *mother.*)

soft constraint A constraint is soft if the ungrammaticality of its violation depends on alternative computations. If representation A violates soft constraint C, that violation does not necessarily result in ungrammaticality, so long as alternative representations to A violate constraints that are ranked higher than C. (See *Optimality Theory, rigid condition.*)

source See *thematic role.*

spandrel Name given to the spaces remaining between arches supporting a dome; the term is used as a metaphor in biology for evolutionary by-products, whose function was not crucial in a process of *adaptation* but that are nevertheless present in the morphology or behavior of a species because they produce no harm. Musical abilities are a likely instance. (See *exaptation.*)

specifier *Sister* of an intermediate *projection.*

Spell-Out Rule that relates the *PF* and *LF levels* of representation, as the end of a partial computation that starts in the *numeration* and the beginning of two other partial computations, one branching off to PF and one branching off to LF.

strong feature A sort of "viral" *feature* that triggers *overt movement* or, in some instances, *merger,* so as to *check* the intruder feature out of the syntactic computation. An unchecked strong feature produces an immediate *derivational cancellation.*

(strongly) constructive Property of a system whose complex objects are obtained by relating simpler objects through the application of certain simple operations.

structural conservation Fundamental property of linguistic processes, whereby structures that are formed as computations unfold are not destroyed in the course of the *derivation.*

Subcase Principle Learning strategy, reflex of the *Elsewhere Condition,* whereby the learner is conservative in the acquisition process; in particular, in learning circumstances involving a condition C that is a subcase of a condition C′, the learner will acquire only C.

sublabel   A *feature* of a zero-level *projection* of a *head*.

suffix   *Affix* that follows the lexical stem of a *word*.

suppletive (form)   Form that replaces a basic lexical stem to express an inflectional contrast. For example, *went* expresses the past tense of *go*. (See *Elsewhere Condition*.)

symmetry breaking (of equilibrium states)   Disturbance in a spatially uniform state of equilibrium that may, often spontaneously, induce the *phase transition* of a system.

syntactic object   Basic building block of linguistic computations. All *lexical items* are syntactic objects, as are the results of *Merge, Move,* and *Adjoin*.

systematicity   Property of syntactic structure that its import is independent of the context it appears in.

target   a. A *transformation* T is said to target a *phrase marker* K to take place; thus, K is equivalent to the *structural description, b.* of T. b. A category that a movement transformation T creates is often referred to as the target of T.

tense marker   Grammatical element that expresses the location of events in time.

term   Building block of linguistic representations. All *syntactic objects* are terms, but terms can also be more complex than syntactic objects (e.g., *chains*).

thematic role   The semantic role that different participants play in events. For instance:

> **agent** Volitional initiator of action. (*Janice kissed Phil*).
> **patient** Object or individual undergoing action. (*The boy ate the food.*)
> **instrument** Object or individual that causes some event that in turn causes the event to take place. (*Phil opened the door with his key.*)
> **location** Place at which the event is situated. (*Mary stood in the middle of the room.*)
> **source** Object or individual from which something is moved by the event, or from which the event originates. (*The inheritance passed from Jill to Kate.*)
> **goal** Individual toward whom action is directed. (*Phyllis gave a book to John.*)
> **experiencer** Individual experiencing some event. (*Melissa felt sick.*)
> **theme** Object or individual moved by action. (*The doctor donated some money.*)

theme   See *thematic role*.

trace   Each *link* of a *chain* other than the first, which is also the one pronounced at *PF*; traces are not pronounced at PF, but they are interpreted at *LF*, and may also have PF reflexes.

transformation   A *mapping* from one *syntactic object* to another syntactic object by way of any application of the operations of the computational system (*Merge, Move, Adjoin, Delete, Erase*).

transitive   A relation R is transitive if and only if for all ordered pairs <*x, y*> and <*y, z*> in R, the pair <*x, y*> is also in R. For example, the relation *is an ancestor of* is transitive in the set of human beings.

transparency   Property of syntactic structure that it is visible for adverbial *modification*.

triggering information   An encounter with *primary linguistic data,* which determines some aspect of the *grammar* of children who are learning a language.

truth conditions   The truth conditions of a statement are the conditions the world must meet if the statement is to be true.

uniformity   a. Property of the *projection* of syntactic structures, which yields constant results given constant *syntactic objects.* b. Property of *chains,* which obey a specific condition on *chain uniformity.*

uninterpretable features   *Features* that cannot be interpreted at the interface *levels* and thus make a *derivation crash* unless *checked.* (See *interpretable features.*)

union   The union of two sets A and B is the set whose members are just the objects that are members of A or of B or of both.

U(niversal) G(rammar)   a. A theory of the *principles* and properties that underlie the *grammars* of all human languages. b. Informally, the initial state of the language faculty.

usability   The output of a *derivation* is usable if the *performance systems* can assign an interpretation to it. (See *interpretable representation, b.*)

variable   A symbol used to represent an unspecified member of some set; a placeholder or a blank for the name of some member of the set.

variation (biological)   The differences between the offspring of a single mating or reproduction.

variation (linguistic)   The differences between languages, explained in terms of the setting of linguistic *parameters.*

word   a. An element from the *lexicon.* b. Technically, a *syntactic object* that obeys the *Wording Law.*

Wording Law   A is a *word* if and only if A has phonological content and obeys the requirements on phonological words, and A is formed around a *pivot.*

Sources of Illustrations

Jacket
P. Prusinkiewicz and A. Lindenmayer. 1990. *The algorithmic beauty of plants,* 103. New York: Springer-Verlag.

Chapter 1

Onset
J. D. de Heem, *Still life with flowers.* Private collection of Mr. and Mrs. Hornstein, from Montreal; reproduced by permission of the owners.

Figure 1.4
Private collection; reproduced by permission of the artist.

Figure 1.8
C. Darwin. 1840. *The voyage of the Beagle.* Reprinted from H. Robin. 1992. *The scientific image,* 32. New York: W. H. Freeman.

Figure 1.9
K. Meinzer. 1994. *Thinking in complexity,* 67. New York: Springer-Verlag.

Figure 1.10
D'A. Thompson. 1917. *On growth and form,* 479. Cambridge: Cambridge University Press.

Figure 1.17
Courtesy of the Junta de Castilla y León.

Figure 1.18
G. A. Borelli. 1680–81. *De motu animalium.* Reprinted from L. C. Bruno. 1989. *The landmarks of science,* 84. New York: Facts on File.
R. Descartes. 1644. *Principia philosophiae.* Reprinted from L. C. Bruno. 1989. *The landmarks of science,* 265. New York: Facts on File.

Figure 1.20
G. Halder, P. Callaerts, and W. J. Gehring. 1995. Induction of ectopic eyes by targeted expression of the *eyeless* gene in *Drosophila. Science* 267, 1790. © 1995 American Association for the Advancement of Science.

Figure 1.22
R. Hooke. 1665. *Micrographia.* Reprinted from L. C. Bruno. 1989. *The landmarks of science,* 86. New York: Facts on File.
G. Cuvier. 1836–49. *Le règne animal.* Reprinted from L. C. Bruno. 1989. *The landmarks of science,* 95. New York: Facts on File.

Figure 1.23
B. M. French and S. P. Maran, eds. 1981. *A meeting with the universe,* 29. Washington, D.C.: National Aeronautics and Space Administration.
X. D. Shi, M. P. Brenner, and R. Nagel. 1994. A cascade of structure in a drop falling from a faucet. *Science* 265, cover photo. © 1994 American Association for the Advancement for Science.

Figure 1.25
Reproduced by permission of the photographer.
Courtesy of the Zoo de la Casa de Campo, Madrid, Spain.

Figure 1.26
K. Klivington. 1989. *The science of mind,* 106. Cambridge, Mass.: MIT Press.

Figure 1.28
R. A. Kerr. 1995. Timing evolution's early bursts. *Science* 267, 34. Reprinted by permission of A. H. Knoll.

Figure 1.29
I. Newton. 1672. *Philosophical transactions.* Reprinted from L. C. Bruno. 1989. *The landmarks of science,* 274. New York: Facts on File.

Chapter 2

Onset
M. López Castro, *The photographer and her child.* Private collection; reproduced by permission of the owner.

Figure 2.4
Courtesy of the Prints and Photographs Division, Library of Congress, Washington, D.C.

Figure 2.6
Courtesy of the Prints and Photographs Division, Library of Congress, Washington, D.C.

Figure 2.7
Based on an image by R. Lichtenstein; drawn as an homage to characters by J. Siegel and J. Schuster; reproduced by permission of the artist.

Figure 2.9
Reproduced by permission of the photographer.
R. Owen. 1838. *Memoir on the pearly nautilus.* London: Royal Society. Reprinted from H. Robin. 1992. *The scientific image,* 63. New York: W. H. Freeman.

Figure 2.10
M. Halle and G. N. Clements. 1983. *Problem book in phonology,* 29. Cambridge, Mass.: MIT Press.

Figure 2.11
M. Halle and G. N. Clements. 1983. *Problem book in phonology,* 31. Cambridge, Mass.: MIT Press.

Figure 2.16
M. Halle and G. N. Clements. 1983. *Problem book in phonology,* 33. Cambridge, Mass.: MIT Press.

Figure 2.22
Spectrograms and data analysis courtesy of J. C. Castillo and B. Moren.

Figure 2.24
Spectrograms and data analysis courtesy of J. C. Castillo and B. Moren.

Figure 2.28
D. Perlmutter. 1992. Sonority and syllable structure in American Sign Language. *Linguistic Inquiry* 23, 412, 414. Courtesy of the artist and D. Perlmutter.

Figure 2.31
Paradigms provided and analyzed by B. Moren.

Figure 2.35
P. Lieberman and E. S. Crelin. 1971. On the speech of Neanderthal man. *Linguistic Inquiry* 2, 208, 211.

Chapter 3

Onset
Chaos Group (University of Maryland at College Park), *Close-up of water flow.* Reproduced by permission of group coordinator C. Gebrogi.

Figure 3.1
Reproduced by permission of the artist.

Figure 3.8
Private collection; reproduced by permission of the owner.

Figure 3.12
Images executed by Advanced Visualization Lab, University of Maryland at College Park.

Figure 3.13
Images executed by Advanced Visualization Lab, University of Maryland at College Park.

Figure 3.14
Images executed by Advanced Visualization Lab, University of Maryland at College Park.

Figure 3.16
Images executed by Advanced Visualization Lab, University of Maryland at College Park.

Figure 3.25
Reproduced by permission of the artist.

Chapter 4

Onset
C. Álvarez, *Tree rings.* Reproduced by permission of the photographer.

Figure 4.3
Courtesy of J. C. Castillo and B. Moren.

Figure 4.4
S. Kuno. 1987. *Functional syntax,* 9. Chicago: University of Chicago Press.

Figure 4.5
S. Kuno. 1987. *Functional syntax,* 10. Chicago: University of Chicago Press.

Figure 4.6
S. Kuno. 1987. *Functional syntax,* 9, 10. Chicago: University of Chicago Press.

Figure 4.15
Reproduced by permission of the artist.

Figure 4.19
Courtesy of the Earth Science Museum at Brigham Young University, Utah.

Figure 4.23
Reproduced by permission of the artist.

Chapter 5

Onset
Image executed by Advanced Visualization Lab, University of Maryland at College Park.

Figure 5.9
L. Carroll. 1865. *Alice's adventures in Wonderland.* Reprinted from M. Gardner. 1960. *The annotated Alice,* 116. New York: New American Library. (In memory of Baron Hans Maximilian von Nichts)

Figure 5.33
Courtesy of the Prints and Photograph Division, Library of Congress, Washington, D.C.

Figure 5.38
Image executed by Advanced Visualization Lab, University of Maryland at College Park.

Figure 5.39
Image executed by Advanced Visualization Lab, University of Maryland at College Park.

Figure 5.40
Image executed by Advanced Visualization Lab, University of Maryland at College Park.

Chapter 6

Onset
Akerra, *Diptych.* Private collection. Reproduced by permission of the artist.

Figure 6.27
R. Jackendoff. 1994. *Patterns in the mind,* 166. New York: Basic Books.

Figure 6.30
Reproduced by permission of Dave and Pam Lebeaux, the artist's parents.

Epilogue

Coda
Adolphe Lalauze. From *M. de Cervantes, Don Quixote.* Courtesy of the Prints and Photographs Division, Library of Congress, Washington, D.C.

References

Abe, J. 1993. Binding and scrambling without A/A-bar distinction. Doctoral dissertation, University of Connecticut.

Abe, K.-I. 1994. Difference in adverbial behavior between English and French: A minimalist approach. In *Harvard working papers in linguistics* 4, edited by S. D. Epstein, H. Thráinsson, and S. Kuno. Department of Linguistics, Harvard University.

Abney, S. 1987. The English noun phrase in its sentential aspect. Doctoral dissertation, MIT.

Akmajian, A., R. A. Demers, A. K. Farmer, and R. M. Harnish. 1990, 1995. *Linguistics: An introduction to language and communication*. 3rd and 4th eds. Cambridge, Mass.: MIT Press.

Anderson, S. R. 1985. *Phonology in the twentieth century*. Chicago: University of Chicago Press.

Anderson, S. R. 1992. *A-morphous morphology*. Cambridge: Cambridge University Press.

Aoun, J., N. Hornstein, D. Lightfoot, and A. Weinberg. 1987. Two types of locality. *Linguistic Inquiry* 18, 537–577.

Aoun, J., and Y.-H. A. Li. 1993a. *Syntax of scope*. Cambridge, Mass.: MIT Press.

Aoun, J., and Y.-H. A. Li. 1993b. *Wh*-elements in situ: Syntax or LF? *Linguistic Inquiry* 24, 199–238.

Arbib, M. A., A. J. Kfoury, and R. N. Moll. 1981. *A basis for theoretical computer science*. New York: Springer-Verlag.

Arends, J., P. Muysken, and N. Smith. 1995. *Pidgins and creoles: An introduction*. Amsterdam: John Benjamins.

Arnold, M. 1995. Case, periphrastic *do,* and the loss of verb movement in English. Doctoral dissertation, University of Maryland.

Atlas, J. D. 1989. *Philosophy without ambiguity*. Oxford: Oxford University Press.

Auger, J. 1994. Pronominal clitics in Quebec colloquial French: A morphological analysis. Doctoral dissertation, University of Pennsylvania. (Distributed as IRCS Report 94–29.)

Ausín, A., and E. López, eds. 1996. *Cuadernos de lingüística IV*. Madrid: Instituto Universitario Ortega y Gasset.

Avise, J. C. 1994. *Molecular markers, natural history, and evolution*. New York: Chapman & Hall.

Bach, E. 1964. *An introduction to transformational grammars*. New York: Holt, Rinehart and Winston.

Bach, E. 1968. Nouns and noun phrases. In *Universals in linguistic theory,* edited by E. Bach and R. Harms. New York: Holt, Rinehart and Winston.

Bach, E., A. Kratzer, B. H. Partee, and E. Jelinek. 1995. *Quantification in natural languages*. Dordrecht: Kluwer.

Bach, E., R. T. Oehrle, and D. Wheeler, eds. 1988. *Categorial grammars and natural language structure*. Dordrecht: Reidel.

Baek, Y.-K. J. 1995. Anti-superiority and scrambling. In Pensalfini and Ura 1995.

Baker, M. 1988. *Incorporation: A theory of grammatical function changing.* Chicago: University of Chicago Press.

Baker, M. 1995. *The polysynthesis parameter.* Oxford: Oxford University Press.

Baker, M., K. Johnson, and I. Roberts. 1989. Passive arguments raised. *Linguistic Inquiry* 20, 219–251.

Baltin, M., and A. Kroch, eds. 1989. *Alternative conceptions of phrase structure.* Chicago: University of Chicago Press.

Barbosa, P. 1994. A new look at the null-subject parameter. Paper presented at Console III, University of Venice.

Barinaga, M. 1994. Watching the brain remake itself. *Science* 266, 1475–1476.

Barss, A. 1986. Chains and anaphoric dependence. Doctoral dissertation, MIT.

Barwise, J., and R. Cooper. 1981. Generalized quantifiers and natural language. *Linguistics and Philosophy* 4, 159–219.

Bate, M., and A. Martínez Arias, eds. 1993. *The development of Drosophila melanogaster.* Cold Spring Harbor, N.Y.: Cold Spring Harbor Laboratory Press.

Beghelli, F. 1993. A Minimalist approach to quantifier scope. In *NELS 23,* edited by A. J. Schafer. GLSA, University of Massachusetts, Amherst.

Behnke, H., F. Bachmann, K. Fladt, W. Süss, and H. Kunle. 1987. *Fundamentals of mathematics.* Cambridge, Mass: MIT Press.

Belazi, H. M., E. J. Rubin, and A. J. Toribio. 1994. Code switching and X-bar theory: The Functional Head Constraint. *Linguistic Inquiry* 25, 221–237.

Belletti, A. 1990. *Generalised verb movement: Aspects of verb syntax.* Turin: Rosenberg and Sellier.

Benincà, P., ed. 1989. *Dialect variation in the theory of grammar.* Dordrecht: Foris.

Benmamoun, E. 1992. Functional and inflectional morphology: Problems of projection, representation, and derivation. Doctoral dissertation, University of Southern California.

Benton, M. J. 1995. Diversification and extinction in the history of life. *Science* 268, 52–58.

Benveniste, E. 1971. *Problems in general linguistics.* Coral Gables, Fla.: University of Miami Press.

Berlin, B., and P. Kay. 1969. *Basic color terms.* Berkeley and Los Angeles: University of California Press.

Berwick, R. 1985. *The acquisition of syntactic knowledge.* Cambridge, Mass.: MIT Press.

Besten, H. den 1989. *Studies in West Germanic syntax.* Amsterdam: Rodopi.

Bickerton, D. 1984. The language bioprogram hypothesis. *Behavioral and Brain Sciences* 7, 173–221.

Bickerton, D. 1990. *Language and species.* Chicago: University of Chicago Press.

Bittner, M., and K. Hale. 1996. Ergativity: Toward a theory of a heterogeneous class. *Linguistic Inquiry* 27, 531–604.

Blevins, J. 1990. Syntactic complexity. Doctoral dissertation, University of Massachusetts, Amherst.

Bloom, P., ed. 1994. *Language acquisition: Core readings.* Cambridge, Mass.: MIT Press.

Bobaljik, J. D. 1995. Morphosyntax: The syntax of verbal inflection. Doctoral dissertation, MIT.

Bobaljik, J. D., and D. Jonas. 1996. Subject positions and the roles of TP. *Linguistic Inquiry* 27, 195–236.

Bobaljik, J. D., and C. Phillips, eds. 1993. *Papers on Case and agreement I.* MIT Working Papers in Linguistics 18. MITWPL, Department of Linguistics and Philosophy, MIT.

Boolos, G. 1984. To be is to be a value of a variable (or to be some values of some variables). *Journal of Philosophy* 71, 205–223.

Borer, H. 1984. *Parametric syntax.* Dordrecht: Foris.

Borsley, R., and I. Roberts, eds. Forthcoming. *Celtic and beyond.* Cambridge: Cambridge University Press.

Bošković, Ž. 1995. Principles of economy in nonfinite complementation. Doctoral dissertation, University of Connecticut.

Bošković, Ž. Forthcoming. Superiority effects with multiple *wh*-fronting in Serbo-Croatian. *Lingua.*

Bošković, Ž., and D. Takahashi. Forthcoming. Scrambling and last resort. To appear in *Linguistic Inquiry.*

Bouchard, D. 1984. *On the content of empty categories.* Dordrecht: Foris.

Bradley, D. 1980. Computational distinctions of vocabulary type. Doctoral dissertation, MIT.

Brandon, R. N., and N. Hornstein. 1986. From icons to symbols: Some speculations on the origin of language. *Biology and Philosophy* 1, 169–189.

Branigan, P. 1992. Subjects and complementizers. Doctoral dissertation, MIT.

Bresnan, J. 1972. Theory of complementation in English syntax. Doctoral dissertation, MIT.

Bresnan, J. 1993. Locative inversion and the architecture of Universal Grammar. *Language* 70, 72–131.

Brody, M. 1993. Theta-theory and arguments. *Linguistic Inquiry* 24, 1–24.

Brody, M. 1995. *Lexico-Logical Form.* Cambridge, Mass.: MIT Press.

Bromberger, S., and M. Halle. 1989. Why phonology is different. *Linguistic Inquiry* 20, 51–70.

Browning, M. A. 1987. Null operator constructions. Doctoral dissertation, MIT.

Bruno, L. 1987. *The tradition of science: Landmarks of Western science in the Library of Congress.* Washington, D.C.: Publications of the Library of Congress.

Bryson, J. W., S. F. Betz, H. S. Lu, D. J. Suich, H. X. Zhou, K. T. O'Neil, and W. F. DeGrado. 1995. Protein design: A hierarchic approach. *Science* 270, 935–941.

Buering, D., and K. Hartmann. Forthcoming. Doing the right thing: Extraposition as a movement rule. *The Linguistic Review.*

Burge, T. 1974. Demonstrative constructions, reference, and truth. *Journal of Philosophy* 71, 205–223.

Burnie, D. 1994. *Life.* Eyewitness Science series. London: Dorling Kindersley Ltd.

Burzio, L. 1986. *Italian syntax.* Dordrecht: Reidel.

Burzio, L. 1991. The morphological basis of anaphora. *Journal of Linguistics* 27, 81–105.

Burzio, L. 1995. The rise of Optimality Theory. *Glot International* 1, 6:3–7.

Burzio, L. 1996. Anatomy of a generalization. Ms., Johns Hopkins University.

Cairns, H. S. 1991. Not in the absence of experience. Commentary to Crain 1991.

Cann, R. 1993. Patterns of headedness. In *Heads in grammatical theory,* edited by G. Corbett, S. McGlashan, and N. Fraser. Cambridge: Cambridge University Press.

Cann, R., and M. E. Tait. 1994. Raising morphology. In *Functional categories, argument structure, and parametric variation,* edited by C. S. Rhys, D. Adger, and A. von Klopp. Edinburgh Working Papers in Cognitive Science 9. Centre for Cognitive Science, University of Edinburgh.

Cardinaletti, A. 1995. Agreement and control in expletive constructions. Ms., University of Venice.

Cardinaletti, A., and M. Starke. 1995. The typology of structural deficiency. In *Clitics in the languages of Europe,* edited by H. van Riemsdijk. The Hague: Mouton de Gruyter.

Carlson, G. N. 1977. Reference to kinds in English. Doctoral dissertation, University of Massachusetts, Amherst.

Carnie, A. 1995. Non-verbal predication and head movement. Doctoral dissertation, MIT.

Carroll, S. B., J. Gates, D. N. Keys, S. W. Paddock, G. E. F. Panganiban, J. E. Selegue, and J. A. Williams. 1994. Pattern formation and eyespot determination in butterfly wings. *Science* 265, 109–114.

Carstairs, A. 1987. *Allomorphy in inflexion.* London: Croom Helm.

Cazden, C. B. 1972. *Child language and education.* New York: Holt, Rinehart and Winston.

Chametzky, R. Forthcoming. *A theory of phrase markers and the extended base.* Buffalo, N.Y.: SUNY Press.

Changeux, J. 1981. Genetic determinism and epigenesis of the neuronal network: Is there a biological compromise between Chomsky and Piaget? In Piattelli-Palmarini 1981.

Chao, W. 1988. *On ellipsis.* New York: Garland.

Cheng, L. 1991. On the typology of *wh*-questions. Doctoral dissertation, MIT.

Cheng, L., and H. Demirdache. 1994. External arguments in Basque. In *Syntactic theory and Basque syntax,* edited by J. I. Hualde and J. Ortiz de Urbina. University of the Basque Country.

Cherniak, C. 1992. Local optimization of neuron arbors. *Biological Cybernetics* 66, 503–510.

Chierchia, G. 1995. *Dynamics of meaning.* Chicago: University of Chicago Press.

Chomsky, N. 1955. *The logical structure of linguistic theory.* Chicago: University of Chicago Press (1975).

Chomsky, N. 1957. *Syntactic structures.* The Hague: Mouton.

Chomsky, N. 1959a. On certain formal properties of grammars. *Information and Control* 2, 137–167.

Chomsky, N. 1959b. Review of B. F. Skinner, *Verbal behavior* (New York: Appleton-Century-Crofts, 1957). *Language* 35, 26–58.

Chomsky, N. 1964. *Current issues in linguistic theory.* The Hague: Mouton.

Chomsky, N. 1965. *Aspects of the theory of syntax.* Cambridge, Mass.: MIT Press.

Chomsky, N. 1968. *Language and mind.* New York: Harcourt, Brace & World.

Chomsky, N. 1970. Remarks on nominalization. In *Readings in English transformational grammar,* edited by R. Jacobs and P. Rosenbaum. Waltham, Mass.: Ginn.

Chomsky, N. 1972. *Studies on semantics in generative grammar.* The Hague: Mouton.

Chomsky, N. 1973. Conditions on transformations. In *A festschrift for Morris Halle,* edited by S. R. Anderson and P. Kiparsky. New York: Holt, Rinehart and Winston.

Chomsky, N. 1975. *Reflections on language.* New York: Pantheon.

Chomsky, N. 1977. On *wh*-movement. In *Formal syntax,* edited by P. Culicover, T. Wasow, and A. Akmajian. New York: Academic Press.

Chomsky, N. 1980. *Rules and representations.* New York: Columbia University Press.

Chomsky, N. 1981. *Lectures on government and binding.* Dordrecht: Foris.

Chomsky, N. 1982. *Some concepts and consequences of the theory of government and binding.* Cambridge, Mass.: MIT Press.

Chomsky, N. 1986a. *Barriers.* Cambridge, Mass.: MIT Press.

Chomsky, N. 1986b. *Knowledge of language.* New York: Praeger.

Chomsky, N. 1988. *Language and problems of knowledge: The Managua lectures.* Cambridge, Mass.: MIT Press.

Chomsky, N. 1990. On formalization and formal linguistics. *Natural Language & Linguistic Theory* 8, 143–147.

Chomsky, N. 1992. Explaining language use. *Philosophical Topics* 20, 205–231.

Chomsky, N. 1993. *Language and thought.* Wakefield, R.I.: Moyer Bell.

Chomsky, N. 1994a. Bare phrase structure. MIT Occasional Papers in Linguistics 5. MITWPL, Department of Linguistics and Philosophy, MIT. (Also published in *Government and Binding Theory and the Minimalist Program,* edited by G. Webelhuth. Oxford: Blackwell (1995).)

Chomsky, N. 1994b. Language and nature. *Mind* 104, 1–61.

Chomsky, N. 1995. *The Minimalist Program.* Cambridge, Mass.: MIT Press.

Chomsky, N. 1996. Some observations on economy in generative grammar. Ms., MIT.

Chomsky, N., and M. Halle. 1968. *The sound pattern of English.* New York: Harper and Row.

Chomsky, N., and H. Lasnik. 1977. Filters and control. *Linguistic Inquiry* 8, 425–504.

Chomsky, N., and H. Lasnik. 1995. The theory of principles and parameters. In Chomsky 1995.

Chomsky, N., and G. A. Miller. 1963. Finitary models of language users. In *Handbook of mathematical psychology,* edited by R. D. Luce, R. Bush, and E. Galanter. New York: Wiley.

Chung, S., and C. Georgopoulos. 1988. Agreement with gaps in Chamorro and Palauan. In *Agreement in natural language,* edited by M. Barlow and C. A. Ferguson. Chicago: University of Chicago Press.

Church, A. H. 1920. *On the interpretation of phenomena of phyllotaxis.* Botanical Memoirs, no. 3. Oxford: Oxford University Press.

Churchland, P. S., and T. J. Sejnowski. 1992. *The computational brain.* Cambridge, Mass.: MIT Press.

Cinque, G. 1990. *Types of Ā-dependencies.* Cambridge, Mass.: MIT Press.

Cinque, G. 1993. A null theory of phrase and compound stress. *Linguistic Inquiry* 24, 239–297.

Clark, R. 1995. Finitude, boundedness, and approximate learning of natural languages. Ms., University of Pennsylvania.

Clark, R., and I. Roberts. 1993. A computational model of language learnability and language change. *Linguistic Inquiry* 24, 299–345.

Cohen, J., and I. Stewart. 1994. *The collapse of chaos.* London: Penguin.

Cole, P., and L.-M. Sung. 1994. Head movement and long-distance reflexives. *Linguistic Inquiry* 25, 355–407.

Collins, C. 1993. Topics in Ewe syntax. Doctoral dissertation, MIT.

Collins, C. 1994. Economy of derivation and the Generalized Proper Binding Condition. *Linguistic Inquiry* 25, 45–61.

Collins, C. Forthcoming. *Local economy.* Cambridge, Mass.: MIT Press.

Comorovski, I. 1989. Discourse linking and the *Wh*-Island Constraint. In *Proceedings of NELS 19,* edited by J. Carter and R.-M. Déchaine. GLSA, University of Massachusetts, Amherst.

Comrie, B. 1981. *Language universals and linguistic typology: Syntax and morphology.* Chicago: University of Chicago Press.

Cormack, A., and N. Smith. 1994. Serial verbs. In *U.C.L. working papers in linguistics,* edited by J. Harris. Department of Phonetics and Linguistics, University College London.

Corver, N., and D. Delfitto. 1993. Feature asymmetry and the nature of pronoun movement. Talk presented at GLOW 16, University of Lund.

Covington, M. 1984. *Syntactic theory in the High Middle Ages.* Cambridge: Cambridge University Press.

Crain, S. 1991. Language acquisition in the absence of experience. *Brain and Behavioral Sciences* 14, 597–650.

Crain, S., and H. Hamburger. 1992. Semantics, knowledge, and NP modification. In *Formal grammar: Theory and implementation,* edited by R. Levine. Vancouver, B.C.: University of British Columbia Press.

Crain, S., and M. Nakayama. 1986. Structure dependence in grammar formation. *Language* 63, 522–543.

Crain, S., W. Ni, and L. Conway. 1994. Learning, parsing, and modularity. In *Perspectives on sentence processing,* edited by C. L. Clifton, L. Frazier, and K. Rayner. Hillsdale, N.J.: Lawrence Erlbaum.

Cronin, H. 1991. *The ant and the peacock.* Cambridge: Cambridge University Press.

Culotta, E. 1994. A boost for "adaptive" mutation. *Science* 265, 318–319.

Cunqueiro, A. 1981. *Ollar Galicia.* Barcelona: Destino.

Curtiss, S. 1977. Genie: A psycholinguistic study of a modern-day "wild child." New York: Academic Press.

Davidson, D. 1967a. The logical form of action sentences. In *The logic of decision and action,* edited by N. Rescher. Pittsburgh, Pa.: University of Pittsburgh Press.

Davidson, D. 1967b. Causal relations. *Journal of Philosophy* 64, 691–703.

Davis, L. 1984. Arguments and expletives. Doctoral dissertation, University of Connecticut.

Dawkins, R. 1987. *The blind watchmaker.* Harlow: Longmans.

Déchaine, R. M. 1993. Predicates across categories. Doctoral dissertation, University of Massachusetts, Amherst.

DeGraff, M., ed. Forthcoming. *Creolization, language change, and language acquisition.* Cambridge, Mass.: MIT Press.

Demirdache, H. 1991. Resumptive chains in restrictive relatives, appositives, and dislocation structures. Doctoral dissertation, MIT.

Déprez, V. 1989. On the typology of syntactic positions and the nature of chains: Move alpha to the specifier of functional projections. Doctoral dissertation, MIT.

Dikken, M. den 1995. Binding, expletives, and levels. *Linguistic Inquiry* 26, 347–354.

Dikken, M. den, ed. Forthcoming. *The syntax of possession and the verb "have."* Special *Lingua* volume, n. 655.

Di Sciullo, A. M., and E. Williams. 1988. *On the definition of word.* Cambridge, Mass.: MIT Press.

DiVincenzo, D. P. 1995. Quantum computation. *Science* 270, 255–261.

Dixon, R. M. W. 1972. *The Dyirbal language of North Queensland.* Cambridge: Cambridge University Press.

Dobbs, B. J. T. 1975. *The foundations of Newton's alchemy.* Cambridge: Cambridge University Press.

Dobrovie-Sorin, C. 1992. *The syntax of Romanian.* Dordrecht: Foris.

Doczi, G. 1994. *The power of limits: Proportional harmonies in nature, art, and architecture.* Boston: Shambhala.

Donald, M. 1991. *Origins of modern mind.* Cambridge, Mass.: Harvard University Press.

Douady, S., and Y. Couder. 1992. Phyllotaxis as a physical self-organized growth process. *Physical Review Letters* 68, 2098–2101.

Dowty, D., R. Wall, and S. Peters. 1981. *Introduction to Montague semantics.* Dordrecht: Reidel.

Duarte, I., and G. Matos. 1995. Romance clitics and the Minimalist Program. Ms., University of Lisbon.

Ducrot, O., and T. Todorov. 1979. *Encyclopedic dictionary of the sciences of language.* Baltimore, Md.: Johns Hopkins University Press.

Duffield, N. 1995. *Particles and projections in Irish syntax.* Dordrecht: Kluwer.

Edelman, G. 1987. *Neural Darwinism.* New York: Basic Books.

Edelman, G. 1992. *Bright air, brilliant fire.* New York: Basic Books.

Eimas, P. D., E. R. Siqueland, P. W. Jusczyk, and J. Vigorito. 1971. Speech perception in infants. *Science* 171, 303–306.

Eldredge, N. 1995. *Reinventing Darwin.* New York: Wiley.

Eldredge, N., and S. J. Gould. 1972. Punctuated equilibria: An alternative to phyletic gradualism. In *Models in paleobiology,* edited by T. J. M. Scopf. San Francisco: Freeman.

Emmeche, C. 1993. *The garden in the machine: The emerging science of artificial life.* Princeton, N.J.: Princeton University Press.

Emonds, J. 1976. *A transformational approach to syntax.* New York: Academic Press.

Epstein, S. D. 1991. *Traces and their antecedents.* Oxford: Oxford University Press.

Epstein, S. D. 1992. Derivational constraints on $\overline{\text{A}}$-chain formation. *Linguistic Inquiry* 23, 135–159.

Epstein, S. D. 1993. Superiority. In *Harvard working papers in linguistics* 3, edited by H. Thráinsson, S. D. Epstein, and S. Kuno. Department of Linguistics, Harvard University.

Epstein, S. D. Forthcoming. Unprincipled syntax and the derivation of syntactic relations. In *Working minimalism,* ed. M. A. Browning. Cambridge, Mass.: MIT Press.

Epstein, S. D., E. Groat, Y. Kitahara, and R. Kawashima, eds. Forthcoming. *Non-representational syntax: A derivational theory of syntactic relations.* New York: Oxford University Press.

Everett, D. L. 1995. *Why there are no clitics.* Summer Institute of Linguistics, University of Texas, Arlington.

Fabris, A. 1992. Portinari e os Tupinamba: A antropofagia recusada. *Ciencia Hoje,* December 1992, 82–89.

Falk, D. 1990. Brain evolution in *Homo:* The "radiator" theory. *Behavioral and Brain Sciences* 13, 333–381.

Ferguson, K. S. In preparation. A feature-relativized shortest move requirement. Doctoral dissertation, Harvard University.

Ferguson, K. S., and E. Groat. 1994. Defining "shortest move." Ms., Harvard University. (Presented at GLOW 17, Vienna.)

Fiengo, R. 1977. On trace theory. *Linguistic Inquiry* 8, 35–62.

Fiengo, R., C. -T. J. Huang, H. Lasnik, and T. Reinhart. 1988. The syntax of *wh*-in-situ. In *Proceedings of the Seventh West Coast Conference on Formal Linguistics,* edited by H. Borer. Stanford, Calif.: CSLI Publications. (Distributed by Cambridge University Press.)

Fiengo, R., and R. May. 1994. *Indices and identity.* Cambridge, Mass.: MIT Press.

Fillmore, C. 1964. The case for case. In *Universals in linguistic theory,* edited by E. Bach and R. Harms. New York: Holt, Rinehart and Winston.

Finegan, E., and N. Besnier. 1989. *Language: Its structure and use.* New York: Harcourt Brace Jovanovich.

Fodor, J. A. 1970. Three reasons for not deriving "kill" from "cause to die." *Linguistic Inquiry* 1, 429–438.

Fodor, J. A. 1975. *The language of thought.* New York: Crowell.

Fodor, J. A. 1983. *The modularity of mind.* Cambridge, Mass.: MIT Press.

Fodor, J. A. 1987. *Psychosemantics.* Cambridge, Mass.: MIT Press.

Fodor, J. D. 1995a. Comprehending sentence structure. In *Language: An invitation to cognitive science,* vol. 1, edited by L. Gleitman and M. Liberman. 2nd ed. Cambridge, Mass.: MIT Press.

Fodor, J. D. 1995b. Fewer but better triggers. Ms., City University of New York.

Fong, S. 1991. Computational properties of principle-based grammatical theories. Doctoral dissertation, MIT.

Fox, D. Forthcoming. Economy and scope. *Natural Language Semantics*.

Frampton, J. Forthcoming. Expletive insertion. In *The role of economy principles in linguistic theory*, edited by C. Wilder, H. M. Gärtner, and M. Bierwisch. Berlin: Akademie Verlag.

Frampton, J., and S. Gutmann. In preparation. Eliminating non-local computation in Minimalist syntax. Ms., Northeastern University.

Frank, R. 1992. Syntactic locality and Tree Adjoining Grammar: Grammatical, acquisition, and processing perspectives. Doctoral dissertation, University of Pennsylvania.

Frank, R., and A. Kroch. 1993. Generalized transformations and the theory of grammar. Ms., University of Delaware and University of Pennsylvania.

Freidin, R. 1986. Fundamental issues in the theory of binding. In *Studies in the acquisition of anaphora*, edited by B. Lust. Dordrecht: Reidel.

Freidin, R., ed. 1993. *Principles and parameters in comparative grammar*. Cambridge, Mass.: MIT Press.

Freidin, R., ed. 1995. *Current issues in comparative grammar*. Dordrecht: Kluwer.

Freidin, R., and L. Babby. 1984. On the interaction of lexical and syntactic properties: Case structure in Russian. In *Cornell working papers in linguistics* 6, edited by W. Harbert. Department of Modern Languages and Linguistics, Cornell University.

Fromkin, V., and R. Rodman. 1993. *An introduction to language*. New York: Harcourt Brace Jovanovich.

Fukui, N. 1986. A theory of category projection and its applications. Doctoral dissertation, MIT.

Fukui, N. 1993. Parameters and optionality. *Linguistic Inquiry* 22, 155–184.

Fukui, N. 1996. On the nature of economy in language. *Cognitive Studies* 3, 51–71.

Fukui, N., and M. Saito. 1995. Order in the theory of phrase structure and movement. Ms., University of California at Irvine and University of Connecticut.

Gabelentz, G. von der 1891. *Die Sprachwissenschaft: Ihre Aufgaben, Methoden, und bisherigen Ergebnisse*. Leipzig: Weigel.

Gamut, L. T. F. 1991. *Logic, language, and meaning*. Chicago: University of Chicago Press.

García-Bellido, A. 1994a. How organisms are put together. *European Review* 2, 15–21.

García-Bellido, A. 1994b. Towards a genetic grammar. Paper presented at the Real Academia de Ciencias Exactas, Físicas y Naturales.

Gazdar, G., E. Klein, G. Pullum, and I. Sag. 1985. *Generalized Phrase Structure Grammar*. Cambridge, Mass.: Harvard University Press.

Gelderen, E. van 1993. *The rise of functional categories*. Amsterdam: John Benjamins.

Gell-Mann, M. 1994. *The quark and the jaguar: Adventures in the simple and the complex*. New York: W. H. Freeman.

George, A. 1989. *Reflexions on Chomsky*. Oxford: Blackwell.

Gibbons, A. 1995. Languages' last stand. *Science* 267, 1272.

Gibson, C. 1981. *The Facts on File dictionary of mathematics.* New York: Facts on File, Inc.

Gibson, E., and K. Wexler. 1994. Triggers. *Linguistic Inquiry* 25, 407–455.

Gibson, K., and T. Ingold. 1993. *Tools, language, and cognition in human evolution.* Cambridge: Cambridge University Press.

Givnish, T. J. 1994. The golden bough. A review of Jean 1994. *Science* 266, 1590–1591.

Givón, T. 1971. Historical syntax and synchronic morphology: An archeologist's field trip. In *Papers from the Seventh Regional Meeting of the Chicago Linguistic Society,* edited by D. Adams et al. Chicago Linguistic Society, University of Chicago.

Gleason, J. B., and N. Bernstein Ratner. 1993. *Psycholinguistics.* New York: Harcourt Brace Jovanovich.

Gleick, J. 1987. *Chaos: Making a new science.* New York: Penguin.

Gleitman, L. 1990. The structural sources of verb meanings. *Language Acquisition* 1, 2–55.

Gleitman, L., and B. Landau, eds. 1994. *The acquisition of the lexicon.* Cambridge, Mass.: MIT Press.

Goldsmith, J. 1993. *The last phonological rule: Reflections on constraints and derivations.* Chicago: University of Chicago Press.

Goodall, G. 1984. Parallel structures in syntax. Doctoral dissertation, University of California, San Diego.

Goodwin, B. 1994. *How the leopard changed its spots.* London: Weidenfeld & Nicolson.

Gould, S. J. 1991. Exaptation: A crucial tool for evolutionary psychology. *Journal of Social Issues* 47, 43–65.

Gould, S. J., and R. C. Lewontin. 1979. The spandrels of San Marco and the Panglossian paradigm: A critique of the adaptationist programme. *Proceedings of the Royal Society of London* 205, 281–288.

Gould, S. J., and E. Vrba. 1982. Exaptation—a missing term in the science of form. *Paleobiology* 8, 4–15.

Grewendorf, G. 1989. *Ergativity in German.* Dordrecht: Foris.

Grice, J. P. 1989. *Studies in the way of words.* Cambridge, Mass.: Harvard University Press.

Grimshaw, J. 1979. Complement selection and the lexicon. *Linguistic Inquiry* 10, 279–326.

Grimshaw, J. 1990. *Argument structure.* Cambridge, Mass.: MIT Press.

Grimshaw, J. 1995. Economy and minimal violation. Ms., Rutgers University.

Grimshaw, J., and R. -A. Mester. 1988. Light verbs and theta-marking. *Linguistic Inquiry* 19, 205–232.

Grimshaw, J., and S. Pinker. 1989. Positive and negative evidence in language acquisition. *Behavioral and Brain Sciences* 12, 341–342.

Groat, E. 1995. English expletives: A Minimalist approach. *Linguistic Inquiry* 26, 354–365.

Groat, E. In preparation. Pure derivation: Against syntactic representations. Doctoral dissertation, Harvard University.

Gruber, J. S. 1965. Studies in lexical relations. Doctoral dissertation, MIT.

Haegeman, L. 1991. *Introduction to Government and Binding Theory.* Oxford: Blackwell.

Haegeman, L. 1995. The syntax of negation. Cambridge: Cambridge University Press.

Haken, H. 1983. Synergetics: An introduction. New York: Springer-Verlag.

Hale, K. 1983. Warlpiri and the grammar of non-configurational languages. *Natural Language & Linguistic Theory* 1, 5–47.

Hale, K., and S. J. Keyser. 1993. On argument structure and the lexical expression of syntactic relations. In *The view from Building 20: Essays in linguistics in honor of Sylvain Bromberger,* edited by K. Hale and S. J. Keyser. Cambridge, Mass.: MIT Press.

Hall, S. S. 1995. Protein images update natural history. *Science* 267, 620–624.

Halle, M., and G. N. Clements. 1983. *Problem book in phonology.* Cambridge, Mass.: MIT Press.

Halle, M., and A. Marantz. 1993. Distributed Morphology and the pieces of inflection. In *The view from Building 20: Essays in linguistics in honor of Sylvain Bromberger,* edited by K. Hale and S. J. Keyser. Cambridge, Mass.: MIT Press.

Harley, H., and C. Phillips, eds. 1994. *The morphology-syntax connection.* MIT Working Papers in Linguistics 22. MITWPL, Department of Linguistics and Philosophy, MIT.

Harris, R. A. 1993. *The linguistics wars.* Oxford: Oxford University Press.

Harris, Z. S. 1952. *Methods in structural linguistics.* Chicago: University of Chicago Press.

Hawking, S. 1993. *Black holes and baby universes.* New York: Bantam.

Herburger, E. 1996. In the event of focus. Doctoral dissertation, University of Southern California.

Heycock, C. 1991. Layers of predication: The non-lexical syntax of clauses. Doctoral dissertation, University of Pennsylvania.

Hideki, M. 1995. The syntax of particles. Doctoral dissertation, University of Connecticut.

Higginbotham, J. 1985. On semantics. *Linguistic Inquiry* 16, 547–593.

Higginbotham, J. 1987. Indefiniteness and predication. In Reuland and ter Meulen 1987.

Higginbotham, J. 1988. Contexts, models, and meanings. In *Mental representations: The interface between language and reality,* edited by R. Kempson. Cambridge: Cambridge University Press.

Higginbotham, J. 1996. GB Theory: An introduction. In *Handbook of logic and language,* edited by J. van Benthem and A. ter Meulen, 311–360. Amsterdam: Elsevier.

Hoffman, J. 1996. Syntactic and paratactic word order effects. Doctoral dissertation, University of Maryland.

Hofstadter, D. R. 1979. *Gödel, Escher, Bach.* New York: Vintage.

Holland, J. 1995. *Hidden order.* Reading, Mass.: Addison-Wesley.

Holm, J. A. 1988. *Pidgins and creoles.* New York: Cambridge University Press.

Hopper, P. J., and E. C. Traugott. 1993. *Grammaticalization.* Cambridge: Cambridge University Press.

Horgan, J. 1995. From complexity to perplexity. *Scientific American,* June 1995, 104–109.

Horn, L. 1989. *A natural history of negation.* Chicago: University of Chicago Press.

Hornstein, N. 1990. *As time goes by.* Cambridge, Mass.: MIT Press.

Hornstein, N. 1994. An argument for Minimalism: The case of antecedent-contained deletion. *Linguistic Inquiry* 25, 455–480.

Hornstein, N. 1995a. *Logical Form: From GB to Minimalism.* Oxford: Blackwell.

Hornstein, N. 1995b. Putting truth into Universal Grammar. *Linguistics and Philosophy* 18, 381–400.

Hornstein, N., S. Rosen, and J. Uriagereka. Forthcoming. Integral existentials. In *Proceedings of the Fourteenth West Coast Conference on Formal Linguistics,* edited by J. Camacho, L. Choueiri, and M. Watanabe. Stanford, Calif.: CSLI Publications. (Distributed by Cambridge University Press.)

Hornstein, N., and A. Weinberg. 1990. The necessity of LF. *The Linguistic Review* 7, 129–167.

Horvath, J. 1981. Aspects of Hungarian syntax and the theory of grammar. Doctoral dissertation, UCLA.

Horvath, J. 1995. Structural focus, structural Case, and the notion of feature-assignment. In Kiss 1995.

Huang, C.-T. J. 1982. Logical relations in Chinese and the theory of grammar. Doctoral dissertation, MIT.

Huang, C.-T. J. 1993. Reconstruction and the structure of VP: Some theoretical consequences. *Linguistic Inquiry* 24, 103–138.

Hyams, N. 1986. *Language acquisition and the theory of parameters.* Dordrecht: Reidel.

Ingria, R. 1981. Sentential complementation in Modern Greek. Doctoral dissertation, MIT.

Ishii, Y. 1991. Operators and empty categories in Japanese. Doctoral dissertation, University of Connecticut.

Jackendoff, R. 1969. Some rules of semantic interpretation for English. Doctoral dissertation, MIT.

Jackendoff, R. 1977. *X̄ syntax.* Cambridge, Mass.: MIT Press.

Jackendoff, R. 1983. *Semantics and cognition.* Cambridge, Mass.: MIT Press.

Jackendoff, R. 1989. A comparison of rhythmic structures in music and language. In *Rhythm and meter,* edited by P. Kiparsky and G. Youmans. New York: Academic Press.

Jackendoff, R. 1990. *Semantic structures.* Cambridge, Mass.: MIT Press.

Jackendoff, R. 1992. Parts and boundaries. In *Lexical and conceptual semantics,* edited by B. Levin and S. Pinker. Oxford: Blackwell.

Jackendoff, R. 1994. *Patterns in the mind.* New York: Basic Books.

Jacob, F. 1982. *The possible and the actual.* Seattle, Wash.: University of Washington Press.

Jacobson, M. 1991. *Developmental neurobiology.* New York: Plenum.

Jaeggli, O., and K. Safir, eds. 1989. *The null subject parameter.* Dordrecht: Kluwer.

Jakobson, R. 1960. Linguistics and poetics. In *Style in language,* edited by T. A. Sebeok. Cambridge, Mass.: MIT Press.

James, G., and R. James. 1992. *Mathematics dictionary.* New York: Van Nostrand Reinhold.

Jean, R. V. 1994. *Phyllotaxis: A systematic study in plant morphogenesis.* Cambridge: Cambridge University Press.

Johannessen, J. B. 1993. Coordination: A Minimalist approach. Doctoral dissertation, University of Oslo.

Johnson, K. 1991. Object positions. *Natural Language & Linguistic Theory* 9, 577–636.

Jonas, D. 1995. Clause structure and verb syntax in Scandinavian and English. Doctoral dissertation, Harvard University.

Jou, D., and J. E. Llebot. 1989. *Introducción a la termodinámica de procesos biológicos.* Barcelona: Labor.

Kaan, E. 1992. A Minimalist approach to extraposition. Master's thesis, University of Groningen.

Kahane, H. 1986. *Logic and philosophy.* Belmont, Calif.: Wadsworth.

Kaplan, D. 1975. Dthat. In *Pragmatics,* edited by P. Cole. New York: Academic Press.

Katz, J. J. 1972. *Semantic theory.* New York: Harper and Row.

Katz, J. J. 1981. *Language and other abstract objects.* Totowa, N.J.: Rowman and Littlefield.

Katz, J. J., and J. A. Fodor. 1963. The structure of a semantic theory. *Language* 39, 170–210.

Kauffman, S. 1991. Antichaos and adaptation. *Scientific American,* August 1991, 78–84.

Kauffman, S. 1992. *Self-organization and selection in evolution.* Oxford: Oxford University Press.

Kauffman, S. 1995. *At home in the universe: The search for laws of self-organization and complexity.* New York: Oxford University Press.

Kawashima, R. 1994. The structure of noun phrases and the interpretation of quantificational NPs in Japanese. Doctoral dissertation, Cornell University.

Kawashima, R., and H. Kitahara. Forthcoming. Strict cyclicity, linear ordering, and derivational c-command. In *Proceedings of the Fourteenth West Coast Conference on Formal Linguistics,* edited by J. Camacho, L. Choueiri, and M. Watanabe. Stanford, Calif.: CSLI Publications. (Distributed by Cambridge University Press.)

Kayne, R. 1984. *Connectedness and binary branching.* Dordrecht: Foris.

Kayne, R. 1989. Facets of past participle agreement in Romance. In Beninca 1989.

Kayne, R. 1991. Romance clitics, verb movement, and PRO. *Linguistic Inquiry* 22, 647–686.

Kayne, R. 1993. Toward a modular theory of auxiliary selection. *Studia Linguistica* 47, 3–31.

Kayne, R. 1994. *The antisymmetry of syntax.* Cambridge, Mass.: MIT Press.

Kelly, D. 1995. *Automata and formal languages.* Englewood Cliffs, N.J.: Prentice-Hall.

Kelso, S. 1995. *Dynamic patterns: The self-organization of brain and behavior.* Cambridge, Mass.: MIT Press.

Kim, S. W. 1990. Scope and multiple quantification. Doctoral dissertation, Brandeis University.

Kingsolver, J., and M. Koehl. 1985. Aerodynamics, thermoregulation, and the evolution of insect wings: Differential scaling and evolutionary change. *Evolution* 39, 488–504.

Kiparsky, P. 1970. Metrics and morphophonemics in the Kalevala. In *Linguistics and literary style,* edited by D. Freeman. New York: Holt, Rinehart and Winston.

Kiss, K., ed. 1995. *Discourse configurational languages*. Oxford: Oxford University Press.

Kitagawa, Y. 1987. Subjects in Japanese and English. Doctoral dissertation, University of Massachusetts, Amherst.

Kitagawa, Y. 1995. An optimalist approach to binding and coreference. Ms., Indiana University.

Kitahara, H. 1992. Checking theory and scope interpretation without quantifier raising. In *Harvard working papers in linguistics* 1, edited by S. Kuno and H. Thráinsson. Department of Linguistics, Harvard University.

Kitahara, H. 1993. Deducing superiority effects from the Shortest Chain Requirement. In *Harvard working papers in linguistics* 3, edited by H. Thráinsson, S. D. Epstein, and S. Kuno. Department of Linguistics, Harvard University.

Kitahara, H. 1994. Target alpha: A unified theory of movement and structure-building. Doctoral dissertation, Harvard University.

Kitahara, H. 1995. Target alpha: Deducing strict cyclicity from derivational economy. *Linguistic Inquiry* 26, 47–77.

Klima, E. 1964. Negation in English. In *The structure of language,* edited by J. A. Fodor and J. J. Katz. Englewood Cliffs, N.J.: Prentice-Hall.

Klima, E., and U. Bellugi. 1979. *The signs of language*. Cambridge, Mass.: Harvard University Press.

Klivington, K. 1989. *The science of mind*. Cambridge, Mass.: MIT Press.

Koizumi, M. 1995. Phrase structure in Minimalist syntax. Doctoral dissertation, MIT.

Kondo, S., and R. Asai. 1995. A reaction–diffusion wave on the skin of the marine angelfish *Pomacanthus. Nature* 376, 765–771.

Koopman, H. 1984. *The syntax of verbs*. Dordrecht: Foris.

Koopman, H., and D. Sportiche. 1991. The position of subjects. *Lingua* 85, 211–258.

Kornfilt, J. 1985. Case marking, agreement, and empty categories in Turkish. Doctoral dissertation, Harvard University.

Kosko, B. 1993. *Fuzzy thinking: The new science of fuzzy logic*. New York: Hyperion.

Koster, J. 1978. *Locality principles in syntax*. Dordrecht: Foris.

Koster, J. 1987. *Domains and dynasties: The radical autonomy of syntax*. Dordrecht: Foris.

Kripke, S. 1972. *Naming and necessity*. Cambridge, Mass.: Harvard University Press.

Kroch, A. 1989a. Asymmetries in long distance extraction in a tree adjoining grammar. In Baltin and Kroch 1989.

Kroch, A. 1989b. Reflexes of grammar in patterns of language change. *Language Variation and Change* 1, 199–244.

Kuno, S. 1987. *Functional syntax: Anaphora, discourse, and empathy*. Chicago: University of Chicago Press.

Laka, I. 1990. Negation in syntax: On the nature of functional categories and projections. Doctoral dissertation, MIT.

Laka, I. 1993. Unergatives that assign ergative, unaccusatives that assign accusative. In Bobaljik and Phillips 1993.

Lakoff, G. 1972. Linguistics and natural logic. In *Semantics for natural language,* edited by D. Davidson and G. Harman. Dordrecht: Reidel.

Lakoff, G. 1986. Classifiers as a reflection of mind. In *Noun classes and categorization,* edited by C. Craig. Amsterdam: John Benjamins.

Lakoff, G. 1987. *Women, fire, and dangerous things: What categories reveal about the mind.* Chicago: University of Chicago Press.

Lakoff, G., and J. R. Ross. 1967. Is deep structure necessary? Ms., MIT.

Land, F. 1960. *The language of mathematics.* New York: Doubleday.

Langacker, R. 1969. On pronominalization and the chain of command. In *Modern studies in English,* edited by D. Reibel and S. Schane. Englewood Cliffs, N.J.: Prentice-Hall.

Langacker, R. 1977. Syntactic reanalysis. In *Mechanisms of syntactic change,* edited by C. Li. Austin, Tex.: University of Texas Press.

Lappin, S. 1996. The interpretation of ellipsis. In *Handbook of contemporary semantic theory,* edited by S. Lappin. Oxford: Blackwell.

Larson, R. 1988. On the double object construction. *Linguistic Inquiry* 19, 335–391.

Larson, R., and G. Segal. 1995. *Knowledge of meaning.* Cambridge, Mass.: MIT Press.

Lasnik, H. 1972. Analyses of negation in English. Doctoral dissertation, MIT.

Lasnik, H. 1976. Remarks on coreference. *Linguistic Analysis* 2, 1–22.

Lasnik, H. 1981. Restricting the theory of transformations: A case study. In *Explanation in linguistics: The logical problem of language acquisition,* edited by N. Hornstein and D. Lightfoot. London: Longman.

Lasnik, H. 1989. *Essays on anaphora.* Dordrecht: Reidel.

Lasnik, H. 1990. *Essays on restrictiveness and learnability.* Dordrecht: Reidel.

Lasnik, H. 1992. Case and expletives. *Linguistic Inquiry* 23, 381–405.

Lasnik, H. 1993. Lectures on Minimalist syntax. University of Connecticut Occasional Papers in Linguistics 1. (Distributed by MITWPL, Department of Linguistics and Philosophy, MIT.)

Lasnik, H. 1995a. Case and expletives revisited: On Greed and other human failings. *Linguistic Inquiry* 26, 615–633.

Lasnik, H. 1995b a. Last Resort. In *Proceedings of the First Numanzu Conference on Formal Linguistics,* edited by S. Haraguchi and M. Funaki. Tokyo: Hituzi Syobo Publishing.

Lasnik, H. 1995c. A note on pseudogapping. In Pensalfini and Ura 1995.

Lasnik, H. Forthcoming. Verbal morphology: *Syntactic Structures* meets the Minimalist Program. In *Evolution and revolution in linguistic theory: Essays in honor of Carlos Otero,* edited by H. Campos and P. Kempchinsky. Washington D.C.: Georgetown University Press.

Lasnik, H., and J. Kupin. 1977. A restrictive theory of transformational grammar. *Theoretical Linguistics* 4, 173–196.

Lasnik, H., and M. Saito. 1984. On the nature of proper government. *Linguistic Inquiry* 15, 235–289.

Lasnik, H., and M. Saito. 1991. On the subject of infinitives. In *CLS 27.* Part 1, *The General Session,* edited by L. M. Dobrin, L. Nichols, and R. M. Rodriguez. Chicago Linguistic Society, University of Chicago.

Lasnik, H., and M. Saito. 1992. *Move alpha.* Cambridge, Mass.: MIT Press.

Lasnik, H., and J. Uriagereka. 1988. *A course in GB syntax.* Cambridge, Mass.: MIT Press.

Lawrence, P. A. 1992. *The making of a fly.* Oxford: Blackwell.

Lebeaux, D. 1983. A distributional difference between reciprocals and reflexives. *Linguistic Inquiry* 14, 723–730.

Lebeaux, D. 1988. Language acquisition and the form of the grammar. Doctoral dissertation, University of Massachusetts, Amherst.

Lebeaux, D. 1991. Relative clauses, licensing, and the nature of the derivation. In Rothstein 1991.

Lebeaux, D. 1996. Determining the kernel. In Rooryck and Zaring 1996.

Lees, R. B. 1960. *The grammar of English nominalizations.* The Hague: Mouton.

Legendre, G., P. Smolensky, and C. Wilson, eds. Forthcoming. *Proceedings of the MIT Workshop on Optimality.* Cambridge, Mass.: MIT Press.

Lenneberg, E. H. 1967. *Biological foundations of language.* New York: Wiley.

Lerdahl, F., and R. Jackendoff. 1983. *A generative theory of tonal music.* Cambridge, Mass.: MIT Press.

Levin, B., and M. Rappaport Hovav. 1995. *Unaccusativity: At the syntax–lexical semantics interface.* Cambridge, Mass.: MIT Press.

Lewontin, R. C. 1990. The evolution of cognition. In *An invitation to cognitive science.* Vol. 3, *Thinking,* edited by D. Osherson and E. Smith. Cambridge, Mass.: MIT Press.

Liberman, A. 1996. *Speech: A special code.* Cambridge, Mass.: MIT Press.

Lieberman, P. 1984. *The biology and evolution of language.* Cambridge, Mass.: Harvard University Press.

Lieberman, P., and E. S. Crelin. 1971. On the speech of Neanderthal man. *Linguistic Inquiry* 2, 203–222.

Lightfoot, D. 1979. *Principles of diachronic syntax.* Cambridge: Cambridge University Press.

Lightfoot, D. 1982. *The language lottery.* Cambridge, Mass.: MIT Press.

Lightfoot, D. 1989. The child's trigger experience. *Brain and Behavioral Sciences* 12, 321–375.

Lightfoot, D. 1991. *How to set parameters: Arguments from language change.* Cambridge, Mass.: MIT Press.

Lightfoot, D. 1995. Empty categories, adaptationism, and the spandrels of San Marco. Talk presented at Developments in Evolutionary Biology, Istituto di Scienza e Arti, Venice.

Lightfoot, D. Forthcoming. Creoles and cues. In DeGraff, forthcoming.

Lincoln, R. J., and G. A. Boxshall. 1987. *The Cambridge illustrated dictionary of natural history.* Cambridge: Cambridge University Press.

Linebarger, M. 1980. The grammar of negative polarity. Doctoral dissertation, MIT.

Longobardi, G. 1994. Reference and proper names. *Linguistic Inquiry* 25, 609–665.

Lyons, J. 1968. *Introduction to theoretical linguistics*. Cambridge: Cambridge University Press.

Mahajan, A. 1990. The A/A-bar distinction and movement theory. Doctoral dissertation, MIT.

Manzini, M. R. 1992. *Locality: A theory and some of its empirical consequences*. Cambridge, Mass.: MIT Press.

Maor, E. 1994. *The story of a number*. Princeton, N.J.: Princeton University Press.

Marantz, A. 1984. *On the nature of grammatical relations*. Cambridge, Mass.: MIT Press.

Maratsos, M. 1988. Innateness and plasticity in language acquisition. In *The teachability of language*, edited by M. Rice and R. L. Schiefelbusch. Baltimore, Md.: Paul H. Brooks.

Marcus, J. F., S. Pinker, M. Ullman, M. Hollander, T. J. Rosen, and S. Xu. 1992. *Overregularization in language acquisition*. Monographs of the Society for Research in Child Development, vol. 57.

Marden, J., and M. Kramer. 1994. Surface-skimming stoneflies: A possible intermediate stage in insect flight evolution. *Science* 266, 427–429.

Markman, E. 1989. *Categorization and naming in children* Cambridge, Mass.: MIT Press.

Markman, E., and G. Wachtel. 1988. Children's use of mutual exclusivity to constrain the meanings of words. *Cognitive Psychology* 20, 121–157.

Martin, R. 1996. A Minimalist theory of PRO and control. Doctoral dissertation, MIT.

Martinich, A. P., ed. 1985. *The philosophy of language*. Oxford: Oxford University Press.

Martins, A. M. 1994. Clíticos na história do Português. Doctoral dissertation, University of Lisbon.

Martins, A. M. 1995. A Minimalist approach to clitic climbing. In *CLS 31*. Vol. 2, *The Parasession on Clitics,* ed. by A. Dainora, R. Hemphill, B. Luka, B. Need, and S. Pargman. Chicago Linguistic Society, University of Chicago.

Mattingly, I., and M. Studdert-Kennedy, eds. 1991. *Modularity and the motor theory of speech perception*. Hillsdale, N.J.: Lawrence Erlbaum.

May, R. 1977. The grammar of quantification. Doctoral dissertation, MIT.

May, R. 1985. *Logical Form*. Cambridge, Mass.: MIT Press.

Mayr, E. 1982. *The growth of biological thought*. Cambridge, Mass.: Harvard University Press.

Mayr, E. 1991. *One long argument*. Cambridge, Mass.: Harvard University Press.

McCarthy, J. 1979. Formal problems in Semitic phonology and morphology. Doctoral dissertation, MIT.

McCawley, J. 1968. The role of semantics in a grammar. In *Universals in linguistic theory,* edited by E. Bach and R. Harms. New York: Holt, Rinehart and Winston.

McDaniel, D. 1989. Partial and multiple *wh*-movement. *Natural Language & Linguistic Theory* 7, 565–604.

McGinnis, M. J. 1995. Fission as feature-movement. In Pensalfini and Ura 1995.

Mehler, J., and E. Dupoux. 1994. *What infants know*. Oxford: Blackwell.

Meillet, A. 1912. L'évolution des formes grammaticales. *Scientia* 12, No. 26, 6. Reprinted in *Linguistique historique et linguistique générale,* 159–174. Paris: Champion (1958).

Meinhardt, H. 1995. *The algorithmic beauty of sea shells.* New York: Springer-Verlag.

Meinzer, K. 1994. *Thinking in complexity.* Berlin: Springer-Verlag.

Mendikoetxea, A., and M. Uribe-Etxebarria. Forthcoming. *Theoretical issues on the morphology/syntax/interface.* Special issue of ASJU, International Journal of Basque Linguistics and Philology. Bilbao: University of the Basque Country.

Michaels, D. 1977. Linguistic relativity and colour terminology. *Language and Speech* 20, 333–343.

Milsark, G. 1977. Toward an explanation of certain peculiarities of the existential construction in English. *Linguistic Analysis* 3, 1–29.

Mitchell, M. 1996. *An introduction to genetic algorithms.* Cambridge, Mass.: MIT Press.

Moore, J. 1994. Romance cliticization and Relativized Minimality. *Linguistic Inquiry* 25, 335–344.

Moro, A. 1996a. Dynamic antisymmetry. Talk presented at GLOW 19, University of Athens.

Moro, A. 1996b. *The raising of predicates: Predicative noun phrases and the theory of clause structure.* Cambridge: Cambridge University Press.

Munn, A. 1993. Topics in the syntax and semantics of coordinate structures. Doctoral dissertation, University of Maryland.

Munn, A. 1994. A Minimalist account of reconstruction asymmetries. In *NELS 24,* vol. 2, edited by M. González. GLSA, University of Massachusetts, Amherst.

Murasugi, K. 1992. Crossing and nested paths: NP movement in accusative and ergative languages. Doctoral dissertation, MIT.

Muromatsu, K. Forthcoming. The classifier as a primitive. In *University of Maryland working papers in linguistics* 3, edited by R. Echepare and V. Miglio. Department of Linguistics, University of Maryland.

Muysken, P. 1982. Parametrizing the notion head. *Journal of Linguistic Research* 2, 57–75.

Nakamura, M. 1997. Object extraction in Bantu applicatives: Some implications for Minimalism. *Linguistic Inquiry* 28.

Neale, S. 1992. *Descriptions.* Cambridge, Mass.: MIT Press.

Nespor, M., M. T. Guasti, and A. Christophe. 1996. Selecting word order: The Rhythmic Activation Principle. Working Paper: Periodico trimestrale 12. Istituto Scientifico H. San Raffaele, Milan.

Newmeyer, F. 1980. *Linguistic theory in America: The first quarter century of transformational generative grammar.* New York: Academic Press.

Nijhout, H. F. 1994. Genes on the wing. *Science* 265, 44–45.

Nishigauchi, T. 1986. Quantification in syntax. Doctoral dissertation, University of Massachusetts, Amherst.

Nishioka, N. 1994. On negative polarity items in English and Japanese: An analysis in terms of movement for feature checking. In *Harvard working papers in linguistics* 4, edited by S. D. Epstein, H. Thráinsson, and S. Kuno. Department of Linguistics, Harvard University.

Niyogi, P., and R. C. Berwick. 1995. A dynamical systems model of language change. Ms., MIT.

Nunes, J. 1995a. The copy theory of movement and linearization of chains in the Minimalist Program. Doctoral dissertation, University of Maryland.

Nunes, J. 1995b. On why traces cannot be phonetically realized. In *NELS 26,* edited by K. Kusumoto, 211–227. GLSA, University of Massachusetts Amherst.

O'Grady, W., M. Dobrovolsky, and M. Aronoff. 1993. *Contemporary linguistics: An introduction.* New York: St. Martin's Press.

Oka, T. 1993. Minimalism in syntactic derivation. Doctoral dissertation, MIT.

O'Neil, J. 1993. A unified analysis of superiority, crossover, and scope. In *Harvard working papers in linguistics* 3, edited by H. Thráinsson, S. D. Epstein, and S. Kuno. Department of Linguistics, Harvard University.

Ordóñez, F. In preparation. Antisymmetry and the clausal structure of Romance. Doctoral dissertation, City University of New York.

Ormazabal, J. 1995. The syntax of complementation. Doctoral dissertation, University of Connecticut.

Ormazabal, J., J. Uriagereka, and M. Uribe-Etxebarria. 1994. Word order and *wh*-movement: Towards a parametric account. Talk presented at the 17th GLOW Colloquium, Vienna.

Ortiz de Urbina, J. 1989. *Parameters of Basque syntax.* Dordrecht: Foris.

Osherson, D., ed. 1995. *An invitation to cognitive science.* 3 vols. 2nd ed. Cambridge, Mass.: MIT Press.

Panganiban, G., A. Sebring, L. Nagy, and S. Carroll. 1995. The development of crustacean limbs and the evolution of arthropods. *Science* 270, 1363–1366.

Papathomas, T. V., C. Chubb, A. Gorea, and E. Kowler. 1994. *Early vision and beyond.* Cambridge, Mass.: MIT Press.

Papavero, N. 1992. A descoberta da biota americana pelos europeus. *Ciencia Hoje,* December 1992, 50–55.

Parsons, T. 1990. *Events in the semantics of English.* Cambridge, Mass.: MIT Press.

Parsons, T. 1995. Thematic relations and arguments. *Linguistic Inquiry* 26, 635–662.

Partee, B. H., A. ter Meulen, and R. Wall. 1990. *Mathematical methods in linguistics.* Dordrecht: Kluwer.

Patel, N. H. 1994. Developmental evolution: Insights from studies in insect segmentation. *Science* 266, 581–590.

Pena, J. 1994. Spanish negation and negative concord: A Minimalist approach. Doctoral dissertation, University of Massachusetts, Amherst.

Penrose, R. 1989. *The emperor's new mind.* Oxford: Oxford University Press.

Penrose, R. 1994. *Shadows of the mind.* Oxford: Oxford University Press.

Pensalfini, R. 1995. Malagasy phrase structure and the LCA. In Pensalfini and Ura 1995.

Pensalfini, R., and H. Ura, eds. 1995. *Papers on Minimalist syntax.* MIT Working Papers in Linguistics 27. MITWPL, Department of Linguistics and Philosophy, MIT.

Perlmutter, D. 1983. *Studies in Relational Grammar.* Chicago: University of Chicago Press.

Perlmutter, D. 1992. Sonority and syllable structure in American Sign Language. *Linguistic Inquiry* 23, 407–442.

Pesetsky, D. 1982. Paths and categories. Doctoral dissertation, MIT.

Pesetsky, D. 1987. *Wh*-in-situ: Movement and unselective binding. In Reuland and ter Meulen 1987.

Pesetsky, D. 1995. *Zero syntax*. Cambridge, Mass.: MIT Press.

Petroski, A. 1993. *The evolution of useful things.* London: Butler and Jammer.

Phillips, C., ed. 1993. *Papers on Case and agreement II.* MIT working papers in linguistics 19. MITWPL, Department of Linguistics and Philosophy, MIT.

Phillips, C. In preparation. Partial structures. Doctoral dissertation, MIT.

Piattelli-Palmarini, M., ed. 1981. *Language and learning: The debate between Jean Piaget and Noam Chomsky.* Cambridge, Mass.: Harvard University Press.

Piattelli-Palmarini, M. 1989. Evolution, selection, and cognition: From "learning" to parameter setting in biology and in the study of language. *Cognition* 31, 1–44.

Piattelli-Palmarini, M. 1994. *Inevitable illusions.* New York: Wiley.

Pica, P., and W. Snyder. 1995. Weak crossover, scope, and agreement in a Minimalist framework. In *Proceedings of the Thirteenth West Coast Conference on Formal Linguistics,* edited by R. Aranovich, W. Byrne, S. Preuss, and M. Senturia. Stanford, Calif.: CSLI Publications. (Distributed by Cambridge University Press.)

Pierce, A. 1992. *Language acquisition and syntactic theory: A comparative analysis of French and English child language.* Dordrecht: Kluwer.

Pinker, S. 1979. Formal models of language learning. *Cognition* 7, 217–283.

Pinker, S. 1984. *Language learnability and language development.* Cambridge, Mass.: Harvard University Press.

Pinker, S. 1994. *The language instinct.* New York: Morrow.

Pinker, S., and P. Bloom. 1990. Language and selection. *Behavioral and Brain Sciences* 13, 707–784.

Pollock, J. -Y. 1989. Verb movement, Universal Grammar, and the structure of IP. *Linguistic Inquiry* 20, 365–424.

Poole, G. 1994. Deriving the X′-structure of syntactic adjunction. In *Harvard working papers in linguistics* 4, edited by S. D. Epstein, H. Thráinsson, and S. Kuno. Department of Linguistics, Harvard University.

Poole, G. Forthcoming. Optional movement in the Minimalist Program. In *Minimal ideas: Syntactic studies in the Minimalist framework,* edited by W. Abraham, S. D. Epstein, H. Thráinsson, and C. J.-W. Zwart. Amsterdam: John Benjamins.

Port, R., and T. van Gelder. 1995. *Mind as motion: Explorations in the dynamics of cognition.* Cambridge, Mass.: MIT Press.

Postal, P. 1970. On the surface verb "remind." *Linguistic Inquiry* 1, 37–120.

Postal, P. 1972. The best theory. In *Goals of linguistic theory,* edited by S. Peters. Englewood Cliffs, N.J.: Prentice-Hall.

Postal, P. 1974. *On raising: One rule of English grammar and its theoretical implications.* Cambridge, Mass.: MIT Press.

Prince, A., and P. Smolensky. Forthcoming. *Optimality Theory: Constraint interaction in generative grammar.* Cambridge, Mass.: MIT Press.

Prusinkiewicz, P., and A. Lindenmayer. 1990. *The algorithmic beauty of plants.* New York: Springer-Verlag.

Pullum, G. 1991. *The great Eskimo vocabulary hoax and other irreverent essays on the study of language.* Chicago: University of Chicago Press.

Pustejovsky, J. 1993. Type coercion and lexical selection. In *Semantics and the lexicon,* edited by J. Pustejovsky. Dordrecht: Kluwer.

Pustejovsky, J. 1995. *The generative lexicon.* Cambridge, Mass.: MIT Press.

Putnam, G. 1973. Meaning and reference. *Journal of Philosophy* 70. Reprinted in Martinich 1985.

Quine, W. V. O. 1953. *From a logical point of view.* Cambridge, Mass.: Harvard University Press.

Quine, W. V. O. 1960. *Word and object.* Cambridge, Mass.: MIT Press.

Quine, W. V. O. 1969. *Ontological relativity and other essays.* New York: Columbia University Press.

Quiring, R., U. Walldort, U. Kloster, and W. J. Gehring. 1994. Homology of the eyeless gene of drosophila to the small eye gene in mice and aniridia in humans. *Science* 265, 785–788.

Radford, A. 1990. *Syntactic theory and the acquisition of English syntax: The nature of early child grammars of English.* Oxford: Blackwell.

Radin, S. H., and R. T. Folk. 1982. *Physics for scientists and engineers.* Englewood Cliffs, N.J.: Prentice-Hall.

Raposo, E. 1987. Case theory and Infl-to-Comp: The inflected infinitive in European Portuguese. *Linguistic Inquiry* 18, 85–109.

Raposo, E. 1995. Romance clitic placement as Move F. Ms., University of California, Santa Barbara. Presented at Going Romance, University of Utrecht.

Raposo, E., and J. Uriagereka. 1990. Long-distance Case assignment. *Linguistic Inquiry* 21, 505–537.

Raposo, E., and J. Uriagereka. 1995. Two types of small clauses. In *Small clauses,* edited by A. Cardinaletti and M. T. Guasti. San Diego, Calif.: Academic Press.

Raposo, E., and J. Uriagereka. Forthcoming. Indefinite *se. Natural Language & Linguistic Theory.*

Reinhart, T. 1981. A second Comp position. In *Theory of markedness in generative grammar,* edited by A. Belletti, L. Brandi, and L. Rizzi. Pisa: Scuola Normale Superiore.

Reinhart, T. 1995. *Interface strategies.* Research Institute for Language and Speech, Faculty of Arts, Utrecht University.

Reinhart, T., and E. Reuland. 1993. Reflexivity. *Linguistic Inquiry* 24, 657–720.

Reuland, E., and A. ter Meulen, eds. 1987. *The representation of (in)definiteness.* Cambridge, Mass.: MIT Press.

Ritter, E., and S. Rosen. 1993. Deriving causation. *Natural Language & Linguistic Theory* 11, 519–555.

Rizzi, L. 1982. *Issues in Italian syntax.* Dordrecht: Foris.

Rizzi, L. 1986. On chain formation. In *The grammar of pronominal clitics,* edited by H. Borer. New York: Academic Press.

Rizzi, L. 1990. *Relativized Minimality.* Cambridge, Mass.: MIT Press.

Roberts, I. 1993. *Verbs and diachronic syntax.* Dordrecht: Reidel.

Roeper, T., and E. Williams, eds. 1987. *Parameter setting.* Dordrecht: Reidel.

Rooryck, J. Forthcoming. Prepositions and Minimalist Case-marking. In *Studies in comparative germanic syntax, vol. II,* edited by H. Thráinsson, S. D. Epstein, and S. Peter. Dordrecht: Kluwer.

Rooryck, J., and L. Zaring, eds. 1996. *Phrase structure and the lexicon.* Dordrecht: Kluwer.

Rosenbloom, P. 1950. *The elements of mathematical knowledge.* New York: Dover.

Ross, J. R. 1967. Constraints on variables in syntax. Doctoral dissertation, MIT.

Rozenberg, G., and A. Salomaa, eds. 1986. *The book of L.* New York: Springer-Verlag.

Rudin, C. 1988. On multiple questions and multiple *wh*-fronting. *Natural Language & Linguistic Theory* 6, 455–501.

Safir, K. 1985. *Syntactic chains.* Cambridge: Cambridge University Press.

Saito, M. 1985. Some asymmetries in Japanese and their theoretical implications. Doctoral dissertation, MIT.

Sapir, E. 1921. *Language: An introduction to the study of speech.* New York: Harcourt Brace Jovanovich.

Sauerland, U. 1995. Early features. In Pensalfini and Ura 1995.

Saussure, F. de 1959. *Course in general linguistics.* New York: McGraw-Hill.

Schein, B. 1993. *Plurals and events.* Cambridge, Mass.: MIT Press.

Schmidt, K. 1994. A puzzle: How similar signals yield different effects. *Science* 266, 566–567.

Schmitt, C. 1995. Aspect and the syntax of noun phrases. Doctoral dissertation, University of Maryland.

Searle, J. R. 1983. Proper names and intentionality. In *Intentionality.* Cambridge: Cambridge University Press.

Seidenberg, M., and L. Petitto. 1987. Communication, symbolic communication, and language. Comment on Savage-Rumbaugh, McDonald, Sevcik, Hopkins, and Rupert 1986. *Journal of Experimental Psychology: General* 116, 279–287.

Selkirk, E. 1984. *Phonology and syntax.* Cambridge, Mass.: MIT Press.

Shapiro, R. 1991. *The human blueprint.* New York: St. Martin's Press.

Sigler, M. In preparation. Topics in the syntax of Western Armenian. Doctoral dissertation, MIT.

Silk, J. 1980. *The big bang.* New York: W. H. Freeman.

Sloan, K. 1991. *Wh*-quantifier ambiguity. In *More papers on wh-movement,* edited by L. Cheng and H. Demirdache. MIT Working Papers in Linguistics 15. MITWPL, Department of Linguistics and Philosophy, MIT.

Smith, J. 1995. People eaters. *Granta,* Winter 1995, 69–84.

Smolensky, P. 1994. Constituent structure and explanation in an integrated connectionist/symbolic cognitive architecture. In *The philosophy of psychology: Debates on psychological explanation,* edited by C. Macdonald and G. Macdonald. Oxford: Blackwell.

Soames, S. 1989. Semantics and semantic competence. *Philosophical Perspectives* 3, 575–596.

Speas, M. 1990. *Phrase structure in natural language.* Dordrecht: Kluwer.

Speas, M. 1994. Null arguments in a theory of economy of projection. Ms., University of Massachusetts, Amherst.

Spelke, E., K. Breinlinger, J. Macomber, and K. Jacobson. 1991. Origins of knowledge. *Psychological Review* 99, 605–632.

Sperber, D., and D. Wilson. 1986. *Relevance: Communication and cognition.* Cambridge, Mass.: Harvard University Press.

Spielberg, N., and B. D. Anderson. 1987. *Seven ideas that shook the universe.* New York: Wiley.

Steen, E. B. 1971. *Dictionary of biology.* New York: Harper and Row.

Stevens, C. 1995. *The six core theories of modern physics.* Cambridge, Mass.: MIT Press.

Stewart, I. 1995. *Nature's numbers.* New York: Basic Books.

Stowell, T. 1981. Origins of phrase structure. Doctoral dissertation, MIT.

Suh, S. K. 1993. The syntax of Korean multiple nominative constructions. In *University of Maryland working papers in linguistics* 1, edited by C. Mason, S. Powers, and C. Schmitt, 105–120. Department of Linguistics, University of Maryland.

Swinney, D., M. Ford, U. Frauenfelder, and J. Bresnan. 1988. On the temporal course of gap-filling and antecedent assignment during sentence comprehension. In *Language structure and processing,* edited by B. Grosz, R. Kaplan, M. Macken, and I. Sag. Stanford, Calif.: CSLI Publications.

Takahashi, D. 1993. Movement of *wh*-phrases in Japanese. *Natural Language & Linguistic Theory* 11, 655–678.

Takahashi, D. 1995. Minimality of movement. Doctoral dissertation, University of Connecticut.

Tancredi, C. 1992. Intonation semantics. Doctoral dissertation, MIT.

Terzi, A. 1995. Two types of clitic climbing from finite clauses. Ms., City University of New York.

Thelen, E., and L. Smith. 1994. *A dynamic systems approach to the development of cognition and action.* Cambridge, Mass.: MIT Press.

Thompson, D'A. W. 1917. *On growth and form.* Cambridge: Cambridge University Press.

Thompson, D'A. 1961. *On growth and form.* Abridged edition, edited by J. T. Bonner. Cambridge: Cambridge University Press.

Thompson, E. In preparation. The syntax of tense. Doctoral dissertation, University of Maryland.

Thompson, J. N. 1994. *The coevolutionary process.* Chicago: University of Chicago Press.

Thornton, R. 1991. Adventures in long distance moving: The acquisition of complex *wh*-questions. Doctoral dissertation, University of Connecticut.

Todd, L. 1990. *Pidgins and creoles.* New York: Routledge.

Torrego, E. 1984. On inversion in Spanish and some of its effects. *Linguistic Inquiry* 15, 103–129.

Travis, J. 1994. Wiring the nervous system. *Science* 266, 568–570.

Travis, L. 1984. Parameters and the effects of word order variation. Doctoral dissertation, MIT.

Tsai, W.-T. D. 1994. On economizing the theory of $\overline{A}$-dependencies. Doctoral dissertation, MIT.

Turing, A. 1952. The chemical basis of morphogenesis. *Philosophical Transactions of the Royal Society* B 237, 37–72.

Ura, H. 1995. Towards a theory of "strictly derivational" economy condition. In Pensalfini and Ura 1995.

Ura, H. 1996. Multiple feature-checking: A theory of grammatical function splitting. Doctoral dissertation, MIT.

Uriagereka, J. 1988. On government. Doctoral dissertation, University of Connecticut. (Distributed by MITWPL, Department of Linguistics and Philosophy, MIT.)

Uriagereka, J. 1994. Government restrictions on Basque movements. In *Syntactic theory and Basque syntax*, edited by J. I. Hualde and J. Ortiz de Urbina. University of the Basque Country.

Uriagereka, J. 1995. Aspects of the syntax of clitic placement in Western Romance. *Linguistic Inquiry* 26, 79–123.

Uriagereka, J. 1996. Warps: Some thoughts on categorization. In Ausín and López 1996.

Uriagereka, J. Forthcoming a. Formal and substantive elegance in the Minimalist Program. In *The role of economy principles in linguistic theory*, edited by C. Wilder, H. M. Gärtner, and M. Bierwisch. Berlin: Akademie Verlag.

Uriagereka, J. Forthcoming b. Multiple Spell-Out. In *Working Minimalism*, edited by M. A. Browning. Cambridge, Mass.: MIT Press.

Uriagereka, J. Forthcoming c. Senderos que se bifurcan. In *Cuadernos de histórica e filosofía da ciência, serie 3, volume especial 1995*, edited by V. Ruben. Universidade Estadual de Campinas, São Paulo.

Uribe-Etxebarria, M. 1994. Licensing conditions on negative polarity items. Doctoral dissertation, University of Connecticut.

Valian, V. 1993. Parser failure and grammar change. *Cognition* 46, 195–202.

Varlokosta, S. 1994. Issues on Modern Greek sentential complementation. Doctoral dissertation, University of Maryland.

Veron, J. E. N. 1995. *Corals in space and time*. Ithaca, N.Y.: Cornell University Press.

Vogel, H. 1979. A better way to construct the sunflower head. *Mathematical Bioscience* 44, 179–189.

Wainwright, P. C., and S. M. Reilly, eds. 1994. *Ecological morphology*. Chicago: University of Chicago Press.

Waldrop, M. M. 1992. *Complexity: The emerging science at the edge of order and chaos*. New York: Simon and Schuster.

Walker, B. 1983. *The woman's encyclopaedia of myths and secrets*. San Francisco: Harper.

Walker, P. M. B. 1989. *Chambers biology dictionary*. Cambridge: Chambers.

Watanabe, A. 1992. Subjacency and S-structure movement of *wh*-in situ. *Journal of East Asian Linguistics* 1, 255–291.

Watanabe, A. 1993. AGR-based theory and its interaction with the A/Ā system. Doctoral dissertation, MIT.

Watanabe, A. 1995. Conceptual basis of cyclicity. In Pensalfini and Ura 1995.

Webelhuth, G. 1989. Syntactic saturation phenomena and the modern Germanic languages. Doctoral dissertation, University of Massachusetts, Amherst.

Webelhuth, G., ed. 1995. *Government and Binding Theory and the Minimalist Program.* Oxford: Blackwell.

Wesson, R. 1991. *Beyond natural selection.* Cambridge, Mass.: MIT Press.

Wexler, K., and P. Culicover. 1980. *Formal principles of language acquisition.* Cambridge, Mass.: MIT Press.

Whitaker, H. 1976. A case study of the isolation of the language function. In *Studies in neurolinguistics II,* edited by H. Whitaker and H. A. Whitaker. London: Academic Press.

Wilder, C. 1994. Coordination, ATB, and ellipsis. In Zwart 1994.

Wilder, C. 1995. Rightward movement or leftward deletion. In *On extraction and extraposition in German,* edited by U. Lutz and J. Pafel. Amsterdam: John Benjamins.

Wilder, C., and D. Cavar. 1994. Word order variation, verb movement and economy principles. *Studia Linguistica* 48, 46–86.

Williams, E. 1984. *There*-insertion. *Linguistic Inquiry* 15, 131–152.

Williams, E. 1994. *Thematic structure in syntax.* Cambridge, Mass.: MIT Press.

Williams, E. 1995. Review of *Indices and identity. Language* 71, 572–576.

Williams, G. 1966. *Adaptation and natural selection.* Princeton, N.J.: Princeton University Press.

Wittgenstein, L. 1953. *Philosophical investigations.* Oxford: Blackwell.

Wolpert, L. 1994. Do we understand development? *Science* 266, 571–572.

Wolynes, P. G., J. N. Onuchic, and D. Thirumalai. 1995. Navigating the folding routes. *Science* 267, 1619–1620.

Wray, G. 1995. Punctuated evolution of embryos. *Science* 267, 1115–1116.

Wright, R. 1991. Quest for the mother tongue. *The Atlantic Monthly,* April 1991, 39–68.

Wu, A. 1994. The Spell-Out parameters: A Minimalist approach to syntax. Doctoral dissertation, UCLA.

Xu, J. 1993. An I-parameter and its consequences. Doctoral dissertation, University of Maryland.

Zanuttini, R. 1991. Syntactic properties of sentential negation: A comparative study of Romance languages. Doctoral dissertation, University of Pennsylvania.

Zubizarreta, M. L. 1994. Prosody, focus, and word-order. Ms., University of Southern California.

Zushi, M. 1995. Long-distance dependencies. Doctoral dissertation, McGill University.

Zwart, C. J.-W. 1993. Dutch syntax: A Minimalist approach. Doctoral dissertation, University of Groningen.

Zwart, C. J.-W., ed. 1994. *Minimalism and Kayne's antisymmetry hypothesis.* Groninger Arbeiten zur germanistischen Linguistik 37. Department of Linguistics, University of Groningen.

Index